MANAGING
INFORMATION
IN ORGANIZATIONS

For JAC, P. M.

With All My Love Always

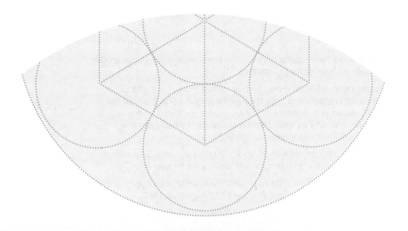

MANAGING INFORMATION IN ORGANIZATIONS

A PRACTICAL GUIDE TO IMPLEMENTING AN INFORMATION MANAGEMENT STRATEGY

SHARON COX
Professor of Information Systems,
Birmingham City University

palgrave
macmillan

First published 2014 by
PALGRAVE MACMILLAN

Palgrave Macmillan in the UK is an imprint of Macmillan Publishers Limited, registered in England, company number 785998, of Houndmills, Basingstoke, Hampshire RG21 6XS.

Palgrave Macmillan in the US is a division of St Martin's Press LLC, 175 Fifth Avenue, New York, NY 10010.

Palgrave Macmillan is the global academic imprint of the above companies and has companies and representatives throughout the world.

Palgrave® and Macmillan® are registered trademarks in the United States, the United Kingdom, Europe and other countries.

ISBN: 978–0–230–29884–2

This book is printed on paper suitable for recycling and made from fully managed and sustained forest sources. Logging, pulping and manufacturing processes are expected to conform to the environmental regulations of the country of origin.

A catalogue record for this book is available from the British Library.

A catalog record for this book is available from the Library of Congress.

Printed in China

BRIEF CONTENTS

DETAILED CONTENTS

LIST OF FIGURES

LIST OF TABLES

LIST OF SCENARIOS

LIST OF QUIZZES

LIST OF DEFINITIONS

ACKNOWLEDGEMENTS

The ideas presented in this book have been developed through experience with a number of organizations. My thanks to Professor Hanifa Shah for discussions related to her work on legacy systems, to Dr Jan Krasniewicz for his comments on the coding presented, and to my research student Stephen Murphy for discussing ideas on open source software.

I would like to thank the reviewers for their constructive comments on draft chapters and I thank June Cox for reading the completed manuscript.

My thanks also to Ursula Gavin at Palgrave Macmillan for her support in producing this book. I am grateful to Cathryn Easthope for designing Figure 15.3, and to Pauline Rafferty and Rob Hidderley for permission to use the indexing template in Table 15.1.

Finally, my thanks to JAC without whose patience, support, and encouragement this book would not have been possible.

PREFACE

Consider the following scenario:

Match Lighting is a lighting manufacturer and has recently been bought by Watts Electrical UK. A meeting is being held to discuss the integration of the data files and computer systems in the two organizations.

Mr Alvis, director of Match Lighting, opens the meeting. 'We have to start using Watts Electrical's enterprise resource planning system. They want us to integrate all customer accounts into the system as soon as possible. Let's start by looking at the scale of the problem. How many customers do we have?'

Ms Bevan, the sales manager of Match Lighting, answers confidently, 'We have 16,327 customers.'

The IT manager, Mr Cook, flicks through a report in front of him. 'No, there are more than that. There are 68,722 customer records on the customer master file.'

'That can't be right,' replies the sales manager. 'The sales teams do not deal with that many customers.'

'I can show you the figures; there are definitely over 68,000 records held on the customer file used by all the sales and finance systems,' explains the IT manager.

'So what are you telling me?' asks Mr Alvis. 'Do we have 16,000 or 68,000 customers?'

How does this scenario happen?
What should be done about it?

Information has been described as the lifeblood of organizations (Sherif, 1988). As an organization conducts its business transactions, information is created, recorded, shared, and acted upon. Rogerson (2008) has suggested that the powerful lifeblood of information has become polluted by the sheer volume of information available and concerns regarding the accuracy of information.

As organizations continue to increase their reliance on information technology (IT), the ability to integrate information between disparate business processes and computer systems is essential. The difficulties of information management often come to the fore with the introduction of new computer systems or the merger of organizations.

Managing information requires a partnership between the IT function and the business. The business functions create, use, and give meaning to information such as purchase orders, delivery notes, and sales invoices. The IT function provides the technological infrastructure to capture, record, and provide access to this information. The responsibility for managing the information needed by an organization cannot be devolved to the IT function. This book discusses the joint responsibilities of the business and IT function in managing information. It explains the business needs for information which affect decisions taken by the IT function relating to how data can be created, stored, and accessed.

This book aims to provide a practical approach to managing information to enable:

○ Business managers to understand the role of IT in managing information.
○ IT managers to understand the role of information within the business.
○ Business managers and IT managers to work together to create and implement an information management strategy for their organization.

The book is divided into four parts:

Part I Fundamentals of Information Management. The first part of the book introduces the organizational context for information and the basic elements of information in the form of the information life cycle. The information life cycle is discussed from the perspectives of both the business and IT functions. The roles of the business and IT functions in managing information are defined.

Part II Information Management Strategies. The second part of the book outlines common problems in organizations, such as inconsistent information, and provides practical guidance on how to address the problems. The main components of an information management strategy, including policies such data governance and data ownerships, are then introduced. Guidance is given on how staff in the IT function and business functions work together in formulating and implementing a practical strategy for managing information.

Part III Challenges to Managing Information. Organizations are not static; changes to the organization can be initiated by the introduction of IT (such as e-business) or by organizational developments (such as corporate mergers). Such changes challenge organizational strategies for managing information. The third part of the book discusses a range of technological and business developments that an organization may encounter and discusses the impact of the developments on managing information in the organization.

Part IV Developments Affecting Information Management. Developments in IT and business management continue to offer new opportunities and challenges to managing information. The final part of the book discusses a range of technological themes (such as enterprise resource planning and cloud computing), and business and social themes (such as social networking and multimedia information). Each theme is discussed in terms of the opportunities it offers for using information in the business and the information management challenges that need to be addressed by the IT function working in collaboration with the business. The book concludes by summarizing the key issues in information management and discussing the ongoing challenges.

Welcome to Business Students

You already know that information is important to organizations. You also have a good understanding of how information is used in the main business functions. You may have heard about online procurement, but that's an IT thing, isn't it? Information is used in the business functions and belongs to the business. You need to be able to work with the IT function to ensure that the information is available to you when you need it and in a form that you can easily use. You therefore need to understand what information the IT function requires from you so they can do whatever it is they do to make the information appear on your computer screen.

If the IT manager asked to talk to you about how the business could benefit from cloud computing, would you know what he meant? Some concepts in the book,

particularly in Part I, will be familiar to you. For example, the value chain model is presented as a way of helping to identify the information the business needs and to communicate these requirements to the IT function. Other sections of the book will explain how the information needs of the business are translated into models with which the IT function is familiar. This book explains how IT can be used to manage the information you need in your organization. It will also help you understand how to communicate with, and get the best support from, your IT function to ensure that information is effectively managed in your organization.

Welcome to IT Students

You are familiar with data models and process models. You can design a database and write a computer program; the users just have to tell you what their requirements are, don't they? When focusing on variable names and field types it becomes easy to forget that the systems you develop provide an organization with all the information it needs to function. If a customer receives an invoice with the wrong information or a manager cannot access a sales report, the computer gets the blame. Who developed the computer system? That would be you. You need to be able to work with the business users to ensure that you understand what information they require. You therefore need to understand the business context of the information so you can understand how to define the information that users need to see on their computer screen.

Some concepts in the book will be familiar to you, particularly in Part III and Part IV. For example, the entity model is presented as a way of helping to identify the information the business needs and the business rules that will affect the design of the database. Other sections of the book will explain how the information you need, such as who can authorize field changes to master files, can be derived through data governance. It will also discuss how developments, such as the proliferation of mobile technologies, impact information management. This book explains how you can work with the business to manage the information needed in the organization. It will also help you understand how to communicate with business users to determine how best IT can support the organization.

The concepts of information management are situated in this book within a longitudinal case study based on Match Lighting, its customers, suppliers, and collaborative partners. Each chapter focuses on the information management problems of a particular organization. The story evolves through the book as these organizations develop trading relationships and further problems of information management are identified. This enables the particular problems of organizations of differing size and technical maturity to be discussed. All chapters follow the format used here: a scenario is first introduced; concepts of information are explained, and then the scenario is reviewed at the end of the chapter.

Reviewing the Scenario

The situation at Match Lighting is extremely common and highlights a number of issues that are addressed in this book. First, there is the inability of the director to get a correct answer to what appears to be a simple question. The organization needs to be able to access accurate and consistent information to answer such questions. This is discussed within Part I, where consideration is given to the organization's need for information and the technical issues that affect access to information.

Second, there is confusion about what is meant by *customer*. The sales manager refers to a customer as someone with whom the sales team currently interacts. The IT manager refers to a customer as someone about whom information is held in a record in the customer master file. It is likely that the customer master file contains details of individuals or organizations who have previously made a purchase from Match Lighting. It therefore includes details of customers who have previously ordered products but may no longer do so, as well

as the details of current customers. Part II discusses how such different definitions of business terms can affect information management.

Third, the IT manager has assumed that every customer has one entry on the customer master file. Further investigation may reveal that one customer has more than one record in the customer master file. For example, a name may have been misspelt resulting in the customer having two entries in the customer master file. Procedures for cleaning, verifying, and validating information are outlined in Part II.

Finally, the parent organization, Watts Electrical UK, wants Match Lighting to use their enterprise resource planning system. Part III briefly explains this type of technology and discusses its impact on information management.

Note: There is a difference between data and information. Data are defined as raw figures and characters; information is data that have been given meaning within a specific context. To interpret data we need to know the rules and conventions for understanding the data. For example, 570 are data. When we know that 570 are the quantity of light bulbs Match Lighting has in stock, data becomes information that the organization can use to make decisions (such as whether to order any more bulbs). The terms *data* and *information* are often used interchangeably. In this book, *data* will be used to refer to the characters that are stored electronically, and *information* will be used to refer to business information.

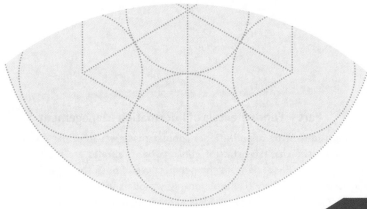

PART

I

FUNDAMENTALS OF INFORMATION MANAGEMENT

Part I Fundamentals of Information Management

Part I introduces the organizational context that gives information meaning, and defines the characteristics of information. Examples are used to discuss the information life cycle from the perspectives of both the organization and information technology (IT) functions. Key models used in later chapters are introduced, such as systems models and the entity-relationship model. The relationships among organizations, information systems, and IT are discussed in terms of how each influences information management.

Chapter 1 Organizational Context of Information

Chapter 1 discusses the need for information in organizations and introduces a generic business model that provides the context for information in organizations. The chapter explains how internal and external factors influence the organization's requirements for information and presents an organizational architecture that is used in later chapters to explore how changes to organizations impact information management.

Chapter 2 Role of Information Systems in Organizations

Chapter 2 discusses the organization as a system and explains the processes needed to provide the organization with the information it needs. The chapter demonstrates how different definitions of an entity reflect business rules, determining how information is managed in the organization. The information life cycle is introduced that is used in later chapters to assess the impact of organizational transformation on the information required by the organization.

Chapter 3 Role of Information Technology in Managing Information

Chapter 3 provides an introduction to IT to collect and store different types of data in a database. The relationship between information systems and IT is explained, demonstrating how IT can support each of the processes in the information life cycle. It explains how IT can influence the characteristics of information and considers the business value of IT. An outline for an information systems and IT plan is presented.

Chapter 4 Role of Business in Information Management

Chapter 4 demonstrates a socio-technical approach to developing an information architecture based on Wilson's soft systems method. The chapter explains how the information requirements of an organization can be extracted from a range of modelling tools and discusses the use and limitations of models. An enterprise architecture is presented demonstrating the relationship between the organizational architecture, information architecture, information systems architecture, and IT architecture to support each stage of the information life cycle.

ORGANIZATIONAL CONTEXT OF INFORMATION

Scenario 1.1

Organizational Context of Bright Spark

Bright Spark is a UK-based retailer selling light fittings (such as bulbs, lamps, and lampshades) to the general public. The retailer started as a small shop with a staff of three and now, 50 years later, has a chain of 63 stores and two warehouses across Europe. The organization also has a growing customer base in Australia and South America through Internet sales. Over the years the organization has experienced many changes as Bright Spark has been forced to adapt and evolve in order to survive. Sometimes change has been triggered by information technology (IT), such as the introduction of e-business, while other changes have been initiated by management to increase market presence and expand the organization. Bright Spark has changed and grown, transformed from its original shop but still retaining key values. As the organization has transformed, the context within which it collects, uses, and manages information has changed.

How has the organizational context changed?
How has the organization changed and how has this affected the information the organization needs?

Learning Outcomes

The learning outcomes of this chapter are to:

○ Examine the need for information in organizations.
○ Develop a business model within which to analyse the context of information in organizations.
○ Define the dimensions of transformation in morphing organizations.
○ Critically evaluate the impact of organizational transformation on the information requirements of the organization.

○ Identify the components of an organizational architecture.
○ Explain the scope of information management in organizations in a changing context.

Introduction

All organizations need information to trigger business processes and form the basis for decisions. This chapter defines what is meant by the term *information* and explains why information is so important to all organizations. The context in which the organization operates and gives information meaning is explored within a business model. Morphing organizations are then defined. The chapter discusses how organizations evolve over time, changing the way in which they operate and their need for information. An organizational architecture is presented which is used to explore how organizations change and how change affects an organization's need for information.

1.1 ▶ Business Needs for Information

An organization is a social entity within which a series of processes take place in order to achieve a specific purpose (Senior & Swailes, 2010). Information is described as the lifeblood of organizations (Rogerson, 2008) flowing through the business processes and providing a permanent record of the many transactions that take place on a daily basis. All organizations need information to trigger events, make decisions, and communicate actions to enable the organization to achieve its purpose.

Information is intended to be acted upon by the person receiving it (Davenport & Prusak, 1998). It is the sender's intention that the message being transmitted to the recipient will have meaning to the recipient and that the recipient will take action after receiving the information. For example, when Bright Spark receives information from a customer the information may trigger the start of a process to make a decision on how much discount to give the customer or to respond to a query raised by the customer.

The amount of information flowing through an organization can become excessive. If a recipient receives too much information they become overloaded, unable to interpret its meaning and unable to act on the information, resulting in information paralysis. Information technology (IT) enables information to be sent quickly and easily from the sender to the recipient(s). As the ease with which information can be sent increases, organizations, and individuals need to take more responsibility for information to avoid information paralysis.

Although IT has become ubiquitous, it must be remembered that organizations can exist without IT, but they cannot exist without information. Information provides the trigger for processes within the business. For example, information received from a customer who wishes to purchase a light fitting from Bright Spark triggers a series of business processes. The customer information triggers business processes to take payment from the customer, add payment to Bright Spark's accounts, amend the stock records to show that a light fitting has been sold, and processes to arrange for the light fitting sold to be dispatched to the customer.

Information provides the basis for decisions to be taken in the organization. Bright Spark needs information to help inform decisions and ensure the short-term operation and long-term survival of the organization. Organizational decisions include:

○ Operational decisions that require immediate action, such as do we need to order more stock? This decision will be informed by information relating to current stock levels, typical sales levels in the same time period, expected sales levels, and external factors such as competitors' pricing strategies.
○ Tactical decisons relating to the medium term, such as by how much should we reduce the price of products in the end-of-year sale? The decision to reduce prices will be informed by stock levels, sales targets, profit margins, and predicted customer demand.
○ Strategic decisions relating to the long-term development of the organization, such as should we open a new store? This will be informed by projected sales figures, predicted customer demand, competitor analysis, and expected returns on investment.

The information needed by organizations to inform decisions is derived from data. *Data* and *information* are different although sometimes the terms are used interchangeably.

DEFINITION: The term **data** generally refers to raw strings of letters and numbers that have been captured in some way. **Information** is data that have been processed to give the data meaning. An understanding of the units of measure to which the data refers and the context in which the data were collected are needed to add value to data and convert the data into information. Information can be numerical, textual, visual, or audial.

This is a string of data:

8, 4, 7, 8, 7, 7

If
    the units of measure are marks out of 10
and
    the context in which the data were collected was an in-store survey about customer service satisfaction
then
    the information provided by the data is that:
        Two people rate the customer service as being 8 out of 10.
        Three people rate the customer service as being 7 out of 10.
        One person rates the customer service as being 4 out of 10.

Bright Spark can use this information about customer service satisfaction to inform decisions such as do we need to improve customer service in the store?

The context in which data are interpreted transforms the data collected into information, which can inform decision-making and be acted upon.

DEFINITION: Context is the setting that gives information meaning. Context emerges from the dynamic set of interrelated conditions that exist at a particular instance within a defined situation.

Information only has meaning in context (Galliers, 1992). A business model provides the context which gives information meaning to the business.

1.2 ▶ Context of Business Information

A business model is a way of identifying the main components of a business (Hedman & Kalling, 2003) and structures the context for information in the organization. The following business model analyses the context in which an organization functions. The business model is a useful tool for analysts to use to define the organizational context and identify key terminology used in the business. The model is also used with business owners to reflect on the organization's mission and assess information requirements.

1.2.1 Overview of Business Model

Figure 1.1 presents a generic business model in which to analyse an organization, the organization's relationship with the environment, and the organization's information requirements. The model prompts key questions concerning fundamental elements of the organization. Information to compile the model can be derived from interviews and documentation. The business model defines the context of the organization and focuses on the key question *what business are we in?* The model identifies three main intersecting sets of concern: the *organization*, the *market(s)* in which the organization trades, and the *business environment* in which the organization operates. These three sets are influenced by, and must operate within, the overall *business climate*. Analysis of these sets assists in developing an appreciation of the organizational context within which information is needed. The model provides a structure based on set theory to identify the main individuals and organizations with whom the organization needs to communicate and to analyse the information flows to and from the organization.

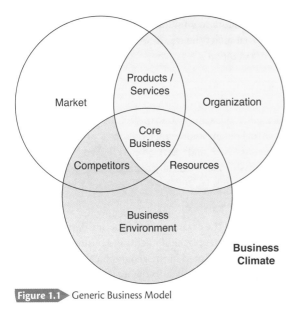

Figure 1.1 Generic Business Model

1.2.2 Organization

The organization set of the business defines the boundary separating the organization from the world surrounding the organization and includes the following elements:

> {mission, internal structure, geographic structure, business processes, organizational culture, history}

Mission

The mission element defines the intention of the organization in relation to other components of the business model such as customers and markets. The mission includes the purpose of the organization (the reason it exists), its values (what is important to the organization), its beliefs (the assumptions about itself and the environment), and a definition of where it operates (de Wit & Meyer, 2010).

Johnson *et al.* (2008) describe the mission as being the premise of the organization that provides the focus of the organization that is used to align components and guide actions and decisions, to enable the mission to be achieved and sustained. The mission provides the overall rationale, the justification for the existence and operation of the organization. The mission focuses on the present context while the vision focuses on the future desired state of the organization. The organization requires information to help communicate, achieve, and measure progress towards achieving its mission.

Internal Structure

The formal internal structure considers the way in which the organization arranges people, processes, and resources to achieve the organization's mission. The formal structure allocates responsibilities for completing, coordinating, and controlling activities (Senior & Swailes, 2010), seeking to identify the optimum grouping of resources and activities. The structure may involve arranging business processes to maximize efficiency or to improve the organization's ability to respond to the needs of customers and other external influences (such as new technological developments and changes in legal requirements). The internal structure defines the formal paths for communicating information between people and processes.

Typical hierarchical organizational structures group people and processes by:

○ Key function such as purchasing, production, sales, finance, and human resources, to form functional hierarchies in which staff develop specialist skills in business processes. Functional structures can lead to fragmentation and the loss of information as work is passed over the wall to the next function (Anumba *et al.*, 2002). Information needs to be managed to coordinate activities between functions and avoid delays where one function may be waiting for information from another function.

○ Product or service offered by the organization, such as the bulb department and lamp department in Bright Spark. Product-based structures enable staff to develop expert product knowledge but business processes may be duplicated across departments. Information management is needed to reduce administration costs and satisfy the different information needs of specialist areas in the product structure.

○ Location-based structures group people and processes to enable an organization to respond to the needs of the local community. Information is needed to coordinate activities between the different geographical locations.

Matrix structures provide an alternative to hierarchical organizational structures superimposing a set of horizontal divisions onto the hierarchical structure (Senior & Swailes, 2010). Matrix structures adopt a flexible project-based structure suited to innovative and problem-solving activities, but the structures can become complex. Information is needed to prioritize competing demands and maintain communication between managers in the structure.

The structure of the organization determines the lines of communication and spans of control between people. The organizational structure therefore affects the way in which information is used and managed in the organization. A number of factors influence the design of organizational structures including the nature of the work to be undertaken, the location of the work, size of the organization, and the degree of power and control to be retained centrally (Senior & Swailes, 2010).

In addition to the formal organizational structure, an informal structure emerges through interactions that are not defined or constrained by the formal structure. An informal structure evolves from the interactions between people in the organization and emerges through friendships and common interests. The informal structure can support, and at times work against, the formal communication paths established in the formal organizational structure. Informal structures can highlight deficiencies in the formal communication channels (Mullins, 2010b) for sharing information. The informal communication flows are powerful information arteries in the organization and should not be neglected in information management policies.

Geographical Structure

The organizational structure operates across the geographical structure of the organization, which considers the physical locations around the world where the organization has a presence. Bright Spark has retail stores in the United Kingdom and warehouses elsewhere in Europe, in addition to Internet sales in other countries. The geographical structure defines the boundary of the organization, identifying where information is needed.

Separate buildings in a physical location, and floors within buildings, isolate departments and functions in the organizational structure. The physical location of resources and expertise seeks to improve coordination and communication within specialized activities. Location also promotes the development of cooperative working practices and cultural values within departmental groupings. However, the strengthening of departmental identities through shared values and goals can lead to friction between departments. As staff identify with their department, creating a *we* group, a separation is identified between those outside the *we* group. The separation can lead to departmental barriers being formed that hinder the effective flow of information needed in the organization. Dingley *et al.* (2000) suggest that departments in organizations can adopt the same characteristics as a tribe, possessing a shared culture, maintaining boundaries, engaging in social rituals, adopting a common language, and defending their territory when it is perceived to be under threat. Differences in values, cognition, language, terminology, and behaviour between departments can lead to cultural communication barriers (Dingley *et al.*, 2000) that affect the way in which information is used in the organization.

The increasing use of IT enables individuals to communicate with colleagues, share information, and collaborate in business processes without the need to be physically located in the same place. This has led to the formation of virtual organizations: organizations that are geographically dispersed and electronically linked (Pedersen & Nagengast, 2008) that can adapt to changes in the environment (Lin & Lu, 2005).

Business Processes

Traditionally, the organizational structure determines the way in which people, equipment, and business processes are physically located in the geographical structure. The business processes relate to the main activities required in the organization to transform resources into the products and services to sell to customers. The business processes relate to the primary activities of the organization, which can be identified using the value chain model. The value chain model distinguishes between primary activities directly involved in the development of a product or service, and secondary activities that support the production process (Porter & Millar, 1985). In Bright Spark, primary activities include inbound logistics (receiving light fittings ordered from suppliers), operations (displaying products and providing advice to customers), outbound logistics (packaging and dispatching lighting products to customers), marketing (advertising light fittings and creating special offers), and after-sales service (exchanging faulty lights and providing an installation service). Support activities in Bright Spark include the organizational infrastructure of management, finance and legal services, human resource management, technology development (involving the website), and procurement (negotiating packaging contracts and purchasing shop display equipment), which provide an infrastructure to support the primary activities. Information is needed to trigger business processes, to be input into business processes, to control business processes, and to be delivered as an output from business processes in the value chain, informing organizational decisions.

Organizational Culture

The culture of the organization is the way in which the people in the organization engage in business processes to achieve the organization's mission. Cultural analysis considers the beliefs and value systems that underpin the philosophy of the organization. Schein (2010) likens the culture of an organization to the personality of an individual, guiding and constraining behaviour. Organizational culture can be evidenced through:

○ Artefacts, including physical signs such as the organizational structure, providing a physical representation of cultural values.
○ Beliefs and values providing the basis for the organizational strategy.
○ Assumptions guiding the decisions and actions of the people in the organization (Schein, 2010).

Culture evolves from the shared history of the members of the organization, providing stability and a sense of identity (Schein, 2010). Brown (1998) suggests that there are three sources of organizational culture: the national culture of the organization's location, the vision and management styles of the key leaders in the organization, and the nature of the business and the environment in which the organization operates. Mullins (2010b) describes organizational culture as providing a pervasive context for everything that happens in the organization.

The organizational culture provides the context within which data are interpreted, giving information meaning. Table 1.1 lists a number of categories, which Schein (2010) suggests can be used to describe culture,

Table 1.1 ▶ Role of Culture in Information Management

Category for Describing Culture (Schein, 2010)	Impact on Information Management
Interpersonal Behaviour and Interaction	The *language* used in communication articulates the information needed by the organization and identifies the terminology with which information is identified. The patterns of interaction between the organization's members highlight the information flows that need to be supported through information management processes.
Group Norms	The organization, and the groups within the organization, will hold minimum *standards* of acceptability relating to the accuracy, frequency, and timeliness of information, which need to be addressed by information management policies.
Espoused Values	The characteristics of the information provided to the organization and to the groups within the organization must reflect the organization's *values* in terms of content, quantity, quality, and presentation to support goals.
Philosophy	The organization's philosophy determines the *policies* that direct business processes and define standards of behaviour. Information management needs to be aligned with the organization's philosophy to provide the content and quality of information needed by business processes.

Table 1.1 Continued

Category for Describing Culture (Schein, 2010)	Impact on Information Management
Implicit Rules	New members of the organization need to learn the *rules* of the informal organization. Information management needs to consider any deficiencies in the formal lines of communication that are addressed in the informal structure, and identify how the implicit rules of working in the informal structure contribute to the management of information in the organization.
Climate	The organizational climate, the *feel* of the organization, is influenced by factors including the physical use of building space and the interactions between staff. Information management needs to consider the flow of information in the organization including how information is communicated and the opportunities and barriers for communicating information. The emphasis on formal information flows through organizational hierarchies that can overlook the informal channels through which information is shared.
Embedded Skills	In the formal organizational structure, explicit business procedures are documented and the information needed by the procedures can be identified from documentation. In the informal structure, implicit *skills* and business practices operate ensuring the effective functioning of the organization; the information needs of these practices must also be identified.
Mental Models	A mental model is a personal construct through which the world is perceived. Members of the organization evolve *shared perceptions* defining the way information is used in work practices. Shared mental models need to be understood to ensure that information is presented in a manner consistent with the perceptions of the organization.
Shared Meanings	The language of a social group creates a *sense of unity* separating the group from others. Within an organization, different departments attribute different meanings to key terms about which information needs to be managed, such as product, item, and component. Different definitions of information can be the source of many problems in information management.
Root Metaphors	Root metaphors are *shared views* of the world characterizing a group. Metaphors can become embedded in physical artefacts, reinforcing a group's view of the world. Information management needs to understand the view of the world held by members of the organization as the views provide the context within which information will be interpreted and used.
Formal Rituals	Rituals are the *actions* taken by a group that are not required by business processes but are needed to maintain the culture of the group. For example, a ritual is the way in which a group celebrates the success of a project or an individual being promoted. Rituals demonstrate the values of the organization that need to be embedded within information management.

Source: Based on Schein (2010).

and shows how the categories may impact on information management.

History

Culture is informed by the history of the organization. The history of the organization considers how the organization has evolved and the current state of business transformation. Bright Spark has a strong history that explains how the retailer has grown from small beginnings by trajectory growth; other organizations may have experienced strategies of diversification, acquisition, downsizing, or dissolution of mergers. The history of the organization has led to the current status and has left an imprint on the organization influencing structure, processes, culture, and information needs. Scenario 1.2 presents a brief history of Bright Spark.

Scenario 1.2

History of Bright Spark

Larry Hughes completed an apprenticeship as an electrician but did not wish to spend his life working for someone else. As he was growing up, he helped out at the local market at weekends and during the holidays so after he completed his apprenticeship he opened his own market stall selling small electrical components. In 1961 he opened the first Bright Spark shop employing two people: Mrs Lewis was responsible for managing the accounts and John Edwards served customers. Larry designed and fitted the shop himself. The main counter included a fitting so that light bulbs could be tested and customers could see how lampshades would look when lights were switched on. Larry also organized the buying of stock. A key success factor for the shop was that Larry provided customers with technical advice and occasionally completed electrical work for customers.

When Larry opened his second shop he wanted to replicate the same level of customer service. Larry employed a manager, shop assistant, and bookkeeper and Larry tried to divide his time between the shops. As more shops opened, the structure of Bright Spark needed to change to coordinate activities. Larry realized that he needed to give managers some flexibility to manage their stores in their own way as the store managers were in a better position to understand the specific needs of their customers. Larry remained in charge of selecting stock and ensured that additional functions of logistics, human resources, and IT were managed to support the retail shops. As more shops opened, area managers were appointed to assist in meeting the changing needs of customers throughout the United Kingdom.

1.2.3 Market

The market set of the business model considers the target audience(s) for the organization's products and services. McDonald and Dunbar (2012) emphasize that markets should be defined from the customer's perspective, rather than the organization's perspective, as the range of products or services that the customer perceives as satisfying the same need.

Three levels can be defined in a market including the:

○ Totally available market of the needs that can be satisfied by all alternative products and services.
○ Potentially available market, focusing on potential uses of the organization's and competitors' portfolio of products and services.
○ Realistically available market of the need which can be satisfied by the organization's portfolio (McDonald & Dunbar, 2012).

The scope of the potentially available market is increased by e-business, which enables organizations to trade in global markets with an online international presence. Although IT enables global transactions to be easily coordinated, global trading has existed for hundreds of years (Lipsey & Chrystal, 2011). The market set of the business model considers the elements:

{customers, consumers, channels}

Customers and Consumers

The market set of the business model distinguishes between customers who buy the product or service directly from the organization, and consumers who use the product or service purchased. Organizations need to communicate and exchange different information with customers and consumers. In retail, the customer and consumer may be the same organization or individual; however, it is important to recognize when and how these roles differ. For example, Match Lighting is a lighting manufacturer who supplies lighting products to Bright Spark. Bright Spark is therefore a customer of Match Lighting. People who purchase Match Lighting's products from a Bright Spark shop are a customer of Bright Spark and a consumer of Match Lighting.

Organizations serve the needs of different types of customers. Lynch (2006) suggests that the main categories of customers include:

○ Domestic customers: Individuals make a purchase for themselves or their family. Demand for the product or service is a primary demand that is not dependent on the demand for a product later in the supply chain.
○ Large commercial customers: Organizations make a purchase for use in their business but the purchase is dependent on demand for their own products and services, which may be in a different market.
○ Small commercial customers: Organizations make a purchase for use in their business, and demand is derived from demand in other markets.
○ Large service customers: Organizations sell products direct to domestic customers for immediate consumption.
○ Public service customers: Public sector organizations use the products to provide a service direct to domestic customers for immediate consumption.
○ Not-for-profit customers: Purchases made for use in the delivery of a product or service to domestic customers within a clearly focused value system.

Different customers have different requirements for the products and services offered by an organization. Market segmentation is based on the premise that groups of customers can be defined that require a similar marketing approach (Jenkins & McDonald, 1997). There is an underlying assumption that market segments objectively exist; however, Jenkins and McDonald (1997) propose that the definition of market segments needs to consider the organizational structure and its capabilities in terms of how the organization makes sense of the marketplace.

Market segments are defined by identifying a collection of variables for categorizing customers with similar needs (McDonald & Dunbar, 2012). For example, Chelsom *et al.* (2005) suggest that variables may include:

○ Geographic features such as region and population density.
○ Demographic features such as age, family size, income, education, and occupation.
○ Psychographic features such as social class and personality.
○ Behavioural aspects such as loyalty, use, and awareness of the organization's offerings.

An understanding of customers and market segmentation requires a range of information to be managed relating to customer profiles and the frequency of product purchase (McDonald & Dunbar, 2012). Customer profiling categorizes customers using variables to identify the primary characteristics of customers who are profitable or have potential for profitable growth in the future. This enables organizations to focus their marketing activities and use resources efficiently.

Channels

The market sector of the business model also considers the channels that the organization uses to transfer products and services to customers and consumers in the marketplace. This includes, for example, selling direct to customers, wholesalers, or intermediaries. The use of the Internet as a channel and the use of IT to coordinate information between channels are discussed in Chapter 10.

1.2.4 Business Environment

The business environment is the main source of inputs to the organization over which the organization has some influence. The business environment includes suppliers of equipment and raw materials, as well as other organizations within the industry (or industries) in which the organization trades, who can affect the business processes and decisions of the organization. The business environment includes:

{industries, suppliers, strategic alliances, parent company, trade unions, professional institutions}

Industries

An industry is a category of business activity in which the organization and its suppliers operate in the business environment. The specific industry or industries with which an organization is associated will influence the information needs of the organization. For example, information will need to be collected and retained to demonstrate Bright Spark's adherence to industry standards on issues relating to quality and safety of electrical products. The North American Industry Classification System (NAICS, 2007) defines 20 main industry categories, including construction, manufacturing, and information. Industries are defined within each category, such as industrial building construction, fruit and vegetable canning and news syndicates. NAICS is used to collect and publish statistics relating to the American economy. Similar systems are used in the United Kingdom, the United Kingdom Standard Industrial Classification of Economic Activities (SIC, 2007), and in Europe, the Eurostat System (2008).

Suppliers

Suppliers are organizations that provide products and services to the organization, including the direct raw materials that the organization needs to create its outputs, as well as resources such as equipment, staff, and consumables. The supply chain focuses on the activities that cross the boundary between the organization and its supplier's organization from initial procurement (including determining need for resources and identifying potential suppliers) through to ordering, receiving, and paying for resources supplied (Wagner *et al.*, 2003). Match Lighting is one of Bright Spark's main suppliers. A regular, reliable supply of quality resources is essential to Bright Spark and this requires accurate and timely information to be exchanged between the trading partners.

Strategic Alliances

A strategic alliance may exist between two or more organizations that have formally agreed to cooperate in some way for mutual benefit. Chen *et al.* (2008) suggest that motivations for forming a strategic alliance may be:

○ Resource-oriented: Seeking the acquisition of, or access to, resources, knowledge, skills, and marketing channels.
○ Cost-oriented: Seeking efficiency savings through sharing the costs of research and development.
○ Strategy-oriented: Tactics to increase market share or shorten time to market to extend barriers to competition.

○ Learning-oriented: Sharing information to support research and development and business growth.

The cooperation can take many forms, such as subcontracting and licensing agreements, joint ventures, acquisitions, and mergers (Johnson *et al.*, 2008). Strategic alliances rely on the exchange of information between organizations creating additional requirements and challenges for information management. Information is also needed to help organizations select potential partners. Chen *et al.* (2008) suggest that information is needed in relation to:

○ Corporate compatibility including size, resources, strategy, culture, and working practices.
○ Technology capability including skills and expertise.
○ Resources such as equipment, knowledge, and investment in research and development.
○ Financial conditions such as profitability and growth potential.

Some of this information can be identified through the comparison of business and information models for each organization.

Link 1.1
Example of Strategic Alliance

Parent Company

An organization may be owned by another organization, called a parent company. Information will be exchanged between the organization and the parent company. The parent organization may limit the autonomy of the organization, imposing restrictions on the actions and decisions the organization can take without prior agreement of the parent organization. The level of autonomy permitted will affect the information requirements of managers at different levels in the organization. Levels of autonomy will also influence the business rules that direct organizational processes and the way in which information is used. Information management needs to be aligned with the requirements of the parent company (where it exists) to ensure that information can be effectively shared and communicated within a common frame of reference. Table 1.1 introduced the importance of shared meaning of information within the organization. A framework of shared meaning needs to be extended to incorporate the views of the parent company.

Trade Unions

Workers in many industries have established trade unions (also known as labour unions) to establish collective bargaining power. This power is used to develop agreements with the management of organizations on issues regarding pay, employment benefits, working conditions, and human resource policies such as recruitment and promotion. Information management is needed to support negotiation, communication, and implementation of such agreements.

Professional Institutions

Characteristics of a profession include specialist knowledge and skills gained through training, high standards of behaviour, and adherence to ethical codes of practice (Professions Australia, 1997). Membership of a professional body is restricted to practitioners who demonstrate the required specialist knowledge and training, and agree to comply with codes of conduct (Bott, 2005). Professions cannot exist without clearly defined ethical guidelines (Presidents & Fellows of Harvard College, 2009) and are governed by a professional body. Professional bodies seek to establish and promote high standards of conduct within a community of professionals. Examples of professional bodies include the British Computer Society, South African Institution of Professional Accountants, American Advertising Federation, and Fédération Internationale de l'Automobile (the world governing body for motor sport).

A professional body differs from a regulatory body. Professionals are members of a professional body; a regulatory body does not have members as it has a legal mandate with the primary purpose of protecting the public (Quality Research International, 2009). Professional bodies have an important role in facilitating interaction between professionals, enabling agreed meanings to be derived and shared to shape and redefine practice, and to monitor compliance in accordance with agreed standards (Greenwood *et al.*, 2002) within the culture of the profession. The influence of the professional body will impact on organizational processes and the information required. In addition, information will need to be collected, managed, and presented on demand to demonstrate that the organization is complying with the requirements of the professional body. The specific requirements of the professional bodies and relevant regulatory bodies with which an organization may be associated need to be considered when developing an information management strategy.

1.2.5 **Products and Services**

The products and services produced as outputs from the organization are made available to customers in the market:

{product portfolio, services}

Product Portfolio

An organization may offer a range of tangible products to one or more potential markets of customers. Different products provided by the organization may be aimed at different customer segments. For example, Bright Spark has identified regional differences in relation to sales of its products; different products are in higher demand in different stores. Customer segments may differ in terms of profitability, degree of competition, and stage of growth of the market (Lynch, 2006). Organizations providing products to customers provide an indirect benefit to the customer; the benefits to the customer are derived from their consumption or use of the product.

Services

Services are less tangible than products but offer a direct benefit to the customer. Unlike products, services cannot be stored to be sold at a later time (Mullins, 2010b). Macdonald (1994) suggests that products and services differ in terms of:

- Timing of consumption, as services are consumed at the point of delivery.
- Scheduling of production and delivery, which are separated for products but may be undertaken at the same time in the provision of a service.
- Role of the customer in the production process as the customer is directly involved in the production of a service.
- Liability as deficient products can be replaced but the provision of a deficient service at the time of consumption cannot be directly replaced.
- Transportation as products are transported to the point of sale and services are transported to the point of delivery.
- Quality measures as products may be more objectively evaluated against agreed criteria than the perceived quality of a service with which a customer may not be satisfied.

The information needs of products and services therefore differ.

1.2.6 Competition

The organization experiences competition from the providers of products and services against which its outputs must compete and includes:

> {competitors, direct substitutes, indirect substitutes}

Competitors

Competitors are organizations that are targeting the same markets and customer groups as the organization.

Johnson *et al.* (2008) suggest that organizations need information about the basis of the competition, the intensity of the competition, and how competition can be influenced. Information is needed about the products and services offered by competitors and the percentage share of the market held. This information is needed to inform corporate strategy, product development, marketing campaigns, and pricing initiatives.

Direct Substitutes

A direct substitute satisfies the need of a consumer in the same way as the need is satisfied by the organization. Rival organizations offer products or services that provide the same function, differentiated by price, perceived quality, or branding.

Indirect Substitutes

An indirect substitute satisfies the need of a consumer in a different way from how the need is satisfied by the organization. It is an alternative rather than a direct replacement for the product or service. For example, candles are an indirect substitute for electrical lighting products therefore Amy's Candles (an independent store) is an indirect substitute for the lighting products of Bright Spark.

Johnson *et al.* (2008) differentiate between two further forms of substitute; substitution of need and generic substitution. Substitution of need occurs when the need for a product or service becomes redundant due to new developments in technology. Generic substitution arises when different types of products are in competition within a larger market, for example, holiday companies and furniture retailers compete for the available income of households (Johnson *et al.*, 2008).

Product cannibalization occurs when a new product is launched and gains sales by diverting sales from an existing product (Srinivasan *et al.*, 2005). Product cannibalization can result from the introduction of multipacks of the same product, multipacks of complimentary products (for example, computer and printer), indirect substitutes, and product variants (such as new colours launched within the same brand). Organizations need to capture and manage information about the product, services, and organizations with which it competes for customers.

1.2.7 Resources

Resources are the materials, skills, and equipment taken as inputs from the business environment into the organization to enable the organization to engage in its core business and provide the products and services to the market. Resources include:

> {finance, people, technology, skills, raw materials, assets, information}

Finance

A wealth of financial information needs to be managed in the organization with high degrees of accuracy, integrity, security, and adherence to relevant legislation. The sources of finance need to be identified and monitored, particularly in relation to any specific conditions about how money can be used or the nature of the return expected by an investor.

People

People are the most important asset in any organization (Mayo, 2006), providing the capability and creativity for an organization to be formed, sustained, and developed. The electrical expertise of Bright Spark's founder differentiated the first shop from competitors in the market. Specialist knowledge is core to a profession. Quinn *et al.* (1996) suggest that specialist knowledge forms the intellectual capital of an organization and includes:

- Cognitive knowledge (know-what) that forms the basic knowledge of the profession.
- Advanced skills (know-how), the ability to apply knowledge within the standards required by the profession.
- Systems understanding (know-why), a deep knowledge of the interrelationships between concepts which enables professionals to develop insight from their experience.
- Self-motivated creativity (care-why) that refers to the ability of highly motivated staff to outperform their peers.

The terms *human capital* and *intellectual capital* refer to the skills and knowledge within an organization which, if supported by appropriate organizational structure, culture, and systems can support the development of core competencies and innovation (Coakes & Bradburn, 2005). Within the business model it is necessary to identify the range of people and professions that comprise the human resources in the organization. Information management then must identify the information that people in the organization need in their work to support knowledge management activities.

Technology

Most organizations will use technological resources to create, manage and distribute their products and services. The use of the word 'technology' is not restricted to IT and considers the use of:

- Heavy machinery such as that used in production lines and on construction sites.
- Diagnostic equipment such as heart monitors in hospitals, temperature monitors used in catering, and on-board diagnostics used in motor vehicles.
- Specialist tools such as stethoscopes, chefs' knives, artists' brushes, and power tools.

Information needs to be managed about each type of technology, such as calibration parameters, maintenance schedules, and depreciation rates. In addition, many types of technology provide data on production rates, error detection, and quality indicators. These data need to be effectively captured and communicated within the organization for use in appropriate business processes and to inform decision-making.

Skills

A skill is an ability to perform a task. Skills may be measured in terms of the performance of the task or the deliverable achieved from the task. Some tasks require skills in the speed and accuracy of motor movement, other tasks require skills in content abilities (such as verbal, mathematics, and spatial abilities) and domain knowledge (Ackerman, 2007).

Employees have two types of skills to offer organizations: subject skills, which are specific to an area of work, and transferable skills (such as communication skills and team working), which can be used in a range of activities crossing professions and organizations during a career (Cox & King, 2006). The business model identifies the range of skills needed by the organization to define and conduct the business processes needed to support the development of products and services. Information needs to be managed about the skill base of the organization and the further development of staff skills to support the growth of both the organization and its employees.

Raw Materials

The organization takes raw materials from suppliers in the business environment to transform through a series of business processes thus creating the products and services offered in the marketplace. The term *raw materials* includes both the direct ingredients needed to create the product or service, and the indirect materials needed for support activities such as marketing and distribution. Information is needed to coordinate regular communication between business processes and suppliers in the business environment to ensure a timely supply of materials.

Assets

Assets are used to transform the raw materials into the products and services offered by the organization. Fixed assets are tangible and intangible items owned by the organization that are not regularly offered for sale (Chelsom *et al.*, 2005) within the portfolio of products and services presented to customers in the market. Tangible assets in Bright Spark include land, buildings, equipment (including warehousing equipment, packaging equipment, IT, and transport vehicles), and fixtures (including office furniture and shop displays). Although an organization may have physical buildings, it is an abstract concept, and virtual organizations can exist without occupying a physical building (Senior & Swailes, 2010). Intangible assets include intellectual capital (such as patents and trademarks), the human capital of knowledge and expertise of staff, and the goodwill developed through the organization's reputation. Current assets can be converted into cash to pay liabilities within 12 months and include cash, debtors, and stocks of raw materials (Chelsom *et al.*, 2005). Information is needed relating to the nature of each asset to calculate depreciation. This includes the original cost of the asset and its expected life span before replacement (Chelsom *et al.*, 2005).

Information

Quality information is an essential business resource (Hannula & Pirttimäki, 2005) providing the basis for business processes and decisions affecting all areas of the business model. Hannula and Pirttimäki (2005) categorize business information in terms of the:

○ Source of the information, whether the information comes from an external source (such as its suppliers) or whether the information is generated internally within the organization.

○ Subject of the information, whether the information refers to something external to the organization (such as the percentage share of the market the organization currently holds) or whether the information refers to something internal within the organization (such as the range of new products being developed).

○ Type of information, whether the information is quantitative (objectively measurable, such as physical measurements of bulb wattage) or qualitative (subjective, such as the aesthetic quality of a lighting design).

Scenario 1.3 shows how these categories can be used to map the current types of information in the organization and to identify further information needed to improve decision-making.

Scenario 1.3

Business Information Cube in Bright Spark

Bright Spark is reviewing its product portfolio. One of the manufacturers has increased its prices and Bright Spark needs to decide whether to keep stocking lampshades from this manufacturer. The information collected to help Larry Hughes make a decision has been categorized using the business information cube in Table 1.2.

Source of Information	Subject of Information	Type of Information	Information Collected
Internal	Internal	Quantitative	Selling price of lampshade to customers. Number of lampshades sold in the last six months.
Internal	Internal	Qualitative	The extent to which the lampshade complements or completes the product range offered to customers.
Internal	External	Quantitative	Number of competitors stocking the same product.
Internal	External	Qualitative	Need information about the anticipated demand for the product based on sales trends.
External	Internal	Quantitative	Not required.
External	Internal	Qualitative	Not required.
External	External	Quantitative	Purchase price of lampshade from manufacturer.
External	External	Qualitative	Need information about expected new products to be launched.

Table 1.2 ▶ Information Cube to Inform Product Portfolio Decision

Table 1.2 highlights some types of information that Bright Spark currently has and would like to have in order to inform the decision about whether to continue stocking a particular lampshade. This helps Bright Spark identify the information to be collected to help support the decision.

A further column could be added to Table 1.2 to distinguish between formal and informal sources of information. Formal sources of information include that derived from organized reporting structures, externally such as annual reports, and internally such as weekly sales meetings. Informal information is derived from unauthorized sources, externally such as salesmen from different organizations commenting on sales trends during lunch at a trade event; internally such as gossip shared between colleagues passing in the corridor.

1.2.8 ► Core Business

An organization may engage in a range of activities, offering a diverse portfolio of products and services in a number of markets. The core business focuses on the main type of business pursued by the organization and considers the organization's:

{purpose, strategy, core competencies}

Purpose

The core purpose of the organization can be considered to be a subset of the mission statement, the fundamental reason for the organization to exist. Over time an organization may diversify the product portfolio to meet customer needs in new markets, but the core of what the organization does provides the basis for the organizational strategy.

Johnson *et al.* (2008) suggest that the purpose of the organization has four main influences:

- Corporate governance: Who the organization aims to serve, how it provides the services, and who is the arbiter of these decisions.
- Stakeholders: Who the organization serves and the power they have to influence the purpose of the organization.
- Corporate social responsibility: Who the organization should serve directed by ethical concerns.
- Cultural context: Prioritization of who the organization serves driven by cultural values.

Information about the purpose of the organization needs to be clearly communicated to provide a focus for the implementation of the organizational strategy.

Strategy

Organizational strategy provides direction to the organization outlining how the organization seeks to engage in the core business to achieve the defined mission in different markets (Johnson *et al.*, 2008). The strategy provides the overall context, constraining and guiding all formal activity in the organization. The alignment of activities in the organization with the organizational strategy may be explicit, for example, through the use of balanced scorecards, or implicit in the actions and directions of business leaders. The information management strategy needs to be aligned with the organizational strategy to ensure information is available to use, and is used, to support the business processes and decisions needed to action the organization's strategy.

Core Competencies

Core competencies are situated at the centre of the business model, in the intersection of the organization, market, and business environment. An organization will have many skills that can be used to provide a range of products and services to the market. Core competencies focus on the skills, knowledge, and expertise at which the organization excels and which can be leveraged to provide a competitive advantage in the market against its competitors. Competencies may arise from (Johnson *et al.*, 2008):

- Cost efficiency, achieved through economies of scale, supply chain management, efficient processes, and experience.
- Value-added features of the product or service derived through expert staff, customer service processes, and timely communication of information. For example, the electrical expertise available in Bright Spark adds value to the sales process.
- Managing links between processes in the organization.
- Robustness of the competence, achieved through the organization's ownership of the competence and the degree to which the competence is difficult to transfer to other organizations.

Information needs to be managed to strengthen and support the core competencies of the organization.

1.2.9 ► Business Climate

The business climate is the wider environment that influences the organization but over which the organization has no direct control. Mullins (2010b) defines the organizational climate as the atmosphere in the organization, reflected in the morale of the community within the organization. Similarly, the business climate is the atmosphere within which the organization operates. The organizational climate is internal, while the business climate is external to the organization, customers, and suppliers. The business climate is shown outside the boundaries of the sets in Figure 1.1 and affects the organization, its customers in the market, and its competitors and suppliers in the business environment. The business climate includes factors relating to:

{legislation, economy, culture}

Legislation

All organizations are required to adhere to a range of legal policies that constrain activities in the organization, the market, and business environment. Legislation relates to the way in which employees are treated; the way in which products and services are created, marketed, and sold; and the environmental impact of the organization. Information is needed to ensure that business processes adhere to current legislation and that, where necessary, information is available to provide evidence of adherence to legislation. Where an organization trades in more than one country, adherence to the legislation of those countries is also necessary. As changes to legislation come into force, organizations need to capture information relating to the new legislation and adapt business processes as required by the legislation.

Economy

The economic system of the country or countries in which the organization trades can significantly impact the organization. Harbury and Lipsey (1993) identify the following features with which to examine an economy:

○ Resources: The availability of physical resources of an economy including land (minerals and energy sources), labour (size and distribution of the human population providing human resources), and capital (tangible assets such as factories and intangible assets such as human capital).

○ Production: The types of production in an economy such as: primary production (the harvesting of natural resources); secondary production (manufacturing and construction of finished goods); and tertiary production (services to support producers, such as finance, or to provide entertainment, such as hospitality).

○ Foreign trade: The balance of payments documents the payments made and received for imported and exported goods and services, and the earnings from investments. It is affected by exchange rate of currencies.

○ Economic growth: Employment indicators measure the production capacity of the economy. The gross national product (GNP) and gross domestic product (GDP) measure the output value of goods and services produced. GDP measures the output values within the boundary of the national economy and GNP includes the value of outputs in foreign countries. For example, the GNP would include Bright Spark's sales in South America but these sales would not be included in the GDP.

○ Money and banking: The outputs of the economy are affected by pricing. Inflation is the level with which prices are increasing. Interest rates indicate the cost of

borrowing money for organizations needing to invest in, for example, equipment.

○ Government: The degree to which governments directly or indirectly influence resource allocation through government expenditure and nationalization.

These economic indicators affect demand for the organization's products and services, and the costs incurred in producing them. Information about these indicators is needed in the organization to support strategic decisions.

Culture

The organization, market, and business environment operate within national and international cultures. Awareness of cultural differences is needed as organizations, such as Bright Spark, increasingly engage in international trade. Differences in cultural values and codes of behaviour need to be considered in terms of how a customer's perception of the product or service offered by the organization may be influenced. Cultural differences relating to, for instance, differences in conversational style between nationalities can affect the way in which trading takes place. An understanding of other cultures can help to appreciate the different views adopted within negotiations (Senior & Swailes, 2010), providing the context for information to be interpreted and to be given meaning. Information management needs to recognize the different ways in which information may be perceived, gathered, used, and interpreted within different national cultures.

Quiz 1.1
Business Model

Link 1.2
Checklist for Developing a Business Model

1.3 ▶ Morphing Organizations

Morphing is a verb meaning to gradually change from one image to another. Over time Bright Spark has morphed through a series of phases to change the face that it presents to its customers. A face is the surface image presented for external view. The face of an organization presents a surface image of the organization to be viewed externally. The face of Bright Spark has transformed from personal service provided at a counter, through to personal service provided via Internet technology. The organizational face covers the underlying structures and systems which maintain the image of the face, in the same way that a clock face covers the inner working of the oscillating wheel, gears, and springs that move the hands around the clock face. Beneath the face lies a network of interacting components that are continually adjusting in response to internal and external triggers in order to achieve the organization's objectives.

Peters and Waterman Jr. (2004) proposed that this network of components comprise dynamic interactions between the components of structure, strategy, systems (including formal and informal procedures), style of management, and culture, skills, staff (including morale, attitude, behaviour, training, and appraisal), and shared values. These internal components change in response to triggers from the external environment (such as the introduction of new legislation or the development of technology) or internal changes (such as the appointment of new managers). The interrelationships between components mean that a change in one component is likely to initiate a series of changes rippling through the organization. Changes to the underlying organization may be reflected in changes to the face of the organization. The morphing organization gradually changes its external image in response to adjustments in the relationships between its internal components while retaining key features which provide its identity.

DEFINITION: A **morphing organization** is an organization that gradually changes the external image it presents to the world while retaining its own identity.

The following sections examine the triggers driving organizational transformation, the phases of transformation, and the dimensions of the morphing organization that may be affected by transformation.

1.3.1 Triggers of Organizational Transformation

Organizational transformation can be triggered by internal or external information (Senior & Swailes, 2010). External triggers for change may come from the business climate, which is influenced by a range of factors, identified using PEST analysis (Johnson et al., 2008), also referred to as PESTEL analysis (Mullins, 2010b). The factors include:

○ Political: National and international priorities and policies can limit or facilitate trade, such as import quotas. Political triggers such as a government's decision to increase fuel duty may affect the ability of an organization to compete internationally (Senior & Swailes, 2010). This could lead to Bright Spark opening or closing stores to reduce transportation costs.

○ Economic: Financial indicators such as inflation, interest rates, currency rates, and unemployment affect the demand for the organization's products and the organization's ability to compete in the marketplace. For example, Bright Spark may be unable to compete on price in certain countries due to exchange rates so will need to change the basis of competition.

○ Sociocultural: Sociocultural triggers such as changes in demographics and standards of living will affect demand for particular types of products. For example, concerns for the environment increase demand for lighting products that are energy efficient and are manufactured from sustainable materials.

○ Technological: Speed, frequency, and uptake of development of new technologies relating to, for example, production techniques, materials, and IT trigger change in organizations. For example, the development of low-energy light bulbs has triggered changes in Bright Spark such as the need to source different light bulbs from new suppliers.

○ Environmental: Issues that affect the natural environment such as energy consumption and waste disposal may require the organization to change production processes.

○ Legal: Legislation such as employment law, health and safety regulations, and the data protection act trigger changes to business processes.

Senior and Swailes (2010) suggest that internal triggers for change include changes of: leadership, structure, strategy, power (of unions or departments), processes, and equipment. Information triggers change and the resulting transformation changes the future information needs of the organization as the architecture of the organization changes.

1.3.2 Stages of Organizational Transformation

Organizational transformation is essential for survival, enabling organizations to adapt to changes in the business environment and become realigned internally and externally (Bryson, 2011). Dixon et al. (2010) identify three stages in organizational transformation:

○ Break with the past: This involves introducing the need to change from the existing organizational architecture.

○ Exploitation and deployment: Developing the dynamic capabilities to redesign and reconfigure the organization to support organizational survival.

○ Exploration and innovation: Engaging in organizational learning, promoting creativity and innovation to create sustained competitive advantage in the longer term.

These stages operate in cycles as an organization continually adapts to survive in its changing environment.

The retailer Bright Spark has transformed through a number of morphing phases. Bright Spark started out as a small shop with a counter. A few products were displayed on the ceiling and behind the counter, but the main stock was held in a stockroom, which was only accessible to staff. Customers came into the shop and asked the sales assistant for the product they were looking for. The sales assistant listened to the needs of the customer and used her knowledge to identify the products that would meet the customer's requirements.

Phase 1: From Counter Service to Self-Service

Bright Spark moved the counter to the side of the shop and put more products on display in the shop. Customers were allowed to take items directly from the display shelves and take the items to a cashier to pay for them. Bright Spark moved from counter service to self-service.

Phase 2: From Self-Service to Internet Service

In 1998, Bright Spark recognized the opportunity offered by the Internet, which triggered the next phase of organizational transformation. Bright Spark created a website to use as a new marketing channel to encourage potential customers to visit the stores. A product catalogue was later added to the website, which increased the functionality of the website enabling customers to buy products online. The Internet provides Bright Spark with a virtual store that customers can access from any location where they can connect to the Internet. The main activities of selecting products, putting products into a basket, and paying for them at the checkout of the store are replicated online.

Phase 3: From Internet Service to Internet Collaboration

In phase 2 Bright Spark focused on the changes needed in the organization to replicate standardized business processes in an online trading environment. In phase 3, Bright Spark seeks to add greater value to the standardized processes by facilitating more engagement with customers and suppliers. From a customer perspective, this means a return to the more personalized service that Bright Spark provided through counter service in the original stores. Customers can enter into a dialogue with sales assistants online to discuss their needs and receive expert knowledge on the lighting options available. Bright Spark's suppliers can also discuss the development of new product ideas with Bright Spark and negotiate order quantities online.

The following section identifies the areas of Bright Spark that were affected at each phase of the organization's transformation.

1.4 ▶ Dimensions of Organizational Transformation

Cox *et al.* (2006) identify dimensions that can be used to analyse the way in which an organization transforms. The dimensions shown in Figure 1.2 are used in the following sections to discuss the internal changes that occurred within Bright Spark as it moved through transformations from: counter service to self-service; self-service to Internet service; Internet service to collaboration. The morphing dimensions illustrate how information is affected when organizations undergo such transformations.

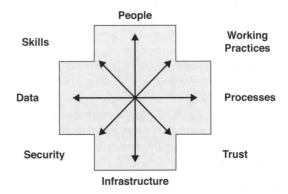

Figure 1.2 ▶ Morphing Dimensions

1.4.1 Transforming from Counter Service to Self-Service (Phase 1)

As Bright Spark moved from providing counter service to allowing customers to serve themselves, the *infrastructure* of the store was first changed by the introduction of new shelving units and checkouts. *Security* was affected as previously the sales counter acted as a physical barrier separating the customer from the stock held behind the counter and in the stockroom. Self-service required customers to be given direct access to the shelves where products were displayed. As customers took the products from the shelves, the price of each product had to be more clearly displayed so the *data* about products had to be changed. Self-service was a different way of shopping and the shopping *practices* were changed both for customers and staff. As customer service changed, the *processes* of sales, purchasing, and payment changed with more autonomy being given to the customer. Bright Spark had to *trust* customers; trust that customers would pay for the products taken from the shelves before leaving the store. This new way of shopping dramatically affected the *people* employed by the stores. The role of the sales assistant was redefined and the *skills* assistants needed changed. Previously sales assistants developed specialist knowledge of the products to help them advise customers of the different products available. Self-service reduced the personal interaction between customers and sales assistants, requiring sales assistants to have a broader but less specialized knowledge of products in the store. These changes are summarized in Figure 1.3.

approach to self-service. For organizations, *practices* such as order fulfilment have had to change considerably. Almost all back-office *processes* are affected by the introduction of Internet sales, including stock control, packing, distribution, and finance. As processes change, the *people* employed have had to adapt to online procedural working; the use of the Internet changed the skills that *people* needed. Internet service can be impersonal and the skills needed for online communication are different from those of sales assistant in a physical store. These changes are summarized in Figure 1.4.

People: Redefining roles and staff levels.

Skills: Less personal, wider scope, new equipment.

Practices: New way of shopping, change to service.

Data: Display pricing information.

Information systems

Processes: Sales, checkout.

Security: Access to shelves.

Trust: Organization trusts customers.

Infrastructure: New shelving, checkouts.

Figure 1.3 Organizational Transformation: Counter Service to Self-Service

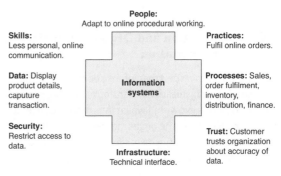

People: Adapt to online procedural working.

Skills: Less personal, online communication.

Practices: Fulfil online orders.

Data: Display product details, caputure transaction.

Information systems

Processes: Sales, order fulfilment, inventory, distribution, finance.

Security: Restrict access to data.

Trust: Customer trusts organization about accuracy of data.

Infrastructure: Technical interface.

Figure 1.4 Organizational Transformation: Self-Service to Internet Service

1.4.2 Transforming from Self-Service to Internet Service (Phase 2)

When Bright Spark sought to replicate the self-service shopping experience online, a technical *infrastructure* was developed providing a technical interface to interact with customers. The absence of direct physical contact with the products to be purchased meant that further consideration had to be given to the *data* that needed to be presented to the customer about the product for sale, and the terms and conditions of the purchasing transaction. Attention also had to be given to the *data* to be captured from the customer in making the purchase.

In stores, *security* focused on the products for sale. Online, *security* focuses on information, including information about transactions, with the aim to maintain security for customers. Previously, *trust* lay with Bright Spark that customers would not take products from the store without paying for the products. Online, *trust* lies with customers that the information provided by the online store is accurate (for example, if the website states that a product is in stock, the product really is in stock) and the transactions will be honoured as agreed (for example, that the correct product will be delivered on time). For the customer, the *practice* of shopping online adopts a similar

1.4.3 Transforming from Internet Service to Internet Collaboration (Phase 3)

Figure 1.5 summarizes the transformation from replicating self-service processes online to engaging in collaboration online with customers, suppliers, and business partners. Bright Spark uses a collaborative Internet-based system to place orders with its main supplier, Match Lighting. Collaborative systems require issues of computer system compatibility to be addressed to provide the *infrastructure* for the online communication. However, the *data* issues that need to be addressed are also extremely significant to ensure that data can be accessed and understood. The *data* issues relate to both technical compatibility and business semantics within the supply chain. While in Internet service *security* focuses on restricting access, in collaborative systems the emphasis is on facilitating authorized access to data. As organizations seek to share data, both parties have to *trust* that the data are accurate and will not be misused. Sharing data requires a change in *practices* to share the data and a change in *processes* to act on the data exchanged. Working with trading partners affects the *people* in both organizations who are required to work together, develop *skills* in online communication, and develop trusting relationships.

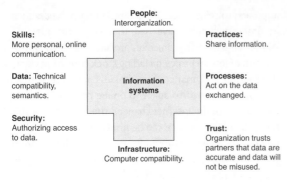

People:
Interorganization.

Skills:
More personal, online
communication.

Practices:
Share information.

Data: Technical
compatibility,
semantics.

Information
systems

Processes:
Act on the data
exchanged.

Security:
Authorizing access
to data.

Trust:
Organization trusts
partners that data are
accurate and data will
not be misused.

Infrastructure:
Computer compatibility.

Figure 1.5 Organizational Transformation: Internet Service to Collaboration

1.5 Information and Organizational Transformation

Earlier it was emphasized that information has meaning in context but as organizational transformation takes place, the business context within which information derives its meaning changes. As the organizational context changes, the organizational requirements for information and the challenges of managing information also change.

1.5.1 Information and the Business Model

The business model introduced in Section 1.2 provides a means of examining the business context (Figure 1.1). The model helps organizations to identify which elements stay the same and which need to change as the business context changes. For example, if an organization decided to trade in a new market, the subsets under the market set would change. The organization would have different competitors in the new market and additional information would be needed about the competitors, trading requirements, and customer expectations within the market. The core values of the organization (within the organization set) would need to remain unchanged to ensure that the organization's identity is maintained in the new market. The business model can therefore be used to identify the initial changes needed to the information required by the organization.

1.5.2 Information and the Dimensions of Organizational Transformation

The morphing dimensions illustrated in Figure 1.2 represent the components of an organization that may need to change in response to changes proposed in the business model. The morphing dimensions may initiate changes to the information needs of the organization. For example:

O Infrastructure: Changes to the geographical, organizational, or technological infrastructure may

require additional information or additional types of information to be captured. For example, opening a new store will require Bright Spark to capture information about the stock levels in the store. Bright Spark already captures information about stock levels in other stores, therefore the new store will increase the volume of information to be managed. If the new store is to operate in a different market, additional information will need to be captured about the customer preferences and trading restrictions in the new market. If changes are made to the organizational structure, the way in which information flows through the organization will also change. Changes to the technological infrastructure may require changes to the way in which information is captured, stored, and used in the organization.

O Security: Changes to the organizational infrastructure may introduce additional risks to the organizational resources. Information may be needed to monitor aspects of security, such as the unauthorized entry into buildings. The changes may introduce new physical or electronic threats to information security. For example, information may be at risk of loss during a theft in a store or at risk from unauthorized modification of an electronic file.

O Trust: Changes to the infrastructure or business processes may affect the nature of trust in the organization. For example, in online transactions customers trust that the information provided is correct. As unreliable information can quickly erode trust, the importance of accurate information becomes more important.

O Data: Changes to business processes may require additional data to be captured. Changes to the infrastructure may increase the points in the organization where data are captured. This increases the risk that data may be captured incorrectly or inconsistently, affecting the quality of the information in the organization.

O Processes: Business processes are initiated by information and involve the processing of information. Changes to the way the organization operates may therefore change the information required to initiate processes. Changes may also be required to the way in which information is processed or presented to support decisions taken in the organization.

O People: Changes to the staff required in the organization may require changes to the type and format of information. For example, the creation of a new post, such as area manager, will require information to be created about the sales and trends in a specific regional area. The appointment of a new person to an existing role may require the existing information to be presented in a different way. For example, some area managers may prefer graphical information about sales trends rather than detailed numerical information.

○ Skills: Information is needed about the skill base in the organization. Changes to business processes may require different skills to be acquired in the organization. Skills are also needed to manage information effectively in the organization. For example, changes to the technological infrastructure may require new technical skills to be developed.

○ Practices: As business processes, infrastructures, people, and skills change, the way in which organizational processes are conducted may change. Changes to business practices may require additional information to be available, or may change the requirements relating to when and where information is needed, or how the information is accessed and used.

These dimensions of change are discussed further within the organizational architecture.

1.6 ▸ Organizational Architecture

Architecture refers to the process and result of designing a structure which establishes boundaries for the suggested use of space (Gerstein, 1992). In designing a building architecture, the architect will consider, for example, purpose, aesthetics, light, materials, and land usage. In the same way that walls in a building delineate space for certain activities to take place (such as kitchen, bathroom, and bedroom), the architecture of an organization delineates space for business processes to take place (such as production, marketing, and stock control). While a building architect considers physical space, the organizational architect considers both physical and virtual space. Bright Spark has physical stores and warehouses, a virtual store to support Internet sales, and conceptual boundaries separating business functions. The organizational architecture creates behavioural space, which provides opportunities and constraints for action (Gerstein, 1992).

The business model provides the context for the organizational architecture and identifies the external stakeholders, which may provide opportunities and constraints for achieving the organization's vision. The organizational architecture is a holistic representation of the formal and informal elements of an organization and the interactions between them, shown in Figure 1.6.

The formal elements of the organization architecture include:

○ Strategy: The current direction being taken by the organization to achieve its desired position in defined markets.

○ Processes: The main activities required to transform resources to products and services offered by the organization.

○ Systems: The integration of business processes required to achieve the aims of the organization's strategy, including the information systems required to provide the information needed to support the business processes.

○ People: The job roles defined within the organizational structure.

○ Technology: The equipment required to undertake the business processes, including the IT required to support the implementation of information systems.

○ Security: The actions taken to minimize and detect risks to the organization's assets and resources

These formal elements are organized within the organizational infrastructure and operate within the organizational culture. For example, Bright Spark possesses a range of resources, including people, finance, stock, and equipment. The organizational structure groups resources together, in a meaningful way, to support the mission of the organization and defines hierarchical paths for communicating information. Data are needed about each of the elements in the formal structure and are needed to integrate the elements to support the performance of the organization.

Bright Spark needs to undertake a range of business processes to achieve the organization's mission. The business processes need to be planned and logically structured before being allocated to staff in the organizational structure. The organizational structure enables the processes to be coordinated and controlled. There is a difference between process and practice; process relates to defined routines of what should happen in the organization and practice refers to what actually happens in the organization, building on the knowledge and experience of the people involved. Business processes and working practices are situated within the organizational culture, influenced by history, management styles, and leadership styles. Business processes, practices, and the artefacts used within them are components of a human activity system (Engeström, 2001) where activity emerges within the situational context (Cox et al., 2006).

Beneath the formal organizational architecture are the informal elements of:

○ Vision: The future state which the organization aspires to achieve.

- Practices: The way that activities are performed to complete the business processes.
- Human activity systems: The integration of business practices performed by people in the organization, recognizing how the participants attribute meaning and purpose to the practices.
- Skills: The physical, cognitive, and interpersonal abilities needed in defined job roles to perform the business processes.
- Socio-technical: The interaction between people and technology in the organization during engagement in business practices.

- Trust: The degree of belief that the practices of the organization are conducted with honesty, fairness, and transparency.

The organizational architecture structures the interactions between these elements, providing the context within which information is interpreted and used in the organization. Different models can be used to analyse, represent, and communicate elements of the organizational architecture that constructs the behavioural space within which organizational activity takes place.

Saucer and Willcocks (2004) emphasize that defining the organizational architecture is not a one-off task (like designing a building); it is a continuous process of adjustment to meet the changing needs of the business environment. The organizational architecture provides the bounded space to facilitate and constrain business activity but does not define the business activity (in the same way that an architect may provide space with the recommendation that the space is used as a bedroom but the residents use the space as an office, games room, or storage room). Most organizational architectures have emerged from a series of transformations over a period of time. The organizational architecture provides the structure, shape, and form within which information is needed to inform and record business activity.

1.7 ▶ Scope of Information in Organizations

Information and the need for information management existed before the proliferation of IT in organizations, however, technology has created a new awareness of information management. Information is needed for an organization to make and communicate decisions, take action, and assess the effectiveness of actions. The information the organization needs can be generated internally within the organization or can be derived from external sources. The business model provides a structure within which to identify the key sources and subjects of information needed by the organization. The business model provides the organizational context for information management.

The context within which organizations operate is continually changing. Organizations need information about their external environment for two main reasons. First, organizations need information as feedback on performance to determine whether changes are needed in order to attain the organization's goals. Second, organizations need information on how the context in which they operate is changing in order to be able to respond to opportunities and threats. Information about changes

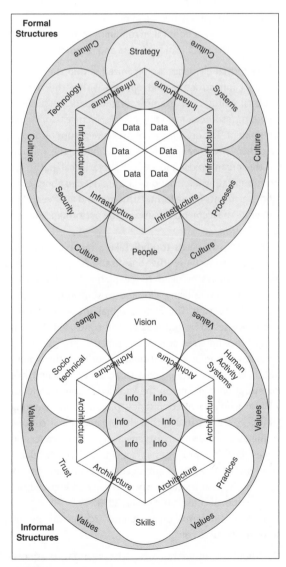

Figure 1.6 ▶ Organizational Architecture

in the external environment may trigger internal changes in the organization which may affect components of the formal structure (including strategy, processes, systems, security, technology, people, infrastructure, and culture) and informal structure (including vision, practices, human activity systems, socio-technical aspects, skills, architecture, and values). Changes to these components will change the information needed by the organization. Information management is needed to support the current information needs of the organization and to provide the flexibility to support future changes to the organization.

Summary

Data are strings of characters that have been captured in some way. Information is derived from an understanding of what the characters represent and the context in which the characters were collected. Information is needed to trigger business processes, record transactions, and inform decision-making at all levels in an organization.

The business model is a tool to analyse the context in which an organization trades. An organization needs to continually adapt to changes in the trading environment. Internal and external opportunities and pressures drive organizational transformation. A morphing organization changes the way it interacts with external parties. The organizational architecture comprises a series of interacting components in the formal and informal structures of the organization. Changes to the morphing organization require changes to be made to one or more components in the organizational architecture. The organizational architecture provides the context within which information is used in the organization. Changes to the organizational architecture therefore change the information needs of the organization.

Reviewing Scenario 1.1

How has the organizational context changed?

In its 50-year history, Bright Spark has evolved from one small shop to a chain of stores. It now also sells its products internationally using e-business systems. The changes to the context in which Bright Spark collects, uses, and manages information can be explored using the business model in Figure 1.1. For example:

○ Organization: The internal structure, geographic structure, processes, and culture of Bright Spark have changed as the organization has grown and moved into e-business.
○ Core business: The purpose of Bright Spark has remained the same and the core competencies are

embedded in the specialist knowledge of the staff. The strategy of the organization has evolved in response to fierce competition from major stores.
○ Resources: The range of skills and technology required by Bright Spark has increased over time. The opening of new stores has increased the volume of information that needs to be managed about Bright Spark's resources.
○ Products and services: The type of products sold by Bright Spark has remained the same, though the range of products has changed to reflect market trends.
○ Market: The Internet has provided an additional channel for Bright Spark to sell its products and opened up new markets for the organization. Information about the different needs and expectations of different customer groups needs to be regularly maintained.
○ Competition: As Bright Spark has moved into new international markets, the range of competitors it needs to be aware of has increased. This has required the organization to continually assess the basis on which it is able to compete.
○ Business Environment: Bright Spark remains a lighting specialist within the home furnishings industry. The retailer purchases lighting solutions from a number of manufacturers such as Match Lighting.
○ Business Climate: Bright Spark must keep up to date with relevant legislation relating to electrical lighting in the countries in which the retailer trades. Bright Spark must also monitor information on economic and social issues that may affect the organization. For example, a combination of factors, such as an increase in home design television programmes and a poor economic climate, has encouraged homeowners to update the lighting in their homes. Bright Spark has therefore seen an increase in sales of lamps and sculptural light fittings.

How has the organization changed and how has this affected the information the organization needs?

The dimensions shown in Figure 1.2 provide a structure within which to analyse the transformation that Bright Spark has experienced.

○ Infrastructure: The infrastructure of the organization has transformed at a number of levels including:
  • Geographically, through the opening of stores and warehouses.
  • Organizationally, in terms of the structure needed to monitor, control, and coordinate operations at multiple locations.

- Technologically, to manage information and communication across locations and to enable e-business processes.

The opening of new stores increases the volume of information to be managed in Bright Spark and changes the structures in which information is communicated. The introduction of e-business changes the way information is captured, communicated, and used.

○ Security: The physical security of products and resources has changed in response to advances in security technology (such as surveillance cameras and monitored alarms) and the demands of insurance companies (such as specification of locks). The security of information has evolved from the storage of paper records in one shop to electronic storage and transmission of information between stores and in e-business. The communication of information across a geographically dispersed organization and in e-business systems introduces risks relating to the loss or corruption of information.

○ Trust: The owner of Bright Spark initially trusted a small number of staff to provide expert knowledge to customers. Larry now has to trust staff in all stores in the chain to adopt and reflect the cultural values of the organization. Online customers have to trust that the information provided by Bright Spark is accurate and that the organization will deliver products as agreed. Customers also have to trust that Bright Spark will keep personal information secure and ensure that personal information is not misused.

○ Data: The volume of data in Bright Spark has increased as the opening of each store widens the business context within which the organization operates. This requires more data to be maintained relating to customers, sales, products, and employees. More information is also needed about competitors in different customer markets and international trading regulations. As the number of places where data are captured has increased, policies and controls are needed to ensure that data are entered accurately and consistently throughout the organization.

○ Processes: The growth of Bright Spark has led to the formalization of business processes to ensure that customers experience consistent levels of service through the chain of stores and to facilitate communication of information throughout the growing organization. The introduction of e-business requires information to be managed to integrate the processing of online transactions with existing business systems, enabling orders

and enquiries received via e-business systems to be actioned.

○ People: Bright Spark has sought to retain its key value of personalized service through the appointment of experienced staff. New roles, such as store and area managers, have been introduced into the organizational structure as the retailer has grown. Bright Spark is required to maintain information about staff it employs.

○ Skills: In the first shop, Bright Spark needed staff with sales and accounting skills. As the retailer has grown, it has needed a wider range of skills including, marketing, IT, and logistics. The organization manages information about the skills of its staff in order to assist in identifying any additional training requirements.

○ Practices: The fundamental working practice of selling lighting products to customers in the store has remained relatively unchanged. The main changes in the store relate to the actions and equipment used to capture information at the point of sale. However, the back-end processes relating to ordering, finance, stock control, and distribution have changed extensively through the formalization of processes needed to capture, store, and use information from across the chain of stores.

Exercise 1.1

1 List four reasons why information is needed in organizations.
2 What is meant by information paralysis?
3 Is IT necessary to manage information in an organization?
4 What two things are needed to add value to data and convert data into information?
5 What is the key question that the business model answers?
6 What is the purpose of the business model?
7 What is the role of the formal organizational structure in information management?
8 Identify the four roles of information in relation to business processes.
9 How do group norms affect the requirements for information?
10 What is a meant by a root metaphor?
11 Give two examples of features which may be used to categorize information about customers.
12 If an organization wanted to capture demographic information about its customers, give two examples of data that the organization would need to collect from customers.

13 What is strategic alliance?

14 What is the difference between a direct and indirect substitute?

15 What information is needed to calculate the depreciation of assets?

16 What information can be derived from the factors identified using PEST analysis?

17 List the areas that are analysed in morphing organizations.

18 What are the three categories of information in the business information cube?

19 Information is reported at the weekly staff meeting. Is this an example of formal or informal information? Why?

20 How does an organizational architecture differ from an organizational structure?

Link 1.3
Answers to Exercise 1.1

Activities 1.1

Apply the following steps to create a business model of Bright Spark.

1 Replace the following labels from Figure 1.1:
- Organization: What is the name of the organization?
- Market: What is the collective name for the field in which the organization's customers are located?
- Business Environment: What is the name of the industry in which the organization trades?

2 Prepare a list of:
- Products and services the organization offers to customers.
- Resources the organization needs to provide the products and services. Provide examples of sources of finance, equipment, skills, assets, and information.
- Competitors who provide the same or similar products and services to the organization's customers.

3 State the core business of the organization, that is, what is its main purpose?

4 Provide more information about the organization under the following headings: mission, internal structure, geographic structure, processes, culture, and history.

5 Identify the customers and consumers in the market.

6 Identify the following organizations in the business environment (where they exist): suppliers, strategic alliances, parent company, trade unions, and professional institutions.

7 Identify factors in the business climate in each of the following categories that may affect the organization: political, economic, legal, social, and technical.

8 Add the main information to the business model replacing the following labels with relevant information:
- Products and Services.
- Core Business.
- Resources.
- Competitors.
- Business Climate.

Discussion Questions 1.1

1 What are the possible motivations for a strategic alliance?

2 How important is the organization's culture in managing information?

3 Why is the source of information considered in information management?

4 What information will Bright Spark need to inform the decision of whether to open a store in Australia?

5 Why do organizations need to change?

6 How does organizational transformation affect information management?

7 Consider the analogy that information is the lifeblood of an organization. To what extent do you agree with this analogy? Can you suggest an alternative analogy?

8 How do the components in the formal structure of the organizational architecture relate to the components in the informal structure of the architecture?

2

ROLE OF INFORMATION SYSTEMS IN ORGANIZATIONS

Scenario 2.1

Information Needed in Amy's Candles

Amy has made candles for her family and friends for several years. After leaving university, she has decided to develop her hobby into a business. Amy knows that keeping accurate and up-to-date information in a business is very important, but *what information does she need to record? How should she record this information?* Amy has purchased a range of stationery, including ring binders and box files. She has labelled separate folders for customer orders, customer accounts, supplier orders, and delivery notes. One of her suppliers has sent her a letter to inform her that they are moving their premises later in the year.

Where should she file this information?
What other information does she need to keep? How should she organize the information?

Learning Outcomes

The learning outcomes of this chapter are to:

○ Examine the role of information in organizations.
○ Critically assess the value of information to organizations.
○ Define the information life cycle.
○ Apply appropriate models and concepts to demonstrate how information is acquired and used in organizations.
○ Describe the role of information architectures and information systems architectures in organizations.
○ Analyse the information flows into, out of, within, and between organizations.

Introduction

An organization can be regarded as a system that receives inputs from the environment, performs some processing, and produces outputs into the environment.

DEFINITION: A **system** is a collection of interrelated elements that interact to form a whole. An element of a system can be a system in its own right. A system can therefore comprise interrelated subsystems working together to meet the aims of the whole system.

The business model shown in Figure 2.1 represents an organization as a system. The circle around the organization represents the boundary of the organization, the boundary of the system. The organization receives information from, and sends information to, individuals and organizations outside the boundary of the organization. This includes information sent to and from the:

○ Market in which the organization competes, comprising customers, consumers, and competitors.
○ Business environment in which the organization trades, including its suppliers, business partners, relevant trade unions, professional associations, and industrial bodies.
○ Business climate in which the organization, market, and industry reside, incorporating local and national government, media organizations, and financial intuitions.

The value of information crossing the organizational boundary in the business model is first discussed in terms of the characteristics of information that influence the perceived value of the information exchanged. Information systems models are then presented to coordinate the

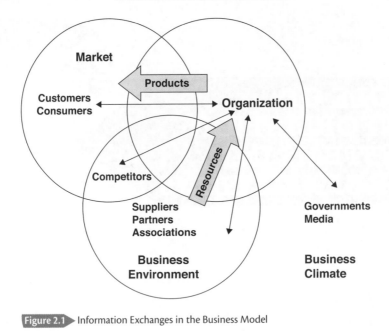

Figure 2.1 Information Exchanges in the Business Model

activities that support the flow of information in the business model throughout the information life cycle. The role of the information architecture in structuring the information that needs to be managed by information systems is explained. The chapter concludes by examining the relationship between information architecture and the information systems architecture in the organization.

2.1 Information and Information Systems

Information is a corporate resource incurring costs to acquire or create, store, retrieve, use, and share. The value of information to the organization relates to the perceived usefulness of the information to inform decisions and prompt appropriate and timely actions.

2.1.1 Business Value of Information

Information has a value but the value is subjective, dependent on the context and intended use of the information. The business value of information relates to who uses the information, when, for what purpose, and the expected outcome anticipated. Information has characteristics that can be defined and measured, which influence individual perceptions of the value of information. The characteristics include:

○ Timeliness: Information needs to be available when the information needs to be used. If information is not available when needed or arrives out of date, the

information is of little use. If information arrives too early, before the information is needed, it may be overlooked.

○ Frequency: Consideration needs to be given to how often information is presented and updated. Too often in organizations regular reports are created and not used because they are produced at arbitrary intervals without considering the time cycle of the activity. For example, weekly reports can convey little information to the recipient.

○ Appropriateness: Information needs to be relevant to meet the specific requirements of the task in which the information is to be used and of the individual performing the task.

○ Accuracy: The degree of accuracy needed in information depends on the purpose for which the information is to be used. Actions taken to increase the accuracy of information consume time and other resources; information needs to be sufficiently accurate to meet the requirements of the particular task.

○ Action: Information requiring action to be taken in response to information must be directed to the individual who can initiate the appropriate action. Information should include sufficient detail to enable appropriate and immediate action to be taken in response to the information received.

○ Understandability: If information is not understood by the recipients, the information is of no use to them. The style and format of information must be suitable for the recipients' technical knowledge, numeracy, and literacy skills, as well as being suitable for the required task.

○ Brevity: The level of detail included in the information must be appropriate for the specific task. Too much information may mean that vital facts can be overlooked.

○ Rarity: The degree to which information is unusual affects the importance of the information for a particular task. Information that reports anomalies may highlight problems or opportunities that require further investigation.

○ Presentation: The format of the information should reflect the needs of the recipient and the task for which they require the information. Natural language is ambiguous and it is necessary to consider how information may be interpreted and misinterpreted by the recipient. Information presented clearly and simply is often the more valued.

Increasing the quality characteristics of information incurs costs. Information needs to be fit for purpose but improving the quality of information does not necessarily increase the value of information. For example, striving for 100 per cent accuracy incurs additional time and costs, and this level of accuracy may not be needed. A sales manager needs to know that the value of an order is around £200 but the accountant needs to know that the value of the order is exactly £207.56.

It is important to provide the right amount of information at the right time, to an acceptable standard of quality in a format appropriate to meet the needs of the recipient (James, 2004). Information must be effectively communicated and reduce entropy (that is, uncertainty) to be consumed and inform decision-making. Information is consumed through processing, refinement, summation, and integration with other information in information systems.

2.1.2 Information System Processes

The organization needs processes to support the exchange of information in the business. Processes are needed to:

○ Capture information the organization receives from external parties and capture information the organization sends to others.

○ Store the information the organization has captured in such a way that the information can be easily retrieved and accessed by authorized personnel when the information is needed.

○ Use and generate information within the organization's functions to inform decision-making.

○ Share information with authorized personnel and departments in the organization and with approved third parties such as shareholders, business partners, and other stakeholders.

○ Maintain information to ensure that the information is complete, accurate, and up to date.

○ Secure information so that the information does not become lost, corrupted, irretrievable, or accessed by unauthorized personnel.

○ Archive historical information to preserve evidential records and organizational history.

○ Destroy information when the information is no longer needed.

These information processes are conducted by information systems.

DEFINITION: An **information system** is an interrelated collection of structured processes that are concerned with capturing, storing, retrieving, using, generating, sharing, maintaining, securing, archiving, and destroying information. An information system may include subsystems and may incorporate manual processes, computer-based processes, or a combination of manual and computer-based processes.

Figure 2.2 shows a system model for a customer information system; the boundary of the system separates the customer information system from its environment. Information input to the system crosses the boundary from the environment into the customer information system. For example, the request for customer details comes into the customer information system from the environment. A trigger comes from the environment to start the process to archive information. The trigger may be an event, such as the end of the financial year. Information generated from the customer information system is output from the information system into its environment. For example, the customer report is output from the customer information system into the environment. The system model is a dynamic model of some of the information needed in the organization.

The system model in Figure 2.2 shows the main systems processes in the customer information system and the flows of information between the systems processes but does not show how the processes are implemented. For example, the model shows that customer information needs to be stored; the model does not specify how or where the information is

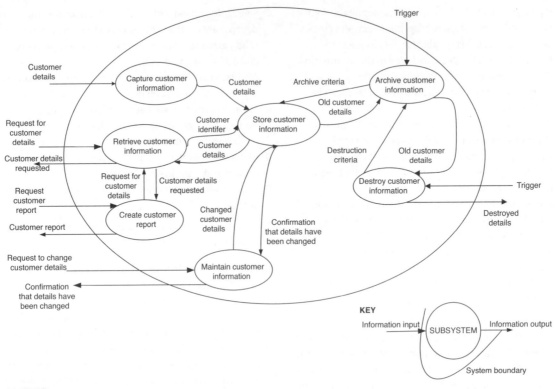

Figure 2.2 System Model for a Customer Information System

stored. The information might be stored on paper or might be stored electronically.

2.1.3 Subsystems of an Information System

An information system comprises subsystems; the systems processes in Figure 2.2 can be considered to be systems themselves. Figure 2.2 shows the main subsystems that are needed to manage customer information, such as *capture customer information*. A data flow diagram can be created for each subsystem, which shows the main flows of information in the customer information system and the flows between the customer information and other parties, such as customers.

Data flow diagrams are used in the development of information systems to identify the flow of information and processes needed to manage the information in the organization. The main subsystems in Figure 2.2 have been defined in more detail using data flow diagrams in Figure 2.3. For example, the subsystem *retrieve customer information* can be decomposed into processes to *receive*

the request, retrieve the information requested from where the information is stored, and *return the retrieved information* in response to the request. Figure 2.3b shows the boundary of the system *retrieve customer information*. The trigger for the system to start is when a member of staff initiates an enquiry and sends a request for information about a specific customer to the system. The system receives the enquiry, retrieves the required information from where the information is stored, and returns the required information to the member of staff. Breaking the subsystems into more detailed processes ensures that all steps required to manage customer information are identified.

Further processes need to be added to the data flow diagrams in Figure 2.3 to support data verification and to maintain an audit trail tracking the changes made to customer information. For example, in Figure 2.3b a verification process can be added so that when a request for information is received, a check is made to ensure that the person making the request is authorized to access the information requested.

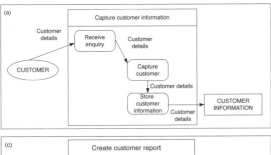

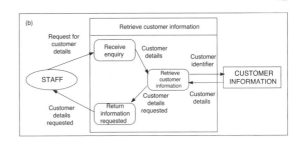

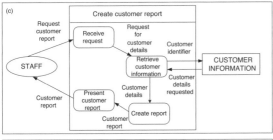

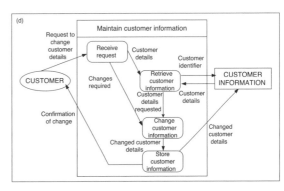

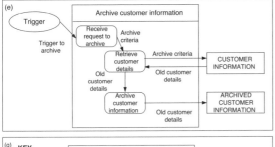

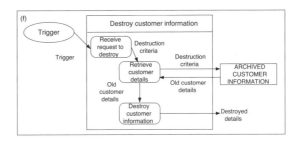

Figure 2.3 ▶ Data Flow Diagrams for a Customer Information System (a) Data Flow Diagram to Create Customer Information; (b) Data Flow Diagram to Retrieve Customer Information; (c) Data Flow Diagram to Create Customer Report; (d) Data Flow Diagram to Maintain Customer Information; (e) Data Flow Diagram to Archive Customer Information; (f) Data Flow Diagram to Destroy Customer Information; (g) Key to Notation Used in Data Flow Diagrams

2.2 ▶ Information Life Cycle

Information systems incorporate all the processes required to support information throughout the information life cycle. Life cycles are used to identify the events that happen to something during its existence, from when it first came into being, through to its final demise. All life cycles consist of three main stages: creation, existence, and termination. The initial stage considers the events and activities involved in the creation of the item being represented. The middle existence stage identifies the events that trigger change and development in the item,

and the final termination stage shows the events that initiate the end of the item's life. Examples of life cycles are shown in Figure 2.4.

Information starts life in an organization by either being captured from an external source or being created internally within the organization. During its lifetime, information will be retrieved from where it is stored, used, and maintained (changed and corrected). As the usefulness of information becomes reduced, information will be archived from regular use and eventually destroyed.

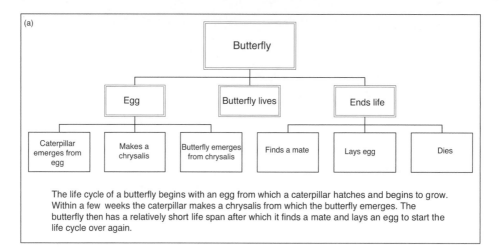

(a) The life cycle of a butterfly begins with an egg from which a caterpillar hatches and begins to grow. Within a few weeks the caterpillar makes a chrysalis from which the butterfly emerges. The butterfly then has a relatively short life span after which it finds a mate and lays an egg to start the life cycle over again.

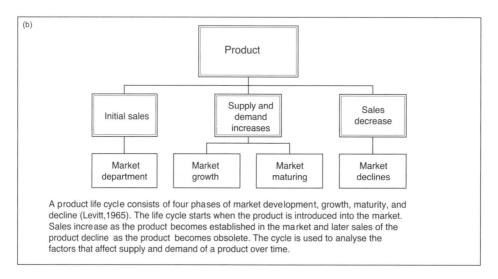

(b) A product life cycle consists of four phases of market development, growth, maturity, and decline (Levitt,1965). The life cycle starts when the product is introduced into the market. Sales increase as the product becomes established in the market and later sales of the product decline as the product becomes obsolete. The cycle is used to analyse the factors that affect supply and demand of a product over time.

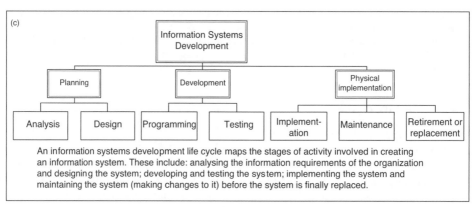

(c) An information systems development life cycle maps the stages of activity involved in creating an information system. These include: analysing the information requirements of the organization and designing the system; developing and testing the system; implementing the system and maintaining the system (making changes to it) before the system is finally replaced.

Figure 2.4 Examples of Life Cycles (a) Life Cycle of a Butterfly; (b) Life Cycle of a Product; (c) Life Cycle of Information Systems Development

DEFINITION: An **information life cycle** is a representation of the stages through which information passes during its life, from being created through to finally being destroyed.

The information life cycle shown in Figure 2.5 begins when information becomes first present in the organization. In contrast, Bryson (2011) suggests that as information is a resource, it has a life cycle similar to other resources, starting with planning the information needed and then progressing with acquisition, maintenance, exploitation, evaluation, and retirement of information. Although the names of the phases may differ, all life cycles focus on the main stages of activity that information experiences during its existence.

Organizations need to have processes in place to manage information throughout the information life cycle. The phases in the life cycle can be used as a checklist to develop information management policies to keep information secure (Bernard, 2007). Figure 2.6 shows a life cycle for customer information that can be used to ensure that processes are in place to manage customer information from its collection to its destruction. In Chapter 3 the role of information technology (IT) is considered in terms of how technology supports information through the information life cycle.

2.2.1 ▶ Life Cycle Assessment

Life cycles adopt the approach of from cradle to grave; however, the pressure to consider the environment and its resources has led to what McDonough and Braungart (2002) refer to as the concept of cradle to cradle. This reconceptualizes product disposal as product retirement (Ellis & Desouza, 2009), emphasizing recycling and reuse. Life cycle assessments consider the environmental impact of processes that take place during the existence of a product or service (Balkau & Sonnemann, 2010). Life cycle assessments include three stages (Vigon *et al.*, 1993): inventory (collecting facts such as quantity of raw materials used and levels of emissions), impact analysis (assessing the impact on the environment of the resource requirements and emissions identified), and improvement analysis (identifying the opportunities for reducing the environmental impact).

Within the context of information management life cycle assessment needs to consider three main areas. First, organizations need to have information available to assess the environmental impact of the organization's products and services. Second, organizations need to collect information to assess the sustainability of the processes used within the information life cycle. Third, organizations need to preserve the sustainability of information, ensuring the

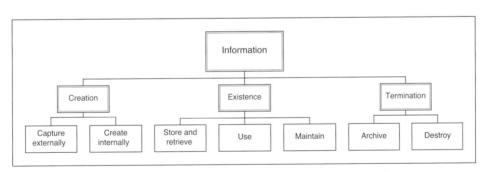

Figure 2.5 ▶ Generic Information Life Cycle

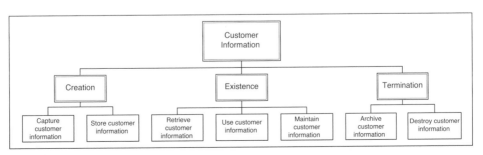

Figure 2.6 ▶ Customer Information Life Cycle

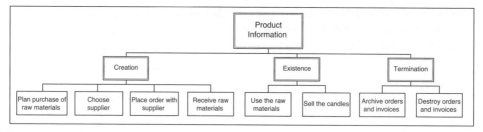

Figure 2.7 Product Information Life Cycle

long-term availability and preservation of information. This includes maintaining the climate for delicate historical documents and digital preservation to ensure that access to information can be maintained as IT continues to develop and older technologies become obsolete.

Life cycle assessment focuses on how information is used in the organization to support the life cycle of the business. This involves analysis of the chain of activities within the core business of the organization. For example, the product life cycle for Amy's business includes the stages of: plan purchase of raw materials, receive raw materials, make the candles, sell the candles (Figure 2.7). Life cycle assessment focuses on the business of the organization and does not consider the current organizational structure of functions and departments (Anonymous, 2006). The assessment moves away from the artificial boundaries imposed by organizational structures and adopts a holistic view of information in the organization, rather than a view of information that is segmented into the information used by individual departments.

2.2.2 Information Life Cycle Management

Information life cycle management identifies the value of information at each stage in the life cycle and develops actions to protect and manage information depending on its value (Tallon & Scannell, 2007). Life cycle management is based on the principle that, over time, the value of information and the frequency with which the information is accessed are reduced. For example, three days after information is created or captured the probability that the information will be used falls by 50 per cent (Moore, 2004). The stages in the information life cycle are explained in the following sections.

2.3 Capture Information

The information life cycle starts with the capture of information. Organizations need to capture information from three main sources: information received from outside the organization, information created within the

organization, and information sent from the organization to the external environment.

First, Amy needs to capture information from the following external areas that are outside the boundary of the organization:

○ The market: To identify whether the markets in which the organization competes are in a period of growth or decline, and to calculate the percentage of the market share that the organization holds. Information is captured from:
  ● Customers relating to enquiries, orders, and payments for products and services.
  ● Consumers who provide feedback about products and services.
  ● Competitors to identify details of current and proposed products and services that compete with those offered by the organization.
○ The business environment: To identify trends that may have a positive or negative effect on the organization from:
  ● Suppliers about equipment, raw materials, terms and conditions of delivery, and pricing.
  ● Business partners to form the basis for plans and collaborative agreements.
  ● Trade unions to develop and commit to agreements relating to, for example, pay and conditions of employment.
  ● Professional bodies about the codes of conduct and working practices in the domain(s) in which the organization operates.
○ The business climate: To identify trends and regulations that may have a positive or negative effect on the organization, its market, and business environment from:
  ● Local, national, and international government about current and proposed legal regulations to which the organization must adhere.
  ● Local, national and international media to identify consumer, cultural and business trends that may

affect the demand for products and services either positively or negatively.

- Financial institutions, such as the Bank of England in the United Kingdom, about financial trends, which may affect the availability of finance to the organization to fund investments, and the availability of disposable income enabling customers to purchase the organization's products and services.

Bryson (2011) suggests that information can be captured from an external source by demand, through unsolicited correspondence, by employing a person who has the information or through activities to collect and collate information. Examples of the information that an organization needs to capture are shown in Figure 2.8.

Second, Amy needs to capture information that is generated internally within the organization, such as details relating to manufacturing processes, sales figures, stock levels, staffing levels, and management reports, illustrated in Figure 2.9.

Third, Amy needs to capture information that is sent from her organization to external parties. For example, the organization will create and send information to:

- Customers about special offers, orders, and payments for products and services the customer has purchased, or may wish to purchase in the future, from the organization.
- Consumers to promote special offers and new products and services or to respond to a complaint.
- Suppliers about orders and payments for products and services the organization has purchased.
- Business partners with whom the organization collaborates.

- Trade unions to explain the organization's position relating to pay and conditions of employment.
- Professional bodies demonstrating the organization's compliance to the required standards of working practices.
- Local, national, and international government about how proposed legislation and taxation may affect the organization.
- Local, national, and international media to promote the organization's products and services.
- Financial institutions about investments.

Capturing information involves four main stages:

1 Identify the things – the *entities* – about which information is needed (for example, *customers, products, suppliers*).

2 Define the *attributes* of the entities, the details of the information needed about each thing (for example, *name of customer, address of customer*).

3 Create a structured format in which to capture the information (for example, *an order form*).

4 Develop a procedure for capturing the information (for example, *when a telephone call is received from a customer wishing to place an order, complete an order form and pass the form to the finance department and warehouse*).

These four stages are discussed in the following sections.

2.3.1 ▶ Identify Entities

An organization needs to capture information about its raw materials, products and services, assets, finances, business processes, staff, customers, suppliers, and investors. These are *entities* that need to be managed in the organization.

Figure 2.8 ▶ Capturing Information from External Sources

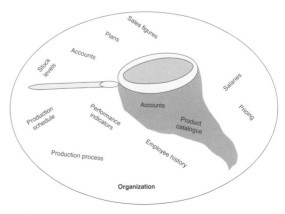

Figure 2.9 ▶ Capturing Information from Internal Sources

DEFINITION: An **entity** is something about which information is needed in the organization. An entity is represented using a singular noun.

Some of the information that an organization needs to capture can be identified from the business model. Table 2.1 identifies potential entities from the business model (Figure 2.1).

Organizations need to capture details of the products and services ordered by, and sold to, customers. In Scenario 2.1, Amy needs to capture details about the products she has available to sell to customers. Amy will need to capture information relating to her customers and about the manufacturing process she uses to create the candles. Amy will therefore need to capture information about entities such as *product, customer, manufacturing process, material*, and *product sale*.

Amy needs to capture information about the:

○ Candle materials coming into her business, where the materials are from, and the price she has paid.
○ Candles she has in stock ready to decorate and candles decorated that are ready to sell.
○ Candles sold, going out of her business, who bought them, and how much they paid.

As Amy's organization grows, the complexity of the information she needs to maintain will increase. In addition to this information needed by the primary processes directly involved in creating and selling the candles, Amy will need to maintain information needed by the support processes of her business. For example, Amy will need processes relating to the staff she employs; she will need to capture

information about their contract details, experience, holidays, absences, and salaries. Scenario 2.2 identifies some further information that Amy needs to capture in her business relating to the resources required to make her candles.

Scenario 2.2

Supplier Information Needed in Amy's Candles

Amy needs to buy a range of raw materials such as:

Wax, dyes, moulds, scents, wicks, and *wick pins.*

She buys paraffin wax from a number of different suppliers and needs to record the contact details for each supplier. This includes the supplier's:

Name, address, telephone number, fax number, website address, email address.

For each supplier she also needs to capture information such as:

Contact person: The name of the person she usually deals with and their direct contact details (for example, email address and mobile telephone number).

Payment method and payment terms: These are the payment arrangements Amy has agreed upon with the supplier. For example, some suppliers allow her up to 28 days to pay for stock while other suppliers demand cash on delivery.

Products stocked: The range of products, sizes, and colours stocked by each supplier, as some suppliers specialize in specific products. For example, Zadok Waxes supply wax but do not stock candle moulds.

Table 2.1 ▶ Information Areas Identified in the Business Model

Area in Business Model	Potential Entities
Organization: The organization itself.	{mission, internal structure, geographic structure, process, culture, history}
Products: The products or services produced as outputs from the organization to the market.	{product portfolio, service}
Core Business: The main type of business pursued by the organization.	{purpose, strategy, core competence}
Resources: The material taken as inputs from the business environment to allow the organization to engage in the core business.	{finance, people, technology, skill, raw material, asset, information}
Competition: The products and services against which the outputs of the organization must compete.	{competitor, direct substitute, indirect substitute}
Market: The target audience for the outputs of the organization.	{customer, consumer, channel}
Business Environment: The source of inputs to the organization over which the organization has some influence.	{industry, supplier, strategic alliance, parent organization, trade union, professional institution}
Business Climate: The wider environment which can influence the organization but over which the organization has no direct influence.	{legislation, economy, culture}

Delivery information: This will include details such as opening times, delivery arrangements, and the time taken to receive items once they have been ordered. For example, Zadok Waxes usually delivers orders within five working days, while Yumil National Supplies offer a same-day delivery service.

Other information: Amy also needs to note other information about suppliers, such as that Zadok Waxes provides good quality wax and Yumil National Supplies has delivered the wrong order on two occasions.

Amy will need to capture information about the raw materials that she has purchased from suppliers. The information will differ for each type of material. For example:

For dyes, Amy needs to know:

Type of dye, colour of dye, volume of dye, supplier of dye, quantity of dye purchased, quantity of dye in stock.

For candle moulds, Amy needs to know:

Type of mould, size of mould, number of candles that can be made in the mould at the same time, the supplier of the mould, the quantity of moulds she has purchased.

Information about suppliers and raw materials can be captured in different ways. Some suppliers will provide, or provide access to, a product catalogue that gives information about the range of products they sell. For example, Yumil National Supplies sends Amy a product catalogue twice a year. Delivery and pricing information may be included in the product catalogue, may be written into a trading agreement with major customers, or may only be available on request. Some information about raw materials purchased will be included on invoices or delivery notes provided by suppliers. Amy will need to capture information herself about the level of stock of raw materials she has available to use.

Organizations need to identify the entities that need to be captured and managed. Each entity must be defined by a short description so that everyone in the organization understands what is meant by the name of the entity. For example, the entity named *supplier* may be defined as:

Supplier Definition 1	An organization that stocks raw materials that may be used in the making of candles.

The *supplier* entity could be defined in other ways, for example:

Supplier Definition 2	An organization from which Amy has previously purchased raw materials.
Supplier Definition 3	An individual or organization that sells materials, which might be purchased in the future.

These alternative definitions reflect the business rules in an organization that determine when information is captured. In definition 1, information about a potential supplier is captured when an organization is identified that sells materials from which Amy may purchase in the future. In definition 2, information about a supplier is only captured when Amy has purchased materials from the supplier. Definition 3 recognizes that Amy may also purchase from private individuals as well as organizations. As Amy will use the information about suppliers, she needs to define how the entity is defined in her organization.

2.3.2 ▶ Define Attributes

When the organization has identified the entities about which it needs to capture information, the *attributes* of each entity have to be defined.

DEFINITION: An **attribute** describes an aspect, a characteristic of the entity, providing more information about the entity.

For the entity *supplier*, attributes may include:

Supplier name.
Supplier address.
Supplier telephone number.
Supplier fax number.
Supplier website address.
Supplier email address.
Supplier sales contact name.
Organization's account number.
Payment terms.

Each of the attributes identified has to be defined; this includes a brief description of the attributes shown in Table 2.2.

Each attribute is further defined in terms of its:

○ Length: The maximum number of characters needed to capture the attribute.
○ Type: The range of alphabetical, numerical, and special characters that may be used in the attribute.
○ Structure: The arrangement of alphabetical, numerical, and special characters that may be used in the attribute.

Table 2.2 Attribute Definitions for the Entity Supplier

Attribute Name	Attribute Definition
Supplier Name	The name of the organization supplying resources.
Supplier Address	The postal address of the organization from where resources may be sourced.
Supplier Telephone Number	The telephone number of the main switchboard for the supplier.
Supplier Fax Number	The number to be used to send faxes to the supplier.
Supplier Website Address	The uniform resource location (URL) of the website for the supplier.
Supplier Email Address	The main address to send emails to the supplier.
Supplier Sales Contact Name	The name of the person who the organization usually contacts to place an order or raise a query.
Organization's Account Number	The customer number of the organization issued by the supplier.
Payment Terms	The agreement of when and how payment should be made to the supplier.

For example, a *supplier email address* may be defined as being:

O Length: Maximum of 32 characters.
O Type: A mix of alphabetical, numerical, and special characters.
O Structure: The special character @ is required within the address.

2.3.3 Create a Structured Format to Capture Information

A structured format needs to be created to capture the entities and attributes defined by the organization. Paper-based or computerized forms provide a structured format in which to capture information. A form ensures that the same information is collected each time, in the same way, and in the same level of detail. The form also ensures that all the required information is captured. Figure 2.10 provides an example of a paper-based form from a supplier directory, which Amy uses to capture information about suppliers. When Amy identifies an organization that sells materials that she might wish to purchase in the future, she captures the information about the supplier by completing the form. The form captures the attributes of the *supplier* entity.

The attribute definition provides the specification of the form, identifying the information to the captured. If additional attributes were defined, such as *town, county, post code,* and *country,* the supplier's address could be captured in separate fields on the form. This would encourage the full details of the supplier address to be captured by the person completing the form.

The attribute length specifies the space required to capture the information, for example, how much space does Amy need to write the name of the supplier? If Amy

Figure 2.10 Form to Capture Supplier Information

defined the attribute *supplier name* to be 12 characters long this would be fine for the supplier *Zadok Waxes* as the name is 11 characters long (a space between words is counted as a character).

Z	A	D	O	K		W	A	X	E	S	
1	2	3	4	5	6	7	8	9	10	11	12

However, the supplier name *Yumil National Supplies* is 23 characters long so only the first 12 characters of the supplier's name could be captured.

Y	U	M	I	L		N	A	T	I	O	N
1	2	3	4	5	6	7	8	9	10	11	12

The attribute type and attribute structure provide further detail about the information to be captured. The attribute type and attribute structure can be used in computerized information systems to provide validation checks on the information captured. For example, a validation check could test whether a *supplier email address* entered into a system includes the required special character. Validation checks help to improve the quality of information captured in the organization but care is needed when defining attributes. For example, the attribute *supplier telephone number* could be defined as comprising a maximum of 12 digits. Implementing this definition would prevent people from entering letters into a telephone number in error. However, the definition would also prevent international codes being entered as, for example, +44, because + is not a numerical character. Figure 2.11 defines the length and type of the attributes for a computer-based form to capture information about suppliers. X is used to indicate an alphanumeric character and 9 is used to indicate a numerical character. The organization's account number is defined as 9(10); this means that the account number can comprise a maximum of 10 numerical characters.

Structured forms can be annoying and inflexible to complete. For example, Amy's supplier details form allows her to capture one contact name and one telephone number for each supplier. Mrs Brown, a secretary at Zadok Waxes, informs Amy that the person she usually deals with will be unavailable for a few months. Mrs Brown provides Amy with the name of the person Amy should contact in the short term. Amy should capture this information; however, the form only allows for one contact name to be captured. A range of situations, which could occur in the future, needs to be considered when designing a form. Situations will inevitably arise that were not foreseen, therefore procedures need to be developed to ensure that information can always be captured.

2.3.4 ▶ Develop Procedures to Capture Information

Organizations need to have procedures in place to capture the information that the organization needs. Information should be captured as close to the source of the information as possible to ensure the accuracy and completeness of the information (Bryson, 2011). After creating a form to capture information about suppliers, a procedure needs to be developed to ensure that the form is completed to capture the information about each new supplier. The definition of the entity *supplier* encapsulates the business rules that determine the procedure of when

---

Supplier Details

Supplier Name: X(20)   Account Number: 9(10)

Address: X(20)

Town: X(20)   Contact Name: X(20)

County: X(20)   Telephone Number: 9(12)

Post Code: X(8)

Country: X(10)   Fax Number: 9(12)

Website: X(30)

Email Address: X(45)

Payment Terms: X(50)

                  X(50)

                  X(50)

                  X(50)

                  X(50)

Figure 2.11 ▶ Attribute Types to Capture Supplier Information

to capture information. An example procedure for capturing supplier information is:

> When a new supplier of candle-making resources is found, complete a supplier details form to capture information about the supplier.

Additional procedures relating to suppliers may include:

> Request a new product catalogue from each supplier at the start of the financial year.
>
> Update payment terms when a new agreement is confirmed.
>
> When a sales contact leaves, change the contact name and telephone number in the supplier directory.

Procedures also need to be defined to ensure that the information captured is accurate and complete.

2.4 ▶ Store and Retrieve Information

When information has been captured it needs to be stored in such a way that the information can easily be located and retrieved when needed. Information comes into Amy's organization in many ways: for example, Amy receives a telephone call from a customer who wishes to order her candles; a printed delivery note accompanies a parcel of dyes sent by Zadok Waxes; Amy receives an email from a potential customer enquiring about whether Amy could produce a specific design for an event. Information goes out of Amy's organization in many ways too. Amy must store copies of the information she receives from outside the organization, the information she creates within her business processes, and the information she sends to others.

Information has to be stored as it comes into the organization. When Amy receives a telephone call from a customer wishing to purchase her candles, Amy needs to capture details about the customer and the order, and then store the details so that at a later date she can retrieve the information and process the order. Despite advances in technology and the promise of the paperless office, all organizations have to develop procedures for storing and retrieving paper documents. Some organizations scan paper documents to create an electronic copy of the documents but the paper documents then have to be stored, archived, and later destroyed. Paper documents can be stored in files in filing cabinets but the key concern is how to find the document when the information is needed. Information needs to be indexed so that information can be retrieved easily, whether the information is stored electronically or on paper.

Storing information involves three steps discussed in the following sections:

1. Define categories to index information.
2. Develop procedures to store information.
3. Develop procedures to retrieve information.

2.4.1 ▶ Define Categories to Index Information

Most items of information can be categorized and indexed in a number of ways. For example, all orders sent to suppliers could be stored in one file; alternatively, separate files could be created for orders for which materials have been received and for orders that have not yet been received; or a separate file could be created to store all supplier orders created each year. Within each file, orders could be arranged by any of the attributes of a supplier order, such as by the name of the supplier, the date the order was placed, the date the order is due to be delivered, whether the status of the order is open (the materials ordered have not yet been received) or completed (the materials ordered have been delivered). How information is categorized and indexed depends on how the information is to be retrieved. For example, if Amy wants to check on the status of an order she has sent to a supplier, will Amy find the information by searching through two files of orders (open and completed)? or by searching through orders sequenced by supplier name? or by the date the order was placed? What would happen if Amy could not remember the date that she placed the order?

Entities identify the main groupings of information that need to be captured and stored in the organization such as suppliers, customers, orders, and products. Further analysis is needed to determine the most effective way of organizing the information to meet the specific needs of the organization. Factors to take into consideration include:

> Who is likely to need the information? Where are they located? In one case, analysis of the steps taken by staff to respond to a query received via a telephone helpline in an organization highlighted problems with information access. Staff had to: write down the details of the query, leave their desk and walk to an area in the centre of the office to access the required information, write down the information required, and then return to their desk to convey the information to the caller (Ackerman & Halverson, 2000). It is therefore important to analyse the structures and working practices of an organization to ensure that information is easily accessible to the person who needs the information, when and where they need the information.

How may someone search for the information? An order may be allocated a unique order number to track the order within the organization. However, procedures need to be in place to ensure that the order can still be retrieved in instances where the number of the order is unknown.

How much information is there to search through? The volume of information needs to be considered. If Amy sends 12 orders a month to suppliers, she could search through each order to find a specific order. However, if Amy sends 100 orders to suppliers every month, it would not be practical for her to search through each order individually; an alternative way of searching for an order would be needed.

Amy could create three categories for supplier orders: *current supplier orders* (orders she has sent and she is waiting for the order to be delivered); *completed supplier orders* (orders for which she has received the materials ordered); *archived supplier orders* (orders for which she received the materials ordered over 12 months ago). Amy could index these categories alphabetically by name of supplier or chronologically by the date the order was placed with the supplier.

IT provides greater flexibility for searching, retrieving, and accessing electronic information but thought still has to be given to how information should be stored and retrieved in order to optimize searches.

DEFINITION: Optimization refers to improving the efficiency with which the required information is located and retrieved. The way in which information is organized affects the volume of information to be searched in order to locate a specific item of information.

2.4.2 ▶ Develop Procedures to Store Information

When an organization has defined categories to index the information captured, a system of procedures must be developed to store the captured information. This involves creating procedures for filing information in the correct place. For example, when Amy sends an order to a supplier, she must correctly file the order in the *current supplier orders* folder, which is sequenced alphabetically by supplier name. Storing information in the wrong place is the easiest way to lose information and can incur huge amounts of wasted time and effort in searching for the lost information. Establishing detailed procedures for indexing and storing information takes time but is an investment in managing information effectively. If information is important to an organization, detailed procedures are needed to ensure that the information can be stored and retrieved when needed. If information cannot be located and retrieved when the information is needed then the information has no value to the organization.

Procedures to store information need to consider both the short-term and the long-term requirements of the organization. Short-term procedures may be that:

a. After an order is sent to a supplier, place the order in the *current supplier orders* folder, which is indexed by supplier name.

b. When the order is completed, take the order out of the *current supplier orders* folder and place the order in the *completed supplier orders* folder, which is indexed by supplier name.

Over a period of time, the completed supplier orders folder may become very full. Long-term procedures are needed to manage information to ensure that the information can still be retrieved when needed. This may include:

c. At the end of the financial year, create a new *completed supplier orders* folder.

d. Move the previous year's *completed supplier orders* folder to the basement in an *archived supplier orders* file.

2.4.3 ▶ Develop Procedures to Retrieve Information

Storing information is a waste of time unless the information can be easily retrieved when needed. Staff need to know where to find information when they need it. This requires indexing systems to be visible and intuitive; locating information where the information is needed and ensuring that the index is logically and clearly labelled. Table 2.5 presents an extract from an information map showing where Amy can find information.

DEFINITION: An **information map** can be created to help staff in an organization locate the information they need. An information map shows the electronic and paper-based information stored in the organization, and indicates where the information can be found.

When the location of the information is identified from the information map, the information can be retrieved. Information retrieval includes the following elements (Manning *et al.*, 2008):

○ Information need: The subject about which a person is seeking information (for example, supplier).

○ Query: The statement posed by a person to convey the information they are seeking (for example, find the address of supplier where the name of the supplier is Yumil).

○ Relevance: The degree to which a person perceives that the information retrieved satisfies their information need.

○ Effectiveness: The degree to which the query resulted in the retrieval of relevant information. This is measured by precision (the number of results returned in response to the search query that are relevant to the person's needs) and recall (the number of documents returned in response to the search query in relation to the total number of relevant documents held by the system).

Procedures for retrieving information require an understanding of the information available and the location of the information (shown on the information map). An understanding is also needed of how the information is categorized and indexed in order to structure queries to retrieve the required information.

Particular consideration needs to be given to confidential information to ensure that the information is stored in an appropriate way to avoid the information being retrieved by unauthorized personnel. Access to information can be restricted so that the information is only accessible to certain staff grades in the organization or via security controls, such as passwords, to ensure that the information is only accessible to authorized personnel.

2.5 ▸ Use, Generate, and Share Information

Information is generated by business processes, used as the basis for decision-making, input into business processes, shared with staff within the organization, and shared with approved external parties. Traditionally organizations are considered to comprise three broad levels of activity that have different information needs: strategic level, tactical level, and operational level.

The strategic level of the organization is the highest level of the organization, focusing on the long-term direction and survival of the organization. This level involves:

○ Formulating the mission statement and strategic objectives for the organization. Amy's mission statement might say that:

'Amy's Candles creates high-quality bespoke candles and wax sculptures for individuals and small businesses. We specialize in intricate designs and offer a range of styles for every budget. We work closely with customers to produce handmade candles to your personal design. We also provide a service to create a unique design especially for you'.

The organization's objectives are to:

1. Develop at least eight designs within three budget categories of under £5, under £30, and over £30.

2. Accrue 60 per cent of income from the custom-design service.

○ Quarterly organization and management control to coordinate the activities required to achieve the strategic objectives. This could include planning a marketing campaign to increase revenue from the custom-design service.

○ Long-term planning to organize resources, including staff, materials, money, and information in order to achieve organizational objectives. This may include negotiating contracts with suppliers of raw materials and developing collaboration with manufacturers to design bespoke wax moulds.

These strategic activities require summarized information captured at lower levels in the organization. At the strategic level, Amy needs to know that orders this year for custom-designed products totaled £1,250.

The tactical level of the organization lies between the operational and strategic levels. It focuses on implementing the strategic plans and involves:

○ Formulating medium-term plans to ensure that the organization meets the strategic objectives. This may include planning and implementing the detailed activities for the marketing campaign needed to increase revenue from the custom-design range in order to meet the organization's strategic objective.

○ Monthly organization and management control to coordinate the activities required to process the transactions and implement plans. This may include reviewing the reliability and quality of materials purchased from suppliers and monitoring finances.

○ Medium-term planning to organize resources, including staff, materials, money, and information in order to process transactions and implement plans. This may include ensuring that resources are in place to process the additional orders anticipated from the planned marketing campaign.

Tactical activities require less detailed information than activities at the operational level but require more detailed information than activities at the strategic level. For example, at the tactical level it is important to have the information that the total value of sales in June was £2,400 and that custom designs accounted for 30 per cent of the total sales.

The operational level of the organization focuses on the main core business of the organization and involves:

○ Processing the transactions between the organization and its customers, and between the organization and its suppliers. This includes receiving supplies ordered from Zadok Waxes, sending payment for supplies received, receiving orders from customers, making candles, sending the candles to customers, and taking payment for customer orders.

○ Daily organization and management control to coordinate the activities required to process transactions. This may include checking that customers have paid for their orders and planning the type of candles to make based on the number of customer orders received and the range of materials in stock.

○ Short-term planning to organize resources, which may include ordering materials from suppliers and scheduling staff workloads.

Operational activities require very accurate and detailed information. For example, on 1 June the Cute Cats Rescue Centre ordered 50 white 12 cm pillar candles. The value of the order was £159.90. The candles are created using mould number C12, with the Cat in Basket Design number CB836. The order is to be collected on 28 June for a fund raising event on 30 June. Amy uses this detailed information to plan the materials she needs to order and the candles she needs to make.

The activities of an organization consist of a series of transactions; information provides a permanent record of each transaction. Each level of activity uses and generates information that is shared between the levels in the organizational hierarchy and shared across business functions. The operational level of the organization uses information about customers, orders, available materials, and manufacturing instructions to decide what type, design, and quantity of candle to make on a specific day. In processing a customer's order, information is generated about the candles made, resources used, and costs incurred. This information is shared with the customer, informing them that their order has been completed and requesting payment. The information is shared with the tactical level of the organization to report the quantity and value of items created, and resources used each month.

The tactical level of the organization uses the information generated by the operational level to determine whether the strategic-level objectives have been met. The tactical level generates detailed plans to improve the organization's performance, which are shared with the operational level to be implemented. The tactical level generates information about the performance of the organization, which is shared with the strategic level of the organization.

The strategic level of the organization uses the information generated by the tactical level to determine whether the strategic objectives have been met, and if not decide what action should be taken. The strategic level also uses information captured from external sources, such as financial markets, suppliers, and competitors, to make decisions about the direction of the organization. For example, if a supplier has developed a new type of wax mould or if a competitor is reducing their prices, the strategic level will generate information in the form of plans to share with the tactical level in response to the information received (for example, develop a design to trial the new mould or review pricing). As well as sharing information internally, organizations have to share information with external parties, such as finance information with banks, product information with customers and the media, and product design requirements with suppliers.

2.6 ▶ Maintain, Archive, and Destroy Information

After information has been captured and stored, the information needs to be maintained to ensure that it is kept up to date. Changes within the organization may require additional information to be captured or created. Procedures need to be developed to:

1 Identify when information changes.
2 Preserve an audit trail.
3 Update information.
4 Archive information.
5 Retrieve archived information.
6 Destroy information.

These activities are discussed in the following sections.

2.6.1 ▶ Identify When Information Changes

Chapter 1 discussed a number of dimensions of organizational change. As organizations change, the requirements for information in the organization change. This may mean that additional entities are identified about which information needs to be captured and stored, or additional attributes may be identified that need to be captured or created for existing entities.

Over time the data value of the attributes of entities are likely to change. For example, a customer may change their address, suppliers may change the price of materials, and the organization may change the products available for sale. Information needs to be correct to be of value. Organizations therefore need to recognize when information needs to be changed. A supplier may report that they have moved premises or a customer may report that the information on an invoice is incorrect. When these events occur, staff in the organization need to know what needs to be done to correct the information. A procedure is needed to change information that identifies:

○ How the information has changed?
○ Who in the organization has changed the information?
○ Any additional information needed to confirm changes to the information. For example, if a customer is changing their name legal documentation may be required to verify the information.

2.6.2 Preserve an Audit Trail

A record of the changes made to information needs to be kept because information may have been changed when the information should not have been changed, either by mistake or through a malicious act. For example, a disgruntled employee might seek to embezzle money from customer accounts. An audit trail provides historical documentation of events that can be reviewed when problems arise. This is illustrated in Scenario 2.3.

2.6.3 Update Information

In Scenario 2.3 Jyoti neglected to inform Amy that her order had been cancelled. When modifying information it is important to consider who will be affected by the change and ensure that they are aware that the change has taken place. However, sometimes changes to information have wider implications and more people need to be notified. For example, when Zadok Waxes reduces prices by 20 per cent in a sale, the price attributes of all products need to be temporarily changed. Customers, sales staff, and finance staff, among others, then need to be notified of this price change.

2.6.4 Archive Information

The volume of information an organization captures, creates, and stores grows at an alarming rate. Although computer-based systems enable vast volumes of information to be stored and retrieved relatively easily, storage of information incurs costs. As the volume of information stored increases, the time taken to retrieve the information also increases. Information systems should only contain the information needed for day-to-day business to minimize the time taken to retrieve information. Information should be regularly reviewed to determine whether the information is needed on a regular basis, or whether the

Scenario 2.3

Audit Trail for Orders Placed by Amy's Candles

Amy placed an order for 20 kg of dip-and-carve wax from Xena's Craft Supplies but Amy did not receive the wax. Amy checked her files, which confirmed that she placed order number EM52855 on 4 April for wax to be delivered on 8 April. Amy telephoned Xena's Craft Supplies and spoke to Gil to find out why she had not received the order. Gil retrieved the information about order number EM52855. Gil explained to Amy that the order was placed on 4 April but then the order was cancelled on 5 April. Amy explained that she did not cancel the order and that she did not know the order had been cancelled. Gil checked the audit trail which provides a history of the order EM52855 shown in Table 2.3.

The audit trail showed who cancelled the order, when and why; Jyoti cancelled the order on 5 April because the wax was out of stock.

Date	Time	Event	Staff	Comment
4 April 2013	12:58	Order created	Farooq	
4 April 2013	13:03	Payment authorized	Farooq	
4 April 2013	13:05	Order approved	Farooq	
5 April 2013	09:22	Order cancelled	Jyoti	Dip-and-carve wax out of stock.

Table 2.3 Audit Trail of Order

information is still needed at all. This means reviewing the currency of information and deciding what information is no longer required. The decision then needs to be taken whether the information can be destroyed or archived. This will depend on both organizational requirements and legislation. Organizations such as the Inland Revenue in the United Kingdom require organizations to keep certain information for specific periods of time. For example, the current requirement of HM Revenue and Customs is for financial records to be kept for a minimum of five years from the end of the submission deadline when a tax claim has been submitted. Although information must be kept, information does not have to be kept with current information. For example, Amy may decide that orders for a 12-month period must be stored in such a way that she can retrieve them quickly, while orders which are more than 12 months old may be archived.

Archived orders can still be retrieved, but cannot be retrieved as quickly as current orders as archived information may be stored in an off-site location or may be stored on different electronic media. However, archived information should be stored in the same way that current information is stored (Ashley & Ashley, 2007). This is because information is archived rather than destroyed because the information may need to be restored (that is, retrieved for use) at some time in the future. Particular care is needed when archiving confidential information to ensure that confidentiality is maintained both when the information is archived and when the archived information is accessed to be used or to be destroyed.

2.6.5 ▶ Retrieve Archived Information

The information map for the organization shows what information is archived, where the information is archived, and how the information can be accessed when needed. This is particularly important when archived information is stored at different locations. If an organization receives a request for information that has been archived, staff need to:

○ Check whether the information is available or whether the information has been destroyed.
○ Check that the person requesting the information is authorized to use the archived information.
○ Locate the information from the archive.
○ Retrieve the information from the archive and, if necessary, restore the information into a computer system to enable the information to be accessed. This can be problematic if computer-based systems have changed since the information was archived.

○ Document the request to retrieve archived information in the audit trail.
○ Return the information to the archive and update the audit trail.

2.6.6 ▶ Destroy Information

Information must have a defined retention period otherwise information is kept forever, incurring unnecessary storage costs, hindering access to other information, and contributing to information overload.

DEFINITION: A **retention period** defines how long information needs to be stored before the information can be destroyed.

When information is no longer needed and legislation permits, information can be purged (that is, destroyed). Care is needed to ensure that confidential information is destroyed in an appropriate manner. This typically involves shredding documents that contain confidential information. A record of information destroyed should also be maintained to avoid searching for information that is no longer available. Organizations need clear procedures relating to what information can be purged, when, how, and by whom. The destruction of information is the final stage in the information life cycle.

2.7 ▶ Information Architecture and Information Systems Architecture

Organizations need both a static and a dynamic view of information. The information architecture provides the static view of information. The static view represents the logical information structures used in the organization; the dynamic view is based on the information life cycle, which shows the processes that use the information (Fisher, 2004). The information systems architecture (including system models and data flow models) shows how information is created and used in the organization providing a dynamic view of information.

2.7.1 ▶ Information Architectures

An information architecture shows the relatively static structure of information that an organization needs to meet the requirements of the business model.

DEFINITION: An **information architecture** is a logical representation of the information that an organization needs to operate. Information is shown independently of the information systems and IT in which the information might be embedded.

An understanding of how information is related in an organization helps to identify details about the information required by the organization. An extract from a high-level information architecture is shown in Figure 2.12.

Figure 2.12 identifies some of the main entities of information that Amy needs to manage in her business and the relationships between them.

For example, a customer places an order for a product. The relationship *places* joins together information about a *customer* and an *order*. The relationship *places* shows that information is needed about customers, orders, and about the placing of an order (such as, which customer placed the order? When did the customer place the order?) This is particularly important to inform decisions about how information should be stored so that the information can easily be retrieved to answer questions, such as on what date did the customer place the order for 100 candles? Figure 2.12 shows that:

> A customer places orders.
> An order is for products.
> Products are dispatched via deliveries.
> A delivery is received by a customer.
> Products comprise materials.
> Materials are provided by suppliers.

Each of the entities in the information architecture in Figure 2.12 has a life cycle. Processes are needed within the organization to respond to the stages in the life cycle of each entity. Processes are organized within an information system.

Information ecology is a term used by Morville and Rosenfield (2007) to encompass the interdependent elements that inform the information architecture: context, content, and users. The context is provided by the organization and is influenced by the market, business environment, and business climate shown in the business model (see Figure 2.1). The content is the information that is captured or created by the organization, identified by examining the information flows between the organization, its market, its business environment, and the wider business climate. Information created in the organization is identified by examining the business processes that contribute to the information life cycle. Information is only of value if the information is used. Individuals have different requirements for information based on their preferences, behaviours, and use of information. The development of an information architecture needs to consider all of these issues. Chapter 4 outlines an approach to develop an information architecture.

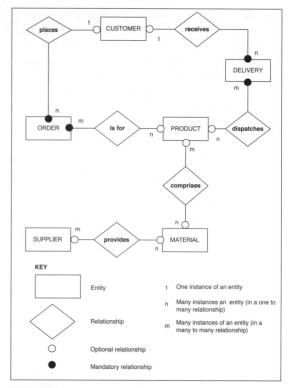

Figure 2.12 Example of a Static Information Architecture

Link 2.1
Reading the Information Architecture

2.7.2 Information Systems Architecture

The information architecture defines the structure of information needed by the organization. Information systems organize business processes to manage the information identified in the information architecture as the information flows through an organization and through the stages of the information life cycle. The information systems architecture implements the business rules defined in the information architecture to maintain the integrity of the organization's information resource.

DEFINITION: An **information systems architecture** is a logical representation of the high-level business processes required to provide the organization with the information specified in the information architecture.

Figure 2.6 shows the life cycle of the *customer* entity. Processes are needed to respond to each of the events in the life cycle of the *customer* entity such as *capture customer details* and *store customer details*. Figure 2.2 outlines an information system to support these processes in the organization. Additional information systems will be needed to support other entities in the information architecture.

The information systems architecture specifies the groupings of business processes that respond to events in the life cycles of the information identified in the information architecture. The individual information systems required in the organization and the flow of information between the information systems are identified independently of the IT and paper-based artefacts that may be used to implement the information systems.

2.8 ▶ Scope of Information Systems in Organizations

Information belongs to the organization therefore business functions need to define the information required to meet the needs of strategic, tactical, and operational processes. An information map shows the physical location of the information in the organization. The information architecture shows the entities about which information is needed and the relationships between the entities, providing a static view of information in the organization. Each entity in the information architecture has a life cycle. The entity life cycle identifies the events that happen to an entity from creation to termination. Processes are needed to support all the events in the life cycle, including capture, storage, use, sharing, maintaining, archiving, and destruction. An information system encompasses the processes to manage information. A systems model shows the main subsystems that are needed to respond to the events defined in the entity life cycle. A data flow diagram can be used to show the specific processes that are needed in each subsystem of the systems model to perform the function of the system and support all stages of the entity life cycle.

The implementation of the information systems architecture is governed by information management. Information management is at the intersection between people, information, and technology (Ellis & Desouza, 2009).

DEFINITION: **Information management** is a set of activities to:

O Define the information needs of the organization.
O Formulate policies for managing information through its life cycle, ensuring that quality information is available to support decision-making.
O Develop and implement processes that adhere to the information management policies.

Information management improves the flow of information to those that need information in the organization to make decisions (Rowley, 1998).

The customer information system (see Figure 2.2) requires information management to:

O Determine what customer information needs to be captured.
O Define the entity of *customer information* and its relationship to other entities.
O Define the attributes of *customer information* (including attribute length and type).
O Develop processes for capturing *customer information* and verifying that the information is correct.
O Develop processes for storing *customer information*.
O Develop processes for retrieving, using, and maintaining *customer information*.
O Develop processes to keep *customer information* safe and recover the information if the information should become lost or corrupted.
O Agree policies on who has access to *customer information*.
O Agree policies for how long *customer information* should be retained.
O Develop processes for archiving and destroying *customer information*.

The role of IT to support the implementation of information systems in the organization is explored in Chapter 3.

Summary

Information is essential to organizations triggering events, such as order processing and informing decision-making at all levels in the organization to ensure that the organization can survive against external pressures, for example, competition. An information architecture presents the logical structure of information required by the organization. Information has a number of characteristics, such as timelines, accuracy, and relevance. The value of information to the organization is subjective and depends on the characteristics of information required by a specific task and the requirements of the individual performing the task. Information has a life cycle comprising activities of capture, store, use, maintain, share, archive, and destroy. An information system is a set of business processes that structure the activities in the information life cycle.

A systems model shows the business processes required in an information system. Data flow diagrams decompose the processes in an information system and model the flow of information through the system. An information systems architecture represents the business processes that are needed to provide the organization with the information specified in the information architecture. The information system implements the business rules defined in the information architecture and structures processes to provide the organization with information that possesses the characteristics required to meet the needs of business functions.

Reviewing Scenario 2.1

As Amy starts her candle-making business she has to identify the information she will need using the following eight steps.

Step 1: Complete a Business Model

A business model will help Amy to define the main flows of information into and out of her business. For example, Amy will receive information about raw materials and equipment from suppliers in the business environment. An extract from Amy's business model is shown in Figure 2.13.

Step 2: Identify Entities

Amy needs to identify the entities about which she needs to capture and store information. From analysis of the business model in Figure 2.13, Amy will need to manage information about key entities such as *supplier*, *equipment*, and *material*. (Note: This list is not complete and further information can be identified from the model.)

Step 3: Define Entities and Attributes

Each of the entities identified in Step 2 have to be defined with their attributes. This defines the information that

Amy will need to capture and manage. The entities *supplier*, *equipment*, and *material* will need to be defined. Amy will then need to define the attributes of each of these entities. Example definitions are included in Table 2.4.

Step 4: Define the Life Cycle for the Entities

Each of the entities identified has a life cycle that needs to be defined. Figure 2.14 presents two life cycles: the life cycle for the entity *equipment* and a life cycle for the entity *equipment information*. The two life cycles show how information relates to physical transactions in organizations, such as ordering equipment from suppliers. Entity life cycles will also need to be developed for the entities *supplier* and *material*.

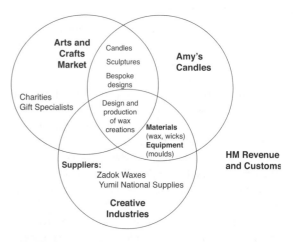

Figure 2.13 Extract from Business Model for Amy's Candles

Table 2.4 Example Entity and Attribute Definitions for Supplier, Material, and Equipment

Entity Name	Entity Definition	
Supplier	An individual or organization that sells materials that might be purchased in the future.	
Material	Items directly consumed within the production of the wax products, such as dye.	
Equipment	Items used but not consumed within the production of the wax products, such as a wax mould.	
Attributes of Material	**Definition of Attribute**	**Format of Attribute**
Type of Material	The composition of the material, such as 100% wax.	X(15)
Expiry Date	The date by which the material must be consumed.	9(8)
Attributes of Equipment	**Definition of Attribute**	**Format of Attribute**
Name of Equipment	A unique code to identify the equipment.	X(5)
Type of Equipment	The nature of the equipment, such as mould or knife.	X(10)
Size of Equipment	The dimensions of the equipment (such as diameter of mould).	9(3)

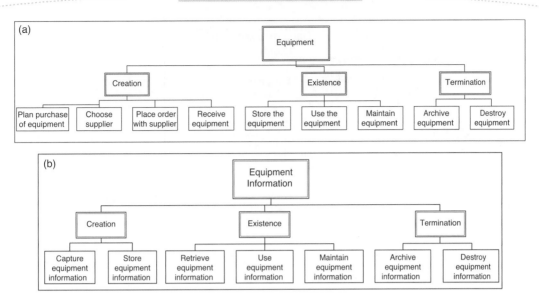

Figure 2.14 Entity Life Cycle for Equipment and Equipment Information (a) Entity Life Cycle for Equipment; (b) Entity Life Cycle for Equipment Information

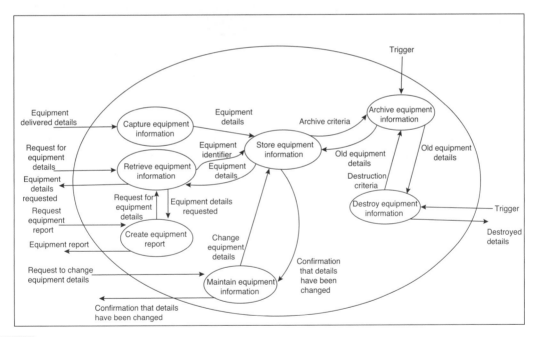

Figure 2.15 Equipment Information System

Step 5: Design Information Systems

Processes are needed to manage information at each stage of an entity's life cycle. Initially, a system is defined for each entity; the systems can later be combined into a larger system. Figure 2.15 outlines an *equipment information system*.

Step 6: Define Processes in Subsystems

Each information system incorporates a number of subsystems. The processes in each subsystem can be defined in a data flow diagram. Figure 2.16 shows the processes of the subsystem *capture equipment information*, which relates to events identified in the entity life

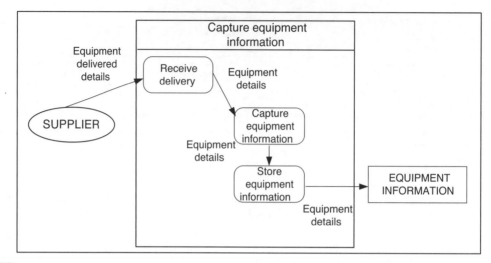

Figure 2.16 Data Flow Model for Subsystem of Equipment Information System

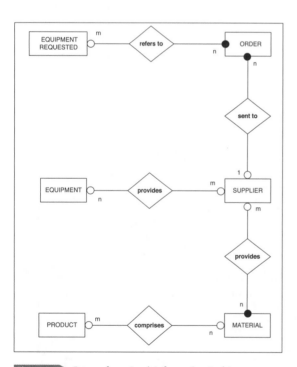

Figure 2.17 Extract from Amy's Information Architecture

cycle (Figure 2.14). Systems will need to be defined to support all the stages in the life cycles for *supplier, equipment*, and *material*.

Step 7: Develop an Information Architecture

The entities identified will be included in an information architecture that shows the relationships between the entities (Figure 2.17).

Link 2.2
Description of Amy's Information Architecture

Step 8: Prepare an Information Map

An information map shows where information can be physically located in the organization. An example of how paper-based information may be stored is given in Table 2.5, however, an information map can also show information held on computer systems.

In Scenario 2.1 information management is required to:

○ Determine what supplier, material, and equipment information needs to be captured.
○ Define the entities and attributes of supplier, material, and equipment.
○ Develop processes for capturing, verifying, storing, retrieving, using, and maintaining supplier, material, and equipment information.
○ Develop processes to keep information safe and determine who can access the information.
○ Agree policies for how long information should be retained and archived before being destroyed.

Cloze Exercise 2.1

Complete the following paragraph by choosing the correct word from Table 2.6 to fill in each gap.

Information is needed in organizations to inform _____ and _____ events. Information can be _____ from external sources, such as _____, suppliers and competitors. It can also be _____ internally within the

Table 2.5 Extract from Amy's Information Map

Equipment Orders	Current	Recent	Archive
Description	Orders sent to supplier awaiting delivery. File order when delivery received and checked.	Orders for equipment which has been received from suppliers since April 2010. Archive completed orders on 31 March each year.	Orders for equipment that have been received from suppliers between April 2007 and March 2010. Destroy orders six years after delivery date.
Location	Purchasing Desk Tray 3, indexed by supplier name.	Supplier Order File, Filing Cabinet A, indexed by supplier name.	Archive Box 42, indexed by financial year and supplier name. Stored off site.
Access	Purchasing Officer.	Purchasing and Accounting Staff.	Accounting Manager.
Supplier Directory	**Current**	**Recent**	**Archive**
Description	Details for potential supplier to be added to supplier directory when a supplier has been approved.	Contact book of previous, current, and potential suppliers of materials and equipment, indexed alphabetically by supplier name. When a supplier has not been used for two years, the entry can be archived.	Details of suppliers previously used, indexed alphabetically. Destroy details four years after last order received from supplier.
Location	Purchasing Desk Tray 1, indexed by date details received.	Red directory on Purchasing Desk.	Archive Box 8, in basement, indexed by year added to box and then indexed alphabetically by supplier.
Access	Purchasing Officer.	All staff.	Purchasing Staff.

Table 2.6 Words to Complete Cloze Exercise 2.1

Appropriateness	Characteristics	Decisions	Policies	Storage
Architecture	Costs	Entities	Relationships	Stored
Archived	Created	Existence	Restored	Termination
Audit	Creation	Life	Retention	Trigger
Captured	Customers	Maintained	Retrieving	Unauthorized

main business processes. Information has a _____ cycle which comprises three main stages _____, _____, and _____. In the first stage, information is captured or created. In the second stage, information is used and _____. In the final stage, information is _____ and destroyed. A _____ period defines how long information needs to be kept in an organization. Archived information should be _____ in the same way as the live information so that it can be _____ when needed. Storing information incurs costs of the physical _____

medium and increases the time and cost incurred in _____ information. Security procedures are needed to protect information from being accessed or changed by _____ personnel. An _____ trail records who modified the information and when it was modified. The value of information to a business depends on the _____ of information such as the information's accuracy and the _____ of the information to the task in which it is to be used. Improving the accuracy of information incurs _____ and may not improve the quality of the information. An information _____ provides a high-level model of the _____ about which the organization needs to manage information. It also shows the _____ between information. Information management defines the information needs of the organization and formulates information _____ to manage information effectively in the organization.

Link 2.3
Answers to Cloze Exercise 2.1

Activities 2.1

1 The business model for Amy's Candles is shown in Figure 2.13. Identify the information that Amy may need to capture from *customers* in the *market*.
2 Section 2.1.1 lists a range of characteristics of information. Use the list to specify the characteristics of information that Amy needs about *customer orders* to inform material purchasing decisions relating to the purchasing of materials.
3 Define the entity *customer order*.
4 Define the name, length, and type of attributes for the entity *customer order.*
5 Develop a form for Amy to capture order details from her customers.

6 Add the relationship *a customer may cancel an order* to Figure 2.12.
7 Draw the life cycle for the entity *customer order*.
8 Develop a system model, similar to Figure 2.2, to support the life cycle of the entity *customer order*.

Discussion Questions 2.1

1 Why is information important to organizations? Is information important to all organizations? Does the importance of information differ in different types of organizations?
2 What factors should be considered when storing information?
3 Explain what is meant by information management and justify why organizations should invest in managing information.
4 Briefly explain the characteristics of information and discuss to what extent perfect information is desirable and attainable.
5 Critically evaluate the value of information to organizations. Illustrate your evaluation with appropriate examples.
6 Choose an organization with which you are familiar and identify examples of the different information needed by the strategic, tactical, and operational levels of the organization.

3

ROLE OF INFORMATION TECHNOLOGY IN MANAGING INFORMATION

Scenario 3.1

Cost of IT in Match Lighting

Match Lighting is a lighting manufacturer specializing in domestic light fittings, which it sells to major retail outlets such as Bright Spark. Mr Cook, the Information Technology (IT) Manager, has prepared a strategy outlining the investment Match Lighting needs to make in IT over the next five years. The strategy includes annual budgets for hardware acquisition, a rolling programme of desktop upgrades, software licensing, systems maintenance, and new systems development projects. Mr Cook presented the strategy to the Director of Match Lighting, Mr Alvis.

'You want how much to spend on IT!' exclaims Mr Alvis. 'I don't understand. I can go online and buy a desktop computer for a few hundred pounds so why do we need to spend so much on IT?'

'A desktop computer costs £400 plus £200 for a monitor and then we install £400 of software on it. So that is £1,000. We replace desktops every five years so the cost is £200 per computer per year. Then there are the annual software licences, the network costs, the mobile devices, and ...'

'Stop, I get the idea', interrupts Mr Alvis, 'but tell me, why do we need all this IT equipment?'

What value does it bring to the business? How does the IT strategy justify this level of investment?'

Learning Outcomes

The learning outcomes of this chapter are to:

O Define the relationship between information systems and information technology.

O Explain how information technology supports the management of information.

O Outline technical considerations in information life cycle management.

O Critically assess the business value of information technology in organizations.

O Describe the purpose of information technology architectures in organizations.

O Demonstrate the role of technology in managing information in organizations.

Introduction

The need for organizations to capture, store, retrieve, use, generate, share, maintain, secure, archive, and destroy information from a range of sources was explained in Chapter 2. The role of information technology (IT) in supporting the processes in the information life cycle to manage information in organizations is considered, showing how the IT manager can justify the proposed IT expenditure in Match Lighting.

The chapter starts by clarifying the relationship between information, information systems, and IT. The role of IT in supporting the management of information throughout the information life cycle is then discussed, demonstrating the relationship between information systems and IT. Approaches are introduced to measure the business value of IT in organizations, which can be used in an IT plan to align investment in technology with an organization's objectives. The purpose of an IT architecture and the relationship between the IT architecture and an IT plan are explained. The chapter concludes by reviewing the role of IT in managing the organization's information resource.

3.1 Information in Information Systems and Information Technology

Information flows through an organization. Figure 3.1 shows the business model with examples of information flowing into and out of the organization. For instance, Match Lighting sends information about its lighting products to potential customers in the market and receives information relating to orders for lighting products from customers.

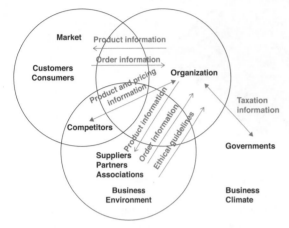

Figure 3.1 ▶ Example Information Flows in the Business Model

Information systems are concerned with the processes in the organization required for the collection, use, and storage of information in the information life cycle. As a system, an information system will have a boundary that separates the system from its environment. Information will cross the boundary as input to and output from the information system. Information systems consider *what* the business processes need to do with the information and do not consider *how* the business processes may be implemented using IT.

Figure 3.2 illustrates an information system in Match Lighting to receive customer orders. This system includes three main processes:

○ Provide a means for a customer to place an order.
○ Capture the information about the order from the customer.
○ Store the information about the order from the customer.

This information system has:

○ Two information inputs crossing the boundary into the information system (*order information requirements* and *customer order*).
○ Two information outputs crossing the boundary out of the information system, these are: (1) *request customer order information*, which leaves the system to go to the customer, and (2) *customer order*, which leaves the information system to be stored in some format.
○ Three business processes (*provide means to place order*, *capture customer order information*, and *store customer order information*). In Figure 3.2 the data received from the customer is not checked to confirm the validity of the data.
○ Information flowing between business processes (such as, *customer order* information flows out of the process *capture customer order* and into the process *store customer order information*).

One way to implement this information system (Figure 3.3) would be for Match Lighting to:

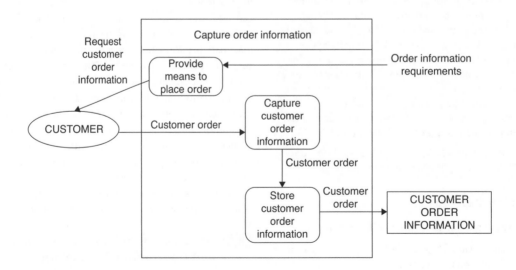

Figure 3.2 ▶ Information System to Capture Customer Order

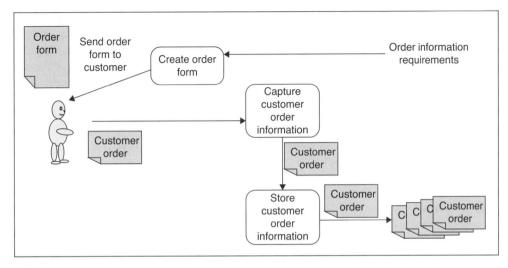

Figure 3.3 ▶ Implementation of Information Systems to Capture Customer Order

○ Provide Bright Spark with a paper order form.
○ Receive the completed order form from Bright Spark in person or via the postal service.
○ Store the customer order form in a folder.

Information systems are concerned with the business processes relating to the capture, storage, and use of information in the organization. An IT system is a set of technologies that implement the business processes to capture, store, and use information.

DEFINITION: Information technology (IT) is a combination of equipment (hardware) and a set of programmed instructions (software) for manipulating data. IT is a broad term that includes, for example, mainframe computers, computer servers, desktop personal computers, tablet computers, printers, storage media, and smart telephones.

Information and communication technology (ICT) incorporates IT and the telecommunications needed to transfer digital data signals between it devices.

IT provides the means to implement information systems. For example, IT could be used to implement the information systems shown in Figure 3.3; Match Lighting could:

○ Provide Bright Spark with access to an online order form.
○ Receive the completed order form from Bright Spark online.
○ Store the customer order form in a shared database or in an electronic folder.

Information systems provide a means for communicating information within and between organizations. IT provides equipment that can improve the efficiency and effectiveness of information systems.

3.1.1 ▶ **Types of Information Systems and Information Technology Systems**

Information systems can be classified as:

○ Formal manual information systems, which are structured ways of working that do not require the use of IT, such as searching for the definition of a word using a paper dictionary.
○ Informal manual information systems, which are evolving patterns of human behaviour that emerge to meet social and cultural needs and sometimes overcome inadequacies with formal systems. An example of this type of system is asking a colleague for advice.
○ Computer-based information systems that incorporate IT and may interface with manual systems. For example, Match Lighting has a computer-based system that generates and prints delivery notes to accompany orders dispatched to Bright Spark. At the Bright Spark warehouse there is a manual system which involves the warehouse supervisor checking that the products listed on the delivery note match the products delivered.

Computer-based information systems can be further categorized by the type of processing performed on the data and information. Lucey (2004), for example, proposes the following categorizations of information systems:

- Data processing systems collect large volumes of data and perform a structured series of actions (often mathematical calculations) to create information for use at the operational and tactical levels of the organization. An example of a data processing system is a payroll system, which calculates and arranges payment of employee salaries.
- Office automation systems collect data to create a range of documentation and assist in administrative tasks. Examples include systems to generate emails and word process documents at all levels in the organization.
- Management information systems categorize and summarize data collected from information systems throughout the organization to support senior managers in making decisions. For example, a management information system may collect data from different systems and provide functions to compare total sales for specific months and analyse sales patterns for individual products in geographical regions.
- Decision-support systems also use data collected from different information systems to generate predictive models, which allow managers to explore 'what if' scenarios. For example, based on consideration of a range of factors, the decision-support system could predict the impact on sales if Match Lighting increased prices by 10 per cent.

Other types of computer-based information systems provide processing functions for specific types of data, such as image-processing systems and geographic information systems.

Another way of categorizing computer-based systems relates to the type of IT used to implement the information systems. For example:

- Desktop information systems are computer-based systems that can only be accessed by using IT devices at a fixed location. For example, at his office Mr Alvis can use office automation systems, management information systems, and decision-support systems.
- Web-based information systems allow information to be accessed using Internet technologies. Information can be accessed from anywhere with any device that provides a web browser. A web browser is a software application that allows a person to access and search the Internet. A person enters an address, a uniform resource locator (URL), into the browser to access public websites such as www.google.com. A URL can also be an address to an organization's web-based information systems. For example, Mr Alvis can use a laptop computer to access the Internet at his home and use his management information system to review sales figures in the same way as if he were in his office.
- Mobile information systems allow information systems to be accessed remotely using devices such as mobile telephones and tablet computers. Such devices have a smaller screen size and less processing power than desktop computers therefore the functionality of the system may be reduced. For example, Mr Alvis can access annual sales figures from a management information system using his mobile telephone but he cannot compare sales figures by type of product although this feature is available when he uses the desktop management information system.
- Mobile applications are information systems that are specifically designed for use on mobile devices. Some applications only access and process information on the device while others allow information to be transferred to remote information systems.

3.1.2 ▶ Relationship between Information Systems and Information Technology Resources

Information systems and IT are resources that organizations can use to create and sustain competitive advantage. IT provides a means to improve the efficiency and effectiveness with which information can be entered, processed, and accessed in information systems. IT provides the means for implementing information systems with technology; however, an information system does not have to be implemented using IT.

Organizations will only invest in IT if the technology is likely to contribute relevant benefits to the organization. For example, mobile computing devices enable employees to access data away from the workplace; however, this will only be of benefit to Match Lighting if employees regularly need to access data away from the workplace. Investment in information systems and IT therefore has to be aligned with the organizational strategy and information needs of the organization.

An understanding of the organization, the problems it must address, and the goals that the organization wants to achieve, is needed to identify the information the organization currently has and the additional information that the organization requires.

An understanding of the information required by the organization is needed to identify the information systems that the organization requires. This includes identifying what information needs to be output from information systems, what processing the information systems need to perform, and what inputs the information system need to receive for the processing to take place.

An understanding of the requirements of the information system is needed to define the technical specification of the IT required to implement the information systems. For example, how much data storage is needed? How many concurrent users need to be accommodated? What operating systems and software packages should be used?

Investment in information systems and IT is aligned with the strategic direction of the organization. There is debate about the extent to which IT should direct or influence organizational strategies. For example, the design of an organizational structure focuses on the flow of information between people in the structure and how the processing of information is coordinated (Nadler, 1992). IT could be implemented to support the existing channels of communication. Information systems enable information to be shared and controlled throughout the organization, therefore IT can provide an alternative to the traditional top-down reporting and control hierarchical organizational structure. IT has the potential to influence, as well as support, the design of the organizational structure and the flow of information through the organization. The following sections explain how technology can support the information processes within the information life cycle introduced in Chapter 2.

3.2 ▶ Capture Information with Information Technology

Section 2.3 explained that organizations need to capture information from external sources and capture information that organizations send to external sources. This implies that information is a thing that can be captured. The concept that information can be captured and shared as an object underpins traditional approaches to information management (Rafferty & Hidderley, 2005). In contrast, Boisant *et al.* (2007) describe information as a pattern that is extracted from data through some form of processing. Buckland (1991) proposes three views of information:

○ Information as a tangible object.
○ Information as a process that changes what a person knows.
○ Information as a person's intangible knowledge.

Information systems capture, store, retrieve, process, use, and communicate information. IT is used to capture, store, retrieve, process, use, and transmit data and objects that contain information (such as documents and pictures).

Information systems can capture information, such as customer order information, at the boundary of the organization. The systems provide the interface between the organization and external sources in the market and business environment (Figure 3.1). Information systems provide the interface between business processes and functions within the organization's internal structure.

Capturing information using an IT system has four elements that are discussed in the following sections:

1 The type of data to be captured.
2 A technical device to capture the data.
3 Instructions relating to what data to capture, what form to capture the data in, and what to do with the data when the data have been captured.
4 A method of transmitting the data to where the data need to be stored or used.

3.2.1 ▶ Types of Data

For many organizations the majority of the data captured from both internal and external sources is text-based. This includes data formed by alphabetical characters (such as customer name), numerical data (such as quantity ordered), and data which include both numerical and textual characters. Match Lighting supplies products to major retail outlets that often have a number of individual stores worldwide. A *store code* is used to identify specific stores owned by a retailer. The *store code* includes both alphabetical characters – a string of three letters to indicate country – and numerical characters, relating to the account number. Other types of data an organization may need to capture include:

○ Image data: Both static and moving images, such as photographs of products and surveillance video, may be needed depending on the type of organization and the industry in which the organization operates. For example, construction organizations use building plans and the aerospace industry uses meteorological images.
○ Audio data: Speech, music, and other forms of natural and manmade sounds can be captured, analysed, and used in organizations. Audio data has four main roles in an organization: audio data may (1) be the product of the organization (such as music downloads), (2) be used to help present and market the product (such as audio used in advertisements), (3) be captured or generated to denote warnings (such as security announcements), or (4) be captured to understand the natural environment or detect potential problems.
○ Sensor data: Sensors capture a range of data (listed in Table 3.1) to support the needs of health and safety, security, and facilities management. For example, manufacturing systems incorporate sensors to detect

machinery malfunctions and to warn when critical levels of temperature, noise, or weight are recorded. Sensors are often used to monitor and control access to buildings, and to areas within buildings; for example, cards containing a magnetic strip or tokens can be read by sensors in door-entry systems.

○ Biometric data: Biometric scanners capture physiological data to identify individuals for security purposes. Examples of biometric systems include fingerprint analysis, face recognition, and iris detection.

○ Movement data: Data relating to the physical movements and gestures made by humans and animals can be captured using cameras and sensors. Data can be analysed to provide information in areas such as healthcare, product design and retail. For example, eye-tracking systems capture eye movement to assess consumer responses to package design (Tonkin *et al.*, 2011).

Information in electronic communications may have current significance or future significance for the organization. For example, historical data may be used for analysis, evidence in legal proceedings, or to demonstrate compliance with standards. Although the data content is clearly visible in structured documents, such as order forms and invoices, valuable data are also embedded in unstructured documents such as letters and reports, which also need to be effectively managed. Electronic communication such as email, Twitter, and messaging services communicate information to different audiences.

Link 3.1
Types of Electronic Communication

3.2.2 Data Capture Devices

Input devices provide an interface to enable data to be captured using an IT system. Data can be captured using different types of input devices. Devices can be categorized in terms of whether the device needs human intervention to capture the data (such as pressing keys on a keyboard) or whether no (or limited) human intervention is required (such as barcode reader). Devices requiring human intervention to capture data include keyboards and composite devices. A composite device provides more than one method for entering data. A computer mouse is an example of a composite device; a computer mouse can be moved to control a cursor on a display and the mouse has buttons that can be pressed to send data commands.

Developments in technology continually seek to improve input devices to avoid input devices forming a barrier to the usability of technology. Technology should be invisible, in the same way that while focusing on the task of writing, the writer becomes unaware of the pen being used (Norman, 1998). Mobile devices enable data to be entered into computer systems using, for example, mobile telephones, tablet computers, and computer game consoles. These devices replace the physical keyboard with other types of interface such as touch screens, which display keyboards or support handwriting recognition.

Sensors can capture speech, gesture, and movement, enabling individuals to interact with technology more directly. Speech can be used to capture data to control devices in cars to reduce accidents due to driver distraction (Maciej & Vollrath, 2009). Gesture capture is used to capture data in situations where a person is unable to directly input data due to physical or situational impairment. For example, gesture capture can be used to support data capture in sterile environments (Rose *et al.*, 2009). Movement-capture devices are used in computer-gaming consoles to make gaming more intuitive and immersive, introducing computer gaming to new markets in well-being, healthcare, and rehabilitation.

Technology can also be embedded in wearable textiles to allow data to be sent and received in smart clothing (Cho *et al.*, 2010). Smart clothing incorporates input devices, such as pressure-sensitive buttons, motion detectors, physiological sensors (such as heart-rate monitors) and speech recognition; output devices convey data using

Table 3.1 Data Collected Using Sensors

Environment	Object Data	Movement Data	Flow
Temperature and humidity	Density	Speed	Water
Light (luminosity and pressure)	Weight	Force	Gas
Air quality (contaminates such as carbon dioxide and ozone)	Size	Pressure	Electrical current
Water quality (pH level, heavy metals and chemical analysis)	Surface area	Angle	Radio waves
Sound (decibels, pressure, intensity)	Volume	Proximity	Microwaves
Weather (wind, rain, sun, atmospheric pressure)	Mass	Vibration	Chemicals

visual, auditory, and tactile interfaces (such as lights, beeps, and vibration).

Devices requiring no or limited human intervention to capture data include: (1) image-capturing devices such as cameras, document scanners, and medical-imaging equipment; (2) audio-capturing devices such as microphones; and (3) sensing devices, for example, radio frequency identification (RFID) that supports the tracking of resources such as cars in a car park.

3.2.3 ▶ Data Capture Instructions

Section 2.3 explained that procedures are needed to specify what information needs to be captured, when, and in what format. If information is to be captured using a data-entry device requiring human intervention, instructions need to be provided to inform the person about what data to enter and how the data should be entered. For example, if Match Lighting plans to capture customer orders using an online form, Match Lighting needs to:

a. Identify the entities about which information is needed (such as *customer, product, order*).
b. Define the attributes of the entities (such as *name of customer, address of customer*).
c. Create a structured format in which to capture the information (such as an online order form). This will include:
  i. Arranging the sequence in which information is requested (for instance, should customer name be entered first or should product details be entered first?).
  ii. Dividing the form into suitable pages so that the form can be easily displayed on a screen. It is particularly important to consider how information is displayed on mobile devices.
  iii. Ensuring that accessibility requirements are met.
d. Develop a procedure for capturing the information; for example:
  i. Provide a link to the online order form and provide instructions on how to complete the form.
  ii. Telesales staff must complete the online order form when a customer telephones Match Lighting to place an order.

Match Lighting provides the information system that enables the information to be captured (Figure 3.2); IT is used to implement the information system. Some of the IT is owned by the customer and some of the IT is the responsibility of Match Lighting. In this example of an online customer order form, the customer needs to use a physical data-entry device, such as a keyboard, to enter data into the online form. The customer will need a device with a screen, such as a desktop computer, netbook, or smart telephone, and the device must be connected to the Internet. Match Lighting needs IT to create and display the order form, receive the data transmitted from the customer, store and process the order data, and send data back to the customer about their order (Figure 3.4).

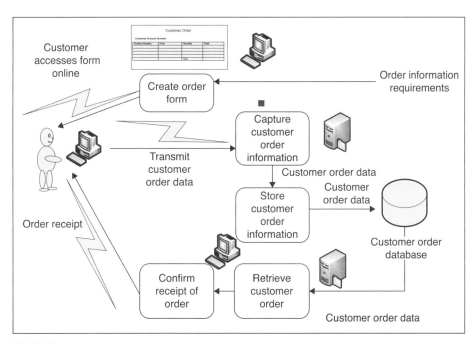

Figure 3.4 ▶ IT-based Implementation of Information System to Capture Customer Order

If information is to be captured using a data-entry device that requires little or no human intervention, the device needs to be programmed with instructions of when, and how, to collect data. For example, Match Lighting will need to keep track of products leaving their warehouse. RFID tags could be added to pallets. When a pallet passes an RFID receiver, the position of the pallet will be logged. The RFID receiver will need to be given instructions such as:

○ Search for RFID signal.
○ When RFID signal is in range, capture data from signal.
○ Transmit data from signal to be stored.

The information collected from the data of the RFID signal will then be used by information systems. For example, the pallet number will be checked against the log of pallet movements. If a problem is detected – perhaps a pallet has left the warehouse but has not triggered the RFID receiver on the delivery lorry – an error message can be created and sent to the warehouse manager to investigate the problem.

3.2.4 ▶ Data Transmission

Once captured, data need to be transferred or transmitted to a storage medium for later use. There is a difference between transmission of data and communication of information. Data transmission transfers a copy of the data from a sending device to a receiving device. Effective communication does not merely reproduce a copy of what is in the sender's mind into the recipient's mind. Effective communication is meaningful communication that modifies the thinking of the recipient (Boisant et al., 2007). Information therefore needs to be targeted to the recipient for whom the information is relevant, presented in an effective manner, with a degree of accuracy and timeliness appropriate to the requirements of the recipient (Curtis & Cobham, 2008).

The business perspective considers what information is needed by whom, when, and in what format. The IT perspective focuses on how the information can be transmitted to meet the needs of the organization in a timely, efficient, and effective manner. Telecommunications and networking technologies are needed to transmit data to and from Match Lighting, as well as to transmit data between people and departments in the organization. For example, the order information entered by a customer needs to be transmitted to Match Lighting and the signals from the RFID receiver need to be transmitted to the logistics management system.

Data transmission involves the following steps:

a Identify the data and recipient.
b Define when and where the data need to be transmitted from and to.
c Select the most appropriate method of transmission.
d Prepare the data to be transmitted. This includes encoding the data to preserve the integrity of the data and to optimize the transmission speed of the specific transmission medium.
e Transmit the data using appropriate protocols to initiate the transmission, transmit the data, verify that the data have been transmitted, and end the transmission.

Security issues need to be considered to ensure that the data transmitted:

○ Arrive at the intended destination and are not intercepted by unauthorized means.
○ Arrive in the intended form, and are not corrupted either accidentally or maliciously.

IT networks are collections of devices and communication channels (such as servers and fibre-optic cables) that enable data to be transmitted between devices. Networks enable data to be transmitted from a sender to a recipient device, sending the data to where the data need to be stored, retrieved, processed, and used. Networks also enable both information and physical IT resources to be shared. For example, each desktop computer at Match Lighting previously had a printer connected to it. Individual printers have been replaced as desktop computers are now connected to Match Lighting's network, enabling staff to transmit documents to centralized printers.

Ward et al. (1996) identify four levels of using IT to transmit data between organizations:

Level 1: Transaction Processing. A batch of transactions is sent to an organization for processing. For example, a retail customer may send a collection of orders to Match Lighting.

Level 2: Enquiry or Information Exchange. Customers and suppliers can enquire directly on data held in each other's computer systems.

Level 3: Transaction-driven Interaction Systems. A customer or supplier conducts an online transaction that initiates an automatic response to process the transaction at the other organization.

Level 4: Interactive Processing Systems. A customer or supplier conducts an online transaction that is processed interactively, that is, the transaction is processed and information on both the customer's and supplier's computer is updated.

Each of these levels requires a greater degree of cooperation between the trading parties as the complexity and dependency of the relationship increases at each level. Customers and suppliers need to cooperate to define data standards and interpret the information processed (Cox et al., 2006). These levels are demonstrated in Scenario 3.2.

Scenario 3.2

IT in the Supply Chain of Match Lighting

Bright Spark is a regular customer of Match Lighting. In the early days, Larry Hughes (the owner of Bright Spark) sent individual orders to Match Lighting, via the postal service, to purchase stock for his stores. When Match Lighting received the paper orders from Larry, staff at Match Lighting manually typed the order data into the order processing system. Match Lighting created paper invoices that were sent to Bright Spark via the postal service (Figure 3.5).

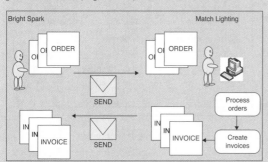

Figure 3.5 Transaction Processing

As the number of orders increased, Larry started to use electronic data interchange (EDI). EDI is an approach to transfer data between computer systems in different organizations using an agreed format so that the data can be received and processed without the need for human intervention (Curtis & Cobham, 2008). Larry entered the orders into his computer system and used EDI to transmit the orders to Match Lighting, reducing the volume of paper being sent in the post. When the computer systems at Match Lighting received the data transmission from Bright Spark, the electronic orders were automatically input directly into the order processing system without human intervention. Invoices were then automatically generated by Match Lighting and sent to Bright Spark via EDI (Figure 3.6).

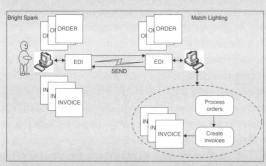

Figure 3.6 Transaction Processing with EDI

When Larry sent orders to Match Lighting, Larry did not know if the products he wanted to order were in stock. Match Lighting then gave Larry limited access to their stock management system. This allowed Larry to check whether products were in stock before he placed an order (Figure 3.7).

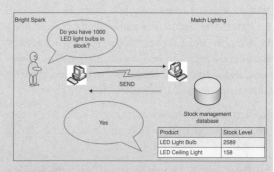

Figure 3.7 Information Enquiry

As the use of technology at Bright Spark increased, Match Lighting was also given access to some of Bright Spark's information systems. This access allowed Match Lighting to update stock levels in Bright Spark's information systems when products were dispatched to Bright Spark (Figure 3.8).

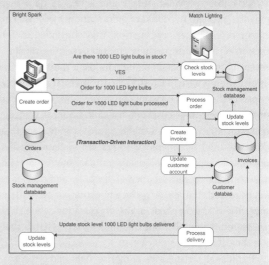

Figure 3.8 Interactive Processing

3.3 ▶ Store and Retrieve Information with Information Technology

When data have been captured and transmitted to the intended recipient, the data need to be stored in a form that will allow the data to later be retrieved by authorized personnel. Data are stored in a database in an IT system.

3.3.1 ▶ Databases

Data are stored electronically in a database. Traditional databases store textual and numerical data; multimedia databases electronically store audio clips and images; and specialist databases store, for example, satellite images, maps, and weather data needed by geographical information systems (Elmasri & Navathe, 2010).

DEFINITION: A **database** is a structured collection of data that are stored electronically on physical data-storage media.

Databases enable data to be stored and retrieved, but a database is more than an electronic filing cabinet. A database is not just a collection of data (Figure 3.9a) or an organized collection of data (Figure 3.9b); a database is a structured collection of data (Figure 3.9c). The way in which the data are stored allows the data to be sorted, to be linked, to be aggregated, and for calculations to be performed on the data in order to generate information. Data are structured and organized in the database so that specific items of data can be found when needed to satisfy the different retrieval requirements of business processes.

A database provides storage and access to data that may be needed by different information systems. For example, customer information may be needed for processing orders, dispatching products, creating invoices, receiving payments and issuing refunds. If these separate information systems each stored customer data, multiple copies of the same data would be stored. This would incur unnecessary storage costs and it would be more difficult to ensure that the data were accurate. Storing data in a database used by different information systems enables organizations to enforce quality standards and maintain the consistency and security of data. In addition, it is easier to add, change, or replace information systems to meet the changing needs of the organization when data are stored separately from the information systems that use the data.

Traditionally, databases comprise fields and records. A field is a storage unit for an attribute such as *customer name*. A record is a collection of fields that has a unique identifier and stores a set of attributes about an entity, such as *customer*. A table is a set of records, such as all

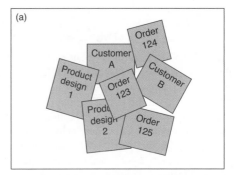

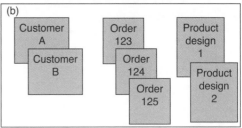

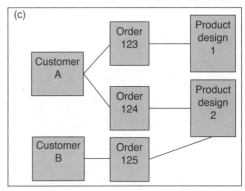

Figure 3.9 ▶ A Database is a Structured Collection of Data (a) Collection of Data; (b) Organised Collection of Data; (c) Structured Collection of Data

customer records in the organization. Queries are structured enquiries to retrieve information from the database. A report provides the collection of data retrieved in response to a given query. Figure 3.10 shows a table of *order* records in Match Lighting and example reports that may be generated in response to queries.

A database can be viewed from a number of different perspectives; some focus on the information needs of the organization and others focus on the technical details of where and how data are stored on the physical storage medium. Figure 3.11 illustrates four views of a database: the external view, the conceptual view, the logical view, and the internal view.

The external view of a database is the view(s) of the database seen by different business processes. For example, the customer account manager responsible for overseeing

Order Number	Date Order Placed	Customer Number	Delivery Date
110190	20-05-2013	BS0567	25-05-2013
110191	20-05-2013	LA1093	23-05-2013
110199	21-05-2013	BS0567	27-05-2013

FIELD

RECORD

QUERY:	List order numbers placed by Customer Number List LA 1093.		
REPORT:	110191		
QUERY:	List the customer number and delivery date for all orders placed in May 2013.		
REPORT:	Order Number	Customer Number	Delivery Date
	110190	BS0567	25-05-2013
	110191	LA1093	23-05-2013
	110199	BS0567	27-05-2013

Figure 3.10 ▸ Example of Database Elements

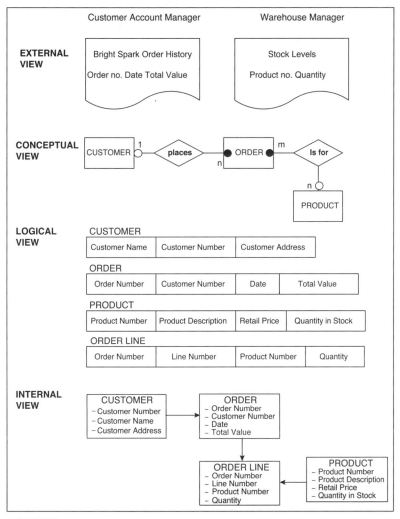

Figure 3.11 ▸ Views of a Database

orders from the retailer Bright Spark will need to access the order history for the retailer. The warehouse manager will need access to the data held in the database relating to the current levels of stock in the Match Lighting warehouse, but the warehouse manager is not interested in the orders of individual customers. Neither the customer account manager nor the warehouse manager needs to be aware of how or where the data they need are physically stored in the database.

The conceptual view of a database is the representation of the data that are required to meet the needs of all the external views, that is, all the data required by the organization (or part of the organization). It is a model of the universe of discourse (also referred to as the domain of discourse), which forms the scope of the areas of interest about which data are needed in the organization. A key feature of the conceptual view of the database is that the conceptual model is both externally and physically independent. The model is externally independent in that the data needed by the organization are represented in a manner that is not influenced by who needs the data or where in the organization the data are needed. This means that the model is relatively stable and does not need to change when new staff are employed or the structure of the organization changes. The model is physically independent in that the model is not influenced by how or where the data are stored on the physical storage medium, nor the type of logical data model that will be used to structure the data in the physical database. The conceptual model represents the data in a manner that is independent of the type of database that will be used to store the data. This means that the physical database and storage medium can be changed without changes being made to the conceptual data model.

The logical view of a database, referred to by Elmasri and Navathe (2010) as the representational model, provides a description of how data are stored in the database. The model, called a schema, is concerned with how the data should be physically structured in the database to meet the business needs identified in the external views. For example, in Figure 3.11 an additional grouping of data order line is added to provide a link between order and product because an order could refer to more than one product. The grouping is not needed in the higher levels of the database design, but becomes significant when considering the physical storage of the data. However, the schema still has a degree of physical independence in that the schema is not concerned with where the data will be stored on the storage medium. There are a number of ways that data can be organized in the database using different types of data model.

Database designers select the most appropriate way to structure data in the database to meet the different information requirements throughout the organization. An aim of a database design is to minimize data redundancy; data redundancy occurs when the same data are stored in different places in the organization. For instance, a number of functions in Match Lighting, such as sales, finance, and dispatch, need to know the name and address of customers. If each of these functions stored customer addresses, when a customer moves to new premises, each of these functions would need to separately change the customer address. This is a duplication of effort as each function updates their copy of the data; there is also potential for the data to become inconsistent. For example, if the Bright Spark store manager informs the finance function of Match Lighting about a change of address and does not tell the other functions, Match Lighting will be storing and using inconsistent data across its business functions. Duplication of data also incurs increased costs to Match Lighting in terms of physically storing the same data in multiple locations, and in the time taken by multiple staff creating and maintaining the data.

Sometimes database designers need to incorporate controlled redundancy in the design of the database to improve the performance of the database response times (that is, how quickly information can be retrieved in response to queries). In such cases, the additional work needed to create and maintain multiple copies of the same data is offset by the reduction in the time taken to retrieve data. A database management system ensures that all copies of the data are updated and that inconsistencies are prevented. A database management system is a set of programs that enable the database to be created, populated, used, and maintained.

The internal view, also known as the storage-level view, represents the way data are held on the physical storage media. The view considers the format of the data and the access paths needed to support efficient retrieval of the data to meet the needs of the organization.

The separate levels of database abstraction provided by the external, conceptual, logical, and internal views provide the following benefits:

○ Different views of the data in the database can be created to meet the needs of different departments and restrict access to data where appropriate.
○ Users can access data without having to know how and where the data are stored.
○ The physical structure and storage of the data can be changed without affecting other layers of the database architecture.

3.3.2 Data Warehouses

Databases store the operational data needed to support the general day-to-day activities in the organization. This is referred to as online transaction processing. Organizations also need to use information to support strategic decision-making. Although the data in transaction databases can be used to support strategic decision-making, organizations often create a separate data warehouse for this purpose. Data warehouses are used to analyse complex relationships between data in the warehouse, described as online analytical processing.

DEFINITION: A **data warehouse** contains summaries of data extracted from transactional databases at regular intervals to provide a single source of data to support decision-making processes.

DEFINITION: A **data mart** is a small data warehouse; a specialized database to support decision-making processes in a specific area of the organization.

A data warehouse receives summaries of data that can be manipulated in data cubes to support organizational decisions. Figure 3.12 shows that during the day separate databases in Match Lighting are continually updated with data about payments, changing stock levels, and orders received. Summary data about weekly sales are extracted from the separate databases and stored in the data warehouse. The data warehouse is then used to create a cube of data, which can be used by the senior management of Match Lighting, to explore the patterns of product sales over time. The advantage of the data warehouse is that the warehouse supports a range of functionality that can be used to analyse the data, such as:

○ Roll-up: Grouping data into larger sets for analysis (such as annual sales of lampshades over the last five years).
○ Drill-down: Increasing the detail of the data for analysis (such as quarterly sales of lilac lampshades in region A).
○ Slice and dice: Grouping the data in different ways for analysis to create different perspectives of the data (for example, sales of products last year grouped by geographical region [slice]; sales of lampshades and switches in all regions over the last four years [dice]).
○ Pivot: Rotating the data cube.
○ Sort: Sorting the data cube by different attributes (Elmasri & Navathe, 2010).

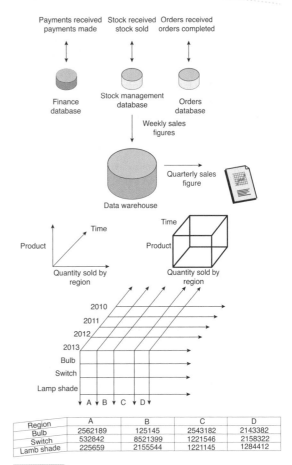

Region	A	B	C	D
Bulb	2562189	125145	2543182	2143382
Switch	532842	8521399	1221546	2158322
Lamb shade	225659	2155544	1221145	1284412

Figure 3.12 ▶ Data Warehouse

3.3.3 Data Storage Devices

A database stores the data needed by the organization and metadata (data about data) which describes the data in the database.

Physical data-storage media differ in terms of:

○ Portability: The ease with which the storage medium can be transported.
○ Capacity: The volume of data that can be stored on the medium.
○ Speed: The time taken to access the medium, find the data, and retrieve the data stored.
○ Volatility: The permanence of the data stored. Volatile memory devices require a constant supply of power to store the data and if power is lost, the data are lost. In contrast, nonvolatile memory, such as a DVD, does not require constant power to store the data but data retrieval is slower than from volatile memory.
○ Primary and secondary storage: Storage determines how data are accessed. Primary storage is a volatile

memory that is directly accessible to the central processing unit of the computer. Secondary storage is nonvolatile and peripheral to the central processing unit. Data are transferred from secondary storage to primary storage for processing.

○ Storage method: There are three main ways to store data on physical media: magnetic storage, optical storage, and solid state. Optical storage media, such as DVDs, store data as marks that can be read by light shining on the spinning disk. Magnetic storage media, such as hard disks, store data as patterns of magnetized particles which are read as the medium moves under a read-and-write head. Solid state disks do not have any moving parts and use electrical current to store data as electrical pulses in transistors. This reduces the time taken to access the data but there is a limited number of times that data can be written to the disk.

The key priority when planning data storage is to ensure that data are not lost (Mullins, 2010a). When selecting a cost-effective data-storage strategy it is necessary to consider:

○ Capacity: Is there adequate capacity for current and anticipated future storage needs?
○ Scalability: Can additional storage capacity be added when needed?
○ Speed: Is the time taken to access the data appropriate to meet the needs of the information system?
○ Fault tolerance: How resilient is the storage medium? How long will it take to address any problems that may arise? Are the resilience and time taken to address any problems that may arise acceptable to the organization?
○ Level of autonomy: Can the storage medium be replaced without affecting access to data in other storage areas? (Mullins, 2010a)

3.3.4 Information Retrieval

Storing data is pointless unless the data can be retrieved when needed. Information retrieval is a set of techniques to help extract data from the database and present the data to authorized staff when needed. Information retrieval involves selecting one or more records from the database that satisfy a selection or filtering condition (Elmasri & Navathe, 2010) such as *select all customers where the customer account manager is Fiona Jones*. In a database application, programs are used to provide an interface to users so that they can access the data in the database. For example, a structured query language is used at the logical level to specify the data to be retrieved from relational databases. The query specifies the tables

or files in the database path, and follows the access path defined in the physical data model to extract the data that are needed.

Figure 3.13 provides an example of how a query could be constructed to retrieve a list of customers who have *Fiona Jones* as their account manager at Match Lighting. The information required can be retrieved from the *Cust_Acc* table in the database (Figure 3.13). However, in order to retrieve the names and addresses of customers who have *Fiona Jones* as their account managers, two tables have to be accessed (Figure 3.14).

The query:
SELECT CName
FROM Cust_Acc
Where AName = 'Fiona Jones';

retrieves the name of all the customers *CName* from the customer accounts table *Cust_Acc* in the database where the name of the account manager *AName* is Fiona Jones.

The customer accounts table *Cust_Acc* stores two fields, the name of customers *CName* and the name of their customer account manager *AName*. The table *Cust_Acc* contains the following records:

Table: *Cust_Acc*	
CName	*AName*
Bright Spark	Fiona Jones
Flash Light Ltd	Jim Lake
Lo-Watts Ltd	Fiona Jones
Cornish Light	Jim Lake

The query would return the names of the following customers who have Fiona Jones as their account manager:

Bright Spark
Lo-Watts Ltd

Figure 3.13 Example of Information Retrieval from a Table

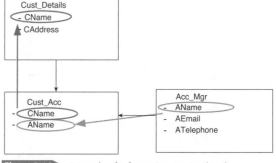

Figure 3.14 Example of Information Retrieval Paths

Sometimes the same information can be retrieved from a database using a different series of operations. Query optimization is used to identify the most efficient strategy for searching the database to retrieve the data required. This assumes that the data are alphanumeric; the challenges of retrieving multimedia information are discussed in Chapter 15.

3.3.5 Data Mining

Information retrieval involves extracting known data from the database to provide information to support operational and tactical business processes in the organization. Data mining aims to discover new unknown information from the data in the database, or data warehouse, to support strategic decisions relating to resource allocation and customer profiling (for instance, sequential purchasing patterns may indicate that customers who purchase product A also purchase product B). Data mining can also support predictive analysis, such as assessing the probable effect on sales of reducing or increasing prices (Elmasri & Navathe, 2010).

In addition to detecting patterns in the data, data mining can be used to recognize anomalies in the data patterns. For example, data mining may detect unusual purchasing patterns that may suggest that a credit card has been stolen and is being used fraudulently. Patterns can be also identified in the way data are accessed, which can then be used to detect potential unauthorized access by intruders trying to gain access to data.

3.4 Use, Generate, and Share Information with Information Technology

Section 2.5 explained that information is:

- Used as the basis for decisions and is input into business processes.
- Generated by business processes.
- Shared with staff both internal and external to the organization.

The following sections discuss the role of IT in each of these activities.

3.4.1 Using Information with Information Technology

Information is used throughout the organization at different levels to support the day-to-day operations, short-term planning at the tactical level, and long-term planning and decision-making processes at the strategic level of the organization. Different levels of the organization have different requirements for information. At the strategic level the Director, Mr Alvis, needs to have access to summarized information that has been captured and generated from the

operational levels of the organization. For example, Mr Alvis needs information about the quarterly sales of the organization and the total amount the IT manager has spent in the last year. This information can be provided by the use of IT. Queries can be constructed to extract the requested information from the organization's databases. For example, daily sales transactions are recorded in a database. A management information system constructs a query to extract details about the daily sales during a defined period. The sales data are then totalled to present the quarterly sales information in the form required by Mr Alvis. Data warehouses may be used to provide historical information to enable Mr Alvis to compare sales this quarter with the same quarter over the last five years. Data mining techniques can be used to support the simulation of future scenarios to predict, for example, sales over the next two years.

IT enables different views of the data in the database to be provided to meet the different needs of departments in the organization. A key requirement of information is that in order for information to be of use to a particular individual, the information needs to have specific characteristics. IT can be used to provide information that has the required characteristics when needed and therefore improve the quality of information. Table 3.2 shows how IT can be used to influence the characteristics of information defined in Section 2.1.

Information systems and IT *can* support attainment of the characteristics listed in Table 3.2, however, the IT staff need to first understand the requirements of the business in relation to these characteristics in order to provide information exhibiting the required quality characteristics.

3.4.2 Generating Information with Information Technology

Davenport and Prusak (1998) suggest that value can be added to data to generate information in five main ways:

- Correction: Information can be generated by removing errors in the data collected. IT can be used to automatically detect errors in the data captured through the use of validation checks.
- Categorization: Information systems enable data to be easily organized in different ways. Manipulation of the data can provide new insights into the relationships among the data, generating new information. Data mining is one approach to identifying patterns in the data collected to generate information.
- Condensing: Summarizing the data stored can provide information for decision-making processes and support the analysis of trends over periods of time.
- Calculation: Information systems can perform mathematical calculations on the data to generate

Table 3.2 ▶ Role of IT in Improving the Quality Characteristics of Information

Characteristic	Role of Information Technology
Timeliness	Information can be retrieved from a database when needed, or programs can be written to send information to an individual at a specific time (such as weekly report of sales) or when a specific event occurs (for example, alert the operations manager immediately if a fault develops on the production line).
Frequency	IT enables both regular and ad hoc reports to be generated relatively quickly. However, this has led to many regular reports being produced because the report can be produced rather than because the report is required. Greater understanding of the information required in an organization is therefore needed to avoid the technical costs of producing unnecessary information and to avoid the people-related costs associated with receiving information that is not required.
Appropriateness	Information can be extracted from the database to meet the specific needs of the task for which the information is to be used.
Accuracy	The accuracy of the information accessed is dependent on the accurate capture of data. Information systems can help maintain the accuracy of data through the use of data validation checks and the implementation of business rules. IT ensures that the accuracy of the data is maintained as data are transmitted, stored, and maintained by authorized staff.
Action	IT can transmit information directly to the individual in the organization who can take action on the information. However, too often information can be transmitted around organizations in search of the most appropriate person who can respond to the information.
Understandability	Information systems enable the style and format of information to be changed to support the specific requirements of different staff. For example, sales figures for different products manufactured by Match Lighting over the last 12 weeks could be presented in a graph.
Brevity	IT stores data in a database, allowing information systems to extract different views of the data to meet the requirements of the different areas of the organization. For example, some staff will need to access the name and telephone extension of an account manager; other staff will need to access the name of the account manager and their list of customers. Information systems and IT enable different levels of detail to be presented to meet different needs.
Rarity	Information systems can be used to identify anomalies or highlight events that require further investigation, such as an attempt to gain unauthorized access to data.
Presentation	Information systems and IT can change the format of the information presented to meet the different needs of recipients. This may include adapting the presentation of the information so that the information is more easily displayed on a small screen or to improve the accessibility of the information.

new information. For example, the total expenditure on consumables can be calculated by adding together individual orders for consumable items. Statistical analysis, such as risk analysis, can also be applied to the data; IT provides the means to undertake such analysis on large volumes of stored data.

○ Contextualization: Chapter 1 explained that information can be generated from data by understanding the units that the data represent and the context in which data are collected. Information systems can help provide the recipient with details of how the data were collected, however, contextualization requires human intervention to interpret data within a specific context to generate information.

IT provides the means to capture, store, retrieve, and manipulate large volumes of data. Information systems provide the processes to enable the business to access and manipulate data, to generate information needed, and to support the operations and plans of the organization.

3.4.3 ▶ Sharing Information with Information Technology

An organization is a system of interconnected business processes. The information generated by, and output from, one process is used as input by other business processes. Information needs to be shared between individuals and business functions to (1) provide instruction (such as, pack this product and send the product to Bright Spark), (2) communicate policies (such as a code of conduct), (3) communicate procedures (such as how to deal with a customer complaint), and (4) communicate facts (such as the annual profits of Match Lighting have increased this year). Information is shared internally to communicate the vision and mission of the organization, maintaining and developing the organizational culture. The interpretation of this shared information relies on a shared understanding of concepts and values that form the culture of the organization.

IT provides the means to store data in a way that allows the data to be accessed by different business processes. IT provides the means to share information quickly in the organization through information systems such as email, instant messaging, and shared filing systems accessed by the organization's intranet. IT also enables information to be shared with external parties, including customers, suppliers, and collaborating organizations in order to promote products and develop relationships using Internet systems (discussed in Chapter 10).

Before information can be shared the following agreements are needed:

- Agreement of what information is to be shared, including the characteristics of the information (such as the level of detail, quantity, and frequency) and the reciprocal arrangements.
- Agreement of how the information will be shared, including the format of the data and the means of access or transmission.
- Agreement of how the information will be used and how security and confidentiality will be maintained. This includes ensuring that the information can be shared without breaching data protection laws.

IT provides the means for data to be transmitted to parties outside the organization and to allow external parties to access specific data held in the organization. However, a degree of technical compatibility between the sending and receiving parties is needed to ensure that the data can be accurately received, interpreted, and used. Beyond the technical compatibility, semantic compatibility is needed to ensure that the receiving party interprets the information correctly.

3.4.4 ▶ Structuring Information Exchange with Information Technology

Extensible markup language (XML) is a way of coding data so that data can be exchanged between computer systems. XML is referred to as being self-describing as the information needed to decode the data is included in the XML document. A key feature of XML is that the language is nonproprietary and therefore XML is independent of specific vendors.

The XML language uses pairs of tags, which describe the content of the information between the tags. For example, *<name> Mr Cook </name>* could be used to show that *Mr Cook* is a *name*. A schema document defines the tags and attributes of the tags. The schema document is then used to check the XML document to ensure that the tags appear in the correct order and with the correct attributes.

Figure 3.15 provides an example of a completed supplier details form.

Supplier Details

Supplier Name:	Zadok Waxes
Address:	Unit 15 Oak Tree Estate
Town:	Birmingham
County:	West Midlans
Post Code:	B17 0LK
Country:	UK
Website:	www.zadokwaxes.com
Email Address:	orders@zadokwaxes.com
Payment Terms:	Order usually delivered within 5 working days. Payment required within 14 working days of delivery being received.

Account Number:	0003258951
Contact Name:	Jake
Telephone Number:	01211415832
Fax Number:	01211415833

Send Cancel

Figure 3.15 ▶ Completed Supplier Details Form

Link 3.2
XHTML of Supplier Details Form

Link 3.3
XML Schema for Supplier Details]

The data included in Figure 3.15 can be represented in XML (Figure 3.16) to enable the data to be transferred across the Internet.

An XML Document Type Definition (DTD) is used to specify the structure of the document. Table 3.3 shows the definition for the XML shown in Figure 3.16. XML can be used to structure information retrieved from a database or provide a structure to documents that contain large sections of text to improve storage, retrieval, and transmission of data.

An XML schema is an XML document that describes another XML document and specifies more constraints on the data than is possible with the DTD. For example, in the DTD (Table 3.3), *supplier account* is specified as being a data string; however, it is known that the account number is numeric and this can be documented in an XML schema. A further advantage of an XML schema is that additional detail can be given to impose business rules on the data, helping to keep data clean by preventing inappropriate values being stored.

```xml
<?xml version="1.0" standalone="no"?>
<!DOCTYPE Supplier Details SYSTEM "supplier.dtd">
<supplierdetails>
    <supplier>
    <name>Zadok Waxes</name>
    <account>0003258951</account>
    <address>Unit 15 Oak Tree Estate</address>
    <town>Birmingham</town>
    <contact>Jake</contact>
    <county>West Midlands</county>
    <tel>01211415832</tel>
    <postcode>B17 0LK</postcode>
    <country>UK</country>
    <fax>01211415833</fax>
    <website>www.zadokwaxes.com</website>
    <email>orders@zadokwaxes.com</email>
    <payterms>Orders usually delivered within 5 work-
    ing days. Payment required within 14 working days
    of delivery being received.</payterms>
    </supplier>
    <supplier>
    <name>Xena's Craft Supplies </name>
...
</supplier>
</supplierdetails>
```

Figure 3.16 XML of Supplier Details

Table 3.3 XML Document Type Definition for Supplier Details

XML Document Type Definition	Comments

`<!DOCTYPE supplierdetails[`
`<!ELEMENT supplier (supplier+)>`
`<!ELEMENT supplier (name, account, address, town, contact, county,`
`tel, postcode, country, fax, website, email, payterms?)>`
`<!ELEMENT name (#PCDATA)>`
`<!ELEMENT account (#PCDATA)>`
`<!ELEMENT address (#PCDATA)>`
`<!ELEMENT town (#PCDATA)>`
`<!ELEMENT contact (#PCDATA)>`
`<!ELEMENT county (#PCDATA)>`
`<!ELEMENT tel (#PCDATA)>`
`<!ELEMENT postcode (#PCDATA)>`
`<!ELEMENT country (#PCDATA)>`
`<!ELEMENT fax (#PCDATA)>`
`<!ELEMENT website (#PCDATA)>`
`<!ELEMENT email (#PCDATA)>`
`<!ELEMENT payterms (#PCDATA)>`
`]>`
	The + indicates that there can be a number of suppliers in the document.
	The details about a supplier include their name, account, address, town, contact name, post code, country, telephone, fax number, website address, email address, and payment terms.
	The question mark next to pay_terms means that this may be left blank if the payment terms of the supplier are unknown.
	PCDATA means parsed character data and identifies the type of data relating to the element. For example, it means that the supplier name is a string of data.

The generation, sharing, and use of information can and does occur without the use of IT. However, IT enables larger volumes of data to be processed than would be possible manually. In addition, data can be transmitted between business processes and shared between authorized personnel much faster and more efficiently with IT.

3.5 ▶ Maintain, Archive, and Destroy Information with Information Technology

Data may change due to a change of circumstances or to correct errors. The role of IT in maintaining information is to ensure that the most recent version of the data is readily available to all authorized personnel across the organization and to ensure that an audit trail is maintained of the changes made to data through the life cycle. An audit trail is needed to identify the events that triggered changes to the data, who changed the data, when the data were changed, and how the data were changed.

An audit trail can be used to identify changes to data that may be incorrect, or may be the result of a malicious act by staff inside the organization, or by unauthorized modification of the data from outside the organization. An accurate audit trail also enables the data to be restored to a previous version of the data when needed, for example, after a system failure has occurred.

Maintaining the accuracy, availability, and security of data involves:

o Keeping the data safe and accurate.
o Providing access to allow authorized personnel to make changes to the data stored.
o Preventing unauthorized personnel from changing the data.
o Preventing the data from being changed or deleted by accident.
o Restricting the changes that can be made to the data using validation rules to improve the quality of the data, for example, checking that a post code that has been entered is valid.
o Retaining a copy of the data before any changes are made in case the data need to be restored to how the data were before the change was made.
o Keeping an audit trail of changes made to the data.
o Backing up the data regularly; keeping copies of data at a particular point in time in case the data cannot be retrieved from the main storage location. Data may become lost or corrupted for a number of reasons, such as: (1) the data are deleted by accident, maliciously, or through defined purging policies, (2) the medium on which the data are stored becomes faulty,

and (3) the location of the storage device becomes damaged through, for example, fire, flood, natural disaster, war, or terrorist attack (Matthews *et al.*, 2009).

Regular data backups are needed to ensure that the current data, required by the organization on a daily basis, are available. In contrast, data archives store data that are not used frequently but need to be retained to satisfy the requirements of retention legislation. Organizations may need to retain information for over 10 years. Archiving provides a valuable source of data for data mining. Removing data from live systems to data archives reduces storage costs by moving the data to cheaper storage media and reduces the volume of data to be searched and maintained.

IT can provide the means to store and index data so that data can be retrieved when needed, and protect archived data so that data are not changed. However, as technology, software systems, programming languages, and data-storage formats continue to evolve, key factors in data archiving include ensuring that:

o Devices are available to read the medium on which archived data are stored. This is akin to individuals replacing compact disk players with iPods and no longer having the facility to play compact disks.
o When the archived data are read from the medium, the data can be input into information systems, which enable the data to be displayed, analysed, and used as required by the organization. Often organizations archive data and later replace their information systems; the archived data are then no longer in a suitable format to be input into the information systems. This means that the archived data cannot be accessed by the business areas that need the information.

When the retention period for data has expired, the data can be destroyed. Approaches to destroy data include shredding of paper files, overwriting electronically stored data, and the shredding and destruction of physical storage media. Care is needed to ensure that the security and privacy of data are not breached during this last phase in the information life cycle.

3.6 ▶ Information Life Cycle Management with Information Technology

Information life cycle management focuses on meeting the changing storage, access, and retrieval needs of information throughout the life cycle. Storage costs can consume a significant percentage of the IT budget. The value of information to the business has to be considered at each stage in the information life cycle to ensure that the storage, access, and security provision are appropriate and in proportion to the value of the information.

One approach to assessing the value of information is in terms of the frequency with which the information is accessed. Hierarchical storage management automatically migrates (that is, moves) less frequently accessed data to slower and cheaper forms of data storage, such as magnetic tape or optical storage. The data can still be accessed, and the recipient does not need to know where the data are stored, but data cannot be retrieved as quickly as data stored in current databases.

Archiving data to slower and cheaper storage media was thought to be the final step before the data were deleted (Moore, 2004), however, historical data potentially has a higher value to organizations. Historical data are needed in data mining to perform trend analysis to detect patterns, particularly in financial, retail, and medical applications. Data also need to be retained to meet the demands of data-retention legislation. Although the cost of data-storage media has fallen, IT departments have not benefited from a reduction in expenditure on data storage. This is because it can be cheaper for organizations to keep data just in case the data are needed later rather than risking fines which may be levied if the organization is not able to provide the data when required to do so by legislative acts.

Information life cycle management ensures that data are available when needed by identifying, assessing, and mitigating the risks that may affect the availability of data. This includes taking regular backups of data and creating restore points so that access to data can be restored in the event of a system or media failure. Data may also be mirrored, that is, identical synchronized copies of data may be maintained by the organization. Mirroring data storage increases storage costs but minimizes the time taken to recover from problems that may affect the ability of the organization to access information when needed. Tallon and Scannell (2007) emphasize that managing risk rather than reducing cost should be the main driver in managing data and that this should include consideration of the time taken to recover from a system or device failure and the cost to the organization of this delay.

Green computing aims to minimize the impact of IT on the environment throughout the IT life cycle (including the stages of production, use, and disposal). Data centres are a major source of energy consumption and with increasing volumes of data to be stored, the cost of managing data centres continues to rise. Energy consumption is therefore a further factor to consider in data storage. This includes the energy costs of storing rarely used data on readily accessible disks versus the costs of increased data transmission in migrating data between storage media so that data can be accessed when needed (Moore, 2004).

3.7 Business Value of Information Technology

IT incurs costs to the organization during the IT life cycle in terms of the acquisition of equipment; the running costs including energy consumption, physical space, technical staff to install, operate, and maintain the IT equipment and the purchase of consumables; and the costs involved in the legal and ethical disposal of the equipment. Information life cycle management aims to reduce these costs; however, all IT costs need to be justified in terms of the value IT contributes to the organization.

The business value of IT is derived from the impact technology has on the performance of the organization, measured in terms of productivity, cost savings, and competitive advantage (Melville et al., 2004). Figure 3.1 showed some of the information transmitted between an organization and its customers and suppliers. IT provides the medium for data to be transmitted but IT is more than a transport system. IT structures the capture of data, according to business rules, to capture the information required by business processes. IT then securely transmits the data, checks that the data have been transmitted correctly, and stores the data. Technology enables business processes to access data; technology restricts unauthorized access to data and protects the data from modifications that would reduce the quality of the data.

When IT is working well in an organization it becomes invisible, providing access to accurate information when needed. The benefits of technology to the organization are based on:

○ Improving access to information.
○ Providing location-independent access to information.
○ Increasing the speed with which information can be accessed.
○ Manipulating large volumes of information.
○ Reducing the direct costs of information handling.
○ Improving the accuracy of the information.
○ Enforcing security and integrity controls to improve the quality of the information.

IT improves the transmission speed, quality, and timely access to data. The value of technology to the organization is therefore reflected in:

○ Availability of information, of the appropriate quality, when needed.
○ More informed decisions.

○ Efficient operation of business processes.

○ Effective use of resources, including information, people, equipment, and space.

○ Transformation of the organization architecture.

Such benefits can be difficult to quantify.

3.7.1 Role of Information Technology in Morphing Organizations

Information flows within the organization and between trading partners outside the organization. IT facilitates the transmission of data among interested parties but technology also provides the means to access, analyse, and interact with data, adding value to data to provide information that has value to organizational processes. The different ways in which information can be used and accessed, facilitated by IT, has changed the way organizations operate and compete. Although a task determines the requirements of an artefact (such as IT) needed to support the task, the artefact itself offers new opportunities to perform the task differently or change the task to be performed (Carroll & Rosson, 1992). The transformation of organizations, including how an organization interacts with external partners, and how organizations operate internally, was discussed in Chapter 1. Gregor *et al.* (2006) propose that the degree to which an organization is transformed by the use of IT is a measure of the value of IT to an organization. IT has transformed organizations by changing the accessibility of information within and among trading partners.

The degree to which IT can transform an organization is dependent on the relationship between IT and change management processes in the organization. Installing new technology will not add value to the organization unless the technology is used; technology will not be used unless the technology supports the needs of the organization. Table 3.4 explains how IT triggers and facilitates change in the dimensions of organizational transformation (from Section 1.4).

Table 3.4 Role of Information Technology in Morphing Dimensions

Dimension of Organizational Transformation	Role of Information Technology
Infrastructure	Technology facilitates flexible access to information, people, and business processes, removing barriers such as location and opening hours. This enables structural changes to take place within and among organizations, affecting the formal structure, informal structure, physical location plans, IT infrastructure, and trading networks of the organization.
Security	IT can be used to impose security controls to restrict electronic access to data (such as by the use of passwords) and physical access to resources, buildings, and parts of buildings (for example, using magnetic card readers). IT can monitor patterns of behaviour and detect potential threats to organizational security. Developments in technology change the way resources can be accessed and used.
Data	Huge volumes of structured and unstructured data can be captured, transmitted, stored, analysed, and presented in different ways by IT. New technologies change requirements for how data are managed. For example, smart telephones impose different requirements on how data are presented and securely transmitted than a desktop computer at a fixed location. Technological developments continue to remove limitations on how data can be managed in organizations, facilitating new ways of working.
Processes	Business processes capture and use information to meet the goals of the organization. As technology removes the barriers to what information is available, when, and where, new opportunities arise for how organizational goals can be achieved through changes to business processes. For example, social networking technologies provide new communication channels to allow organizations to communicate with their customers. This requires new business processes to be developed in order to engage effectively within these communication channels.
Working Practices	Working practices are continually changed by the advent of new technologies. Changing the technology used in the organization initiates different ways of working, supported by changes to formal business processes. This includes changing when, where, and how work is performed, which has a wider impact on society in terms of work-life balance. While technology can improve working practices, poorly designed information systems can have an adverse effect on organizations too. Working practices are embedded in the culture of the organization and changes therefore impact upon morale, productivity, and the effective operation of the organization.

Table 3.4 ▶ Continued

Dimension of Organizational Transformation	Role of Information Technology
Skills	Developments in technology require technical staff to continue to develop new skills in the latest hardware, software, operating systems, and networks. This includes keeping up to date with standards, protocols, software updates, hardware upgrades, and security threats. The impact of changes to technology on the organization is not limited to the IT department. As working practices change in response to technology, different skills are required in working practices. For example, Match Lighting's sales team previously spent most of their time visiting retailers to promote new product ranges. This required staff to have excellent oral communication and negotiation skills. Now much of their time is spent communicating to retailers via email, which requires different communication skills. The skill profile of an organization changes in response to changes in technology.
People	People are the most important resource in any organization and are constantly challenged to adapt to technological changes. New business processes require new ways of working and different skills sets to be developed. As technology initiates changes to processes and structures, roles in the organization may expand or contract. The staffing profile of the organization evolves and staff may need to be deployed in different areas of the organization as teams are re-formed. This impacts both the formal and informal structure of the organization, affecting the culture of the organization, its vision, philosophy, and values.
Trust	Relationships between people within and between organizations are dependent on trust. Technology can facilitate the development of trust by facilitating communication. Technology can also destroy trust by failing to secure, maintain, and process information appropriately. IT changes structures and processes that impact on how trust can be developed and destroyed.

Quiz 3.1
Role of Information Technology

3.7.2 ▶ Strategic Role of Information Technology

As information is a strategic resource, information systems and IT need to be aligned with the organizational strategy. Information systems can change both the product and service provided by the organization and the manner in which the organization competes in its industry (Ives & Learmonth, 1984). There are three main generic strategies for seeking competitive advantage (Porter, 1980): cost leadership, product or service differentiation, and focus on a niche market.

IT can support an organization in seeking and maintaining competitive advantage by:

○ Reducing costs through efficient business processes supported by effective information management.
○ Providing information to support product innovation and added-value service differentiation.
○ Providing a means to engage with customers in a specialized market to identify their specific needs.

Parsons (1983) identifies the following areas in which information systems and IT can contribute to establishing competitive advantage:

○ Increasing the cost for a customer to switch suppliers.
○ Reducing dependence on a single supplier by reducing the cost of switching suppliers.
○ Identifying the potentially most profitable customers.
○ Supporting product innovation.
○ Sharing information and IT with rivals.
○ Reducing production and distribution costs.
○ Gaining greater appreciation of customer base.
○ Providing barriers for new entrants into the market.

Although IT is described as a competitive necessity, its ability to improve competitive advantage (for example, by market access, product differentiation, and cost efficiency) is only temporary (Reddy & Reddy, 2002).

3.7.3 ▶ Measuring the Value of Information Technology

Section 3.1 introduced a number of types of information systems, supported by different technologies, to capture, transmit, store, and process data. Different measures of value need to be used depending on the type of information system being evaluated. Farbey *et al.* (1995) categorize information systems within eight rungs of a ladder (shown in Figure 3.17) to reflect varying levels of potential value to the organization.

Farbey *et al.* (1995) suggest that as the potential benefits to the organization increase up the ladder, the potential risks associated with the implementation of the information systems and the importance of risk assessment also increase. Different methods are therefore needed to evaluate the risks and benefits associated with information systems on different rungs of the ladder (Farbey *et al.*, 1995). The evaluation methods range from quantifiable measures of improvements in process efficiency at the lower rungs, through to more qualitative and holistic assessments at the higher levels (Figure 3.17).

3.7.4 Importance of Information Technology to the Organization

Information is as important to an organization as the goods the organization produces because the effective use of information can reduce costs and improve services (Sudalaimuthu & Raj, 2009). IT provides the means to manage information efficiently and effectively to support attainment of the organizational strategy, adding value to business processes

Rung	Information System	Focus of Evaluation
8	Business Transformation: The introduction of IT initiates widespread change in business processes and working practices in the organization.	Focus holistically on the impact of the change using process modelling techniques and socio-technical analysis.
7	Strategic Information Systems: Designed to change the product or service provided, or the manner in which the organization competes in its industry.	Focus on the business benefits in relation to the competitive position of the organization.
6	Interorganizational Systems: Support the exchange and processing of information between organizations.	Focus on the trade-off between the loss of independence and the benefits of shared systems from the perspective of both partners.
5	Infrastructure: The platform of hardware and software that provides the foundation for information systems in the organization. The infrastructure includes for example, the physical networks required to link computer systems and the standard level of information systems to be provided to everyone in the organization.	Focus on flexibility and new opportunities provided by the investment.
4	Management Information and Decision Support Systems: Provide information to support planning activities.	Focus on added value through probability measures and scenario analysis.
3	Direct Added Value Systems: Business processes are changed with direct added value systems to improve business performance.	Focus on value and new capability generated through focus groups and pilot studies.
2	Automation Systems: Provide IT support to existing business processes with the aim of increasing production and reducing costs.	Focus on efficiency using work measurement and simulation modelling techniques.
1	Mandatory Systems: Systems that the organization must have to satisfy legal or regulatory requirements, or to meet a standard level of accepted practice to compete in an industry.	Focus on cost and productivity using cost accounting and work measurement techniques.

Figure 3.17 Information Systems Evaluation Ladder

Source: Based on Farbey *et al.* (1995).

and providing opportunities to gain competitive advantage. IT changes competition by changing industry structures, providing opportunities to improve performance and develop new forms of business (Porter & Millar, 1985).

Despite these potential benefits, the importance of IT to organizations is perhaps most apparent when things go wrong. Table 3.5 highlights some of the situations that have been blamed on computer errors. In many of these examples, poor information management and lack of business processes to check the information produced by technology may have been at the root of these problems.

Organizations often complain that the computer is slow, information is wrong, information is difficult to access, information has been lost, and information has been stolen or accessed by unauthorized parties. IT generates unnecessary costs to the business through poorly designed information systems that hinder, rather than facilitate, access to the organization's information. Too much or too little information and poor quality

information adversely affect decisions that can have a direct financial impact on the organization. These problems are discussed in Part II.

3.8 Information Technology Architecture

The organizational architecture (discussed in Section 1.6) provides the boundaries for using space in organizations; the IT architecture provides the boundaries for using IT in the organization. The IT architecture provides a set of policies and guidelines to ensure that technology can be effectively integrated across the organization. This enables different business functions to share data among compatible IT systems. The guidelines help departments to select equipment and packaged software that meets their functional needs while ensuring that data can be can sent and received in a form that is compatible with other IT systems used in the organization. The IT architecture also ensures that the organization's systems are compatible with those of its business partners to support collaboration and e-business activities. For example, the IT policy may require all software to be open source. An example of the scope of the IT architecture is shown in Figure 3.18.

The IT architecture is different from the IT infrastructure. The IT architecture establishes the policy and procedures for selecting hardware and software to be used in the organization.

DEFINITION: The **information technology (IT) architecture** defines the policies relating to the purchase, development, and implementation of hardware and software in an organization to facilitate data integration within compatible IT systems.

The IT infrastructure refers to the organization of IT equipment in the organization.

DEFINITION: The **information technology (IT) infrastructure** is a diagrammatic representation of the

Table 3.5	Examples of Problems Caused by the Wrong Information
2010	After sending a passport to be renewed, the passport was returned to its owner with the birth certificates of two strangers.
2011	22,000 people were wrongly informed that they had been granted US visas.
2011	450 prisoners were wrongly released from prison in California.
2012	Two gas explosions were caused by workers being misinformed that gas pipes had been decommissioned in the United Kingdom.
2013	1,000 customers received the wrong property tax bill in the United States.

Link 3.4
More Examples of Problems Caused by the Wrong Information

Mobile Devices Desktop	Applications	Servers Processors Storage Media Printers	Operating Systems Database Management Systems	Local Area Network Wide Area Network Security	Protocols	Offsite Data Archive
		Policies	Standards	Guidelines		

Figure 3.18 Information Technology Architecture

systems, databases, data centres, computer processors, servers, printers, and desktop computers needed to implement the information systems required by the organization.

The relationships between the organizational architecture, information architecture, information systems architecture, and IT architecture are discussed in Chapter 4.

Scenario 3.3 provides an example of how IT policies support the IT architecture at Match Lighting.

supporting the implementation of information systems for strategic advantage. The information management strategy provides the framework in which the information systems and IT strategies can be implemented.

Earl (1996) makes the following distinction between information systems strategy and IT strategy:

○ Information systems strategy is demand-oriented, business-focused, identifying **what** information and information processes are needed by the organization.

Scenario 3.3

IT Policies in Match Lighting

Mr Cook has developed a set of IT policies for Match Lighting, which aims to provide a consistent and sustainable infrastructure to meet the needs of all departments. The Head of the Sales Department, Mr Selas, wants to purchase six desktop computers for staff in his department but Mr Cook has stopped the purchase. This has led to the following conversation:

Mr Selas:	'Why have you cancelled my purchase order? My staff need those computers urgently. Their old computers are useless and I want them to install the Make-It-Up software package I bought at the weekend.'
Mr Cook:	'The hardware policy clearly states that all computers have to be purchased through the IT department.'
Mr Selas:	'But you always buy the same standard computer and my staff need something different.'
Mr Cook:	'The hardware policy provides an agreed standard level of equipment for all staff. The standardization ensures that all equipment can be easily maintained and that automated software updates can be implemented with minimum disruption to staff.'
Mr Selas:	'My staff all need to install this copy of the software that I have bought.'
Mr Cook:	'You cannot buy and install your own software. The software policy states that all software must be purchased by the IT department and thoroughly tested before the software is installed to ensure that the software is stable and free from viruses. By installing your own software you are putting the whole network at risk. In addition, the IT department tracks licences to ensure that software is installed legally. The hardware and software policies are published on the intranet.'

Link 3.5
Example IT Policy

The IT infrastructure is the implementation of the architecture, the technical layer of specific devices needed to support the information systems architecture introduced in Chapter 2.

3.9 ▶ Scope of Information Technology in Information Management

Managing information means ensuring that information is available and accessible when needed by business functions to inform actions and decisions in the organization. IT is the means for communicating information and

○ IT strategy is supply-oriented, technology-focused, identifying **how** the information needs identified in the organization may be satisfied through the use of IT.

The organization's corporate strategy determines **why** an information system is required. An information systems plan outlines how the transition from strategy phase (vision) to implementation (reality) will take place, outlining:

○ What information systems are needed.
○ Why the information systems are needed.
○ How the information systems will be provided.
○ When the information systems will be provided.
○ What actions are required to provide the information systems.

Figure 3.19 provides the headings for Match Lighting's information systems and IT plan. The mission of the

1. Challenges and Objectives
   This includes the mission, strategic objectives and business requirements.
2. Major Achievements
   This outlines how information systems and IT have contributed to the corporate and business requirements in the previous year.
3. Business Alignment of the Information Systems and IT Programme of Projects
   The information systems and IT response to business requirements such as:
   ○ Integrating operational systems.
   ○ Establishing a single version of data in management information systems.
   ○ Planning infrastructure projects to support mobile computing devices.
4. Information Systems and IT Contribution to Strategic Plan
   ○ Data Strategy
   ○ Systems Strategy
   ○ Technical Strategy
5. Resource Requirements
   ○ Revenue Budget (including software licenses)
   ○ Capital Budget (including servers)
   ○ Staffing Requirements
6. Information Systems and IT Programme of Projects
   This is a plan of projects with timescales for each project.
7. Architectures
   ○ IT Architecture
   ○ Information Systems Architecture
   ○ Information Architecture

Figure 3.19 Headings for an Information Systems and Information Technology Plan

organization and its strategic objectives provide the business context with which to align the information systems and IT plan, justifying expenditure. The strategic value of information systems and IT to Match Lighting in the previous year is evaluated before the future information systems and IT priorities, aligned with the organization's objectives, are identified.

Summary

IT provides a means of implementing information systems, which coordinate business processes in the information life cycle. IT enables data to be captured using data input devices and sensor technologies. Data are stored in databases and can be retrieved to support operational decisions. Summarized data are stored in a data warehouse to support strategic decisions and data mining techniques can be used to identify patterns in data to discover new information.

The value of IT to the organization relates to the benefits derived from implementing information systems using technology. Information systems can be categorized in terms of their value to organizations, supporting operational processes, providing information to inform tactical decisions, and offering opportunities to facilitate organizational transformation. The introduction of IT can change ways of working in the organization, changing communication structures, cultural practice, and the way the organization interfaces with external parties in the market and business environment. The IT architecture defines the policies and processes relating to the purchase and use of IT. The IT infrastructure is a diagrammatic representation of the hardware devices and operating systems that comply with the IT architecture to meet the needs of the information systems architecture.

Reviewing Scenario 3.1

Match Lighting needs IT equipment to support the information processing needs of the organization. IT enables data to be effectively captured, stored, transmitted, used, and archived when and where needed by all business functions. While a desktop computer can be purchased relatively cheaply, it is just one part of the technological infrastructure needed by Match Lighting. For example, a range of data capture devices are needed throughout the organization; data-storage media and a database management system are needed to enable data to be stored, accessed, and shared; networks are needed to transmit data among the database and devices such as desktop computers, laptops, and handheld computers; and software is needed to support information systems that facilitate data processing, office automation, and management information systems.

The value of IT to Match Lighting relates to improvements in the management of information to support the organizational strategy and facilitate business transformation. IT implements security and integrity controls to improve the quality of data and provides authorized staff with access to the data when and where they need it, in the format required. IT enables business processes to access and process data efficiently and effectively, providing decision-makers with accurate information when needed to meet the organizational objectives. IT continues to transform the way Match Lighting operates. For example, sales staff communicate with retailers via email and Mr Alvis is able to retain control of decision-making processes when he is out of the office by remotely accessing internal information systems.

The information systems and IT strategy justifies investment by aligning proposals with Match Lighting's strategic objectives, focusing on:

○ Improving core operations.
○ Supporting the information management needs of the organization.
○ Examining the potential role of new IT in the organization.
○ Assessing the future information needs of the organization.

The strategy considers the technical infrastructure needed to meet the information requirements of the organization. The IT architecture provides a range of policies to promote standardization of hardware and software acquisition in order to facilitate effective integration of data and technology throughout Match Lighting.

Exercise 3.1

1 What is the difference between a formal and an informal information system?
2 What does URL mean?
3 What are the three views of information proposed by Buckland (1991)?
4 What is the role of a network in information management?
5 What is EDI?
6 Which view of a database is seen by the business processes?
7 Why are there different views of a database?
8 What is the difference between a database and a data warehouse?
9 Do XML or HTML tags refer to how the information is to be displayed without considering the content of the information?
10 What is the purpose of data mining?
11 List three reasons why data need to be backed up regularly.
12 What is the purpose of hierarchical storage management?
13 What is meant by green computing?
14 Why is green computing relevant to information management?
15 How does IT assist an organization in implementing a strategy of cost leadership?
16 Match Lighting has had to implement an information system to demonstrate that equipment from the asset register has been disposed of in accordance with legislative requirements. Where would this information system be positioned in the evaluation ladder?

17 In Scenario 3.3, why is Mr Selas prevented from purchasing desktop computers?
18 How does IT affect trust in an organization?
19 How does an information architecture differ from an information infrastructure?
20 Explain the relationship between information systems and IT.

Link 3.6
Answers to Exercise 3.1

Activities 3.1

1 Apply the data transmission steps to explain how to send a message to someone in the same room using only paper.
2 Mr Cook needs a monthly report providing information on the computer equipment purchased in Match Lighting. Apply the characteristics of data listed in Table 3.2 and produce a specification of the requirements of this monthly report.
3 Develop an information life cycle for information relating to IT equipment purchased by Match Lighting. Map the use of IT to each event in the life cycle to show how IT can be used to manage the information.
4 Slice and dice the data cube in Figure 3.12 in different ways to create new information for Match Lighting.
5 Section 3.7.2 listed a number of ways that information systems and IT can contribute to establishing competitive advantage. Provide an example of each to show Mr Alvis the potential value of IT to Match Lighting.
6 Map the example information systems identified in Activity 3.1.5 to the appropriate rungs in the information systems evaluation ladder shown in Figure 3.17.

Discussion Questions 3.1

1 When creating an online order form for customers to use, should the customer first be asked to enter their personal details or the details of the item they wish to order? Why?
2 Discuss the business implications, both positive and negative, of allowing an external organization such as a supplier to directly access the information systems in an organization.

3 Explain the different circumstances in which you would use email and Twitter to communicate with a friend.

4 Data can be input into an IT system in different ways. What factors should be considered when selecting the IT to be used to capture data?

5 Summarizing data is one approach to add value to data. To what extent can summarizing data be supported by IT?

6 Mirroring data improves the availability of data. What factors need to be considered to assess whether mirroring is needed?

7 Discuss the benefits and problems relating to the ability to access information remotely.

8 To what extent can the value of IT to an organization be assessed by quantifiable measures?

ROLE OF BUSINESS IN INFORMATION MANAGEMENT

Scenario 4.1

IT in Amy's Candles

Amy realized that in setting up her business, Amy's Candles, she will need to capture, store, and manage a vast quantity of information. Amy has already identified that she will need information relating to her customers, suppliers, orders, product range, stock, and finances; the list seemed endless. At the moment, Amy does not have many customers and she can manage all the information she needs using paper-based systems. Amy hopes that her business will grow and she realizes that she will need to use information technology (IT) to store and retrieve information quickly and easily.

Amy visited her local computer superstore and explained to a sales representative that she wanted something to help her manage the information in her business. The sales representative talked about database packages and spreadsheets, hard drives and printers, memory and storage capacity; it all seemed so confusing.

Amy decided to hire someone to advise her about the technology she needed and to set up the equipment for her. Bob, a consultant, quickly took charge, buying a computer and a range of software for her. Within two months, Bob had put Amy's current customer details in a database and showed her how to store information about customers, products, and materials.

At first everything seemed fine but then Amy began to notice some peculiarities with the systems that Bob had set up. A customer requested a quote for a wax sculpture for a wedding reception and Amy wanted to store the customer's details in the customer database. The program would not allow her to store the customer details without a valid order number, but the customer had not yet placed an order. Amy gave up and wrote the details on paper. The system also keeps displaying a message stating that Amy should reorder midnight moon dye; stock of this dye is low but it is no longer manufactured and has been replaced by deep space blue dye, which Amy has plenty of in stock.

Why have these peculiarities arisen? How could they have been avoided?

Learning Outcomes

The learning outcomes of this chapter are to:

○ Describe the stages in developing an information architecture.
○ Apply a socio-technical approach to developing an information architecture.
○ Identify information requirements using a range of business models.
○ Structure information with business rules.
○ Define information access, security, and integrity requirements with business rules.

○ Describe an enterprise architecture.
○ Explain the important role of the business in information management.

Introduction

The increasing complexity and ubiquitous presence of information technology (IT) has led to businesses delegating the responsibility of information management to IT departments. The aim of this chapter is to outline the activities that the business needs to undertake, with guidance from IT professionals, to provide the IT function in the organization with information about how information is used in the organization. The IT function will use the information provided by the organization to inform decisions about how technology can be used to manage the information required by business functions. The important role of the business in leading information management is emphasized.

Information has meaning in context and the organization provides the context for information. Section 3.9 explained that the corporate strategy of an organization provides the context and justification for the development of information systems; it explained why information systems are needed, justifying investment. Chapter 3 also outlined the role of IT in providing the means to implement the information systems required to improve the management of information; improving the quality, security, and integrity of information as well as facilitating and restricting access to information. IT provides the means to implement the business processes to manage information throughout the information life cycle. However, information belongs to the organization and the business functions must seize control and accept responsibility for the organization's information. This chapter explains how the organization can achieve this by developing an information architecture. The information architecture specifies the organization's requirements for information. IT can then be used to help the organization to capture, to generate, and to manage the information required by business functions. The chapter concludes by explaining the relationship between the information architecture, organizational architecture, information systems architecture, and IT architecture.

4.1 ▶ Develop the Information Architecture

Information architectures were introduced in Chapter 2 as a means to define the information to be managed in an organization. There are a number of approaches to developing an information architecture. Some approaches are data-driven, led by the IT function, focusing on developing a conceptual model of the data needed to provide information in the organization. Other approaches adopt a broader view of architecture as a visual representation of an organization's information systems strategy and IT strategy. For example, Earl (1989) refers to architecture as a framework incorporating computing, communication, data, and applications for constructing an IT infrastructure. Earl (1989) proposed the following approaches to developing this architecture:

○ Mapping: A bottom-up approach incorporating an inventory of current information provision and an assessment of the current strengths and weaknesses.

○ Steering: A top-down approach establishing the strategic goals, values, and policies to which the architecture will need to adhere.

○ Updating: An inside-out approach developing links between the information systems strategy and the IT strategy.

○ Shaping: A distillation approach of collecting the information from the previous stages to define the principles on which the architecture will be based.

There is a lack of clarity between the roles of architectures and strategies in the literature. In this context an information architecture is used to identify the current and potential future information needed by the organization. The information systems strategy and IT strategy consider how information systems and IT are deployed in the organization, aligned with the priorities of the organizational strategy, to implement the information architecture. An information management strategy (Part II) is formulated to manage the information identified in the information architecture throughout the information's life cycle. The development of the information architecture should be led by the business (Martin *et al.*, 2010). The information architecture provides a model of the information needs of the business, which can be mapped to the technological infrastructure needed to satisfy the organization's information requirements.

4.1.1 ▶ Introduction to Principles of Socio-Technical Approach

Martin *et al.* (2010) suggest that a socio-technical approach is needed for developing an information architecture. A socio-technical approach is concerned with the relationship that emerges between technology (such as IT) and the social context in which technology is used. The approach recognizes that although it is necessary to consider technical issues such as efficiency and response times, the impact on the people who use the technology also needs to be considered.

A purely technical approach to developing an information architecture focuses on information as objects of data that can be organized in an objective manner. Information management is measured in quantifiable terms relating to the data objects, such as the time taken to retrieve data, network transmission speeds, and the storage capacity of IT.

A social approach recognizes that the cultural values of the organization are embedded in the context within which information is interpreted and IT is used. The management of information is subjectively measured as people interpret information and the characteristics of information differently.

A socio-technical approach considers the interrelationships between the:

○ Task to be undertaken.
○ Structure of the organization, including lines of authority, responsibility, and communication.
○ Management style.
○ People involved in the task; their perceptions, skills, and values.
○ Technology available to support the task.

The information requirements of an organization emerge from the interactions among these elements.

The socio-technical approach is embedded in soft systems methods. There are two main approaches to information systems development: hard systems approaches and soft systems approaches. Hard systems approaches start with a defined, agreed upon problem; the approaches aim to solve the problem in an objective, systematic and reductionist manner. Hard systems approaches are based on the philosophy that everyone sees things the same way, that everyone is in agreement with what the problem is and how the problem should be solved (that an IT system needs to be developed). In contrast, soft systems approaches adopt the stance that people see things differently. Soft systems approaches use techniques that help to explore different views of the same situation and expose areas of conflict, which may be the root cause of problems in the organization. Agreements then emerge about the information needs of the organization and the information systems that need to be developed. Soft systems approaches do not seek to solve problems; they seek to develop understanding of problematic situations.

Soft systems tools can be used to explore different views of the organizational context that need to be accommodated in the information architecture. The approach to developing an information architecture presented in Section 4.1.3 uses tools from Wilson's (1990, 2001) soft systems method. The use of soft systems tools supports a holistic approach to information management that helps to ensure that the information needs of the whole business are met; if the information needs of the whole organization are not met, the business will not have the information needed to make decisions and support business processes.

4.1.2 ▶ Overview of Wilson's (1990) Soft Systems Method

Wilson's (1990) soft systems method comprising eight stages shown in Table 4.1, extends the soft systems method proposed by Checkland (1981). Some of the stages involve activities that include modelling aspects of the real world. Other activities require a separation from the real world, stepping back from the problem, constraints, and structures of the real world to explore the context more freely. The first four stages are iterative; they explore different views about the problem situation and seek to develop a consensus conceptual model of activities that will effectively address the situation identified. The later stages explore the information needed to support the activities in the consensus conceptual model and compare the model with the current situation in the real world. Table 4.2 lists soft systems tools from Wilson's (1990) soft system method that have been incorporated into the approach to developing an information architecture presented in Section 4.1.3.

Table 4.1 ▶ Stages in Wilson's Soft Systems Method

Real World	Thinking about the Real World
1. Find out about Situation and Express the Situation.	
	2. Formulate Potential Root Definitions.
	3. Develop Conceptual Models.
4. Compare Conceptual Models with Real World and Develop Consensus Model.	
	5. Derive Information Categories.
	6. Map Activity to Activity Information Flows.
7. Map Current Information Provision.	
8. Map Organization Structure.	

Source: Based on Wilson (1990).

Link 4.1
Description of the Stages of Wilson's (1990) Soft Systems Method

Table 4.2 ▶ Soft Systems Tools

Tools	Definition
Rich Picture	A diagrammatic representation of different views within a problem situation, using free-form notation.
Root Definition	A textual description of the activity system that represents one view of the world shown in the rich picture.
CATWOE	Elements that provide the foundation of a root definition (customer, actor, transformation, Weltanschauung, owner, environmental constraints).
Conceptual Model	A diagrammatic representation of the activities, and the relationships between activities, required to satisfy the transformation process identified in the root definition.
Consensus Model	A conceptual model of activities that encompasses a shared view of the world, agreed to by those involved in the problem situation.
Information Categories	The groups of data that are needed as input to, output from, or to monitor activities within the system represented by the consensus conceptual model.
Maltese Cross	A matrix mapping the information categories input to and output from: A) Activities included in the consensus conceptual model. B) Equivalent existing information processes in the real world. It enables the completeness of the information requirements needed to support activities in the consensus model to be verified and then compared with the existing implemented systems.

4.1.3 ▶ Approach to Developing an Information Architecture

Developing an information architecture includes the following stages:

Stage 1: Analyse the organizational context.
Stage 2: Define information requirements.
Stage 3: Structure information with business rules.
Stage 4: Specify information access.

Stage 1 adopts a top-down approach to define the context within which the information architecture will be situated. The stage is based on the premise that as information has meaning in context, the context needs to be understood and the boundary of the context needs to be defined. The organizational architecture provides the overall context for the information architecture. The business model is developed to establish the overall view of the organization and its position in its market(s), business environment(s), and business climate. The fundamental information needed by the organization is then defined. Further detailed information requirements can be derived using additional analytical models in the organization.

Stage 2 adopts an inside-out approach in which different views of the organization (or parts of the organization) are explored to define detailed information requirements. This stage focuses on key processes in the organization and the information that the processes need and generate. A bottom-up approach is then adopted; a data to process mapping is conducted to assess the completeness of the information requirements that have been identified. An audit is taken to assess the limitations of the existing information provision in the organization.

Stage 3 defines the structure of the information identified in stage 2 by analysing the relationships between categories of information. In this stage business rules are defined, which specify the restrictions on how data are captured, stored, and used, that will be implemented using information systems and IT.

Stage 4 focuses on identifying the access that the organization requires to the information. Checks are made to ensure that the information required by the organization can be derived from the structure proposed in stage 3. The security requirements of the information, such as access restrictions to confidential information, are then agreed to and documented in a data dictionary. The four stages adopt a socio-technical approach and use soft systems modelling tools, listed in Table 4.2. Table 4.3 provides an overview of the stages to develop an information architecture.

Table 4.3 Approach to Develop an Information Architecture

Stage 1	**Analyse the Organizational Context**
	Step 1.1: Define the Context
	1.1.1 Apply the business model.
	1.1.2 Identify the external parties who send information to the organization.
	1.1.3 Identify the external parties who receive information from the organization.
	1.1.4 Identify the key terminology used in the organization.
	Step 1.2: Identify Master Data
	1.2.1 Identify the information that flows into or out of the organization.
	1.2.2 List the interactions that take place between the organization and each external party.
	1.2.3 Identify the entities, the core data groupings, about the information exchanged in the interactions between the organization and external parties.
	Step 1.3: Define Strategic Information Requirements
	1.3.1 Select modelling tool(s) (from the mapping of tools to the business model).
	1.3.2 Apply the modelling tool(s) in accordance with the tool's guidelines.
	1.3.3 Analyse the completed model(s).
	1.3.4 Extract the information requirements identified from the model(s).
	1.3.5 Combine the information requirements with the information requirements identified from the business model.
Stage 2	**Define Information Requirements**
	Step 2.1: Identify Different Views within the Context
	2.1.1 Develop a rich picture of the situation.
	2.1.2 Prepare a set of CATWOE for each world view.
	2.1.3 Construct a root definition for each world view.
	2.1.4 Develop a conceptual model for each root definition.
	2.1.5 Form an agreed upon consensus model.
	Step 2.2: Define Information Categories
	2.2.1 Identify the inputs and outputs to each activity in the consensus model.
	2.2.2 Specify the information needed to measure the performance of the system represented in the consensus model.
	2.2.3 Extract potential information categories from the root definitions.
	2.2.4 Create a brief description of each information category.
	Step 2.3: Data to Process Mapping
	2.3.1 Complete the top half of the Maltese Cross.
	2.3.2 Check the completeness of the Maltese Cross to ensure that all the information categories are identified and used.
	2.3.3 For each information category, check that the life cycle activities are supported.
	2.3.4 Complete the bottom half of the Maltese Cross.
	2.3.5 Compare the top and bottom halves of the Maltese Cross.
	2.3.6 Combine the information categories from the Maltese Cross with the information requirements identified from stage 1.
Stage 3	**Structure Information with Business Rules**
	Step 3.1: Identify Hierarchies
	3.1.1 Create a category association table.
	3.1.2 Review candidate relationships to ensure that they are complete and meaningful.
	Step 3.2: Define Integrity Constraints
	3.2.1 For each relationship specify whether an occurrence is optional or mandatory in each direction.
	3.2.2 For each relationship specify whether one or more than one instance of an entity can be associated with an instance of the other entity.

Table 4.3 ▶ Continued

Stage 3	Structure Information with Business Rules
	Step: 3.3: Model Business Rules
	3.3.1 Draw the entities and relationship from the candidate relationships identified.
	3.3.2 Add the determinacy constraints for each relationship.
	3.3.3 Add the cardinality constraints for each relationship.
	3.3.4 Check the accuracy of the business rules represented.
Stage 4	**Specify Information Access**
	Step 4.1: Identify Access Paths
	4.1.1 Develop a list of typical queries.
	4.1.2 Identify example data for each entity.
	4.1.3 Map the access path through the model to answer each query.
	Step 4.2: Specify Access Requirements
	4.2.1 Identify who needs to access each entity.
	4.2.2 Assign access restrictions for each entity.
	Step 4.3: Define Security Requirements
	4.3.1 Define the legal and ethical requirements that affect access to each entity.
	4.3.2 Identify who is authorized to perform each activity in the entity life cycle.
	4.3.3 Ensure integrity constraints are sufficient.
	Step 4.4: Construct Data Dictionary
	4.4.1 Define entities and attributes.
	4.4.2 Document the entity relationships.
	4.4.3 Specify the access and usage requirements of each entity.
	4.4.4 Define archive and retention policies.

4.2 ▶ Stage 1: Analyse the Organizational Context

The first stage in developing an information architecture is to determine what information the organization needs so that the information can be captured, stored, and used to support business processes. A context-oriented approach is adopted, focusing on the organizational context that gives information meaning. Context emerges from the dynamic interactions between the internal components of the organization and the organization's reactions to information about changes in the market, business environment, and business climate in which the organization is situated. Morphing organizations are continually changing in response to information generated both internally and externally. Internal and external factors are identified to shape the holistic context of the organization from which information requirements can be determined.

The organizational architecture (introduced in Section 1.6) captures the internal context within which information is interpreted in the organization. Table 4.4 shows how the organizational architecture defines the information needed in the organization. For example, the mission of Amy's Candles is to create high quality, bespoke candles, and wax

sculptures. Information is therefore needed about the creation of candles, the creation of wax sculptures, and quality monitoring processes. Amy's full mission statement (Section 2.5) provides further insight into the nature of the organization and its information needs.

4.2.1 ▶ Step 1.1: Define the Context

Applying the business model (step 1.1.1), introduced in Chapter 1, addresses the fundamental question of *what business are we in?* The market, business environment, and business climate identify the external sources of pressures, opportunities, and constraints within which the organization is required to operate. In the organization set of the business model, the main business processes, structure, and culture are identified that provide the internal context in which activity takes place in the organization.

A strength of the business model is that the model captures the external context within which the organization is situated. The model helps to *identify the external parties who send information to the organization (step 1.1.2)* and to *identify the external parties who receive information from the organization (step 1.1.3)*, including customers, suppliers, and national and international authorities. For example, the Association of European Candle Manufacturers

Table 4.4 Information Derived from the Organizational Architecture

Organizational Architecture	Information Requirements
Strategy	The terms used in the mission statement identify fundamental information required by the organization to measure the extent to which the mission is being attained.
Business Processes	Key processes indicate core information needed.
Systems	Information is needed to integrate business processes and measure the performance of business systems.
People	Job descriptions provide an indication of the range and type of information required by the role.
Technology	Information is needed about the range of equipment used in the organization, such as calibration requirements.
Security	The specific type of security risks to the organization identifies information that needs to be captured and monitored.
Organizational Structure	The structure of the organization, in terms of locations and functions, defines the boundaries of information.
Culture	Cultural values indicate key characteristics of information valued by the organization.
Informal Structure	The communication paths that are in operation indicate where information is currently used and located in the organization.
Vision	The terms used in the vision statement identify the information and values that are important to the organization and the information needed to enable the organization to achieve its future ambitions.
Working Practices	How tasks are performed will identify the information used within them.
Human Activity Systems	The characteristics of information needed help employees attribute meaning to business practices and the information required to integrate business practices.
Skills	Information is needed to identify the key skills required by business processes.
Socio-Technical	Information is required to facilitate meaningful interaction between people and technology during business processes.
Trust	The characteristics of information that engender trust in the quality of the information.

Table 4.5 Example Information Derived from Step 1.1

Step 1.1.2 Amy Sends Information To:	Step 1.1.3 Amy Receives Information From:	Step 1.1.4 Key Terminology Used
Customers (private individuals, charities, gift specialists). Suppliers. Local newspaper.	Customers. Suppliers. Professional bodies. Government offices.	Candle Wax sculpture Material Equipment Customer Supplier

(a professional body in the business model for Amy's Candles) recommends that members do not use lead wicks; Amy needs to capture such information from the association.

The construction of the business model helps to *identify the key terminology used in the organization (step 1.1.4).* For example, the beneficiaries of the organization in the market may be referred to as customers, clients,

guests, patients, students, or visitors depending on the organizational context. Table 4.5 shows an example of the information derived from step 1.1.

4.2.2 Step 1.2: Identify Master Data

Master data management is a key area within data management.

DEFINITION: Master data are the key data entities in an organization that are critical to the organization.

Master data are normally used by a number of business functions therefore improving the quality of master data is likely to have the largest impact on the business in terms of improvements to decision-making. Scenario 4.2 explains the background to master data management.

Scenario 4.2

Master Data in Match Lighting

The IT Manager at Match Lighting, Mr Cook, regularly received complaints that the information reported from *his* computer system was wrong. His response was that *his* systems only stored *their* business data. The problem was that over time different departments had developed information systems to meet their specific functional requirements. Almost all the information systems in the organization included some data about its products or customers. For example, the:

○ Sales department maintained a list of products available to be purchased by customers.
○ Market research department created a list of products that are on trial with pilot groups of customers.
○ Manufacturing department maintained a list of products currently in production.

These departments each stored and used some information about products. This led to a number of problems; for example:

○ Gathering together all the information about products required information to be collected and merged from different systems.
○ Merging information from different systems was difficult as each department had a different way of identifying products. Attempts to merge the data from the different departments resulted in the same product appearing more than once in the final list.
○ Changing product information was difficult as all copies of the product information held in different departments had to be changed. Storing and maintaining multiple copies of the same data also incurred unnecessary costs.

Mr Cook therefore created two master files: *product* and *customer*. A policy was implemented which meant that no data relating to products or customers could be held in departmental systems. All computer systems that now need to create, access, update, or delete information relating to products or customers must use the centralized files. These centralized files provide a single source of information about products and customers for use across the organization.

Master data management considers the transaction data surrounding key entities. This provides the ability to move from account-based to customer-centric provision (Berson & Dubov, 2011). A customer-centric approach reflects how the customer converses with the organization and enables an organization to provide more joined-up services to meet the overall needs of customers. Customer information is integrated from across the organization to provide a richer holistic service to customers.

The aim of master data management is to improve the quality of the key data that are critical to the organization. From the business model, Amy needs to *identify the information that flows into or out of the organization (step 1.2.1)* and then *list the interactions that take place between the organization and each external party (step 1.2.2)*. This will help to show the domain surrounding the master data that Amy needs to manage. For example, her *customer* data need to support a range of interactions as her *customers* adopt different roles as they:

○ Enquire about products (design, cost, availability, colours, material, sizes, and safety).
○ Order products (design, quantity, colour, size, and delivery date).
○ Query product orders (verifying order status, quantity, and price).
○ Complain about products (quality, quantity, and price).
○ Complain about product processes (delivery times).
○ Return products.
○ Request discounts on products.
○ Compliment products.
○ Comment on competitors' products.

Focusing on the interactions between key elements of the business model provides a richer understanding of the information required and the links between information sources. The interactions can be used to *identify the entities, the core data groupings, about the information exchanged in the interactions between the organization and external parties (step 1.2.3)* such as *product* and *order*. Table 4.6 shows some of the information derived from step 1.2.

4.2.3 Step 1.3: Define Strategic Information Requirements

Organizations use a range of models to assist in analysing the current strategic situation of the organization from both internal and external perspectives. Models provide information that will inform decisions relating

Table 4.6 ▶ Example Information Derived from Step 1.2

Step 1.2.1 Information Flows (from Steps 1.1.2 to 1.1.3)	Step 1.2.2 Interactions (from Steps 1.1.2 to 1.1.3)	Step 1.2.3 Potential Entities
Customer requirements. Order for materials and equipment. Special offers. Health and safety regulations. Annual accounts.	Customer places order for candles. Customer enquires about product design. Request quote for price of materials from supplier. Annual accounts submitted to tax office.	Customer Requirement. Order. Special Offer. Regulation. Product Design. Enquiry. Quotation. Annual Accounts.

to the organization's strategy and monitor progress towards achieving strategic targets. Each model provides one view of the organization. Models provide a filter to reduce the complexity of a situation to support analysis. Models consist of a set of constructs to be applied to a situation to help focus attention on key aspects of the situation. The completion of a model is not the end; the model then needs to be analysed to determine the information that can be derived from the application of the model. The process of analysing a situation using models is extremely valuable as the process improves understanding and facilitates insights into a situation.

Figure 4.1 maps a range of analytical models that are commonly used in organizations to the business model. This mapping can be used to help to **select modelling tool(s) (step 1.3.1)** to analyse different aspects of the organization and its trading environment.

Link 4.2
Information Content of Strategic Analysis Models

When the modelling tool has been selected from Figure 4.1, the next step is to **apply the modelling tool(s) in accordance with the tool's guidelines (step 1.3.2)** and record any questions, issues, and insights that arise during the application. Next, **analyse the completed model(s) (step 1.3.3)** to determine what can be learnt about the situation from the model and **extract the information requirements identified from the model(s) (step 1.3.4).** Finally, **combine the information requirements with the information requirements identified from the business model (step 1.3.5).** Figure 4.2 shows how Amy uses an analytical model to identify information to contribute to achieving her mission.

4.3 ▶ Stage 2: Define Information Requirements

Detailed analysis of the business processes provides an understanding of the operational information requirements of the organization. However, there can be disagreement about what the business processes are and what information a process requires. Data are intrinsically meaningless, only becoming information when invested with meaning by people (Mingers, 1988). All information modelling therefore implies inter-pretation (Hitchman & Bennetts, 1994). Information is interpreted within a context by people; however, individuals interpret information differently within the same context. Chapter 2 explained that information has a subjective value dependent on, for example, who uses the information and the task they are undertaking. This is because individuals view the world through a cognitive filter formed by their past experiences, values, and beliefs. In the same way that applying a model filters

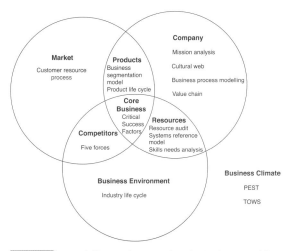

Figure 4.1 ▶ Modelling Tools Mapped to the Business Model

Step 1.3.1 Select Model

Amy needs to grow her business by focusing on the needs of customers. The customer resource process model is selected from Figure 4.1.

Step 1.3.2 Apply Model: Customer Resource Process

The model consists of 13 steps that a customer takes in purchasing a product from a company. For each step:

A. Identify what information is needed by the customer.
B. Explain how the information is currently provided to the customer.
C. Suggest how the information could be provided to the customer.
D. Define the business processes needed to provide the information required.

For example:

Step in Customer Resource Process Model	A: What Information is Required by Customer?	B: How is the Information is Currently Provided?	C: How Information Could be Provided?	D: Business Processes Needed to Provide the Information
Specify requirements for product or service.	Products available. Special offers. Location of shop. Telephone number.	Advert in local newspaper paper.	Leaflet. Catalogue. Radio. Web page.	Plan special offers. Maintain product catalogue. Prepare adverts. Liaise with newspaper.

Step 1.3.3 Analyse Model	**Step 1.3.4 Information Requirements**
The model shows that Amy currently relies on advertising her candles in newspapers. She could improve the information she provides to potential customers by creating a catalogue of the products and services she offers.	Product catalogue Special offers Location of shop Advertisements

Step 1.3.5 Combine Information Requirements

Information Requirements From Step 1.1.4	Information Requirements From Step 1.2.3	Information Requirements From Step 1.3.3
Candle Wax sculpture Material Equipment Customer Supplier	Customer requirement Order Special Offer Regulation Product Design Enquiry Quotation Annual Accounts	Product Catalogue Special Offers Location of Shop Advertisements

Figure 4.2 Example Information from Step 1.3

reality focusing on key aspects relevant to the modelling constructs, an individual's cognitive filter filters reality and interprets it within the context of his or her knowledge and experience.

Batra *et al.* (1990) define two distances in a model: a semantic distance between a person and the model; and an articulatory distance between a model and the area of reality being represented. Semantic distance is concerned with the difference between the meaning of the model and the person's knowledge of reality. Articulatory distance is the difference between the abstraction of reality represented in the model and actual reality. Figure 4.3 illustrates these distances between a house, a model of a house, and a cognitive model of a house. The goal of any

model is to minimize cognitive effort. A good model is therefore one that minimizes both semantic and articulatory distance.

Semantic distance can be bridged by the preparation of rich models, which minimize the scope for interpretation by the use of a clear notation, reducing cognitive effort. The articulatory distance can be reduced by balancing the degree of the complexity captured in a model against the abstraction required to support understanding and communication.

Figure 4.3 shows the relationships between reality, a cognitive model, and a model of reality which correspond to the three worlds defined by Popper (1968):

○ *Reality:* Physical environment of objects.

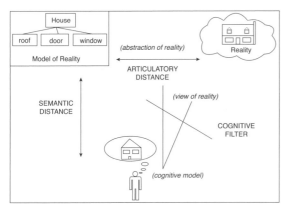

Figure 4.3 Semantic and Articulatory Distance
Source: Dingley (1996).

○ *Subjective view of reality:* Social environment of subjective experience.
○ *Models:* Knowledge of statements and theories.

Tsichritzis and Lochovsky (1982) suggest that people-oriented modelling consists of two mappings. The first maps the real world into some basic human concepts that describe the application in a natural manner; this is called an infological approach. The second maps the basic infological concepts into a corresponding datalogical representation. Some information may be lost in the translation between these mappings. In this stage, some soft systems techniques from Wilson's (1990, 2001) soft systems method are used to explore different views of a situation and create the two mappings suggested by Tsichritzis and Lochovsky (1982).

4.3.1 Step 2.1: Identify Different Views within the Context

Everyone sees the world through their own cognitive filter, which evolves over time, based on their knowledge, experiences, and cultural values. This causes disagreements about what the organization should do, how it should be structured, what business processes are needed, how the processes should be performed, what information is required, and the characteristics of the information required. Soft systems tools provide a means to explore different views held within a situation, which forms a basis for developing a shared understanding of the activities and information needed in the organization.

Scenario 4.3 briefly outlines the situation at Amy's Candles.

Scenario

Opportunity for Amy's Candles to Work with Match Lighting

Amy's Candles is a small business that makes bespoke candles and wax sculptures by hand. Amy sells her products in her shop and exhibits her work at local craft fairs and summer fetes. Much of her current trade is from local organizations, such as charities, that buy personalized candles from her in large quantities. Two people work for Amy. Brian mainly looks after the accounts and deals with the suppliers, though he often has to take orders and help out in the shop too. Chris answers the telephone and works in the shop. The staff work together well and often socialize outside of work.

Sales of candles have risen nationally. The major supermarkets and the greeting card chains Clumptons and Great Ideas have started to stock a range of standard candles. Amy's main competitor is the specialist chain of Wicked Wax Works, which sells sculptured scented candles. As Amy is a member of the British Candle Makers Federation and the National Candle Association, she is required to follow their regulations, in addition to standard consumer legislation.

Match Lighting is a lighting manufacturer who specializes in designing and manufacturing domestic light fittings stocked by the major retail outlets. The director, Mr Alvis, has approached Amy to stock her products. This would enable Amy to sell her products to major retail outlets such as Bright Spark, but she would need to invest in new equipment to increase production capacity. Amy would also need to use more IT as the major retail outlets expect online order processing and order-tracking facilities.

Working with Match Lighting would provide a major opportunity for Amy's Candles. It would enable Amy's designs to be sold on a much larger scale; however, it would also change the focus of the organization, emphasizing the design and manufacture of candles for the mass market rather than the design of bespoke wax sculptures. Increasing production and sales would secure the long-term future of Amy's Candles, but it would also be difficult to reconcile large-scale mass production with the organization's current philosophy of unique handcrafted designs.

Developing a rich picture of the situation (step 2.1.1) helps to explore the different views within an organizational context. A rich picture is a diagram that represents one or more views of a situation and can include opinions, cultural values, pressures, opportunities and areas of conflict. The picture can also include information extracted from analysis of the organizational architecture and the master data previously identified. A rich picture differs from analytical models as it does not have a defined set of notation; it is a free-form diagram to capture the rich complexity of the problem situation. Symbols are created, which are meaningful to the creator, to communicate the opinions and beliefs about a situation. A rich picture does not consist of a predefined set of concepts that provide a lens through which the situation must be interpreted; the lack of prescribed notation provides freedom to represent the specific features of the unique situation being considered.

Figure 4.4 presents a rich picture of the problem situation described in Scenario 4.3. The rich picture shows the tension between remaining a small creative organization and moving to mass production. A rich picture provides a means of allowing key stakeholders to surface and question their perceptions of a situation (Delbridge, 2008). Although Mr Alvis provides an opportunity for Amy to expand candle production, the opportunity challenges the philosophy and culture of her existing organization. The picture also emphasizes the pressures that are challenging the way Amy currently works, such as the increasing price of raw materials and the pages of regulations to which she must adhere. In Figure 4.4 there are a number of potential world views to explore, including:

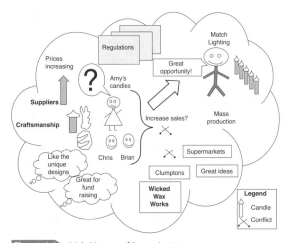

Figure 4.4 Rich Picture of Scenario 4.3

○ Mr Alvis who values mass production.
○ Amy who values creativity and individuality.
○ Chris and Brian who are happy working in a family-style culture.
○ Current customers who like the unique designs.
○ Current customers who need to buy candles cheaply to make a profit when they are resold for charity.

○ Competitors who recognize the potential growth in the candle market.

From the rich picture, Amy now needs to **prepare a set of CATWOE for each world view (step 2.1.2)**. CATWOE is a tool, consisting of six elements, which provides the constructs for defining a system needed to satisfy one view of the world from the rich picture. The elements of CATWOE are:

○ Customer: The individuals or groups of people who will be affected, either positively or negatively, by the outputs of the system. The word *customer* is not used here to refer to someone who buys goods and services from an organization. Although in some situations customers of an organization may also be identified as beneficiaries of the system, a broader view of beneficiaries is adopted in CATWOE.
○ Actor: The individuals or groups of people who undertake the activities needed to complete the transformation process of the system.
○ Transformation Process: The main conversion of inputs to outputs required by the system.
○ Weltanschauung: The specific view of the world, identified in the rich picture, which incorporates the assumptions on which the system is to be based.
○ Owner: The individuals or groups of people who have the power to create or remove the system.
○ Environmental Constraints: Factors external to the system over which the system has no control, which affect and constrain how the transformation process can be performed.

Table 4.7 provides two completed CATWOEs, one based on Amy's world view and the other based on the view of Mr Alvis. When completing CATWOE it is sometimes easier to complete the elements in the order shown in Table 4.7.

The completed CATWOE can be used to **construct a root definition for each world view (step 2.1.3)**. A root definition specifies a system that represents the underlying assumptions of one view of the world expressed in the rich picture. All the elements of CATWOE are combined into one sentence to form a root definition. Root definitions, which capture the separate world views of Amy and Mr Alvis, are shown in Table 4.8.

A conceptual model is developed for each root definition (step 2.1.4) to identify the activities needed to achieve the transformation process included in each root definition. The term *conceptual model* is used in soft systems to refer to activities, in contrast to the term *conceptual data model* that refers to data. An extract from the conceptual model relating to Amy's world view is shown in Figure

Table 4.7 ▶ CATWOEs for Scenario 4.3

CATWOE	Amy's View	Mr Alvis's View
Weltanschauung: What is the world view, from the rich picture, on which the CATWOE is to be based?	People appreciate bespoke design and craftsmanship.	Mass production is cost effective.
Transformation Process: What should a system do in order to support the chosen world view?	To satisfy the need for uniquely designed wax products.	To satisfy the need for mass-produced candles.
Customers: Who will be affected by the transformation process?	Amy, Brian, Chris, charities, recipients of candles.	Amy's Candles, Match Lighting, supermarket chains.
Actors: Who will perform the transformation process?	Amy, Brian, and Chris.	Amy, Match Lighting staff.
Environmental Constraints: What are the limitations on the transformation process?	Regulations from professional bodies, production techniques, trading laws.	Production equipment constraints, trading laws, minimum cost.
Owners: Who has the power to create or remove the transformation process?	Amy.	Match Lighting.

Table 4.8 ▶ Root Definitions for Scenario 4.3

Root Definition Based on Amy's World View	Root Definition Based on Mr Alvis's World View
A system owned by Amy, which is operated by Amy, Brian, and Chris, to satisfy the need of charities and individuals for uniquely designed wax products, which will benefit Amy, Brian, Chris, charities, and the recipients of candles who appreciate bespoke design and craftsmanship, within the constraints of the regulations from professional bodies, production techniques, and trading laws.	A system owned by Match Lighting, which is operated by Amy and the staff of Match Lighting, to be cost effective by satisfying the need for mass-produced candles, within the constraints of minimum costs, the production equipment, and trading laws, for the benefit of Amy's Candles, Match Lighting, and customers such as the supermarket chains.

Table 4.9 ▶ Potential Measures of Performance

	Amy's Root Definition	Mr Alvis's Root Definition
Efficacy	Is the need for uniquely designed wax products being met?	Is the need for mass-produced candles being met?
Efficiency	How much time is taken in designing each bespoke product?	What is the production cost of each candle? What is the profit margin?
Effectiveness	Is the craftwork being appreciated?	Is mass production minimizing costs?

4.5, which emphasizes the creative process of designing bespoke products with the client. In contrast, Figure 4.6 represents the world view of Mr Alvis, which emphasizes the constraints imposed on the design process by production equipment and manufacturing costs. The conceptual model represents the system defined by the root definition. All systems need to include control mechanisms to check that they are meeting their objectives and to take corrective action if necessary. Performance measures therefore need to be defined for both systems. Wilson (1990) suggests that performance measures relate to:

○ Efficacy: Does the system successfully achieve its transformation process?
○ Efficiency: Does the system satisfy its objectives using the minimum number of resources required?
○ Effectiveness: Does the system achieve its longer term objectives? Does the system achieve the objectives which underpin the worldview?

Table 4.9 suggests potential measures of performance for the models shown in Figure 4.5 and Figure 4.6.

The conceptual models in Figures 4.5 and 4.6 are then reviewed in the real world to *form an agreed consensus*

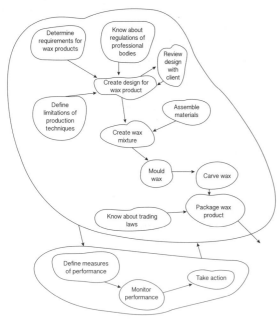

Figure 4.5 Conceptual Model Based on the World View of Amy

Figure 4.6 Conceptual Model Based on the World View of Mr Alvis

model (step 2.1.5). The conceptual models provide a starting point for discussion about the activities required in a system founded on the beliefs and values captured in the root definitions. For example, both conceptual models include an activity to determine the needs of the customer. In Amy's model, she wants to work closely with customers to design a unique product that reflects her creative values. In Figure 4.6, customers are less involved in the design process and the design process is more constrained by the physical requirements of the production equipment. The models provide the opportunity to discuss the different perceptions Amy and Mr Alvis have about customers and the different types of customers they can serve.

A potential consensus model is presented in Figure 4.7. The model incorporates activities to support collaborative design with customers that meets Amy's needs; it also incorporates activities to design and produce candles for the mass market that meets the needs of Mr Alvis. The consensus model may provide additional benefits to Amy's existing customers; for example, it may be possible to reduce the production costs of candles, which would benefit charity organizations.

4.3.2 Step 2.2: Define Information Categories

The activities in the consensus model need and generate information. The data modelling techniques introduced

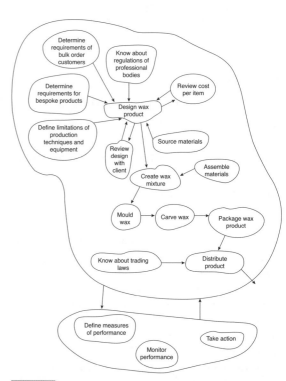

Figure 4.7 Consensus Conceptual Model for Amy and Mr Alvis

in Chapter 2 seek to capture an objective view of reality in terms of the information needed in a situation. This is difficult to achieve as information is interpreted rather than objectively recognized. The boundary of Weltanschauung can be used to replace the objective view that other forms of data analysis attempt to capture (Lewis, 1994). Using Weltanschauung to define information categories recognizes that relevant systems are only meaningful with respect to a set of cognitive categories. An information category is a collection of data that provides a means of classification, which has meaning within the conceptual system being described. The boundary of an information category is defined by specifying the data items that the category contains (Wilson, 1990). For example, within the context of Table 4.7, *wax product* may be considered to be an information category that includes data about candles (such as size, colour, and design motif). Lewis (1994) suggests that if a value can be assigned to something, it is an attribute rather than an information category. For example, *quantity of candles* required could be given a value; it is therefore an attribute of an information category, such as *customer requirement*.

There are two approaches to identifying information categories using soft systems tools. First, Wilson (1990) suggests that a table is created documenting the data required as input to and output from each activity in the consensus model. The data items can then be grouped into meaningful information categories. Second, Lewis (1994) suggests that the words used in CATWOE and the root definition can form the initial list of cognitive categories. By agreeing on the meaning of the cognitive categories, a data model can be prepared to complement the conceptual model in the soft systems methodology.

Combining the two approaches ensures that all the information categories required to support the activities in the consensus model are appropriately identified.

Identifying the inputs and outputs to each activity in the consensus model (step 2.2.1) records the information required by the model. It is necessary to also *specify the information needed to measure the performance of the system represented in the consensus model (step 2.2.2)*. Table 4.10 provides an example of the data needed by some of the activities in the conceptual model from Figure 4.7. Information categories can be defined from Table 4.10; for example, potential information categories include *customer requirement, regulation, wax specification*, and *materials list*.

An alternative approach to defining information requirements is to *extract potential information categories from the root definitions (step 2.2.3)*. Table 4.11 identifies candidate information categories from the root definitions of Amy and Mr Alvis.

A candidate list of information categories identified from analysis of the root definitions and the information requirements of activities in the consensus conceptual model is shown in Table 4.12. An information category may be an entity or attribute in the organization's information architecture. Each category needs to be given a brief description to define the category. For example, *material* may be defined as the physical elements that are combined to form a wax product; *customer requirement* may be defined as a unique set of design specifications for one or more wax products, to be delivered on a specific date. The information categories identified from the business model and organizational architecture can be added to the list of information categories. *Create a brief*

Table 4.10 Extract of Information Required by Activities in the Consensus Conceptual Model

Role of Information	Activities from Conceptual Model	
	Design Wax Product	**Create Wax Mixture**
Input to the Activity.	Customer requirements (type of product, size, colour, quantity, design). Production line restriction. Cost of materials. Regulations.	Wax specification (quantity, colour, density). Production instruction.
Output from the Activity.	Design specification (wax, mould, carving, decoration, and packing specifications). Wax specification. Production instruction.	Quantity created. Colour created.
Measure the Performance of the Activity.	Design specification. Cost of materials. Cost of design process.	Colour, quantity and density of wax. Cost of creating wax.

Table 4.11 ▶ Identifying Candidate Information Categories from Root Definitions

Root Definition Based on Amy's World View	Root Definition Based on Mr Alvis's World View
A system owned by Amy, which is operated by Amy, Brian, and Chris, to satisfy the need of charities and individuals for uniquely designed WAX PRODUCTS, which will benefit Amy, Brian, Chris, charities, and the RECIPIENTS of CANDLES who appreciate BESPOKE DESIGN and crafts-manship, within the constraints of the REGULATIONS from PROFESSIONAL BODIES, PRODUCTION TECHNIQUES, and TRADING LAWS.	A system owned by Match Lighting, which is operated by Amy and the staff of Match Lighting, to be cost effective by satisfying the need for mass-produced CANDLES, within the constraints of minimum costs, the PRODUCTION EQUIPMENT, and TRADING LAWS, for the benefit of Amy's Candles, Match Lighting, and CUSTOMERS such as the supermarket chains.

Table 4.12 ▶ Candidate Information Categories

Information Categories Identified from Consensus Model (Table 4.10)	Information Categories Identified from Root Definitions (Table 4.11)
Customer Requirement	Wax Product
Production Line Restriction	Recipient (Customer)
Material	Candle
Regulation	Bespoke Design
Design Specification	Regulation
Wax Specification	Professional Body
Production Instruction	Production Technique
Wax	Trading Law
	Production Technique
	Production Equipment

description of each information category (step 2.2.4) to ensure that there is a clear understanding of the meaning of each category.

4.3.3 ▶ Step 2.3: Data to Process Mapping

All approaches to developing an information architecture include some form of data to process mapping (Brancheau *et al.*, 1989). The purpose of the mapping is to identify any anomalies, ensuring that all the data needed by the business processes have been identified and that all the processes needed to manage the data through the life cycle have been identified.

Wilson (1990) proposes the construction of a Maltese Cross to support two phases of data to process mapping. The Maltese Cross is at the boundary that separates the systems thinking environment from that of the real world. In the systems thinking world, a conceptual model has been defined which shows the activities required to perform the transformation process specified in the root definition. The top half of the Maltese Cross considers the information that is needed as input to these activities and the information generated from, or modified by, these activities. The list of candidate information categories (Table 4.12) is mapped to the activities from

the consensus conceptual model to form the top half of the Maltese Cross.

Complete the top half of the Maltese Cross (step 2.3.1) by:

- Listing all the activities from the consensus model in the north section of the cross.
- Listing all the information categories in the west section of the cross.
- Listing all the information categories in the east section of the cross.
- Inserting X in the west section to identify the information categories input to each activity.
- Inserting X in the east section to identify the information categories modified by, or output from, each activity.

Figure 4.8 shows an extract of the top of the cross that comprises three sections: information categories needed as input to one or more activities, the activities from the consensus model, and the information categories that are produced or modified by the activities.

Check the completeness of the Maltese Cross to ensure that all the information categories are identified and used (step 2.3.2). All the activities from the consensus

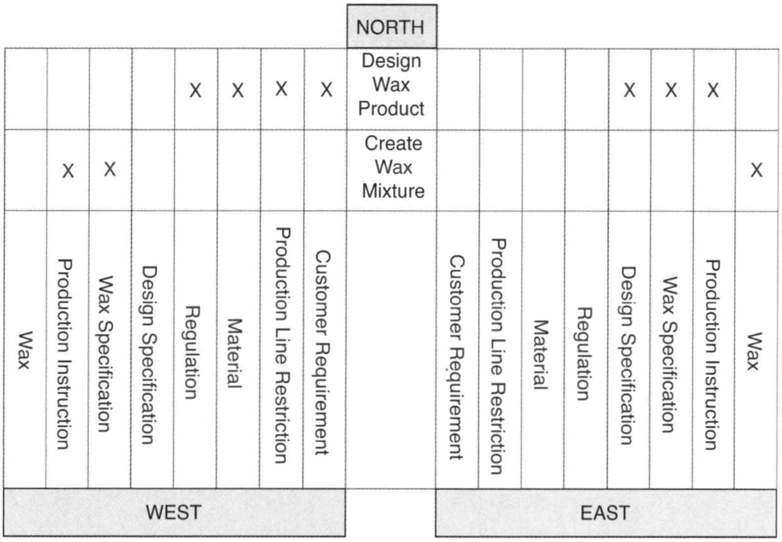

Wax	Production Instruction	Wax Specification	Design Specification	Regulation	Material	Production Line Restriction	Customer Requirement	NORTH	Customer Requirement	Production Line Restriction	Material	Regulation	Design Specification	Wax Specification	Production Instruction	Wax
				X	X	X	X	Design Wax Product					X	X	X	
	X	X						Create Wax Mixture								X

WEST   EAST

Figure 4.8 ▶ Extract from Top Half of Maltese Cross

conceptual model and all the related information categories should be included in the Maltese Cross. Table 4.10 shows that the activity *design wax product* takes four information categories as input and creates (or modifies) three information categories as outputs of the activity (*design specification*, *wax specification*, and *production technique*). Two of the information categories, which are created as outputs from the activity *design wax product*, are taken as input to the activity *create wax mixture*.

The information life cycle (Section 2.2) identifies the main events that occur, triggering change in information, including its creation. **For each information category, check that the life cycle activities are supported (step 2.3.3)** in the Maltese Cross. The mapping in Figure 4.8 shows that the information category *wax specification* is created by the activity *design wax product* and is then used by the activity *create wax mixture*. However, other information categories such as *customer requirement* are needed as input to the activity *design wax product* but the Maltese Cross does not show where this information is created. Such anomalies need to be investigated and further refinement may be needed of the consensus model, information categories, and Maltese Cross. In some cases an activity may need an information category as input that is created by activities that are outside the scope of the current system being modelled. Further investigation would be needed to ensure that the required information is created elsewhere.

The bottom half of the Maltese Cross is completed by returning to consider the real world. The activities that are currently taking place in the real world are listed in the

bottom, or south, section of the cross. For each current activity, the information that is input into the activity is identified and the information categories that are currently created or modified as outputs from the current activities are shown on the cross.

Complete the bottom half of the Maltese Cross (step 2.3.4) by:

○ Listing all the activities from the current system in the real world in the south section of the cross.
○ Adding X to show which information categories are needed as input to each activity.
○ Adding X to show which information categories are modified by, or output from, each activity.
○ Adding any additional information categories to the west and east sections of the cross that are used in the real world but were not identified in the top half of the cross.

Figure 4.9 shows the Maltese Cross from Figure 4.8 with the bottom section of the cross added.

When the Maltese Cross is complete, **compare the top and bottom halves of the Maltese Cross (step 2.3.5).** The current activities and information categories in the organization are compared with the activities and information categories proposed by the modelling in the systems thinking environment. The comparison provides a basis for discussion and can lead to the formation of a plan for change, identifying the information needs of the organization.

Figure 4.9 shows that in the current system Amy has an activity *consult with customer* that captures the customer's

NORTH

Wax	Production Instruction	Wax Specification	Design Specification	Regulation	Material	Production Line Restriction	Customer Requirement	Activity	Customer Requirement	Production Line Restriction	Material	Regulation	Design Specification	Wax Specification	Production Instruction	Wax
				X	X	X	X	Design Wax Product					X	X	X	
	X	X						Create Wax Mixture								X
			X		X			Consult with Customer	X							
				X			X	Design Candle			X		X	X	X	
	X	X						Mix Wax								X

SOUTH

Figure 4.9 Extract from Top and Bottom of Maltese Cross

requirements. Amy also has an existing activity to *design candle* which takes the information categories *customer requirement* and *regulation* as inputs. In contrast, the equivalent activity identified from the consensus model, *design wax product*, takes additional inputs of *production line restriction* and *material*. This reflects the different information requirements which will be needed if the system represented in the consensus model is implemented (that is, if Amy decides to design candles for Match Lighting).

The soft systems approach can therefore be used to identify the information needed by morphing organizations. The Maltese Cross is a useful tool to illustrate how business processes and their information requirements may need to be changed. The last step in this stage is to **combine the information categories from the Maltese Cross with the information requirements identified from stage 1 (step 2.3.6)** shown in Table 4.13.

Table 4.13 Candidate Entities Identified from Stage 1 and Stage 2

Advertisement	Production Instruction
Annual Account	Production Line Restriction
Candle	Production Technique
Customer	Professional Body
Customer Requirement	Quotation
Design Specification	Regulation
Enquiry	Special Offer
Equipment	Supplier
Location of Shop	Trading Law
Material	Wax
Order	Wax Product
Product Catalogue	Wax Sculpture
Product Design	Wax Specification
Production Equipment	

4.4 ▶ Stage 3: Structure Information with Business Rules

In Chapter 3, a database was defined as a structured collection of data. An information architecture represents the structure of the information needed by the organization. The structure of information is determined by business rules that define how the information categories relate to one another. The business rules define the limitations of how the data can be changed by business processes, in order to ensure that the integrity of the data is maintained. In stage 3, information categories are used to form the basis of an entity model. The business rules and entity definitions specify the relationships between entities in the information architecture.

An entity model identifies the main items of information that an organization needs to manage in order to support the business processes. The business rules explain how the items of information are related, that is, how they make sense to different areas of the business. At the top level the business rules explain the processes that relate to the information. For example, the rule that *a customer can place an order* defines the relationship between a *customer* and an *order*. The business rules go further in that they define, for example, whether an order can exist without a customer. Can an order be placed by more than one customer? Can a customer place more than one order? Are there restrictions on the type of customers that can place an order? Are there limits on the type, or the value, of the orders that can be placed by specific customers? These rules are defined by the business and are then implemented by the IT department. The rules help to keep the data clean (that is, complete and accurate) and also help to define the input screens (forms) needed to capture the information, the reports needed to present the information and to inform design of how the data should be stored in the database to support the needs of the business.

The terms *data model*, *conceptual model*, and *semantic model* are used interchangeably in literature, although each term emphasizes a specific aspect of representation. The term:

○ *Data model* emphasizes data structure.
○ *Conceptual model* indicates installation independence.
○ *Semantic model* incorporates the meaning attributed to the data.

Information categories identify the data needed by the activities in the consensus conceptual model to support the root definition. Entities are a conceptualization of the data that need to be stored in a database to support the

information requirements of an organization in the real world. Entity modelling has extended from a database design model to managing the organization's information resource (Lewis, 1993). The progression of data modelling from a technical to a business technique reflects the evolution of IT from supporting data processing tasks to providing management information that should be driven by business requirements.

Business rules determine how information relates to other information. For example, the business rule that *materials must be supplied by a registered supplier* means that information cannot be captured about a new material unless the material is supplied by a registered supplier; that is, a supplier code must be entered that matches an existing record for a supplier. Business rules define the integrity of the data; the rules specify structures, determinacy, and cardinality relationships among data. The rules are implemented in business processes and enforced through software programs to preserve the quality and integrity of the organization's data.

4.4.1 ▶ Step 3.1: Identify Hierarchies

Two entities are related to one another if the removal of one makes a significant difference to the other. Relationships among entities can be stable relationships relating to structures, or transient relationships relating to processes (Carter *et al.*, 1984). Structural membership relationships, such as *is a* or *is part of*, are identified through structural roles (for example, *a candle is a wax product*) or composition (for example, *a candle consists of material*). Structural relationships impose constraints on subsets that specify generalization and specialization within categories. Specialization relationships are a specific type of membership where a subtype entity inherits all the attributes and business rules involved with an associated supertype. For example, *candle* and *wax sculpture* are subtypes (specialist instances) of the entity *wax product*. Subtypes inherit the attributes and rules of the entity *wax product*, but they will have additional attributes and rules that are specific to them. For example, a *candle* may have attributes such as *length of wick* and *burning time*, which are not relevant to a *wax sculpture*.

Process relationships promote change in one or more of the entities in the relationship. Causal relationships such as *is controller of*, and contractual relationships such as *is the supplier of*, are identified through the potential for action within business processes. Lewis (1994) suggests that relationships can be identified by **creating a category association table (step 3.1.1)** in which all possible pairs of information categories are examined to identify a potential relationship within the context of the system.

Table 4.14 ▸ Candidate Relationships from Category
Association

Information Category	Relationship	Information Category
Customer	States	Customer Requirement
Design Specification	Fulfils	Customer Requirement
Candle	Is a	Wax Product
Candle	Is made from	Material
Materials	Are specified in	Design Specification
Production line Restriction	Limit	Design Specification
Design Specification	Specifies	Wax Specification
Design Specification	Specifies	Production Instruction
Production Instruction	Relate to	Wax Product
Regulations	Limit	Design Specification
Production Equipment	Is specified in	Production Instruction
Trading Law	Restrict	Wax Product

Examples of potential relationships among some of the information categories identified in Table 4.13 are shown in Table 4.14. When the relationships have been identified, *review candidate relationships to ensure that they are complete and meaningful (step 3.1.2)* within the boundary of the consensus conceptual model and organizational architecture. The determinacy and cardinality of each relationship can then be defined.

4.4.2 ▸ Step 3.2: Define Integrity Constraints

Determinacy constraints specify whether a relationship between two entities is optional or mandatory. The constraints govern whether an instance of an entity can exist without being directly associated with another entity. *For each relationship specify whether an occurrence is optional or mandatory in each direction (step 3.2.1):*

○ If the relationship is optional, instances of the one entity can exist without being related to an instance of the other entity. For example, a business rule may state that a customer may be associated with an order but a customer does not have to be associated with an order. Specifying this optional relationship allows the details of a customer to be captured without the need for a customer to immediately place an order with the organization.

○ If the relationship is mandatory, instances of the one entity cannot exist without being related to an instance of the other entity. For example, a typical rule might be that an order cannot exist without being associated with a customer.

Determinacy asks the questions:

○ Can an instance of entity A exist without being associated with entity B?
  ● The relationship is optional if an instance of entity A can exist without being associated with an instance of entity B.
  ● The relationship is mandatory if an instance of entity A cannot exist without being associated with an instance of entity B.
  ● For example, in Table 4.14 the question is asked *can a customer exist without being associated with customer requirement?* (Can customer data be captured and stored without any customer requirements for a candle being captured at the same time?). It is possible that Amy may wish to store customer details about a customer who has not yet specified any requirements or, perhaps, cancelled their requirements. The relationship is therefore optional.

○ Can an instance of entity B exist without being associated with entity A?
  ● The relationship is optional if an instance of entity B can exist without being associated with an instance of entity A.
  ● The relationship is mandatory if an instance of entity B cannot exist without being associated with an instance of entity A.
  ● For example, *can customer requirement exist without being associated with a customer?* (Can customer requirements be captured and stored without any customer details being captured at the same time?) This is perhaps unlikely so the relationship is mandatory.

Cardinality constraints specify the type of membership that the entity has in the relationship. A cardinality constraint specifies whether more than one instance of an entity can be associated with more than one instance of another entity. *For each relationship specify whether one or more than one instance of an entity can be associated with an instance of the other entity (step 3.2.2).* The possibilities include:

○ One to one (1:1) where only one instance of entity A can be associated with only one instance of entity B. For example, Amy may decide that a customer has one customer account, and a customer account is held by only one customer.

○ One to many (1:N) where one instance of entity A can be associated with more than one instance of entity B. For example, a customer may specify many sets of requirements, but a set of requirements must be specified by only one customer.

○ Many to one (N:1) where many instances of entity A can be associated with only one instance of entity B. For example, a number of candles can be made from one mould, and one mould may be used to make many candles.

○ Many to many (M:N) where many instances of entity A can be associated with many instances of entity B. For example, a candle comprises many materials and a material may be used in a number of candles.

Cardinality poses the questions:

○ Can an instance of entity A be related to more than one instance of entity B?
  • The relationship is one if an instance of entity A can be related to only one instance of entity B.
  • The relationship is many if an instance of entity A can be related to more than one instance of entity B.
  • For example, in Table 4.14, the question is asked *can a customer be associated with more than one instance of customer requirement?* (Could a customer place multiple requests for wax products over a period of time?) Yes, so the relationship is many (N).

○ Can an instance of entity B be related to more than one instance of entity A?
  • The relationship is one if an instance of entity B can be related to only one instance of entity A.
  • The relationship is many if an instance of entity B can be related to more than one instance of entity A, and only one instance of entity A can be associated with entity B.
  • For example, *can an instance of customer requirement be associated with more than one instance of customer?* (Could a set of customer requirements be placed by more than one customer at the same time?) No, so the relationship is one.

The business rules coded within the determinacy and cardinality restrictions are implemented in business processes and information systems to ensure that the integrity of the data is maintained. For example, if a relationship between two entities is defined as being mandatory, one instance of entity A cannot be deleted without also deleting the associated instance in entity B (as the instance of entity B cannot exist without being associated with an instance in entity A).

4.4.3 ▶ Step 3.3: Model Business Rules

Constructing a model of the business rules provides a diagrammatic relationship of the structure of information required in the organization. The first step is to **draw the entities and relationship from the candidate relationships identified (step 3.3.1).** There are a number of different notations for representing entity relationships in a model. The choice of notation is usually specified by the in-house style of the organization or by a proprietary systems development methodology. The notation used in this book is defined in Table 4.15.

When the initial model has been drawn, **add the determinacy constraints for each relationship (step 3.3.2), add the cardinality constraints for each relationship (step 3.3.3)**, and then **check the accuracy of the business rules represented (step 3.3.4).**

Table 4.15 ▶ Entity-Relationship Notation

Symbol	Meaning
ENTITY	Entity
◇ Relationship	Relationship
ENTITY ──○──	Optional Relationship
ENTITY ●────	Mandatory Relationship
ENTITY ──1──	One Instance in Relationship
ENTITY ──N──	Many Instances in a 1:N Relationship
ENTITY ──M──	Many Instances in a M:N Relationship
SUBTYPE / SUPERTYPE	Subtype and Supertype Entities

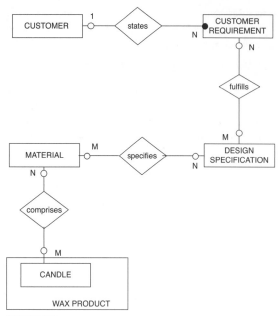

Figure 4.10 Extract from Entity-Relationship Model

An extract from an entity-relationship model that includes six entities from Table 4.14 is shown in Figure 4.10.

Figure 4.10 illustrates a number of business rules that will be implemented in the information systems developed to manage the information identified in the model. For example:

- A customer may state zero, one, or many customer requirements.
- A customer requirement must be stated by one customer.
- A customer requirement may be fulfilled by zero, one, or many design specifications.
- A design specification may be fulfilled by zero, one, or many customer requirements.
- A design specification may state zero, one, or many materials.
- A material may be stated in zero, one, or many design specifications.
- A candle may comprise zero, one, or many materials.
- A material may be used in zero, one, or many candles.
- A candle is a type of wax product.
- A wax product may be a candle.

These business rules enable and restrict access to the organization's information.

4.5 ▶ Stage 4: Specify Information Access

The information architecture formed by the entity-relationship model needs to be examined to ensure that the model can provide access to the information required across the organization. Further business rules then need to be defined to specify who is authorized to access specific data. Access authorization may be determined by the organizational structure; for example, only staff employed in the payroll department may be allowed to access information about employee tax codes. The complete information architecture is then documented to form a data dictionary for the organization.

4.5.1 ▶ Step 4.1: Identify Access Paths

The information architecture provides a diagrammatic representation of the structured data needed to provide the information required by the organization. When the initial structure of the data has been defined, checks need to be made to ensure that the structure will enable the different departments in the organization to access the information required.

Develop a list of typical queries (step 4.1.1) that different departments in the organization may pose, to test the completeness of the information architecture. For example, typical queries that Amy may ask are:

Query 1: What materials are specified in design specification J0209?

Query 2: Which customers have ordered design specification J0209?

Identify example data for each entity (step 4.1.2) in the architecture and *map the access path through the model to answer each query (step 4.1.3).* Figure 4.11 shows the access paths through the model in Figure 4.10 to provide the information needed to answer the queries. For example:

Answer 1: The materials specified in the design specification J0209 are: wax, blue dye, and wick.

Answer 2: Customers who ordered the design specification J0209 are: Suki, Vicky, Jimmy, and S I Liv.

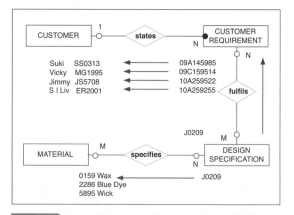

Figure 4.11 Access Paths to Facilitate Information Retrieval

4.5.2 Step 4.2: Specify Access Requirements

The information architecture identifies the information needed to meet the diverse needs of business processes and people, in different parts of the organization, at different levels in the organizational hierarchy.

Identify who needs to access each entity (step 4.2.1) as not everyone in the organization will need access to all information included in the information architecture and then *assign access restrictions for each entity (step 4.2.2)*. Limitations of information access need to be defined in order to:

- Satisfy privacy and confidentiality requirements.
- Minimize threat of inappropriate use of information.
- Reduce risks of information being corrupted or destroyed.
- Increase the effectiveness of business processes by limiting information overload.
- Reduce risks of information disclosure to unauthorized sources.
- Ensure the security of the organization and its staff.
- Protect commercial interests.
- Avoid prejudice in the detection of illegal activity.

Consideration therefore needs to be given to:

- Who needs access to the information? Restrictions must be defined to identify the staff, functions, and processes that need access to specific information.
- What type of access is needed? The type of access permitted to the data can be restricted to help to improve the quality of the data. For example, some members of staff may need to be able to access specific items of data but do not need to have access to make changes to the data or have authority to delete data. Organization structure charts, job titles, and employment grades (captured in the organizational architecture) provide a means of defining authority rules for accessing and modifying information.
- What information do staff (and other authorized parties) need to access? Different departments will need to be able to follow different access paths in the information architecture. For example, sales staff will need to access customer details and customer requirements but may not need to access information about materials. Further restrictions can be defined on the attributes of an entity, that is, the specific items of data which describe an aspect of the information. For example, if a report was needed to identify the names of customers that had purchased candles in the last 12 months, the report would not need to include all the information stored about customers. The report would only need to include some of the attributes of the entity *customer* (such as *customer name*). Different views of the data in the entity-relationship model can therefore be specified to meet the needs of different business functions.

- How frequently will the information need to be accessed? Some information will need to be accessed perhaps several times a day while other information may only be needed once a week, once a month, or perhaps less often. The frequency and regularity with which specific data items will be accessed need to be defined as this may affect how the information architecture is implemented by the IT department. There is a difference between frequency and regularity; a regular event occurs at a defined interval but the interval may not be frequent; for example, an annual report is a regular report that is generated on a yearly cycle. A frequent event occurs often but may not necessarily occur at regular intervals.

4.5.3 Step 4.3: Define Security Requirements

Define the legal and ethical requirements that affect access to each entity (step 4.3.1). Legal and ethical requirements influence the information security measures that need to be imposed to protect the organization's information. Information security addresses four main issues. First, security is needed to prevent unauthorized access to information from both within the organization and from external individuals or organizations. Second, information security prevents unauthorized operations on the information. For example, security measures are needed to ensure that information is not destroyed, accidentally or maliciously, before the defined retention period has expired. Third, security is needed to ensure that authorized staff only perform operations on the information that conform to their authorization level. For example, a member of staff may have authorization to access specific information but not have authorization to change or delete the information. Fourth, security is needed to ensure that information is not corrupted or lost due to technical issues (such as physical storage device breaking), power issues (such as a power outage), physical issues (such as the theft of equipment devices), or disasters (such as flooding). Security issues are discussed further in Part II.

Within the information architecture, security requirements need to be determined for each stage in the information life cycle. *Identify who is authorized to perform each activity in the entity life cycle (step 4.3.2).* Key questions to consider at each stage in the life cycle include:

Table 4.16 ▶ Security Requirements in the Customer Information Life Cycle

Stage in Life Cycle	Actors	Access	Restriction
Capture	Sales and customer service staff.	All customer attributes.	Integrity constraints.
Retrieve	Sales and customer service staff.	All customer attributes.	
Use, Generate, and Share	Sales supervisor.	All details.	
	Accounts staff.	All details.	
	Dispatch department.	Delivery address.	
Maintain	Sales and customer service staff.	Attributes entered for the accounts they manage.	Integrity constraints.
Archive	Sales supervisor.	All customer attributes.	After three years of no contact with customer.
Destroy	Sales manager.	All customer attributes.	After 10 years from last payment received.

○ Who is authorized for the activity?

○ What are the limitations of a person's authorization? For example, can a person create, change, read, print, copy, archive, or delete information?

○ What are the integrity constraints defined by the business rules associated with the activity? *Ensure integrity constraints are sufficient (step 4.3.3).* For example, Figure 4.10 shows that a customer requirement cannot be created without being associated with a valid customer record.

Table 4.16 provides an example of some of the security requirements that Amy may specify to ensure the security of customer information.

4.5.4 ▶ Step 4.4: Construct Data Dictionary

All the information gathered about the information systems requirements of the organization, the structure of the information, and the access required to the information, is documented in a data dictionary. The data dictionary is a database that stores metadata, that is, data about the data in the organization (Date, 2004). The data dictionary provides a central reference for the organization documenting the information architecture and the associated business rules, which will be implemented by business processes, information systems, and IT. Detailed descriptions of the information resources needed by the organization increase the efficiency and effectiveness of information management (Batley, 2007).

The data dictionary includes:

○ Name of the entity: The name assigned to the entity taken from the entity-relationship model.

○ Entity code: A shortened way of identifying the entity.

○ Definition of the entity: Different definitions may need to be documented to capture different views of the entity used by different business processes.

○ Attributes of the entity: The characteristics that describe the entity and form the template for capturing data about the entity. The following details are defined for each attribute:

• Attribute name: The name of the characteristic of the entity.

• Attribute definition: A description of the characteristic of the entity.

• Attribute length: The maximum number of characters that can be captured for the attribute.

• Attribute type: The range of alphabetical, numerical, and special characters that may be used for the attribute.

• Attribute structure: The arrangement of alphabetical, numerical, and special characters that may be used in the attribute.

• Attribute default value: Initial value of the attribute until another value is entered for the attribute. An attribute does not have to be assigned a default value.

• Attribute mandatory indicator: A code that indicates whether a value must be recorded for the attribute when the data for the entity is captured or whether the attribute is optional.

• Attribute unique indicator: A code that specifies if the attribute value is unique across all instances of the entity. A unique attribute could be used as a key to retrieve an instance of the entity.

○ Relationships of the entity: The relationships shown on the entity-relationship model that preserve the structure and integrity of the information. The following details are defined for each relationship:
- Entity name: The name of the entity that is related to the entity being defined.
- Relationship name: The nature of the relationship between the entities.
- Determinacy constraints: An indicator of whether the relationship is optional or mandatory.
- Cardinality constraints: The degree of the relationship, that is, the number of instances of an entity that can be related to another entity.

○ Access requirements: Identify who is authorized to create, access, modify, and delete the entity.

○ Usage requirements: An indication of the frequency and regularity with which the information is likely to be used in the organization. It may also include details of the volume of information that may be needed.

○ Views of the entity: Any business rules that restrict access to some of the attributes of the entity.

○ Archive policy: The minimum time span for retaining details of the entity on live systems before the details can be archived.

○ Retention policy: The minimum time span for retaining details before they can be destroyed and guidance relating to how the data need to be destroyed.

Creating a data dictionary involves **define entities and attributes (step 4.4.1), documenting the entity relationships (step 4.4.2), specifying the access and usage requirements of each entity (step 4.4.3), and defining archive and retention policies (step 4.4.4).** An example data dictionary entry is shown in Figure 4.12. Further information may be added to the data dictionary, such as data owners, which is discussed in Part II.

Entity Name: Customer
Entity Definition: A person or organization who has expressed an interest in purchasing goods or services from Amy's Candles. Details can be captured in *customer* without the need for a purchase to be made.
Entity Code: CUST

Attribute Name	Attribute Definition	Attribute Length and Type	Attribute Structure	Default Value	Mandatory Indicator	Unique Indicator
CUST_Name	Name of Customer.	X(30)	String of characters.		Y	N
CUST_Number	Unique number to identify a customer and their address.	X(2)9(4)	The first two characters refer to a customer category, the remaining digits are automatically generated.		Y	Y
CUST_Crd_Lim	Credit limit assigned to the customer.	9(4)	String of digits.	250	Y	N

Relationships FROM CUSTOMER TO

Entity	Relationship Name	Determinacy	Cardinality
CUSTOMER_REQUIREMENT	States	Optional	1:N

Data Views:

○ All attributes can be viewed by: Staff in sales, accounts and customer service function.
○ All attributes except CUST_Crd_Lim: Staff in dispatch function.

Access Requirements:

○ CUST_Crd_Lim: Can only be changed by accounts staff.

Usage Requirements:

○ Daily access may be needed with a maximum volume of 9999 customer records.

Archive Policy: Archive after three years of no contact with customer.
Retention Policy: Retain for 10 years from last payment received.

Figure 4.12 ▶ Extract from Data Dictionary Entry for Customer Information

4.6 ▶ Scope of Business in Information Management

Three levels of architecture have been introduced in the previous chapters.

Chapter 1 introduced the organizational architecture, which:

○ Provides the bounded space in which organizational activity can take place, determining the requirements for information.
○ Is situated within the business model that provides the context for the information requirements of the organization.
○ Incorporates a number of levels including: mission, organizational structure, business processes, culture, working practices, informal structures, and vision.

Chapter 2 defined the information architecture, which:

○ Provides the foundation for capturing and generating the information that an organization needs.
○ Is situated in the context of the organizational architecture.
○ Represents the logical structure of information needed to support the operational processes, tactical planning, and strategic decision-making in the organization.

Chapter 2 also discussed the information systems architecture which provides the systems and processes to support information throughout the life cycle.

Chapter 3 outlined the IT architecture, which:

○ Provides the boundaries for selecting and implementing IT in the organization.
○ Is situated in the context of the information architecture, implementing the business rules to maintain the security and integrity of information.
○ Specifies the policies, standards, and guidelines for IT, ensuring compatibility and integration of IT through the organization.

A common feature of these architectures is that they specify boundaries, providing frameworks in which decisions and actions can be taken. Hanseth and Braa (2000) emphasize that infrastructures focus on connection, ensuring that the different elements of an organization can work together effectively towards common goals. The architectural structures aim to retain organizational integrity so that, for example:

○ Changes to organizational hierarchies and processes do not make the organization unrecognizable.

○ Changes to information do not adversely affect areas of the organization.
○ Changes to IT do not hinder the ability to share information between departments and functions.

The architectures define the limitations in which an organization can morph, ensuring that the organization retains its identity. As IT becomes increasingly heterogeneous the need to integrate information and business processes within an architecture becomes more important and more challenging (Martin *et al.*, 2010).

The architectures each provide a unique view of the organization, modelling specific aspects. For example, the organizational architecture defines the organization in its environment and the IT architecture provides the platform for implementing technology to support information systems (Aerts *et al.*, 2004). The architectures can be considered as defining layers of the organization and collectively form the enterprise architecture. The enterprise architecture framework reflects the alignment of the organizational architecture, information systems architecture, and IT architecture (Pessi *et al.*, 2011). The information systems architecture provides a layer of systems and processes that capture, use, and maintain the information in the information architecture to meet the needs of the organizational architecture by using the technology defined in the IT architecture.

Table 4.17 provides an enterprise architecture which structures the organization, information, information systems, and IT architectures within the stages of the information life cycle. The organizational architecture drives information management through the enterprise architecture. The organization determines the need for information, the characteristics of information, and access requirements. The business rules are documented in the information architecture, which is used as the foundation for implementing information systems and IT. IT provides the technology to enable the organization to capture and access the information needed. Information systems implement the business rules to enable and restrict access to information and ensure that the integrity of information is maintained, providing quality information to meet the information needs of the entire organization. It is therefore essential that the business defines its requirements for information and the rules for using the information within the specific organizational context, which gives the information meaning.

Table 4.17 ▶ Life Cycle Approach to Enterprise Architecture

	Information Life Cycle			
	Capture	**Store and Retrieve**	**Use, Share, and Maintain**	**Archive and Destroy**
Organizational Architecture	Specifies the need for information and the characteristics of information.	Specifies where information is needed in the organization.	Specifies the need for information to support operational, tactical, and strategic activities.	Specifies the time periods when access to the information is likely to be needed.
Information Architecture	Defines the structure of information needed.	Defines the structure of information and access rights.	Defines the business rules to maintain information integrity.	Defines the business rules for archiving and destroying information.
Information Systems Architecture	Provides processes to capture the required information.	Provides processes to enable access that is independent of storage details.	Provides processes to use the information in accordance with the business rules.	Provides processes to facilitate access to archived information.
IT Architecture	Provides the means to capture data and the characteristics of the data required.	Provides a means to facilitate authorized access to stored data.	Provides a means to facilitate and restrict changes to data by implementing the business rules.	Provides a means to store and facilitate access to archived data and to delete data at the end of the retention period.

Summary

The information architecture is a layer in the enterprise architecture that joins together the organizational architecture and the information systems architecture. The information architecture outlines the structure of the information needed in the organization which will be used in the information systems specified in the information systems architecture. The IT architecture relates to the hardware and software to be used in the organization to support the information systems in providing the organization with access to the information needed.

A socio-technical approach has been outlined for developing an information architecture that uses the business model discussed in previous chapters, established analytical modelling tools, and soft systems tools from Wilson's (1990) soft systems method. Stage 1 of the approach explores the context of the information architecture using the organization architecture and business model to identify the master data and initial information requirements of the organization. Rich pictures, root definitions, conceptual models, and a Maltese Cross are used in stage 2 to define information categories needed to support different views of the organization. The structure of the information categories is represented in an entity-relationship model in stage 3 and business rules are defined to maintain the integrity of information in the organization. In stage 4, access requirements and access restrictions to information are agreed to and the information architecture is documented in a data dictionary. Information is used by the business functions, therefore the business must take responsibility for identifying and defining the information required in the organization.

Reviewing Scenario 4.1

The problems Amy experienced with the system occurred because she devolved responsibility for managing the information needs of her business to Bill. Bill made what he thought were reasonable assumptions about information in Amy's business. Amy told him she needed to keep information about her customers. Bob took *customer* to mean someone who had placed an order with Amy to buy her candles. Bob therefore defined the business rule that a customer is only a customer if they have placed an order with Amy's Candles. He then implemented this business rule by only allowing a new entry to be created and stored in the customer database if they had a valid order number. Bob implemented integrity checks to check that a number had been entered into the order number field of the customer record and that the order number was valid (an order number is valid if it corresponds to an order in the order database). This would mean that an order could not be placed by someone whose details were not captured in the customer database.

Bob also set predefined limits to alert Amy when stock of her raw materials was running low. However, he did not consider the possibility that materials could be substituted and did not provide Amy with an easy facility to change or stop the reorder reminders triggered by low stock levels.

Amy should have spent time with Bob to explain how information was used in her business. Sometimes it seems obvious what information is needed so it is not stated explicitly. Unfortunately, something is only obvious within a specific context, and without detailed knowledge of the context, information needs can be misinterpreted. Amy was familiar with suppliers regularly changing the names of dyes and it was obvious to her that dyes could be substituted. Bill was not familiar with the details of her business and so to him this was not obvious. Sometimes the possibility of a situation arising is not thought of in advance. For example, Bob did not think about the possibility of Amy needing to store information about potential customers. Even if Bill had asked Amy if she needed to capture information about potential customers, she may not have thought it necessary until the specific situation arose. Sometimes the implication of a decision is not fully understood at the time. Bill implemented validity and integrity checks to ensure that a customer record could not be created without a customer being associated with a valid order. Amy may not have realized that by agreeing to the business rule that *a customer is someone who has placed an order with the organization,* she would not be able to capture details of potential customers who had not yet placed a confirmed order.

Cloze Exercise 4.1

Complete the following paragraph by choosing the correct word from Table 4.18 to fill in each gap.

Information is owned by the _____ and therefore the management of this important resource should not be delegated to technical functions. An _____ architecture is a framework that demonstrates the alignment among the organizational, information, information systems, and IT architectures. An _____ architecture provides a diagrammatic representation of the information needed by the organization. A _____ systems approach has been proposed for developing an information _____. This approach recognizes that people view the same situation differently, through their own _____ filter. The first stage in developing an information architecture is to analyse the organizational _____. The organizational architecture provides the context that gives information meaning. The _____ model is used to _____ some of the general information that the organization will need. The existing strategic _____ models used in organizations can contribute to identifying the information needed by different _____ of the business. The second stage involves _____ information requirements by analysing the activities that the organization needs to undertake. A data to process _____ is then conducted to ensure that all the information needed has been identified. In stage _____ the structure of the information is defined using an entity-_____ model. Determinacy and _____ constraints define the relationships among entities specifying the _____ of information. The constraints provide the business _____ which aims to preserve the _____ of information. This prevents changes to the information which may _____ affect how the information can be used in other areas of the organization. The _____ of the model is reviewed in stage 4 to ensure that the required information can be derived by _____ paths through the model. A _____ dictionary is then created which defines the _____ data, documenting the information architecture and the business rules which will be _____ by information systems and IT.

Link 4.3
Answers to Cloze Exercise 4.1

Table 4.18 ▸ Words to Complete Cloze Exercise 4.1

Access	Business	Data	Information	Relationship
Adversely	Cardinality	Defining	Integrity	Rules
Analysis	Cognitive	Enterprise	Mapping	Soft
Architecture	Completeness	Identify	Meta	Structure
Areas	Context	Implemented	Organization	Three

Activities 4.1

1 Identify the information that Amy needs from her suppliers. List the interactions Amy may have with suppliers and then suggest potential entities that may be needed to store the information Amy receives (following the example in Table 4.6).

2 Figure 4.2 presents an extract from a customer resource process model. Another step in the customer resource process is *place order*. Complete columns A to D to show the information that Amy needs to provide to customers to help them to place an order for her products.

3 Prepare a set of CATWOE and a root definition to reflect the view of Brian, an employee of Amy's Candles.

4 Table 4.10 shows an extract of the information requirements for the consensus conceptual model shown in Figure 4.7. Complete Table 4.10 to include all the activities in the consensus conceptual model and the information requirements for each activity.

5 Complete the Maltese Cross in Figure 4.8 by adding all the activities from the consensus conceptual model shown in Figure 4.7 and complete the mapping of information categories.

6 Extend Table 4.14 to include the potential relationships between all the candidate entities listed in Table 4.13.

7 Complete the data dictionary for all the entities shown in Figure 4.10.

8 Define the business rules that Amy needs in order to resolve the problems she has identified in Scenario 4.1.

Discussion Questions 4.1

1 Consider the advantages and disadvantages of creating an order before creating a new customer record.

2 Discuss the arguments for and against everyone in the organization being given complete access to all the organization's information.

3 Discuss the relationship between the organizational architecture and the information architecture. Consider the different roles of the two architectures, how they relate to one another, and whether both architectures are needed in an organization.

4 Why does a rich picture not have defined notation? How might this affect its use?

5 Should information requirements be identified from existing business processes or should information be defined independently of existing processes? Why?

6 Review the semantic and articulatory distances shown in Figure 4.3. How do these differences affect the way information is managed in organizations?

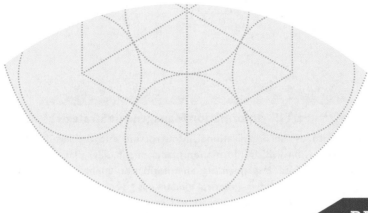

INFORMATION MANAGEMENT STRATEGIES

Part II Information Management Strategies

Part II outlines the organizational infrastructure and the legal and ethical framework within which information management takes place. An approach to developing and implementing an information management strategy is presented, with examples. Practical guidance is given on how business and IT functions can work together to address common information management problems in organizations.

Chapter 5 Information Management and Governance

Chapter 5 defines types of governance and explains the relationship between information governance and information management. It outlines the responsibilities of information management roles and identifies risks to information security. The ethical issues that underpin legislation relating to information are discussed, including privacy, ownership, accessibility, and retention. The chapter demonstrates how information management tools can be used to address typical information issues that arise in organizations.

Chapter 6 Information Management Strategy

Chapter 6 explains the relationship between an information management strategy, organizational strategy, information systems strategy, and IT strategy. It defines the components of an information management strategy and outlines an approach to formulate and implement an information management strategy. Example strategies are presented. The critical success factors for implementing an information management strategy are discussed and the need to evaluate the progress and impact of an information management strategy is considered.

Chapter 7 Improving Information Access

Chapter 7 explores factors that impede access to meaningful information in organizations, such as the formation of information silos. Barriers to sharing and defining data are discussed and approaches to overcome the barriers are suggested. The chapter demonstrates how different data definitions affect the quality of information and explains how business rules embedded in data definitions influence each stage of the information life cycle.

Chapter 8 Improving Information Consistency

Chapter 8 discusses a range of problems that affect the quality and reliability of information in organizations. The causes of dirty data are explained and guidance is given about how to clean data. The problems of fragmented and conflicting information are considered, demonstrating how information becomes fragmented and explaining how data from different sources can be reconciled. The chapter identifies how information may become corrupted and presents an example of data recovery.

INFORMATION MANAGEMENT AND GOVERNANCE

Scenario 5.1

Information Overload in Match Lighting

Mr Alvis, the Director of the lighting manufacturer Match Lighting, surveyed his desk. The desk held piles of unread annual reports from departmental managers, trade journals, and invitations to conferences and events. The mountain of information was in danger of slipping off the desk and into the waiting recycling bin. He had exceeded the storage limit on his email box and was unable to send any further emails. He had contacted the IT department and asked for his storage limit to be increased but he was advised to send an email to confirm his request – if only he could! He scanned the list of email addresses and subject headings in search of emails that could be deleted quickly but found few that could be discarded without a response. The inbox included emails from:

○ A customer complaining that they had been incorrectly charged three times.
○ The head of sales exchanging emails with the IT manager about communication of the IT policy.
○ The director of Bright Spark about problems with accessing information relating to past orders on the collaborative e-business system.
○ A sales manager and a distribution manager who were disagreeing about the accuracy of the report analysing order completion times.
○ Someone in accounts asking who had authorized the change of the *supplier credit code* field.
○ Mr Cook asking if the purchase orders from 12 years ago were still needed or whether the purchase orders could be destroyed.

Mr Alvis sighed, *'How can I take control of all this information?'*

Learning Outcomes

The learning outcomes of this chapter are to:

○ Explain the purpose of governance.
○ Outline roles and responsibilities for managing information.
○ Identify the ethical and legal issues relating to information management.
○ Define data security classifications.
○ Recommend actions to maintain information security.
○ Identify tools used in information management.

Introduction

Staff throughout the organization encounter the problems caused by poor information management on a daily basis. The impact of poor information management is a long-term insidious degradation of organizational performance rather than an immediate crisis. Rogerson (2008) suggests that the powerful lifeblood of information in organizations has become polluted by the sheer volume of information available and concerns relating to the accuracy of information available. Information management is needed to effectively manage the second most critical resource in organizations (people being the most important resource in any organization). This chapter outlines the infrastructure of policies to improve information management in organizations. The relationship between information management and information governance is first considered and then the responsibilities for information management are identified. Legal and ethical issues that need to be considered in relation to information management are discussed. The chapter concludes by identifying tools to help manage the information resource.

5.1 Types of Governance

Corporate governance in Europe was initiated by the Cadbury Report (Parum, 2006), which describes corporate governance as directing and controlling the actions of an organization (Cadbury Committee, 1992). Corporate governance incorporates three main factors: direction, leadership, and accountability (Willis, 2005). A governing council explores the conflicting needs of different stakeholders, establishes the expectations of the organization, and defines the strategic aims of the organization. Governance also institutes controls, defining the limitations of acceptable behaviour to achieve these aims, focusing on the responsibilities for accountability of the organization in relation to legal compliance and ethical behaviour. Monks and Minow (2011) describe corporate governance as an element of risk management, which aims to ensure that appropriate controls are in place to protect the value of the organization for stakeholders. Corporate governance seeks to foster ethical behaviour and ensure compliance to statutory legislation by establishing due process and accountability of the actions of the organization (Willis, 2005).

DEFINITION: **Corporate governance** is the infrastructure of policy, structures, and systems to direct, manage, and monitor an organization, defining the boundaries of acceptable behaviour in an ethical and legal context.

The corporate governance framework has a number of subsets focusing on the specific needs of different organizational resources such as information technology (IT), information, and data.

5.1.1 Information Technology Governance

The accountability of corporate governance is embedded in IT governance, which focuses on the strategic role of IT in organizations. It seeks to maximize the business value of the IT resource (Webb *et al.*, 2006) and align IT with the needs of the organization (Ko & Fink, 2010). IT governance considers key questions relating to decisions about the IT resources, how the decisions will be made, and who will be involved in the decisions (Weil & Ross, 2004).

DEFINITION: **Information technology (IT) governance** is the infrastructure of policy, structures, and systems to direct, manage, and monitor the organization's IT resource, establishing accountability for the way the IT resource is used.

IT governance defines the role of IT in the organization and the priorities for IT investments (Weil & Ross, 2004). Ko and Fink (2010) suggest that IT governance

incorporates the three views of structure, processes, and people. The structure view considers the degree to which control of IT is centralized, decentralized, or federated. The process view defines the processes needed to ensure that IT is aligned with, and contributes to, adding value to the organization. The people view focuses on the roles and responsibilities of staff in the organization for implementing the processes in the defined structure. These views are used to determine the IT architecture and IT infrastructure needed in the organization.

5.1.2 Information Governance

Information governance focuses on monitoring an organization's information assets and poses new challenges to organizations than other forms of governance due to the subjective value of information (Kooper *et al.*, 2011). It is a framework of policies, structures, and systems within which information can be managed in the organization. Information governance involves establishing processes to control and account for actions relating to information (Lomas, 2010) to ensure that information management policies are enforced (Martin *et al.*, 2010) and that decisions taken reflect the needs of the whole organization.

DEFINITION: **Information governance** is the infrastructure of policy, structures, and systems to direct, manage, and monitor the organization's information resource. Information governance establishes accountability for the processes relating to information throughout the information life cycle and seeks to encourage a culture of responsible behaviour.

Information governance establishes the environment for managing information effectively throughout the information life cycle. A framework of information governance is shown in Figure 5.1 that incorporates:

○ A series of policies to guide and control how information is captured, used, accessed, and destroyed in the organization.
○ A structure of information management roles, which cut across the formal organizational structure and have specific responsibilities for governing the use of information.
○ Business processes and procedures to implement the information management policies.

Information governance provides the authority to mobilize resources to formulate and implement an information management strategy.

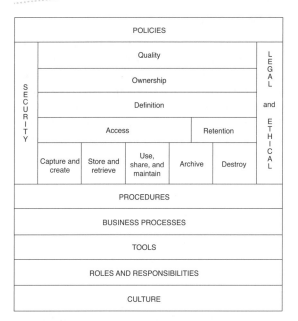

POLICIES					

Figure 5.1 ▶ Framework of Information Governance

5.1.3 ▶ Data Governance

Data governance refers to the introduction of processes to improve the quality of data by making people accountable for data (Sarsfield, 2009). Thomas (2011a) suggests that a data governance programme comprises three main elements: creation of rules for the capture and use of data, development of processes for resolving issues relating to data, and provision of ongoing services to achieve the organization's vision for data.

DEFINITION: Data governance is the infrastructure of policy, structures, and systems to direct, manage, and monitor data in the organization. Data governance establishes accountability for the quality and availability of data.

The implementation of data governance requires data management policies and processes to be defined (Griffin, 2010). Khatri and Brown (2010) propose five domains in a data governance framework: data principles, data quality standards, metadata definitions, data access requirements, data life cycle inventory. Thomas (2011a) suggests that the focus of the data governance framework may differ in organizations and may include: policies and standards, data quality, data privacy and security, data integration, business intelligence, and management support for routine decisions. All of these areas are important but implementing a governing framework to improve the management of data takes time and needs to be implemented in stages. These stages include:

Stage 1: Establish a governing council and an Information Management Committee.
Stage 2: Define structural responsibilities.
Stage 3: Formulate policies and standards.
Stage 4: Develop management processes to implement the policies.
Stage 5: Create tools to support management processes.
Stage 6: Propose projects to improve data quality, access, security, and integration.

A key process of data governance is changing the attitude towards data in the organization (Sarsfield, 2009). This requires a change in organizational culture, demonstrating that everyone in the organization has a responsibility for the data with which they interact.

5.1.4 ▶ Relationship between Information Governance and Information Management

Corporate management focuses on planning and organizing resources to achieve the strategic aims of the organization within the requirements of the corporate governance framework. Effective information management is needed to facilitate corporate governance by demonstrating accountability and demonstrating the organization's adherence to due process and legislative compliance through documented information (Willis, 2005). Table 5.1 summarizes the relationship between governance and management.

Table 5.1 ▶ Relationship between Information Governance and Information Management

Information Governance	Information Management
Establishes the requirements of stakeholders.	Organizes resources.
Protects the value for stakeholders as a whole, rather than individual interests.	Implements the vision. Operates within the governing framework.
Provides the vision.	Develops processes and procedures to action the governing controls.
Formulates strategic objectives.	
Defines the limitations of acceptable activity.	
Identifies potential risks to the organization's value.	Addresses issues that arise with reference to the governing framework.
Establishes controls to protect the organization's value.	
Provides a framework of structures, processes, and policies to direct acceptable actions.	
Seeks to facilitate ethical behaviour.	

5.2 ▶ Information Management Roles

Everyone who handles personal information needs to take responsibility for handling the information appropriately. However, clearly defined roles and responsibilities are needed to improve the quality of data (Umar *et al.*, 1999) and roles such as data ownership need to be defined (Silvola *et al.*, 2011). A number of specific roles are needed to address the immediate problems in the organization and take responsibility for maintaining the quality of information as the information needs of the organization change over time.

5.2.1 ▶ Information Governing Council

An information governing council, comprising senior managers representing all areas of the organization, prepares the information governance framework within which information management processes can be implemented. Alternative names for the council include Information Governing Committee, Management Forum, Steward Council, and Corporate Information Group. The governing council provides an integrated business perspective on the information resource and is concerned with other aspects of information management including definition, integrity, validity, availability, and security. The council addresses internal political issues to overcome barriers to achieving strategic aims of information management. In some organizations the same council has responsibility for both information governance and information management, while other organizations have a separate Information Management Committee. This is usually dependent on the number and location of divisions in the organization.

5.2.2 ▶ Information Management Committee

The Information Management Committee comprises senior staff from across the organization, reinforcing the requirements for the business to take responsibility for the information resource. The committee is responsible for organizing and mobilizing resources to implement the information management strategy within the requirements of the governing framework. The committee meets regularly, usually monthly, and is a practical forum in which to address information management issues. Members of the committee are called information stewards and work together to adopt an integrated approach to managing information across the organization. This includes taking action to ensure that appropriate procedures and training programmes are developed to implement information management policies.

5.2.3 ▶ Information Steward

An information steward is appointed to the Information Management Committee to represent the interests of a specific area of the business. Stewards need to have a good understanding of how information is used in their area and a willingness to investigate issues when required. The stewards are responsible for communication between their business area and the Information Management Committee. Information stewards:

○ Raise information management issues at the committee that are causing problems in their area and pursue the issues to resolution.
○ Report back to staff in their area about the actions and decisions taken by the committee.
○ Represent the interests of their area at the committee.
○ Investigate the impact on their area of proposals discussed at the committee.

The information stewards collaborate with the information manager to ensure that the information needs of all areas of the organization are appropriately supported.

5.2.4 ▶ Information Manager

The information manager is responsible to the Information Governing Council and Information Management Committee. The information manager has overall responsibility for establishing the policies and processes required to effectively manage information as a corporate resource to meet the needs of the entire organization. The information manager works closely with senior managers to ensure that all staff are aware of the importance of data and know how to handle business-critical data. The information manager will identify and secure the resources needed to address the immediate information-related problems in the organization, and to establish structures and processes to minimize the opportunity for problems to reoccur.

It is unrealistic for one person to fully understand how information is used in the entire organization. The information manager will therefore first establish an excellent team of staff across the organization with whom they can work to understand the different information requirements of the organization. The team will include the roles of data owners, data authors, and data maintainers.

The information manager, working with data owners, will start to define the data in the organization, developing the information architecture and data dictionary. A number of separate projects will be needed to define data and take action to improve the quality of data. Each of these projects will require a project manager and will involve staff from different business areas.

The information manager aims to take control of the processes that manage information through the information life cycle and establish new processes to maintain and improve the quality and integrity of the information resource. The needs of the organization change over time. The information manager will therefore need to continually review the suitability of the information management processes to ensure that the processes satisfy the changing context of information in the organization.

The information manager needs to possess an understanding of both the business and technical aspects of information management in order to effectively communicate with all aspects of the organization. Knowledge of data models and technical systems will help the information manager to communicate the needs of the business to IT staff. It will also help the manager to understand the specific requirements of IT staff seeking to implement the business rules to improve the quality and integrity of information. A hybrid manager is therefore needed who has excellent communication skills and is committed to addressing the challenges of improving the quality of information.

5.2.5 Data Owner

The information manager works with data owners. A data owner has overall responsibility for specific items of data and is usually a member of a business function.

DEFINITION: Data Owner has overall responsibility for defining an item of data and for formulating policies relating to data capture, use, and destruction. All queries relating to the data item, such as requests to change the data item's structure or to seek access to data values, are addressed to the data owner.

Scofield (1998) criticizes the term *ownership*, suggesting that the term implies a hoarding of data that works against the principle that data are owned by the organization as a whole, rather than an individual person or department. Scofield (1998) proposes the alternative term of *data steward*. The organization does own the data and everyone in the organization needs to accept responsibility for how his or her role affects the quality of data. However, in practice, an individual needs to be identified as the main contact to make decisions and provide guidance on the effective use of individual data items. The term *ownership* reflects the need for the business to take responsibility for defining the business rules that determine how data are used effectively in the organization. In practice, ownership roles have demonstrated a clear responsibility for ensuring that the information needs of all areas of the organization are addressed.

Data Owner Responsibilities

The data owner is the primary contact for specific items of data. Data owners need to understand how data are used within business processes to ensure that data are used effectively. Data owners control who can access and change data based on the organization's use of the data and the specific definition of a data item. The aim of controlling access to data is to prevent data from being used in a way that is inconsistent with data definitions; this could lead to data being misinterpreted or could lead to changes to the data that reduce its quality and adversely affect other areas of the organization.

The responsibilities of data owners include:

○ Identifying the data needed to support the continued operation of the organization and raise requests for the capture or purchase of additional data.
○ Defining the data and identifying any changes needed to the data definitions documented in the data dictionary.
○ Implementing the business rules defined for using and maintaining the data.
○ Establishing procedures to maintain data integrity.
○ Investigating data issues arising in the organization and proposing recommendations to resolve them.
○ Participating in project meetings about the data items for which they are responsible.

The role of data owner is an ongoing task. During the initial phase of information management as an organization takes control of data, a data owner will need to work with the information manager to define data, improve the quality of data, and develop policies to ensure that the quality of data is maintained. The data owner is responsible for creating and maintaining the data definition in the data dictionary. The data owner is the primary contact for any queries relating to data in the organization. Queries may include: Can an additional attribute be added? Can an attribute be removed? Can a division have access to read or change the data? Can the structure of an attribute be changed from numerical to alphabetical characters? Data owners do not need to know the answers to these questions, but they do need to be willing to work with others to investigate the queries. It is important that such queries are investigated thoroughly to ensure that the full impact of any changes to both business and IT systems are identified before any changes are agreed.

Table 5.2 summarizes the role of data owners in the data life cycle.

Table 5.2 ▸ Role of Data Ownership in the Data Life Cycle

Capture	Store and Retrieve	Use, Share, and Maintain	Archive and Destroy
Defines the data and data attributes to be captured. Formulates the policies of what data are to be captured, when, and by which business function. Specifies the validation and verification rules to be applied to the data captured. Agrees the business rules to maintain the integrity of the data.	Defines the data to be stored. Specifies the roles within the organization (and any external parties) that may retrieve the data and specifies what attributes a role can access.	Formulates the policies regarding the use, sharing, and maintenance of data. Defines the business rules for using and maintaining data to preserve the integrity and quality of the data. Specifies who may use the data. Identifies who may change the data and the limitations of the changes permitted.	Formulates the policies relating to archiving, retention, and deletion of data. Defines when data can be archived, how long data must be retained, when and how data can be destroyed.

Skills of a Data Owner

While data owners have ultimate responsibility for the data assigned to them, they are expected to consult and work with staff across the organization to ensure that the policies developed, and decisions and actions taken, meet the needs of the whole organization. It is therefore important that the assignment of data owners is carefully considered.

A data owner needs to have a good understanding of how data are captured and used both within their own functional area and in other areas of the business. Good communication skills, social skills, and a willingness to work effectively with colleagues across the organization are essential to facilitate discussions and resolve issues when they arise. For example, data owners will discuss the data validation and verification controls required to maintain data integrity.

Data owners also need to understand the importance of data management in the organization. A data owner is an ambassador for improving the quality and accessibility of information in the organization. In practice, establishing responsibility for data items is difficult. Some people may not want the responsibility of being accountable for the data, while others may seek the responsibility for political reasons (Martin *et al.*, 2010).

5.2.6 ▸ Data Author

Although the data owner has responsibility for specific data items, a data owner does not work in isolation. A data author has responsibility for implementing the definitions and policies approved by the data owner. Although there is one data owner for each data item, there will be a number of data authors assigned to a data item. Data authors may raise queries with the data owner and assist the data owner in defining data and data structures. Typical decisions relate to who has authority to access and change data, and policies relating to the controls needed to protect data integrity.

DEFINITION: Data Authors implement the definitions and policies defined by the data owner. This includes specifying the valid values and coding systems for data items. There are likely to be several data authors accountable to a data owner.

Data authors are responsible for implementing the policies relating to the use of data. A combination of both business rules and physical IT controls are used to enforce the policies and standards defined by the data owner. Data authors will therefore be situated in different departments, including the IT department. For example, as product data are used in many divisions in Match Lighting there will be a number of data authors for product data across the organization. For example, in Scenario 5.2 the *prod_handling* attribute has a set of agreed values that the attribute can possess. The data author is responsible for ensuring that only these values are used for the attribute. This will require business rules to be defined about the meaning of the attribute *prod_handling* code. The warehouse supervisors will be given access to the required information system to change the data value of a *prod_handling* code for a specific product. IT systems used for capturing product details will need to have an additional field added so that the *prod_handling* attributes can be captured when details of a new product are created.

Scenario 5.2

Information Management Roles in Match Lighting

The warehouse staff in Match Lighting want to add an attribute *prod_handling* to the *product* entity. The attribute will be a code used to inform warehouse staff of any particular handling requirements of the product, such as *do not store by heaters* or *fragile: handle with care.* The request to add the attribute is considered by the data owner for *product* data who will consult staff in business and IT departments to assess the impact of adding this attribute to *product* data. If the new attribute is approved, IT staff will add a field on files, forms, reports, and labels to enable the handling code to be entered, read, and changed as required.

The data owner, with staff from the warehouse, will:

○ Define the data item.
  • *Prod_handling* is defined as a code to indicate any specific requirements that need to be considered when handling the product in the warehouse and when the product is in transit.
  • The length of the data attribute is X(4).
○ Formulate the policies relating to the data item.
  • When a new product is created, a value for this code must be recorded. The default value of the attribute code *NORM* is recorded, unless another value is entered.
  • The code can be accessed by all internal divisions of Match Lighting.

• The value of a code can only be changed by supervisors in the warehouse.

The data author will:

○ Define the data values for the attribute *prod_handling*.
  • Acceptable values for *prod_handling* are *NORM, FRAG, COOL, WARM*.
○ Implement the policies relating to *prod_handling*.
  • Implement controls to ensure that when a new product is created, a default value of *NORM* is entered if one of the other acceptable codes is not entered.
  • Ensure that all internal divisions within Match Lighting have access to read the code but cannot modify the code.
  • Implement controls so that only warehouse supervisors can change the value of the product-handling code.
  • Implement controls so that the product-handling code cannot be changed to any value except the values *NORM, FRAG, COOL,* or *WARM*.

The data maintainer will:

○ Create product data.
  • Add a value of *NORM, FRAG, COOL, WARM* to the field *prod_handling* when a new product is entered into the system.
○ Change the value of a product's handling code.
  • Warehouse supervisors can change the value of the attribute *prod_handling* for a product to any of the defined values of *NORM, FRAG, COOL,* and *WARM*.

Link 5.1

Actions Associated with Data Management Roles

Data authors for an individual data item support the work of data owners; the data author directs queries to the data owner and works with the data owner to investigate the impact of potential changes proposed to the definition, structures, and management of the data for which he or she has a direct responsibility.

5.2.7 Data Maintainer

Data maintainers have responsibility for creating, maintaining, and using data on a daily basis. There are likely to be a number of data maintainers for each item of data, who are identified by their job role in different business

areas. For example, supervisors in sales and marketing and manufacturing functions in Match Lighting have authority from the data owner for product data to maintain certain values in relation to a product.

DEFINITION: Data maintainers have responsibility for the values of a data item. Data maintainers create instances of the data item and change data values when authorized to do so, within the limits imposed by the coding structure defined by data authors. There will be several data maintainers for a data item.

In Match Lighting, warehouse supervisors have been given responsibility for changing values of the attribute *prod_handling*. IT staff will implement controls to ensure that only warehouse supervisors have access to change the values of the attribute. As data maintainers for the attribute *prod_handling*, warehouse supervisors are responsible for ensuring that the value of the attribute is correct for all products. When a warehouse supervisor receives a request to change the *prod_handling* code for a specific product, the supervisor needs to consider the request to ensure that an accurate *prod_handling* value is allocated to the product. If a product has an incorrect *prod_handling* code, damage could be caused to the product or to staff handling the product in the warehouse. If the warehouse supervisor suggests that the current range of valid *prod_handling* codes is inadequate, they will need to seek agreement from the data author to approve the addition of further values.

Data maintainers are responsible for maintaining the quality of the data captured, modified, and used. A data maintainer works at the operational level of the data and may identify changes needed in the way data are captured to improve data quality. For example, if *prod_handling* codes are continually entered incorrectly, additional validation checks may be needed when the code is entered. The data maintainer has a responsibility to suggest this to the data author. Data maintainers need to understand the importance of their role in information management and recognize that they have a responsibility for improving the quality of information in the organization.

Quiz 5.1
Information Management Roles

5.2.8 Relationship between Information Management Roles

Table 5.3 provides examples of the authorization levels of data owner, data author, and data maintainer in response to common requests in Match Lighting.

Clarity of data definitions and identification of data owners provide the foundation to enable data to be effectively shared and integrated across the organization. A data ownership matrix provides a record of the individuals who have been assigned the roles of data owner, data author, and data maintainer for each data item in the information architecture. Initially the matrix identifies organizational roles from the organizational structure that are positioned to have the knowledge required for a specific information management role. The matrix is then completed by adding the names of specific individuals in the organization who have been allocated the information management roles.

The data ownership matrix provides an essential document identifying staff to contact when any queries arise relating to specific data items. A key priority of the information manager is to create and maintain this matrix. As individual staff change roles in the organization or staff leave the organization, replacement data owners need to be allocated immediately. It is essential that data owners are clearly identified and that if necessary temporary data owners are assigned to data rather than leaving entries as *to be appointed*. Table 5.4 shows an extract of a data ownership matrix for Match Lighting.

5.2.9 Responsibilities for Information Management

The business owns the data held in information systems in the organization and is responsible for defining the business rules to maintain the quality and integrity of data. Overseeing and preserving data quality should be undertaken by everyone in the organization as custodians of the data resource, recognizing the need to have accountability for actions. There is a tendency for the individual or team who captured or created the data to feel that they own the

Table 5.3 Examples of Information Management Authorization Levels

Request	Authorization Level
A new product has been approved by the product design team and head of manufacturing. Who can enter the product details?	Data Maintainer
Who can change the *prod_weight* from 84g to 96g for *prod_num* 124165871?	Data Maintainer (manufacturing supervisor)
Can the *prod_handling* code for *prod_num* 124165871 be changed from *WARM* to *FRAG*?	Data Maintainer (warehouse supervisor)
Can a new *prod_handling* code be created called *CARE*?	Data Author
How can a new warehouse supervisor get access to product data?	Data Author
Can a new attribute be created for the *PRODUCT* entity to capture the colour of the product?	Data Owner

Table 5.4 Data Ownership Matrix Entry

Data Item	Data Owner	Data Author	Data Maintainer	Status
Product	Lee Mullins (Head of Product Development)	James Eldwidge (Warehouse Supervisor)	James Eldwidge (Warehouse Supervisor) Fa Chen (Manufacturing Supervisor) June Giles (Sales and Marketing Supervisor)	Draft definition 02–07–12

Table 5.5 Issues Concerning the Individual in the Information Life Cycle

Capture	Store and Retrieve	Use, Share, and Maintain	Archive and Destroy
What information do you want from me and why?	Who will you allow to access the information about me? Will you keep the information safe to ensure that no one else can access it?	How will you use the information? Who will you share the information with? How do I know if the information you have about me is accurate? How can I correct the information if the information held about me is inaccurate?	How long will you keep the information about me? How will you ensure that the information remains safely secured? How will you destroy the information to ensure that it cannot be accessed again?

data and there can be reluctance to share data with other business areas. Information management aims to change the organizational culture to reflect that information is a corporate resource that must be shared with those in the organization who need the information and who are authorized to access the information. It is important that the organizational culture supports data management practices and the work of data owners (Silvola *et al.*, 2011).

Some organizations introduce further specialist information management roles, especially in the early stages of developing an information governance framework. For example:

○ An information architect is responsible for leading the design of the information architecture.
○ An information quality manager implements information quality policies and ensures that information is appropriately classified in the data classification framework.
○ A data steward works with staff in the IT department, such as database administrators, to ensure that data meet the requirements of defined quality metrics (Berson & Dubov, 2011). A data steward identifies potential problems with existing information systems that may adversely affect the quality of data.
○ A digital archivist oversees the creation and preservation of electronic information assets needed for historic and legislative purposes.

○ A project manager is responsible for coordinating resources and activities to achieve defined information management objectives in a specific period of time.

Information management needs to:

○ Establish commitment and support for the role of data ownership.
○ Outline the responsibilities of data owners.
○ Develop the infrastructure to support data owners.
○ Establish processes to maintain the data ownership matrix.
○ Secure the resources for data ownership activities.
○ Regularly review the effectiveness of the data ownership matrix.

5.3 Legal and Ethical Issues

Information management incorporates a range of information-related legislation to which the organization must adhere. Table 5.5 maps key concerns that individuals may have about the information they provide to organizations to the information life cycle in order to show where the concerns can be addressed.

Legislation regularly changes and differs between countries. Table 5.6 provides examples of legislation relating to the information management concerns highlighted in Table 5.5. General principles incorporated in legislation relating to the management of information are introduced in the following sections.

Table 5.6 Sample Legislation Relating to Information Management

Act	Focus	Country
Environmental Information Regulations 2004	Access to environmental information held by public authorities.	United Kingdom
Freedom of Information Act 2000	Access to information held by public bodies.	United Kingdom
Right to Information Act 2005	Access to information held by public authorities.	India
Regulation of Investigatory Powers Act 2000	Interception and disclosure of communication data.	United Kingdom
Data Protection Act 1998	Capture, use, access, and disclosure of personal data.	United Kingdom
Privacy Act 1993	Collection, use, and disclosure of personal information.	New Zealand
The Electronic Commerce Directive Regulations 2002	Information to be provided when engaging in e-commerce.	European Community
Patent Law of the People's Republic of China 2009	Intellectual property of inventors.	China
Copyright Law of the People's Republic of China 2001	Intellectual property.	China
Regulation on the Protection of the Right to Network Dissemination of Information 2006	Intellectual property.	China
Intellectual Property Rights	Ownership of patents, designs, trademarks, and copyright.	United Kingdom
The Children's Online Privacy Protection Act of 1998	Personal information relating to children online.	United States of America
Health Insurance Portability and Accountability Act of 1996	Privacy of personal health information.	United States of America
Human Rights Act 1998	Privacy.	United Kingdom
Security Breach Notification California 2002	Requirement to notify individuals in the event of the security of personal information being compromised.	United States of America
Federal Information Security Management Act of 2002	Responsibilities of information security.	United States of America
The Data Retention Regulations 2009	Retention of communications data.	European Community
Electronic Communications Act 2000	Use and encryption of electronic data communication.	United Kingdom

Link 5.2
Information Management Legislation

Information legislation is founded on ethical principles. Ethics refers to moral standards of behaviour expected by a community in specific circumstances. Judgements relating to acceptable behaviour are based on different philosophical standpoints relating to the rights of individuals and values such as honesty and integrity.

Difficulties arise because there are different views of moral rights. For example, online consumers in Germany and America have different attitudes towards marketing and privacy; organizations require prior permission from an individual in Germany before sending a marketing email whereas America adopts an opt-out, rather than an opt-in, policy on email marketing (Singh & Hill, 2003). At the core of information ethics is the question of who should have access to specific information (Fallis, 2007). Key ethical issues relating to information management include privacy, accuracy, property, and accessibility (Mason, 1986).

5.3.1 ▶ Right of Privacy

Aristotle asserted that 'privacy is a basic human desire' (Gayton, 2006). Information privacy is generally accepted as referring to the right of individuals to control who has access to data regarded as being personal to them and how the information may be used. This includes information relating to heath, finance, and employment. Information privacy incorporates three dimensions: (1) confidentiality relating to access, storage, and destruction of the information; (2) consent for the use and disclosure of the information provided; and (3) trust that the information will be accessed, stored, used, and disclosed within the conditions agreed upon when the information was provided. The moral dimension of privacy is complex as some philosophers suggest that privacy is a human right while others suggest that an individual's right to privacy must be balanced against the greater good of a community (Singh & Hill, 2003). Different cultures also address privacy differently; for example, there is no word for privacy in the Thai language (Capurro, 2008).

A distinction is therefore made between confidential data, such as an individual's health record, and data that may be considered to breach an individual's right of privacy, such as monitoring his or her whereabouts. The Human Rights Act 1998 gave individuals a legal right to privacy (Warren, 2002). Legislation such as the Data Protection Act 1998 requires organizations to consider the information they need to capture about individuals. Organizations have to clearly state what personal data will be captured and for what purpose the data will be used. The legislation is not restricted to text-based data and incorporates other forms of data such as visual recordings. For example, ICO (2008) provides a code of conduct on the use of CCTV images to meet the requirements of the Data Protection Act.

Information held in different computer systems poses challenges to information privacy (Clarke, 1994). While it may seem reasonable for government agencies to cross-check the data they hold to verify the accuracy of data, Clarke (1994) points out that cross-checking requires the disclosure of data between departments. This disclosure of data may be taking place without the knowledge or consent of the individual to whom the data relate (Clarke, 1994). The right of individuals to control who has access to data about themselves has to be viewed in the context of the rights of authorities to verify information for the purposes of detecting, for example, fraudulent behaviour.

Tavani (2011) discusses the need to preserve contextual integrity within privacy, that is, information given by a person on the understanding that the information will be used for one purpose, should not be used for another purpose for which consent has not been given. For example, Match Lighting may ask consumers to provide information about their lifestyle, such as their income, employment, and family situation in order to design lighting products that meet their needs. If Match Lighting's retail customers asked Match Lighting to provide information about the lifestyle of consumers so consumers could be sent marketing literature, Match Lighting would be violating the privacy of the consumers if retail customers were provided with the information Match Lighting had collected. The consumers consented for the information to be used within one context and the integrity of the context is violated if the information is passed to another organization without consent. Social contract theory asserts that customers and organizations engage in a social contract; customers may provide an organization with information in exchange for incentives (Singh & Hill, 2003) and the organization has a responsibility not to breach customers' trust.

Privacy is continually challenged as every interaction with an organization leaves an information audit trail of the transaction (Gayton, 2006). IT enables data to be captured relating to the actions and whereabouts of an individual and this also needs to be considered in the context of an individual's right to privacy. Clarke (1988) created the term *dataveillance* to refer to the use of technology to monitor and record data. IT can be used to capture data from a range of devices including door-access systems, car park systems, and mobile devices. Each system will have been designed to gather data for a particular purpose, for example, a door-access system can be used to restrict entry to authorized personnel. However, the data collected from such systems could be used to track the movements of individuals.

The development of IT to identify the location of an individual in order to provide location-based services has led to concerns about the extent to which this may be considered a breach of privacy. Location-based services send information to an individual, which is relevant to their current geographical location. The current location is determined by detecting the geographical location of an individual's device, such as their mobile telephone. Examples of location-based services include notification of traffic reports and offers at nearby retailers. It is generally accepted that the provision of location-based services does not breach an individual's privacy; however, the ability to capture data about the location of an individual does raise further issues relating to the security of such data. For example, Bettini *et al.* (2009) refer to the risk of sensitive association occurring when an authorized party can infer information about the identity of an individual and information about the individual, which they may consider to be private, through the information collected from location-based services.

A significant limitation with current legislation is that it only covers explicitly stored confidential data; it excludes the personal data that can be derived from analysis of explicit data (Tavani, 2011). Techniques such as data mining can be used to discover new information and determine patterns of behaviours through analysis of data that may be used for consumer profiling and direct marketing. Personal information derived from such techniques is not currently addressed by legislation.

Radio frequency identification (RFID) technology was mentioned in Chapter 3 as a means of capturing data to monitor the location of stock. Concerns have been raised about the extent to which RFID can be accessed after an item has been sold to an individual customer and how this impacts on individual privacy. Garfinkel *et al.* (2005) discuss the need for a bill of rights for RFID, which would give individuals the right to know whether items purchased include RFID tags and the opportunity to have the tags deactivated.

Much of the data collected by organizations is exchanged with other organizations (Tavani, 2011) that may be located in different countries and are therefore subject to different legislation. The Data Protection Act requires organizations to check that the rights of an individual will remain protected before sharing an individual's data with organizations in different countries. European Union (EU) laws governing e-business require consumers to give consent for their information to be transmitted outside the EU (Singh & Hill, 2003).

Maintaining information privacy encourages consumer trust and employee satisfaction with an organization, enhancing the organization's reputation (Gayton, 2006). The implementation of privacy legislation requires organizations to (Hewett & Whitaker, 2002):

○ Identify staff authorized to disclose information to authorized parties.
○ Ensure staff are aware of the limits of the information they may disclose.
○ Ensure the security of data within internal departmental systems is maintained and that data are not put at risk by practices such as sharing passwords.
○ Provide tracking information to identify when data have been changed and by whom.

○ Educate new staff on actions that may be taken against them if procedures for managing data privacy are not followed.
○ Check that IT systems do not capture unnecessary data.

5.3.2 Accuracy of Information

Inaccurate information can lead to wrong decisions being taken, which have a significant effect on both individuals and organizations. Responsibility and accountability for the accuracy of information are key ethical issues that organizations need to address (Mason, 1986). The Sarbanes-Oxley Act 2002 in the United States (www.soxlaw.com) requires organizations to present financial information as a complete, accurate, and true reflection of the financial situation of the organization. Fines and imprisonment are imposed for concealing or falsifying information. The accuracy of information extends beyond correctness to incorporate dimensions such as validity, honesty, completeness, and accountability for the quality of the information.

When entering and editing volumes of data displayed on computer screens the relevance of the information being handled can become overlooked. Staff have a moral responsibility to ensure that data are correct at the point the data are captured. IT can be used to process the data according to the business rules and then staff have a moral responsibility for using the information correctly and reporting the information accurately.

5.3.3 Information Property

Mason (1986) uses the term *property* to refer to the ownership of information. Attributing ownership of creative information is based on the ethical view that an individual owns the ideas that they create. Ownership seeks to protect the owner's rights relating to financial gains that may arise from his or her work. Legislation relating to intellectual property seeks to protect ownership of information created by individuals and organizations. Intellectual property has two roles: assigning ownership of ideas and regulating use of those ideas (Boldrin & Levine, 2002).

While legislation exists to clarify the assignment of intellectual property, some argue that legislation is unethical, preventing the free distribution and use of information. For example, Seadle (2004) raises the issue of whether an individuals have a right to claim ownership of their creations or whether by doing so they are stealing property that should be freely available to others. Boldrin and Levine (2002) suggest that while the originator should have the initial right of sale, they should not be entitled to downstream licencing as this hinders competition. Current trends suggest the balance of rights is being moved more towards the owners of the intellectual property rather than its users (Oppenheim, 2011).

In the United Kingdom, the Intellectual Property Office (www.ipo.gov.uk) provides guidance on the legislation available to secure ownership of intangible assets. For example, ideas about how an object or a process works are protected by patents; trademarks identify a brand associated with an organization; visual designs relate to the visual appearance of a product; the creation of other artefacts, such as computer software, information on websites, musical compositions, and film and artistic works, are protected by copyright.

Ethical issues relating to the ownership of information include the organization's responsibility for restricting the dissemination of information and limiting the use of confidential information for the purpose that the information was intended. The organization needs to protect intellectual property generated by the organization through the registration of trademarks and patents as well as the use of nondisclosure agreements. Organizations also need to ensure that they use information owned by others appropriately.

5.3.4 Information Accessibility

The ability to access information requires:

○ The information to be available.
○ Knowledge that the information exists.
○ Literacy skills to find out how to access and use the information.
○ Financial and physical resources to access the information.
○ Freedom to access the information.
○ Physical and mental capacity to use information systems.
○ Cognitive capacity to interpret the information.

Individuals have a right to access information, irrespective of age, gender, physical or mental abilities, nationality, or position in society, but barriers may deliberately or inadvertently infringe this right. Barriers preventing an individual from accessing information include literacy skills, availability of libraries and IT, cost of technology, and cost of information access (Mason, 1986). A more fundamental barrier to accessing information in organizations is the lack of awareness of the existence of the information. A further barrier to information access is censorship. Ethical arguments for and against the censorship of information include the potential adverse consequences that may arise from lack of censorship and the desire for intellectual freedom (Fallis, 2007).

There are a range of legal issues that need to be considered in relation to accessibility to ensure that reasonable adjustments are made to accommodate the needs of individuals with disabilities. Disabilities can be categorized as visual, auditory, cognitive, and motor (Peters & Bradbard, 2010). The World Wide Web Consortium (W3C) develops open standards to improve technical access and interoperability of data. The web accessibility initiative (WAI) develops international standards to improve access to digital resources (W3C, 2011). The standards include guidance for improving accessibility of information to ensure that access to information is not restricted due to issues of disability. The Americans with Disabilities Act, the UK Disability Discrimination Act, and the eEurope Action Plan recommend that public sector websites in EU member states adopt the WAI web content accessibility guidelines (Peters & Bradbard, 2010).

IT provides the ability for employees to access organizational information outside the workplace and outside their working hours. Although information access offers opportunities for flexible working, it can also have an adverse effect on work–life balance. For example, in some organizations it is considered unacceptable to call staff on their home telephones outside working hours yet it is considered acceptable to contact colleagues at home on their mobile telephones (Prasopoulou *et al.*, 2006). Appropriate guidelines are needed to address the impact of mobile technology on employees to maximize the benefits offered by technology while protecting employees from inappropriate demands (Cox, 2009). Access to information therefore needs to consider the ethical use of IT to contact individuals to obtain information from them.

5.3.5 Data Retention

The UK Data Protection Act states that data must only be stored for as long as necessary. Some organizations set a maximum retention period of five years for data unless there are reasons for a longer retention period. Data may need to be retained for longer periods if there is a potential need for the data in litigation, for longitudinal analysis, or for historic or research purposes.

Organizations seek to retain information to assist in historical analysis and the identification of trends but may not need to include data that identifies individuals. For example, if Match Lighting wishes to analyse retail customer trends, the organization would not necessarily need information such as the name and address of each retail customer; information could be analysed by attributes such as type or size of the retail customer. Organizations need an information management policy on data retention that clearly states the duration for which different types of data must be retained and how the information will be stored and destroyed. For example, financial data, such as salary data, are usually required to be retained for six years.

The EU Data Retention Directive of 2006 (EU, 2006) requires telecommunication providers to retain data relating to telephone calls, text messages, and emails for between six months and two years. The data retained include the sender, recipient, time, duration, type, equipment, and location of the communication so that these data are available if required.

Data retention periods are defined by data owners and documented in the data dictionary. Data owners assess the value of data in the organization and consider how data may be used in the future, both in the organization and by external parties. Care is needed when determining retention periods to ensure that the future potential value of the data to the organization is fully considered. The data may no longer be required by operational systems but may be needed later elsewhere in the organization for legal reasons or to support longitudinal analysis. The value of data to the organization at the end of the life cycle can therefore increase, particularly if fines are imposed if data cannot be retrieved when needed.

The future value of data, after the immediate needs of operational systems have been met, is difficult to predict. Historic data may record precedents, facilitate trend analysis, identify best practice, or provide evidence for use in legal proceedings. For example, in the future:

○ A previous customer or employee may allege that they have suffered health problems as a result of the organization's products, emissions, or working practices.
○ Past medical records may be used to investigate the source of a disease (Moore, 2004).
○ The introduction of a new industry standard may be used as an example of a turning point in industrial development.

Data are archived so that data can be restored to information systems in the future if required. It is therefore important to define and test procedures for recovering data from archived storage. However, during the time the data have been archived, changes may have been made to information systems in relation to data structures and business rules; data formats; data definitions, verification, and validation checks; and IT. Restoring archived data may therefore be difficult.

Link 5.3
Problems Restoring Archived Data

Although organizations often specify data retention periods, action is not taken to delete the data no longer required. Regular purges are needed to delete archived data no longer required, including any backup copies of the data. Data need to be securely destroyed in accordance with the classification requirements. For example, confidential data need to be disposed of in such a way that the data cannot be accessed accidentally or deliberately by unauthorized parties. Specialist companies can be used to securely shred both paper and storage devices containing electronic confidential data. Audit trails need to be maintained to record what data have been destroyed, when, how, and by whom. This includes recording the chain of activities, the people involved, and the secure transportation of data from archived storage to where the data are destroyed.

Information management needs to:

○ Identify the data retention legislation to which the organization must comply.
○ Ensure that data retention periods are assigned to data in compliance with legislative requirements.
○ Outline an archiving policy that ensures data are archived using the current data structures and that the data can be retrieved when required.
○ Ensure that archived data are stored in accordance with data classifications.
○ Specify the procedures for purging data in accordance with the data classification allocated to maintain data security.

5.3.6 Ethical Information Management

Information provides evidence of an activity; information is therefore a resource that organizations need to protect (Shepherd, 2006). Protecting information requires information to be ethically managed throughout all stages of the life cycle. Key ethical issues to consider through the life cycle are shown in Table 5.7.

An ethical code of conduct is a key characteristic of professions and professionals. Professional bodies such as the Association for Computing Machinery (ACM), the Institute for Electrical and Electronics Engineers (IEEE), and the British Computer Society (BCS) provide codes of conduct to which their members are expected to adhere. An ethical code of conduct seeks to inspire, educate, and guide members to adopt good practice, in addition to defining the accountability and responsibility of members (Tavani, 2011). Ethical

Table 5.7 Ethical Issues in the Information Life Cycle

Capture	Store and Retrieve	Use, Share, and Maintain	Archive and Destroy
What data to collect? Who owns the data? Should the data be captured? Who is responsible for the accuracy of the data? How are the data collected? (For example, with consent, with the use of surveillance equipment).	Who can access the data? Are confidential data identified?	How are the data processed? (For example, accurately and with proper use of procedures). How are the data presented? (For example, complete, accurate, with consent). How are the data used? What are the consequences of using the data?	Who can access the data? How is confidentiality maintained? How will the data be securely destroyed?

Table 5.8 Legal Issues in the Information Life Cycle

Information Life Cycle	Capture	Store and Retrieve	Use, Share and Maintain	Archive and Destroy
	Permission to capture data. Capture only data necessary for the purpose for which permission has been granted. Do not disclose information to unauthorized parties. Record ownership of intellectual property.	Store data securely to avoid unauthorized access to the data. Only disclose data to authorized parties.	Do not share data with unauthorized parties. When using data, ensure that confidentiality is maintained where applicable. Ensure permission is sought to use data where applicable.	Keep data for the minimum required retention period. Keep archived data secure. Do not disclose archived data to unauthorized parties. Destroy data securely to ensure that confidentiality of data is maintained.
Area of Legislation	*Data Protection*	*Data Privacy* *Data Security*	*Data Protection* *Data Privacy*	*Data Retention* *Data Privacy* *Data Security*

codes have a role in enforcing good practice through regulation and initiating disciplinary action where behaviour is considered to breach the code of conduct.

The ability to gain access and share information using IT devices continually raises ethical issues. For example, cookies are one approach used to collect data about an individual. Cookies are files on an individual's computer that store data about the use of a specific website and the data entered into the website. When the website is next visited, it retrieves the information from the file on the computer. This allows organizations to capture information relating to an individual. The organization owns the information collected and can sell the information to a third party (Tavani, 2011). In Europe, the use of online tracking technologies such as cookies requires prior informed consent from the individual (van Eijk *et al.*, 2012) before the cookie can be stored on his or her computer.

Ethical behaviour requires staff in organizations to take more responsibility for the way in which they interact with

information. This includes using information honestly and competently, being accountable for the effect of their actions. A lapse of ethical treatment of information can seriously damage an organization's reputation. Before taking action it is necessary to consider three questions. First, who may be affected by the action? Second, to what extent may the effect be regarded as positive or negative? Third, what are the potential consequences of not taking the action?

Information management needs to incorporate policies to ensure that issues of information privacy, accuracy, ownership, and accessibility are appropriately addressed at all levels of the organization, throughout the information life cycle. Organizations also need to ensure that internal information about colleagues and external information about customers are treated with equal ethical concern.

Table 5.8 summarizes the legal issues relating to information during the life cycle and identifies the main areas of legislation to address the concerns raised in Table 5.5.

5.4 ▶ Information Security

When an organization has captured data, the organization has a responsibility to keep the data and resulting information securely. Storing information securely involves protecting data from unauthorized access, loss, and damage. This means protecting the data from accidental or deliberate acts that will modify the data, delete the data, or allow the data to be accessed, changed, or processed by unauthorized parties. IT enables organizations to easily collect and disseminate copies of digital information and this provides increased opportunities for information to be accessed by unauthorized personnel (Sun *et al.*, 2011). Although much attention is given to incorporating security measures in IT systems using methods such as data encryption, breaches of data security are often the result of human error.

5.4.1 ▶ Data Breaches

A data breach occurs when the policies relating to who can legitimately access specific data are contravened. The contravention of access policies may occur due to inadequacies in the design or implementation of security procedures, or the violation of security procedures.

DEFINITION: A **data breach** is the voluntary or involuntary disclosure of data to unauthorized personnel within, or external to, the organization responsible for maintaining the security of the data.

Data breaches can be accidental or deliberate from authorized or unauthorized personnel. Deliberate authorized actions occur when someone with legitimate access abuses their authorized access to the data and changes the data values for fraudulent purposes. Accidental actions that cause the loss or corruption of data include fire, theft, and negligence, such as leaving a laptop unattended.

Garrison and Ncube (2011) define five types of data breaches that can affect personal information. These are:

○ Stolen: The theft of hardware such as laptops and flash drives in which data are stored.
○ Hacker: Unauthorized access to information systems usually from remote sources.
○ Insider: Unauthorized access, or misuse of authorized access, to information systems from current or former employees of the organization.
○ Exposed: Data are made publicly accessible through electronic communications such as emails or careless disposal of data records.
○ Missing: Mobile technology and storage devices that have been lost or mislaid such that the security of the data on them may have been compromised.

Table 5.9 provides examples of data breaches which affect the quality of the data stored in the organization.

While organizations actively seek to minimize the occurrence of data breaches, data are often exposed to unauthorized sources through careless actions. Table 5.10 identifies recent incidents that have led to information security breaches.

Link 5.4
Examples of Information Security Breaches

Employee oversight and poor business processes are the most common causes of data loss (Tarzey, 2010). Poor workspace design can provide the opportunity for information breaches through, for example, shoulder surfing. When Anya was creating the report on part sales, for example, her line manager brought Mr Reynolds to her

Table 5.9 ▶ Types of Data Breaches

	Accidental	**Deliberate**
Authorized	Changing a data value, which a person is authorized to change, by mistake. For example, mistakenly changing Mr Smith's credit limit instead of Mr Smyth's credit limit.	Changing a data value, which a person is authorized to change, intentionally, in order to deceive. For example, deliberately changing a friend's credit limit from £200 to £2,000.
Unauthorized	Changing a data value, which a person is not authorized to change, by mistake. For example, when accessing the data about the number of parts in stock, Anya mistakenly changed the stock of part 12154421 from 30 to 3 by pressing the wrong key on the keyboard. Anya does not have authorization to change stock levels and should not have been able to change the stock level.	Changing a data value, which a person is not authorized to change, intentionally, for fraudulent purposes. For example, an employee gaining access to their salary data and increasing their salary.

Table 5.10 ▸ Breaches of Information Security

Information Breach	Cause
Patient medical records.	Memory stick found in car park.
Details of prisoners.	Lost memory stick.
Classified information.	Lost laptop.
Names and addresses.	Papers found in a skip.
Patient medical records.	Paper records found in abandoned building.
Command codes for the international space station.	Stolen laptop.

desk. Mr Reynolds was from S. D. Fittings, one of Match Lighting's main suppliers. Organizational data about sales performance was therefore potentially exposed to an unauthorized source. As the proliferation of technical devices on which data can be displayed continues to increase, individuals using data need to be more aware of their surroundings to limit the risk of exposing data to unauthorized sources.

DEFINITION: **Shoulder surfing** is a data breach occurring when an unauthorized individual gains access to data by looking over the shoulder of an authorized individual who is accessing data legitimately. A typical example occurs at cashpoints (automated teller machines) when someone deliberately observes a customer entering their personal identification number (PIN) in order to use the PIN themselves to attain money or goods fraudulently.

When a data breach occurs there is understandable anger and outrage from the individuals directly affected, fuelled by the seemingly careless actions that led to the data breach. Part of the problem is perhaps that in manipulating data through a series of keystrokes and mouse clicks, the operator is distanced from the personal nature of the data being manipulated. Organizations provide training on how to use computer systems but often neglect to provide training on the responsibilities of staff in handling personal information using technology. The examples in Table 5.10 emphasize the need for information management to seek to generate a culture of responsibility for the information in the organization. This may include statements in the information management security policy to prohibit confidential data being copied to mobile storage devices.

5.4.2 ▸ Information Security Risks

Actions to maintain data security depend on the probability of a threat occurring and the potential severity

of subsequent consequences. The perceived adequacy of security measures relates to the perceived value of the information (Sun *et al.*, 2011). The probability and severity of a security risk are balanced against the cost of securing the data and the impact that securing the data has on the organization. For example, limiting data access to a few individuals increases data security but can mean that the data may not be accessible during periods of staff absence, which may affect the operation of the organization.

Risk assessments need to be conducted to:

○ Identify the nature of a potential threat.
○ Quantify the probability of the threat occurring (for example, high: probable; medium: possible; low: remote).
○ Define the potential consequences from a threat occurring.
○ Quantify the severity of the potential consequences that may arise from the threat.
○ Define actions to minimize the threat occurring.
○ Define actions to minimize the impact of the threat if it were to occur.

There are a number of standards to support risk assessment such as ISO 27005 (ISO, 2008) and the UK Risk Management Standard (IRM, 2002). Moreira *et al.* (2008) propose an ontology of vulnerabilities that provides a common language for security planning. The ontology includes four elements: (1) range of potential impact of the threat (local, remote, data interception); (2) significance of potential consequences of the threat (high, medium, low severity); (3) potential loss of features from the threat (availability of data or systems, integrity of data); and (4) the nature of the systems that may be affected (operating systems, hardware, software, networks). The ontology provides a means of capturing incident data for later analysis. Match Lighting employ Angel Security Solutions to provide a range of consultancy and security services. Table 5.11 provides an extract from an incident log at Match Lighting using the security ontology. The log is used by Angel Security Solutions to demonstrate the effectiveness of its services and identify areas of vulnerability that need to be addressed.

In addition to attempts to gain unauthorized access to data, security risks also include actions to disrupt IT services, such as denial of service attacks. Denial of service attacks are deliberate acts targeting the IT systems in organizations with the aim of disrupting the daily operations of the organizations. Attacks may slow down the performance of IT systems or completely debilitate a system, for example a website may be withdrawn from service resulting in

Table 5.11 Extract from Incident Log

Date of Incident	Scale of Impact	Significance of Potential Consequences	Features of Threat	Systems Affected	Description of Incident
03–03–13	Data Interception	High	Integrity of data compromised.	Network transmission	Hacker attempt identified and prevented.
15–06–13	Local	Low	Availability of internal system.	Software	Virus identified and removed.

Table 5.12 Threats to Data Security in the Data Life Cycle

	Capture	Store and Retrieve	Use, Share, and Maintain	Archive and Destroy
Phishing, impersonating a trusted source to gain access to confidential information such as user names and passwords.	X	X	X	X
Eavesdropping, intercepting authorized network data transmissions.	X	X	X	X
Spyware, malicious software collecting data accessed by authorized individuals.		X	X	
Spoofing, falsifying data to impersonate an individual or program to gain unauthorized access to data.		X	X	X
Loss or theft of devices that store data.		X		X
Unauthorized data retrieval from internal or external sources.		X		X
Corruption or loss of stored data due to virus or malware (malicious software).		X	X	X
Authorized or unauthorized changes to data values for fraudulent purposes.			X	
Unauthorized access to data storage equipment.	X	X	X	X
Inappropriate disposal of data or data storage equipment.				X
Inability to access or use data systems due to: <ul><li>Spam attacks (sending large volumes of unsolicited emails).</li><li>System hacks (unauthorized access to computer systems, usually from external sources).</li><li>Denial of service attacks (deliberate concentrated actions to overload servers by transmitting large data streams).</li><li>Code injection attacks (unauthorized access gained by program code entered into data capture fields).</li></ul>	X		X	

potential loss of business. Table 5.12 maps threats to data security to stages of the data life cycle.

The value of data can be difficult to quantify but the loss or unauthorized disclosure of data can have serious consequences for the organization. The impact of threats shown in Table 5.12 can range from adversely affecting the performance of networks and IT systems, through to data breaches and financial loss (Shirtz & Elovici, 2011).

The costs of security breaches to the organization include:

Table 5.13 ▸ Example Data Security Classification Framework

Classification	Description
Classification 1 (highest)	**Top secret:** Internal data that would adversely affect an organization's plans if the data were disclosed externally. Examples include plans to merge with another organization. This classification requires the highest level of security to prevent business-critical data being released to external sources.
Classification 2	**Highly confidential:** Critical internal data that would impede the organization's operation if disclosed externally or to unauthorized sources internally. Examples include financial information and medical records. This classification requires high security with authorization given prior to copying or removing the data from the organization's premises.
Classification 3	**Proprietary:** Internal information relating to the operational procedures and product designs that should only be available to authorized internal and external sources. This requires high security with limited access given to internal staff and trusted external partners (following the completion of a nondisclosure agreement).
Classification 4	**Internal use:** Internal information generated and used within the conduct of normal business operations where disclosure may adversely affect the credibility of the organization. Examples include meeting minutes and emails. This classification requires normal security where staff are not expected to disclose information to external parties unless as part of agreed working practice.
Classification 5 (lowest)	**Public information:** Information which is available externally, such as annual financial reports. This classification requires minimal security to ensure data are only released through authorized channels with prior approval.

○ Loss of business through the unavailability or poor performance of IT systems.

○ Loss of business while the security issue is being addressed, which may require the withdrawal or reduced functionality of IT systems.

○ Time and resources needed to resolve the data breach, recover the data, restore the IT systems, and take action to minimize the risk of the incident reoccurring.

○ Direct costs of the loss of the data, including fines imposed by legal or professional bodies and compensation claims.

○ Indirect costs of the loss of the data including loss of business or opportunities due to not having the data to inform decisions, loss of custom, and loss of reputation.

5.4.3 ▸ Data Security Classifications

Data classification is a key element of information security (Collette & Gentile, 2006). A data classification framework is a set of categories that define the value of specific data to the organization. Data classification frameworks are used to assess the nature of the data and assign a classification relating to the actions that need to be taken to maintain security of the data. All computer-based data should be classified. A data classification framework needs to include a definition of categories, examples of common data items in each category, and the permitted access level for each category. For example, details of new products that Match Lighting is currently developing would be categorized as being business critical. It would have a serious impact on Match Lighting if information about new products under development was disclosed, deliberately or accidentally, to competitors. The classifications determine the sensitivity of data and specify the actions to be taken to minimize risks to the data. Data security classifications may also provide guidance on the minimum period that data need to be retained. Care is needed to ensure that archived data adhere to the requirements of the data security classifications. Table 5.13 provides an example of a data security classification framework commonly used in organizations.

Link 5.5
Example Data Security Classification Framework

Scenario 5.3 outlines how the security classifications were used to assess the implications of a data beach in Match Lighting.

Scenario 5.3

Data Breach in Match Lighting

Before leaving the office, Alexander, a sales analyst at Match Lighting, downloaded data to a laptop so that he could finish a report while on the train going home. The train was very busy and there was no room for Alexander to work so he put the laptop in the luggage rack. When he arrived home, Alexander realized that he had left the laptop on the train. He telephoned the train operator but the laptop could not be found.

The next day Alexander reported the missing laptop to the IT manager who reported the loss to Angel Security Solutions, Match Lighting's security consultants. Angel Security Solutions took a statement from Alexander about exactly what had happened, what data he had downloaded to the laptop, and what data were already stored on the laptop. The security classifications for the data on the laptop were identified. Fortunately, no personal data relating to customers or employees were stored on the laptop. However, the monthly regional sales figures and the draft report that Alexander was writing are classification three data; data that are only available for internal use in the organization. The data breach could result in adverse publicity for Match Lighting and affect product sales.

Angel Security Solutions advised the IT manager to increase the security controls to prevent data being downloaded to laptops. Changes were also recommended to the acceptable usage policy to ensure that staff are aware of the risks and their responsibilities when removing IT equipment from the organization's premises. Match Lighting's press office was alerted to the data breach. Staff prepared a statement to release to the media in case the data breach was publicized.

5.4.4 Acceptable Information Usage Policy

Security problems can be caused through carelessness, mistakes, or malpractice by staff within the organization (Stanton *et al.*, 2005). An acceptable use policy addresses the threat of poor security behaviour (Doherty *et al.*, 2011) and informs staff of their responsibilities relating to IT security. Computer usage policies include: (1) information about the organization's right to monitor how an employee is using its IT systems; (2) a statement of acceptable and unacceptable use of IT systems, such as accessing personal emails and downloading of material from the Internet; (3) the disciplinary procedures to be followed if a breach of the computer usage policy is suspected and the potential consequences that may arise, such as termina-

tion of contracts; (4) the actions employees are expected to take to maintain data security (Holmes, 2003).

Doherty *et al.* (2011) recommend that an acceptable usage policy should also include:

○ Access management: specifying who is authorized to access information.
○ Licence compliance: documenting the rules regulating the sharing of software.
○ Roles and responsibilities: outlining the specific roles relating to access and use of information.
○ Policy management: stipulating how the policy will be reviewed and updated.

However, usage policies are often unread due to apathy, or due to employees believing that the policy is not relevant to them and believing that security staff are solely responsible for data security (Foltz *et al.*, 2008). Data security requires all staff to take responsibility for the data to which they have access. This includes ensuring that staff:

○ Log off a computer when the computer is unattended to prevent anyone accessing the data using their authorization.
○ Do not leave computer disks, flash drives, and other storage media in the computer or on desks.
○ Backup the data on their computer and use shared storage areas that are regularly backed up.

Training needs to be provided in organizations to raise awareness of security issues. However, training can sometimes lack content and not be effective (Lacey, 2010). Other actions to protect data security include off-site data storage to provide contingency against events such as theft, fire, and flood, enabling data to be stored in controlled atmospheric conditions. A chain of custody log needs to be maintained and secure transportation needs to be considered, which conforms to BS4783 and ISO 27001, when moving data between sites. Technical steps can also be taken to avoid and minimize risks to data security, such as the use of anti-virus software, workstation locks, network firewalls, and data encryption software (Shirtz & Elovici, 2011).

5.4.5 Secure Information Management

Moreira *et al.* (2008) suggest that decisions relating to information security need to be taken at the appropriate level in the organization and propose an information security governance framework with the hierarchical layers of:

○ Strategic activities, such as establishing policies relating to the role of information security in the organization.

- Tactical proactive activities to improve security by reviewing and following up operational issues as required.
- Operational activities needed to react to immediate security issues.

Each level includes four elements: (1) processes and controls to implement the security objectives, (2) criteria for measuring the efficiency and effectiveness of the processes, (3) roles and responsibilities for implementing processes, and (4) tools to be used for implementing the security processes. The need for a structured security policy must be balanced with sufficient flexibility to change the policy if required (Harnesk & Lindström, 2011). The security of IT systems needs to be addressed by the IT department, particularly in relation to the physical security of storage devices and access controls to data systems. However, data security is not just the responsibility of the IT department. All staff in the organization have a responsibility to ensure that they do not accidentally or deliberately cause a data breach.

The level of data access and security required for each data item need to be defined to ensure that issues of confidentiality are balanced with the needs of individuals to access the data. Data owners, working with data authors, determine the security classification required for the data for which they are responsible. Data security classifications are documented in the data dictionary. Staff authorized to access or change data, and the controls needed to maintain data security, will be also defined. Data security procedures apply to data at all stages in the life cycle, including the secure disposal of data when the data retention period has expired.

Information management needs to:

- Increase awareness of potential data breaches.
- Define the data classification framework.
- Determine metrics for measuring the impact of data security risks within a risk assessment framework.
- Establish targets to improve data security.
- Encourage a culture of shared responsibility for data security.
- Develop a framework for information security responsibilities at each level of the organizational hierarchy.
- Develop an infrastructure of policies to improve data security including an acceptable IT usage policy, a data recovery plan, and an off-site storage policy.
- Review the effectiveness of actions taken to improve the security of data.

Summary

Information governance provides an infrastructure within which information management can operate to improve the quality and accessibility of the information resource. Although everyone in the organization has a responsibility to ensure that their actions do not adversely affect the accuracy, reliability, or availability of information, specific roles are also needed to manage information. Key information management roles include: the information manager, who is responsible for developing and implementing the information management strategy; data owners who have responsibility for seeking agreement on definitions and usage of specific items of data; and data authors and data maintainers who adhere to data definitions as they capture, maintain, and use data.

Information management takes place within an ethical and legal framework. Policies and training are needed to ensure that information is stored securely and used appropriately within legislative requirements of privacy, accuracy, property, accessibility, and retention. Information management uses a number of tools such as a data ownership matrix and data security classifications. Data classifications determine the level of security controls required to protect data from security breaches. Table 5.14 demonstrates how these tools can be used to direct answers to typical questions that may arise in Match Lighting. The following chapter discusses the formulation and implementation of an information management strategy within a framework of information governance.

Reviewing Scenario 5.1

Mr Alvis is facing information overload; he has too much information to absorb and action. He cannot read the reports and trade journals because much of his time is being spent dealing with emails. The emails highlight underlying problems with the quality and management of information in Match Lighting. The information management problems need to be resolved and a strategy needs to be developed to effectively manage information in Match Lighting.

Match Lighting needs to take control of information by:

- Establishing a framework of information governance.
- Forming an Information Management Committee.
- Assigning roles and responsibilities for information management.
- Conducting a risk assessment and implementing procedures to ensure that Match Lighting's data are secure.

Table 5.14 Information Management Tools in Practice

Frequently Asked Questions	Information Management Tool
Who in the business knows about **X**? For example, who in the business knows about *product handling codes*?	Data owners are documented in the ***data ownership matrix.***
What does **X** mean? For example, what is a *product*?	Data definitions are proposed by data owners and documented in the ***data dictionary.***
How should **X** be used? For example, how should the attribute *prod_handling* be used?	Business rules form part of a data definition documented in the ***data dictionary.*** Some business rules are also shown by relationships between data entities in the ***information architecture***.
Who can I contact to discuss proposing a change to **X**? For example, who can I talk to about adding a field called *product colour variant* to the *product* record?	***Data owners*** are documented in the data ownership matrix and there is a defined process for raising issues to the ***Information Management Committee*** through local ***information stewards***.
What would be the implications of changing **X**? For example, what would be the implications of changing the length of the *product number*?	The ***information architecture*** shows the data entities which may be affected by changes to one entity. The ***data dictionary*** and ***data repository*** provide some functionality to support impact analysis.
Why can't I use **X** in a different way? For example, why can't I use the *prod_name* field to show the colour of the product?	Business rules form part of a data definition documented in the ***data dictionary*** and can be discussed with the data owner identified by the ***data ownership matrix***. The relationships between data entities in the ***information architecture*** can demonstrate the potential implications of changes to data in one area.
When will the problem with **X** be addressed? For example, when will the inconsistent use of *product handling codes* be resolved?	The current activities and planned projects of the ***Information Management Committee*** are documented in the ***information management strategy implementation plan.***
What would be affected if the application package **X** was upgraded? For example, what would be affected if the existing customer relationship management system was upgraded?	The ***information architecture*** shows the data entities which may be affected by changes to one entity and the ***data dictionary*** and ***data repository*** provide some functionality to support impact analysis.
Is there a data management policy about **X**? For example, is there a policy relating to the storage of data on memory sticks?	All agreed ***data management policies*** are documented in the ***data management policy framework.***
Does the organization buy data? For example, where can I find out what data Match Lighting buys from outside organizations?	The ***external data directory*** documents the data that are currently purchased.
We have the opportunity to purchase data directly from **X;** should we buy the data? For example, Bright Spark has offered to sell their sales data; should we buy the data?	The ***external data directory*** documents the data that are currently purchased. These data are also documented in the ***information architecture.*** If the data are not already purchased, consideration needs to be given to how the data would be used by consulting data owners identified from the ***data ownership matrix.***
How can I raise a data issue? For example, the product list contains things which we no longer sell; how can this be changed?	There is a defined process for raising issues to the ***Information Management Committee*** via the committee members in each area of the organization.

○ Agreeing on policies on data retention and purging data at the end of retention periods.

○ Developing projects to improve and maintain the quality of data from which information is derived.

Exercise 5.1

1 What is corporate governance?
2 What is the purpose of information governance?
3 How does a data owner differ from a data author?
4 How does the role of data author relate to data maintainers?
5 What type of intellectual property is protected by a patent?
6 What type of intellectual property legislation protects information published on a website?
7 What is meant by right of privacy?
8 What type of data is currently excluded from legislation relating to privacy?
9 What are ethics?
10 Why are ethics not universally agreed upon?
11 What is the core question of information ethics?
12 Within privacy, what is meant by contextual integrity?
13 List three dimensions of information privacy.
14 What barriers may prevent someone accessing information?
15 What are the two roles of intellectual property?
16 Explain how a cookie is used.
17 What is meant by the term *dataveillance*?
18 Why are historical data needed?
19 What is a data breach?
20 What is a data classification framework?

Link 5.6
Answers to Exercise 5.1

Activities 5.1

1 Review the six emails that Mr Alvis refers to in Scenario 5.1. For each email, identify the underlying information management problem and recommend an approach to address the problem.
2 List processes in each stage of the information cycle to demonstrate how accountability for information can be embedded in the life cycle.
3 Identify the data you have on your computer.
   • List the potential risks to the data security.
   • Assess the implications from a data breach of the data stored on the computer.
   • List the actions you can take to prevent a data breach.
4 Develop a list of the skills and characteristics a person needs to be an effective data owner.
5 Locate examples of information legislation and identify to which stages of the information life cycle they relate.
6 Review the security breaches in Table 5.10 and write policy statements to prevent such breaches reoccurring.

Discussion Questions 5.1

1 What is the relationship between governance and management?
2 How does IT influence an individual's perception of their accountability and responsibility for information?
3 How can the risks of a data breach occurring be reduced?
4 Security cameras capture and monitor visual data about the movement and actions of individuals. Discuss to what extent this is an invasion of personal privacy or a legitimate means of personal security.
5 Consider how an individual's right to privacy may be breached by government departments cross-checking information stored relating to residents of a household.
6 Are cookies a legal and ethical means of information capture?
7 Do the benefits of location-based services outweigh an individual's right to privacy?
8 Discuss the view that intellectual property legislation is unethical.

INFORMATION MANAGEMENT STRATEGY

Scenario 6.1

Need for an Information Management Strategy in Amy's Candles

Amy was sitting at her desk in the office at the back of her shop, Amy's Candles, gazing out of the window. Brian, one of her employees, came into the office.

'You look deep in thought; are you working on a new design?' he asked.

'In a way I guess I am,' explained Amy. 'I have read several management books and they say that every organization needs to design a strategy in order to manage all the information in the organization.'

'The volume of information relating to accounts, sales, and orders is quickly growing so a strategy to manage all the information sounds like a good idea,' agreed Brian.

'The problem is,' replied Amy, 'what does an information management strategy look like and how do I design one?'

Learning Outcomes

The learning outcomes of this chapter are to:

○ Introduce the purpose of an information management strategy.
○ Outline the structure and components of an information management strategy.
○ Develop an approach to formulate an information management strategy.
○ Define critical success factors for implementing an information management strategy.
○ Prepare a plan to implement an information management strategy.
○ Evaluate the progress of implementing an information management strategy.

Introduction

An information management strategy reflects an organization's acknowledgement of the importance of information and the organization's commitment to effectively manage one of its most critical resources. The strategy defines the vision for information management and specifies measurable objectives for improving how information is managed in the organization. Earl (1989) emphasizes that an information management strategy should be written down and includes operational guidance in the form of procedures, actions, and goals. The strategy outlines a planned approach to achieve the information management objectives, establishing a framework of policies and procedures to guide the actions affecting information throughout the life cycle. An information management strategy is a practical and achievable document, demonstrating the organization's full commitment to improving the management of information across the organization. This chapter explains the purpose of an information management strategy and outlines typical components of a strategy. Example information management strategies are then presented. Approaches to formulate, implement, and evaluate an information management strategy are discussed.

6.1 ▶ Purpose of an Information Management Strategy

Overcoming problems relating to information requires the development and implementation of an information management strategy. The organizational strategy defines the purpose and mission of the organization. The information management strategy therefore has to be aligned with the organizational strategy to understand and to influence the information needs of the organization. The information management strategy specifies objectives and policies to ensure that quality information is available to meet the needs of the organizational strategy. The information management strategy is informed by the information systems and information technology (IT) strategy.

DEFINITION: An **information management strategy** outlines the vision and objectives relating to the availability, accessibility, and quality of information in the organization. It specifies policies, responsibilities, and measures for managing the information resource within the framework of information governance.

6.1.1 ▸ Role of Information Management Strategy in the Organization

The organizational strategy provides the context that explains *why* information, information systems, and IT are needed. The information systems strategy defines *what* information systems are needed to meet the information needs of the organization to help achieve the organization's mission. The information systems strategy will also seek to identify opportunities for leveraging the value of information to inform the organizational strategy.

The information systems strategy provides the information processes to manage information in accordance with the information management strategy. The IT strategy defines *how* IT can be used to implement the information systems strategy and may provide opportunities to use information in different ways. The IT strategy includes the hardware, software, and telecommunications needed to implement the information processes and business rules required by the information management strategy. The information management strategy responds to the opportunities and challenges posed by advances in IT.

Scenario 6.2 provides an example of the relationship between these different strategies within Amy's Candles.

Scenario 6.2

Relationship between Strategies in Amy's Candles

Amy employed Louise to work in the shop during the holiday season. As a temporary member of staff, Louise had not been given access to the computer systems. She was employed to help in the shop by stocking the shelves and using the cash register. If a customer had a query, she was to direct the customer to another member of staff.

Amy was visiting a supplier when she received a call on her mobile telephone from Louise. She had been left on her own in the shop while Brian went to lunch. A regular customer, Mr Burton, wanted to know whether he could double his order for pillar candles and still keep to the original agreed delivery date. Amy did not have access to the details of the order or the materials she had in stock. She told Louise to inform Mr Burton that it would probably be possible and that she would call him later to confirm the arrangement. Later, when she accessed the full details of Mr Burton's order, she realized that it would not be possible to create double the quantity of candles for the delivery date. Mr Burton was annoyed at being given the wrong information. He had previously complained that the last two invoices he had received from Amy were wrong and therefore he cancelled the complete order.

Figure 6.1 shows that Amy's organizational strategy includes the objective to sustain customer satisfaction at 96 per cent. Providing customers with the wrong information reduces customer satisfaction. An objective of Amy's information management strategy is to reduce invoicing errors by 60 per cent as reducing invoicing errors will improve the quality of the information given to customers and help to improve overall customer satisfaction. Amy's information systems strategy therefore needs to include an objective to improve the quality of information provided to customers in order to help Amy meet her organizational objective of sustaining customer satisfaction.

Mr Burton was given the wrong information because Amy and Louise did not have access to the information they needed. Amy's IT strategy needs to include an objective to improve the computer network, enabling her to access data remotely. This will allow Amy to access up-to-date customer information when she is not in the shop. This supports the information systems strategy to improve the quality of information provided to customers. The introduction of remote access to data would also provide the opportunity for Amy to consider allowing her customers (and possibly her suppliers) to access data about their orders and the candle designs available. Amy could consider incorporating this step towards e-business in her organizational strategy to improve the service she offers to her customers. The IT strategy could therefore influence as well as support her organizational strategy.

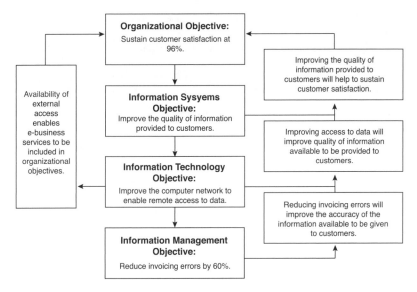

Figure 6.1 Relationship between Strategies in Amy's Candles

Table 6.1 applies the enterprise architecture from Chapter 4 to Amy's objectives relating to the information provided to customers. This shows the role of the information management strategy in the enterprise architecture.

The overall aim of an information management strategy is to ensure that high-quality, reliable information is accessible to authorized personnel, when they need the information, in the format required, irrespective of where personnel are or where the information is located.

An information management strategy seeks to:

- Ensure the organization's staff have access to the information needed to perform their roles effectively and support the organization in achieving its objectives.
- Improve the quality of the information resource.
- Minimize risks of loss or corruption of the information resource.
- Manage the information resource efficiently and effectively.
- Comply with legislative requirements relating to personal information and information accessibility.
- Provide guidance on using IT effectively, cognizant of information management requirements.

The information management strategy cannot exist in isolation. The strategy must operate within the framework of information governance to ensure that the organization is compliant with statutory and ethical requirements.

6.1.2 Requirements of an Information Management Strategy

Problems with information are inherent in organizations and become accepted as the norm. The information management strategy seeks to gain commitment from all levels of the organization to tackle the problems relating to the quality, availability, and accessibility of information. This requires organizations to change the way employees perceive information. A culture needs to be cultivated in which everyone recognizes their role and responsibility towards managing data effectively in the organization. The business needs to take responsibility for data and not seek to relegate responsibility to the IT function.

An information management strategy needs to:

- Demonstrate the importance of, commitment to, and need for effective information management.
- Define the vision and specify targets for improving information management in the organization.
- Establish a framework of policies, controls, and procedures to manage information throughout the life cycle. This includes:
  - Defining data.
  - Improving the quality and reliability of data.
  - Facilitating authorized access to data.
  - Encouraging the sharing of data.
  - Ensuring data are stored and disposed of securely.
  - Complying with legislative requirements.
- Specify the roles and responsibilities for ensuring adherence to the policies and implementing information management procedures.

Table 6.1 Enterprise Architecture Supporting Amy's Information Management Strategy

Information Life Cycle				
	Capture	**Store and Retrieve**	**Use, Share, and Maintain**	**Archive and Destroy**
Organizational Architecture	Specifies the need for customer information and the characteristics of the information.	Specifies where customer information is needed in the organization.	Specifies the need for customer information to support operational, tactical, and strategic activities.	Specifies the time periods when access to customer information is likely to be needed.
Information Architecture	Defines the structured information needed for customers.	Defines the structure of customer information and who can access it.	Defines the business rules to maintain the quality of customer information.	Defines the business rules for archiving and destroying customer information.
Information Systems Architecture	Provides processes to capture the required information for and about customers.	Provides processes to enable access to customer information.	Provides processes to use the customer information in accordance with the business rules.	Provides processes to facilitate access to archived customer information.
IT Architecture	Provides the means to capture customer data and the required characteristics of the data.	Provides a means to facilitate authorized access to stored customer data.	Provides a means to facilitate and restrict changes to customer data by implementing the business rules.	Provides a means to store and facilitate access to archived customer data and to delete the data at the end of the retention period.
	Information Management Strategy Formulates the objectives and policies to guide and coordinate the actions at each level of the architecture.			

- Develop a culture of responsibility towards data.
- Develop an infrastructure of information management resources and processes.
- Provide appropriate staff training.
- Incorporate regular audits to identify problems and review the progress of the information management strategy.

6.1.3 Key Principles of an Information Management Strategy

The key principles of an information management strategy include:

- Justification of the investment to improve information management.
- Active senior management support and commitment to developing and implementing the strategy.
- Direct contribution from all areas of the organization and from all levels of staff in the organizational hierarchy.
- Acknowledgement of the existence of information management problems without directing blame.
- Focus on the specific immediate information management problems in the organization.
- Alignment with the needs of the business while retaining an awareness of how advances in IT may influence and direct the organizational strategy too.
- Identification of the data management priorities for the organization.
- Specification of the legal and ethical requirements relating to information.
- Commitment to addressing issues of data definition, data quality, data ownership, data integration, data security, and data retention.

○ Encompassing the needs of information throughout the life cycle activities of capture, storage, security, retrieval, use, maintenance, archive, and destruction.

6.2 ► Components of an Information Management Strategy

The information management strategy includes six core components. First, the strategy presents the vision for information management in the organization. The vision documents the role of information in the organization in relation to how information supports the organization's business strategy.

Second, the aims and objectives of the strategy are defined. Aims are broad statements that direct actions to achieve the organization's vision for information management. The objectives are specific measureable statements that if achieved would demonstrate that the aims have been satisfied.

Third, the strategy identifies the information management policies needed to meet the requirements of information governance. Information management policies seek to direct and constrain actions to align activities with the direction of the aims and objectives. Policies need to be robust but flexible to meet the changing needs of the organization. Part IV discusses a range of business-driven and technology-driven changes that organizations experience which impact the information needs of the organization. The policies need to be able to remain viable in a changing organizational context.

Fourth, procedures are defined in the information management strategy. Procedures facilitate actions specifying the sequential steps to be taken to complete a task, conforming to the requirements of policies. Procedures

Table 6.2 ► Example Sections in an Information Management Strategy

Section Headings	Key Questions
1. Justification	Why is an information management strategy needed? What problems are being caused in the organization as a result of issues with information management?
2. Purpose and Scope	What is the organization's vision for information management? What information will the strategy cover? What information will be excluded from the information management strategy?
3. Business Benefits	What improvements will be achieved through the information management strategy and how will the improvements affect the organization?
4. Challenges	What difficulties must the organization overcome in developing and implementing the information management strategy?
5. Fundamental Principles	What are the key requirements of information management needed to achieve the organization's vision?
6. Aims and Objectives	What are the specific aims that the information management strategy needs to achieve to attain the defined vision? What are the specific objectives that need to be achieved to demonstrate that the aims have been satisfied?
7. Framework of Policies	What policies need to be defined to guide and constrain actions to ensure that the principles, aims, and objectives are achieved?
8. Roles and Responsibilities	What new roles will need to be defined to implement the policies? What will the new roles do? What will be the responsibilities of each role?
9. Statutory Compliance	What regulations relating to information management must the organization follow? How are regulations reflected in the information management policies?
10. Performance Measures	How will the information management strategy be evaluated? What targets and measures will be used? What mechanisms will be implemented to review performance of the strategy?

provide detailed guidance, demonstrating how policies are to be implemented in the organization.

Fifth, the strategy outlines the specific roles and responsibilities needed to implement and govern the information management policies. Finally, the information management strategy defines performance measures to monitor both the implementation of the information management strategy and the impact of the strategy on the organization.

The six components are fundamental to an information management strategy and additional components may also be included. Table 6.2 shows typical section headings that may be included in an information management strategy to incorporate these six components. Key questions to be addressed in each section of the strategy have also been included in Table 6.2.

6.2.1 Justification

The information management strategy starts by explaining why the strategy is needed. Staff in the organization are aware of the problems of data management that they encounter every day but the strategy needs to demonstrate that senior management are also aware of the problems and are committed to resolving the problems. The justification section of the information management strategy should include specific examples of problems in the organization to which employees can relate, demonstrating the importance of data in the organization. The rationale for the strategy should also refer to the consequences that arise as a result of data management problems. For example, Scenario 6.2 shows that data management problems affected the quality of information given to customers, which adversely affects customer satisfaction and could lead to loss of custom. The legal penalties that may be incurred, in addition to the damage to the organization's reputation, if data legislation is breached, need to be documented in the strategy.

At the operational level, data management issues are often blamed on the actions or inactions of other departments or the failings of information systems and IT systems. The information management strategy needs to demonstrate that the purpose is not to allocate blame, nor to introduce policies and procedures that will be an unnecessary burden to staff. The strategy demonstrates action and commitment to improving the accessibility and reliability of information to ensure that staff have access to the quality information they need to perform their role in the organization. Developing and implementing the strategy will require staff resources to be diverted from other aspects of the organization; the strategy therefore needs to justify this investment.

6.2.2 Purpose and Scope

The information management strategy must have a clearly stated purpose, partly derived from the need to address the specific issues identified, though the strategy must also consider the broader vision of information management in the organization. There is likely to be agreement that the problems with data management need to be addressed but this may be balanced by the view that the organization is managing sufficiently. Problems are worked around when they occur so perhaps there is not an urgent need to take the widespread action that an information management strategy will initiate. The organization's vision for information management therefore needs to be considered. For example, timely and accurate information may improve the organization's ability to respond to customers and improve customer service.

The scope of the strategy specifies the range of information to which the strategy applies. The strategy may include all the information in the organization but specific consideration needs to be given to all sources and types of information. For example, decisions will need to be taken about whether externally sourced data, paper-based data, and informal data should be included in the strategy. The implications of the decisions to include or exclude data need to be assessed. For example, including externally sourced data in the strategy means that data must be subjected to the same controls and quality standards as internally generated data, which may not be possible to achieve.

6.2.3 Business Benefits

The benefits of the information management strategy are derived from addressing the problems identified and the business benefits arising from access to reliable quality data. The business benefits will include quantifiable cost savings such as reduction in the volume of rework required. Cost savings can also be achieved by reducing data redundancy as only one version of a data item needs to be captured and maintained. Staff will not need to spend time searching for information and seeking ways to work around the limitations of information systems.

Less tangible benefits may include improvements to customer service, higher employee morale, more timely decisions, and better quality decisions. This section of the strategy aligns the potential benefits that can be derived from improvements to information management, with the specific objectives and critical success factors defined in the organizational strategy.

6.2.4 Challenges

Implementing an information management strategy is a complex task and it will take time for the organization to achieve all the anticipated benefits of the information management strategy. The strategy needs to identify the specific challenges that the organization may encounter in implementing the strategy. Potential challenges for an organization seeking to develop and implement an information strategy may include:

○ Limited understanding of the data in the organization. The organization may have inherited information and information systems with sparse documentation through a series of corporate mergers or acquisitions. Many organizations are using legacy computer systems that are often inadequately understood and difficult to change, though vital to the organization's daily operations.

○ Lack of awareness and education of data management practices. Training in organizations often focuses on entering and extracting data from IT systems and lacks a broader understanding of how the data will be used and why the data are needed. Training is a core part of an information management strategy as organizations seek to raise awareness of the importance of data quality issues. The importance of reliable and high quality data to the organization and the role of individuals in improving data quality need to be communicated as part of the strategy.

○ The need to change the organizational culture. There can be reluctance by staff in the organization to take responsibility for data. As data are entered into computer systems using IT, data can be regarded as belonging to the IT department. Data belongs to the business, not the IT department, and responsibility for the quality and security of data lies with everyone in the organization. The implementation of the information management strategy may involve actions to facilitate a change of culture in which everyone

recognizes their responsibility for data and shares data appropriately.

○ The overwhelming scale of the task. When data management issues are identified the scale of the work needed to resolve the issues quickly starts to grow. The work needed crosses the physical boundaries of organizational structures and technical structures. Changes to one item of data may affect several departments and IT systems. The information management strategy needs to recognize the scale of the problem, commit the resources required, and prioritize problems to be addressed.

6.2.5 Fundamental Principles

The information management strategy specifies the core principles on which the vision for managing information in the organization is based. The principles reflect the role of information in the organization and the relationship between information and the organization's business strategy. For some organizations information is a commodity to sell. For example, The Nielsen Company (www.nielsen.com) is an international market research company that sells data to manufacturers relating to the sale of their products by consumers. The company also conducts market research for events such as the Olympics and Paralympics Games. In other organizations information provides the resource for core business processes. The role of data and information in the organization will influence the principles of information management. The principles in the information management strategy reflect the organization's culture and priorities relating to the characteristics of quality information. General information management principles may relate to adherence to legislation, data quality, and data security. Figure 6.2 provides an example of how Amy may tailor these principles for Amy's Candles.

All staff, whether full-time or part-time, have a responsibility to ensure that:

○ The information they use is:
  • Complete, accurate and up to date.
  • Available in a form that can be shared with authorized staff.
  • Accessible to authorized staff (for example, part-time staff need to ensure that information can be accessed by other staff when they are not at work).
○ The security of information is not put at risk by theft, loss or unauthorized disclosure through careless or deliberate acts.
○ Details of the candle designs and design processes observed or documented are not disclosed to third parties.
○ Legal requirements relating to the security and disclosure of personal data are understood.
○ Issues with the accuracy or security of data are raised with Amy as soon as they arise.

Figure 6.2 Information Management Principles for Amy's Candles

6.2.6 Aims and Objectives

The information management strategy outlines the vision for information in the organization and specifies the aims and objectives to achieve the vision. Aims are broad statements that reflect the organization's business strategy. An aim of Amy's Candles is to improve the quality of information provided to customers. Objectives are specific and measurable statements which when achieved support the intention of the aim. For example, Amy has an objective to reduce invoicing errors by 60 per cent. The objective is measurable; the current number of invoicing errors can be calculated and compared over time. If the objective was achieved, it would demonstrate an improvement in the quality of information provided to customers and therefore contribute to Amy's aim.

6.2.7 Policy Framework

Policies outline how information in an organization should be managed in practice. A policy documents the rules to be followed in situations that may arise in the organization. Policies are supported by procedures. Procedures are practical instructions of the actions to take in specific circumstances to ensure adherence to the relevant policies. For example, in most organizations a policy states that details about an employee's performance may not be disclosed to a third party, such as a future employer, without prior permission being obtained from the employee or former employee. The policy provides a rule to follow when an employer receives a request for information about current or previous staff. Procedures list the specific actions to follow when a request for information about an employee is received, such as to check whether the employee has provided consent for information to be disclosed to a third party.

Chapter 5 identified a generic framework of information governance outlining policies, roles, and processes needed to govern the information resource. The information management strategy specifies the policies needed to manage information throughout the life cycle within the governing framework.

6.2.8 Roles and Responsibilities

The strategy defines the roles needed to define, implement, and monitor the information management policies required in the organization. The roles of data owner, data author, and data maintainer (defined in Section 5.2) are needed to implement the information management strategy.

6.2.9 Statutory Compliance

The legal regulations relating to information management to which the organization must adhere are documented in the information management strategy. The organization needs to identify the specific regulations relating to the nature of the information it captures and the countries in which the organization operates. A range of legal issues is discussed in Section 5.3.

6.2.10 Performance Measures

The information management strategy needs to be reviewed to assess the extent to which its aims and objectives have been achieved and to determine changes required to the strategy, or its implementation. Performance measures are defined in the information management strategy to monitor the progress and effectiveness of the strategy. Potential measures may refer to the implementation of the strategy, such as the volume of data items that have agreed definitions documented in the data dictionary. Performance measures may also directly relate to the objectives of the strategy, such as the number of invoicing errors reported or the number of parcels returned as being undeliverable. The measures should be meaningful to the organization and relate back to the specific problems in the organization cited to justify the information management strategy.

6.3 Information Management Strategies in Practice

Figure 6.3 provides an example of extracts from an information management strategy for a fictitious local council in the United Kingdom, listing a range of government recommendations and regulations which all local councils are required to follow. The UK Freedom of Information Act 2000 requires public authorities to provide access to the information they have, which requires authorities to manage information effectively, specifically being able to identify the information held and have mechanisms in place to enable information to be accessed (Shepherd & Ennion, 2007). Figure 6.3 highlights the council's concerns that a limited ability to promptly respond to freedom of information requests is adversely affecting public opinion of the council. The council has recognized that a better understanding of the information available is needed and that the council could pre-empt some information requests if the quality of information provided on the council's website was improved.

The Lightpark Council's Information Management Strategy

Justification

Local councils in the United Kingdom are under significant pressure to improve efficiency of service provision. The Freedom of Information Act has resulted in a significant number of requests for information from the Council. Difficulties in finding the information requested are adversely affecting the public's opinion of the Council and impact on staff workload. Improving the management of information and improving the accessibility of information to the public would reduce Freedom of Information requests, improving public opinion and service efficiency.

The Council has received a number of complaints relating to the inconsistent handling of services. This is caused by different departments duplicating information collection. Improved management of information is needed to understand the overlap of information between departments and to provide joined-up customercentric services. This will provide the platform for meeting the public's expectations and government targets for the electronic provision of Council services.

Purpose and Scope

The purpose of the information management strategy is to ensure that the Council uses the information available efficiently to meet the needs and expectations of the public. The Council will strive to capture information once and provide customercentric services. Information will be used to enable the Council to engage with the public and encourage active participation in the community. The strategy is to be followed by everyone working for, or providing services to, the Council.

Business Benefits

The Council seeks to achieve service efficiency and increase its public reputation in four main ways:

1. Reducing the duplication of information capture and storage will enable the Council to make significant cost savings. This will be achieved through reduction in storage costs and reduction in the work needed to recreate information already held by the Council.
2. Providing access to one accurate source of information will enable queries from members of the public to be addressed effectively the first time, reducing the need to transfer calls between multiple departments.
3. Mapping the information the Council holds against the Council's information needs will ensure that all information needed is captured. This will assist in the Council's ability to promptly respond to requests for information under the Freedom of Information Act.
4. Improving information security, supported by a programme of training, will improve public confidence in the Council and ensure that legislative requirements are satisfied.

Challenges

It is recognized that the Council will need to invest resources to achieve the benefits outlined. For example, the rationalization of duplicate information will require staff in different departments to work together to identify and address issues of duplication. An extensive training programme will be required to ensure that all staff that handle data are aware of the legal and ethical responsibilities to which they are required to adhere. The Council's long-term strategy to move to electronic delivery of services has been met with some reluctance. The Council will therefore need to address a number of issues, such as the suitability of existing processes and the existing IT infrastructure to support remote access to information services.

Fundamental Principles

The Council's information management strategy is founded on the following principles:

○ All information belongs to the council and the use of information will not be limited to the department that captured the information.
○ Information will be centralized where possible to promote ease of accessibility and security.
○ Action will be taken to capture information from the public once and share the information with other services in the Council.

Aims and Objectives

The Council aims to:

○ Improve efficiency and effectiveness of service delivery.
○ Improve ability to share information with both internal and external parties where legitimate access can be proven.
○ Deliver holistic customercentric services.

The following objectives have been identified to support attainment of these aims:

○ Create a centrally shared information repository.
○ Map information required by Council services to information in the repository.
○ Create a directory of information resources.

 **Figure 6.3** Continued

- ○ Provide electronic delivery of all Council services.
- ○ Initiate a programme of staff training.
- ○ Develop guidelines for the communication of information on the Council's intranet and Internet sites.

Framework of Policies

The Council's information management strategy includes the development of the following policy documents:

- ○ Information ownership.
- ○ Information sharing.
- ○ Information security.
- ○ Digital signatures for email authentication.
- ○ Information retention.
- ○ Intranet publishing.
- ○ Internet publishing.

Roles and Responsibilities

The following roles will be created to support the formulation and implementation of the information policies:

- ○ Data Owner: Data owners will be allocated to each data entity. The data owners will be responsible for ensuring that the data for which they are responsible are complete, accurate, and up to date.
- ○ Data Protection Officer: The data protection officer will be responsible for maintaining the Council's registration with the Data Commission.
- ○ Information Security Manager: The information security manager will oversee staff training to ensure that the requirements of the Data Protection Act are maintained.
- ○ Project Team: A project team will be established to respond to Freedom of Information requests. The team will advise the Council about the information that needs to be made available to the public via the Internet.

The Council will invite applications to tender from consultants and information service providers in accordance with the Council's procurement services policy.

Statutory Compliance

The Council will comply with the government technical standards, in addition to compliance with:

- ○ British Standard BS7799 Code of Practice for Information Security.
- ○ Computer Misuse Act 1990.
- ○ Copyright, Designs and Patents Act 1988.
- ○ Data Protection Act 1998.
- ○ E-government metadata standard.
- ○ Environmental Information Regulations 2004.
- ○ Freedom of Information Act 2000.
- ○ Local Government Access to Information Act 1985.
- ○ Modernising Government White Paper 1999.
- ○ Public Records Act 1958 and 1967.
- ○ Recommendations of the Disability Discrimination Act and World Wide Web Accessibility Initiative.
- ○ Re-Use of Public Sector Information Regulations 2005.

Performance Measures

Quarterly reports will be provided on the performance of the information management strategy against the following measures:

- ○ Progress on policy development and implementation.
- ○ Number of requests for information under the Freedom of Information Act.
- ○ Time taken to respond to requests made under the Freedom of Information Act.
- ○ Progress made on:
  - Creation of a centrally shared information repository.
  - Mapping information required by Council services to information in the repository.
  - Creation of a directory of information resources.
  - Electronic delivery of all Council services.
  - Staff training.
  - Guidelines for the communication of information on the Council's intranet and Internet sites.

The Council will review the strategy annually and revise the strategy as appropriate in response to the changing demands of local government.

Figure 6.3 ▶ Information Management Strategy for Lightpark Council

Figure 6.4 shows extracts from the information management strategy for Match Lighting. Match Lighting has identified specific examples of current issues caused by problems with information management to which staff will be able to relate. Match Lighting's information management strategy refers to some of the components of information governance. The strategy includes an initial policy framework and identifies key roles that need to be established to implement the information management strategy.

Match Lighting's Information Management Strategy

Justification

Match Lighting has achieved recognition as a leading manufacturer of domestic light fittings through a series of corporate acquisitions. The effective amalgamation of people, information, processes, and systems in Match Lighting's infrastructure remains challenging. Inconsistent coding systems between different product brands continue to cause problems on a daily basis. In addition to the extra work such problems create, they also have a direct financial cost to Match Lighting through:

- Wrong orders delivered.
- Inaccurate sales forecasts.
- Poor stock management.
- Production shortages.

The recent pilot use of e-systems with some suppliers has highlighted the urgent need to address issues of information management before extending the use of e-systems in the supply chain. If Match Lighting is to maintain its position at the forefront of the industry, it needs to maximize the use of e-business systems to secure long-term collaborative relationships with both suppliers and customers.

Purpose and Scope

The information management strategy includes all information coming into or out of Match Lighting using IT systems. The strategy will therefore address the issues arising from the information received from suppliers via the e-systems such as item code and unit conversion. The strategy seeks to reconcile the diverse information assets that Match Lighting has acquired to provide a coherent information resource which can be used to support:

- Effective decision-making.
- Development of e-business systems.
- Sustainable collaborative relationships with customers and suppliers.
- Demonstration of compliance.

Business Benefits

Improvement in the management of information will:

- Reduce the number of wrong orders delivered, reducing wastage and increasing customer satisfaction.
- Reduce stock outages and improve stock management through more accurate information on which to base sales forecasts.
- Reduce machine downtime through more effective production schedules and improved availability of components.
- Reduce order queries and improve invoice reconciliation.
- Reduce the number of different information systems needed.
- Improve the ease with which accurate information can be accessed.
- Improve the information available with which to inform decisions.
- Enable the further development of e-business systems.
- Simplify coding systems to improve customer ordering processes.

Challenges

The main challenge for Match Lighting is the reconciliation of the information inherited through acquisitions. A clear coding system needs to be defined and applied to all products. Purging of out-of-date information will also be required; for example, the parts catalogue still refers to lamps with high mercury content that have been obsolete for a number of years. Purging data is a complex task as care is needed to ensure that data integrity is maintained. Business and IT staff will need to work together to review data, clean data, and reload data into appropriate systems.

Fundamental Principles

The following principles provide the foundation for Match Lighting's information management strategy:

- All data will be clearly defined with consistent coding structures.
- Data will be accurate and available when needed.
- Confidentiality of data will be maintained.

 **Figure 6.4** Continued

Aims and Objectives

The information management strategy aims to:

○ Improve the quality of data available to add value to the organization and enable Match Lighting to achieve competitive advantage.
○ Improve the availability of data to ensure that data are accessible at the appropriate time to the individuals that need the data.
○ Develop consistent procedures for managing data effectively throughout Match Lighting.
○ Establish an information architecture to support e-business collaboration with customers and suppliers.

The following objectives have been identified to support attainment of these aims:

○ Develop an agreed upon product-coding mechanism.
○ Clean the data, remove redundant data, and improve data integrity.
○ Define procedures for managing data consistently and ensuring data integrity.
○ Review the accessibility of data and develop procedures to enable authorized personnel to access data as required.
○ Design a sustainable information architecture to support e-business systems.
○ Rationalize the information systems architecture.

Framework of Policies

The achievement of Match Lighting's information management strategy will require a number of policies to be developed including:

○ Information definition.
○ Information ownership.
○ Access to information.
○ Information security.
○ Information dissemination.
○ Information exchange.

Roles and Responsibilities

A range of additional roles have been identified to improve the management of information at Match Lighting, including:

○ Information Manager: The information manager will be responsible for ensuring that the information management strategy is implemented and that Match Lighting achieves its vision for effective information management.
○ Information Stewards: An information steward will be appointed within each division to liaise with the information manager and ensure that the information management issues in their areas are addressed.
○ Data Owners: Data owners will be assigned to master data and will be responsible for defining the data, and ensuring that the data are accessible when required by authorized individuals.
○ Data Authors: Data authors will be appointed in each division to work with data owners and manage the dissemination of information on the Internet and intranet.
○ Project Team: Intradivisional project teams will be established to undertake the work required by the information manager and information stewards. Projects will include data cleaning, data definition, and data access.

Statutory Compliance

The implementation of the information management strategy will comply with appropriate legislation and professional standards including:

○ Data Protection Act 1998.
○ The Electronic Commerce Directive Regulations 2002.
○ British Standard BS7799 Code of Practice for Information Security Management.
○ International Organization for Standardization ISO 9000:2000 International Standard for Quality Management.

Performance Measures

Information stewards will meet with the information manager monthly to review implementation of the strategy against the following measures:

○ Appointment of data owners and data authors.
○ Development of information management policies.
○ Percentage of data items defined.
○ Status of the coding system and information architecture.
○ Number of wrong orders delivered.
○ Percentage of stock outages.
○ Machine downtime.

The Board of Directors will review the progress of the information management strategy with the information manager at six monthly intervals.

Figure 6.4 ▶ Information Management Strategy for Match Lighting

Both strategies recognize that there is a need to address problems with information management to support the electronic provision of services via the Internet. However, the strategy priorities differ, reflecting the specific challenges in each organization.

6.4 ▶ Formulating an Information Management Strategy

The information management strategy is a physical document, founded on developing a culture of responsible behaviour towards the management of information. Everyone in the organization plays a role in the life cycle of information and therefore widespread participation is needed in the development of the strategy. Participation in formulating the strategy will help encourage participation in the strategy's implementation and ensure that the strategy addresses the practical information management issues in the organization.

6.4.1 ▶ Critical Success Factors for Formulating an Information Management Strategy

Formulating a viable and practical information management strategy requires four main critical success factors to be addressed. First, the organization needs to be aware of the current problems relating to information in the organization and the impact that the problems have on organizational performance. This provides the initial justification for the information management strategy to be formulated.

Second, practical support from senior management in the organization is needed to formulate the strategy. It is extremely difficult to formulate an information management strategy without management commitment as staff will not be motivated to participate and may consider the strategy to be a waste of time on the basis that the resources to implement the strategy will not be provided. Management commitment demonstrates the importance of the information management strategy to the success of the organization. The management support needs to be more than a written statement; senior staff need to be involved in initiating the strategy and in mobilizing resources to formulate the strategy.

Third, formulating an information management strategy requires an interdepartmental team, comprising senior staff, to represent the information needs and concerns of their area of the organization. All areas of the organization must be represented to ensure that the strategy meets the needs of the entire organization, acknowledging that information is a corporate resource.

Finally, the members of the interdepartmental team need to thoroughly understand how information is used in their area of the organization and be committed to improving the quality of information. Members must be motivated to thoroughly investigate and address the underlying problems that affect information management. The enthusiasm of the team for improving information in the organization can help to motivate others in the organization to contribute to improving the quality of information. Members of the team therefore need to possess good communication skills to convey information between the team and their department and must be relied on to complete the actions required by the team.

6.4.2 ▶ Steps in Formulating an Information Management Strategy

Figure 6.5 outlines an approach to formulating an information management strategy that starts by collecting examples of the problems caused by poor information management to justify investment in the strategy. When support from senior management has been attained, an infrastructure is developed to coordinate information management activities. This enables the problems experienced in the organization to be discussed. The vision for improving information management is then agreed upon and the policies needed to achieve the vision are identified. Performance measures must be developed to regularly evaluate the progress and effectiveness of the information management strategy.

Developing the information management strategy is not a one-off task. The strategy will need to be reviewed and adapted in response to the changing needs of the organization and business climate. An information management strategy outlines the structures and policies to support information management. The implementation of the strategy focuses on the processes and tools that need to be adopted to adhere to the policies, discussed in Chapter 5.

6.4.3 ▶ Internal Analysis

Developing and implementing an information management strategy incurs costs and diverts resources away from other areas of the organization's operating processes. A strong business case must therefore be formed to justify investment in the strategy. The organization needs to first assess the current situation with regard to information management. This involves identifying the particular information management problems in the organization and assessing the potential impact of these problems. The internal analysis of current problems is accompanied

1   Gain senior management support:
    1.1   Collate an initial set of examples that highlight problems with information management and the impact of the problems on the organization.
    1.2   Arrange a meeting with senior management from all areas of the organization to:
       1.2.1   Discuss the impact of data management problems on the performance of the organization.
       1.2.2   Acknowledge that the underlying causes of the problems may be complex and are likely to take time to resolve.
       1.2.3   Gain agreement that the problems need to be addressed.
       1.2.4   Seek commitment to secure the resources to develop and implement an information management strategy.
       1.2.5   Agree on the purpose and scope of information management in the organization.
2   Establish a mechanism to enable all areas of the organization to actively participate in formulating the information management strategy:
    2.1   Establish a team representing all areas of the organization to lead development of the information management strategy.
    2.2   The team should meet regularly.
3   Engage all areas of the organization. In each area of the organization:
    3.1   Communicate the organization's commitment to addressing problems with information.
    3.2   Collate examples of problems experienced relating to information and the implications of the problems.
    3.3   Regularly communicate the progress of the team.
    3.4   Identify issues to raise with the team.
4   Assess the current situation:
    4.1   Identify current problems.
    4.2   Assess the impact of current problems on the organization.
    4.3   Identify the legal and ethical issues that need to be considered.
5   At the team meeting:
    5.1   Discuss the problems identified in each area.
    5.2   Categorize the underlying cause of the problems.
    5.3   Agree on priorities that need to be addressed.
    5.4   Identify any quick actions that can be taken to alleviate specific problems.
    5.5   Plan a series of data audits based on the priorities identified to analyse the internal situation.
    5.6   Assign tasks to analyse the external environment, identifying the legislative and ethical requirements to which the organization must adhere.
    5.7   Allocate resources and agree on a timescale to complete tasks, taking into consideration any training needed.
6   As information from the internal and external analysis is gathered:
    6.1   Document the justification for the information management strategy.
    6.2   Identify the business benefits of improved information management for each area of the organization.
    6.3   Review the challenges that need to be addressed to improve information management.
    6.4   Discuss opportunities to address the challenges identified.
7   Define the vision for information management in the organization:
    7.1   Document the legislative requirements to which the organization must adhere.
    7.2   Define the fundamental principles on which the information management strategy will be founded.
    7.3   Formulate the aims and objectives of the strategy.
    7.4   Ensure members of the team discuss drafts of the principles, aims, and objectives within their individual areas before they are finalized.
8   Design the structures and policies needed to support effective information management in the organization:
    8.1   Identify the policies that need to be developed relating to the management of information.
    8.2   Establish working groups to define the policies identified.
    8.3   Identify the roles and responsibilities needed to manage information.
    8.4   Define each role.
    8.5   Identify staff with appropriate skills for the roles across the organization.
9   Review the challenges to achieving the objectives.
10   Develop performance measures:
    10.1   Agree measures for evaluating the effectiveness of the strategy.
    10.2   Define a timescale for monitoring the progress of the strategy.
    10.3   Communicate the strategy and improvements to information management achieved by the strategy to staff in the organization.

Figure 6.5 Steps in Formulating an Information Management Strategy

by an external review of the information management requirements and expectations of parties outside the organization. This includes consideration of the legislation relating to information to which the organization must adhere; the minimum standards and ethical requirements required by relevant professional bodies; and the expectations of customers, suppliers, and collaborating partners in relation to the quality and management of information. The combination of internal and external analysis helps to identify the consequences that may arise from poor information management, such as financial penalties, loss of reputation, and loss of custom. This provides the justification for the information management strategy to be developed and can support the development of a cost–benefit analysis.

Most organizations experience problems relating to the completeness, accuracy, reliability, integrity, and availability of data on a daily basis. Short-term actions are taken to work around the problems. The formulation of an information management strategy provides the opportunity to initiate steps towards a longer-term solution that resolves information management problems and seeks to prevent problems reoccurring. Assessing the current situation requires the current information problems to be captured. This may require a mechanism to be established for staff to document issues when they arise. A log provides direct evidence of the problems arising but has the limitation that only problems arising during a specific period may be identified. There is the potential for less frequent but perhaps more significant issues to be omitted from the log. Workshops are a useful way of capturing a wider range of issues. Workshop facilitators avoid discussions becoming too restricted to one problem and can help staff to:

○ Recall specific examples of how tasks are adversely affected by problems with information.
○ Identify the underlying issue with information management that caused the problem to arise.
○ Recommend the actions that need to be taken to avoid the problem reoccurring.

Such discussions must not merely blame other departments but focus on identifying the improvements needed to information management throughout the organization. When the issues from across the organization have been collected, analysis can be undertaken to identify the nature or cause of the problem to assist in categorizing the issues identified. Scenario 6.3 shows some of the information management problems found in Amy's Candles.

Scenario 6.3

Information Management in Amy's Candles

Amy asked her staff to log any problems they encountered relating to information for a period of six weeks. The list included:

Problem 1	An order was sent to the wrong address because the card index in the shop was used rather than the new computer-based system.
Problem 2	A customer list was printed to send out details of sales items. The same customer appeared on the list twice.
Problem 3	Dr Kio complained that the parcels he orders are always left on the doorstep. He has repeatedly asked for parcels to be put in the porch and this information is always included on his order.
Problem 4	Brian asked Mrs Green for her customer number and she asked, 'Which one?' Mrs Green has two customer numbers.
Problem 5	Mr Ayelton complained that a delivery went to his previous address. His new address had been updated in the address book but not on the delivery system.
Problem 6	There is no more room to store the delivery notes received from suppliers.
Problem 7	Yumil National Supplies queried an invoice from two years ago and Amy could not find the invoice.
Problem 8	Zadok Waxes has changed some of their colour codes and the wrong coloured dye was ordered.

Each of the problems listed was discussed to identify the root cause of the problem and the problems were categorized (shown in Table 6.3).

Scenario 6.3 Continued

Data Management Category	Data Management Problem
Redundant Data	Problem 1, both the card index and computer-based system store customer addresses. Problem 2, customer details are printed twice. Problem 4, a customer has two customer numbers. Problem 5, customer address was updated in the address book but not on the delivery system.
Data Retention	Problem 6, retention period needs to be reviewed and delivery notes received from suppliers need to be purged. Problem 7, retention and retrieval of invoices need to be reviewed.
Data Integrity	Problem 3, the notes field is used on orders for delivery instructions rather than the delivery instructions field. Delivery instructions usually have more local information about the address but the notes field is not printed out on the delivery note. Problem 8, supplier colour codes are inconsistent.

Table 6.3 ▶ Categorization of Data Problems

In Amy's small organization, all employees were directly involved in the process of identifying data problems. In larger organizations a team needs to be created with representatives from all areas of the business. Representatives undertake a review of the specific problems in their local area to discuss with the team. This ensures that data issues from across the organization are identified and emphasizes the corporate role of data in the organization.

6.4.4 ▶ Information Audits

An information audit is the process of identifying and evaluating the information resource in organizations to improve information management (Buchanan & Gibb, 1998). The audit is more than an inventory of the information resources available and the information an organization requires; the analysis shows how information flows through the organization and improves understanding of the organizational context in which information is interpreted. Organizational analysis is needed to develop an integrated strategy and to identify opportunities for the organization to gain competitive advantage through the use of information (Buchanan & Gibb, 2007).

An information audit identifies four elements: (1) the data collected; (2) the source of the data, where the data comes from and who collects the data; (3) the use of the data, who uses the data, who owns the data and how frequently the data are updated; and (4) the location of the data storage, where data are stored and for how long. A template for an information audit based on the information life cycle is shown in Table 6.4. This information can be used to populate a data dictionary and create the information architecture (outlined in Chapter 4).

Link 6.1
Example Information Audit

Buchanan and Gibb (2007) outline three approaches to conducting an information audit: strategic approach, process-based approach, and resource-based approach. The strategic approach is a top-down approach starting with the mission of the organization. It subsequently considers the objectives, critical success factors, and business processes needed to support the mission of the organization. The information needed for each business process is then identified. Information is also needed to monitor the critical success factors and to demonstrate achievement of the organization's objectives. Any gaps are identified between the information available and the information needed to support the organization's mission. This approach ensures that the information resource is aligned with the strategic direction of the organization. However, there is a risk that opportunities to use information to influence the organizational strategy or to use information to gain competitive advantage will be overlooked. Table 6.5 shows the mission of Amy's Candles, three of her objectives, and related critical success factors from her strategic business plan.

The objectives and critical success factors in Amy's strategic plan require information to monitor progress and demonstrate their attainment. For example, objective 2 requires information about the income generated from different ranges of candle designs. The critical success factors to attract new customers and retain existing customers require information about Amy's customer base. Business processes are needed to support attainment of the critical success factors. For example, a process is needed to promote Amy's Candles and her design service in order to attract new customers; a process is needed to offer discounts to regular customers and maximize the potential for sequential purchasing in order to retain current customers. These business processes require information about customer profiles and manufacturing costs.

Table 6.4 ▶ Template for Information Audit

Data Identifier: *unique identifier for data item.*	
Data Item: *the data identified.*	**Data Owner:** *individual responsible for defining the data item if applicable.*
Capture	What attributes of the data are captured? *Attributes of the entity.* Who captures or creates the data? *Role, system, process, or department.* Where does the data come from? *Source.* Where are the data captured or created? *System, process, or department.* How are the data captured? *System or process.* When are the data captured? *Triggering event.*
Store	Where are the data stored? *System or department.* What are the data security classifications? *Classifications listed in Section 5.4.*
Retrieve	What data are retrieved? *List of attributes.* Who retrieves the data? *Role, system, process, or department.* Where are the data retrieved? *System, process, or department.* How are the data retrieved? *System or process.* When are the data retrieved? *Triggering event.* How frequently are the data retrieved? *For example, daily, weekly, or monthly.*
Use	For what purposes are the data used? *Process.* Who uses the data? *Role, system, process, or department.* Where are the data used? *System, process, or department.* How are the data used? *System or process.* When are the data used? *Triggering event.* How frequently are the data used? *For example, daily, weekly, or monthly.*
Maintain	What data are maintained? *List of attributes.* Who maintains the data? *Role, system, process, or department.* Where are the data maintained? *System, process, or department.* How are the data maintained? *System or process.* When are the data maintained? *Triggering event.* How frequently are the data maintained? *For example, daily, weekly, or monthly.*
Archive	What data are archived? *List of attributes (in some instances only aggregated data may be archived).* Who archives the data? *Role, system, process, or department.* Where are the data archived? *System or location.* How are the data archived? *System or process or department.* When are the data archived? *Criteria for archiving data.* How frequently are the data archived? *Frequency that the data are compared against the archiving criteria; for example, monthly or annually.*
Destroy	Who destroys the data? *Role, system, process, or department.* Where are the data destroyed? *Location.* How are the data destroyed? *Process.* When are the data destroyed? *Retention period.*

The process-based approach to developing an information audit identifies the information needed as input to and output from business processes, independently of current departmental structures. All processes are considered throughout the internal value chain and external supply chain of the organization, including the support functions and management processes needed alongside operational activities. The focus on processes adopts a practical approach to the information audit but there is a risk that analysis can be constrained by examining current ways of working rather than seeking improvements to processes.

Table 6.5 ► Extract from Strategic Plan for Amy's Candles

MISSION		
'Amy's Candles creates high-quality bespoke candles and wax sculptures for individuals and small businesses. We specialize in intricate designs and offer a range of styles for every budget. We work closely with customers to produce handmade candles to your personal design. We also provide a service to create a unique design especially for you.'		
OBJECTIVE 1 Develop at least eight designs within three budget categories under £5, under £30, and over £30.	**OBJECTIVE 2** Accrue 60% of income from the design range.	**OBJECTIVE 3** Sustain customer satisfaction at 96%.
CRITICAL SUCCESS FACTORS 1. Source quality resources within pricing variables. 2. Develop collaborative relationships with current suppliers.	**CRITICAL SUCCESS FACTORS** 1. Attract new customers. 2. Retain current customers.	**CRITICAL SUCCESS FACTORS** 1. Retain staff. 2. Train new staff.

The resource-based approach focuses entirely on identifying and evaluating the existing information in the organization. The approach considers what information exists, how and where the information is used, and by whom. Each information resource can then be assigned a value to indicate whether the information is critical to the organization providing direct or indirect support to business processes (Buchanan & Gibb, 2007). This value may affect the categorization of data for security purposes discussed in Section 5.4. The resource-based approach focuses on the content of the information available to the organization and assesses the extent to which the resource is being utilized, identifying further opportunities to leverage value from the existing resource base.

A further approach to undertaking an information audit is the actor-based approach. This approach focuses on the people in the organization and the information they need to perform their role and conduct their responsibilities. The actor-based approach recognizes that information is interpreted; as individuals interpret information differently their specific information requirements will differ. Focusing on the people who will use the information is particularly important when defining the information used in management and planning processes. Chapter 4 discussed how the business model and organizational architecture introduced in Chapter 1 could be used to explore the information needs of the external and internal context of the organization. The business model adopts an actor-based approach to identify the partners with whom the organization interacts and the information sent to and received from them. The organizational architecture can be used to explore the role of information in the formal and informal working practices of the organization. The architecture also reveals the cultural

values of the organization that influence the qualities of information required, such as quantity and frequency of information.

The four approaches (strategic, process-based, resource-based, and actor-based) are complementary approaches and combinations of the approaches can be used to audit the information resource, assessing the use of information in the organization.

6.4.5 ► External Analysis

The identification of existing information issues and the construction of an information audit mainly focus on internal data. Data also need to be considered from an external perspective. The business model introduced in Chapter 1 supports external data analysis. The industry set of the business model identifies professional bodies relevant to the organization. Professional bodies specify codes of conduct that represent the minimum standards to which both organizations and individual members are expected to adhere. The standards may include reference to the security, quality, and use of information.

The business climate section of the business model identifies the national and international legal requirements relating to data to which the organization must adhere. The external analysis provides strong justification for an information management strategy to be developed, identifying legislative issues and potential consequences of failure to comply. It also provides a richer understanding of the qualities of information that the organization is expected to provide.

In addition to the legislative and professional requirements, organizations have to satisfy the cultural expectations of customers, consumers, suppliers, and partners. This requires the organization to understand the expectations of the different communities. For example, the expectations of the online customer are different from those of the traditional customer (Martin, 1999). The increase in social media and the speed with which information can be transmitted increases expectations of the time taken to respond to electronic communications such as emails. Organizations need to understand the expectations of their customers in relation to the quantity and quality of information. This requires consideration to be given to how different groups of people value and prioritize different measures of data quality.

The assessment of the current situation in relation to information management in the organization identifies the problems in the organization that are caused by poor quality information and highlights the need for the information management strategy. The assessment provides evidence of the impact of poor information management on the organization, documents the potential penalties that may be incurred if information management legislation is breached, and justifies investment in developing an information management strategy. The analysis identifies the benefits to the organization of improving information management and specifies the requirements of information management from internal and external perspectives, including regulatory mandates in addition to ethical and social expectations. The assessment also identifies the current status of policies, processes, and tools to support information management, which informs the vision and objectives of the information management strategy.

6.5 Implementing an Information Management Strategy

The plan to implement the information management strategy considers a number of factors, such as the availability of resources, the information issues that are causing the organization most concern, the priorities identified during the formulation of the information management strategy, and the performance measures specified in the strategy.

6.5.1 Approach to Implementing an Information Management Strategy

There are four main stages in implementing an information management strategy. First, the organization needs to define a structure of roles, responsibilities, processes, and tools in which information management can be conducted. Second, the organization needs to prepare a planned approach to manage information. The approach needs to be broken down into specific actions that can be achieved and time frames allocated to achieving them. Third, the implementation of the information

management strategy will require a number of projects to be initiated over a period of time. The implementation plan should be aligned with IT project plans in the organization as this will help to align information management with the current work in the organization. For example, if Amy was planning to develop a customer relationship management system, this would provide an opportunity to improve the quality of customer data as part of the systems development project. Finally, processes need to be established to regularly review both the progress of the strategy's implementation and the impact of the strategy on the organization.

Figure 6.6 presents an approach to develop a plan for implementing an information management strategy for an organization.

Figure 6.7 shows an implementation plan developed for Lightpark Council. A named individual will be assigned responsibility for completing the action and a date by which the action must be completed. This facilitates accountability for the actions that need to be taken.

6.5.2 Barriers to Implementing an Information Management Strategy

Barriers hindering implementation of the information management strategy are likely to be resource-based, culture-based, or fear-based. Lack of resources may be a barrier to implementing the information management strategy as staff may not be available to undertake the work required (such as participating in discussions to agree on data definitions) due to existing workloads. This may require senior management to intervene and resolve any underlying political or financial issues preventing staff from participating in information management tasks.

Staff may be reluctant to participate in information management tasks as they believe information management to be a waste of time, or that information management is the IT department's problem, or another department's problem, or that nothing will change. Improving information management in an organization requires a change of culture to be facilitated. Changing the culture will take time and requires senior staff to demonstrate and communicate their active commitment to implementing the information management strategy. Regular communication is needed about the importance of information, the problems caused by poor quality information, and the improvements that have been achieved through information management projects.

Information management projects, such as creating agreed upon definitions of information used in an organization, are challenging. Staff may be concerned that they may make a mistake or may not know the

1   Establish an Information Governing Council and Information Management Committee. This will ensure that there is senior management commitment for information management and will help to promote a collaborative approach to implementing the strategy.

2   Define the roles and responsibilities for information management. This includes:
  2.1   Terms of reference for the Information Management Committee.
  2.2   Job description for the information manager.
  2.3   Responsibilities of information stewards, data owners, data authors, and data maintainers.

3   Set up tools to support information management, including the data dictionary, data ownership matrix, and information architecture. Consideration needs to be given to:
  3.1   The structure of these tools (for example, the metadata the tools will store).
  3.2   The location and accessibility of the tools. (For example, if the information manager maintains a spreadsheet of data owners, where will the spreadsheet be stored so that others can access it?)
  3.3   Who can have access to information management tools and how will access be facilitated? (For example, will the data dictionary be accessible to staff working remotely via the Internet?)

4   Specify the overall approach to be taken to implement the strategy. This may include, for each data item:
  4.1   Assigning data owners and data authors.
  4.2   Agreeing on data definitions.
  4.3   Specifying business rules.
  4.4   Defining policies on how the data are used.
  4.5   Cleaning the data to implement the policies and rules agreed.
  4.6   Implementing controls to ensure adherence to policies and rules.

5   Agree on the priorities for information management. This will include consideration of the:
  5.1   Problems and priorities identified when the strategy was formulated.
  5.2   Performance measures specified in the information management strategy.
  5.3   Master data items.
  5.4   Plans for new information systems or changes to existing information systems.
  5.5   Resources available.
  5.6   Opportunities for quick wins. These are relatively small tasks which can be undertaken in a short period of time that will have a positive impact on information management.

6   Develop six tiers of work for each 12-month period to include:
  6.1   Development of the information management infrastructure of structures, policies, processes, tools, and procedures.
  6.2   Preparatory work to define terms and policies for data. This provides the foundation for later work to clean data and implement the policies.
  6.3   Defined projects with cross-departmental teams working to clean data and implement controls so that data stay clean.
  6.4   Small working groups to investigate and resolve problems raised by members of the committee.
  6.5   Participation in planned business and IT projects to assess any impact on information, such as what information is needed or how information is accessed.
  6.6   Development of training programmes and communication of the committee's work.

7   Define the projects to be undertaken in each tier and include:
  7.1   Objectives of each project.
  7.2   Timescales for when the work is to be completed.
  7.3   Allocation of resources.
  7.4   Performance measures to be used to report progress each month.
  7.5   Assignment of project manager.

8   Establish the reporting format for meetings of the Information Management Committee. This is likely to include:
  8.1   Ongoing actions from the previous meeting.
  8.2   A report from each current project.
  8.3   Progress made against the performance criteria specified in the information management strategy.
  8.4   Reports from information stewards about issues arising or resolved in their area.
  8.5   A report on the development of training and communication activities.

Figure 6.6   Approach to Develop an Implementation Plan for an Information Management Strategy

answer to the questions asked about how information is used in their areas. In addition, staff may be anxious and defensive when aspects of the work environment, which are taken for granted, are questioned as this questions a person's perception of reality (Shekleton, 1991). Staff therefore need to be given appropriate training to understand the processes and skills required in information management.

Plan to Implement Lightpark Council's Information Management Strategy

Stage 1: Establish an Information Management Committee

1.1 Outline the purpose of the Information Management Committee.
1.2 Identify information stewards to represent each area of the council.
1.3 Appoint the information manager to chair the committee.
1.4 Agree on the dates for monthly meetings of the committee for the current year.

Stage 2: Define the Roles and Responsibilities for Information Management

2.1 Define the responsibilities of the information manager.
2.2 Agree on the terms of reference of the Information Management Committee.
2.3 Define the roles of data owners, data authors, and data maintainers.

Stage 3: Set-up Information Management Tools

3.1 Specify the data to be held in the data dictionary.
3.2 Define the columns in the data ownership matrix.
3.3 Agree on the notation to be used for the information architecture.
3.4 Agree on where policy documents and tools, such as the data ownership matrix, should be stored.
3.5 Agree on access rights to the information management tools.
3.6 Specify the requirements of the data dictionary and information architecture.
3.7 Evaluate software tools needed to create and maintain the data dictionary and information architecture.
3.8 Implement the data dictionary, information architecture, and data ownership matrix.

Stage 4: Agree on Approach to Implementing the Strategy

4.1 Identify the information management processes needed.
4.2 Prioritize the information management processes, identifying any interdependencies.
4.3 Agree on approach to be adopted.

Stage 5: Agree information Management Priorities

5.1 Identify the problems and priorities captured when the strategy was formulated.
5.2 Extract the performance measures specified in the information management strategy.
5.3 Identify the main data objects used in the Council.
5.4 Document the current information systems and IT plan.
5.5 Assess the resources available in each area of the Council to participate in information management processes.
5.6 Identify current information management issues in each area of the Council.
5.7 Outline a list of priorities for the next 12 months.

Stage 6: Develop Six Tiers of Work

6.1 Agree on the priorities for defining data in the Council.
6.2 Agree on the priorities for cleaning data.
6.3 Agree on the priorities for investigating issues in each area of the Council.
6.4 Identify where information management will need to participate in current information systems and IT projects.
6.5 Agree on a programme of training to support the objectives of the committee.
6.6 Develop a communication strategy to disseminate the work of the committee.

Stage 7: Define the Projects in Each Tier of Work

7.1 Assign a project manager and information steward to have responsibility for each project.
7.2 Develop the project specification for each project.

Stage 8: Establish Reporting Mechanisms

8.1 Agree on the standard agenda for the Information Management Committee.
8.2 Agree on the process of raising issues at the committee.
8.3 Develop the forms to be used to submit reports to the committee.

Figure 6.7 ▶ Implementation Plan for an Information Management Strategy

6.5.3 ▶ Critical Success Factors for Implementing an Information Management Strategy

Four key requirements are essential to address barriers to implementing the information: (1) commitment to the strategy, (2) intraorganizational collaboration, (3) focusing the implementation plan on practical issues, and (4) the regular communication of the benefits derived from implementing the strategy.

Commitment to the Strategy

Improving information management must be a strategic objective of the organization. Active senior management commitment to developing and implementing the information management strategy is essential. Senior management's support for, and commitment to, formulating and implementing an information management strategy needs to be directed into practical actions to implement the strategy. This includes providing the resources required and creating the infrastructure to implement the information management strategy, which will provide long-term benefits to the organization. For example, effective information management helps organizations avoid fines, maintain their reputation, and avoid loss of custom through nonadherence to information privacy regulations.

The work involved in auditing, cleaning, and improving the quality of data in the organization incurs costs and the benefits of these activities may only be fully realized in the long term. The allocation of resources to implement the strategy will involve diverting resources from other areas of the organization and this will be met with resistance. Senior managers may therefore need to instruct divisional managers to release staff from other activities or provide funding for temporary staff to be employed so that experienced staff can be seconded to specific projects to implement the information management strategy. Funding will also be needed to make changes to existing information systems to improve the integrity of information. For example, program code will need to be changed to implement new business rules to improve the verification and validation of data entered into computer systems. The information management strategy cannot be achieved without support from senior management; the support needs to go beyond words of encouragement and include practical action to provide the resources needed to implement the strategy.

Intraorganizational Collaboration

The objectives of the information management strategy can only be met by intraorganizational teams working together. Representatives from all areas of the business will need to be included in project teams to ensure that the implications of changes agreed upon have been identified. The business staff need to help determine how the data are currently used in different departments and define the changes required to the data. The IT staff can help determine how data are integrated in IT systems. Together, the IT and business staff can assess the implications of the changes proposed. The IT staff implement the changes agreed upon and raise any issues that need to be resolved with the business staff. The business staff define the business rules needed to ensure that data are used consistently; the IT staff implement the business rules.

Link 6.2
Example of How Business and IT Work Together

The success of information management projects is dependent on assigning the right people to the project team. Members of the project team need to possess:

○ Good knowledge of how information is used in their area of the organization.
○ An awareness of how the information used in their areas flows to and from other areas of the organization.
○ Effective communication skills.
○ Willingness to work in a cross-divisional team.

In addition, members of the project team need to be fully supportive of the information management strategy. The team needs to recognize that there will be problems to be addressed and have a willingness to work with others to overcome the problems to improve information management in the organization. Commitment to the strategy and a positive attitude are essential for project team members to become ambassadors, promoting the changes needed to implement the strategy.

Practical Planning

Implementing the information management strategy is a large, complex task. The implementation plan therefore needs to be realistic and focus on resolving current problems in the organization identified from the assessments completed during the formulation of the strategy. It is easier to gain access to resources if benefits of the project can be specified and the timescales can be defined, identifying when staff will need to be seconded to the project team. The implementation plan therefore needs to specify a programme of projects with planned activities and resource requirements. The progress of individual projects and the aims of the information management strategy should be monitored and reported regularly.

The implementation plan will involve resolving current information management problems and then introducing systems (both human and computer-based) to ensure that the aims of the information management strategy are attained and sustained in the future. This will require IT staff to implement validation and verification checks to be applied when data are input into computer systems. Staff must adhere to these checks and not seek ways to circumvent them. This may require a change of culture in the organization, which will focus on accepting responsibility for information, its quality, and use. A communication strategy is a key tool in changing organizational culture.

Regular Communication

The implementation of the information management strategy will require considerable investment over a long period of time. As data become defined and cleaned, confidence in the quality of data should increase, enabling data to be shared across divisions in the organization. It is therefore important that the progress of the strategy and its achievements are regularly communicated throughout the organization for a number of reasons.

First, regular communication of the aims of the strategy and current achievements reinforces the importance of information management in the organization. It shows that managers have listened and are taking action to address the information management problems reported when the strategy was being formulated. Communication shows that issues raised are being addressed, though they are often complicated and take time to resolve.

Second, communicating the practical and quantitative benefits achieved as a direct result of improvements in information management demonstrates the return on the investment from the strategy and justifies further investment in information management projects. For example, after deleting obsolete data Amy may be able to quantify the storage space that is no longer required and the associated annual cost savings.

Third, communication raises awareness of the range of issues that can be caused by problems with information and shows how problems with information in one area of the organization can affect other areas of the business. Communicating the achievements of information management projects demonstrates how addressing problems with information can have a positive impact on the daily work of staff across the organization, such as reducing complaints and making it easier to access information. It demonstrates that staff can make a difference and encourages staff to participate in improving the quality and reliability of information. In particular, it shows what can be achieved when the business and IT staff work together.

Finally, regular communication contributes to cultivating a culture that recognizes the importance of information management, is willing to share information, and takes responsibility for the quality and security of information. The transition from a culture of data hoarding to one of openness is challenging and takes time to evolve. The information manager will identify specific areas where training is needed and opportunities to raise awareness of information management. Improving awareness of the importance of information management provides the foundation for improving the quality of information in the organization required by corporate governance.

The information manager will work with data owners and data authors to:

○ Develop a strategy for communicating the work to improve information management.
○ Identify the need for training in specific areas of information management.
○ Create materials for communicating the work and achievements of information management.

Figure 6.8 summarizes the critical success factors that need to be addressed to implement the information management strategy:

1. Demonstrate practical leadership and commitment to the strategy.
2. Provide resources, including releasing staff from day-to-day activities as required.
3. Ensure that the right people are in key roles to drive the strategy forward.
4. Set a realistic time frame for the implementation.
5. Resolve current problems in information management.
6. Establish both technical and human activity systems to implement the strategy.
7. Plan actions to direct the culture towards the management of information in the organization.
8. Establish controls to ensure that new systems and business practices implemented by the strategy are not circumvented or subverted.
9. Regularly review the progress of the strategy implementation and monitor the impact of the strategy on the organization.
10. Develop a communication strategy to inform staff of the information management strategy, its progress and staff responsibilities.
11. Celebrate successes resulting from the implementation of the strategy.
12. Make the strategy real; bring it to life by addressing recurring problems and seeking opportunities for a quick win.

Figure 6.8 ▶ Critical Success Factors for Strategy Implementation

Link 6.3
Tasks to Implement an Information Strategy

6.6 ▶ Evaluating Progress of the Information Management Strategy

Organizations need to regularly evaluate the progress of implementing the information management strategy. There is a risk that strategy documents remain neglected and unimplemented unless specific action is taken to follow through with the commitment to implement the strategy. As the strategy is implemented the effectiveness of the strategy should be reviewed, identifying and resolving problems that arise. The strategy may need to be revised if the expected benefits are not being achieved.

6.6.1 ▶ Status of Information Management Strategy Implementation

The progress towards implementing the information management strategy is reviewed regularly by the information manager and reported to the Information Management Committee. Progress of the strategy implementation may include quantitative measures such as the number of data owners appointed and the number of data definitions agreed upon. In reviewing the progress that has been made in implementing the strategy, it is necessary to identify any barriers that are hindering implementation. The Information Management Committee is required to identify barriers that are hindering progress to implement the strategy and take action to overcome them.

6.6.2 ▶ Impact of Information Management Strategy

The organizational benefits arising from improvements in information management should be identified and communicated, demonstrating the value that effective information management has on the organization. The information management strategy outlines performance measures against which the impact of the strategy will be reported to the Information Management Committee. The information management strategy in Figure 6.4 identifies key performance measures such as the number of wrong orders delivered and the percentage of time stock was unavailable. The information manager will report these figures each month and seek to demonstrate that improving the quality of product data has contributed to a reduction in both of these areas.

In addition to quantitative measures, the process of implementing the information management strategy has a qualitative impact on the organization. For example, it can have a positive effect on the organizational culture and staff morale as senior managers demonstrate that action is being taken to address problems with information. As the quality of information improves and security breaches are avoided, the confidence suppliers and customers have in the organization will also increase. This will provide the foundation for supporting the development of long-term relationships in the supply chain.

6.6.3 ▶ Review of the Information Management Strategy

An information management strategy is developed in response to the current problems in the organization and to address the challenges, opportunities, and legislative requirements identified in the external business environment. The performance measures in an information management strategy reflect the organization's current situation, which justifies the development of the information management strategy. The problems caused by poor quality information are easily identified, and as the problems are resolved the benefits to the organization are recognized. As problems are addressed, the next set of priorities can be defined.

Continued investment is needed in information management to avoid similar problems arising in the future. However, it can become more difficult to justify investment in information management without measurable benefits being identified. It is therefore important to establish information management as a core continuous activity to implement information governance in the organization. The process of implementing the strategy will trigger changes in the organization and therefore the organization's information requirements will also change. The information management strategy needs to be reviewed and revised in response to changes in the organization and the achievement of initial performance measures.

Formulating and implementing an information management strategy are not one-off tasks; they are continuous processes responding to the changing information needs of the organization. The organization and its environment are continually changing and the continued suitability of the strategy must be periodically reviewed. The information manager and data owners need to be regularly consulted when any changes to the organization are considered that may impact the requirements for information or the way in which data are managed. Part III examines a range of changes which take place in organizations including business-led change, such as merger and acquisitions, and IT-led changes such as the opportunities offered by Internet technologies. The potential impact of such changes on existing information management policies needs to be assessed before the changes are implemented. This ensures that any changes relating to information can be planned and resourced appropriately. The information governance framework needs to incorporate procedures to ensure that the potential impact on the information resource is appropriately considered when changes to the organization are proposed.

Summary

An information management strategy formulates the objectives and policies to coordinate actions affecting the information resource at all levels in the enterprise architecture. The strategy aims to ensure that staff across the organization have timely access to quality information to support the organization's mission. Investment in information management must be justified by direct benefits to the organization. Formulating an information management strategy involves establishing structures and policies to manage the information resource within the framework of information governance.

One of the main barriers to implementing an information management strategy is the availability of sufficient resources. Implementing the strategy has to be undertaken alongside the daily operations of the organization. Additional staffing resources are therefore needed as existing staff have to be diverted from their usual tasks to contribute to the strategy. Senior management commitment to support the information management strategy is essential to ensure that appropriate resources can be allocated to implement the strategy.

Staff may be resistant to implementing the strategy as they may feel that things will not change or that other areas of the organization are to blame for poor quality information. A key process in the information management strategy is communication, highlighting the benefits that are achieved through improving the quality and availability of information in the organization. The impact of the information management strategy must be regularly evaluated against organizational performance measures and reviewed as changes in the internal and external environments change the organization's requirements for information.

Reviewing Scenario 6.1

An information management strategy defines an organization's objectives for managing information and documents the approach to be adopted to achieve the objectives. Amy first needs to identify the specific issues with information in her store. This will involve undertaking an information audit and identifying current problems that arise with information, such as any difficulties accessing information. Amy will also need to understand the ethical and legal issues relating to information to ensure that her organization adheres to appropriate legislation. An internal analysis of how information is used in Amy's Candles and an external review of relevant legislation will help direct the objectives of the information management strategy.

Amy then has to plan the approach needed to achieve the objectives. The plan will include policies and procedures to help Amy and her staff effectively manage the information resource. Policies relating to data ownership, data quality, data security, and data retention provide a framework in which information can be managed. Amy can then develop specific procedures to implement each policy. For example, Amy may define a policy for data ownership that specifies that a data owner must approve changes to the definition of data. This requires procedures to be developed to ensure that definitions cannot be changed without the approval of the data owner and to outline how approval from the data owner can be attained. Amy therefore needs to develop an information management strategy that sets out her objectives for information management and the framework of policies and procedures to achieve the objectives. Headings to use in an information management strategy are given in Section 6.2, and Section 6.4 outlines a plan that Amy could use for developing her strategy. When the strategy is implemented, Amy should regularly review whether the objectives are being met and make changes to the strategy as the organization and business climate change. Table 6.6 outlines the tasks Amy needs to undertake to design her information management strategy.

Cloze Exercise 6.1

Complete the following paragraph by choosing the correct word from Table 6.7 to fill in each gap.

An information _____ strategy demonstrates the organization's _____ to improving the quality and accessibility of information in the organization. The strategy defines the _____ and specifies _____ for improving information management, establishing a framework of _____, controls, and procedures to manage information throughout the _____. The strategy _____ the required investment in information and demonstrates that poor information management may lead to _____ penalties and loss of custom. Business _____ of information

Table 6.6 ▸ Strategy Development Plan for Amy's Candles

Task	Contribution to Strategy
1. Collect data about current problems through a log book or workshop.	Provides justification for strategy.
2. Assess the current internal and external situation by conducting an internal information audit and completing the business model.	Identifies the information requirements and problems to be addressed. This can be used to form the basis for the aims, benefits, and key principles of the strategy.
3. Identify legal and ethical issues.	This can be documented in the statutory compliance section of the strategy.
4. Define the vision for information management to overcome the problems identified and support the overall strategy of the organization.	The vision informs the purpose and scope of the strategy.
5. Define the aims and objectives. 6. Identify the challenges that need to be overcome to achieve the objectives. 7. Specify the policies needed to support attainment of the objectives. 8. Identify key performance measures to monitor the implementation and impact of the strategy.	This is based on the analysis of the internal and external situation which informs sections of the strategy.

Table 6.7 ▸ Words to Complete Cloze Exercise 6.1

Architecture	Commitment	Justifies	Policies	Resource
Assessment	Communication	Legal	Practical	Strategy
Audit	Continuous	Life Cycle	Problems	Systems
Benefits	Cost	Management	Process	Targets
Collaboration	Dictionary	Performance	Quantitative	Vision

management may be tangible such as _____ savings or intangible such as improvements to decision-making and customer service. The information _____ strategy provides the information processes to manage information in accordance with the information management strategy.

Formulating a strategy requires _____ support from senior management and _____ from interdepartmental teams. An _____ of the current situation with regard to information management is needed to identify the specific information management _____ in the organization. An information _____ can then be undertaken to identify existing information resources available and the information that the organization requires. There are four complementary approaches to conducting an audit; these are strategic, _____ -based, resource-based, and actor-based. The results of the information audit can be used to populate the data _____ and create the information_____.

Barriers hindering implementation of the information management strategy are likely to be _____ -based, culture-based, or fear-based. Barriers to implementing the strategy can be addressed by organizational commitment, intraorganizational collaboration, _____ strategy, and by focusing the _____ on practical issues. The progress of implementing the strategy can be reported using _____ measures such as the number of data owners appointed. The impact of the strategy is evaluated using meaningful _____ measures defined in the information management strategy. Formulating and implementing an information management are _____ processes responding to the changing information needs of the organization.

Link 6.4
Answers to Cloze Exercise 6.1

Activities 6.1

1   Prepare a presentation to Amy to persuade her that she needs an information management strategy.

2   Define the business processes Amy needs to support the critical success factors for objectives 1 and 3 shown in Table 6.5. Identify the information required for each business process.

3   Identify the similarities and differences between the information management strategies shown in Figures 6.3 and 6.4.

4   Develop an information management strategy for Amy's Candles.

5   List the barriers Amy needs to overcome to implement an information management strategy.

6   Recommend actions for Amy in order to overcome barriers to developing an information management strategy.

7   Develop a set of fundamental principles for Amy's information management strategy.

8   Draft a standard agenda that could be used by Amy to evaluate the progress of implementing the information management strategy.

Discussion Questions 6.1

1   Why is a separate information management strategy needed?

2   How does the information management strategy relate to the organizational strategy, information systems strategy, and IT strategy?

3   How and why do the objectives of information management differ between organizations?

4   To what extent is it possible to develop a generic information management strategy?

5   Why is it difficult to implement an information management strategy?

6   What is the role of a communication strategy in information management and why is it important?

IMPROVING INFORMATION ACCESS

Scenario 7.1

Implementing the Information Management Strategy at Match Lighting

Following the Board's approval of Match Lighting's information management strategy, the lighting manufacturer has appointed Mrs Kerry Winters as their information manager. Mrs Winters has been given responsibility for implementing the information management strategy. The first problem to overcome is that the information manager does not have any authority relating to the management of staff in Match Lighting's organization structure. Mrs Winters does not directly manage any staff so *how can she access the staff resources she needs to implement the strategy?* Secondly, Match Lighting is a large organization with high volumes of data flowing between divisions through diverse information systems. *Where should she start?*

Learning Outcomes

The learning outcomes of this chapter are to:

- Review the causes of information overload.
- Improve the accessibility of information.
- Assess the barriers to sharing data.
- Define measures of data quality.
- Implement approaches to define data.
- Identify opportunities for implementing the information management strategy.

Introduction

Information is often taken for granted in organizations until something goes wrong. Information is referred to as being the lifeblood of organizations (Rogerson, 2008) and, like blood in the human body, information is usually not considered until there becomes too much information, not enough information, information is leaked, or the information is of poor quality. An information management strategy aims to take control of the information resource and minimize the occurrence of future problems. This chapter discusses some of the organizational challenges that need to be addressed to implement the information management strategy.

Staff in the organization need to be able to access accurate information. The problems of having too much information or too little information are discussed. If staff cannot access the data they need or do not trust the reliability of the data available, staff will purchase, capture, or create their own version of the data. This can lead to inconsistent data being used in different areas of the organization. The barriers to sharing data in the organization are assessed and measures of data quality are defined. Before data can be shared, the data must be understood; approaches are outlined in the chapter to define data so that the data are used and interpreted consistently throughout the organization.

7.1 Reducing Information Overload

Toffler (1970) predicted information overload, a time when the volume of information would be so excessive it would not be possible to act on the information and make decisions. Information technology (IT) and the Internet have exponentially increased the volume of digital information available to an organization; the volume of digital information doubles in UK firms every two years (Parnell, 2001). Klausegger *et al.* (2007) suggest that 60 per cent of time in organizations is spent reading and processing information. IT facilitates the accessibility of people and information, contributing to information overload. Mobile devices provide the means for employees to receive and access information continually both inside and outside of the workplace. The continued *connectivity* can be beneficial and provide the opportunity for flexible and mobile working. However, the constant *accessibility* can also invade family life, adversely affecting work–life balance, and be a source of stress.

Information overload increases stress and requires staff to work longer hours and take work home (Klausegger *et al.*, 2007), which has a negative impact on individuals and work performance. Responses to information overload include confusion, irrational behaviour, and decision stress due to the inability to process all the information available (Toffler, 1970).

Miller (1956) showed that human cognitive capabilities are limited and that as the volume of information transmitted to a recipient increases, his or her ability to accurately recall and act on the information decreases, with the optimal level being seven (plus or minus two) elements. As information volumes increase beyond the limitations of cognitive capabilities, the ability to perform tasks efficiently and effectively decreases. Savolainen (2007) describes information overload as having insufficient time to respond to the information being presented. This can lead to poor decision-making or the inability to make decisions at all.

DEFINITION: Information overload occurs when the volume of information presented to an individual exceeds their cognitive capacity, and there is insufficient time available to analyse and use information effectively. When a person feels overloaded, they can become stressed and unable to carry out their work to an appropriate standard.

Information is only meaningful if the information informs the appropriate person so that the necessary action can be taken in response to the information received. When the volume of information becomes excessive, it is no longer possible to act on the information. The cost of creating, storing, and transmitting information escalates, yet the information has no value to the organization.

7.1.1 Causes of Information Overload

The problem of having too much information is caused by technical and social factors. IT has increased the ease with which information can be created and transmitted contributing to the volume of information received from a range of internal and external sources. Society contributes to information overload by poor information responsibility. Broadcasting information to people who do not need the information, and adopting a just-in-case policy to sending information, unnecessarily overloads individuals with information they do not need.

Three typical aspects of organizational life can contribute to information overload. First, volumes of information are associated with meetings. Before the meeting, emails are circulated to arrange the meeting and the minutes of the previous meeting are circulated with additional documents to read in advance of the meeting. During the meeting, the minutes of the previous meeting will be corrected and agreed upon, the action list will be discussed, the main items on the agenda will be actioned, and further information may be circulated. Each meeting generates a range of information to be used, stored, and retrieved when necessary. Meetings can take place for a range of reasons – to inform, to gain agreement, to action – but they can deteriorate to merely reporting. In many cases meetings are used as means of management control in organizations dictating regular reporting cycles. In such cases the cost of the meeting (the hourly wage of staff attending the meeting multiplied by the length of the meeting) outweighs the value of decisions taken and the work completed during the meeting.

Second, information systems often generate reports on a regular cycle, for example, weekly, monthly, or quarterly. The value of regular reports varies and the reports may not be effectively used. Regular reports will be automatically sent to named recipients who may be unable to act on the information due to the number of reports received or may not need to act on the information.

Third, most managers have a pile of information pending, waiting to be read. Industry reports, trade journals, and white papers may include relevant information, if only there was time to read them. There is a tendency to adopt squirrelling behaviour, gathering information which may not be used (Rowlands *et al.*, 2008).

Table 7.1 lists a number of common problems with information that cause individuals to feel that they have too much information to comprehend, resulting in information paralysis, the inability to act on information received.

7.1.2 Approaches to Reducing Information Overload

Actions to manage information overload are both technical and personal (Parnell, 2001). At the technological level, information systems must provide timely information of the appropriate quality. At the personal level, individuals select sources of information based on their personal judgement and adopt adaptation mechanisms such as delegating responsibilities, skimming information, storing information for future reference, ignoring information, and prioritizing information (Klausegger *et al.*, 2007).

Table 7.1 ▶ Problems and Recommendations for Information Overload

Problems	Recommendations
Volume of information being received.	Define information needs. Eliminate regular reporting. Filter information. Develop a culture of using information responsibly.
Volume of emails being received.	Develop a policy on acceptable email usage.
Unable to find information when needed.	Improve usability of information tools. Implement search optimization tools. Develop a policy on the centralized storage of documents.
Time spent searching for, using, and acting on information.	Prioritize information needs. Plan activities.
Information generated for meetings.	Plan agenda. Close actions quickly. Centralize storage of minutes. Use tools, such as a central repository, to enable documents to be accessed.
Mountain of unread information.	Only print information when necessary. Skim read documents, highlighting key articles; remove key articles and discard remainder. Schedule time to read information.
24x7 accessibility.	Switch off IT devices off-hours.
Quality concerns.	Assess credibility of data and develop quality categories. Identify issues and develop an action plan to improve the quality of information using a single source of data.
Regular reports.	Eliminate unnecessary regular reports. Use exception reporting and meaningful reporting cycles.

Managing information overload involves providing people with the information they need (Meglio & Kleiner, 1990). A clear understanding of the information required by individuals to perform their work effectively is first needed. Information can then be targeted to the individuals who need and can act on the information. The frequency and regularity of information reporting should be reviewed to ensure that it is aligned with business processes.

IT can be used in two main ways to improve the alignment between the information and the people who need the information. Pull technology refers to tools that help to refine searches for relevant information and filter out less relevant information; the recipients choose to pull the information towards them. However, there is a risk that relevant information may also be mistakenly filtered out (Savolainen, 2007). Push technology sends (pushes) information to the recipient based on predefined preferences. Rich site summary feeds (RSS) are an example of push technology, notifying subscribers when information has changed on an Internet or Intranet site. Push technology has the advantage that the recipient does not have to

search for the information but the technology contributes to the increasing volume of information received by an individual. Personalization systems use personal profiles and browsing history to filter the results of information searches with the aim of providing more relevant information to an individual (Ferran *et al.*, 2005).

Table 7.1 provides recommendations to address some of the causes of information overload; however, a fundamental change in the attitude and approach to information is needed, both at an individual and organizational level, to use information more responsibly.

7.1.3 Role of Information Management Strategy in Reducing Information Overload

Overcoming information overload requires the information management strategy to:

○ Review information from an individual perspective, including:
  • What information is received?
  • When is the information received?
  • Where is the information from?

- Why is the information being sent?
- Is the information needed?
- Could the information be provided in a different way? This may include changing the timing of the information, the format of the information, or the way the information is accessed (for example, making the information accessible when needed rather than sending the information to the recipient on a regular basis).
- Review how IT is used in the organization to provide access to information, including:
  - Use of intranets, shared storage areas, information systems, and extraction tools, which enable individuals to gain access to the information (pull information) when needed.
  - Use of email, instant messaging, social media, paper memos, reports, minutes, newsletters, and other circulated documentation, which push to individuals whether or not the information is needed.
- Streamline information provision to balance the use of IT to push and pull information to meet the information needs of individuals in the organization.
- Develop policies to generate a culture of information responsibility to ensure that:
  - IT is not abused by circulating information to people who do not need the information.
  - Information is provided to the people who need the information, when they need it.
  - The value of information and the costs incurred by generating and circulating information of poor value are understood.

7.2 ▶ Improving Information Accessibility

Information needs to be accessible to the right people in the organization, at the time and place they need the information, and in a form that meets their needs. This incorporates a number of factors relating to the:

- Interoperability of the devices being used to store and access the information.
- Availability of the information, the content of the information, and the organization's rules relating to the appropriate use of the information.
- Compatibility of the specific needs of the person requesting the information and the information that can be provided.

Table 7.2 lists factors that affect information accessibility, which can be examined from both technical and practical perspectives.

7.2.1 ▶ Availability of Information

The first question to consider is whether the required information currently exists. An investigation is needed to determine whether the organization captures the information required or could generate the information from existing data. Separate consideration then needs to be given to feasibility and acceptability: feasibility considers whether it is possible to generate the information; acceptability considers whether the cost of generating the information is proportionate to the value of the information and whether it is acceptable to the organization to expend the effort needed to generate the information.

Second, if the information exists, the information then has to be located. Despite advances in IT to support information retrieval, employees spend significant time searching for information in organizations. In one study it was reported that 60 per cent of employees spend 15 minutes a day looking for information (Parnell, 2001). Attention therefore needs to be given to the range of tools available to help locate information stored in the organization. Information only has value when used; collecting and storing data that cannot be accessed when needed incurs unnecessary costs.

Third, when the information has been located the next factor to consider is whether the individual requesting the

Table 7.2 ▶ Factors Affecting Information Accessibility

	Availability	Interoperability	Compatibility
Technical Perspective	The location where the information is stored. The location where the information is needed. The ability to gain access to the information.	The format of the information at source. The format the information needs to be in to be transferred to the appropriate device.	The content of the information at source. The presentation restrictions of the device.
Individual Perspective	The ability to find the information.	The format the individual requires the information to be in.	The presentation requirements of the individual.

information has the appropriate level of authorization to access the information. Access rights may be defined by an individual's position in the organization's hierarchy or may be constrained within the boundaries of, for example, a project, sales area, or product type. Further legal restrictions need to be considered in relation to data privacy and the transmission of data internationally.

From a technical perspective, consideration needs to be given to bridging the gap between where the information is located and where the information is needed. Despite advances in telecommunications there can still be barriers to transmitting the information requested. Such barriers include:

○ Volume restrictions on the quantity of data that can be physically transmitted between devices and locations.

○ Physical restrictions on transmitting data, such as the lack of ability to obtain a sufficient transmission signal within buildings or remote locations. Widespread, uniform, and reliable access to power sources, wireless communications, and the Internet are not available in some areas, especially in developing countries.

○ Security restrictions such as firewalls blocking data transmissions. Although the purpose of such restrictions is to protect computer systems from unauthorized access they can occasionally hinder legitimate access to data via specific network ports.

7.2.2 ▶ Interoperability of Information

Interoperability refers to the ability of two or more different IT devices to exchange data transmissions. Interoperability is dependent on the format of the data and the communication protocols of each device. If the format of the source data is not the same as the format of the data required by the receiving device, a conversion process is needed. The communication protocols of each device need to correspond so that the data can be transmitted and received accurately without being corrupted.

Link 7.1
Interoperability Model

Beyond the technical considerations relating to the format and communication of data, consideration needs to be given to the format of the source data and the format in which the recipient requires the information. For example, the information could be retrieved and sent as a noneditable file in portable document format (PDF) but the recipient may need to edit the information.

The recipient may have specific requirements about the format of the information to meet his or her personal requirements, such as the need for large text, text to audio conversion, and the use of specific colours of text and backgrounds. The source data have to be in a form that can be converted to meet these specific requirements.

7.2.3 ▶ Compatibility of Information

Continued development of standards has improved interoperability (the ability to transmit and receive data between devices) but issues of compatibility (the ability to use the data transmitted) remain. It is technically possible to transmit large text documents to be accurately received by a mobile device without any issues of interoperability arising. However, large text documents are not *compatible* with small screens, and limited *usability* hinders use of the information.

Access to information needs to be provided that is compatible with the needs of the recipient in relation to:

○ Timeliness of when the information is needed and the frequency that the information needs to be updated.

○ Appropriateness, accuracy, and brevity required for the task.

○ Format, language, and presentation required so that the information is understood and used by the recipient.

Improving accessibility of information therefore involves both analysis of the information requirements of the task and the requirements of the context in which the information will be used to ensure compatibility. There is a difference between accessibility and usability. Accessibility focuses on providing the information required to the individual who needs the information. Usability refers to providing the information in a manner which meets an individual's needs, enabling the information to be used effectively. Nielsen (1994) describes usability of an information system interface as including properties such as the ease with which a person can learn how to use the interface, the ability of a person to remember how to use the interface because of cues in the design, the efficiency with which tasks can be completed, and the number of errors that may be made when using the interface. Improving the usability of information systems by removing technical barriers and making access more intuitive improves the accessibility of information.

7.2.4 ▶ Approaches to Improving Information Accessibility

Information must be useful to the recipient; this depends on matching the characteristics of information to requirements of the authorized recipient within the

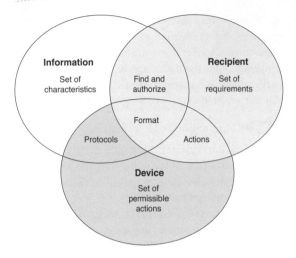

Figure 7.1 ▶ Key Components of Information Accessibility

permissible actions of the IT device (Figure 7.1). The protocols of the device the recipient is using to access the information need to be interoperable with the protocols used by the technology where the data are stored. The format of the information and the actions that can be performed on the information using the recipient's device need to be compatible with desired actions of the recipient.

Approaches to improve access to information relate to improving:

○ Information availability by the design of software tools that aid in the search and retrieval of relevant information.
○ Data interoperability through the development of open standards to support transmission of data between technological devices by agreed upon protocols.
○ Data compatibility by adherence to guidelines on interface design, which enable the recipient to access and use the information required.

These approaches focus on using technology to facilitate access to the organization's information by authorized individuals. Underpinning these approaches is a fundamental need to understand:

○ What information is needed.
○ Who needs the information.
○ Where the information is needed.
○ When the information is needed.
○ How the information is needed (in terms of presentation, granularity, and technical format).

This requires a detailed understanding of how the information is used in the organization and the specific needs of the individuals in the organization.

7.2.5 ▶ Role of Information Management Strategy in Improving Information Accessibility

Improving access to information in the organization requires information management to address the availability, interoperability, and compatibility of information.

The information management strategy needs to:

○ Identify the information available in the organization and specify who can access the information.
○ Document the location of information and provide training to help authorized individuals access available information.
○ Agree on standard data formats to facilitate data interoperability.
○ Define standard data structures to ensure data compatibility.
○ Ensure adherence to legislation and where possible implement recommendations on information accessibility.

7.3 ▶ Sharing Data

A key aim of an information management strategy is for data to be shared across business functions. IT enables data to be stored, shared, and transmitted across geographical, organizational, and departmental boundaries; however, without careful management there is a risk that islands of inconsistent data develop. Haug and Arlbjørn (2011) suggest that IT has had an adverse effect on data quality because the complexity of data management increases with the volume of data collected. For example, if several applications store customer data there is a risk that details may not be updated across all applications.

There is a tendency in organizations for individuals and departments to hoard data, perhaps believing that data provide a source of power, or due to fear that sharing data will highlight inaccuracies and limitations. As technology continues to make sharing data easier, the need to share data, and the expectation that data will be made available to others, is increasing. Organizations are finding that sharing data through e-business and social networking applications adds value, improves service, and initiates opportunities through the creation of trading relationships that were not previously apparent. Sharing data requires agreements on what data are to be shared, when, how, and by whom. There is also an expectation that the sharing of data will be reciprocated by other parties; however, there are both cultural and technical barriers to sharing data.

7.3.1 ▶ Problems of Sharing Data

An initial barrier to sharing data is a lack of awareness of the data available in the organization. The lack of visibility of data in organizations may be due to the formation of information silos. A key feature of a silo is that data and information are kept for the sole use of a limited area of the organization such as a team or department.

DEFINITION: An information silo occurs where data are captured, stored and used but the information is not readily accessible to other parts of the organization. The owners of the data prevent others accessing the data and therefore other areas of the business may be unaware of the existence of the data stored.

Silo is an agricultural term referring to separate independent grain stores. The term is also used to refer to staff working in silos, that is, working on their own and not sharing information with others. A silo culture reduces the ability for data to be shared in the organization so data are often recreated or purchased externally by other departments. This duplication of data incurs unnecessary cost and there is a risk of inconsistent data being used in different areas.

A silo culture is difficult to eradicate. Although technological solutions can be implemented to enable data to be accessed more widely in the organization, changing the organization's culture to encourage staff to share data is more difficult. Some areas of the organization may be accused of hoarding data and other areas of the organization may be reluctant to use data created by others, questioning the quality of the data and preferring to buy or create the data themselves. A lack of awareness of the availability and location of data in the organization can be a significant problem embedded in the organizational culture that the information management strategy needs to address. The technical problems can often be overcome much more easily and quickly than the social problems in an organization, which limit the ability to share information between departments, systems, and external collaborating partners.

When a willingness to share data has been established, the data need to be clearly understood in order to be used effectively. The context in which the data were captured or created, the units that the data represents, and the definition that forms the business rules acting on the data, need to be unambiguous.

Barriers to sharing data therefore include:

- Differences in definition and interpretation of terms.
- Lack of awareness of the data available in the organization.
- Lack of awareness of how to access the data available. This includes not knowing who to ask to gain authorization to access the data and how to physically access the data via different IT systems.
- Concerns relating to the quality of the data, which may be based on a poor understanding of how the data have been captured and maintained.
- Concerns that the data will not meet specific needs, which relate to the different ways departments may interpret data.
- Inconsistencies in the data due to different timescales used in the collection and analysis of data in different departments.
- Difficulties in reconciling data from different sources due to different coding systems.
- Lack of trust in the data captured from other departments.
- Length of time required to gain access to the data.

Sharing data is likely to highlight inconsistencies in information. This may be due to inconsistent data definitions or the use of different time frames. Such differences need to be understood and documented if data are to be effectively shared between organizational functions.

7.3.2 Processes for Improving Sharing Data in the Life Cycle

Improving the processes in the data life cycle outlined in Table 7.3 can help to overcome barriers to sharing data in the organization.

Table 7.3 Role of Data Sharing in the Data Life Cycle

Capture	Store and Retrieve	Use, Share, and Maintain	Archive and Destroy
Identifies the data captured in the organization to reduce duplication of effort and to record the data available to be shared. Establish common definitions and coding systems to enable data to be shared and integrated with data from other sources.	Provides guidance on who may access the data (defined by the data owners) and the procedures for requesting access to the data.	Encourages the sharing of data and the use of agreed upon data definitions to ensure data are interpreted appropriately.	Ensures the potential data requirements of the whole organization are considered by the data owner before archiving or purging data.

7.3.3 ▶ Role of Information Management Strategy in Sharing Data

The information management strategy creates the expectation that data will be shared, forcefully breaking down the silo culture. This involves facilitating cultural change and instigating barriers to prevent information silos being developed. For example, an organization can implement policies to prevent departments purchasing external data without authorization from the information manager. Policies are also needed to ensure that new information systems make use of existing data sources and enable data captured to be used in other systems across the organization.

The information management strategy needs to:

- Formulate a vision of an information-sharing culture.
- Initiate cultural change away from information silos.
- Develop barriers to the formation of information silos.
- Provide a means of increasing the visibility of the data available in the organization.
- Develop an infrastructure to support data sharing, which provides guidance on how to gain access to available data in the organization, subject to issues of security and privacy.
- Promote the benefits of sharing data between business functions and external collaborating partners.
- Review the opportunities and benefits for sharing data throughout the organization, its supply chain, and customer relationships.

The quality of the data becomes more prominent as data are shared. Staff will be more willing to use data from other departments if there is confidence in the quality of the data available. Issues of data quality need to be addressed to avoid the problems of poor quality data disseminating through the organization.

7.4 ▶ Improving Data Quality

Information management aims to improve the quality of data available in organizations. If the data are of poor quality, the data cannot be relied on, which will affect how data are interpreted to inform actions and decisions. *Data quality* is a subjective term, interpreted in different ways in different contexts.

7.4.1 ▶ Measures of Data Quality

One view is that the quality of data is intrinsic to the data (Inmon *et al.*, 1997). Measures of data quality, such as relevance and usefulness, depend on the particular context in which data are being used (Haug & Arlbjørn, 2011). Data need to be fit for purpose but different people will have different preferences and different needs in relation to the characteristics of data. Fitness for purpose is therefore subjective, depending on both the purpose for which the data are being used and the individual using the data. For example, different levels of accuracy of data are needed for decisions at different levels in the management hierarchy. Problems of data quality occur when data are collected for one purpose but later used for purposes for which the data were not intended (Olson, 2003).

Defining measures of data quality is difficult as both the definition of a measure and the application of a measure is subjective. For example, O'Donoghue *et al.* (2011) define timeliness as the frequency with which data are captured. Eurostat (2003) defines timeliness in relation to the time taken from an event occurring to the time when data about the event is available. A further interpretation of timeliness is the availability of up-to-date data in an appropriate format such that the data can be acted on.

Eurostat (2003) defines the following additional quality measures for statistical data:

- Relevance to the needs of the individual.
- Punctuality in relation to the time when the data were predicted to be available and the date the data were made available.
- Accessibility in terms of the actions needed to obtain the data which, in the context of the European Union, may involve the ordering of reports.
- Clarity of the data, including the use of diagrams and metadata.
- Comparability of the data in different periods and geographical areas.
- Coherence, the reliability in which the data can be used for different purposes.

Chapter 2 listed a range of characteristics of information that can be used to evaluate the quality of information. Table 7.4 provides further definitions of criteria used to assess data quality.

7.4.2 ▶ Processes for Improving Data Quality in the Life Cycle

The quality of data can be influenced throughout the stages of the data life cycle. For example, consistency in the approach used for data collection and the completeness of all the required data parameters being collected are data quality measures (O'Donoghue *et al.*, 2011) in the first stage of the data life cycle. At the data capture stage, the correctness and validity of the data become imprinted. Data can be considered to be of poor quality if inaccurate, invalid, or incomplete data are captured. For example, inaccurate data may be deliberately entered into a computer system to work around business rules

Table 7.4 ▶ Definitions of Data Quality Criteria

Quality Criteria	Definition
Accuracy	Data value resembles the true value of the element represented and satisfies the degree of variance required for the purpose in which the data are to be used.
Trusted	Belief that the data are correct based on the subjective understanding of the way in which the data have been collected and maintained.
Understood	Data values can be correctly interpreted and used to inform decisions.
Validity	Compliance with the accepted values identified in the data definition.

preventing a process being completed. The data capture stage is the most appropriate place to check the accuracy of the data, at the source. Validation and verification procedures are therefore needed at the data collection stage to ensure that the data captured are accurate and complete, improving the quality of data in the organization.

When data are transmitted and stored, validation procedures can be used to check that data are transmitted accurately. For example, a parity bit can be added to the binary digits that comprise the electronic data transmitted between IT systems so that the bit value of the data transmitted is either set to an odd or even number. The receiving device then confirms that the parity of the data transmission received is as expected.

When data have been stored securely, controls are needed to prevent any changes to the data that may adversely affect data quality. The quality of data needs to be maintained during data processing to ensure accuracy, particularly in calculations. When data have been accurately processed, the data need to be interpreted and used effectively. The accuracy with which the data are interpreted (O'Donoghue *et al.*, 2011) is a measure of quality relating to the use of data.

Table 7.5 categorizes criteria for assessing the quality of data within the main stages of the data life cycle. Some criteria, such as appropriate volume, apply to data in all stages of the life cycle; other criteria, such as ease of interpretation, are more relevant when sharing and using data.

Quiz 7.1
Data Quality Measures

7.4.3 ▶ Approaches to Improving Data Quality

Quality data are needed to ensure that the decisions made in an organization are based on accurate data, however, organizations need to balance the requirement to improve

the quality of data against the costs involved in achieving the quality improvements. For example, it may be possible to achieve 100 per cent accuracy in data collection but the cost to the organization may be excessive. Inmon *et al.* (1997) argue that accuracy should not be the main characteristic of data quality and suggest that simple and consistent data are more important than complete accuracy. While much attention is given to data accuracy, accuracy needs to be considered in relation to completeness too.

In Scenario 7.2 the *part stock levels* and *sales dates* in the report are accurate. The report correctly states that starter sockets have not been sold. It would be reasonable to consider not purchasing any more starter sockets based on this report, however, further data show that starter sockets are used by Match Lighting in the manufacture of fluorescent tube lighting units. The decisions based on the information derived from this report could be inappropriate because the data in the report are accurate but incomplete. The lack of consistent data definition for *part* has led to poor quality information being reported. The significance of the impact of poor data quality varies in different industries but all organizations need quality data.

Link 7.2
Consequences of Poor Decisions Based on Poor Quality Data

Improvements in data quality can have a range of positive impacts on an organization including:

○ Cost savings by reducing operating costs, rework, and fines (Loshin, 2010).
○ Improved customer satisfaction and service quality (Umar *et al.*, 1999).
○ Productivity through improvements to business processes, reduction in delays of raw materials, and removal of bottlenecks in the value chain.
○ Reduction in risks and increased compliance (Loshin, 2010).

Table 7.5 Quality Characteristics in the Data Life Cycle

Capture	Store and Retrieve	Use, Share, and Maintain	Archive and Destroy
Accuracy.	Accessibility.	Accessibility.	Accuracy.
Appropriate volume.	Accuracy.	Accuracy.	Appropriate volume.
Authority.	Appropriate volume.	Appropriate volume.	Appropriateness of the format.
Clarity.	Authority.	Appropriateness of the format.	Authority.
Cohesiveness.	Availability.	Authority.	Cohesiveness.
Completeness.	Comparability.	Availability.	Comparability.
Comprehensive.	Completeness.	Awareness of bias.	Completeness.
Consistency.	Conciseness.	Believability.	Comprehensive.
Convenience.	Consistency.	Clarity.	Consistency.
Correctness.	Consistent representation.	Cohesiveness.	Consistent representation.
Currency.	Content.	Comparability.	Content.
Efficiency.	Contextual.	Completeness.	Contextual.
Format.	Convenient.	Comprehensive.	Correctness.
Freedom from bias.	Correctness.	Conciseness.	Efficiency.
Granularity.	Currency.	Consistency.	Format.
Importance.	Ease of understanding.	Consistent representation.	Granularity.
Information to noise ratio.	Efficiency.	Content.	Importance.
Informativeness.	Flexibility.	Contextual.	Latency.
Latency.	Format.	Convenient.	Level of detail.
Level of detail.	Granularity.	Correctness.	Objectivity.
Objectivity.	Information to noise ratio.	Currency.	Orientation.
Orientation.	Interpretability.	Ease of interpretation.	Portability.
Portability.	Latency.	Ease of manipulation.	Precision.
Precision.	Level of detail.	Ease of understanding.	Privacy.
Privacy.	Meaningful.	Efficiency.	Relevancy.
Quantitativeness.	Objectivity.	Flexibility.	Reliability.
Relevancy.	Orientation.	Format.	Representation.
Reliability.	Portability.	Freedom from bias.	Response time.
Representation.	Precision.	Granularity.	Secure.
Reputational consistency.	Privacy.	Importance.	Sufficiency.
Response time.	Relevancy.	Information to noise ratio.	Timeliness.
Scope.	Reliability.	Informativeness.	Traceable.
Secure.	Representation.	Interpretability.	Usability.
Sufficiency.	Representational consistency.	Latency.	Well-defined.
Timeliness.	Reputation.	Level of detail.	
Traceable.	Response time.	Maintainability.	
Unambiguousness.	Scope.	Meaningful.	
Understandability.	Secure.	Objectivity.	
Validity.	Timeliness.	Orientation.	
Verifiable.	Traceable.	Popularity.	
Well-defined.	Understandability.	Portability.	
	Usability.	Precision.	
	Verifiable.	Privacy.	
	Well-defined.	Quantitativeness.	
		Relevancy.	
		Reliability.	
		Representation.	
		Representational consistency.	
		Reputation.	
		Response time.	
		Scope.	
		Secure.	
		Sufficiency.	
		Timeliness.	
		Traceable.	
		Unambiguousness.	
		Understandability.	
		Usability.	
		Verifiable.	
		Well-defined.	

Improving the quality of data involves cleaning data and changing the processes that may pollute the data (Umar *et al.*, 1999). This requires the development of quality metrics, monitoring the data life cycle for pollution, and using controls to maintain the required quality standards.

Data quality can be improved by:

○ Controlling the quality of data captured at data entry.
○ Defining and implementing business rules consistently.
○ Maintaining a record of when data were changed and by whom.
○ Assigning ownership and responsibility for data quality.

It is important that all staff who capture, amend, and use data appreciate the potential implications that may arise from their actions. Validation checks can be applied to ensure that a data value entered is consistent with the values expected for the data item; however, a data value may be valid but inaccurate. Verification checks can be used to check that the data entered are believed to be correct, usually by asking for the data to be re-entered.

7.4.4 Role of Information Management Strategy in Improving Data Quality

The information management strategy needs to:

○ Determine metrics to demonstrate the impact of data quality on organizational performance. The metrics may include the volume of rework required, time taken to complete a process, or volume of throughput.
○ Establish targets to improve data quality.
○ Develop an infrastructure to improve the quality of data throughout the data life cycle, which includes definitions of information management roles and responsibilities, and a programme of actions.
○ Facilitate the development of a culture of responsibility for data quality.
○ Review the effectiveness of actions taken to improve the quality of data.
○ Communicate the positive impact on the performance of the organization achieved through improvements in data quality.

The organization needs to maintain the quality of data and ensure that data are captured, transmitted, stored, used, and destroyed appropriately using secure processes. Data definitions play an important role in data quality, specifying the business rules associated with the data to ensure that data integrity is maintained.

Data integrity is an aspect of data quality that is determined by the business rules represented in the information architecture and documented in the data dictionary. The data dictionary and information architecture provide the basis for data quality in the organization. Clean quality data, which can be relied on as being accurate and up to date, are essential for organizations.

7.5 Defining Data

Many of the problems experienced by organizations relating to information management derive from the lack of agreed meanings associated with data items. A clear, unambiguous definition of a data item is an aspect of data quality (Umar *et al.*, 1999). Well-defined data that are used consistently in accordance with the agreed definitions, are essential to ensure that the organization can rely on accurate quality information as a basis for decision-making. If data are misunderstood, information may be interpreted incorrectly, which may result in no action or inappropriate action being taken. Every day in organizations the lack of clear definitions of business terms is skated over and is difficult to eradicate.

7.5.1 Problems of Defining Data

Most data are used in more than one area of the organization, therefore agreed upon definitions are essential to ensure that data are used and interpreted consistently. Agreeing upon data definitions is difficult; the process involves staff from across the organization and takes time. There is an assumption that words used and accepted accurately describe reality. Words are not the most accurate tools for a complete analysis of reality, but if a word works most of the time, the word is not questioned. It is only when words cause problems that their use is scrutinized (Shekleton, 1991; Boisot, 1994). Defining data is inherently difficult as the process requires aspects of the business environment, which are taken for granted, to become questioned. This questions a person's perception of reality and finally reality itself, initiating reactions of anxiety, defensiveness, and avoidance (Shekleton, 1991). McGarry (1981) points out that it is possible to recognize a sparrow without being able to define one. Questioning definitions is often perceived as a threat, particularly in instances where data sharing is required across functional and organizational boundaries. Business areas aggressively defend *their* data, terminology, and definitions.

Definitions are needed to communicate ideas (McGarry, 1981), however, effective communication is not about transmitting and reproducing an image in the mind of the recipient; effective communication modifies the recipient's view of the world (Boisot, 1994). Table 7.6 illustrates different ways in which an employee is defined in Match Lighting and the implications of the different definitions.

The precise definition of an employee is important because the definition will change how the data are used

Table 7.6 Definitions of Employee

Potential Definition: An Employee Is:	Implications of the Definition
Someone who is paid by Match Lighting.	Tungsten UK is paid by Match Lighting to provide tungsten filaments. This definition suggests that a supplier is an employee.
An individual who is paid by Match Lighting.	Mark Edwards was paid compensation by Match Lighting for the inconvenience and loss of custom caused by an incorrect order being delivered. This definition suggests that a customer is an employee.
An individual who is paid by Match Lighting for providing a service to the organization.	May Lee is paid by Match Lighting to work on a project to upgrade the IT network. May is self-employed. This definition suggests that a contractor is an employee.
An individual who is paid by Match Lighting for providing a service to the organization and is not self-employed.	Alfie is a German student at the local university. Match Lighting pays Alfie to help in the distribution department for six weeks during the summer. This definition suggests that temporary staff are employees. This may be true but further investigation is needed to ensure that the business rules relating to employees (such as holiday and pension entitlements) are valid for temporary staff.
An individual who is paid by Match Lighting for providing a service to the organization and has a contract of employment that does not have a fixed end date.	Individuals are employees and remain employees if they are: ○ Absent due to illness or holiday. ○ Retired from Match Lighting. Further investigation of the business rules associated with employees is needed to verify the accuracy of this definition.

Agreed Upon Definition:

An employee is a permanently employed individual who is paid by Match Lighting via the payroll system for providing a service, full-time or part-time, to the organization and has a contract of employment, which does not have a fixed end date, who has a signed contract of employment. An employee is classed as being inactive when they leave or retire from Match Lighting.

in relation to payroll records, tax and national insurance payments, legal rights of staff classed as employees, and the responsibilities of the organization. Different departments will define terms differently. Scenario 7.2 discusses different interpretations of what is meant by a *part* in Match Lighting. A key problem in defining data is that in creating a definition, the thing being defined is to some extent stripped of the context that gives it meaning.

Language is a system of symbols by which members of a community give meaning to their environment (McGarry, 1981). Every area of human activity has its own specialist terminology, separating those in the group from those excluded (Dingley *et al.*, 2000). Over time a tacit understanding of terms in a business area evolves but as staff move between departments or leave the organization, valuable information and tacit knowledge are lost.

Scenario 7.2

Defining a Part in Match Lighting

Anya, a member of the sales staff, created a report to show when parts were last sold. Table 7.7 shows an extract of the report.

Part Sales Report				
Part Number	**Part Name**	**Stock Quantity**	**Stock Units**	**Days Since Last Sale**
12154421	10w light bulb	3,000	3	1
SD8512	Light bulb 10w	1,581	100	
12165871	1m florescent tube	10,000	1,000	5
SD9741	Starter socket	1	1,000	
MLKEYS12	Key ring	250		105

Table 7.7 Extract from Sales Report

Scenario 7.2 Continued

Anya discusses the report with Molly, a colleague in the warehouse.

Anya:	'I ran a sales report to identify when parts had last been sold and the report contained over 50,000 parts.'
Molly:	'The report can't be right. There are only 1,800 parts in the current catalogue.'
Anya:	'That's what I thought but the report includes things like starter sockets.'
Molly:	'We don't sell starter sockets; we buy them and use them to make fluorescent tube lights. Starter sockets are components, not parts.'
Anya:	'The report also includes things like key rings and pens.'
Molly:	'They are merchandise, not parts.'
Anya:	'The report even includes lamps with high mercury content that have been obsolete for a number of years.'

When Anya produced the report, the information system generated a list of part numbers from the part database. The system searched the sales order data to identify the date when the part number was last sold and then calculated the number of days since that date.

The report shows that there are 3,000 packs of light bulbs in stock, which each contain three light bulbs, and that light bulbs were last sold yesterday.

The parts department buys light bulbs in boxes of 100 from the supplier S. D. Fittings. There are 1,581 bulbs in stock and there is no date when this item was last sold. The parts department creates a new part number when a part is purchased for the first time, or purchased for the first time from a different supplier.

There are 10,000 fluorescent tubes that have been manufactured by Match Lighting and loaded into boxes of 1,000 to be used in the manufacture of lighting units or sold separately.

The parts department buys in starter sockets which are used in the manufacture of fluorescent tube lighting units. There is one box in stock containing 1,000 sockets.

The marketing department is responsible for promotional merchandise. When a new item is commissioned, the marketing department creates a new part number and adds an entry to the part database. The marketing department only records the number of items available to be used for promotion and does not enter details of stock units. The figure in the days since the last sale column is therefore misleading as merchandise is not sold.

Match Lighting needs to define what is meant by the term *part*. Anya asked several departments to explain what they understand by the term *part*. The responses are shown in Table 7.8.

Department	Definition
Sales	'A part is something we sell, such as a light bulb, lampshade, or switching disc.'
Parts	'A part is something we buy, such as a tungsten filament, glass, or cardboard.'
Manufacturing	'A part is something we make, such as a ceiling rose or fluorescent tube assembly.'
Engineering	'A part is something we use to make something else, such as a starter socket or tube holder.'
Marketing	'A part is something we brand for publicity, such as a pen, key ring, or baseball cap.'

Table 7.8 Definitions of a Part

After talking to these departments, Anya proposed that:

○ A product is something we sell.
○ An item is something we buy.
○ A part is something we make.
○ A component is something we use to make something else.
○ An item of merchandise is something we brand for publicity.

The proposal was not well received. Eeyo in engineering complained, 'An item, a part, a component and an item of merchandise could also be a product, so why are separate terms needed?'

Anya explained that the definition of the part affects the data attributes collected about a part, the way in which the data are interpreted and used, and the business rules that relate to the data.

Anya needs to identify parts that have not been sold in the last six months to inform decisions about parts to retire from the catalogue. Parts that are not selling well are difficult to identify using the current part records.

7.5.2 Approaches to Defining Data

Data definition is a core process in information management and supports the construction of the information architecture. The initial task of defining all data in the organization can seem impossible and must be tackled in stages. Priority should be given to master data items such as *product*, *customer*, and *supplier* as these items are the most important to the organization. This master data will be the most complex to define as the information derived from these data will be used in different ways in different areas of the organization.

A data owner should be appointed before attempting to define the data. The data owner can then investigate how the data are used in different business processes and seek to derive an agreed upon definition of the data. The difficulty of this task should not be underestimated. It will require careful negotiation and practical support from both the information manager and the Information Management Committee to secure an agreed upon definition for master data.

Figure 7.2 shows the data owner defining where data are used in the organization and how the data maps to physical databases. Different departments will create different definitions of a *part*. A new definition is agreed upon that can be used consistently across the organization and information systems. Although all business functions agree on the *part* definition, each function will only use some of the *part* attributes. The *part* entity will therefore be fragmented, with some attributes stored in different physical locations and used in different information systems.

The process of defining data will seek agreement on attribute length and structure, helping to improve the integration of data across departments and information systems. This will also help to identify data that are not currently captured and data that are needlessly replicated in different departments.

When definitions have been agreed upon, consideration needs to be given to the processes to be followed when a change is proposed to data. The allocation of data owners to data items provides a single point of contact to discuss changes to data definitions. The accuracy and integrity of data rely on the consistent application of the agreed upon data definition; misuse of data fields is a common cause of dirty data. Data authors are responsible for agreeing on the data values that can be entered into data fields, adhering to the attribute definitions and structures defined in the data dictionary by data owners. The data definition and data codes embed the quality characteristics of the data. For example, the attribute length of quantitative data determines the accuracy of the data value to be captured.

The data author will consult staff in all areas of the business to seek agreement of: meaningful coding systems, valid values that an attribute of a data item can store, and guidelines on the use of acceptable abbreviations that can be used in text-based fields. The agreed upon guidelines for valid values of data attributes will be documented in the data dictionary. This will help to improve the consistent use of data fields and reduce misuse, which contributes to data duplication and impedes data integration between departments and systems.

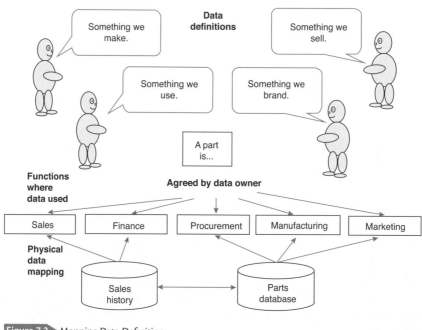

Figure 7.2 Mapping Data Definitions

7.5.3 Documenting Data Definitions

Data owners are responsible for documenting the agreed upon data definitions in the data dictionary. The definitions can be referred to when any queries arise relating to data in the organization. A data dictionary is a centralized repository of metadata about the information in the organization. The data dictionary includes the agreed upon definition of the data; the format and structure of the data; relationships to other data; and business rules specifying how data can be used.

Business Rules

When a data owner defines data, they are specifying how information is used in the organization; they specify the business rules for the information.

DEFINITION: A **business rule** specifies how information is used in the organization and its relationship to other information. It determines the controls that need to be imposed to structure data and maintain data integrity.

Figure 7.3 shows how business rules can be extracted from the definition of a *product* defined by the data owner in Figure 7.2.

The business rules show how items of information (entities) are interrelated and can be shown diagrammatically in the information architecture. Figure 7.4 is an extract from an information architecture, which shows the business rules for a *product* defined in Figure 7.3. Consumers are not included in the information architecture since they are out of the scope of information currently held by Match Lighting. Further information would need to be identified by the data owner to complete the information architecture to define the determinacy and cardinality of the relationships

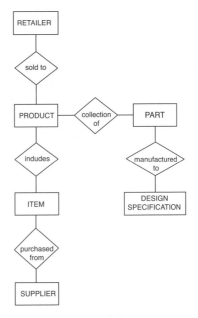

Figure 7.4 Draft Information Architecture of Business Rules

(discussed in Chapter 4). For example, the data owner would need to consider the following questions:

○ Can the details of a product be captured if the product has not yet been sold to a retailer? This would mean the relationship between *product* and *retailer* is optional.

○ Must a part be manufactured by a design specification? This would mean the relationship between *part* and *design specification* was mandatory.

○ Can an item be purchased from more than one supplier? Can more than one item be purchased from the same supplier? This would mean the relationship between *item* and *supplier* is many-to-many.

The information architecture represents the information in Match Lighting at a conceptual level, that is, independent of information systems and physical IT systems in which data are used and stored. The architecture can be used by data owners to identify the potential impact of changes proposed to data items in the future.

Data Repository

Data definitions can be mapped to where data are physically stored so that any potential implications arising from making changes to data definitions and structures can be identified. A data repository provides a mapping between the logical data dictionary used by the business and the physical data dictionary used by IT staff. The physical data dictionary records where data are physically located on storage devices (shown in Figure 7.2). The data repository enables the impact of potential changes to data to be analysed. For example, if the length of the attribute

---

Definition of Product

"A product is a physical thing that is offered *for sale* by Match Lighting to retailers. It *includes* items that are *purchased* by Match Lighting directly from its suppliers, individual *parts* that are *manufactured* by Match Lighting *using* a design specification, and collections of parts that are *packaged* as a final product for retailers to *sell* to consumers."

Key: Potential entity and *business rules*.

Business rules from the definition include:

- A product is offered for sale to retailers.
- A product includes items.
- An item is purchased from suppliers.
- A product includes parts.
- A part is manufactured using a design specification.
- Parts are packaged to form a product.

Figure 7.3 Business Rules in a Data Definition

prod_num changes from a nine-digit integer to a ten-digit one, the logical data dictionary is used to determine the logical data entities that may be affected. The dictionary also identifies the other data owners who will need to be consulted about the proposed change. The data repository is used to identify the physical data records held in different storage systems that the IT staff will need to change in order to implement the new attribute length.

7.5.4 Processes for Defining Data in the Life Cycle

Data definitions are used in processes throughout the data life cycle shown in Table 7.9.

7.5.5 Role of Information Management Strategy in Defining Data

Identifying and defining the information resources currently available in the organization are essential to avoid duplication, to act on the information available, and to respond to requests under the Freedom of Information Act 2000.

The information management strategy needs to:

○ Emphasize the importance of defining data in the organization.

○ Formulate a vision of all data being defined in a central data dictionary, which is used to assess the impact of changes to data and information systems.
○ Develop an infrastructure to support the development and maintenance of the data dictionary.
○ Prepare a practical action plan to define data in the organization. An example plan is shown in Figure 7.5.
○ Establish processes to resolve issues of conflict that arise when defining data.
○ Regularly review the progress of developing the data dictionary.

When data definitions have been agreed upon, a process of data cleaning is needed to ensure that the data definition is applied consistently across the organization to improve the quality of the data. This checks that the existing data adhere to the data definitions and identifies the validation and verification controls required to ensure clean data are captured and maintained in the future.

Defining data is a huge task, but planned information systems and IT projects provide the opportunity to define data and improve the quality of information. This is demonstrated in Scenario 7.3.

Table 7.9 ▶ Role of Data Definitions in the Data Life Cycle

Capture	Store and Retrieve	Use, Share, and Maintain	Archive and Destroy
Specifies the attributes of the data to be captured, when the data are to be captured, and which business function captures the data. Indicates the validation and verification rules to be applied to the data captured. Identifies the business rules to maintain the integrity of the data.	Specifies the data to be stored. Identifies the roles within the organization, who can retrieve the data and the level of detail they may retrieve.	Specifies the business rules for using and maintaining the data to retain the integrity and quality of the data. Identifies the roles within the organization: who can use, share, and change the data.	Specifies when the data can be archived and defines the period for which the data must be retained. Indicates when the data can be deleted and any requirements relating to data purging (for example, the secure destruction of confidential data).

1. Assign data owners to data items.
2. Start with the master data items and define one item at a time, such as *part* or *customer*.
3. Refer to the documentation of existing information systems developed to identify in which information systems the data item is used.
4. Identify the attributes captured about the data item in the different systems.
5. Identify each area of the organization that uses the data item.
6. For each area, identify the specific data attributes the area captures, changes or uses and then develop a definition of the data item for each area.
7. Compare the definitions and investigate differences.
8. Strive to formulate a consensus definition, noting any variances in how the data are used or interpreted in different areas of the organization.
9. Document the agreed upon data definition in the data dictionary.
10. Maintain a record of the status of each definition to indicate the degree to which the definition is approved by all areas of the organization.

Figure 7.5 ▶ Plan for Defining Data

Scenario 7.3

Information Management Committee in Match Lighting

At the first meeting of the Information Management Committee Mrs Winters, the Information Manager, outlines how she plans to implement the information management strategy.

Mrs Winters:	'The implementation of the information management strategy is going to take considerable time. The problems with data have evolved over a number of years and it will take years to undo them and to establish procedures to ensure that similar problems are avoided in the future. We therefore need to identify the priorities for the current year. We will start by establishing data owners and definitions for the key data in the organization. From there we can develop the policies for the data items defined and then initiate the clean-up projects needed to address the problems with the data. Then we need to implement controls to ensure that the cleaned data stay clean. The same approach will be repeated with the next set of data items. It is important to start with the master data items first. These are the main items of information on which the organization depends. Match Lighting needs to have information about products, customers, orders, resources, suppliers, and finance. These are the main inputs to and outputs from Match Lighting. Although these are the most important and most frequently used items of information, they are likely to be the most challenging terms to define as they are used differently across areas of the business. From there, we can start to branch out to other information items. I have asked Mr Cook from the IT department to be a member of this Information Management Committee. He will help with resourcing the IT aspects of information management. He is here today to outline the IT plan for the year. If we can coordinate our activities with the current IT projects, we can use the opportunity to clean data as new systems are being developed and current systems are being maintained. This will provide us with the resources needed to address information management issues. It will also help to ensure that new systems do not start life by using inaccurate data.'
Mr Cook:	'The main project for this year is the deployment of product data in the data warehouse. It would be useful if we could clean the data before the data enter the warehouse. There is also a smaller project which will implement a new interface to the product catalogue for the sales staff. It would be timely if issues surrounding the definition and use of product and product sales data were addressed this year.'
Mr Chen:	'I am a manufacturing supervisor. One of the main issues for us is that product codes are used inconsistently across the different product ranges. Will this be addressed this year too?'
Mrs Winters:	'Yes, when a clear definition of a product has been agreed then it will be possible to agree on the product coding structure. This is one of the priorities identified during the development of the information management strategy.'
Ms Raven:	'I am representing customer services so if customer data are not being considered this year, do I need to be here?'
Mrs Winters:	'Customer data will be defined this year, and your input will also be needed to ensure that the product definitions meet your requirements too. As you work directly with customers you will be very aware of the problems that are caused by the current coding structures.'
Ms Raven:	'It would help if we could easily access a list of the current coding structures. At the moment we have to search the product catalogue and it takes too long when we are talking to a customer.'
Mr Chen:	'We have a printed list of the codes. I can send it to you.'
Ms Raven:	'That would save us so much time.'
Mrs Winters:	'It is small actions such as this that can make a difference to your work, which is why it is so important for all areas of the business to attend these meetings. The plan for this year should include: ○ Assign data owners to products, customers, orders, resources, suppliers, and finance data. ○ Define products, customers, orders, and suppliers. ○ Specify the policy rules for products and customers. ○ Define the cleaning projects needed for product data. ○ Implement the policy rules for products.'

Summary

There are generally three complaints about information in organizations: there is too much information; there is insufficient information; or the information is of poor quality. When there is too much information, information overload occurs as staff are unable to use the information. Information overload can be exacerbated by IT due to the ease with which information can be created and disseminated. Analysis of the information required in organizations enables IT to provide access to relevant and timely information to support organizational goals.

Access to information can be hindered by both technical and organizational factors. Technical factors affecting the accessibility of information include interoperability and compatibility of data. Interoperability relates to the technical format of the data required by the IT devices used to access and store the data. Compatibility of data considers whether the data are compatible with the IT device and usage requirements of the individual accessing the data. A further barrier to sharing data is concern about data quality. Data quality can be improved by implementing validation and verification controls throughout the data life cycle. Organizational factors affecting information accessibility include lack of awareness that the data exist in the organization and staff reluctance to share data. Silos can develop in organizations where data are hoarded. Effective information management encourages data to be shared throughout the organization.

As data are shared, data definitions need to be agreed upon to ensure that data are used and interpreted consistently. Defining data items is difficult as it challenges the way terms are used in different areas of the organization. Planned IT projects provide the opportunity to define data as information systems are changed, replaced, or new systems are implemented in the organization. When data definitions have been agreed on, data must be cleaned to ensure that the data stored in the organization conforms to the data format and agreed-upon structures. Approaches to clean data are discussed in Chapter 8.

Reviewing Scenario 7.1

The information manager, Mrs Kerry Winters, needs to resolve two main issues: how to access staff resources to implement the information management strategy, and how to start implementing the strategy. Match Lighting's Board of Directors have been involved in the formulation and approval of the information management strategy. The directors now need to ensure that Mrs Winters has access to the resources she needs to implement the strategy. The information management strategy (Chapter 6) identified the appointment of information stewards in each division and the need for data owners and data authors. Mrs Winters needs to oversee the appointment of information stewards and work with colleagues to ensure that the information stewards are allocated time to work with her. Data owners and authors can then be appointed by the information stewards.

Mrs Winters will develop an implementation plan for the information strategy. The plan will include specific projects to improve access to information and to improve the quality of information. A number of IT projects will already be planned in Match Lighting. Mrs Winters can take the opportunity provided by these projects to improve information management. She will need to focus on master data as improving the quality of master data will have a significant impact on many areas of the organization.

The information management strategy identified a number of performance measures, reflecting Match Lighting's priorities for improving information management. Mrs Winters will work with the information stewards to identify opportunities for quick wins, relatively small pieces of work that will have an immediate positive effect on information management. This will help to demonstrate the benefits of information management at all levels in the organization.

Exercise 7.1

1 What is information paralysis and how is it caused?
2 Explain the difference between pull technologies and push technologies.
3 What are the effects of information overload?
4 Give an example of how someone may demonstrate poor information responsibility which contributes to information overload.
5 Explain the difference between feasibility and acceptability.
6 If two computer systems are interoperable, what does this mean?
7 Explain the difference between accessibility and usability.
8 What are the three components of information accessibility?
9 What is an information silo?
10 Why is a silo culture difficult to eradicate?
11 List four barriers to sharing data.
12 Why might data be inconsistent?
13 Why is fitness for purpose a subjective measure of data quality?
14 Give two definitions of timeliness of data.

15 Why might inaccurate data be deliberately entered into a computer system?

16 At what stage in the data life cycle should the accuracy of data be checked?

17 Explain how a data value can be valid but inaccurate.

18 Why is defining data difficult?

19 Who is responsible for gaining agreement of a data definition?

20 What is a business rule?

Link 7.3
Answers to Exercise 7.1

Activities 7.1

1 Propose a definition for a *merchandise item* in Match Lighting, discussed in Scenario 7.2.

2 Identify quality measures from Table 7.5 for assessing the quality of the *product* data.

3 Extract business rules from the following definition of an *item*.

'An item is purchased from a supplier and may be used in a product. An item may be presented in a promotional merchandise set given to potential customers'.

4 Extend Figure 7.4 to include the business rules defined for an item defined in Activity 7.1.3.

5 Prepare a presentation to explain to Match Lighting how information overload could be reduced.

6 Apply the definition of employee in Table 7.6 to determine whether Mrs Winters, Alfie, and May Lee are employees of Match Lighting.

Discussion Questions 7.1

1 To what extent do you agree with the statement that there is too much information available?

2 How does the organizational culture influence information overload?

3 In Scenario 7.2, how should the definition of a *part* be resolved?

4 How can information silos be reduced in organizations?

5 What factors affect the usability of an information system?

6 Which are the most important measures of data quality and why?

7 Why does an organization need to develop a data dictionary rather than adopting definitions published in, for example, the Oxford English dictionary?

8 Who is responsible for the accuracy of information?

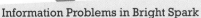

Scenario 8.1

Information Problems in Bright Spark

Larry sat in the boardroom with members of Bright Spark's executive management team accompanied by reams of paper, reports generated from information systems across the organization. The purpose of the meeting was to prepare the annual report outlining the performance across Bright Spark's chain of stores. The report needed to include information about the number of orders received, number of items sold, total sales for the year, the overall operating profit, and the profitability of different products. Finding this fundamental information was proving to be more difficult than first anticipated.

'This report states that every customer placed an order with us last year. That can't be right, can it?' asked Larry.

'Yes,' replied Clare. 'We sent a copy of our latest product catalogue to every customer. The system would not let us print customer address labels without an order so we set up the mail shot as a customer order.'

'Does this mean that we can't tell how many orders were really received last year?' asked Larry.

'We could find the information by running a query on the number of customers who placed orders of more than zero pence,' suggested John.

'More than one penny,' corrected Clare. 'The system would not allow us to enter an order for zero pence so we charged one penny for the product catalogue and then raised a credit note for one penny for each customer.'

'Could we work out what percentage of customers placed an order last year?' asked Larry.

'That would be difficult,' explained John. 'A customer may have more than one account; for example, if they have different stores there may be a separate account for each store so we can only tell if a store ordered in the last 12 months, not a customer.'

Alan then added, 'Customers may have more than one address – a delivery address and an invoice address – so I guess we could run a query on the number of orders that relate to an invoice address. This may take some time.'

'We found that some customers received more than one catalogue at the same address,' said Clare. 'Some customers seemed to have different account numbers for the same address.'

'*Why is it so difficult to find out basic information about the organization?*' asked Larry. '*We invest heavily in computers and database systems. Why can't they produce the reports we need?*'

Learning Outcomes

The learning outcomes of this chapter are to:

- Identify the causes of dirty data.
- Implement approaches to clean data.
- Integrate fragmented data.
- Review causes of inconsistent information.

- Resolve problems of incompatible data and conflicting information.
- Introduce approaches to recover corrupted information.

Introduction

The information management strategy aims to provide a consistent and coherent set of data that can be shared by staff across organizational functions. Defining data provides standard formats and structures for the data in the organization, which enables the data to be more easily shared and used consistently in different areas of the organization. When data definitions have been agreed upon, a programme of data cleaning is needed to ensure that the data values held in the organization conform to the agreed upon data definitions. This chapter explains how to clean data and how to implement controls to avoid data becoming dirty in the future.

Information requires data to be gathered from information systems across the organization and may highlight inconsistencies in data. For example, different attribute names and coding systems may be used by different information systems. Approaches to reconcile data are discussed. As data are integrated to produce reports, conflicting information may be generated. The causes of conflicting information and approaches to recover corrupted information are then outlined. The chapter concludes by reviewing the key information management processes needed to implement the information management strategy.

8.1 ▶ Cleaning Dirty Data

Data definitions determine data structures and data values required by the organization. One way of measuring data quality is in terms of the validity of data values, checking that all data values are present, consistent with one another, not duplicated, and are linked appropriately to other data (Loshin, 2010). Business rules defined in the data dictionary provide a formal specification of the:

○ Range of data values that are valid for an attribute.
○ Type of data that can be stored in an attribute.
○ Number of characters that can be stored in an attribute.
○ Relationships between entities.
○ Cardinality and determinacy of relationships between entities.

Data that are of poor quality, violating business rules, are referred to as being dirty.

DEFINITION: **Dirty data** are data of poor quality that may be inaccurate, incomplete, or inconsistent. Dirty data violate the business rules of data integrity and do not meet the organization's requirements for quality data. Poor quality data may lead to poor business decisions and adversely affect all aspects of the organization's value chain.

Over time, data can become inaccurate and incomplete. This can happen for a number of reasons, for example,

data may be incomplete at the point of capture (a post code may not be known) or mistakes may be made entering the information. In such cases the data become dirty, of poor quality, and need to be cleaned. Cleaning data involves verifying, validating, and correcting the data stored in the organization so that data are consistent with the agreed upon data definitions. Procedures then need to be developed and implemented to ensure that data remain clean by making changes to both manual procedures and information technology (IT) systems.

8.1.1 ▶ Causes of Dirty Data

Data can become dirty or corrupted in organizations in a number of ways, such as through accidental or malicious acts, incomplete data fields, and the workarounds adopted to overcome the inflexibility of information systems or poor systems design.

Accidentally

Data may be entered into a system incorrectly by accident. Accidental errors can be reduced by:

○ Providing guidance on the data that can be included in an attribute value (for example, a policy on the use of capital letters and spaces).
○ Validating data entry against existing data. For example, as a data value is entered the value could be checked against existing values for that attribute and prompt an individual to select an existing value if appropriate.
○ Verifying data entry by asking for data values to be retyped so that inconsistencies between the entries can be identified and corrected. Retyping values to verify data is often used when capturing an email address in online forms.
○ Encouraging a culture of responsibility for data quality.

Data integrity can be adversely affected if business rules are not consistently implemented across all information systems and processes. Staff need to understand business rules to avoid creating workaround solutions that breach business rules and adversely affect the quality of the data. Data may also become dirty by accident if a data value is corrupted as a result of a technical error with the IT equipment.

Deliberately

Data may be deliberately entered into a system incorrectly either by someone within the organization or from a source outside the organization with a malicious intent. Mitropoulos *et al.* (2011) explain that systems developers wrongly assume that individuals will enter the required number and type of characters in data entry fields. Such assumptions can mean that invalid data are processed. Program code can be maliciously entered into a computer system by taking advantage of these assumptions; this is referred to as a code injection attack (Mitropoulos *et al.*, 2011). A code injection attack occurs when program code is entered into a data capture field, such as an address field in an online form. The code entered can allow unauthorized access to locate, change, store, and delete data values in information systems (Pietraszek & Berghe, 2005). Validating data entered to minimize attacks is difficult but prohibiting the use of quotation marks and other syntactic characters (such as −/*;) in data entry fields can help to detect some potential attacks (Pietraszek & Berghe, 2005).

Link 8.1
Valid but Inaccurate Data

Lack of Flexibility

Business rules and processes are designed to restrict actions that may affect the integrity of data. Sometimes these restrictions can be regarded as a barrier preventing what is considered to be logical and reasonable actions. In such situations, analysis of the problem is needed to assess the potential consequences of the required action and, if appropriate, processes can be changed to accommodate the action. In practice this approach is likely to be too time-consuming so staff search for a way to do what is needed within the constraints of the existing systems.

In Scenario 8.1, Clare explained that there was not a business process to print all customer addresses onto a set of labels. When the system was designed the analysis of the business requirements suggested that customer addresses would only need to be printed when

creating a label relating to a specific customer order. This may have seemed a reasonable assumption and would prevent anyone printing customer addresses for potentially malicious purposes. Clare probably thought that requesting a change to the IT systems to enable her to print addresses for the mailshot would take too long, so she found an alternative way to print the addresses. Clare used the existing business processes in a way in which the processes were not intended, to enable her to create the labels she needed. In taking this action, Clare affected the quality of the data because she invalidated the business rules for creating customer orders and credit notes. The data used to derive information about the number of customers who had placed orders in the last year were then of poor quality. The dirty data gave an inaccurate reflection of the number of customer orders because the spirit of the business rules defining the relationship between customers and orders had been violated; the data had been used in a way that had not been intended.

Poor Systems Design

The accuracy and validity of data values can be increased by addressing weaknesses in the design of information systems. For example, a number of websites provide a drop-down list to enable customers to select their title, such as Mr, Mrs, Miss, Ms, Dr, Prof or Rev. At the end of the list, some systems developers include the option of *other* to accommodate the situation when a customer wishes to use a title that has not been listed. However, a number of websites include the option *other* and do not allow the customer to enter the title that is not listed. This means that in future communication the word *other* is displayed before the customer's name, for example, Other Larry Lewis. Scenario 8.2 presents another example of poor systems design.

Scenario 8.2

Data Validation Problems in Bright Spark

Anya Po found the perfect lilac lampshade for her bedroom while browsing Bright Spark's website. She clicked the button *add to basket* and then went to *checkout*. As Anya had not made a purchase from the website before, she had to register as a new customer. She entered her personal details (for example, address and email address) and a message was displayed welcoming her as a new customer. She went to *checkout* again and found the basket was empty. The system had not saved

her order before initiating the process of registering her as a new customer.

Anya located the lampshade again and went to *checkout* for the third time. She entered her credit card details, which were accepted, and she was asked to confirm her order before the process was completed. Anya clicked the *confirm* button. An error message was displayed stating *post code invalid, click here to correct the post code*. Anya was certain she had entered the post code correctly but clicked the button indicated. This action emptied the basket, cleared the address fields, and cleared

Scenario 8.2 Continued

the credit card fields; Anya had to re-enter all the information again. She meticulously selected the product, entered her post code slowly, carefully checked the entry, entered her credit card details, and clicked to confirm the order. An error message was displayed stating *post code invalid, click here to correct the post code*.

Anya knew the post code was valid and she was becoming increasingly frustrated. She went through the whole process again but this time, she entered her home address details and then entered the post code of where she worked. The system did not check that the address line and city details were consistent with the post code entered. The system recognized the post code as being valid and accepted the order.

Anya sent an email to Bright Spark pointing out the problem with the ordering process and

informing them of her correct post code for the order. She received an automated response which thanked her for her email. A few days later when Anya was at work she received a telephone call from the corporate post room. A delivery driver had a parcel with her name on it, the post code related to her workplace but the remainder of the address did not relate to the workplace.

The input data validation checks did not recognize Anya's valid post code and then did not check that the post code, city, and street address were valid as a set of data values. Individually the data values were valid but they were inaccurate as a legitimate address. In addition, the delivery system only used the post code data and did not check the accuracy of the address fields. The data validation checks caused unnecessary problems in the ordering and delivering processes.

8.1.2 Types of Dirty Data

Dirty data may include invalid, inaccurate, incomplete, inconsistent, or non-integrated data values (Adelman *et al.*, 2005).

Invalid Data Values

An invalid data value occurs when an attribute is specified as a value range and the data held against the attribute is not within the specified range. Invalid data values can be prevented by enforcing validation checks when data are captured.

Nonintegrated Data Values

An attribute value may be a valid but inaccurate value due to dependencies between attributes or the specification of business rules. For example, two attributes of an address are city and country. London is a valid value for the attribute city. China is a valid value for the attribute country. However, when the values are used in the same address the data are inaccurate as the city of London is not in the country of China. Inaccurate data can be avoided by enforcing dependency checks through the use of lookup tables at the point of data capture to ensure that the values entered are accurate within a specific context.

Nonintegrated data values can occur when there is a lack of coordination and control in the development of information systems. As Bright Spark opened stores throughout the country, Larry allowed local store managers to make decisions about the information systems and IT needed in each store. Each store independently developed their own computer systems; the lack of coordination has resulted in an inconsistent approach to data

capture, storage, and use with nonintegrated data values. For example, each store defines the data to be captured about a product differently, using different attribute names, definitions, structures, and data types. These differences hinder the ability to integrate the data from the different stores needed to provide an overall view of the organization.

Incomplete Data Values

Incomplete data values can occur when changes are made to data definitions. The data dictionary specifies the attributes that can be captured relating to an entity, such as whether an attribute value is optional or mandatory, and whether the attribute has a default value. A value will not always be captured for an optional attribute. At a later date, a business need may be identified that requires the attribute to be redefined as being mandatory. Future instances of the entity must have a value captured for the attribute, but previous data collected will not have captured a value for the attribute; this will result in incomplete data values. Figure 8.1 shows the data dictionary entry for the entity *electrical item* and some example instances of the entity for which data values have been captured. The attribute *ELECITEM_Country* is optional and has not been captured for all the electrical items. If Bright Spark decides that the attribute should be mandatory to improve the information provided to customers, the data will contain incomplete values as the attribute value does not exist for all electrical items previously captured. This problem often arises when systems are changed and when data from different systems need to be integrated.

Data Dictionary Extract
Entity Name: Electrical Item   **Entity Code:** ELECITEM
Entity Definition: A piece of equipment, which requires connection to a mains power supply, and is available for sale to domestic customers.

Attribute Name	Attribute Definition	Attribute Length and Type	Attribute Structure	Default Value	Mandatory Indicator	Unique Indicator
ELECITEM_Number	Stock code number.	9(8)	String of numbers.		Y	Y
ELECITEM_Name	Name of item.	X(30)	String of characters.		Y	N
ELECITEM_Country	Country in which item can be used.	X(4)	Country code.		N	N
ELECITEM_Amp	Measure of electrical load.	9(3)	String of numbers with leading zeros.	013	Y	N

Example Values

ELECITEM_Number	ELECITEM_Name	ELECITEM_Country	ELECITEM_Amp
01584726	Battery Charger		013
12545844	10m Extension Lead	EURO	013
22159554	15m Extension Lead		013
22361545	Desk Lamp		013

Figure 8.1 Example of Incomplete Attribute Values

Inconsistent Data Values

Attributes of master data are needed in different systems across the organization. Despite the formalized specification of valid attribute values, a degree of flexibility can remain when entering data that requires individuals to make decisions about how to enter the data. Flexibility in data capture introduces a risk of inconsistent data values being captured and stored. A common example is the attribute *name,* such as *customer name, organization name,* and *product name.* A *name* attribute is often defined as a string of characters and the individual entering the data makes a decision about how to format the name. Table 8.1 shows a number of ways the name *Bright Spark* may be entered into an attribute field defined as being X(20). Each of the entries is valid but not all entries are accurate. An organization name may be entered in different ways in different information systems by different individuals. It is therefore difficult to determine whether the data refer to the same organization or a different organization. For example, *Bright Spark* and *Brite Sparks* may be two valid but different organizations; alternatively the data may refer to one organization and the organization's name has been typed incorrectly. Guidance on data entry can help to improve the cleanliness of the data.

Capturing accurate and consistent data values involves:

- Validating the data entered as being intrinsically valid and contextually valid. Intrinsically valid means that the value entered is of the correct type, length, and within a defined value range. Contextually valid means that a set of data values are valid when considered together rather than independently.
- Verifying that the data entered are as accurate as the individual believes the data to be, that is, checking that the data values have not been typed incorrectly.
- Reducing the potential for inaccurate data to be entered. This includes defining precise rules for valid inputs (such as not allowing special characters to be entered) and searching previous data values that can be selected. For example, in Table 8.1, as an individual starts to enter *Bri* in the *organization name* field, a list of potential valid organization names stored could be displayed from which the correct name could be selected; this avoids the name being typed incorrectly.

8.1.3 Approaches to Cleaning Data

Improving the accuracy and consistency of data increases the reliability of data available in different departments and enables data to be integrated from different information

Table 8.1 ▶ Inconsistent Data Values in the Attribute *Organization Name*

Attribute Value	Comment on Data Validity
Bright Spark	Valid and accurate.
bright spark	Requires guidance on the use of capital letters.
Brightspark	Requires guidance on the use of spaces in the name field.
BrightSpark	Requires guidance on the use of spaces and capital letters in the name field.
Bright Spark Ltd	Requires guidance on the use of abbreviations.
Bright Spark limited	Requires guidance on the information to be captured (such as, is the type of the organization part of the name to be captured?)
Bright Sparks	Valid but inaccurate.
Bright Spars	Valid but inaccurate.
Brite sparks	Valid but inaccurate.
Bright_Spark	Requires guidance on the use of underscore characters.

systems more effectively. Cleaning data improves the quality of data in the organization. When data definitions and valid values have been agreed upon, existing data must be cleaned to conform to the agreed upon standards. This will require issues of data duplication, lack of consistent data values, missing data values, and invalid data values to be addressed. When the data have been cleaned, additional controls must be defined to avoid similar problems reoccurring.

Data maintainers work with IT staff and data authors to check the consistency of data against the agreed upon definitions and values, resolve issues of missing or invalid data, and define the guidelines and controls needed to keep data clean. This ensures the availability of valid and consistent data to the organization.

Cleaning dirty data involves:

○ Correcting the problems identified to produce a clean set of data by developing programs to identify and correct incomplete and inconsistent data.
○ Backflushing, returning the cleaned data to where the data are stored and used.
○ Identifying how the data became dirty.
○ Implementing changes to ensure that the cleaned data stay clean, avoiding similar problems arising in the future.

Figure 8.2 provides guidance on the actions to be taken to clean data by removing invalid, inaccurate, inconsistent, and incomplete data values.

The actions listed in Figure 8.2 to clean data and to keep data clean require collaboration between the business and the IT function. The IT function can write programs to highlight and correct attribute values, however, business rules are needed to provide the logic to be included

in the program code. In addition, the business needs to work with the IT function to highlight, investigate, and correct anomalies. For example, the IT staff can write a program to compare the values for a customer name in different systems. A list of attribute values similar to that shown in Table 8.1 can be created but the business then has to inform the IT staff which value is correct. When the correct value has been identified, IT staff can write a program to change all instances of the incorrect value to the correct value.

The amount of time spent cleaning dirty data reflects the organization's need for quality information. In addition to improving the accuracy of data entered directly by staff and customers, consideration also needs to be given to data that are automatically entered into an organization's systems. Migration errors occur when dirty data are migrated into an information system, perpetuating poor data quality. Data need to be stored, validated, and cleaned before being loaded directly into the organization's live systems.

8.1.4 ▶ Problems of Cleaning Data

Cleaning data is a time-consuming and costly activity that requires an intraorganizational team of people to work together to identify, investigate, and resolve problems to create a clean set of data. Cleaning data and taking action to ensure data stay clean are extra activities that have to be carried out in addition to the daily operations of the organization. Project teams or working groups are established to which staff from around the organization can be seconded for some or all of their time, for a defined period, to clean specific items of data. There are three approaches to securing the resources needed to clean data. First, a business case can be developed to initiate

Invalid Data Values:

○ Identify data values that are not in the specified range.
○ Develop a process to either highlight invalid values for manual correction or define a default value to replace the invalid value automatically.
○ Change the data entry validation checks to only allow future data to be entered within the valid range.

Inaccurate Data Values:

○ Identify the logical dependency between attributes, such as between post code and city or city and country.
○ Develop lookup tables for valid values. For example, in the United Kingdom, Royal Mail provides a post code address file (Royal Mail Group Ltd., 2011), which includes 28 million valid addresses in the United Kingdom.
○ Develop a process to check existing data values against the lookup tables and correct values where possible, highlighting anomalies for manual correction.
○ Change the data entry processes to include validation checks using the lookup tables.

Inconsistent Data Values:

○ Identify common attributes used in different systems such as *customer name* and *product name*.
○ Develop a process to compare the attribute values in different systems, highlighting inconsistencies.
○ Define the correct version of the attribute value.
○ Develop a process to change attribute values to match the correct version.
○ Change the data entry processes to include verification checks against existing attribute values stored.
○ Provide guidelines for data entry staff about the content and format of data to be included in text input fields.

Incomplete Data Values:

○ Develop a process to identify null attribute values.
○ Investigate what the correct value should be.
○ Correct the value.
○ Change the data dictionary entries to ensure that the attribute value is mandatory and include a default value if applicable.
○ Change the data entry processes to ensure that a value for the attribute is always entered.

Figure 8.2 Actions to Clean Dirty Data

projects with the specific purpose of cleaning data. For example, an organization experienced problems as several information systems captured and stored customer addresses in slightly different ways. The organization incurred unnecessary costs due to undelivered orders, orders delivered to the wrong addresses, delivery times not being met, orders being returned due to late delivery, and lost custom. A business case was therefore made to clean customer addresses to reduce these costs. A project to clean customer addresses involved:

○ Defining an agreed upon standard use and length for address lines (for example, line 3 town, line 4 county) and agree on the length of address lines.
○ Reformatting address lines to adopt the agreed upon standard.
○ Agreeing upon standard abbreviations, such as *Rd* for *road*.
○ Applying the standard abbreviations.
○ Checking the completeness, validity, and accuracy of post codes.

The project team included representatives from across the organization that created, modified, or used customer addresses. Staff from the IT department identified the information systems that used customer addresses and produced a report showing the different ways that addresses were formatted. The report was used in a series of meetings to define an agreed upon format for customer addresses. When a standard format was agreed upon, the IT staff made the initial technical changes to information systems so that future addresses would be captured and maintained using the agreed upon standard. IT staff produced a series of reports identifying addresses that did not comply with the new standard. The project team worked through the reports to identify how to correct the addresses. In some instances, the IT staff could write program code to implement the changes, such as to change all instances of *road* to *Rd*. Other changes required staff in different business areas to investigate issues. For example, a customer had two addresses, High Road in Kings Lynn and High Hill in King Lin. An investigation was needed to determine which address was correct. When such issues were resolved, the data were corrected either manually or by program code. Verification and validation procedures were then implemented to ensure that the customer address data remained clean.

A second approach to securing resources to clean data is to incorporate data cleaning into planned IT projects. For example, the implementation of a new human resource management system in Bright Spark was planned to improve the management of professional development records. Implementing the new system involved migrating employee data from the old system to the new system. The planned data migration provided the opportunity to clean employee data before the data entered the new system. The project involved defining terms such as *employee*, *contractor*, and *temporary staff* and the data attributes associated with each term.

A third approach to data cleaning relates to the population of data warehouses. Inmon *et al.* (1997) suggest that there are three places to clean data: at the source system before the data are loaded into the data warehouse; during the process of loading data into the warehouse; or after the data are stored in the data warehouse. Cleaning the data at source is the preferred option but this may not always be possible due to limitations of storage and processing capacity. If rules have been developed to reconcile and consolidate conflicting data, programs can be run to, for example, automate the substitution of coding systems and convert units of measure before the data are entered into the data warehouse. Data should not be manually changed in the data warehouse; the source of the problem should be identified, corrected, and the data reloaded (Inmon *et al.*, 1997). However, programs can be run within the data warehouse to address issues of coding consistency.

Link 8.2
IT Function and Business Functions
Working Together to Clean Data

8.1.5 **Processes for Cleaning Data in the Life Cycle**

The processes relating to data cleaning in the data life cycle are shown in Table 8.2.

8.1.6 Role of Information Management Strategy in Cleaning Data

When data have been cleaned, processes are needed to ensure that future proposed changes to the structure of data are consistent with the agreed upon data definition and do not threaten to weaken the quality of the cleaned data. The appointment of data owners provides a single point of contact with authority and overall responsibility for maintaining the quality of data.

The information management strategy needs to:

- Acknowledge the importance of clean data.
- Emphasize the commitment of the organization to clean data.
- Secure the resources needed to clean data.
- Identify the priorities for data to be cleaned.
- Prepare a practical action plan to clean data in the organization.
- Form project teams.
- Establish processes to resolve issues of dirty data.
- Secure the resources to take the actions needed to maintain clean data.
- Regularly review progress of projects to clean data.

8.2 Integrating Fragmented Information

Information is captured and created throughout the organization's information systems, which are geographically, physically, technologically, and cognitively disparate. Decisions, particularly at the strategic level of the organization, require a range of information to be collated and analysed to inform action. In creating the annual report for Bright Spark, Larry needs to integrate information relating to sales and finance from all the retail stores.

At an individual level, information fragmentation occurs when different types of information are stored in different places (Bergman *et al.*, 2006). For example, emails, word processing documents, and links to Internet sites are stored in different structures, which cause inconsistency in managing the information. When working on a particular project, the information needed is

Table 8.2 Role of Data Cleaning within the Data Life Cycle

Capture	Store and Retrieve	Use, Share, and Maintain	Archive and Destroy
Identifies opportunities for improving the quality of the data captured through validation, verification, and integrity controls.	Ensures that the data stored are complete and valid. Minimizes data fragmentation and addresses issues of consistency and integrity if data become fragmented.	Identifies the need for validation, verification, and integrity controls to ensure that changes to the data do not adversely affect the quality of the data.	Ensures that the data archived are complete and valid.

fragmented in different information systems, applications, and storage locations. More time and effort is required to retrieve information scattered between both storage locations and applications (Reimer *et al.*, 2009). This leads to adaptation approaches to deal with this situation such as storing copies of material at different locations with the risk of inconsistent information being created.

DEFINITION: Fragmented information is when elements of the information required are physically stored in different locations and possibly in different formats.

One approach to addressing information fragmentation is to use search tools to find all related information, irrespective of the file format (Bergman *et al.*, 2006). A limitation of search tools is that systems search by keywords but people recall by entities, including time, place, and action (Ma *et al.*, 2007). Organizing information so that the information can be found when needed therefore involves analysis of human behaviour (Ma *et al.*, 2007). Jones and Anderson (2011) suggest that organizing documents by project provides a means of integrating information that reflects how recipients think about and use the information. Collaborative toolsets integrate different types of information stored at different locations to enable project teams and virtual teams to work together. Bright Spark needs a way of bringing together the data needed from different parts of the organization to inform the development of the annual report. Collaborative tools provide a shared space that Larry's executive management team could use to share information and work together preparing the annual report.

8.2.1 ▶ Causes of Information Fragmentation

The proliferation of IT in an organization can lead to a number of different information systems storing part of the information relating to a business object. Data fragmentation occurs when the data attributes related to an entity are not stored together on the physical media storage device. Fragmenting data can be used to maintain data confidentiality by storing confidential data separate from data that will allow individuals to be identified (Samarati & di Vimercati, 2010).

Data fragmentation is used in distributed database systems to minimize data transfer by storing data where data are most needed. Fragmentation is a way of managing large data volumes and improving the response times of data retrieval (Mahboubi & Darmont, 2008). Some applications only need to access part of an entity so fragmenting the entity means that less data are transferred and processed (Ezeife & Barker, 1995). There are three ways to fragment an entity. Horizontal

fragmentation is the division of entities into subsets of instances. Vertical fragmentation is based on subsets of attributes processed by different transactions. Hybrid fragmentation is a combination of both horizontal and vertical fragmentation.

Figure 8.3 provides examples of horizontal and vertical entity fragmentation. Decisions about how to fragment data need to consider where data are needed and the type of queries that will be processed on the data. Details of data fragmentation should be documented in the data dictionary.

8.2.2 ▶ Approaches to Integrate Fragmented Information

There are three main problems to be addressed relating to fragmented information: Where is the information? Where is the information needed? How can the fragments be integrated? Information management aims to provide access to information irrespective of where the information is located or where the information is needed. In practice, individuals often need to have an idea of where the information may be located in order to choose the appropriate information system to use to retrieve the information. Information maps show where information can be found in the organization. Collecting the information required from different sources across the organization can be difficult and problems relating to dirty data may need to be addressed. Data warehouses aim to provide a single source of data to support strategic analysis of the organization by regularly integrating operational data from across the organization.

When Larry's executive management team has located the required data for the annual report, the team can import or upload a copy of the data into a collaborative system. All members of the team can then access and analyse the data to create the information for the annual report. Copying the data involves extracting the data from the original context; care is therefore needed to ensure that the data are interpreted accurately in creating the annual report.

Integrating fragmented data involves reconstructing the fragmented entities. The information architecture, data dictionary, and physical database schemas can be used to identify where data attributes are physically located. A new data file can be created to integrate the data. Figure 8.3 shows horizontal fragments integrated by collating instances of the entity fragments. Vertical fragments are integrated by checking the value of identifying attributes to ensure that data fragments relate to the same instance of the entity.

Entity: Electrical Items Sales

Item_Num	Sale_Date	Qty_Sold	Sale_Value	Unit_Size

Horizontal Fragmentation

Data Storage Area A:

Item_Num	Sale_Date	Qty_Sold	Sale_Value	Unit_Size
01584726	14/10/2012	1	199.99	S
12545844	15/10/2012	10	249.52	S

Data Storage Area B:

Item_Num	Sale_Date	Qty_Sold	Sale_Value	Unit_Size
22195837	14/10/2012	1	199.99	M
34669331	15/10/2012	10	249.52	M

Vertical Fragmentation

Data Storage Area A:

Item_Num	Sale_Date	Qty_Sold	Sale_Value
01584726	14/10/2012	1	199.99
12545844	15/10/2012	10	249.52
22195837	14/10/2012	1	199.99
34669331	15/10/2012	10	249.52

Data Storage Area B:

Item_Num	Pack_Size
01584726	S
12545844	S
22195837	M
34669331	M

Integrated Fragments

Item_Num	Sale_Date	Qty_Sold	Sale_Value	Unit_Size
01584726	14/10/2012	1	199.99	S
12545844	15/10/2012	10	249.52	S
22195837	14/10/2012	1	199.99	M
34669331	15/10/2012	10	249.52	M

Figure 8.3 Entity Fragmentation

8.2.3 Role of Information Management Strategy in Integrating Fragmented Information

Integrating fragmented information therefore requires:

○ An audit to determine where data and information are located in order to:
  • Create an information map.
  • Ensure entity fragmentation is documented in the data dictionary.

○ An understanding of the context in which data are collected, documented in the data dictionary so that data can be interpreted appropriately.
○ Consideration of where information will be needed. This may lead to the development of:
  • A data warehouse to provide a single point of access for management information.
  • Management information systems to integrate information and provide summary analysis.

- Collaborative tools to enable individuals to share information and work together creating shared documents.

8.3 Reconciling Data

Data stored in different systems need to be integrated to provide information. Integrating data requires different views of the same data to be reconciled, which is challenging as different functions or areas of the business may define entities in a slightly different manner and use different coding systems. This section addresses the problem of trying to integrate similar data from different sources where:

O The same attribute name may be used to mean different things.
O Different attribute names may be used to describe the same thing.
O Different measuring systems may be used.
O Different coding systems may be used.
O Not all attributes may be included in each source.

Data dictionaries and information architectures help to identify inconsistencies and record agreed upon standards. A programme of verification and validation is undertaken to reconcile different views, followed by the implementation of agreed upon standards and changes in procedures to avoid problems reoccurring.

DEFINITION: Data reconciliation is the process of investigating and resolving issues with similar data to provide one set of data, which uses consistent data definitions and units of measure.

Reconciling data involves merging files, removing duplicate data, reformatting dates, and cleaning data as required (Inmon, 1996). Larry needs to combine information from his different stores and business functions to generate information about the performance of Bright Spark. Figure 8.4 shows three sets of data and their related data dictionary entries from Store A and Store B in the United Kingdom and Internet sales in Australia. These three sets of data need to be reconciled to calculate the total value of sales for the electrical item identified by the number 01584728.

8.3.1 Problems in Reconciling Data

Four problems in integrating data from different sources relate to encoding data, units of measurement, attribute names, and attribute structures (Inmon, 1996).

Data Encoding

Coding systems represent the legitimate values used for common attributes but different coding systems may be used by different information systems and departments, hindering the ability to reconcile data from different systems. Figure 8.4 shows that the three data sets have different coding systems for the attribute *unit_size*: Store A uses three sizing codes; Store B refers to the number of people needed to carry the item; and the final data set uses an alphanumeric code relating to postage costs. Encoding transformation is needed to convert the codes into a consistent form so that the data values can be integrated.

Dates are another common attribute that can adopt a range of coding structures. Three different date structures are used by the data sets in Figure 8.4. Table 8.3 illustrates possible representations of 31 January 2013. Date structures can differ in terms of the sequential ordering of the components, use of numbers or letters to represent a date component, the length of date components, and the symbol used to separate the components.

Table 8.3 Possible Date Structures

Date Format	Example Date
DD/MM/YY	31/01/13
DD/MM/YYYY	31/01/2013
YY.MM.DD	13.01.31
YYYY.MM.DD	2013.01.31
DD-MON-YY	31-JAN-13
DD-MON-YYYY	31-JAN-2013
MON DD YY	JAN 31 13
MON DD YYYY	JAN 31 2013

Units of Measure

Different systems may use different currencies, such as the attribute *sale_value* in Figure 8.4. The data from the different systems need to be converted into a single currency before data can be integrated. Figure 8.4 also shows that different units of measure are used such as millimeters, centimeters, and inches. Units of measure transformation identifies the units stored in each system and converts them into a common unit of measure. Although each data set in Figure 8.4 stores a value for the attribute *qty_sold*, two of the data sets measure this as being an item, while one of the data sets refers to the quantity of boxes in the item. This is a problem of definition, rather than conversion, that needs to be addressed.

Attribute Names

Different systems may include the same data values for different attribute names. In Figure 8.4 three different attribute

Item 01584728 in Store A in UK

Date	Elecitem_Number	Qty_Sold	Sale_Value	Unit_Size
21–09–12	01584728	3	59.97	S

Data Definitions Used by Store A in UK

Attribute Name	Attribute Definition	Attribute Length and Type
Date	Date order was received.	dd–mm–yy
Elecitem_Number	Stock code number.	9(8)
Qty_Sold	Number of individual items ordered.	9(3)
Sale_Value	Total selling price in pounds sterling.	9(3)v9(2)
Unit_Size	Size of unit for display purposes (S, M, L).	X(1)

Item 01584728 in Store B in UK

Item_Num	Sale_Date	Qty_Sold	Sale_Value	Unit_Size
01584728	21/09/12	1	199.99	01

Data Definitions Used by Store B in UK

Attribute Name	Attribute Definition	Attribute Length and Type
Item_Num	Unique identifier of a product.	9(8)
Sale_Date	Date the product was sold.	DD/MM/YY
Qty_Sold	Number of boxes sold. There are 10 units in each box.	9(3)
Sale_Value	Total value of products sold in pounds sterling.	9(3)v9(2)
Unit_Size	Number of people needed to lift product in accordance with manual handling guidelines.	9(2)

Item 01584728 in Internet Sales in Australia

I_Elecitem_No	I_Order_Date	Qty_Sold	Sale_Value	Unit_Size
01 584 72 8	21.09.2012	2	61.41	A

Data Definitions Used for Internet Sales in Australia

Attribute Name	Attribute Definition	Attribute Length and Type
I_Elecitem_No	Identification code of a product that can be sold via the Internet.	99^999^99^9
I_Order_Date	Date the order was entered on the Internet site.	MM.DD.YYYY
Qty_Sold	Number of products ordered.	9(3)
Sale_Value	Total price of products sold in Australian dollars.	9(3)v9(2)
Unit_Size	Size of product for posting purposes.	X(1)

Figure 8.4 Data Sets to Reconcile

names are used for *ELECITEM_Number* (specified in Figure 8.1) *ELECITEM_Number*, *Item_Num*, and *I_ELECITEM_No*. Attribute name transformation reconciles the attribute names and documents the differences between the attributes names in the data dictionary. This involves checking that similar attribute names refer to the same attribute.

In addition to the structural aspects of data set reconciliation, consideration also needs to be given to semantic transformation. Different systems may use the same attribute name for a different purpose within a specific context. For example, in Figure 8.4, *sale_date* has been defined both as the date an item has been sold and the date an order has been received; consideration needs to be given as to whether these meanings are the same. The attribute *unit_size* has also been used differently to refer to methods of display, handling, and postage. Care is needed to ensure that attributes with the same name have the same meaning and that contextual information is not lost if codes are changed.

Attribute Structures

Different systems may have different attribute types, lengths, and structures specified for a similar attribute. In Figure 8.4, the attributes *ELECITEM_Number* and *Item_Num* are structured as 9(8) but the equivalent number in the third data set is defined as 99^999^99^9 (where ^ refers to a space) to assist with online data entry of orders by customers. Attribute structure transformation identifies attributes that refer to the same instance of an entity in the different systems.

8.3.2 ▶ Causes of Data Reconciliation Problems

The difficulties of data reconciliation emerge over time as the organization evolves. The organization changes, information systems change, opportunities for using IT increase, and the information requirements of the organization become more complex.

Organizational Transformation

Bright Spark has evolved from one store to a chain of 63 stores; each store has been given the freedom to independently define their information systems. The information requirements have been influenced by the knowledge and experience of the staff at each store and by the IT staff participating in the information systems development projects. The disparate systems have resulted in different entity and attribute definitions, different data being captured, different coding systems, different data structures, different storage options, different reports generated, and different archive and retention periods.

Local autonomy provides store managers with the flexibility to operate their stores and manage information in a way that is directly appropriate for the local customers they serve. However, lack of coordination of how information is captured, used, and stored makes reconciling multiple data sets across the chain a difficult task. Similar problems arise when an organization undergoes other forms of transformation, such as when one organization takes over another organization. The data sets in both organizations will have different structures and definitions that need to be reconciled to provide information on the overall corporation (discussed in Chapter 9).

The introduction of e-business has perhaps been the most significant trigger of organizational transformation since the introduction of IT in organizations. Online sales provide a new market, a new context, in which the organization can trade. The Internet changes the context in which information is interpreted. In Figure 8.4, the attribute *sale_date* has a slightly different meaning in the e-business context from that of a sale in the context of a physical store. Trading electronically may involve sharing information electronically with partners in the supply chain who are likely to adopt different data structures and definitions. External data received from partners will need to be correctly interpreted and reconciled with existing internal data to provide useful information for the organization.

Information Systems Transformation

During the last 50 years, the information systems used in Bright Spark have changed many times. Store managers have introduced new business processes to meet the changing needs of their customers. As business processes change, changes are needed to the information input into the processes, the way information is used within the processes, and the information derived as output from the business processes.

Each change to an existing information system, replacement of an existing system, or introduction of a new system affects the way information is managed. In addition to changes in the information required by and produced from the information system, the way the data are defined, named, structured, and stored are likely to change too. This can result in inconsistent data structures between different information systems and between versions of the same information system. For example, additional attributes may be captured in later versions of an information system, making it more difficult to reconcile historical data for analysis.

Information Technology Transformation

The continued developments in IT challenge the way data are captured, transmitted, stored, and used. For example, developments in storage devices change the way data are physically stored and the volume of data that can easily be accessed. New technologies change the way data are consumed and fuel expectations about the availability of, and access to, information. Developments in technology also require the formulation of new standards and protocols relating to how data are structured, stored, and transmitted.

Changing Information Needs

The organization's information requirements change in response to changes of personnel, processes, systems, structures, and technology. Triggers for change can come from both internal and external sources. For example, external pressures in the business climate place significant demands on the management of information in organizations, including the need to provide evidence of compliance to regulatory requirements, retain information for defined periods of time, and protect personal data. IT can be both an enabler and barrier to change. Moving information between different IT systems can introduce problems of information compatibility and can require changes to attribute lengths, types, and structures.

8.3.3 Approaches to Reconciling Data

Reconciling data sets from different sources involves:

- Identifying the data attributes needed to provide the information required.
- Determining the nature of the compatibility (for example, checking that attributes, which appear to be the same, are the same in terms of definition, structure, and value).
- Determining the nature of data incompatibility (for example, coding systems).
- Developing a plan to reconcile incompatibilities where possible.
- Implementing the reconciliation plan to create one data set.
- Defining processes to either change the way data are stored in the source systems or a means of automating the reconciliation plan for future use of the data.

Inmon *et al.* (1999) suggest that reconciling data from different sources may involve five actions. First, the data sets in Figure 8.4 contain similar attributes but the attributes are in a different sequence. **Changing the sequence** of the attributes may help to identify the degree of compatibility between the data sets.

Second, **encoding attributes** requires identifying and defining attributes that include embedded codes, agreeing on a standard form of coding to be used, and then converting codes to the agreed upon standard. In Figure 8.4, a standard coding system needs to be defined for the *date* attribute and the *unit_size* attribute so data values are used consistently across all systems.

Third, **converting units of measure** involves identifying the attributes that include units of measure, agreeing on the standard units of measure to be used, and then applying a formula to convert all units of measure to the same measuring system. In Figure 8.4 a standard unit of measure is needed for the attributes *sale_value* and *qty_sold*.

Fourth, **standardizing attribute names** examines attributes that may have a different name and the same meaning, or have the same name but do not have the same meaning in their original context. The information architecture and data dictionary entries can be used to help identify whether the attributes have the same meaning and are used in the same manner in their source contexts. Standardizing attribute names involves steps to identify attributes that have the same meaning, agreeing on a standard name for the attribute, and then changing the attribute name to show that the attribute used in different data sets is the same attribute.

Standardizing attribute structure compares the structure of attributes with the same meaning in different systems. When attributes with the same meaning are identified, a standard for the structure of the attribute can be agreed upon. The attribute structure is changed so that the same structure is used in all data sets. The attribute values are then converted to adhere to the agreed upon structure.

Fifth, depending on the purpose of the data reconciliation, it may be necessary to add an additional attribute to the data being reconciled to indicate the original source of the data. **Semantic transformation** defines the attributes of the new data created to ensure that data are interpreted correctly. If the data sets shown in Figure 8.4 were merged, the source of the data would be lost, which would mean that the context in which the data should be interpreted becomes unknown. An additional attribute such as *store_number* could be added to show which data related to sales from Store A, B, and the Internet.

Action needs to be taken to avoid the same problems arising each time there is a need to integrate data sets to provide the organization with information. A detailed understanding of the data will have been achieved during the reconciliation process. This information, such as the agreed upon systems of coding and units of measure, needs to be documented in the data dictionary. The data dictionary provides a consistent reference point for how data are used and structured in the organization. If the data dictionary is kept up to date, reconciliation problems should be easier to resolve. Data reconciliation requires collaboration between IT staff and business functions. The IT staff can make reasonable assumptions about how similarly named attributes may be related, but the assumptions may be incorrect. The staff who create the data and use the resulting information are best positioned to understand how data that may appear to be similar are used differently across the organization.

8.3.4 Role of Information Management Strategy in Reconciling Data

As the management of information in the organization progresses, the understanding of how data are defined, generated, stored, and used in different information systems will improve. Over time actions can be taken to implement the agreed upon data definitions and business rules facilitated by data owners. Some changes may be difficult to implement due to technical restrictions, particularly in cases where proprietary software is used in the organization. For example, in Figure 8.4 the attribute *unit_size* is defined as X(1) in the information system used by Store A and defined as 9(2) in the information system used in Store B. Although agreement may be reached that the attribute *unit_size* is defined as X(1), it may not be possible to make changes to the information system in Store B to reflect this decision. The differences in the attribute format need to be documented and a bridging program written to convert the *unit_size* from Store B to the format used by Store A when data from the two systems need to be integrated. In the longer term, when the information system in Store B is updated or replaced, the agreed upon definition of *unit_size* can be implemented.

The information management strategy needs to:

○ Identify differences in attribute name, structure, units of measure, and coding mechanisms used in different information systems.
○ Agree upon data standards to be used across all information systems.
○ Implement the agreed upon standards through attribute name, attribute structure, units of measure, and encoding transformations.
○ Implement validation controls to ensure that the agreed upon data standards are used when data are captured and maintained.
○ Document instances where inconsistencies in attribute name, structure, units of measure, and coding mechanisms remain.
○ Develop bridging programs to translate inconsistent data into a standard format so that data can be integrated with data in other information systems when required.
○ Ensure that agreed upon data standards are implemented when information systems are modified or replaced.

Data reconciliation addresses inconsistencies in the way data are captured and stored in different information systems; however, the situation may arise where attribute names and structures are the same in different systems but the data value stored in the attribute differs. For example, in Figure 8.4 the attribute *unit_size* for item 01584728 is defined as X(1) in Store A and the Internet store, but has the values S and A in the different systems. Consolidation is needed to resolve situations where conflicting information arises.

8.4 ▶ Consolidating Conflicting Information

Organizations require a single version of correct information; however, different information systems in the organization can return different responses to the same query. Inconsistent information leads to a lack of data credibility as the organization loses confidence in the information produced from information systems. This section addresses the problem of trying to integrate similar data from different sources. The same attribute name may store different values in different systems, the context of the data collection may differ, the timing of the data collection may differ, the reporting time frames may differ, and relationships between entities may have become invalid because of dirty data.

These problems are not technical problems; the problems may be caused by different functions of the business defining entities in a slightly different manner. Sometimes data are repeated in different IT systems, which can mean that data are updated in one system but not in all systems where the data are stored. This can result in conflicting information being held in the organization.

8.4.1 ▶ Causes of Conflicting Information

Problems in information management are revealed when two or more reports provide conflicting information about the performance of the organization. This raises two fundamental questions: Which report is correct? And, why do the reports differ? An investigation is needed to address these questions, which considers how the reports were generated and how the data used in the reports were generated.

Generation of Reports

Poor data credibility is caused by three main issues (Inmon, 1996). First, the data may differ due to time differences. Reports generated at different times on different days are likely to give different information because of the continuous nature of organizational life. Second, algorithmic differences may occur as different logic may have been applied to structure the queries used to collect the data incorporated in the reports. Third, reports may have been generated from different data sources and may differ in terms of the degree to which externally sourced data have been included in the analysis presented.

Data Used to Generate the Report

A range of issues with the data used to generate a report can result in different information being reported. Scenario 8.3 outlines some of the situations that have arisen in Bright Spark relating to one source of customer data. Different sources of data are likely to have different:

○ Data definitions: Entity and attribute definitions may vary depending on the requirements of a particular business function. Differences in the way data are defined change the context of the data, affecting how data are captured and used. This may mean that data are misinterpreted. For example, in Scenario 8.3 John assumes that a customer account number has a unique address but this assumption is wrong, therefore any analysis of the data based on this assumption will be wrong.

○ Data types and structures: Different sources of data may define attribute types and structures differently. Care is therefore needed to ensure that coding and measuring systems are correctly interpreted. Figure 8.4 showed that different sources of data captured the attribute *sale_value* using different units of currency. Sales figures would be incorrectly reported if the inconsistent use of units of currency was not recognized.

○ Data time frames: There are three data time frames to consider. First, some data changes constantly; for example, exchange rates fluctuate so data values will vary depending on when currencies were converted. Second, the time period for data collection and storage may vary depending on the data definition. For example, in Scenario 8.3, the customer data included details of customers who had not made a purchase within the last five years. Other data sources may only include customer data where a

customer has made a purchase within the last two years. Reports of customer numbers will therefore vary depending on the source of the customer data used. Third, differences in the data definition may affect how frequently the attribute values are updated. For example, if the total value of orders placed by a customer is calculated weekly in one system and daily in another system, this will result in different sales figures being reported. Janeert (2011) also points out that time flows backwards; for example, when a customer returns an item to Bright Spark, the return triggers changes to data in the stock, sales, order, and finance systems. Reports produced before the item is returned will differ from the reports produced after the item has been returned to the store.

○ Update propagation rates: Multiple copies of the same data may be stored and maintained to satisfy data access and response times. The database management system will propagate changes made to one copy of the data to all copies of the data. The propagation of changes may be completed as soon as possible or scheduled to be completed at a specific time; however, there will be a short time frame when the copies of data are temporarily out of sync, which may result in synchronization errors.

Scenario 8.3

Causes of Poor Customer Data in Bright Spark

John has to produce a report of exactly how many individual customers Bright Spark really has. Three reports list different numbers of customers. John first ran some programs to clean the customer data; this identified any missing or invalid attribute values. He then ran a query on the customer data to ensure that each customer account number related to a unique address. The query highlighted instances where several customer account numbers referred to the same address. John took the list to the sales team to find out more about these specific accounts. The sales manager for the area explained that the situation arose for a number of reasons and gave the following examples.

Historic Data

Customer Mr Eric Gordan has the account number 12574392 and lives at 4 Elm Tree Avenue, London. Mr Gordan has not made a purchase in the last five years.

Customer Mrs Madeline Jameson has the account number 12652455 and lives at 4 Elm Tree Avenue, London. The account opened five years ago.

It is possible that Mr Gordan has moved out of the area.

Two customer accounts appear to have the same address because one of the account numbers refers to an old customer account. One of the reports includes the account number 12574392, the other two reports do not include this account. The reports differ in relation to the inclusion of historic customer data.

Faulty Logic

John assumes that a customer account should refer to a unique address, but this assumption may be incorrect. A new trading estate has 30 factory units, occupied by different organizations. Each organization has the same address: the trading estate. This means that different customer account numbers may have the same address. One report has calculated customers by counting the number of unique customer addresses; the other reports do not identify customers in this way, which has led to different results.

Lack of Clarity Relating to Ownership of Accounts

Mrs Madeline Jameson makes regular purchases from Bright Spark. Her husband visited the local

Scenario 8.3 Continued

store to make a purchase. He did not have a customer account and therefore a new account was created for him. This means that Mr and Mrs Jameson have separate account numbers that relate to the same address. This raises the question of whether an account relates to individuals, organizations, families, or addresses; this will depend on the financial implications relating to the account (such as responsibility for paying the account).

Change of Name

The retailer Daisy Chains had the customer account number 11286544 and occupied a store in the High Street of Aberdeen. Daisy Chains merged with another local business. Daisy Chains changed its trading name to Daisy Chains and Daffodils, and remained at the same premises on the High Street. A new customer account number was issued

to reflect the organizational change. This means that there are two account numbers, with different names, at the same address. This raises the issue of under what circumstances customer names can be changed.

Dirty Data

Mrs Jameson makes a purchase from Bright Spark. The sales staff mistyped her name as Jam*i*eson and therefore cannot find her customer account. Staff create a new account number, 12956624, for Mrs Madeline Jameson, with the same address. The same person now has two customer accounts. The business rules assume that a person has one entry on the customer master file; however, the misspelling of a name has resulted in a customer having two entries in the customer master file, causing dirty data.

Data definitions are at the core of all of the problems in Scenario 8.3. Clarity of how data are defined and used in each area of the business, making any assumptions explicit, can help to avoid problems in information reporting.

8.4.2 Approaches to Consolidating Conflicting Information

Investigation into the causes of conflicting data can determine whether the inconsistencies are caused by the way the reports are generated or by the source data used to generate the reports.

Problems can be addressed in the generation of reports by agreeing on the:

○ Precise content of the information required in the report, including relevant time frames. This will ensure that staff creating the report understand the exact information required in the report.
○ Date and time when the report is to be generated, in order to gain an accurate representation of the data at the same point in time.
○ Source of the data to be used to create the report. Typically a range of different sources of data will need to be used and analysed. Further analysis of the consistency of the data sources is therefore required.
○ Way in which the data are to be collected and analysed.

The underlying problem is that different data are used to create the reports. The data from different systems have to be reconciled to create a consistent data set that can be used for analysis. This involves:

○ Clarifying the data definitions to identify the data needed to generate the report. Queries may need to be structured differently to ensure that equivalent information is extracted from different systems. For example, in Scenario 8.3 different systems store two years of customer data and five years of customer data. A query therefore needs to be executed to extract only customer data where a customer has made a purchase in the last two years. This will ensure that only equivalent information is reported for analysis.
○ Cleaning the data to complete missing attributes values and removing duplicate records (such as the accounts for Mrs Jameson and Mrs Jamieson). This requires detailed analysis of the data from an organizational perspective, rather than a technical perspective, to check that Mrs Jameson and Mrs Jamieson are the same person.
○ Resolving conflicts relating to attribute types and units of measure so that equivalent data values are analysed and reported.

Once the source data have been understood, the information gained about how the data are used in the different source systems should be documented in the data dictionary. The data dictionary can then be used to address similar problems that may arise in the future. In the longer term, the data dictionary can be used to provide guidance on how data are used in the organization so that when information systems are changed or replaced, the organization can move towards implementing consistent data definitions across all information systems.

8.4.3 ▶ Role of Information Management Strategy in Consolidating Conflicting Information

It is frustrating when conflicting information is presented to inform decisions. The situation arises due to lack of clarity and consistency in both the way data are managed in the organization and the way information is requested.

The information management strategy helps to:

○ Define the information required to inform decisions.
○ Understand how data are defined, captured, and created in different information systems.
○ Ensure that consistent information is combined from different information systems to inform decisions.

8.5 ▶ Recovering Corrupted Information

Information is corrupted when integrity has been compromised by an unauthorized change or a technical error. Corrupted information may be inaccurate, unreliable, unreadable, or inaccessible. Information corruption can range in scale from a relative minor error that can easily be corrected through to information being completely destroyed. Information may be corrupted due to human error. For example, an error in an attribute value may occur (intentionally or unintentionally) during data entry or data maintenance. Minor data errors may also occur during data transmission or due to a technical error in data storage (such as an unreadable sector of a disk). These errors involving small volumes of data can usually be quickly identified and corrected.

8.5.1 ▶ Causes of Corrupted Information

Information may be temporarily inaccessible or corrupted due to the inability to read or access the physical storage caused by technical issues (such as malfunction) or environmental issues (such as loss of power). These types of issues may take time to resolve. In extreme cases, information may be inaccessible, corrupted, or destroyed for a prolonged period due to the destruction of IT equipment resulting from, for example, natural disasters or acts of terrorism.

Information can become corrupted by:

○ Accident: Where there is a human element, there is always the risk that data can be changed or deleted accidentally. Information systems seek to embed business rules to prevent data being changed outside specified parameters but mistakes can happen.
○ Malicious attack: Information is at risk from individuals, both within the organization and outside the organization, who seek to deliberately corrupt the

information. This includes acts to corrupt information directly or by sabotaging information systems and IT.
○ Technical malfunction: IT systems can break down or suffer from external events, such as a cut or surge in power delivered to the systems, which can cause data to become corrupted.
○ Computer virus: A virus is a self-replicating program code that can exploit security vulnerabilities in IT systems and may corrupt data or adversely affect the performance of the system.
○ Data transmission: Data may become corrupted when an error occurs during the transmission or storage of the data. For example, checks are needed that data received by an IT device are the same as the data sent to the device.
○ Disasters: Chow and Ha (2009) define a disaster as an event that has a significant impact on the operation of the organization. Disasters can be natural, human, manmade, intentional, or unintentional. Acts such as fire, flood, hurricane, earthquake, and terrorism can damage IT equipment, removing the ability to access information and corrupting the data held on storage devices. A range of disasters are categorized in Table 8.4. Disasters can vary in scale from a minor inconvenience to catastrophic damage and disruption (Matthews *et al.*, 2009).

8.5.2 ▶ Approaches to Recover Data

Events such as technical malfunction and power failure can happen to any organization, adversely affecting the operation of the IT systems and the organization's information resource. A plan is needed to prioritize critical business functions for recovery and define the minimum functions and data needed to operate at an acceptable level (Chow & Ha, 2009).

Keeping the organization operational involves:

○ Identifying the event.
○ Providing operational systems with access to data, even if the data may not be completely up to date.
○ Identifying the data affected during the event.
○ Recovering the data.
○ Repopulating databases with the recovered data.

At any point in time, data are being created, accessed, modified, stored, transmitted, or deleted in the organization. For example, Table 8.5 shows a number of actions that were taking place in Bright Spark at 10:15 a.m. on 11 November when the power to the main IT systems was cut for a period of five seconds.

Data recovery identifies the state of the data before the event occurred, the transactions being performed on

Table 8.4 ▸ Categorization of Disasters

	Intentional	Unintentional
Natural		Weather: O Floods. O Hurricanes. O Snow. O Electrical storm. Ecology: O Earthquake. O Tsunami. O Avalanche. O Volcanic eruption.
Human	Fire. Acts of terrorism. Arson. War. Equipment sabotaged. Information maliciously modified or deleted. Computer virus.	Data deletion. Drilled cable. Unsecured building.
Manmade	Poor maintenance.	Equipment malfunction. Industrial accidents: O Burst pipe. O Electrical fault. O Gas leak.

Table 8.5 ▸ Transactions in Progress

Transaction	Transaction Description
Transaction 1	Person A is accessing the details of customer.
Transaction 2	Person B is closing a customer's account.
Transaction 3	Person C is capturing an order.
Transaction 4	Person D is sending an email.
Transaction 5	Data from the accounts database are being transmitted to the data warehouse.

the data when the event occurred, and the desired state of the data (as if the event had not occurred). Table 8.6 identifies the data recovery information for the transactions in Table 8.5.

In the case of transaction 1, data were only being accessed when the power failed. The customer data stored should be unaffected; however, it is necessary to redisplay the data to Person A in case a data transmission error occurred. This ensures that the data displayed to Person A are accurate and have not been corrupted during the process of accessing, receiving, transmitting, and displaying the data.

In transaction 2, data were being changed when the fault occurred. The data recovery process identifies the original status of the data and the action being performed on the data. If the action has not been successfully completed, the recovery process completes the transaction and changes the customer account status to closed, before confirming to Person B that the transaction has been successfully completed.

In transaction 3, Person C was capturing order data and had not completed capturing the order details when the fault occurred. None of the order details were successfully transmitted to the order database before the fault occurred. It is likely that the order details will have been stored in a temporary file to be transmitted to the order database when all the details had been entered to complete the order. The recovery process therefore has to identify where the order details have been temporarily stored while the order was being captured. The recovery process involves rolling forward the transaction so that the transaction can be stored in the database. The order details will be displayed to Person C so that the remainder of the order details can be captured.

In transaction 4, Larry was in the process of sending an email to Clare when the fault occurred. The recovery process locates the email, sends the email to Clare, and confirms that the email has been sent.

When the fault occurred, 5,000 account records were being transmitted to the data warehouse in transaction 5. The recovery process first checks the status of the transmission. Half of the records have been transmitted to the data warehouse; however, further checks are made to ensure that the records have been transmitted accurately. It may be necessary to delete some (or all) of the accounts from the warehouse or roll back the data in the data warehouse to the state the data were in before the update was sent. The process to transmit the data to the warehouse is then restarted from the beginning.

The specific data recovery activities depend on the cause of the problem. For example, if data have been accidentally deleted or the physical device on which data are stored is damaged, the cost of recovering the data has to be weighed against the recreation of the data. A range of data recovery tools are available that repair data files by extracting information from the damaged file and storing the data in a new file (Cross & Shinder, 2008). The tools can identify changed, corrupted, or deleted files and enable the files to be recovered while preserving the integrity of the data being recovered. Computers keep a list of the files stored. When a file on a computer

Table 8.6 ▸ Data Recovery Information

Transaction Number	Data Status before Event	Type of Transaction	Data Status after Event	Recovery Action
1	Customer Name: Mrs Liz Fox Customer Account Number: 12651308	Accessing record.	Customer Name: Mrs Liz Fox Customer Account Number: 12651308 Data at source unaffected.	No change made to customer data. Redisplay customer details in case transmission error occurred.
2	Customer Name: Mr Eric Gordan Customer Account Number: 12574392 Status: Open	Changing customer status to closed.	Customer Name: Mr Eric Gordan Customer Account Number: 12574392 Status: Open	Change account status to closed.
3	Order Number: 110190 Item Number: 01584726 Quantity: 7 Customer Account Number: 124	Capturing order.	No details stored.	Recover details and roll forward the transaction to store order details.
4	To: Clare From: Larry Re: Status of Annual Report 'Please send me an update on the status of the annual report.'	Sending email.	Email not received.	Recover email and send it.
5	5,000 account records.	Transmitting data.	2,500 account records.	Roll back the data transmission and retransmit.

is deleted, the list is updated to indicate that the file has been deleted. The computer's file allocation table indicates that the space where the file was stored is now available to be used to store other files. Although the file has been logically deleted from the computer (the file list indicates that the file has been deleted), the file may still be physically stored on the computer (that is, the storage space may not yet have been overwritten with another file). File recovery involves the salvaging of data before the data are overwritten.

8.5.3 ▸ Role of Computer Forensics

Computer forensics is the process of gathering electronically stored data from electronic devices, which may provide evidence that illegal activity has taken place. Every interaction with IT devices creates a trail of data, a footprint, such as the date and time a website was accessed. Securing, locating, and recovering data to be used as evidence requires a series of e-discovery protocols to be followed.

DEFINITION: A **digital footprint** is the collection of data, which records the interactions that have taken place in a digital environment. **E-discovery** is the process of searching for electronically stored information that may be used as evidence in legal proceedings.

Information can be viewed as an informative object, equating to evidence; evidence comprises artefacts that provide information of facts, independent of inference (Buckland, 1991). Events can be informative but the facts about the event – the evidence – include objects (such as a footprint) and representations of the event (such as a film) (Buckland, 1991).

Cybercrime is a broad term to include criminal acts where computer technology has a role. The computer may have a role as the target of the crime, the direct tool used in the crime, or as a secondary tool in managing the crime (Cross & Shinder, 2008). For example, a computer network could be the target of cybercrime as the unavailability of a communications network may have a devastating effect on the operation of an organization. Alternatively, an employee could use the internal computer systems, to which they have legitimate access, to deliberately change data values and commit an act of fraud; in this case the computer is being used as a tool of the crime. Finally, computers can be used to access and record information in the planning and execution of criminal acts, such as collecting information to be used in identity theft or using email to communicate with accomplices. Examples of cybercrime include: fraud and illegal money transfers, data interceptions, threatening or offensive behaviour, and offensive content (Vlachos *et al.*, 2011).

DEFINITION: Cybercrime is the use of IT in criminal activity, either as the target of the criminal act, or as a tool to conduct, plan, or co-ordinate the criminal activity.

There are two main information management issues relating to cybercrime. First, when a cybercrime is suspected, action must be taken to preserve the integrity of the organization's information. This involves containing the situation and recovering the corrupted information. Second, action is needed to preserve the digital footprint and evidence that may be required for legal purposes. When an incident occurs it is important to be able to quickly access security information (Cross & Shinder, 2008). Information maps and the information architecture can be used to identify the information that may have been affected by an incident, and can be used to develop plans for containment, recovery, and restoring organizational operation.

8.5.4 ▶ Role of Information Management Strategy in Recovering Corrupted Information

The information management strategy plans actions to assess and avoid threats to the organization's information resource. When an incident occurs, the action taken in response to the incident is documented to facilitate a review of procedures.

Recovering corrupted information involves:

○ Identifying that a problem has occurred.
  ● Assess the situation to determine the degree of the problem.
  ● Take immediate action to limit the effects of the problem. This may involve isolating parts of the IT network to prevent a computer virus from spreading or locking databases to prevent further transactions taking place until the integrity of the data has been verified.
○ Addressing the problem where possible. This may include, for example, using a secondary power source and enabling information systems to continue operation by using a backup copy of data, which may be slightly out of date but whose integrity has not been compromised.
○ Assess the extent of the data corrupted.
  ● Identify the transactions taking place at the time of the incident.

● Decide whether to recover corrupted data using appropriate tools, or recreate the data from transaction files.
○ Recover the information.
  ● Roll back or roll forward transactions to ensure that the transactions have been completed successfully.
○ Take action to minimize future risk; this includes action to:
  ● Avoid the problem reoccurring.
  ● Minimize the future impact if the problem should reoccur.
  ● Improve the approach to identifying and responding to the problem.

Summary

Poor quality information is caused by dirty data or inconsistent data values. Dirty data contain inaccurate, incomplete, or invalid data values. Data become dirty by accident, through deliberate acts or poor systems design. When data are corrupted, action needs to be taken to identify the state of the data before the incident and restore data values to the original state. Steps are needed to clean data and then to implement appropriate validation controls to prevent similar problems reoccurring.

Data captured from different information systems can contain conflicting data values, due to the differences in the way in which data are defined and captured. Reconciling conflicting data requires analysis of the context in which the data were collected. Reports may present conflicting information due to differences in the data used or differences in the way the reports were generated. For example, reports could be produced at different times, using different time periods and different procedures for analysing the data.

The information management strategy aims to improve the quality of data and information in organizations. A range of processes coordinate activities in the information life cycle and support the aims of the information management strategy within the requirements of the governance framework. Information management processes are continuous, seeking to maintain the quality of information as the organization and its requirements for information change. The processes of information management are implemented within a programme of projects scheduled in the strategy's implementation plan. The programme implements the structures for managing information and addresses immediate problems with data quality and data access in the organization. Figure 8.5 illustrates the relationship between key processes in information management.

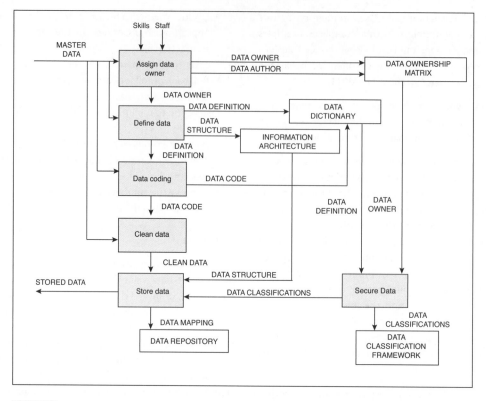

Figure 8.5 Information Management Processes

The previous chapters have provided practical guidance on how to develop and implement a strategy to address the information management problems in organizations.

○ Chapter 5 introduced the governing framework within which information management is undertaken, including the:
  • Ethical and legal issues relating to information management.
  • Roles and responsibilities for managing information.
  • Tools used in information management.
○ Chapter 6 outlined the components of an information management strategy and discussed how to:
  • Formulate an information management strategy.
  • Implement an information management strategy.
  • Evaluate the progress of the information management strategy.
○ Chapter 7 discussed how to improve access to quality information including:
  • Barriers to sharing data.
  • Measures of data quality.
  • Approaches to define data.

In morphing organizations, the context which gives information meaning is continually changing. The information management strategy therefore needs to be sufficiently flexible to address the challenges and opportunities offered by developments in technology and new ways of working. Part III discusses how changes in the organization can be supported by information management.

Reviewing Scenario 8.1

Over time Bright Spark has changed and grown from its one initial store. As the organization has grown the complexity of its information needs has also increased. Individual computer systems have been developed to meet the specific needs of individual departments and stores. This has resulted in duplication of data, flexibility of how data are used and interpreted, and incompatible data held in different systems. Information has become locked in silos in different formats, which makes it difficult for the organization to achieve an accurate and unified view of the information it needs.

A range of data held in different computer systems has to be accessed and integrated to provide a definitive answer to the type of questions required in the annual report. For example, there is not one system which can produce a report of the total sales for the year. Data from the sales systems in different stores need to be collated and this may be complicated if the data captured and stored about sales differ in the different systems. Different views of the data in different systems need to be reconciled in order to produce one consolidated view of the trading performance of Bright Spark. This may require the creation of a data warehouse in which data from operational systems are consolidated to provide one source of data for information reporting.

The preparation of reports is further complicated by dirty data. In Scenario 8.1 a business process was not in place to enable catalogues to be easily sent out to all customers so Clare created an order of one penny for each customer. This order affected the quality of data reporting relating to orders, creating dirty data and creating extra work in relation to the raising of credit notes. If the number of credit notes were taken as a measure of problems with customer orders that were rectified by issuing a credit note, the information would be misleading. In addition, Clare mentioned that some customers have different accounts that relate to the same address. This suggests that additional accounts have been wrongly created for a customer, causing dirty data. The duplicate records need to be reviewed to clean the data.

Cloze Exercise 8.1

Complete the following paragraph by choosing the correct word from Table 8.7 to fill in each gap.

Data _____ occurs when an entity is physically stored in different locations and may be used to improve data _____. The division of entities into subsets of instances is referred to as _____ fragmentation. _____ fragmentation is based on subsets of attributes processed by different transactions. Data in different information systems may use the same attribute name to mean different things or different attribute names to describe the same thing, requiring data _____. This involves standardizing attribute names, attribute structures, units of measure and _____ systems. Two reports may present _____ information due to how the reports were generated and how the _____ used in the reports were generated. For example, different data _____ may have been used to gather the data reported.

Data may be _____ accidentally or deliberately due to natural, human, or manmade actions. For example, data may be lost during a flood, by a computer virus, or an electrical fault. Electronic _____ create a digital _____ that can be used in computer forensics to investigate cybercrime. _____ can be used to perform or plan a criminal act, or may be the target of the crime. When an incident occurs the situation must be contained to preserve the evidence. Information maps and the information _____ can be used to identify the information that may have been affected by an incident. Data _____ involves identifying the state of the data before the

Table 8.7 ▸ Words to Complete Cloze Exercise 8.1

Accidental	Conflicting	Horizontal	Management	Recovery
Architecture	Corrupted	Inaccurate	Procedures	Technology
Backflushing	Data	Inconsistent	Quality	Transactions
Coding	Footprint	Integrity	Queries	Validation
Confidentiality	Fragmentation	Invalid	Reconciliation	Vertical

Dirty data are data that are of poor _____ and may lead to poor business decisions. Dirty data may be inaccurate, incomplete _____, and violate the business rules of data _____. Causes of dirty data include _____ or malicious acts, incomplete data fields, and staff working around existing quality controls. A data value is _____ if the value is not within the value range defined for the attribute. This can be prevented by using _____ checks when data are captured. A data value can be intrinsically valid but _____ due to dependencies between attributes. This can be prevented by using dependency checks. Cleaning data involves identifying and correcting problems, _____ the corrected data and implementing _____ to ensure the data stay clean.

incident occurred. Information _____ aims to maintain the quality of information as the organization and its requirements for information change.

Link 8.3
Answers to Cloze Exercise 8.1]

Activities 8.1

1 Define a set of data entry rules for the attribute *organization name* to avoid the problems listed in Table 8.1.

2   Using the entity *electrical item* in Figure 8.1, demonstrate vertical and horizontal data fragmentation.

3   Scenario 8.3 highlights a number of problems with information in Bright Spark. Explain how information management can be used to address each problem.

4   Reconcile the data sets in Figure 8.4 to create one file. List the actions you take and any assumptions you make that would need to be verified by Bright Spark.

5   Specify the data validation checks needed to implement the date format of DD/MM/YYYY.

6   Explain the steps that would need to be taken if connection to the Internet was lost while a customer was placing an order online with Bright Spark.

7   Keep a diary for 24 hours in which you note your activities, such as logging into an email account, catching a bus, using an ATM machine, and making a purchase in a shop. Review the diary, identifying how you could prove your whereabouts throughout the day based on data captured for each activity (such as receipts, surveillance cameras, and computer-based records).

8   Find examples of cybercrime:
   a   Classify the role of technology as the target, primary tool, or secondary tool in the crime.
   b   Identify the information management issues relating to the incident.

Discussion Questions 8.1

1   How often should data be cleaned?

2   Who is responsible for dirty data: the organization, information systems, or IT?

3   Who is responsible for conflicting information, the organization or the IT department?

4   Can conflicting information be completely eliminated in an organization?

5   To what extent is cybercrime an issue to be addressed within information management?

6   Which poses the most significant threat to data: natural, human, or manmade disasters? Why?

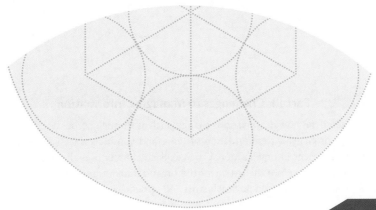

III

CHALLENGES TO MANAGING INFORMATION

Part III Challenges to Managing Information

Part III discusses how organizations change, such as through corporate merger, the use of IT, or changes to information systems, and considers the role of information management in organizational change. Each chapter uses the organizational architecture to explore the extent of the organizational transformation initiated by organizational or technological factors and presents a checklist for assessing the information management challenges introduced by organizational change.

Chapter 9 Organizational Change

Chapter 9 introduces types of organizational change such as business growth, diversification, and dissolution, and explains how organizational change affects information management. Guidelines for assessing the impact of organizational change on the information resource are presented. The role of information management during organizational change is discussed, for example, the role of the information architecture in extracting information to facilitate corporate divestiture and to support the information needs of leaders is considered.

Chapter 10 Information in E-Business

Chapter 10 outlines types of e-business systems, considers the strategic role of e-business systems, and discusses the impact of e-business on the organizational architecture. IT maturity models are introduced and the stages of e-business maturity are explained. The chapter considers the role of information in customer relationship management and supply chain management, and discusses the impact of collaborative systems on the information architecture.

Chapter 11 Changing Information Systems

Chapter 11 explains why and how information systems change in an organization. The chapter outlines the systems development life cycle and explains how information systems development methodologies differ. Barriers to determining information systems requirements are considered and guidance is given about how to overcome the barriers to determine information systems requirements. The information content in a range of models is identified and a black box approach to integrating information systems is introduced.

Chapter 12 Changing Information Technology

Chapter 12 explains how changes in IT in an organization impact the information life cycle. Issues such as data migration, information integration, and interoperability are discussed from an information management perspective. The chapter presents criteria for evaluating packaged software, compares open source and closed source software and explains the stages of introducing packaged software into an organization. The role of information management in managing legacy systems is also discussed.

ORGANIZATIONAL CHANGE

Scenario 9.1

Merger Announced between Match Lighting and Watts Electrical UK

Mr Alvis, Director of Match Lighting, made the following announcement to his management team:

'Match Lighting is a lighting manufacturer specializing in domestic light fittings stocked by the major retail outlets. We have been approached by Watts Electrical UK to discuss the possibility of a merger. The acquisition would further secure the position of Watts Electrical UK as a specialist in the design and manufacture of both commercial and domestic lighting units. Match Lighting would be viewed as a valuable asset strengthening Watts Electrical UK's position in the domestic market. Match Lighting is exploring ways to increase production capacity and this is one of the options being considered.'

If the merger goes ahead, what is the impact of this on Match Lighting's information resource?

Learning Outcomes

The learning outcomes of this chapter are to:

O Define types of organizational transformation.
O Introduce approaches to build organizational capacity.
O Assess the impact of merging or separating information between organizations.
O Identify the information requirements of business diversification.
O Assess the information needs of organizational leadership.
O Develop a model to assess the impact on information management of organizational change.

Introduction

Organizations are required to continually adjust to changes in their internal and external environment in order to survive. The business model (Chapter 1) showed the interrelationships between an organization and the:

O Customers and competitors in the market(s) in which the organization trades.
O Suppliers and professional associations in the industry in which the organization is based.
O Political, economic, and cultural factors within the overall business climate.

The organizational architecture comprises formal and informal structures, incorporating people, processes, practices, trust, skills, data, security, and infrastructure. These internal components of an organization change to pre-empt and respond to changes in the internal and external environments; changes to the components of the organizational architecture change the context in which information is used, changing the organization's requirements for information. This chapter explores how organizational changes affect the management of information. Types of organizational transformation are first explained which differ in terms of the scale of the impact on the organizational architecture. Different ways an organization may change are then discussed, including organizational growth (through internal growth, corporate merger, or diversification) and downsizing. Business leadership is then considered as different leaders require different types and qualities of information. The chapter concludes by summarizing the challenges of organizational change that need to be considered in information management.

9.1 ▶ Types of Organizational Transformation

Changes in an organization can range from relatively minor incremental changes through to the complete destruction of existing structures and systems (Senior & Swailes, 2010). Incremental changes take place in organizations to improve the efficiency of business operations and are a regular part of organizational development, acting upon feedback to continually improve competitiveness and sustain survival. In contrast, transformational changes aim to improve the effectiveness of the organization through redesigning the organizational architecture. Transformational change requires changes to be made to fundamental aspects of the organization, such as the organizational structure, which have a significant impact on all areas of the organization. Transformational changes trigger a series of changes to other elements of the organization (such as systems, processes, and people) in order to accommodate the initial change and complete the new organizational design.

Within this spectrum of change, Dunphy and Stace (1993) identify four types of change that differ in terms of the scope of the change; this is reflected in the number of components in the organizational architecture that change. First, fine-tuning involves adjusting the organizational alignment of strategy, structure, people, and processes. Fine-tuning changes may be restricted to changes in the boundary of a department. Second, increment adjustment involves modifying strategies, structures, and management processes in response to changes in the external environment. The changes may affect one or more departments and aim to improve the operation of the organization. Third, modular transformation incorporates the restructuring of one or more departments. This will impact the coordination of activities in the departments affected and the way the redesigned departments interface with other areas of the organizations. Fourth, corporate transformation involves revolutionary change of the strategy, structures, and systems in the organization, requiring wide-scale redesign of the organization.

Organizational transformation requires changes to be implemented within four main organizational dimensions explored in the following sections: strategy and governance, infrastructure, business processes, and cultural practice.

9.1.1 ▶ Strategy and Governance

Organizational change involves redefining the goals and values of an organization (By, 2005). The organizational strategy states the direction of the organization and encapsulates the intangible qualities that inform the organization's identity. Changing the organizational strategy changes one or more components of the generic business model highlighted in Figure 9.1. The organization may change the markets it trades in or the basis on which it competes (such as price or quality). Changes in one area of the model will require changes to be made in other areas of the model. For example, if Match Lighting plans to sell its products directly to the public rather than to sell to retail outlets, changes would need to be made to the structure and processes in the organization. Corporate governance provides a framework of policies, guiding acceptable behaviour, to achieve the organizational objectives. As the strategic objectives change, the governing principles of the organization may need to be revisited and possibly revised.

9.1.2 ▶ Infrastructure

The organizational infrastructure includes four main elements: the geographical structure of the organization and its trading network; the formal organizational structure of functions; the informal organizational structure that evolves through social relationships; and the technical structures, such as the telephone system and network of information technology (IT) services. The infrastructure implements control mechanisms to manage resources and coordinate interactions between people, business systems, and technology.

A change of strategic direction requires realigning organizational resources with the revised strategy. This will involve changes to the organizational structure, including the division of functional responsibilities, reporting structures, and the allocation of resources. The total level

Figure 9.1 ▶ Changing the Business Model

of resources available to the organization may increase (through corporate merger) or decrease (through the closure of a business branch). There may also be a change in the balance of resources required by different areas of the organization in the new structure. Barbaroux (2011) suggests that an organization can improve its ability to adapt to changing circumstances by decomposing the organizational structure, reducing the coupling between components. This improves the flexibility of the organization and enables the organization to quickly adapt to changes in the market or business environment.

9.1.3 Business Processes

Business processes may be located in a functional division of the organization or cross the boundaries in the formal organizational structure. Changes to the organizational infrastructure may change the location of where processes need to be completed, change the source of inputs to the process, and change the destination of outputs from a process. Changing business processes changes how the organization provides products and services to the marketplace, and can change the range and nature of the product and services offered. Changes to a process may have a positive (or negative) effect on the performance of the process. For example, changes can affect the quality of the output of the process or performance of the process (such as improve the efficiency of the process or increase the time taken to complete the process). Business processes are integrated, therefore changes to one process may require changes to be made to other processes.

Businesses processes coordinate interactions among the organization, its markets, and industry, as well as the internal interactions between departments and systems in the organization. Changes to, for example, customers, suppliers, and business partners may require the processes that interact with these parties to change too. Changing the strategy may require existing processes to be changed or removed, and new processes to be implemented. The interrelationships between processes need to be carefully examined to ensure that improvements in one process do not have an adverse effect elsewhere in the organization. For example, improving the speed with which a process is completed could increase the number of items waiting to be input into a later, slower process creating bottlenecks.

9.1.4 Cultural Practice

Cultural practice emerges from the interaction among people within the formally defined processes and structures of the organization. The recurring events that form common practice become embedded in the organizational infrastructure and are mediated by sociocultural rules (Perkins & Cox, 2004). Chapter 6 identified the need for organizations to cultivate a culture of responsibility towards the management of information, however, cultural change is difficult and progresses slowly.

Cultural change may be initiated by changes to the organization's strategy as the organization seeks to change the values by which the organization operates or how the organization is perceived by those outside the organization. Attempts may be made to impose a change of values through new control systems (such as measures of performance), structures, and processes. Behavioural changes needed to change organizational culture can only partly be achieved through business processes; individuals need to commit to changing behaviour (Bacon, 2007). The success of organizational change is dependent on the acceptance of the change by the people in the organization (Kuntz & Gomes, 2012).

9.1.5 Role of Information in Organizational Transformation

Information is needed to initiate and inform the change process. Information initiates the change process by informing decision-makers of changes in the context, which require the organization to respond. Information is then needed to inform the change process of what needs to be changed and the impact of the change, defining, implementing, and monitoring the process of organizational change.

During the change process, some staff will perceive the change negatively, as a threat to the established ways of working, while others will view the change positively. Kuntz and Gomes (2012) suggest that this difference in attitude is influenced by a number of factors including communication systems, leadership style, individual differences (such as previous experience of changes), and the information made available (including the source of the information and how the information is used).

Soparnot (2011) suggests that change can be analysed in terms of:

○ Content (what changes).
○ Process (how it changes).
○ Context (why change is needed).
○ Interaction between content, process, and context.

Information is one resource, part of the content, which may be affected by organizational transformation. All changes to the organization have the potential to impact the information resource. Information management needs to focus on the potential impact of organizational change on the organization's information resource.

The organizational architecture comprises the interrelated components that form the organizational change context. Information is given meaning within the organizational context, therefore any changes to the organizational context changes the frame of reference that gives information its meaning. Information needs to be redefined within the new context. This can range from the addition of a new attribute that needs to be captured to whole sets of new data that need to be captured and managed from external sources. Table 9.1 lists potential ways in which the information needs of the organization may be affected by changes in the organization.

A number of data management roles were outlined in Chapter 5. The data management processes and tools can be used to help to identify the potential impact of changes needed to information in order to reflect the changing needs of the organization throughout the transformation process. The potential impact of each type of organizational change on the information resource needs to be considered.

Strategy and Governance

The information resource, as other resources, needs to be aligned with the organization's strategy of the organization. Changes to the organization's strategy are therefore likely to impact the type of information that needs to be captured. For example, if Match Lighting's strategy is to move into a new market, the organization will need to capture information about the customer expectations in the market. Match Lighting will also need information to communicate the strategy through the organization and to monitor and review the impact of the strategy. A change of strategy may also affect the qualities of the information to be used in the organization. For example, the organization may seek to improve the accuracy or timeliness of the information provided to customers, requiring improvements to be made in managing and communicating information in the organization.

Infrastructure

The formal organizational structure directs the flow of information among divisions (Barbaroux, 2011). Any changes to the organizational structure are therefore likely to impact on where information is needed and who needs access to information. As the organizational structure defines areas of responsibility, changes to the functional or divisional structures will change the scope of responsibility of departments and divisions. If a new department is created, the information requirements of that department will need to be identified. Changing the locus of control among departments may require changes to be made relating to the level of detail and the specific characteristics of the information managed. The assignment of information management roles may also need to be reviewed.

Business Processes

The business processes are the means by which information is captured, used, and created. Any change to one or more processes is therefore likely to impact the information resource. Changes to a business process may require:

- Different data to be entered as *input to* the process, which may mean that changes need to be made to preceding business processes to capture or create the data required.
- Different data to be created *during* the process, which will require changes to be made to data processing and data storage systems.
- Different data to be *output from* the process, which may mean changes need to be made to proceeding business processes that will use the data.

Table 9.1   Impact on Information Needs of Organizational Transformation in the Life Cycle

Capture	Store and Retrieve	Use, Share, and Maintain	Archive and Destroy
The type, quality, volume, and characteristics of the information that need to be captured.	How the information is to be stored.	Who has access to the information.	How much information needs to be accessible.
When and how the information is captured.	The security of the information.	How the information is retrieved.	Specification of archive and retention policies.
Who the information is captured from and who captures the information.		How the information is to be processed.	
		Who uses the information.	
		How the information is defined in the organization.	
		What business rules maintain the integrity of the information.	

Any changes to data will need to be discussed with the relevant data owners to ensure that the processing requirements are consistent with the agreed upon definition of the data. The business rules agreed upon to maintain the quality and integrity of the data may need to be reviewed to reflect the new requirements.

Data are stored in IT systems and accessed by business processes through information systems. Changes to business processes may therefore require changes to be made to the information systems and underlying IT systems.

Cultural Practice

Information is interpreted by people in the organization; Martins and Martins (2011) refer to individuals as knowledge carriers. Staff in the organization develop a shared frame of reference within which they interpret events and actions. Conflict occurs when the information received from the organization diverges from an individual's frame of reference. Transformational changes challenge the existing frames of reference (Kuntz & Gomes, 2012) requiring a new frame of reference to be developed.

Changes to the organizational structure change the definition of roles and the allocation of staff to those roles. The information required by the roles will therefore change in terms of, for example, the type, quantity, frequency, and accuracy of the information required by the individual in the role. Changes to structure also affect the culture in which information is valued and the responsibility that is given for information. Data management roles must be maintained during the change process, particularly the role of data owners as they will oversee the changes required to information management policies.

9.2 Business Growth

Business growth refers to increasing organizational capacity; capacity refers to the organization's resource base and the limitations on the levels of performance that can be achieved by the current resources available. Capacity also considers the ability of the organization to extend its resource base. The growth of an organization can be considered in terms of three measures of capacity: internal organizational parameters (such as the number of locations, staff, and equipment to which the organization has access); organizational performance (measured by volume of outputs and sales); and the organization's relative performance (indicated by share of the market(s) or number of markets in which the organization trades).

9.2.1 Increasing Capacity

Soparnot (2011) defines change capacity as the ability of an organization to change (content and/or processes)

either proactively or in response to internal or external changes. The organization's ability to change is determined by the organization's absolute capacity.

DEFINITION: Absolute capacity relates to the organization's maximum potential level of achievement that can be attained by its current resources controlled within the current configuration of formal structures.

Capacity can be increased by increasing the number of resources, improving the efficiency of resource utilization, or by modifying the product or service (Meredith, 1992). There may be limitations on the ability of an organization to increase its resource base. For example, in Match Lighting the manufacturing equipment is working at maximum capacity, the equipment cannot work any faster or for longer periods, and therefore the only way to increase capacity would be to increase the number of machines or replace the machinery with new equipment that can produce a higher quantity of output. The upgrade or replacement of machinery takes time and there will be a delay in the organization's ability to increase production capabilities. Alternatively, the organization could outsource some of the work to other organizations. Information would be needed to identify potential organizations, formulate the agreement, and monitor the outsourcing process.

The organization's ability to achieve efficiency improvements in the use of current resources may be limited by the structures in which the resources are controlled. For example, the formal structure of the organization or the geographical location of resources may need to be reviewed to enable resources to be used more efficiently. The organizational processes may also need to be redesigned to improve efficiency and this will affect the information input to, and output from, the processes. Reducing the complexity of a product or service and seeking opportunities for mass production can provide opportunities for improving the production capacity. Changes to the business processes to produce the outputs of the organization may change the information required by the processes.

As Match Lighting wishes to increase its size, the organization can achieve this by increasing the volume of existing outputs, increasing the customer base, entering new markets, or offering new products and services. These options will require different types of information to be stored and different volumes of information to be held. The impact of capacity building on information management needs to be considered in three ways. First, how is the information resource affected by organizational growth? Second, to what extent does the information architecture and IT architecture constrain an organization's capacity for growth? Third, how is information management affected by organizational growth?

9.2.2 Impact of Business Growth on the Information Resource

Increasing the capacity of an organization may require more information to be captured. This may be an increase in terms of the:

○ Quantity of existing information, that is, greater volumes of existing data need to be managed. For example, increasing the volume of customers will require the same data about customers to be captured, but the volume of customer records will increase.
○ Need for different information to be collected, that is, details about different competitors will be captured and stored with existing data about competitors. The same data attributes will be collected with different data values. Data authors will need to ensure that new data values are consistent with the policies specified by the data owner.
○ Need for different types of information to be collected, that is, additional attributes of existing entities or new entities needed to store data about things of interest to the organization. New data owners will need to be identified to define the data. Analysis will need to be undertaken to ensure that the new data are effectively integrated into the existing information systems.
○ Need for different quality characteristics of existing information, that is, greater accuracy or detail needed for existing data attributes. Data owners will need to change the entity and attribute definitions in the data dictionary to reflect the changes required.

9.2.3 Impact of Business Growth on the Information Architecture

The information architecture is designed to meet the current and predicted future needs of the organization. Changes to the information resource may require changes to be made to the information architecture to ensure that the integrity of the relationships between information are retained. The information architecture informs decisions of how data are stored on physical storage devices. The location and organization of data are determined by a number of factors, such as frequency of access required to the information and the access paths to locate data in response to typical information requests. If the organization's information requirements change, the data may no longer be organized in the most optimal manner. The

information architecture may therefore hinder the ability to access certain data more quickly.

The IT infrastructure provides the communications network enabling data to be accessed throughout the organization. The infrastructure is designed to meet the data transmission requirements of the organization in terms of the:

○ Volume of data to be accessed and transmitted.
○ Level of demand for the data, that is, the number of requests.
○ Capability of equipment, such as speed.
○ Location of the data and location of where the data are needed.
○ Paths to be navigated to access and transmit the data.

If any of these factors change, the performance of the communications network may be adversely affected. For example, if Match Lighting increases the number of sites from which the organization operates, this will require information to be accessed and collected from different locations. This presents an additional loading on the IT infrastructure and the technical storage systems that will have a maximum storage volume.

DEFINITION: Loading refers to the volume of data to be captured, transmitted, stored, or processed in a specific period of time. A technical device or information system will have a maximum capacity of data that can be manipulated.

Processing more information, or more demands to access information, will have an impact on the performance of information systems. The information system will take more time to respond to requests for information and response times will increase as the system slows. While it may be technically possible to access an existing database of data from a different location, the number of requests for data may be such that the performance of the whole system becomes excessively slow.

In exploring the capacity of the information resource, the organization needs to consider the ability of the IT infrastructure to grow and the impact that this will have both in terms of data storage and in terms of data access requirements. IT should not limit the growth capacity of an organization but the effective implementation of actions to increase capacity will require an effective IT infrastructure to be in place.

9.2.4 Role of Information Management in Business Growth

In relation to information, capacity needs to consider the ability of the organization to manage more information.

This may include additional types of information or more volume of the existing information used in the organization.

Plans to increase the volume of existing data collected and processed will require the capacity of information systems, storage devices, and the IT infrastructure to be assessed. Consideration will need to be given to the existing retention strategy to assess whether the increased volume of data may pose any challenges to the organization's ability to archive and retrieve data from archived storage when needed.

Plans to collect new types of data will require changes to be made to the information architecture and data dictionary. Data owners will need to analyse how the new data can be integrated with the existing data in the organization to ensure that the data can be correctly interpreted. For example, if data are collected about a new entity, *trade events*, the data may need to be linked to data about products to enable information to be derived about which products were showcased at a specific event.

The potential impact of proposals for business growth on the information resource, information architecture, IT infrastructure, and management of information therefore needs to be considered when the feasibility of proposals is assessed. Figure 9.2 provides guidelines for assessing the impact of capacity building on information management.

9.3 ▶ Corporate Merger

One approach to increasing capacity is to acquire access to resources, skills, expertise, and markets through working with other organizations. This can take a number of forms such as merger, acquisition, or joint venture. Despite the advantages of mergers, such as reducing risk and reducing the time taken to introduce a product to a market, mergers often fail (Raben, 1992). Mergers fail due to integration problems caused by differences in strategy and culture; successful mergers require detailed planning and effective communication (Nguyen & Kleiner, 2003). Information is the key to successful communication at all stages in the merging process.

9.3.1 ▶ Stages of Corporate Merger

Mergers and acquisitions impose internal changes to organizational structures and working environments (Miczka & Größler, 2010). Raben (1992) outlines four stages in the acquisition and merger process: stage 1, assessment; stage 2, planning and design; stage 3, implementation; and stage 4, development.

In stage 1, information is collected to establish the organization's need for a partner and to identify the business opportunities offered by working with another organization. This will include a review of the organization's own strategic plan, operating requirements, and readiness to make the changes required by the proposed

---

1. Determine whether the capacity growth will increase the quantity of existing data managed or whether additional different data attributes and entities will be captured.
2. If additional attributes need to be added to existing entities:
   a. Data owners need to define the attributes and policies relating to them.
   b. Data authors need to define the valid values for the attributes.
   c. Data owners need to use the information architecture to identify how the integrity of the attributes may be dependent on other attributes.
   d. IT staff need to define the new data fields in the storage records and modify existing information systems to enable the new data to be captured, used and integrated with existing data.
3. If changes are required to the quality characteristics of information, for example, to increase the accuracy of data values from one to two decimal places:
   a. Data owners need to define and agree the rules associated with data attributes.
   b. IT staff need to modify existing information systems to capture and validate attribute values.
   c. IT staff may need to make changes to existing data values to ensure that the data can be integrated with new data values collected.
4. If new data are collected, new entities will need to be defined.
   a. A data owner needs to be assigned to the entities.
   b. Data owners need to define the entity, attributes and policies relating to the use of the data.
   c. Data owners need to assess how the new entities can be integrated into the information architecture to maintain data integrity.
   d. IT staff need to define the new data fields in the storage records and modify existing information systems to enable the new data to be captured, used and integrated with existing data.
5. Assess the extent to which the increased data volumes can be accommodated in the spare capacity of the existing IT infrastructure.

Figure 9.2 ▶ Guidelines for Assessing Impact of Capacity Building

venture. Information is then collected to identify and assess the suitability of potential candidate organizations. This assessment of potential partners considers both the formal and informal structures of the partner organization to fully explore the potential degree of compatibility. This should include, for example, the operating styles and organizational culture as well as the degree of commitment to the venture proposed at all the levels in the organization.

In stage 2, the detailed structural issues of the new enterprise need to be agreed upon. This includes the structure of the merged organization, reporting requirements, and the degree of autonomy of individual components. Information about current structures and practices need to be shared and the new structural designs communicated to all parties.

The implementation of the organizational design of the merged enterprise is undertaken in stage 3. The change management process will address issues such as the power dynamics and staff anxiety during the transition. Information is needed to effectively communicate the need for the changes taking place and to monitor the progress of the implementation of the new organizational design.

Stage 4 involves establishing the organizational identity for the new enterprise, moving away from the separate identities of the individual organizations. Information is needed to develop and monitor the plans and performance criteria for the new merged enterprise.

A merger requires the formal and informal organizational architectures of two organizations to be integrated. In stage 1 an alignment and agreement of strategies is sought. The implementation of the agreed strategy will require adjustments to be made throughout both organizations to realign organizational components with the strategy.

9.3.2 ▶ Impact of Corporate Merger on the Information Resource

Merging organizations increases the information resource available to the merged enterprise. The information from the two organizations needs to be effectively integrated and accurately interpreted in order for the information to be of value. However, despite apparent similarities between the organizations (justifying the suitability of the merger) each organization will have a different context from which the information derives meaning. The creation of a merged organization creates a new context within which information will be interpreted. Merging the existing information resources is therefore not a simple

process as it involves reconciling two contexts to create a third, shared context.

People in the organization interpret information and give information value. Merging organizations has a significant impact on people. For example, the structures in which individuals work, the strategy, processes, practices, and control systems change. During this period of change, the knowledge staff have about how each organization operates and how data are used is most valuable. Knowledge becomes embedded in information systems over time (Chun & Whitfield, 2008) and this makes the integration of information resources and processes in the merged enterprise problematic and sometimes impossible. There is a danger that in enforcing standardization, the unique abilities of each organization that prompted the merger become lost.

Within the stages outlined in Section 9.3.1, the feasibility of merging information resources needs to be considered during the initial assessment phase. The information architecture, data definitions, and information management strategy of both organizations will need to be considered. The design of an agreed upon information architecture and the actions needed to merge data from the two organizations are planned in stage 2. Decisions will be taken about the permitted extent of local control of data. For example, after the merger Match Lighting may become a division of Watts Electrical UK retaining control of the manufacturing processes. This would mean that Match Lighting retains control for managing data about the manufacturing processes but that data about Match Lighting's customers, finances and resources need to be merged with that of Watts Electrical UK. Before integrating the data, old data may need to be archived or purged. The remaining data can then be cleaned before being integrated with the data from Watts Electrical UK to form the data resource of the merged organization. Cleaning data and issues with integrating data are discussed in Chapter 8. The implementation of plans to integrate data is completed in stage 3 to contribute to the identity of the new enterprise in stage 4.

9.3.3 ▶ Impact of Corporate Merger on the Information Architecture

Each organization will have an information architecture and an IT infrastructure. Decisions will need to be taken in stage 2 about the extent of the merger and control of information and IT resources. Although there is likely to be duplication of resources, the IT capacity may be reduced due to the need to transfer information between organizational systems. IT infrastructures, which were designed to meet the demands of the individual organizations, may hinder capacity growth and may ideally need to be redesigned to meet the needs of the merged organization.

Merging two organizations will require two distinct information architectures to be united. There are three options:

○ Create a new unified information architecture for the merged organization. This will require the existing architectures to be initially mapped to the new architecture to enable existing data to be imported into the new structure.

○ The existing information architecture of one of the partner organizations is imposed as the standard information architecture to be adopted by the merged enterprise. The information architecture of the second organization will need to be mapped to the new architecture and changes undertaken to integrate the data into the new structure.

○ Develop an intermediate information architecture that maps between the two existing architectures. This allows for data to be shared between the merged organizations but the organizations retain their existing information architecture. This will require detailed analysis of the data to ensure, for example, that data with the same name in both organizations, also have a shared meaning. The impact of the merger on the information resource also needs to be assessed at an early stage. Terms are likely to have different meanings in the two organizations, which will need to be reconciled. This is problematic due to the different data definitions and coding structures used in both organizations.

Implementing a common IT infrastructure is a pivotal point in the merger, providing the foundation for sharing procedures and creating a coherent merged organization (Linder, 1996). The common infrastructure severs the links to the original organizational processes and practices, creating a context and identity for the new enterprise in stage 4. The integration of information systems ratifies the cohesion of the merged organizations (Linder, 1996). Integration requires combining and standardizing data, processes, and systems, but this can be hindered by a lack of integrated data and incompatible hardware and software (Chun & Whitfield, 2008).

9.3.4 ▶ Role of Information Management in Corporate Merger

Information is embedded in the organizational culture. Mental models are developed by staff working together and shaped by cultural values that become embedded in the quality characteristics of information. Addressing the limitations of existing mental models and fully understanding the consequences of a merger are critical to its success (Papadakis, 2005).

There is the potential problem of a power struggle between the merged organizations seeking to retain control of data. This can lead to misunderstandings of how data have previously been captured and used, which will affect the quality of information used in the future. Communication is critical but the lack of a common language between the organizations is a barrier to communication (Granlund, 2003). An understanding of the information architectures and data definitions used in the organizations is needed to develop agreed data definitions for the merged organization, which will provide the basis for effective communication.

Decisions need to be taken relating to the information life cycle in the merged organization, including:

○ What data are needed and how data are defined.
○ When and where data are captured, used, stored, and archived.
○ How security of the data is maintained.
○ Who owns the data, addressing issues such as data policies.
○ Who has access to the data and authority to make changes to the data.
○ How information is accessed, used, and stored.

Information management needs to be considered at each stage of the merger process. In stage 1, the feasibility of merging information resources, the potential benefits and difficulties that may arise are assessed. Further detailed analysis of the information resources is conducted in stage 2 where issues of information governance, strategy, and structures are addressed. An information management strategy for the merged enterprise needs to be agreed upon and plans developed to support implementation of the strategy. The plans are implemented in stage 3, which will include projects to clean and integrate data, supporting the emergence and future development of the merged organization in stage 4.

Figure 9.3 presents guidelines for merging information from two organizations.

9.4 ▶ Business Diversification

An organization diversifies by changing the product or service provided, or changing the trading market. Diversification requires an organization to develop additional capabilities, such as an understanding of customer expectations in a different market. This changes the information required by the organization.

1. Compare the information architecture and data definitions documented in the data dictionaries of both organizations.
2. Recognize that data are interpreted within a social and cultural context and it is from this context that the meaning and value of information is derived.
3. Consult staff in both organizations and involve staff in exploring the impact of potential changes because staff in each organization, creating and using data, are best positioned to understand the impact of proposed changes on the information resource.
4. Define the structure for managing information, establish information policies and allocate staff to information management roles.
5. Develop data definitions and an information architecture for the new organization.
6. Map and reconcile any differences in data definitions to avoid potential problems in misinterpreting information.
7. Agree the new information architecture and data definitions.
8. Assess the impact on the IT infrastructure.
9. Develop a plan for implementing the new information architecture.
10. Define projects for cleaning and integrating data from both organizations.

Figure 9.3 Guidelines for Merging Information

9.4.1 Types of Business Diversification

Diversification can be vertical or horizontal (Liu & Hsu, 2011). Vertical diversification refers to an organization entering a different stage in the product life cycle. This involves moving backward or forward in the supply chain (Porter, 2008). For example, Match Lighting manufactures light fittings so the organization could move backward in the supply chain, taking ownership of activities currently undertaken by suppliers, such as the manufacture of starter sockets currently supplied by S. D. Fittings. Alternatively, Match Lighting could move forward in the supply chain and take responsibility for processes performed by customers, such as selling products directly to the public.

Horizontal diversification refers to entering the same stage of the product life cycle with the same product in a different market (for example, Match Lighting could sell lighting units to car manufacturers) or a different product in the same market (for example, Match Lighting could introduce a new form of lighting to the existing domestic retail market).

Diversification can be achieved by developing internal capacity (internal diversification) or through acquisition (external diversification). Concentric diversification relates to developing existing resources, such as taking an existing product into a new marketplace. This requires some new capabilities to be developed, such as knowledge of the customer expectations and price sensitivity of the market.

9.4.2 Impact of Business Diversification on the Information Resource

Changing the product or service that an organization provides will require new information to be captured, stored, and used. Data owners will need to be assigned to define the new information and the business rules to manage the integrity of the data. This may require changes to be made to information systems and IT systems to capture, store and process the new data.

When an organization seeks to compete in a different market, the information requirements of the customers and consumers in the marketplace may be different. This may require additional information to be captured from the marketplace and change the way information is communicated. Consumers in different markets will have different demands for the quantity and quality of information about a product or service during the purchasing process. Competing in a different market may require changes to the characteristics of information used in the organization. For example, selling products on the Internet requires more information about the product to be provided to the potential customer than when selling the product in a physical store.

Diversification may require changes to the organizational structure, such as the introduction of a new department. The introduction of a new department will need lines of communication to be established and access rights agreed within the communication structure. Such changes are likely to impact on where information is required, when, and by whom. This may require changes to be made to the characteristics of the information provided to meet the needs of individual managers.

9.4.3 Impact of Business Diversification on the Information Architecture

Diversification may require new information to be captured, different values for existing data items to be captured, or a greater volume of existing data to be captured. As the volume of data needed by the organization increases, the impact on the IT architecture will need to be assessed; for example, the capacity of the existing data storage may need to be increased. The arrangement of data on storage devices is determined by factors such as the volume of data and frequency of access required. If the volume of data increases the current arrangement may no longer be appropriate. In addition, increasing the volume of data will reduce the speed that data can be processed and transmitted, affecting the response times of information systems.

If new information needs to be captured to support development of new products and services, changes will need to be made to the information architecture. For example, if Match Lighting started to design lighting installations, the new service would require new entities to be defined in the information architecture to support the data requirements of the activity (such as installation site and illumination unit). Data owners will need to be assigned to define the additional data required and define the relationship between the new data and the existing data to maintain data integrity. Changes to the information architecture will then require changes to be made to the information systems and the IT architecture. Additional changes to the IT architecture may be required to ensure that the capture and use of the additional information does not adversely affect the performance levels of the IT systems (such as time taken to retrieve data from databases).

If different values for existing data items are needed minor changes may be required to the information architecture. For example, if Match Lighting started to offer products for sale in the car components market, the organization would need to capture information about customers in the market. The existing *customer* entity may be sufficient, or additional attributes may need to be added to the *customer* entity with the agreement of the data owner. Any changes will then need to be implemented in the information systems and IT systems that capture and use customer data.

9.4.4 ▶ Role of Information Management in Diversification

The organization responds to changes in demand for products and services, and seeks opportunities for using its capabilities to enter new markets. The organization's products and services have a life cycle and as they come to the end of their life cycle, they need to be reviewed and replacement products and services developed. Information on past sales and customer feedback will be used to inform the redesign process. The new offerings will require changes to be made to the information captured and managed. For example, new attributes may need to be added to the *product* entity. This will have an impact on the organization's ability to compare sales figures for different products over a period of time and issues of data integration will need to be considered.

The information management strategy needs to be sufficiently flexible to respond to the changing information needs of the organization, but the strategy must also ensure that the integrity of the information resource is maintained. The information manager therefore needs to be actively involved as opportunities for diversification are assessed to ensure that the additional information needs are satisfied. Figure 9.4 presents guidelines for addressing the information management issues of business diversification.

9.5 ▶ Company Dissolution

Corporate downsizing, division sell-off (demerger), and corporate closure (dissolution) also have an impact on information management. Information may need to be archived or removed from information systems. The transformation of organizations during periods of business decline creates an uncertain environment for staff. As staff leave an organization, either voluntarily or through redundancy and severance programmes, valuable knowledge is lost (Martins & Hester, 2012). During these periods information can also be lost by accident, carelessness, or through malicious acts. Greater vigilance is therefore needed to maintain the confidentiality and security of information.

---

1. Identify the information needed by the organization to diversify the business.
2. Agree the definitions for the additional data entities that need to be created to support the diversification.
3. Define the data policies relating to the new data to be captured, such as policies relating to data security and retention requirements.
4. Define the attributes of the new entities proposed.
5. Specify the relationships between the new entities and existing entities in the information architecture to integrate the new data and maintain data integrity.
6. Assess the changes required to business processes and practices to use the new data collected.
7. Assess the changes required to information systems to capture, verify and enable authorized access the additional data.
8. Plan the changes to IT to capture, store and maintain the security of the additional data.

Figure 9.4 ▶ Guidelines for Business Diversification

9.5.1 ▶ Impact of Company Dissolution on the Information Resource

Breaches of information security can occur when staff remove paper, laptops, or mobile storage devices from the organization. Clear policies are therefore required to define the restrictions that apply to the removal of information from the organization. The requirements of mobile working need to be balanced against the potential risks to information security.

The impact of divestiture on the information resource will depend on the scale of the reduction in the business operations. When corporate downsizing is restricted to the scaling back of operations, the information resource may be relatively unaffected as all the information resources are likely to still be needed. Opportunities may also arise for further use to be made of the existing information resources in order to gain a more detailed understanding of, for example, trading patterns to stabilize and redirect business growth.

If a division of the organization is closed the information that will no longer be actively used by the organization will need to be identified so that the information can be removed from operational information systems. The information will be retained and archived for the duration dictated by legal requirements. Care will need to be taken to ensure that the archived information can still be accessed if the information is required. There is a tendency in such situations to consider information systems and IT to be obsolete if they are no longer needed by the operational processes in the organization. However, the systems may be needed in the future to provide a means of retrieving and analysing the archived data.

If a division of the organization is established as a separate trading company or sold, the relevant information relating to that division will need to be extracted from the organization. This is challenging as some of the information will still be needed by the original organization. Legal issues will need to be considered in relation to the terms of use of the information, service agreements, and privacy policies. For example, a company privacy policy will state whether the organization has the right to transfer data through the sale of the company or sale of the data alone. The company policy may also state that a company has the right to share information with third parties where there is a business reason to do so.

9.5.2 ▶ Impact of Company Dissolution on the Information Architecture

The information architecture can be used to identify the information that may no longer be needed. When extracting information from the information architecture, care

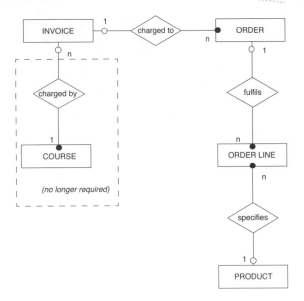

Figure 9.5 ▶ Extracting Course Information from the Information Architecture

is needed to decouple relationships to ensure that data integrity can be retained. These changes will need to be documented in the data dictionary by the data owners. The changes will then need to be implemented in the relevant information systems. For example, if Match Lighting closes its training division, information about *courses* may no longer be needed and could be archived. However, an extract from the information architecture (Figure 9.5) shows that *courses* are related to *invoices*. *Course* data can be removed from the information architecture as further information about *courses* will not be required; however, *invoices* cannot be removed as an *invoice* can either request payment for a *course* or an *order* for a *product*. Removing *course* data from the architecture will reduce the integrity of the information (there will be *invoices* relating to *courses* that can no longer be accessed). The specific *invoices* that relate to the *courses* therefore have to be extracted from the database and archived.

Link 9.1
Explanation of Figure 9.5

Reducing the information resource may mean that the organization can dispose of some data storage devices (once the data have been securely removed). Reducing the size or degree of activity of the organization may also reduce the demand for information in the organization. This may therefore increase response times and the overall performance of information systems.

9.5.3 Role of Information Management in Company Dissolution

During divestiture, responsibility for information must be maintained to avoid papers being left in a disused building or confidential information disposed of inappropriately. When staff leave the organization, care is needed to ensure that the information management roles are reallocated. This will ensure that the information management processes can be retained.

Figure 9.6 outlines the approach of information management in extracting information during corporate dissolution.

9.6 Business Leadership

A change in organizational leadership may initiate a change of strategy, change of structure, or changes to business processes. However, a change of leadership may also have an impact on the information needs of the organization if these components remain unchanged. One of the key factors that determine the information requirements of an organization is the people who use the information. As job roles change in organizations and new staff take on management roles, they often require different information from that of their predecessors.

9.6.1 Styles of Business Leadership

A range of leadership styles has been defined focusing on how a leader communicates and interacts with others. For example, democratic leaders invite staff to participate in decision-making; authoritarian, autocratic, and dictatorial leaders make the decisions themselves and give direction to others; and laissez-faire leaders delegate, empowering others to make decisions.

Bass (1990) differentiates between transactional and transformational leaders. Transactional leaders establish rewards for good performance and manage by exception.

They look for instances where there is a deviation from the standards required and intervene. Transformational leaders provide a vision and communicate their high expectations of staff; they mentor staff and encourage them to become committed to achieving the vision.

Dunphy and Stace (1993) identify four main types of leadership of change. (1) Collaborative: leaders involve staff in decisions relating to both the nature and process of the change. (2) Consultative leaders involve staff in decisions relating to the process of the change. In contrast, (3) directive leaders use authority to decide the nature and process of change, and (4) coercive leaders impose change.

Lussier and Achua (2009) suggest that a leader's style will be influenced by the information available to him or her. For example, if a leader has all the information needed to make a decision, he or she may adopt an autocratic style. If a leader has some of the information needed, a consultative leadership style may be adopted which will enable them to gain more information from others. If a leader has little information, a participative approach to leadership may be adopted, empowering staff to provide the information needed.

Quiz 9.1
Information Requirements of Leadership Styles

9.6.2 Impact of Business Leadership on Information Resource

All leaders need accurate and timely information on which to base their decisions (Lussier & Achua, 2009). Different leadership styles and individual preferences will impose different requirements for the volume, frequency, quality, and range of the information provided to facilitate decision-making.

---

1. Recognize that company divestiture is a difficult period for all staff in the organization.
2. Ensure that the information resource is not forgotten.
3. Identify the information resource needed by the surviving elements of the organization and recognize that information is an asset; identify ways in which information can be exploited in the future.
4. Plan how to break ties with affected areas of the business and maintain information integrity whilst ensuring business continuity during the change period.
5. Clarify legal issues relating to the ownership, confidentiality and retention of information.
6. Identify information to be archived and removed from information systems.
7. Establish plans to extract data and identify issues of integrity.
8. Ensure information management procedures are in place and documented (as knowledge may be lost with staff leaving).
9. Ensure the roles of data owner and data author are reassigned.
10. Maintain information security and adopt greater vigilance on information leaving the organization.

Figure 9.6 Guidelines for Extracting Information in Company Divestiture

This may mean that:

○ The characteristics of existing information need to be changed. For example, existing information may be required more frequently.

○ Existing information needs to be presented in a different format. For example, some people prefer information to be presented as graphs while others prefer to view the information in the form of tables.

○ Existing information needs to be made accessible. For example, monthly sales figures may be currently reported by product type. A different leader may require the sales figures to be reported by customer demographics. Customer profiles may currently be captured (so the data are available) but changes may be needed to existing information systems to enable the required reports to be produced.

○ Different information needs to be captured. For example, a person may require sales figures to be reported by age of customer. If the age of customer is not currently captured, changes will need to be made to the existing information systems to capture and report the age of customers.

Match Lighting's sales manager, Ms Bevan, likes to work with detailed statistics but her predecessor preferred to receive graphical summaries to compare year-by-year sales. Since Ms Bevan's appointment, the sales team have collected more detailed and accurate data about daily sales to produce the information she requests. This required changes to be made to the data collected about sales. The changes were agreed to by the relevant data owners, recorded in the data dictionary, and then implemented by the IT staff.

9.6.3 ► Impact of Business Leadership on Information Architecture

The information architecture is designed to meet the existing and anticipated future information needs of the organization. The architecture should enable information to be derived to meet the needs of a change of leader but sometimes changes to the architecture may still be required. Figure 9.7 shows an extract of Match Lighting's information architecture. The monthly sales figures reported by product type can be generated by following the path indicated in Figure 9.7. The sales figures cannot currently be reported by customer demographics as only the customer name and address are stored. A new attribute of, for example, *customer age*, would have to be added to the *customer* entity. This would require changes to be made to the information systems to ensure

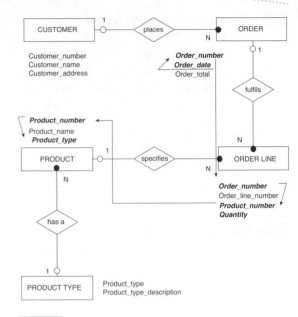

Figure 9.7 ► Access Paths in Information Architecture

that the date of birth of a customer is recorded when the details of a new customer are captured. This would enable sales to be analysed in relation to the age profile of new customers but not existing customers. All existing customers would have to be asked to provide their date of birth. The required sales reports could then be generated but it would take time to make the required changes to the information systems and collect data from existing customers.

Link 9.2
Explanation of Figure 9.7

9.6.4 ► Role of Information Management in Business Leadership

A change in business leadership may require more information or different information to be managed. The information manager and data owners need to determine the information needed by senior staff and to assess whether data are available from which to derive the required information. The specific leadership style will reflect the focus, frequency, regularity, accuracy, type, and level of detail of information required. The information architecture will need to be reviewed to determine if the information can be provided. Changes may need to be made to the information architecture and information systems to provide the quality information required.

9.7 ▶ Information Management Challenges with Organizational Change

Too often the potential impact of organizational change to information is not considered. It is taken for granted that the changes to information will eventually be identified, resolved, and will be insignificant, however, often change processes fail or are hindered because of the lack of consideration that has been given to issues relating to information, information systems, and IT integration.

The scope of organizational change can vary. The impact of small changes taking place in a department may be restricted to the information used by that department. However, as many data items are used across many departments, the wider impact of changes of one department on other departments needs to be considered.

Organizational growth, merger, diversification, and dissolution are initiated by a change to the organization's strategy. This may be in response to changes in the external trading environment, such as customer demand, or changes to the internal capabilities of the organization such as a change in leadership or the resource base. These changes of strategy will directly affect the organizational structure, and the people and business processes whose activity is coordinated using information within the structure.

Changes to business processes are likely to have an impact on the data needed as input to, and output from, the processes. This may require changes to be made to the:

○ Technology that is used to capture, store, and transmit the data to and from the processes where the data need to be created and accessed.
○ Systems that create and use the data.
○ Security required to verify, validate, and restrict access to the data.

Changes to people in the organization are likely to have an impact on the data needed to provide the information required to inform decisions and activities. This may require changes to be made to the values that define the quality characteristics of information required (such as frequency or accuracy); definitions of the data required; and practices adopted for accessing and acting upon information.

Information is a core organizational asset. The information requirements and meanings are determined by the organizational context. Changes to the organization, strategy, systems, structure, people, or processes affect what information is needed, when, how, why, and by whom. Sometimes the subsequent changes to information are easy to implement, but information is accessed via information systems through the application of IT. Changes to how information is needed may therefore require extensive changes to be made to IT systems, which will take time and may cause some interruption of business operation. Any change to the organizational capacity is likely to impact on the type, quality characteristics, and volume of information required by the organization. The impact of changes on the informal organizational structure also needs to be considered. Organizational change creates a period of uncertainty as the organization's structures change and the organization's culture and practices become challenged. This may require new skills to be developed that will need to be supported by different requirements for information. Changes to IT also pose specific challenges to information management and these are considered in later chapters. The areas affected by strategy-led business transformation are shown in Figure 9.8.

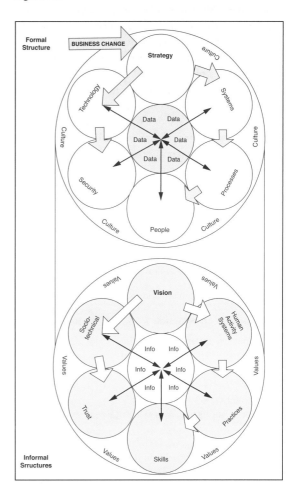

Figure 9.8 ▶ Strategy-led Organizational Transformation

Link 9.3
Checklist for Assessing Information
Management Challenges of
Organizational Change

Summary

Organizations transform in response to changes in the internal and external environments. Organizations may grow, through increasing capacity, merging with other organization, or diversification. Organizations may reduce in size through downsizing initiatives or dissolution. As organizations increase or decrease in size, this affects the information required by the organization and the way in which information is managed in the organization. The changes affect the volume of information needed and the content of the information, the entities and attributes required to provide the information needed by changes to different aspects of the organizational architecture. For example, changes to organizational structures affect who needs information, what type of data need to be captured and maintained, and how information will be needed to coordinate business processes. Changes to processes may require different data to be entered, stored, processed, and analysed. Corporate merger requires the information resource to be analysed in terms of how information can be integrated with the information architecture of another organization. In corporate dissolution the information architecture is used to decouple information. Organizational change is inevitable and the organizational architecture provides a structure in which to analyse the impact of the transformation and determine how the information resource may be affected.

Reviewing Scenario 9.1

The impact of the takeover of Match Lighting by Watts Electrical UK will initially depend on the structure of the merged organization; there are three options. Option 1, Match Lighting could be completely subsumed by Watts Electrical UK. Option 2, Match Lighting could become a manufacturing division of the organization. Option 3, Match Lighting could be allowed to maintain a degree of autonomy and retain its operations and branding.

Option 1 will have the most impact on the information resource as Match Lighting's information will be completely merged with the information of Watts Electrical UK. This is a complex task. There is a high risk that during the merger process seemingly similar data will be merged and problems will later arise as the information is misinterpreted. For example, the definitions of product, item, and merchandise are likely to differ between the organizations, therefore integrating product data may generate conflicting reports.

Option 2 enables Match Lighting to become a reporting division of Watts Electrical UK. The impact on Match Lighting's information resources will depend on the extent to which the information needs to be used by the existing information systems in Watts Electrical UK for reporting purposes.

Option 3 will have the least impact on the information resource as Match Lighting's existing information architecture will be used. Match Lighting will be required to regularly provide information on its performance to its parent company, therefore Match Lighting will need to understand the reporting requirements, particularly the definitions of the terms used by Watts Electrical UK to ensure that the correct information is reported. Relevant data owners in Match Lighting will need to work with staff in Watts Electrical UK to understand the reporting requirements and identify any changes that may be needed to the way data are defined and captured in Match Lighting.

Table 9.2 lists the actions required to implement each of these options.

Table 9.2 ▶ Merging Information in Match Lighting and Watts Electrical UK

Implementation of Option 1	Implementation of Option 2	Implementation of Option 3
1. Gaining an understanding of the information architecture of Watts Electrical UK. 2. Creating a mapping between the information architecture of Match Lighting and Watts Electrical UK. 3. Identifying the legal issues relating to the data held by Match Lighting. 4. Developing a plan to merge the information held by Match Lighting with that of Watts Electrical UK.	1. Determining the information reporting requirements of Watts Electrical UK. 2. Identifying which information systems need to use information from Match Lighting. 3. Gaining an understanding of the information architecture of Watts Electrical UK. 4. Creating a mapping between the information architecture of Match Lighting and Watts Electrical UK.	1. Determining the information reporting requirements of Watts Electrical UK. 2. Identifying which information systems are needed to use information from Match Lighting. 3. Gaining an understanding of the information architecture of Watts Electrical UK. 4. Creating a mapping between the information architecture of Match Lighting and Watts Electrical UK.

Table 9.2 ▶ Continued

Implementation of Option 1	Implementation of Option 2	Implementation of Option 3
5. Archiving historic data from Match Lighting. 6. Cleaning and purging data from Match Lighting's systems. 7. Developing a plan to migrate data from Match Lighting to Watts Electrical UK. 8. Communicating the data definitions and business processes used by Watts Electrical to staff at Match Lighting.	5. Assessing the extent to which the reporting requirements can be satisfied by the current data definitions. 6. Developing bridging systems to extract and reformat relevant information from Match Lighting's databases so that the information can be input into the systems of Watts Electrical UK.	5. Assessing the extent to which the reporting requirements can be satisfied by the current data definitions. 6. Developing systems to extract and reformat relevant information from Match Lighting's databases to produce the reports required by Watts Electrical UK.

Exercise 9.1

1 What is the primary reason for organizational change?
2 What effect does incremental change have on organizations?
3 What is the aim of transformational change?
4 Name the four organizational dimensions that are affected by organizational transformation.
5 Name the four types of organizational infrastructure.
6 Explain the purpose of infrastructure.
7 How might changes to business processes impact information?
8 List the three ways that organizational growth can be measured and provide an example of each.
9 If Match Lighting decides to outsource production, what information will Match Lighting need?
10 How might the information resource be affected if an organization seeks to increase capacity through diversification?
11 List four ways in which information might be affected by an organization's plans to increase capacity.
12 How might the IT infrastructure be affected by an increase in the volume of information to be processed?
13 Explain how information is used in the four stages of merger.
14 Why is merging information from two organizations not a simple process?
15 List three approaches to designing an information architecture for the merged organization.
16 Why is developing an agreed information architecture and IT infrastructure in the merged organization important?
17 Explain the difference between vertical and horizontal diversification.
18 What is the purpose of a company's privacy policy?

19 How does a change of leader impact information management?
20 How is the leadership style influenced by the information available?

Link 9.4
Answers to Exercise 9.1

Activities 9.1

1 With reference to Match Lighting, give an example of the characteristics of information that Mr Alvis might use depending on the style of leadership he adopts.
2 Add the attribute *customer_age* to Figure 9.7 and draw the access path to create a list of all product numbers purchased by customers over 50 years of age.
3 Define the range of information reports that can be produced by using the information architecture in Figure 9.7.
4 Assess the impact on information and the information architecture if Match Lighting diversified to sell light fittings to car manufacturers.
5 Explain the impact of improving the effectiveness of business processes in Match Lighting, with reference to Figure 9.8.
6 Specify the criteria that could be used to assess the impact on the information required when a new production manager is appointed in Match Lighting.
7 Develop a checklist to assess the potential impact on the information resource of organizational transformation.
8 Using Figure 9.8, assess the extent of the changes to Match Lighting if the organization were to become a division of Watts Electrical UK.

Discussion Questions 9.1

1 What type of organizational transformation has the greatest impact on the information resource? Why?

2 What problems might arise if Match Lighting merges with Watts Electrical UK? Do the potential benefits outweigh the problems?

3 How can the capacity of an organization's information resource be measured?

4 Why is security of information a significant concern during organizational divestiture? How can the risks to information security be minimized?

5 Why does a change of leader affect the information required in an organization?

6 How can the compatibility of the information resource of two organizations be assessed as part of the feasibility study to merge the organizations?

7 Which would be the most appropriate option for Match Lighting, vertical diversification with Bright Spark or horizontal diversification with Amy's Candles?

8 Why is it important to consider information management in planning and implementing organizational transformation?

INFORMATION IN E-BUSINESS

Scenario

Collaborative System Opportunity at Bright Spark

Graham George, the IT Manager for the light fittings retailer Bright Spark, has requested a meeting with the owner, Larry Hughes. Graham explained the purpose of the meeting.

'I have been talking with the IT Manager at one of our main suppliers, Match Lighting. They are planning to pilot the use of collaborative systems with some of their customers.'

'What are collaborative systems?' asked Larry.

'You know how customers in Australia can buy our products using the Internet?'

Larry nodded.

'A collaborative system is the same sort of thing. We would use the Internet to buy our supplies from Match Lighting. It would help reduce our transaction costs,' George explained.

Larry was still confused. 'Customers buying lamps from us just choose the one they want and pay for it. We negotiate the purchase of large volumes of lamps with Match Lighting, so how is that going to be done via the Internet?'

How will e-business affect Bright Spark and its relationship with Match Lighting?

Learning Outcomes

The learning outcomes of this chapter are to:

○ Define types of e-business.
○ Assess the organizational transformation required to support e-business.
○ Define the information management responsibilities of intranet systems.

○ Outline the information management issues of collaborative systems.
○ Assess the information management issues relating to email.
○ Develop a model to assess the impact on information management of e-business systems.

Introduction

The phrase *electronic business* embodies the alignment of information systems and information technology (IT) with the needs of the organization (Cox *et al.*, 2001). *E-business* has become a general term to describe business transactions conducted electronically using the Internet.

DEFINITION: E-commerce refers to the conduct of simple business transactions electronically, replacing paper forms and filing cabinets with electronic forms and digital storage. It includes the buying and selling of goods and services on the Internet.

Email is an example of e-commerce as information is sent electronically, replacing paper memos and letters sent via internal and external postal systems. E-business extends the use of the Internet beyond the completion of online transactions.

DEFINITION: E-business refers to the use of IT to support business processes throughout an organization's internal value chain and external supply chain. It involves the use of interorganizational networks.

E-business is more than the automation of existing business processes; e-business uses IT to achieve organizational goals. In addition to enabling the electronic exchange of information, e-business provides support to decision-making that underpins business processes

(Holsapple & Singh, 2000). Organizations engaging in e-business have learnt that conducting business electronically requires more than the introduction of appropriate IT (Cox, 2013). E-business systems change the nature of the business processes, work practices, and communication skills needed in and between organizations, initiating widespread organizational transformation (Cox et al., 2006). E-business changes the organization's outward face, through which the organization interacts with external partners, and requires corresponding changes to take place in the organization to support the information interaction. This chapter explores the challenges to information management initiated by different types of e-business systems.

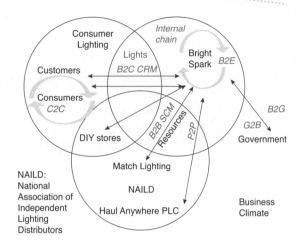

Figure 10.1 E-Business Relationships with Bright Spark

10.1 Types of E-Business Transformation

E-business can support trading relationships between two or more parties. A range of e-business relationships is listed in Table 10.1.

The business model (Figure 10.1) identifies potential relationships which could be strengthened using e-business technology for Bright Spark. Bright Spark currently engages in B2C activities to sell products to customers in Australia and South America. Bright Spark could extend the use of e-business to support additional trading relationships.

10.1.1 Maturity Models

Maturity models represent the business transformation initiated by the introduction of IT in organizations. Models such as Nolan's maturity model (1973) outline the progress and management of IT in organizations (Wilson, 2000). The stages in Nolan's maturity model (1973), shown in Table 10.2, outline an organization's transition between stages of technological maturity. The technological maturity is driven by growth in the number and complexity of

computer applications, growth in specialization of technical staff, and growth in formalization of organizational control of technological systems. Two further stages were later added to represent growth in the integration of technological systems and data prior to reaching maturity (Nolan, 1979).

Table 10.2 reflects the historic position that the introduction of information systems and IT in organizations has been internally focused. The introduction of IT starts with the automation of back-office processes such as accounting. As the organization's IT capability develops, the use of IT extends throughout the organization to include more customer-focused business processes. The organization's maturity with technology is reflected by the move from being internally focused to externally focused.

E-business focuses IT externally and inverts traditional IT maturity models (Cox et al., 2006). Wilson (2000) outlines a four-phase maturity model representing the sequential transformation of an organization's engagement

Table 10.1 E-Business Relationships

E-Business Relationships	Support Business Processes Between
B2C: Business to Customer (also known as Business to Consumer).	An organization and its customers or consumers.
B2B: Business to Business.	Two organizations, usually in different stages of the supply chain.
P2P: Partner to Partner.	Two organizations, usually in different industries, that work together.
C2C: Consumer to Consumer.	Two individuals, such as individuals trading on auction websites.
B2E: Business to Employee.	An organization and its employees.
B2G: Business to Government.	An organization and local or central government.
G2B: Government to Business.	Local or central government and an organization.

Table 10.2 Stages of Maturity

Stage	Description of Maturity
Stage 1: Initiation	IT is introduced to deal with the volume and complexity of data processing applications.
Stage 2: Contagion	Uncontrolled growth in the number and complexity of computer applications.
Stage 3: Control	Management control introduces standards to overcome problems of replication and incompatibility of computer applications.
Stage 4: Integration	Disparate applications are integrated and greater emphasis is placed on planning.
Stage 5: Data Administration	Focus on managing data independently of computer applications, recognizing the difference between information systems and IT.
Stage 6: Maturity	Information systems are used to develop competitive advantage.

Source: Based on Nolan, 1979.

in e-business. In phase one, an organization starts exploring the potential of e-business with the introduction of a noninteractive web page. Interaction is added to the web page in phase two to enable customers to enter orders online for some of the organization's main products. The complete catalogue of products and services is available online in phase three. In phase four, the functionality of the website is extended as back-office processes, such as dispatching, are available online.

Wilson's (2000) model follows Nolan's (1973) model in that the number and complexity of e-business applications increase. However, the final maturity level in Wilson's (2000) model is achieved when back-office processes are available online, which is an initial phase of development in Nolan's (1973) model. E-business maturity adopts an outside-in approach to organizational transformation. This puts more pressure on organizations as external parties are affected by any problems that occur due to the lack of initial internal adjustments in the organization transformation.

10.1.2 Transformation Dimensions of E-Business

The introduction of a B2C system changed the way customer orders are received and processed by Bright Spark. Superficially, introducing B2C applications was considered to simply require a technical solution to capture orders. In practice, the organizational impact was more extensive.

Creating an IT interface between the organization and its customers demanded that back-office processes, such as forecasting, procurement, and delivery, be effectively integrated into online operations. Orders can only be processed and dispatched if all internal operations are integrated and able to respond effectively to online events.

In introducing B2C, Bright Spark followed Wilson's (2000) stages. Bright Spark first created a static web page

to advertise products. A B2C system was then developed to enable customers to order products online. This was viewed as a separate IT system. The orders received by the system were printed and passed to the order processing staff to be processed in the same way as the orders received by post or telephone. This caused problems as sometimes customers placed orders for products that were out of stock. The B2C system was then connected to the stock control system to ensure that customers were aware of current stock levels prior to placing their order. The B2C system automatically updated the stock control system when an order was entered by a customer online. Additional functionality was also added to accept online payment for orders. Customer orders received via the B2C system are now automatically entered into the order processing system directly, without human intervention.

Table 10.3 shows the areas of Bright Spark that were affected by the introduction of the B2C system. The changes extended beyond the IT department.

10.1.3 Role of Information Management in E-Business Transformation

The introduction of B2C in Bright Spark created a new context in which data were captured: the online system. Detailed information had to be provided to potential customers about the products available, payment methods, and delivery options. The data owners responsible for data relating to products, payments, and delivery had to review the data needed by potential customers. Staff were then assigned responsibility for updating the information on the web page.

The data captured by the B2C system about a customer order were the same order data captured via other means. The main impact of the B2C system on the information resource related to the secure capture of data and the integration of data into different IT systems to process orders and payments.

Table 10.3 ▶ Impact of Introducing B2C System

	Stage 1	Stage 2	Stage 3	Stage 4
Strategy	Display products online.	Accept orders online.	Inform customers of stock levels and accept online payments.	Process orders online.
Systems	Separate online system developed to display products.	Functionality of online system extended.	Stock control and finance systems linked to online system.	Order processing system linked to online system.
Processes	Introduce new process to update online system when prices or descriptions of products change.	Introduce new process to print orders entered into online system and pass them to order-processing department. Introduce new process to address issues arising from orders (for example, inform customer that product is out of stock).	No additional requirements.	No additional requirements.
Technology	IT needed to display web page.	IT needed to capture, validate, and store order data.	IT needed to integrate online system with stock control and finance system.	IT needed to integrate online system and order processing system.
People	Skills needed in web design. Staff ensure information on website is up to date.	Skills needed to develop online system.	Skills needed to integrate online system with existing systems.	Skills needed to integrate online system with existing systems.
Security	Security needed to ensure that information on the web page can only be changed by authorized personnel.	Security needed to ensure that order information is captured and stored securely.	Security needed to ensure that payment information is captured and stored securely	No additional requirements.
Data	Detailed data about product specifications and pricing need to be added to web page.	Data required for ordering needed to be clearly defined.	Data required for payments needed to be clearly defined.	Data integration issues between online system and order processing system had to be resolved.
Infrastructure	Additional technology needed to display the web page.	Integration of customer database and online system.	Integration of online system, stock control system, and finance system.	Integration of online system and order processing system.

Source: Based on Wilson (2000).

Information management was therefore required to:

○ Define the data to be displayed on the website, using the data dictionary.
○ Assign responsibilities to ensure data on the website were kept up to date.
○ Define the data to be captured by the online system.
○ Ensure the security requirements relating to data capture and storage were implemented.
○ Use the information architecture to identify the information to be integrated with the online system.
○ Resolve issues relating to the integration of data captured from the online system with the data stored in the existing information systems.

10.2 Intranet Systems

The same technology that is used by Bright Spark to support e-business transactions with customers can be used within the organization to form an intranet.

DEFINITION: An **intranet** is a computer network providing access to data and information systems using Internet technologies. Access to the network is limited to authorized personnel, usually employees and approved partners of the organization.

Masrek *et al.* (2008) suggest that the main use of an intranet is to keep staff informed and to provide a mechanism for sharing knowledge. Intranets provide a means of accessing the organization's information and information systems supporting internal communication, collaboration, and information processing (Baptista, 2009).

Different organizational functions may each have their own intranet site, that is, a set of pages which they are responsible for developing and maintaining. The intranet provides a central repository for storing core information that employees may need to reference, such as a telephone directory, staff handbook, and IT policies. Often in organizations staff will need to collaborate on the preparation of reports, policies, and presentations. Intranet systems can be used to provide access to shared documents and avoid the need for documents to be circulated via emails.

B2E systems can be provided via the intranet to enable the business advantages of e-business systems to be realized with internal transactions as well as external transactions. For example, benefits of online systems can include reduced transaction costs; reduced time to process transactions; instant verification and error checking; and automated authorization of requests. B2E systems in Bright Spark are used by employees to record absences, complete time sheets, and submit expense claims.

10.2.1 Intranet Information Management Policy

Key information management issues relating to intranet publishing include:

- What is the policy for sharing information?
- What information resources can be made available via the intranet?
- Who can see what content?
- Who creates and maintains the content?
- Who controls the quality of the content?
- What is the approval process for uploading content?
- How frequently should the content be updated?
- When can the information be removed from the intranet?
- Should copies of information removed from the intranet be retained?

A series of information management policies are needed to provide guidance on managing the content of material published on the intranet to ensure that the quality, integrity, and availability of material is maintained. This will ensure that the intranet becomes a valuable and usable source of information, preventing it from becoming a store of out-of-date and unvalidated data. An intranet information management policy needs to consider the:

- Content of information published on the intranet.
- Roles and responsibilities for publishing information on the intranet.
- Time period for information published on the intranet.

10.2.2 Intranet Information Content

Information requires consistent data definitions, standards, and values to be agreed for all data items used in the organization. This includes information on the intranet to ensure that information is interpreted appropriately to inform decisions. The intranet policy needs to ensure that all information published on the intranet reflects the definitions and controls agreed to by the organization's data owners documented in the data dictionary. This will ensure that:

- Information published on the intranet can be compared with other information sources because of adherence to agreed upon definitions and formats.
- Information is traceable and has an identifiable data author so that clarification can be sought if needed.
- Responsibility and accountability for information is maintained.
- The content of the intranet is managed by the same data management principles as other forms of data in the organization.
- Information published reflects the organization's requirements relating to the characteristics of information, such as timeliness and accessibility.

10.2.3 Roles and Responsibilities for Managing Intranet Information

Data owners are assigned responsibility for data entities in the organization. The same level of data accountability is needed for intranet publishing. Roles are assigned responsibility and accountability for the accuracy, maintenance, and removal of content from intranet sites.

Data accountability of intranet material is needed to:

- Identify the source of information presented, enabling the source of material to be tracked when necessary and to improve the reliability of the content presented.

○ Identify a named data owner who is accountable for the quality of the information published.

○ Ensure that key terms (such as *product* and *customer*) are used consistently across intranet sites and are consistent with the definitions in the data dictionary.

○ Update information published in a time period appropriate for the specific content.

○ Ensure that information remains available for a time period reasonable for the nature of the content.

Roles of editor, publisher, and author can be assigned to manage intranet content. The responsibilities of these roles are outlined in Table 10.4.

10.2.4 Time Period for Intranet Information

The regular removal of content from the intranet is needed to prevent the intranet from becoming a store of unreliable, out-of-date data. Dated content can adversely affect how the content is used and perceived. A policy is needed to ensure that information published on the intranet

is accurate, updated, and deleted in a timely manner in accordance with the organization's data management policies.

The length of time content needs to be made available on the intranet depends on the purpose of the content. Information can be perishable, such as news announcements, or timeless, such as organizational policies. When publishing information on the intranet, a decision should be made concerning the frequency that the information is to be updated and the date when the information can be removed from the site. Intranet content can be:

○ Static content, unchanged for 12 months or more, such as policy documents.

○ Semi-static content, required for up to one month, such as news items.

○ Dynamic content, with a life span of a maximum of one week, such as staff notices.

Information will need to be archived when removed from the intranet so the information can be retrieved if needed for legal or historic purposes. An intranet information

Table 10.4 Roles and Responsibilities for Intranet Data Management

Role	Responsibilities
Intranet editor has the overall responsibility for an intranet site.	○ Formulate the strategy for the intranet site. ○ Create policies relating to the life cycle of information on the intranet site including how information is created, published, and removed from the site. ○ Ensure that terms used are consistent with those agreed upon in the data dictionary and define additional terms specific to the intranet site when necessary. ○ Assign roles of intranet publishers with authority to approve content for the intranet site.
Intranet publisher implements the intranet site policy defined by the intranet editor and approves information to be published on the intranet site. Several publishers are usually needed for each intranet site.	○ Inform intranet authors of the strategy, purpose, and standards relating to material on the intranet site. ○ Ensure information published supports the strategy of the site and adheres to the standards defined by the intranet editor. ○ Ensure the content of the intranet site remains valid and that out-of-date material is removed in a timely manner. ○ Define and conduct the process for approving content to be published on the intranet site.

Intranet author prepares and maintains the information to be considered by an intranet publisher for inclusion on a specific intranet site.	○ Prepare material to present to the intranet publisher that:
	  • Meets the requirements, standards, and presentation guidelines of the intranet site.
	  • Is accurate and up to date.
	  • Adheres to agreed upon data definitions.
	  • States the source of data used.
	○ Ensure that publishing the information on the intranet does not breach the confidentiality and security policies relating to the information.
	○ Maintain the content of the information published on the intranet.
	○ Propose a retention period for the information, after which information can be archived from the intranet site.

policy needs to define categories that specify the information's life span, including:

- Start date: by which the information needs to be made available on the intranet site.
- Maintenance date: by which the information needs to be updated.
- Review date: when consideration is given to whether the information is still relevant to the intranet site or whether the information should be removed.
- End date: when the information is no longer needed on the intranet site and should be removed.

Table 10.5 provides examples of information with differing life spans on Bright Spark's intranet site.

10.2.5 Transformation Dimensions of the Intranet

The introduction of intranet systems in Bright Spark was driven by the introduction of technology, which provided new opportunities for the internal communication of information. The adoption of new technology required the creation of a:

- Technical infrastructure to enable content to be published on the intranet and for information to be accessed via the intranet.
- Management infrastructure of roles and responsibilities to coordinate the use of the intranet as a communication tool and to be accountable for the information published on the intranet.
- Content structure to organize the information content on the intranet so that information can be located when needed.

Processes and procedures had to be defined for creating, authorizing, publishing, maintaining, and removing information from the intranet. Staff required training to attain the skills needed to create and publish information on the intranet.

The impact of introducing an intranet extends beyond the provision of a means to access information. Baptista (2009) suggests that intranets can be used to support organizational change; for example, the greater visibility of information between departments can inspire improvements in performance. Over time intranets become embedded as an information tool in the organization and social practices relating to information sharing and use adapt and evolve. The electronic communication of information therefore initiates changes throughout the formal and informal organization.

10.2.6 Role of Information Management in Intranet Systems

Intranets provide a means of internal information communication and need to be incorporated into information management policies. Information management is needed to:

- Define and implement policies for managing information on the intranet.
- Assign responsibilities to ensure data on the intranet are of the appropriate quality.
- Establish accountability for information published.
- Ensure that information is communicated consistently with the definitions and security policies documented in the data dictionary and information management strategy.
- Develop processes to ensure that information on the intranet is accurate, timely, and that data that are no longer required are regularly removed.

Table 10.5 Example Life Span of Intranet Content

Category	Event	News	Reports
Example Content	'A health and safety briefing will be held for all staff at 8 a.m. on 1 March.'	'Bright Spark has launched a new range of glass shades.'	'The sales figures for January show a 10% increase compared with the same period last year.'
Start Date	10 days before event.	10 days before product release date.	Within 12 hours of report being available.
Maintenance Date	Only if date or time is changed.	Only if information is inaccurate.	Every month to update the performance figures.
Review Date	Not applicable.	Not applicable.	Every 12 months to determine whether the report is still useful.
End Date	24 hours after event.	Four weeks after announcement.	After 13 months.

○ Ensure that information published reflects the organization's requirements relating to the characteristics of information.

10.3 Internet Systems

The Internet provides opportunities for organizations to interact with individuals and other organizations through exchanging information in innovative ways. There is a distinction between the Internet and the web.

DEFINITION: The **Internet** is a technological network linking computer networks providing access to information and information systems.

The Internet provides the technical infrastructure for the web.

DEFINITION: The **World Wide Web** (WWW) is a collection of information resources, such as multimedia documents, that can be accessed via the Internet.

Technological innovations such as smart phones and tablet computers increasingly offer new ways to interact with information through the Internet. The degree of complexity and levels of interaction that can be supported by Internet systems can be considered on a spectrum ranging from static web pages through to collaborative information systems and include:

○ Static: A one-way presentation of information to those outside the organization. The information may be accessed by going directly to the organization's website using their uniform resource locator (URL) such as www.palgrave.com or through the use of search engines such as www.google.com.
○ Two-way exchange of information: A facility can be added to a website to allow information to be sent to the organization. This could be a form to seek, for example, an email address, so the organization can include an individual on a mailing list.
○ Two-way exchange of transaction information: A more complex form of two-way communication may include the use of online ordering. The organization publishes their product catalogue online, receives online orders, and accepts online payments. The receipt of the order and payment will trigger a series of processes in the organization to complete the order.
○ Two-way process of dynamic transactions: This is when the information presented on an organization's website is immediately updated in response to transactions. It goes beyond presenting static information and includes additional information such as how many units of a product are in stock.

This information is updated when an order is received.
○ Collaboration: Further detailed collaboration can take place using online systems, such as chat systems, that enable two parties to communicate immediately in conversation with limited delay (unlike email where there is a delay until the message has been opened).

The greater the complexity of interaction, the greater responsibility there is to ensure that the information is reliable.

10.3.1 Internet Information Architecture

Every website has an information architecture (Morville & Rosenfield, 2007). Within the context of Internet and intranet systems, the term *information architecture* refers to the physical structure of the information presented. It includes components such as labels and categories that are used to locate information when needed. The design of an Internet information architecture is based on three concepts (Morville & Rosenfield, 2007):

○ Content: The type and structure of the information, and the vocabulary used, reflecting the organization's mission and values.
○ Context: The factors that provide meaning to the information content and which may affect how information can be used. This includes factors such as business goals, culture, and information technology.
○ User needs: The intended recipients of the information, their behaviours and expectations.

The Internet information architecture incorporates (Morville & Rosenfield, 2007):

○ Organization systems that reflect organizational structures, such as roles and departments.
○ Navigation systems that consider how to browse information and use breadcrumbs.
○ Search systems that include how to search for information and execute queries.
○ Labelling systems that categorize information in a meaningful way and use familiar terms.

DEFINITION: Breadcrumbs indicate the current location in a website and the location that is one level higher than the current location in the overall website hierarchy. This provides a navigation trail.

Terminology and its interpretation provide the foundation for the information architecture and are the source of the major challenges in developing an information architecture. Natural language is ambiguous and differences in perception mean that individuals organize information in different ways. An information architecture therefore needs to use a controlled vocabulary based on the organization's data dictionary. This ensures that terms are used consistently throughout the website and that the information can be interpreted and used appropriately. In addition, the use of a controlled vocabulary with thesauri enhances information searching. A search can include synonyms and broader, narrower, or related terms within the search criteria.

Approaches to developing an information architecture for an Internet or intranet site include:

- Top-down approach of defining a hierarchy of categories.
- Bottom-up approach using the controlled vocabulary of the organization's information architecture defined in the data dictionary.
- Social classification approach that enables the users of the information to participate in determining the structure through, for example, free tagging.

10.3.2 Internet Information Management Policy

The organization's information management policy needs to be extended to incorporate the information published on Internet systems. The Internet presents the organization's external face to the outside world and therefore the content of the information and the manner in which information is presented are critical to an organization's reputation. The e-consumer is very demanding; poor quality information, inconsistent information, and information that is difficult to find on a corporate Internet site can lose an organization both potential and existing customers. However, good quality information published on the Internet is also a means of securing new customers and developing relationships with them. The information management policy for Internet information needs to:

- Contribute to designing the information architecture, particularly the use of the controlled vocabulary.
- Provide guidance to ensure that the information is accessible via the Internet when needed and that information can be appropriately navigated and searched.
- Develop policies for controlling the process of authorizing content before information is published externally.
- Define the roles and responsibilities for creating and maintaining the content of the organization's information published on the Internet.
- Provide appropriate training to staff in creating and presenting information to external sources.

- Ensure that the information published on the Internet goes through the same stringent processes as other forms of external communication.
- Ensure staff are aware of the legal and ethical issues relating to information published on the Internet.
- Assign individual accountability for the information published and maintain an audit trail so that the source of information can be determined if necessary.
- Align the use of the information on the Internet with the organization's business strategy and the overall information management strategy. For example, detailed accurate information on the Internet can reduce the number of email queries received.
- Integrate the information content published on the Internet with internal information sources and business processes. If a potential customer raises a query via email, business processes need to be in place to ensure that the customer receives a prompt and meaningful response.
- Ensure the information published is of appropriate quality, particularly in terms of accuracy, consistency, and timeliness.
- Define the security policies relating to the information to ensure confidential information is not inadvertently published.
- Determine the archive policy for information published on the Internet.
- Specify the retention policy for information published on the Internet.

10.3.3 Transformation Dimensions of the Internet

The use of the Internet by an organization needs to be aligned with the organization's business strategy. The IT department implements the technical controls for publishing content on the Internet and provides a means of integrating systems, which can be accessed via the Internet with the existing databases and information systems.

The technological change provides a means of transmitting data to and from an external partner using Internet technologies. The data that are displayed to the other partner need to be identified and extracted from the internal information systems in the organization. The data captured from the external partner need to be stored and used by the organization.

Data in Internet systems need to be used consistently with the data dictionary definitions. Sufficient information has to be provided to third parties to ensure that they have all the information they need to complete their purchase or make the decision to use the services offered by the organization. The information published on web pages must be consistent across web pages and easy to locate. The design of the web pages needs to be considered from both the perspective of being able to navigate between pages and being aesthetically pleasing. The transmission of data raises concerns of security both from a technical perspective and in terms of the risk of information being deliberately or accidentally disclosed to unauthorized parties.

Business processes provide the data that Internet systems publish externally and respond to the data received by the Internet systems. The business processes are conducted by people in the organization and therefore working practices change to accommodate Internet systems. Different skills are required in the working practices to use the Internet systems as they emphasize written (electronic) communication rather than oral communication skills (Dingley & Perkins, 1999).

10.3.4 ▶ Role of Information Management in Internet Systems

The Internet provides a means of capturing and publishing information externally and therefore needs to be incorporated into information management policies. Information management is needed to:

○ Define roles and responsibilities for publishing information and providing access to information via the Internet.

○ Raise awareness of the information management issues, including the legal issues, associated with the use of the Internet.

○ Contribute to aligning the implementation of Internet systems with the organization's information needs and strategy.

○ Integrate the information from Internet systems in the organization's information architecture.

○ Develop policies and processes to manage the information captured and published via the Internet to ensure:

- Accuracy and consistency of information published on the Internet or communicated via Internet systems.
- Information is used accurately and consistently between the Internet systems and internal business systems.
- Accountability for the information published and captured.
- Security and confidentiality of information is maintained.
- Information is easily accessible via Internet systems.

10.4 ▶ Collaborative Systems

Interorganizational cooperation can take many forms requiring different degrees of cooperation and commitment. A collaborative information system ties organizations together by joining their information and business processes using Internet technology to form an extranet.

DEFINITION: An **extranet** is a computer network providing access to data and information systems using Internet technologies to authorized external personnel and approved partners of the organization.

Collaborative systems provide a means of conducting business electronically, offering benefits such as reduced transaction costs. The investment needed in developing the collaborative system demonstrates commitment to the interorganizational partnership, making it more difficult to justify leaving the relationship.

DEFINITION: A **collaborative system** is an Internet-based information system used by more than one organization to conduct e-business and is directly integrated with other information systems in the organizations.

Collaborative systems provide the interface between two or more organizations, joining together the value chains of the organizations; for example, linking the outbound logistics of one organization with the inbound logistics of another (Figure 10.2).

Figure 10.3 shows the interactions that currently take place between Bright Spark and one of their main suppliers, Match Lighting. The sales representative visits Bright Spark with their latest range of light fittings and negotiates an order with the buyer from Bright Spark. The order is processed in Match Lighting using their internal systems and the light fittings are dispatched. Bright Spark receives and checks the light fittings delivered before updating their internal systems to reflect the arrival of the new stock.

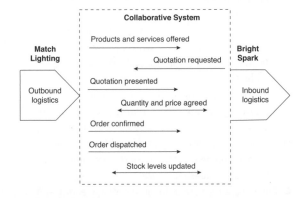

Figure 10.2 ▶ Collaborative Systems in the Value Chain

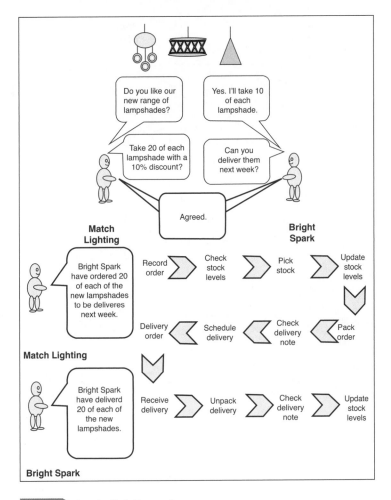

Figure 10.3 Supply Chain Transactions

A collaborative system replaced the physical negotiation process and automates some of the processes in both organizations. Figure 10.4 illustrates how the transactions in Figure 10.3 are conducted in a collaborative system. The face-to-face contact between the staff at Bright Spark and Match Lighting is replaced by text-based communication via the collaborative system. When the order has been finalized the collaborative system triggers the process in Match Lighting to process the order. When the order is delivered the collaborative system updates the stock levels in both organizations.

Collaboration using e-business systems can be regarded as being synonymous with integration (Cox *et al.*, 2006) but the integration extends beyond that of information systems and technology. Staff at Bright Spark need to trust that the items will be delivered on the date and at the price agreed. Incorrect orders, delays in delivery, or inaccurate invoices contribute to eroding trust in the relationship between the two organizations. It is therefore essential that the collaborative system is integrated with internal systems in both organizations. This ensures, for example, that Match Lighting has sufficient items in stock to satisfy the agreed upon delivery date.

10.4.1 ▶ Information in Collaborative Systems

Collaborative systems exchange information between two or more parties. It is therefore essential that the information exchanged is accurate and appropriately interpreted. Each organization will have their own definitions for data and an agreed upon understanding of the terminology used in the collaborative system needs to be developed to avoid problems. The staff at Bright Spark need to understand and trust the information presented to them via the collaborative system. For example, they need to understand what is meant by *product units* to ensure that they are aware of how many items are being purchased

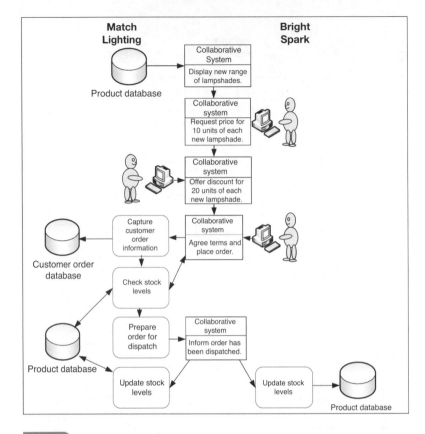

Figure 10.4 Transactions in Collaborative System

(Figure 10.5). Organizations need to cooperate to define data standards and interpret the information processed in collaborative systems appropriately.

When using a collaborative system, the information management strategy in both organizations needs to be reviewed to identify issues that may affect the scope of information that can be included in the collaboration. Examples of issues that may arise include:

○ Legal issues relating to permission required for sharing data with a third party.
○ Regulatory requirements in the trading countries of the organizations.
○ Archiving policies that may limit the range of historical data available for comparative analysis.
○ Differences in data quality and reliability.
○ Availability of data, as an organization may not currently capture the data required by the collaborative system proposed.

Such issues are unlikely to prevent an organization engaging with a collaborative system but may limit the range and depth of data that can be accessed and exchanged.

10.4.2 Transformation Dimensions of Collaborative Systems

Many organizations have incurred problems by approaching the development of collaborative systems as an IT project, merely the implementation of a technical solution to enable the collaborative system to be used in the organization. Implementing collaborative systems requires more than investment in IT; it requires business processes to be re-engineered to use and act upon the intercompany information. In addition to the need to establish a consensual understanding of data, Dingley and Perkins (2000) identified the following issues to consider in collaborative systems:

○ Controlling proliferation of links: Considerable work is needed to implement collaborative systems in terms of the technical integration of the IT systems, gaining an understanding of data semantics, changing business processes, and learning how to use the systems effectively. A major supplier, such as Match Lighting, can dictate that all its customers use its own collaborative system to place their orders. However, for customers such as Bright Spark this may mean that

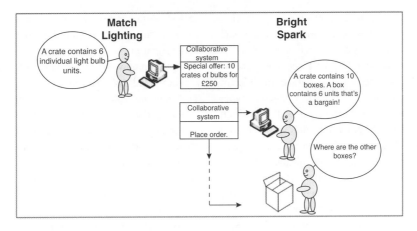

Figure 10.5 Misunderstandings of Data in a Collaborative System

each of their suppliers requires them to use a different collaborative system which becomes impractical.

○ Agreeing on mutually beneficial outcomes from collaboration: The business benefits to all organizations using the collaborative system should be identified before investing in the collaboration.

○ Reinforcing sensitive business processes to support e-business: IT can improve the completion of simple transactions but the complexity of business processes such as negotiation is more difficult to reproduce unchanged using technology.

○ Instituting training for development of new skills: Changing how business processes are conducted requires appropriate training to be given to assist staff in developing the range of skills required to conduct processes in an electronic context.

Figures 10.3 and 10.4 show that the impact of the collaborative system affects:

People: The sales representative from Match Lighting has previously visited the buyers at Bright Spark regularly to negotiate orders. These visits may no longer be required.

Practices: Face-to-face negotiation is replaced by text-based communication via the collaborative system.

Skills: The skills developed for face-to-face negotiation are different from the skills needed for negotiations online.

Trust: A rapport will have been established through the face-to-face negotiations, providing a context of trust. The socialization aspect of negotiation is lost in the sterility of the collaborative system. This creates concern about potential problems that may arise during the transaction (such as, has the order been accepted?). The lack of trust also means that when problems do arise,

such as the wrong product being delivered, they are perceived as being more serious and can have a negative effect on the interorganizational relationship. Previously such problems may have been amicably resolved during the next visit but without the social arena of human contact, problems may be interpreted as incompetence or deliberate intentions to deceive, rather than a simple mistake.

Processes: Business processes need to be adapted to accommodate the collaborative system. Processes may need to be developed to respond to queries and problems arising from the collaborative system. In one case an organization had a query about the order that they had placed with a supplier using the agreed upon collaborative system. They telephoned the supplier to try to resolve the query but neither the sales nor customer service staff were aware of orders being taken by the collaborative system. The orders from the collaborative system were being processed by a separate team. The existing processes in place for addressing order queries were not extended to include orders from the collaborative system and new processes to address the queries had not been introduced.

Systems: Information systems will need to accept and respond to information received from the collaborative system, in addition to providing information to the system. The data definitions used in the collaborative system may differ from those used in the organization. Additional translation processes may need to be developed to effectively process data from the collaborative system. Information systems may need to be changed to generate data that are specifically required by the collaborative system, such as key performance indicators in the supply chain (for instance, on time delivery).

Technology: A collaborative system requires a level of technical integration to be performed to integrate data from internal organization systems (such as performance data and product descriptions) and the collaborative system. The technical integration of data from different systems may be challenging due to differences in data types and formats. Conversion programs may need to be written to translate data received from a collaborative system into the format expected by internal IT systems and back again.

Security: Allowing an external organization to access data held on internal organizational systems via the collaborative system raises issues of security. First, security controls are put in place to prevent third parties from gaining access to the data held by the organization. These controls have to be changed to allow the partner organization to have limited access to data via the collaborative system. Second, security controls will need to be implemented to restrict access to the collaborative system to only the collaborating partners. Within the partner organizations, limitations on the range of access to the system will need to be defined for individual authorized staff. Third, security controls are needed to monitor access and detect instances of unauthorized access and unauthorized actions from authorized staff. Finally, awareness is needed of legal issues arising from sharing data with a third party, particularly if the organizations are based in different countries.

Strategy: The decision to use a collaborative system should be aligned with the aims of the organization's strategy. In many cases, large organizations insist that all their trading partners adopt their collaborative system if other organizations wish to trade with them. An organization may therefore have to adapt their strategy in response to introducing the collaborative system and the metrics against which the organization's performance is measured in the collaboration. Many organizations have found collaborative systems offer benefits, such as improved understanding of future product demand (Sahay, 2003), reduced transaction costs; and reduced time to market (Graham & Hardaker, 2000). However, the collaborative system can create an imbalance of power in the trading relationship (Dingley & Perkins, 2000) and negotiations can become increasingly fierce (Bensaou, 1999). It is therefore important for organizations to clearly define the strategic objectives for engaging with partners using collaborative systems.

10.4.3 Role of Information Management in Collaborative Systems

Collaborative systems facilitate electronic access and exchange of information among trading partners. Information management is therefore needed to:

- Define the scope of information that will be shared with trading partners and the expected reciprocal information.
- Agree on how the data will be used and who will be authorized to access the data.
- Assess the legal issues relating to sharing data and ensure that appropriate permissions and regulatory requirements have been satisfied.
- Agree on the definitions of terminology to be used in the collaborative system.
- Agree on the format, type, and quality of data to be entered and returned in the collaborative system.
- Assess the difference in data definitions, format, and type required by the collaborative system against the definitions documented in the data dictionary.
- Identify the information systems from which the required information will be derived.
- Specify any data conversion required between data sent to and received from the collaborative systems and internal systems.
- Assess the impact of existing archive and retention policies on the collaborative system.
- Formulate and agree on a policy relating to the access and limitations of use for data from collaborative systems.

10.5 Customer Relationship Management

Customer relationship management (CRM) is a business and information systems strategy which focuses on the customer (Bull, 2010), facilitated by the application of IT. It represents a change of focus from customer acquisition to customer retention by seeking to improve customer experience (Öztayşi *et al.*, 2011).

DEFINITION: Customer relationship management (CRM) seeks to assess the value of a customer to the organization and maintain profitable interactions with them after the completion of their initial sales transaction.

Organizations seek to develop long-lasting relationships with profitable customers throughout the customer life cycle. Rajola (2012) identifies the following stages in the customer life cycle:

- First contact between the customer and the organization.
- Reciprocal discovery of the organization's offering and the customer's requirements achieved through collecting information.
- First transaction.

○ Critical periods where the customer complains about the product or service received or where the customer is tempted by competitors.

○ End of relationship either by the customer (taking their custom elsewhere or no longer requiring the products and services offered by the organization) or by the organization (as it changes its offerings).

CRM focuses on three main areas of activity:

○ Customer acquisition focusing on attracting new customers by profiling existing customers and encouraging prospective customers to interact with the organization. This could include activities such as competitions and viral marketing activities. Viral marketing activities include animations, video clips, and games related to an organization and its products, which are circulated using social media (discussed in Section 14.2).

○ Customer retention aims to maintain relationships with existing customers, encouraging customers to return to the store (or website) and make further purchases through promotion management activities.

○ Customer extension (or customer development) seeks to increase the range or quantity of purchases from a customer through, for example, cross-selling related items and recommendations from other customers (Chaffey, 2006).

Electronic communication can be used to increase interaction between the organization and its customers using, for example, targeted promotions through emails.

10.5.1 ▶ Electronic Customer Relationship Management

Electronic customer relationship management (ECRM) is CRM using e-business as the main form of interaction between an organization and a customer. A related topic is mobile customer relationship management (MCRM), which refers to customer-focused activity conducted using a mobile device such as a mobile phone (Sinisalo *et al.*, 2007). The Internet provides the opportunity to gather data from customers using, for example, surveys, forums, customer product reviews, and social networking activities. It can also be used as a means of delivering customer services at a reduced cost, increasing customer profitability. For example, introducing a frequently asked questions (FAQ) section on a website can reduce telephone queries to call centres (Bergeron, 2002).

The customer resource process (Ives & Learmonth, 1984) was introduced in Chapter 4. It identifies the main stages that a customer goes through as they interact with the organization from presale, through to sale,

maintenance, disposal, and finally accounting for cost of the product or service. These stages are also applicable to online sales. Cenfetelli and Benbasat (2002) propose that an e-business system can be evaluated using these stages to assess the extent to which information is provided to the customer to support each stage of the purchasing process. This evaluation can then be used to benchmark ECRM activities and identify opportunities for improvement.

ECRM and MCRM provide opportunities for personalizing communication with individual customers and maintaining active customer interaction. In addition to increasing the number of touchpoints available to customers, the Internet arena provides the opportunity for organizations to offer digital products for customers to download, encouraging customer interaction and sustaining brand awareness. Data need to be captured about these interactions to be incorporated in the overall digital profile of a customer.

DEFINITION: Touchpoints are the interfaces in an organization that provide an opportunity for interaction with customers. They are points of contact that include teams in the organization (such as call centres and help desks); technical interfaces (such as self-service machines and Internet sites); and communication channels (such as newsletters and advertising commercials).

10.5.2 ▶ Role of Information in Customer Relationship Management

Information is key to managing customer relationships. Quality, consistent information about customers is needed that can be aligned with existing information in the organization (Rajola, 2012) to make informed decisions. Finnegan and Willcocks (2007) suggest that CRM involve:

○ Collecting and integrating customer data from different departments and channels.
○ Analysing the data to identify the profit potential of customers.
○ Tailoring information communication to target customers.

CRM collects data from all customer touchpoints and integrates the data to form a single complete picture of the customer.

Table 10.6 shows an example of the interactions between Bright Spark and one of their customers, Mrs Brookes.

The ability to gather information from different touchpoints enables Bright Spark to provide a single view of a customer's interactions with the organization, improving

Table 10.6 Customer Interactions

Date	Interaction	Touchpoint
01–07–2011	Enquiries about products and pricing.	Telephone call to sales team.
10–07–2011	First transaction.	Sales team A.
08–09–2011	Second transaction.	Sales team A.
09–09–2011	Product replaced.	Customer service in store.
28–09–2011	Sent newsletter.	Post.
15–12–2011	Third transaction.	Sales team B.
20–12–2011	Purchased after sales contract.	After sales team A.
10–01–2012	Sent vouchers.	Marketing team.
04–04–2012	Fourth purchase.	Sales team C.
19–12–2012	After sales contract renewed online.	Contract insurance team.
22–12–2012	Fifth purchase via self-service till.	Self-service sales.
23–12–2012	Email received about complaint relating to sales contract renewal.	After sales team C.
13–01–2013	Completed a customer service questionnaire.	Customer service team.

customer service. For example, when Mrs Brookes telephones Bright Spark, the person answering the call will have access to all the information about her previous interactions. They can see the products and services Mrs Brookes has purchased and offer her related products to support customer extension.

Data mining is fundamental in CRM to analyse customer data (Rajola, 2012). This requires data from different organizational systems to be integrated but this can be difficult due to differences in data formats and definitions (discussed in Chapter 8). However, in order to analyse the profitability of a customer, data are also needed about the performance of business processes. CRM focuses on the profitability of all customer interactions and is not limited to the volume or value of subsequent purchases. For example, when a customer uses the organization's after-sales support facility, the customer interaction is problem-oriented, incurring costs to the organization. Organizations may therefore actively dissuade customers from contacting them by ignoring complaints and putting customer telephone calls on hold (Bergeron, 2002). This requires information to be analysed to inform decisions on actions to be taken with specific customers to maximize profitable interactions.

Information is also needed to measure the effectiveness of CRM strategies. Measures of success may include a positive return on investment, increased brand awareness, and enhanced customer experience. Information systems need to be developed to capture data to measure the effectiveness of CRM strategies.

10.5.3 Transformation Dimensions of Customer Relationship Management

CRM is initiated by a change of strategy to focus on sustaining interaction with profitable customers. It triggers changes in business processes to facilitate interaction with profitable customers and hinder interaction with less profitable customers. Information is needed to assess the profitability of customers to the organization and to improve the customer experience. This requires data to be integrated from different business systems and changes may be required to improve the quality and completeness of the data required. Information systems are then needed to support analysis of the integrated data and inform business activities. Business processes need to be created and adapted for use via the Internet, and integrated with existing business processes and information systems.

10.5.4 Role of Information Management in Customer Relationship Management

CRM is dependent on the organization's ability to integrate and analyse data about its customers, independently of when, how, or why the interaction takes place. Effective information management is therefore critical to the success of CRM. Information management is needed to:

○ Identify customer-related information that is captured by an organization. This can be supported by the information architecture and data dictionary.
○ Determine the integration requirements for providing a complete view of a customer's interactions.

- Identify issues arising with integrating data from different information systems.
- Resolve data integration issues. This will require collaboration with data owners to address issues such as data incompatibility.
- Determine the additional data required to support analysis of customer data (such as costs associated with individual business processes).
- Review the information provided to customers via e-business systems to identify opportunities for improving the customer experience.
- Determine the information to be captured from CRM activities.
- Define the information needed to measure CRM activities.
- Review the ethical and legal issues related to the use of data for CRM activities.
- Formulate policies for capturing, using, archiving, and purging CRM data.

10.6 Supply Chain Management

Supply chain management includes all the activities between the original conception of the product or service and its final consumption. It goes beyond logistics, which coordinates the delivery of resources to ensure that they are in the right place at the right time. Logistics occurs *within* an organization, incorporating procurement, distribution, and inventory management activities. Supply-chain management occurs *between* organizations, managing relationships between trading partners for mutual benefit and seeking to add value within and between the activities that take place at all stages in the supply chain. By sharing information, partners in the supply chain can create added value, resulting in competitive advantage, service improvements, and cost savings. Collaborative systems are a component that can be used in supply chain management, although collaborative systems can also be used horizontally between trading partners as well as vertically in the supply chain.

Coordinating activities between levels of activity in the supply incur production costs and transaction costs. Production costs are incurred to create and distribute goods and services. Transaction costs, also referred to as coordination costs, are the costs incurred in exchanging and acting on information to complete an agreement. IT can reduce the information costs in a transaction. More timely and more detailed information can also reduce production costs.

10.6.1 Information in Supply Chain Management

Sharing information between partners in the supply chain enables activities in the supply chain to be effectively coordinated. Hugos (2011) summarizes supply chain management as comprising fundamental questions in the following areas:

- Production: What do people want? When? How can production be scheduled? How can workload be balanced? How can maintenance be scheduled?
- Inventory: How much stock to hold? How much of the inventory should be ready to sell?
- Location: Where should facilities be located?
- Transportation: How should goods be transported? Where are goods transported to? When are goods transported?
- Information: How much information should be collected? With whom should information be shared?

Sharing information among levels in the supply chain enables each partner to gain a better understanding of the needs of other parties, improving the efficiency and effectiveness of the overall supply chain. For example, if Match Lighting has a greater understanding of the sales patterns experienced by Bright Spark, they can more accurately forecast sales. However, supply chain management extends integration between organizations beyond the use of extranets. For example, technology such as RFID (introduced in Chapter 3) enables data to be collected remotely, providing information for real-time tracking and scheduling of activities. Myerson (2007) suggests that RFID can improve inventory control, reduce losses, and monitor actions that have been performed, such as equipment maintenance. This improves product traceability, which is particularly important in areas such as food consumption where mandatory traceability is stipulated by EU General Food Law Legislation.

Link 10.1
Levels in the Supply Chain

Automated systems are available to collect and monitor data from supply chain partners. Supply chain systems analyse data to predict patterns such as sales trends and trigger alerts if a significant increase in demand is forecast. However, it is important to understand the nature of business in order to understand the potential impact of anomalies identified by automated supply chain systems. For example, an infrequent customer who places a very large order could be misinterpreted by an automated system as a signal of increasing market demand for an organization's products. It is therefore important that business expertise is used to interpret the data captured in the supply chain.

Supply chain management systems facilitate the exchange of further types of information. For example, Lee and Cheong (2011) suggest that frameworks are needed to capture and analyse information about the environmental impact of processes linking organizations in the supply chain. A carbon footprint measures the amount of carbon dioxide generated directly and indirectly from the operations of an organization. Information therefore needs to be captured and managed relating to the amount of carbon dioxide that is generated throughout the organization in order to calculate the environmental impact of the complete supply chain.

10.6.2 Transformation Dimensions of Supply Chain Management

The need to coordinate actions among partners in the supply chain has always existed. Suppliers need information to forecast future demand for their products or services. At the strategic level decisions are taken relating to whom to trade with and how much information to share with trading partners. IT provides the opportunity to exchange data between levels in the supply chain more quickly. It also provides the ability to access data that were not previously easily attainable, such as the exact location of an order in transit or road traffic congestion. However, extending the data accessibility also increases concerns relating to data security. Information systems need to be able to send and receive secure data about different agreed upon aspects of the status of activities in the supply chain.

Greater access to information is only of value if the information used and actions taken based on the information are of benefit to the organization. The benefits may be direct to the organization, such as cost savings resulting from improved planning of distribution routes, or indirect, such as added value to customers through the provision of order tracking data. Business processes need to change to act on the information provided from the supply chain. Staff in the organization then need to be able to interpret the information appropriately to inform the decisions taken in response to the information received from the supply chain.

10.6.3 Role of Information Management in Supply Chain Management

Supply chain management relies on information exchange among different levels in the supply chain. One UK retailer calculated that mismatched data in supply chain activities resulted in costs of £2.2 million. Difficulties with data integration among levels in the supply chain arise due to differences of calendar periods and data aggregation. Supply chain management therefore requires all parties to agree on the data to be exchanged, including the:

○ Breadth and depth of the data to be exchanged.
○ Semantic definitions and coding structures adopted.
○ Level of detail and accuracy of the data.
○ Format and type of data.
○ Volume of data.
○ Frequency of exchange.
○ Time period of data.
○ Means of access.
○ Limitations on the use of the data.

Information management is needed to:

○ Define the scope of information that will be exchanged among levels in the supply chain.
○ Agree on how the data will be used and who will be authorized to access the data.
○ Assess the legal issues relating to sharing data and ensure that appropriate permissions and regulatory requirements have been satisfied.
○ Define the metrics required to measure activities in the supply chain.
○ Agree on the requirements of the data to be exchanged (including definition, frequency, and structure).
○ Agree on the definitions of terminology to be used in the collaborative system.
○ Assess the difference in data definitions, format, and type required by the supply chain partner against the definitions documented in the data dictionary.
○ Assess differences in context (such as differences in calendar periods), which may affect how the information exchanged should be interpreted.
○ Identify the information systems from which the required information will be derived and the received information will be used.
○ Specify any data conversion required between data sent and received through supply chain systems.

10.7 Email Communication Systems

Electronic mail provides a means of communication from parties who may be internal or external to the organization. The ease with which an email can be created and sent has led to the increasing volumes of email experienced by staff in organizations. Although emails are quick to send, and therefore *could* initiate a quick response, the volume of email being sent is increasingly delaying responses. Radicati (2010) suggests that 100 emails are sent and received by the average employee per day. The increasing volume of electronic communication, fuelled by developments in new technology, poses significant challenges for information management.

This endless stream of email can have a significant impact on both technology and staff in organizations. Parnell (2001) suggests that email has resulted in a 39 per cent increase in information communicated via organizational computer networks. This adversely affects the performance of information systems and increases IT costs. Email also has an impact on the staff performance. When a person interrupts a task to read an email, it takes 68 seconds to recover from the interruption and refocus on the original task (Marulanda-Carter & Jackson, 2012). Email contributes to feelings of information overload as the volume of information received becomes a burden to staff. However, Burgess *et al.* (2005) suggest that sometimes the burden of email may be partly self-inflicted due to email addiction. Marulanda-Carter and Jackson (2012) report instances of email addiction identified by the occurrence of clinical characteristics (such as feeling preoccupied with emails) and behavioural characteristics, which include prioritizing email over other activities and checking email frequently.

10.7.1 Information in Email Systems

The purpose of email communication can be broadly grouped as providing or requesting information. Valuable information is often embedded in emails and the ability to retrieve the information is a significant concern for information managers. Information storage and retrieval was regarded as a personal data management issue of how an individual organized their email in an inbox and archiving folders. However, the Freedom of Information Act 2000 in the United Kingdom means that organizations frequently have to trawl through emails to gather information to respond to Freedom of Information requests, as well as to gather evidence to resolve legal issues.

Although there is a tendency to react and respond to emails as quickly as possible, care is needed about what is said and what commitments are made when emails are exchanged. The informality of the communication (and the lack of restrictions that often apply to email communication) can mean that staff may communicate information that they would not disclose by other means. Guidelines are needed about when to use email, who can respond to specific types of query, and what information can be given via email to ensure that confidentiality and legal issues are not infringed

10.7.2 Transformation Dimensions of Email Systems

While IT provides the means to send and receive electronic communication, it is the staff in the organization that need to respond to email. Many e-business systems have been set up to include an automated system for sending an immediate response to emails that have been received from outside the organization. The email usually takes the format of 'Thank you for your email; we will reply to the email within 48 hours.' This serves the purpose of confirming that the email has been received by the electronic system, but does not guarantee that the sender will receive a meaningful response. The response is often nonexistent: a general email may provide links to areas of the organization's website that may or may not provide the answer to the original query, or the email may ask the respondent to contact the organization by another means. These types of response are unsatisfactory and are likely to have an adverse effect on the relationship between the organization and the sender of the email.

Organizations need to have business processes in place to:

○ Read email (particularly if the email is sent to a general email address rather than a named individual).

○ Identify the nature of the email, such as a query with a supplier order or a customer asking for more details about the range of service offered.

○ Identify the most appropriate staff to respond to the email. Internal information systems (such as an intranet) can help to identify colleagues who are able to respond to a specific issue raised via email.

○ Respond to the email in a detailed and appropriate manner, within an acceptable time period.

○ Ensure that the follow-up action is taken to prevent emails being continually forwarded through the organization without being resolved.

The organization should have business processes in place to address most queries raised via email. The receipt of emails therefore needs to be embedded into the existing processes. Similarly, processes need to be modified to create and send external email communications alongside other forms of communication. It is the lack of integration between email and business processes that is the main source of customer dissatisfaction with email communication with organizations. This has led to the development of instant messages services and live chat facilities on websites, which attempt to provide an immediate response to simple queries. In addition, the two-way communication can help to clarify queries and seek further information to resolve the issue more promptly.

Email poses a significant security risk to information. Physical security issues need to be addressed to ensure that technology is not used to gain unauthorized access to information. However, information security needs to address the appropriate use of emails to ensure information is not disclosed by thoughtless or careless acts. Emails can easily be sent to the wrong person or department. Staff can also unwittingly provide unauthorized or confidential information via email. For example, email addresses have been unwittingly disclosed to others by entering addresses in the carbon-copied (cc) field rather than blind-carbon-copied (bcc) field where a recipient cannot see the addresses of other recipients.

This requires staff to be given appropriate training in the communication of information via electronic means. Organizations need to carefully consider how email supports their communication needs with both internal and external parties and ensure that appropriate business processes are in place to respond to the communication received via this medium.

10.7.3 Role of Information Management in Email Systems

Increasing volumes of email require organizations to address both technical and management issues relating to the storage and retrieval of email. Burgess *et al.* (2005) identify the following problems with email:

○ Information deficiency: Emails sometimes contain insufficient information for the desired action from the recipient to be undertaken.

○ Poorly targeted: Emails are copied to additional recipients as a record of the communication rather than for action.

○ Media selection: Email is used to avoid social interaction with difficult or intimidating individuals rather than considering whether email is the most appropriate form of communication.

○ Interruption: Email interrupts and delays other tasks.

○ Filing: Emails are often left in the inbox to respond to later or so they can be more easily located due to difficulties in finding emails that have been filed.

Information management can help address these issues by:

○ Developing a policy that specifies the appropriate use of email and cultivates a culture of responsibility towards its use.

○ Providing guidance on remote access to emails to minimize information loss.

○ Specifying regulations for email retention and preservation.

○ Defining the range of information that can be disclosed via email.

○ Identifying staff authorized to disclose information via email and the limitations of their responsibility.

○ Providing guidance on the appropriate use of cc and bcc facilities.

○ Ensuring information communicated via email conforms to the security classification assigned to the information and that legislative requirements are satisfied.

○ Stipulating the acceptable usage policy for personal email.

○ Agreeing on an archiving and retention policy for emails.

○ Ensuring training is available on how to communicate appropriately via email.

10.8 Information Management Challenges with E-business

E-business provides opportunities to change the way in which business is conducted in organizations. The design of e-business systems therefore needs to be aligned with the organization's strategy. Cox *et al.* (2001) suggest that e-business needs to be considered in terms of the:

○ Business strategy, which provides the rationale for the e-business system; it explains *why* the e-business system is needed.

○ Business objectives, providing measurable targets of *what* the e-business system is expected to achieve.

○ E-business activity that determines *how* Internet technology is to be used to achieve the specified objectives.

○ Trading partner *who* will participate in the e-business activity.

Table 10.7 provides an example of how e-business activities can be aligned to an organization's strategy. Bright Spark can use a collaborative system to engage with its supplier, Match Lighting, to improve the management of stock levels. It can also use e-business to reduce transaction costs and improve customer retention through customer relationship management systems. E-business systems change the relationships among links in the supply chain, influencing the balance of power in the relationships, which needs to be considered in relation to the organization's strategy.

The e-business activity in Table 10.7 identifies the initial focus of the information that needs to be managed in the relationship. The degree of information integration

Table 10.7 ▸ Strategic Role of E-Business

Business Strategy (WHY)	Business Objective (WHAT)	E-business Activity (HOW)	Trading Partner (WHO)
Business Process Enhancement	Reduce transaction costs.	Online ordering.	Customers.
	Improve stock management during product promotions.	Collaborative system to support supply chain management.	Suppliers.
Market Development	Advertise brand range.	Static web presence.	New customers and consumers.
	Improve customer retention.	Customer relationship management.	Customers.

Source: Based on Cox *et al.* (2001).

Business Objectives	Business Process Enhancement		Customer Online Ordering	Supply Chain Management Collaborative System for Stock Management
	Market Development	Static Website Email Newsletter	Customer Relationship Management	
		Information Delivery One-Way	Information Transaction Two-Way Asynchronous Exchange	Information Collaboration Two-Way Exchange and Direct Systems Integration

Figure 10.6 ▸ Complexity of Interaction in E-Business

among e-business trading partners is determined by the nature of the trading relationship. Figure 10.6 shows how the organization's strategic objectives need to be considered within the context of the type of communication required with the e-business partners: one-way, two-way, or collaborative interaction with direct access to the internal information systems of each partner.

E-business facilitates international trading therefore consideration needs to be given to legal and ethical issues in the countries in which organizations wish to trade.

While IT provides the infrastructure for information exchange in e-business systems, it is the knowledge and skills of staff who engage in the collaboration that enable organizational benefits to be achieved. Figure 10.7 shows the organizational transformation required to support e-business. Information is at the core of *e* activities and should not be subsumed with the technical challenges of e-business. Information management needs to ensure that e-business activities do not threaten the integrity of the organization's information resource. For example, controls are needed to protect information when direct access to information systems is given to an external organization, allowing information to be

created, modified, or deleted. An understanding is also needed of the e-business context within which the information exchanged will be interpreted to highlight semantic differences and avoid potential problems of communication.

Summary

E-business offers organizations a different way in which to conduct business transactions. The introduction of e-business changes the external face of the organization and how the organization interacts with external parties. However, internal changes to business processes and practices are needed to support this external transformation. The internal transformation of the organizational architecture, initiated by e-business, is summarized in Figure 10.7. Information is at the core of e-business, and information management policies and processes are needed to ensure the accuracy of information published and transmitted by e-business systems. Internal business processes need to change to support the publication of information externally and to act on the information received from e-business systems.

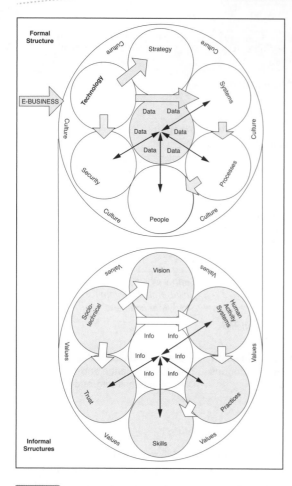

Figure 10.7 E-Business-led Organizational Transformation

Link 10.2
Checklist for Assessing Information
Management Challenges with E-Business

Reviewing Scenario 10.1

Match Lighting expects their major customers such as Bright Spark to use their collaborative system as the main means of trading with them. This requires extensive changes to take place in Bright Spark. Business processes need to change as the placing of orders and the negotiations surrounding price, quantities, and discounts will take place online rather than in person. This will impact upon the socio-technical systems in place as the impersonal nature of conducting business through electronic communications replaces face-to-face negotiation among staff who have become acquainted over a number of years. Online transactions may be more cost-effective in terms of the efficiency of information exchange, however,

both organizations may be adversely affected by the loss of trust that had been previously established through personal relationships.

Staff at Bright Spark will need to be trained in how to use the collaborative system. Match Lighting will provide the training, but staff who are experienced face-to-face communicators will need further training about how to communicate effectively through the electronic medium. IT staff will need to ensure that authorized staff in Bright Spark have access to the system and work with staff at Match Lighting to resolve any technical issues. An understanding of the system will need to be developed from a business perspective to ensure staff entering orders online are fully aware of what they are ordering and the contractual commitment of the transaction being performed. This will require the semantics of the system to be understood, particularly in relation to the difference in terminology from that used in Bright Spark.

Direct links will need to be made between the collaborative systems and the existing IT systems in Bright Spark. For example, if Match Lighting can access Bright Spark's stock records, they can arrange deliveries when Bright Spark needs them. The IT department can arrange access to the relevant IT systems but further consideration will need to be given to the business benefits and additional risks associated with providing this information to Match Lighting.

The negotiation of orders via the collaborative system will be slower than the current processes as each partner will have to wait for a response from the other via the electronic system. While it is technically possible for immediate responses to be provided, delays may occur for a number of reasons. For example, appropriate staff may be unavailable to respond to the electronic communication or the delay can be a deliberate business tactic in the negotiation process. The introduction of the collaborative system changes the trading relationship between the two organizations and triggers a chain of business transformation in Bright Spark.

Cloze Exercise 10.1

Complete the following paragraph by choosing the correct word from Table 10.8 to fill in each gap.

E-business uses Internet technology to support business processes beyond the completion of _____ transactions. The business model can be used to help identify potential _____ which could be strengthened by the use of e-business technology. Historically the introduction of information systems and IT in organizations has been

Table 10.8 ▶ Words to Complete Cloze Exercise 10.1

Acquisition	Editor	Internally	Online	Security
Ambiguous	Externally	Internet	Overload	Touchpoint
Architecture	Extranet	Intranet	Publisher	Value
Collaborative	Information	Logistics	Relationships	Vocabulary
Disseminating	Integrity	Navigation	Retention	WWW

_____-focused. E-business inverts traditional IT maturity models and first focuses IT _____ before using Internet technology to transform internal information systems.

The _____ is a network that provides the technical infrastructure for information resources which form the _____. The Internet information _____ refers to the physical structure of the information presented on an Internet site. It includes _____ and search systems to locate information on a site. However, natural language is _____ and individuals organize information in different ways. A controlled _____, based on the data dictionary, ensures that terms are used and interpreted consistently.

An _____ is a computer network which is only accessible to employees and approved partners of an organization. It provides a means of _____ information and facilitates access to internal information systems. An intranet _____ defines the strategy and policy for an intranet site. The intranet _____ approves the information to be included on the site.

An _____ extends an organization's intranet to enable external access to its information systems. A _____ system joins together the information systems of two or more organizations and requires agreement of the information to be shared. Customer relationship management (CRM) assesses the _____ of a customer to the organization and seeks to maintain profitable interactions with customers. It includes customer acquisition, _____, and extension. CRM is dependent on the organization's ability to integrate and analyse data about its customers irrespective of the _____ used.

Supply chain management coordinates activities between organizations relating to the _____ of resources through to the consumption of the final product or service. _____ coordinates resources within an organization. Sharing _____ in the supply chain enables each partner to gain a better understanding of the needs of others in the chain. The volume of email received can contribute to information _____. Email poses a threat to information _____ as information may be disclosed through thoughtless or careless acts. Information is at the core of e activities; information management needs to ensure that

e-business activities do not pose a threat to the _____ of the organization's information.

Link 10.3
Answers to Cloze Exercise 10.1

Activities 10.1

1 Review the last 10 emails you have sent. If email did not exist, would you have still tried to send the message in another way? If you would have used another method to send the message, what method would you have used?

2 List the business processes that may be supported by a B2E system.

3 Section 10.2 lists four main uses of an intranet. Using an intranet to which you have access, provide examples of each of the categories included in the list.

4 Prepare an outline of a web page for Bright Spark. Identify the information to be included on the web page. For each item of information, specify whether the content is static, semi-static, or dynamic.

5 Identify the organization, navigation, search, and label systems on a web page with which you are familiar.

6 Apply the customer resource process outlined in Chapter 4 to a shopping website. Assess the extent to which the website provides information to support each stage of the customer resource process.

7 With reference to Figure 10.7, explain how e-business initiates organizational transformation.

8 The wayback machine (http://archive.org/web/web.php) creates an archive of the Internet. How might this be used?

Discussion Questions 10.1

1 Is the delay in responding to emails (due to the volume of emails being sent) driving the increase in SMS, instant messaging, and tweets, as electronic communication vies for immediate attention?

2 To what extent has the anonymity and efficient transaction of messages online given rise to the growth of social media? Has society taken back control of personalized communication?

3 In Figure 10.3 the supplier, Match Lighting, types the order from the retailer. In Figure 10.4, e-business has moved the overhead of physically typing the order from the supplier, who wants to make the sale, to the customer, who wants to make the purchase. What are the advantages and disadvantages of this for each partner?

4 What are the disadvantages of a supplier having access to its customers' stock records?

5 Identify the issues for and against removing information from the Internet or an intranet.

6 What problems may arise if an organization has to use different collaborative systems to trade with each of its suppliers?

CHANGING INFORMATION SYSTEMS

Scenario 11.1

Online Ordering System at Amy's Candles

Amy is the owner of Amy's Candles, an independent shop selling handmade candles and wax sculptures. Although Amy prepares bespoke designs for her customers, she has developed a range of standard candle designs. She is considering selling her standard designs online. Amy needs to determine the information requirements of the online system and consider how the information in the online system will be integrated with her existing information systems.

What approach should Amy use to determine her information requirements?
How will the system integrate with her existing systems?
What problems might Amy need to address when integrating her information systems?

Learning Outcomes

The learning outcomes of this chapter are to:

- Outline types of information systems transformation.
- Explain approaches to information systems development.
- Introduce approaches to identify information requirements in information systems development.
- Identify models used in information requirements analysis.
- Assess the problems that arise in integrating information systems.
- Determine the challenges of information management when information systems are changed.

Introduction

The need for information in organizations is met by the development of computer-based and noncomputer-based information systems. Information systems provide processes to support the information life cycle. As organizations change in response to changes in the internal and external environment, the organization's information requirements change too. Information systems then need to change in order to adapt to the changing information requirements of the organization. This chapter explores how the organization's changing requirements for information are determined and documented.

The chapter first considers how information systems change and the potential drivers for change. Approaches to information systems development are then explained. Techniques and models for determining the information requirements of information systems are introduced and problems that may arise in determining requirements are identified. The chapter concludes by discussing the components of the organizational architecture that may be affected by changes to information systems.

Link 11.1
Differences Between Systems, Information Systems, and IT Systems

11.1 Types of Information System Transformation

An information system requires a means of:

- Capturing information as input to the information system.
- Storing information.

○ Accessing the information stored.
○ Processing information.
○ Providing external access to the information created.
○ Sending information out of the information system.

An information system will include a number of components, which include human and physical resources, to support these processes. An information technology (IT) system includes the technological components to support the processes of the information system.

Table 11.1 illustrates the human, physical, and technological resources required by an information system to accept orders from Amy's customers.

11.1.1 ▶ Drivers for Information Systems Transformation

Change to an information system may be initiated by changes in the underlying IT system, the organization(s) in which the system is used, or the organization's external environment. Changes may affect the:

○ Content or qualities of information captured, stored, or processed.
○ Business rules relating to how information is captured, stored, and processed.
○ Location of where the information is processed.
○ Sequence and content of processes applied to the information.

Drivers for changes to an information system can be categorized as being:

○ Top-down drivers relating to changing information needs of the organization. Examples include changes to:
 • An organization's strategy, structure, systems, and people.
 • External legislative requirements, nationally or internationally.
 • Requirements of the industry or market and suppliers, customers and partners.

Table 11.1 ▶ Components of an Information System to Accept Customer Orders

Processes	Human Resources	Physical Resources	Technological Resources
Capturing information.	Specify the information required. Provide the information requested.	A means of capturing the information.	Input devices. Software to display information requested and capture information entered. Communication networks to provide a means of transmitting information from the sender (customer) to the receiver (Amy).
Storing information.	Devise a way of organizing information stored.	Means of recording and storing the information so that the information can be found later.	Storage devices. Software to organize information and keep the information secure.
Accessing the information stored.	Specify the request for information from storage.	Means of retrieving information from storage.	Storage devices. Software to access validity of request, find information required. Communication means to send information to authorized recipient.
Processing information.	Interpret the information. Specify business rules for processing the information.	Apply the business rules to process the information.	Processing devices. Software to perform business rules on the information stored.
Providing external access to the information created.	Specify who can access attributes of the information.	Means to retrieve and present information to authorized recipient.	Software to access validity of request, and locate information required. Means of communications to send information to authorized recipient.
Sending information out of the information system.	Specify what information is required and where it is authorized to be provided.	Means to present or transmit required information.	Means of communications to send information to authorized recipient.

- Bottom-up drivers relating to changes with IT that affect the information systems such as changes to:
  - Devices available to capture or access information.
  - Ability to transmit data between different systems both internal and external to the organization.
  - Application packages used to implement the information system (discussed in Chapter 12).
- Inside-out drivers relating to changes that can be made to the information system to improve the efficiency or effectiveness of the information system. Examples include changes to the sequence of information processes, artefacts used to store information, and the people participating in the information system.

Examples of drivers requiring changes to information systems in Amy's Candles include:

- The organization's strategy. Amy defined a strategic objective to accrue 60 per cent of her income from her design range. Her information systems therefore need to regularly monitor the sales performance of her design range. If Amy changed her strategy to withdraw this range of products and focus on a bespoke design service, the information systems would need to be changed to provide her with the information she needs to implement and monitor her strategy.
- An organizational structure reflects how information is coordinated in the organization. A change in structure will change who in the organization needs specific information. As individuals differ in terms of their preferences and values for information, information systems may need to change the information provided to individuals both in terms of the content and quality of the information (such as frequency, volume, and accuracy).
- National legislative requirements dictate the information an organization is required to provide to government agencies in areas such as taxation, immigration, and the environment. As legislation changes, information systems change to provide the required content and quality of information for defined time periods.
- The information required from Amy's customers and suppliers may change. For example, she may be asked to report the level of carbon dioxide that is generated directly and indirectly from her organization. She will need to capture and process information in order to respond to such requests.

11.1.2 Information Systems Transformation Dimensions

Changes to information systems can be incremental or transformational. Incremental changes seek to develop and extend the existing information systems. These changes may include minor changes such as changes to a data field or changing the way information is presented in a report. Such changes seek to improve the quality of information presented to the recipient to inform business processes and decision-making, but do not significantly impact the way the business processes are conducted. In contrast, transformational changes are likely to involve the complete redesign of an information system and significantly impact other areas of the organizational architecture.

The scale of change to an information system can relate to:

- Changing the length of a data field.
- Capturing more (or less) data.
- Changing the qualities of the data captured.
- How the data are stored.
- Who can access the data.
- How the data are accessed.
- How the data are processed.
- Introducing new processes to be performed on the data.
- Where the data are transmitted to and from.
- When the data are to be transmitted.

Information systems are situated within the context of the organizational architecture. A change to an information system may require changes to be made to:

- Business processes which use the information system to capture or use information.
- People who provide or use the information system in the business processes.
- Security procedures required to maintain the integrity and confidentiality of the information captured, stored, and transmitted in the information system.
- Technology required to implement the information system's processes.

11.1.3 Role of Information Management in Information Systems Transformation

All changes to information systems relate to information. The role of information management is to:

- Determine the impact of the change to the information system proposed.
- Liaise with the IT department to assess the impact of the change on technical systems, which may result in further implications to the information resource.

○ Assess the impact of the change on other information systems in the organization, with reference to the information architecture.

○ Assess whether the change aligns with the requirements of the information management strategy.

○ Assess the legal and ethical issues relating to the change.

○ Check that the security requirements of the information will not be adversely affected by the change.

○ Specify any changes required to the information archive and retention policies.

○ Consult relevant data owners about the change proposed.

○ Ensure that changes agreed upon are documented in the data dictionary and information architecture.

○ Define any changes to information management required (such as the assignment of additional data owners).

11.2 Developing Information Systems

An information system defines the processes needed to satisfy a defined objective of the system (such as capture orders) and specifies the flow of information into the system, among the processes in the system, and the flow of information from the system. The processes in the system which implement the organization's procedures and business rules are performed by people using both IT (such as computers and databases) and nontechnical artefacts (such as paper-based contact lists).

Information systems development refers to the stages of activity that are undertaken to create or change an information system. A range of terminology used in information systems development is defined in Table 11.2.

11.2.1 Approaches to Information Systems Development

The systems development life cycle outlines a general approach to developing an information system which includes the following general stages:

○ Assess feasibility: This determines whether a proposed information system could be developed to meet the organization's needs and considers aspects such as the:
  • Practicality of whether the development is technically possible.
  • Legality of the proposed information system.
  • Economic viability.
  • Availability of resources (such as finance, IT, and expertise).
  • Suitability of information system in terms of its alignment with the organization's strategy.
  • Acceptability of information system to people and culture of the organization.

○ Determine requirements: Information is gathered about what the information system needs to do and the context within which the information system

Table 11.2   Definition of Terminology in Information Systems Development

Term	Definition
Paradigm	A paradigm is the view of the world adopted which provides the focus for the information systems development and can be regarded as a fundamental cognitive filter through which the information system development activity is conducted and guided.
Philosophy	A philosophy is the underlying principles on which the information systems development is based. It determines the priority which will be given to specific components in an information system, directing and influencing the development of the information system.
Approach	An approach defines the general structural framework in which the information systems development activities will take place.
Methodology	A methodology embodies a specific philosophy and approach, within a formalized framework of activities, divided into stages and steps with defined deliverables, and specified methods, techniques, and tools and techniques to be used.
Method	A method outlines a general structured way in which to accomplish a specific activity required in information systems development.
Technique	A technique is a detailed set of actions used to accomplish one or more steps in a method.
Tool	A conceptual or physical device used to assist in the application of one or more techniques.
Model	A limited conceptual or physical representation of some aspect of an information system.

will be used. An understanding is gained about the problems and opportunities in the organization and its trading environment to which the proposed information system will contribute to addressing.

○ Analyse requirements: A detailed description of the proposed system is developed which considers the functions of the system, the information needed by the system, and nonfunctional requirements.

○ Design system: Models of the proposed system are developed, which include the information, processes, IT equipment, network infrastructure, and security controls for the physical information system.

○ Develop and test system: The information systems design is constructed through the writing (or purchase) of software and acquisition of resources (including hardware and people with required skills). Initial testing of the system is undertaken and changes are made to hardware or software as required.

○ Implement system: IT equipment is set up and business procedures are documented to make the designed system available for use in the organization. Further testing of the system is conducted and additional changes are made as appropriate.

○ Review system: When the system has been used for an agreed upon period, the system is assessed to determine whether the original requirements have been satisfied.

○ Maintain system: Further changes to the system will be required through a programme of regular maintenance to respond to the changing needs of the organization and continuous refinement of the IT architecture.

The sequential application of these stages is referred to as the *waterfall* approach to systems development as the deliverables of one stage fall directly into the next stage. The waterfall approach has been criticized as the sequential process can take so long to complete that the organization's requirements for the information system have changed by the time the system is finally implemented. The sequential approach also lacks the flexibility to respond to the changing needs of the organization during the development process. These criticisms have led to the proposal of iterative approaches to information systems development encouraging more active and continuous participation of business staff throughout the development process. Shorter development times and more interaction with the staff who will be using the information system enable the development process to adapt to the changing needs of the organization. Examples of such approaches include:

○ Rapid application development, which is an iterative approach comprising cycles of information systems development. All the stages of information systems development are completed relatively quickly in each cycle to gain a better understanding of the requirements of the system. The stages are then repeated in the next cycle to improve the design and implementation of the system.

○ Prototyping, which constructs a meaningful tangible representation of the information systems with limited functionality relatively quickly. The prototype forms the basis for further exploring the purpose and requirements of the information systems with the business. Prototypes may be low fidelity (lo-fi), which are low cost using low technology such as paper, or high fidelity (high-fi) which are closer in appearance to the final information system and use similar IT.

○ Agile approach to information systems development, which is an iterative approach to construct and deploy a working system. Determining and modelling the requirements of the information system are an iterative and incremental part of the development process. Each iteration of the approach is likely to take no more than two weeks.

11.2.2 Methodologies for Information Systems Development

A range of methodologies have been created which seek to improve the process of developing or modifying an information system. The organization of the methodology differs depending on the approach adopted by the methodology, for example, Structured Systems Analysis and Design Method (SSADM) adopts the waterfall approach, Rational Unified Process (RUP) adopts an iterative approach, Web Information Systems Development Methodology (WISDM) adopts a prototyping approach, and agile systems development uses components of extreme programming (writing program code in a team focusing on the quick completion of discrete coding tasks that meet the requirements of the business) and the SCRUM management process (focusing on two-to-four-week sprints of work in which progress is reviewed daily).

The application of an information system development methodology provides an approach to information systems development, communication mechanisms, specified deliverables, and measures of development progression. Methodologies can be regarded as a problem-solving mechanism, comprising three main phases of problem formulation, solution design, and design implementation (Jayaratna, 1994). Table 11.3 presents a comparison of the characteristics of information systems methodologies which adopt an engineering approach to information systems development (such as SSADM) and those that adopt an approach of continuous learning (such as the Soft Systems Method).

Avison and Fitzgerald (2006) categorize information systems development methodologies as being process-oriented, blended, object-oriented, rapid development, people-oriented, or organizational-oriented. Methodologies also differ in relation to the paradigm,

philosophy, methods, techniques, and tools recommended in the methodology (Avison & Fitzgerald, 2006).

Paradigm

Paradigms that have influenced information systems development methodologies include the:

○ Science paradigm that adopts the view of the scientific method and is based on the principles of reductionism (continually breaking down the complexity of a

Table 11.3 ▶ Comparison of Learning and Engineering Approaches to Information Systems Development

Basis for Comparison	Continuous Learning	Engineering
Systems View	Emergent	Reductionist
World View	Subjective	Objective
Context	Dependent	Independent
Aim	Improvement of situation	Solve the problem
Role of Developer	Participant	Observer
Framework	Iterative	Linear
Problem Definition	Vague	Precise
Process	Flexible and systemic	Strict and systematic
Client Role	Active	Passive
Concepts	Unrestricted	Restricted
Models	Informal	Formal
Automation	Discouraged	Encouraged
Type of Problem	Unstructured	Structured
Scope	Unlimited	Limited
Improvement	Application	Version
Report of Failure	No	Yes
Solution	Creative	Standard
Documentation	Free-form	Prescribed
Cultural Analysis	Rich	Sparse
Change	Agreed upon	Imposed
Template	Guides process	Frames view
Management	By consensus	Formal directive
Approach	Reflective	Clinical
Disciplines	Social	Science
Training	Guidance	Instructive course
Acceptance	Cautious	Enforced
Location	Organization	Development team
Climate	Anticipation	Fear
Ability to Participate	Willing	Unwilling

Source: Based on Dingley (1996).

problem into its smallest elements) and independence (between the observed and observer).

o Systems paradigm that adopts the principle of holism that properties interact with one another (therefore by applying reductionism the inherent properties of a problem are destroyed).

o Objective paradigm that adopts the view that reality exists independently, and therefore everyone views it in the same way.

o Subjective paradigm that adopts the view that reality can only be interpreted and that different views of reality will exist due to the different cognitive filters, developed through experience, by individuals.

o Positivist paradigm that adopts the view of objectivity that people can be observed and manipulated in the same way as other resources.

o Interpretivist paradigm that adopts the view of subjectivity and asserts that people cannot be manipulated in the same way as other resources due their complexity.

Quiz 11.1
Paradigms in Information Systems Development

The differences between the positivist paradigm and the interpretivist view of social systems approaches are shown in Table 11.4.

The paradigm of a methodology determines the way the context of the system is explored in the methodology. For example the:

o Science paradigm deconstructs the context of the information system into smaller and smaller elements to analyse.

o Systems paradigm investigates the interactions between elements in the system and the properties of the system that emerge through the interaction.

o Objective paradigm rejects ambiguity and assumes that the context and requirements of the system are agreed.

o Subjective paradigm explores the different views of the organizational context within which the system will be situated and the different views of people who will be directly and indirectly affected by the information system.

o Positivist paradigm treats people the same as other resources in analysing the requirements and designing the system.

o Interpretivist paradigm accepts that people are more complex than other objects when analysing and designing the system.

Table 11.4 Positivist and Interpretivist Paradigms in Information Systems Development

Characteristics of Positivist Paradigm (Susman & Evered, 1978)	Assertions of Interpretivist Paradigm (Preece, 1994)	Limitations of Positivist Science for Information Systems Development
Knowledge can only be obtained by direct experience of an independent observer.	Knowledge cannot be objectively observed, only subjectively interpreted.	Direct independent observation of information systems is not possible due to the complexity of information systems embedded in socio-technical contexts.
Methods are assumed to be objective.	The act of observation may change the behaviour of the social system.	As information systems concern human activities, engagement with the process of systems development changes the organizational context and the requirements of the information system.
People are treated as objects.	Humans are more complex and variable than inanimate objects.	Human activity is embedded in the information system and cannot be isolated or predicted as it is people who give meaning and value to information.
The role of history in the generation of knowledge is eliminated.	A person's view of the world is influenced by previous experience.	Information systems are used by people whose behaviour cannot be predicted due to the rich personal context in which a person makes sense of their world.
A system is assumed to be defined only to the extent that a denotative language exists to describe it.	The richness of social complexity cannot be captured in language.	Information systems are complex and a range of models can be used to provide limited abstractions; however, the richness and complexity cannot be captured in a model.

Source: Based on Cox *et al*. (2005).

Philosophy

The philosophy on which an information systems development methodology is based focuses the development activity on what is considered to be the most important aspects of the information system. For example, the methodology Information Engineering is based on the philosophy that data are at the core of an information system and that modelling data is a prominent activity of information systems development.

Methods, Techniques, and Tools

The methods, techniques, and tools recommended in an information system development methodology provide guidance on how to undertake the stages of the information systems development approach adopted. They are based on the characteristics of the underlying paradigm and philosophy of the methodology. For example, Wilson's soft system method (2001) adopts the systems interpretivist paradigm and incorporates holistic techniques such as rich pictures. In contrast, Information Engineering is based on the scientific objectivist paradigm and uses techniques of data modelling and data-to-activity mapping.

11.2.3 Information in Information Systems Development

Methodologies differ in terms of how the stages are organized and how the stages are conducted, including the methods and techniques recommended and the degree of involvement of business staff in each stage. However, irrespective of the methodology used all methodologies follow the general broad stages of:

- Finding out the purpose of the information system required.
- Determining the information needed by the system.
- Specifying the processes required to achieve the purpose of the information system.
- Documenting the information system.
- Producing a representation of the information system.
- Checking that the information system satisfies the purpose of the information system.

Within the information systems development process, it is necessary for business staff to work with IT staff to identify, define, model, and review the information requirements of the information systems. This includes:

- Identifying information requirements (Section 11.3). This focuses on exploring the organizational context to determine the purpose of the information system and the information that the organization needs.
- Defining information requirements. This involves attaining agreement of the information and the

characteristics of the information to be delivered by the information system, including the quantity, quality, accessibility, and security of the information.

- Modelling information requirements (Section 11.4). A range of modelling techniques is used to produce a visual representation of the information to be provided by the system. Models are used to improve understanding of the information and its relationship to other information in the organization ensuring that issues of information consistency and integrity are addressed. Models are also used to represent the flow of information in the design of the information system to facilitate discussion about the processes that will act on the information.

- Reviewing the information requirements of the information system. Models and prototypes are used to finalize agreement on the information to be used and provided by the information system. Agreement is sought that the design of the system and final system implemented meet the information needs of the organization.

Within the development process, key issues to be addressed will include:

- What information is needed by whom in the organization? Why do they need the information? When do they need the information (for example, daily, monthly)? Where do they need the information (for example, do they need to be able to access the information when away from the organization)? What are the characteristics of the information required (such as quantity, accuracy, units of measure, presentation issues)?

- What is the life cycle of the information? Who creates, changes, uses the information? How is the information stored? What security controls are needed? What are the archive and retention requirements?

- How does the information relate to existing information systems? What information systems will receive information from and send information to the system? Are there any information integration issues that need to be resolved?

Information systems development is a knowledge-intensive activity (Chou, 2011). Information needs to be managed throughout the information systems development process. During information systems development information is captured by members of the project team relating to the organization architecture, the information architecture, the IT architecture, problems with current information systems, recommendations to improve current information systems, and opportunities for using information to add value to business activities. This information needs to be documented so that it can be shared by other members of the project team. It also needs to be used to update existing documentation in the organization so that it can be used by future project teams. Too often valuable information discovered during the development of an information system becomes neglected, perhaps because it is not considered directly relevant to the specific system being developed. In addition, considerable effort is repeated in organizations to gather the same information about business processes because project documentation is incomplete or difficult to access.

Information management is needed to:

○ Clearly document information gathered during the information systems development process.
○ Agree on coding systems and dissemination mechanisms for sharing information and controlling versions of documents.
○ Share information within the information systems development team.
○ Provide a means of easily accessing information gathered from previous project teams.
○ Ensure key documents such as the data dictionary, information architecture, and IT architecture are kept up to date.

11.2.4 ▶ Role of Information Management in Information Systems Development

Within the information systems development process information management is needed to ensure that the information needs of the organization are satisfied by the design of the information system. Existing documentation relating to the use and implementation of data in the organization is a valuable resource that can be used in systems development.

The aims of information management in information systems development include:

○ Define policies, standards, and procedures to promote data integrity.
○ Provide an information architecture and data dictionary to support systems development.
○ Promote integration of information in an evolving information, information systems, and IT architecture.

The design of the information system needs to adhere to the information management strategy and policies to ensure that the information system enhances, rather than weakens, the organization's information resource. This requires the:

○ Information systems development process to adhere to information management policies and procedures.
○ Information manager and relevant data owners to be involved in the information systems development process.
○ Data dictionary to be used and updated to ensure that data definitions and related business rules are used consistently between information systems. Table 11.5 lists checks that need to be made to ensure that the data models produced during information systems

Table 11.5 ▶ Data Management Checks in Information Systems Development

During Systems Development Check that:	Deliverable
• The entity-relationship model will satisfy the high-level business requirements. • Scope of model reflects the project scope. • Data owners affected have been identified and consulted. • The entity and relationship definitions are coherent and reflect business needs. • Data are normalized. • The model corresponds to the entries in the data dictionary. • New definitions (or agreed upon changes) have been added to the data dictionary. • Data are not duplicated and data integration is supported.	Approved entity-relationship model, highlighting any: • Anomalies between the model and business requirements. • Queries concerning entity definitions, attribute definitions, or business rules. • Inconsistencies between proposed model and existing data structures. • Updated entries to the data dictionary. • Impact on data outside scope of project.
During Systems Development Review Check that:	**Deliverable**
• Attribute specifications against physical element definitions. • The data model logically reflects and supports the physical file definitions. • Data dictionary is up to date.	Fully documented data model, highlighting any: • Differences between logical definition and physical implementation. • Attributes that have not been implemented or additional elements that have been implemented.

development are accurately documented in the data dictionary.

○ New data items to be defined, documented, and assigned to data owners.

○ Information architecture to be used and updated to show where data are used in the organization. It is important that systems affected by the information systems development are identified early in the development process.

○ All potential information issues to be identified as early as possible and addressed appropriately.

○ Legal issues relating to the capture, storage, use, retention, and destruction of information to be identified.

○ Business rules used to maintain the integrity of the information are defined and that controls are implemented to maintain the quality of the information captured and used.

○ Archive and retention policies to be reviewed.

○ Security controls are defined to protect the information from unauthorized access and accidental or deliberate misuse.

11.3 Determining Information Requirements

Unclear, incomplete, misunderstood, and frequently changing requirements are common problems that may result in information systems developed which do not meet the needs of the organization. Determining the information requirements of an information system is a critical stage in information systems development. If the information requirements are not fully understood and implemented, the resulting system cannot satisfy the information needs of the organization. However, there are a number of barriers which can hinder the ability to identify and agree on information requirements, listed in Figure 11.1.

A range of techniques are available to assist in eliciting information requirements. The techniques and models (discussed in Section 11.4) provide a focus for communication through the development of artefacts that help to externalize mental models of the information system. However, the process of identifying information requirements is reliant on effective communication skills and interpersonal skills which enable business and IT staff to establish an open and trusting rapport. Table 11.6 provides guidance for effective communication.

11.3.1 Scope of Information Requirements

The information requirements for an information system include both functional and nonfunctional requirements of the system. Functional requirements refer to the processes the system will perform. Nonfunctional requirements include characteristics and constraints of the system relating to areas such as appearance or performance of the system. Table 11.7 provides examples of questions to determine information requirements of the information system needed by an organization.

---

1. Lack of time available to fully explore requirements.
2. Key staff have limited time to participate in the development process.
3. Poor communication between the business and IT staff.
4. Lack of a common language between information systems developers and business staff.
5. Differences in use of terminology between business users.
6. Use of specialist terminology by both IT staff and business staff.
7. Lack of a means to communicate requirements and check understanding of requirements. Both IT staff and business staff have a mental model of the system which they assume is the same.
8. A lack of willingness of IT staff or business staff to establish a common basis for communication.
9. Some business staff may be reluctant to participate in the development process.
10. Difficulties in explaining detailed processes which are completed automatically by staff without thinking about them.
11. Difficulty in recalling events and situations to be included in the system.
12. Assuming that facts are obvious and do not need to be made explicit.
13. Each business person only knows part of the system and the development team need to piece together incomplete and perhaps conflicting requirements.
14. Lack of agreement about the scope of the information systems requirements.
15. Range of different people with different ideas about what the system should do.
16. Difficulty in identifying who to involve.
17. Difficulty in future thinking of how the system may be used.
18. Reluctance to change the existing systems and working practices.

Figure 11.1 Barriers to Determining Information System Requirements

11.3.2 Approaches to Determine Information Requirements

The scope of information systems development can range from an incremental change of an existing information system to transformative change requiring a new information system to be developed. Approaches to determining information requirements relating to incremental change focus on exploring the current information system. It is necessary to identify the limitations of the current system and consider how the information system could be improved. Transformative change requires a new system to be proposed, therefore existing ways of working need to be set aside to consider alternative business processes.

Table 11.6 Guidance for Business and IT Staff in Determining Information Requirements

Guidance for Business Staff	Guidance of IT Staff
• You know the area of activity in which you work and the information you use; the IT staff does not know this.	• You know the IT system, which databases are used, the operating system, version controls.
• What seems obvious to you is likely to be news to the IT staff.	• You need to find out about how the IT system fits into the business context: What works well and what needs to be improved.
• Explain how you do your work in detail, including any difficulties you have with the existing information you use or weaknesses with the existing IT systems and any ideas you have for improving the system.	• Ask lots of questions to find out how the person works and what artefacts they use to complete tasks (or need to complete future tasks).
• If you do not understand what the IT staff are saying, ask them to explain it.	• If you do not understand what the business staff are saying, ask them to explain it.
• You will use the final system that is delivered. You therefore need to ensure that the IT staff understand what you need and that you understand what has been agreed upon with them.	• It is your responsibility to leave an interview with sufficient information to explain the process you have learnt about in detail to someone else.
• It is your responsibility to check that the IT person fully understands the information and processes you need in your area.	

Table 11.7 Questions to Determine Information Requirements

Information	Data
What information needs to be provided by the information system? Who needs the information? When do they need the information? What format does the information need to be in?	What are the definitions of the key data items? What are the attributes of the data items? How are they defined?
How can the information be provided?	What is the format of the data?
What information is needed as input to the information systems?	What business rules are applied to maintain the integrity of the data?
What actions need to be performed on the information?	What security controls need to be applied to the data?
What information needs to be captured by the information systems? Who is the information captured from? When? How frequently?	How much data are needed? When can the data be archived? How long do the data need to be retained?
Who needs access to the information system? What level of access do they need?	
How is the information defined?	
How does the information need to be presented?	
Business Processes	**Constraints**
What information is needed by the process?	Where does the information system need to be used? (For example, does the system need to be web-based or support mobile devices?)
What does the process need to do?	
What are the steps in the process?	How quickly does information need to be provided?
What business rules need to be applied to the process?	What features relating to the appearance of the system need to be included?
What actions does the information system need to support?	

Table 11.7 Continued

Life Cycle			
Capture	**Store and Retrieve**	**Use, Share, and Maintain**	**Archive and Destroy**
What information needs to be captured? Why? Where is information captured? Who is information captured from? When is information captured? How is information captured?	What information needs to be stored? Why? Where is information stored? How is information stored? Who can retrieve the information? When is the information retrieved? How is the information retrieved? What security is needed to protect the information from unauthorized access?	Who can maintain the information? Who can use the information? With whom can the information be shared? How is the information used? What format does the information need to be in to be used? How often is the information used? What security is needed to protect the information from unauthorized access?	When can the information be archived? When can the information be destroyed? What security is needed to protect the information from unauthorized access? How can the information be destroyed?

There are six main approaches to determining requirements:

○ Reverse engineering: This approach analyses an existing operational system to define how the system interacts with other systems, the information used and generated, and the processes performed. It deconstructs existing systems.

○ Exchange-driven: This approach focuses on the information received that triggers a task and the information which is passed to other people or processes. Document analysis is one technique which can be used in this approach.

○ Goal-oriented: This approach focuses on the purpose of the information system and the specific actions that those using the system aim to achieve (such as identify customers who have not placed an order for the last four months). The approach focuses on the specific demands for information and actions (such as change customer credit limit) that the information system will need to support. A limitation of this approach is that it assumes that the goals are known and can be clearly communicated using techniques such as use cases.

○ Process-driven: This focuses on the business processes and procedures that are currently in place in the organization. Techniques such as interviews and observation are used to capture the current sequence of activities and the flow of information between activities.

○ Scenario-driven: This approach is used when a new system is being developed and there are no existing business processes that can be modelled. Scenarios are also used to encourage exploration of both typical situations and infrequent situations that arise.

○ Context-driven: This focuses on defining the limits of a situation and identifying the activities, components, and interactions within the context from which the information required derives its meaning.

11.3.3 Techniques to Determine Information Requirements

A range of techniques can be used individually or in combination to determine the information requirements of an information system. The choice of technique depends upon the approach adopted to determine requirements and the culture of the organization or department(s). For example, some areas of the organization may be unwilling to be observed and others may prefer to discuss requirements in one-to-one interviews rather than in a focus group with a manager present. There are three main approaches to eliciting information requirements: collecting documentation, asking questions, and observing practice.

Documentation

Existing business processes and information systems may have documentation that explains organizational policies and procedures. This can be used to gain an overview of how current practices should be undertaken; however, the documentation may be out of date or documented procedures may not be followed in practice.

Document analysis is a technique used in an exchange-driven approach to determine information requirements. Document analysis provides a means of understanding the information that is currently captured and used by the organization. It demonstrates the fundamental information requirements of the current business processes

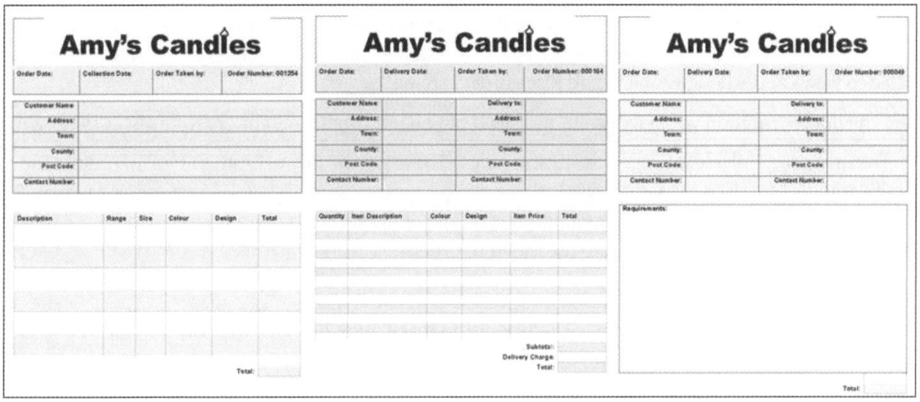

Figure 11.2 Order Documents

(for example, documents used by Amy are shown in Figure 11.2). The documents show key information used by Amy in the ordering process.

Asking for Information

Interviews are a technique used by the process-driven and goal-oriented approaches to determine information requirements. They may be conducted on a one-to-one basis or with a small group of staff. Interviews provide the opportunity to obtain detailed information about how current information systems work in practice and to find out about the workarounds used to overcome the limitations of the existing systems and processes. They rely on establishing a good rapport between the business and IT staff. Interviews should be conducted in business areas. Conducting interviews away from the interviewee's normal working environment (such as a side office) helps to avoid distractions and may encourage a more open disclosure about the current processes. However, there is a risk that the interviewee will explain how the current processes should be used, rather than how they are actually used in practice. It is therefore often beneficial to discuss the current practices in the usual working area to see how current information systems and information artefacts are regularly used. Skill is needed to develop appropriate questions to find out the information needed. Figure 11.3 shows a transcript from part of an interview with Amy and an information systems developer, Mark, discussing the requirements of the online ordering system.

Focus groups enable the views of a number of participants to be sought at the same time. This facilitates a rich source of information as the discussion builds on the ideas and comments made by individuals in the group, prompting responses from others. Focus groups can be used to seek agreement of information requirements and the priorities of the information systems development.

However, the group can become dominated by key individuals and some may be reluctant to participate. Focus groups need to be carefully facilitated to avoid discussions digressing into other areas and to ensure that the objectives of establishing the focus group are satisfied.

Snowden (2003) suggests that 'we only know what we know when we need to know it'. Asking questions is essential to stimulate thinking about information requirements. The language used when framing questions is important as it creates the context for recalling situations (Snowden, 2003) within which the information requirements can be elicited.

Observing Practice

Observation is also a technique used by the process-driven approach that focuses on the current information systems and the current ways of working in the organization. Observing the activities in the organization and, specifically, the actions, conversations, and reminder notes of key staff can reveal deeper insights into the limitations of the existing information systems. Observation provides the opportunity to find out how the existing processes and systems in the organization really work, which is likely to differ from the documented procedures. However, there are also risks with observation as people do not like to be observed and may work differently when watched. In addition, the person conducting the observation has to interpret what they have observed and the interpretation will be influenced by their opinions and beliefs.

Document analysis and observation are limited, providing information about the current working practices. Interviews can be used to explore current practice and future requirements but information only has meaning in context, therefore a shared understanding of the business context for the information systems needs to be formed in order for effective communication to take place.

Amy:	'At the moment, customers come into the shop to buy candles directly or to place an order with me. A few customers place repeat orders by telephone. Several customers have asked if I have a website as they would like to be able to view candle designs online and place orders online.'
Mark:	'From the documentation you have given me I see that you use three different order forms. Is that right?'
Amy:	'Yes. The first is for individual orders for stock candles. These are the most common type of orders. The second is for bulk orders of stock candles, they differ in that the customer is sent an invoice requesting payment 28 days after delivery. Payment on delivery is required for the first type of orders and a deposit is needed for the third type of order. These are bespoke wax sculptures designed to order.'
Mark:	'What do you mean by stock candles?'
Amy:	'They are standard candles I usually have in stock or can make quite quickly. They differ in terms of their size, colour and the design sculpted into them.'
Mark:	'Can you give me an example?'
Amy:	'Pillar candles come in three sizes. There are six main colours (though three additional colours vary between seasons) and then there are 25 set designs to choose from.'
Mark:	'So these stock candles are the ones that customers will be able to buy online?'
Amy:	'Yes. I can't sell design pieces online as I need to discuss the design with customer.'
Mark:	'The website could show that you make bespoke pieces and have a contact form for potential customers to complete so that you can get in touch with them to discuss their requirements.'
Amy:	'That would be fine but I would only need their name and contact details.'
Mark:	'What are the delivery options for the online orders?'
Amy:	'Customers should have a choice of collecting the order in the shop or having it posted to them. At the moment we only deliver bulk orders.'
Mark:	'On the one order form there is a column for range. What does range refer to?'
Amy:	'It is how I classify my designs. A range has a common theme running through all the pieces; it might be a specially mixed colour or a particular carving. Some customers like to collect all the pieces in a range.'
Mark:	'Range is not included on the second form. Why is that?'
Amy:	'The second form is used for bulk orders and these are usually for more simple pieces.'
Mark:	'What sort of customers place bulk orders? Are they retailers?'
Amy:	'A few local shops stock my candles but the main bulk orders are placed by local charities or organizations running events such as a fetes.'

Figure 11.3 Interview Transcript to Determine Information Requirements

Techniques for establishing a shared context to support the elicitation of information requirements include:

○ Joint application development: Workshops are used in iterative approaches to information systems development. Workshops seek to involve all the stakeholders in the information system, including the sponsor of the system, potential users of the final system, and systems developers. Involving stakeholders enables opinions to be shared and helps to establish a consensus of the information requirements.

○ Scenario formation: Scenarios are a sequence of events that form a context within which information requirements can be derived. The scenario can relate to past events to explore the effectiveness of current processes and systems. However, scenarios can also be postulated for future events to explore *what if* situations. Scenarios help in focusing attention on both typical and less frequent events that occur or may occur in the organization.

○ Use cases: A use case also provides an example of a typical situation but focuses on specific aspects of a scenario. A use case identifies the actors in the situation, the goals they aim to achieve (such as *place an order*), and then derives the steps and conditions required for the goal to be achieved. Use cases focus on modelling functional requirements. The completed use case documents show how an information system will be used by representing the interactions that will take place between the system and an individual or between the system and other systems.

○ Task–artefact cycle (Carroll & Rosson, 1992) is a means of exploring how the technical and nontechnical information artefacts are used in an information system. It is based on human activity theory that human activity is mediated by the tools and concepts that are used (Engeström, 1987). The task–artefact cycle is based on two premises: the task being undertaken determines the requirements of the artefact to support the task; the design of the artefact provides additional opportunities (and constraints) relating to how the task is performed. This is particularly evident in IT; for example, developments in mobile technology and social media have changed the way organizations can interact with their customers. The task–artefact cycle can be used in a prototyping approach to systems development, and with scenarios and role plays to explore how an information system may be used in practice.

○ Context analysis focuses on defining the context in which information is needed and given its meaning. It is based on the concept that situations are bounded by structural elements (discussed in Section 15.4).

The information life cycle can be used to assess the completeness of the information requirements identified to ensure that the requirements relating to all stages of the life cycle have been addressed.

11.3.4 ▶ Information Requirements of Web-based Information Systems

A range of web-based systems were introduced in Chapter 10. Yang and Tang (2005) classify web-based information systems as:

○ Intranet systems supporting internal business processes.
○ Web presence sites such as marketing tools.
○ E-commerce sites supporting consumer interactions.
○ Extranets which combine internal and external systems for business-to-business communication and transaction.

Motivations for using web-based information systems include: the acquisition of information, communication of information, exploration of information content, and the acquisition of goods and services (Rodgers & Sheldon, 2002). The main difference between developing a web-based information system and a non-web-based system is that when developing an information system the potential users of the system are known and can be consulted in order to determine the information requirements of the information system. When developing a

web-based system the final users of the information system may be unknown, too many, and too heterogeneous (Wang & Head, 2001) to involve in the information systems development process. In such cases, typical users may be identified to determine the information requirements, but they may not be final users of the systems. The gathering and sharing of information content are the most important requirements for web-based information systems and therefore navigation and data filtering are key issues in web-based information systems design (Yang & Tang, 2005).

11.4 ▶ Modelling Information Requirements

The information requirements identified for an information system need to be documented, agreed upon with the business staff who will use the final information system, and shared with the staff who will develop and implement the information system. In the traditional waterfall approach to information systems development, the information requirements are documented in models and then passed through the stages of analysis, design, and implementation. In iterative and agile approaches to information systems development the information requirements evolve through iterative discussions of both conceptual and physical models which simulate the design and operation of the final information system. The role of the business staff is to ensure that the information requirements are accurately and fully captured in the models developed. The role of the IT staff is to ensure that the models are understood by the business staff and accurately represent the information needs of the business.

11.4.1 ▶ Process of Modelling

All information systems development methodologies advocate the use of models as means of representing information requirements and providing abstractions of the information system. A model provides a simplified view of the information system which focuses on specific aspects of the information system. The completion of a model is required as a deliverable from a stage in the methodology, signalling completion of the stage and representing progress through the development process. The emphasis is therefore often placed on producing a model, which can be agreed upon and signed off demonstrating completion of a stage of development.

Models have a number of roles in information systems development, including providing a basis for discussion and communication, prompting questions, identifying omissions, documenting concepts, and sharing ideas. However, the process of constructing the model is key to

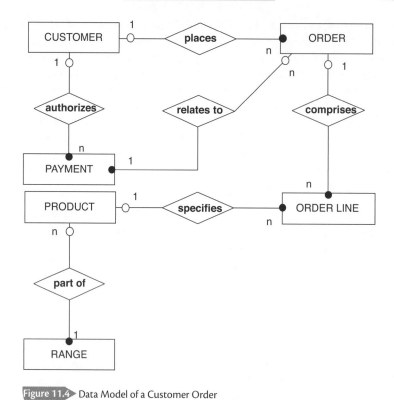

Figure 11.4 Data Model of a Customer Order

the development process. The discussions relating to the construction and refinement of the model provide valuable insights into the context within which information will be interpreted.

Models provide a limited view of the complexity of reality. The modelling notation provides a filter with which to extract key aspects of a situation and produce a simplified representation. Models are therefore inherently incomplete and the integration of different models is needed to provide a more complete understanding of the information system. A range of notations are used by different modelling techniques, which can make models appear complex. Business staff do not need to fully understand the notation used in the model. Most models can be read by focusing on the words used (such as nouns representing information categories and verbs representing information processes) and following the directions of arrows which represent flows of information or activity.

11.4.2 Types of Models

A wide range of models have been proposed to support the modelling of information requirements in information systems development. Different types of models focus on different aspects of the information system, including:

○ Context: Models such as rich pictures provide freedom to explore the context of the information system and elicit different views of the problem situation and the information requirements of the business.

○ Data: Models such as the entity-relationship model show the categories of information used by an information system and the business rules which determine the relationship among the categories of information. An example of a data model is shown in Figure 11.4.

Link 11.2
Description of Data Model for a Customer Order

○ Process: Process modelling techniques such as data flow diagrams focus on business processes which capture or modify information in some way. The models show the flow of information among the business processes. Figure 11.5 shows an example of processes which may take place when a customer places an order for candles with Amy.

○ Events: Models such as state-transition diagrams focus on the events that trigger changes in information.

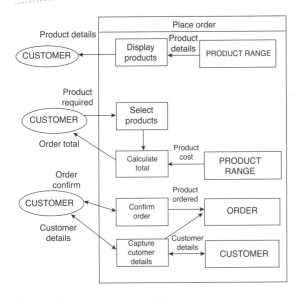

Figure 11.5 Process Model of Customer Ordering

Figure 11.6 shows the events that occur in the life of an order. Processes are needed to recognize that an event has occurred and perform the changes to the information required in response to the event. The information life cycle model is used to identify the key events that trigger changes in information and ensure that processes are identified to support all aspects of the information life cycle from capture through to secure destruction of the information.

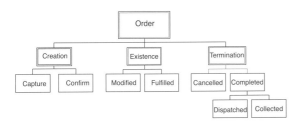

Figure 11.6 Life Cycle of an Order

- Object: Object models encapsulate data and processes into an object, as opposed to being separately represented in data and process models. An object has an identity, state, and behaviour which specify the actions that the object can undertake. Objects that have the same structure and behaviour are grouped into classes.
- Interactions: Models such as social network analysis focus on the interactions among individuals. This is used to show the key sources of information in the

organization and reveals the informal organizational structure in which the information system will operate.
- Use case: A use case represents the actions needed to achieve a specific goal in a scenario in which the system is used. The information needed to trigger and respond to events is defined.
- Simulation models: Most models used in information systems development are static models. Simulation models enable systems to be animated to explore the information in defined scenarios.
- Prototypes: A prototype can be static or partially operational to provide a more realistic representation of the final information system. It helps focus discussion on the system interface, which will provide the means for specific processes to be conducted. An example of a lo-fi prototype for Amy's online ordering system is shown in Figure 11.7.

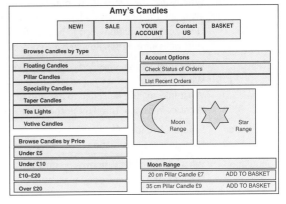

Figure 11.7 Prototype of Ordering System

Table 11.8 provides examples of the information requirements to be captured in different types of models.

11.4.3 Role of Information Management in Modelling Information Requirements

The range of models created during the development of an information system show different but related views of information. For example:

- The information that flows between processes in, for example, a data flow diagram, is defined in information categories in data models.
- The events that trigger changes to information in the information life cycle need to have processes defined to identify and respond to the event. These processes should be included in process models.

Table 11.8 Information Content of Models

Component	Key Questions
Context	Who will use the information? Why is information needed? What are the current limitations of the information resource? What new information is needed? How will the information be used? When is the information needed? Where will the information be used? What are the key categories of information?
Data	What are the information categories? How is the information defined and structured? What are the business rules that affect the data? How are information categories related? What is the cardinality of the relationships? What are the determinancy constraints of the relationships? What are the integrity constraints of the relationship?
Process	What are the processes that are needed to achieve the objectives of the information system? What information does each process need? Where does the information come from? What information does each process provide? How does information need to be stored? How does information flow between processes?
Event	What information is needed to identify that an event has occurred? What processes are needed to identify that an event has occurred? What information is needed to respond to an event? What events occur throughout the life cycle of information to trigger changes to the information?
Interaction	Who is asked for information? How does the information flow between people and processes?
Simulation	What variables affect information stocks? (For example, the number of sales is a variable that affects an activity). What are the minimum and maximum thresholds for variables? In what time period do events take place?
Prototype	What processes are needed? What typical tasks are performed? How is information captured? How is information retrieved? How is information presented? How can information be changed?

- The social network analysis shows who uses information. Information is provided to them through processes included in the process models.
- A prototype shows the interface through which the functionality of the information system can be accessed. The options shown on menus in the prototype should respond to processes documented in process models and actions in use case models. The presentation of the information in the prototype and permitted actions that can be performed on the information should reflect the business rules defined in the data model and data dictionary.

The key role of information management in information systems development is to ensure that the information system developed does not adversely affect the integrity or security of the existing information resource. It therefore needs to ensure that:

- There is consistency between the information content of the different models.

○ The definition of information, its attributes, and application of business rules is consistent with that documented in the data dictionary.

○ The information system does not duplicate the capture of information that is available in existing systems.

○ Appropriate security controls are defined to protect unauthorized access or modification to the information.

○ The impact on other information systems has been identified.

○ Archive and retention policies are addressed in the information system.

○ Relevant data owners have been consulted about the information system.

○ The information system proposed is documented in the data dictionary and information architecture.

11.5 Integrating Information Systems

An information system does not exist in isolation. It receives information from other systems both within and external to the organization. It also provides information to other systems. Information flows through the organization through the information systems. The impact of changing an existing information system, replacing an existing information system, or introducing a new information system on the existing systems in the organization therefore needs to be assessed as part of the information systems development process.

A black box approach can be adopted when exploring the integration of information systems.

DEFINITION: A **black box** approach involves examining an object in terms of its external interface, its inputs and outputs. It does not require analysis of the internal workings of the object.

Systems have a boundary and information flows into the system and out of the system across the boundary. Assessing the integration of information systems does not require analysis of the processes that occur in the information system. Integration issues only need to consider the compatibility between the outputs produced by one system that are used as inputs to another system. The information architecture can be used to identify which information systems may be affected by changes to specific information categories.

11.5.1 New Information Systems

The introduction of a new information system in the organization requires the information system to be embedded in the existing information systems architecture. During the information systems development process, consideration needs to be given to:

○ What information will the information system need? Is the information captured or produced by an existing information systems?

● If the information already exists, checks are needed to ascertain whether the existing information conforms to the requirements of the new information system. For example, is the information in the required format? Is the level of accuracy of the information acceptable? Does the frequency with which the information is updated satisfy the needs of the new system? If not, changes may be required either to the existing system that produces the information or to the new information system to adapt the information to meet its needs. Bridging programs may need to be developed which convert the outputs of one information system into the format required by this system. The use of bridging programs avoids the need to make widespread changes to existing information systems across the organization.

● If the information does not already exist, the new information system will need to incorporate processes to capture the required information.

○ What information will the information system produce and what other systems may use the information produced? The compatibility of the information provided by the new information system will need to be compared with that of the existing systems.

Figure 11.8 shows how a simplified view of some of the current information systems in Amy's candles and how the introduction of a new ordering system would need to be linked to the existing systems.

11.5.2 Existing Information Systems

When making changes to an existing information system, detailed analysis is needed of how the information system integrates information with other systems. Consideration will need to be given to:

○ Whether the changes to the information system mean that the existing information that is input to the system is sufficient. Does the system require further information? Does the system require more or less detailed information? Does the structure, format, quality, or frequency of the information entering the system need to change?

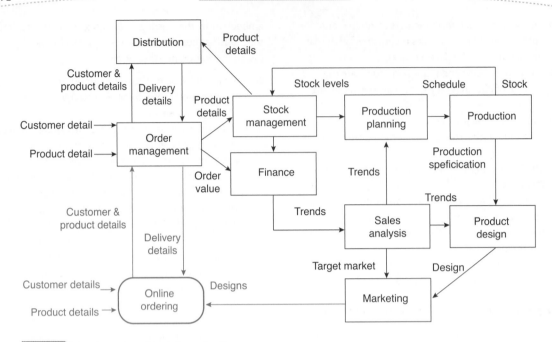

Figure 11.8 Implementing a New Information System

- If additional or different information is needed by the information system, where will the information come from? Additional processes may be needed to capture the information or to change the information that is currently received by the system. For example, the new online ordering system will need to be able to display details of the candles that can be purchased. The marketing system will need to be changed to include additional processes to produce detailed information about the product range which can be displayed online.
- Whether the changes to the information system mean that the existing information that is output from the system will change.
  - If the information output does change, the systems that receive this information as input may need to change too. The online ordering system could be integrated with the existing order management system (as shown in Figure 11.4) or integrated directly with the distribution, stock management, and finance systems. Integrating with the existing order management system reduces the changes needed to other systems.

11.5.3 Role of Information Management in Information Systems Integration

Information management is concerned with establishing and protecting a coherent information resource which meets the requirements of the whole organization.

Changes to existing systems and the development of new information systems must be consistent with the current information definitions and policies in the organization. The impact of information systems development on the existing information systems needs to be thoroughly explored. Information management is needed to ensure that:

- The impact of the proposed changes to existing systems or the introduction of new systems on the information resource has been assessed.
- Information is used consistently in the information systems in line with the definitions agreed upon by the data owners and documented in the data dictionary.
- Additional information created is assigned to a data owner who defines policies relating to the appropriate use of the information, which are documented in the data dictionary.
- Changes to existing information definitions and associated business rules are agreed upon with the relevant data owners and recorded in the data dictionary.
- The integration of information systems does not breach the security requirements defined for the information.
- The integration of systems is documented in the information architecture.
- New information captured or created, and changes proposed to existing information, adhere to appropriate legislative and ethical requirements.

○ The changes proposed have been reflected in the security, archiving, and purging policies. For example, the introduction of a new information system may mean that an archiving policy may need to change. Previously customer records may have been archived after six months of nonactivity. If a system is developed which aims to target offers to nonactive customers, customer data which would previously have been archived after six months of nonactivity is now needed. The archive policy may now need to change so that customer data are archived after 12 months of nonactivity.

11.6 ▶ Information Management Challenges with Changing Information Systems

Information systems are situated within the context of the organizational architecture. Information systems provide the information used to support business processes, therefore changes to the information resource are likely to impact upon business processes. Business processes are conducted by people in the organization who use the information systems; additional training or the development of new skills may be required to use the systems developed. Figure 11.9 reflects the morphing dimensions initiated by changes to information systems in the organization.

Information systems provide the processes for creating, maintaining, and using the information resource. Information management therefore needs to be closely involved when changes are proposed to information systems. The role of information management is to maintain the quality, security, and availability of the information resource to meet the requirements of the entire organization. When changes to an information system are proposed, there is a risk that the changes may adversely affect other systems in the organization. Information systems are integrated, providing the means for information to flow through the business processes, recording transactions, initiating actions, and informing decisions. It is therefore important that a consistent and coherent view of information is maintained. The information manager and relevant data owners need to be involved in information systems development activities to ensure that the impact of changes to the information resource is fully explored. This may require changes to be made to a number of different information systems to accommodate a new information system being developed or changes to an existing information system. Accurate and up-to-date detailed documentation about how and

where information is used in the organization is therefore critical to assess the impact of changes to the information systems. The challenges to information management include:

○ Assessing the impact of proposed changes to the information resource on existing information systems and business processes.
○ Maintaining accurate documentation of how and where information is used.
○ Working with IT staff to identify the IT systems that are affected by the changes to information systems.

The implementation of changes to information systems is likely to require changes to security procedures required to maintain the integrity and confidentiality of the information captured, stored, and transmitted in the information

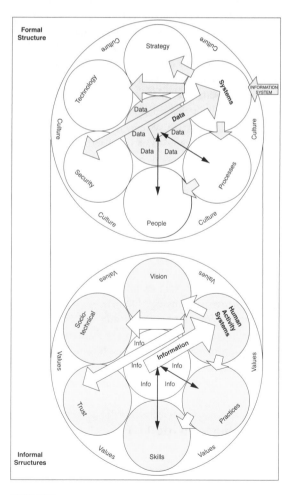

Figure 11.9 ▶ Information Systems-led Organizational Transformation

system. Changes to the underlying IT required to implement the information system's processes are discussed in the following chapter.

Link 11.3
Checklist for Assessing Information Management Challenges with Changes to Information Systems

Summary

Information systems provide the means to support information throughout the life cycle, comprising processes to capture, store, retrieve, use, modify, archive, and delete information in the organization. Changes to an information system can range from the addition of a new data attribute to the captured through to the redesign of the system. Information systems development methodologies provide a structured approach to changing existing information systems and developing new information systems. Methodologies are based on a paradigm (determining how the investigation is approached) and a philosophy (determining the focus of the investigation), which determine the methods, techniques, and tools used. Determining information requirements is a key stage in all information systems development methodologies. A range of models can be used to analyse and communicate information requirements. Each model represents a specific view of the information required; the models are related to provide a coherent view of an information system.

New information systems need to be integrated with existing information systems through information flows to and from the system. Changes to an existing information system may change how information systems are integrated. The role of information management in information systems development is to ensure that changes to information systems, and the development of new information systems, are consistent with the information management policies, business rules, and data definitions. The impact of changes to information systems on the organizational architecture need to be assessed.

Reviewing Scenario 11.1

Although Amy plans to develop a new information system to enable her customers to place orders online, she currently has information systems that enable her to take orders from customers offline. The current processes involved in capturing customer orders could therefore be documented to provide a starting point for determining the information requirements of the new online information system. A scenario-based approach could then be used to identify the changes needed to the existing processes in order for them to be appropriate in an online context. Amy could then use a prototyping approach so that she can visualize how the information system will operate in practice. This is particularly important as the information system will need to accommodate processes that are used by Amy and her customers. For example, customers will need a process that will allow them to select candles that they wish to purchase. Amy will need a process that will enable her to display pictures of her candles in the online system for her potential customers to see. Amy will also need additional processes to update the details of her candles and other products on the online system.

Amy already has systems in place to process the orders she receives. The new online system will therefore need to be integrated with existing systems such as her stock-control system, production system, finance system, and dispatching system. A black box approach can be taken to explore the content, structure, and format of information that the new information system needs to provide to the existing systems. Amy will need to ensure that the terminology used in the new system is used consistently with how information is defined in her existing systems. This will ensure that the integrity of her information resource is maintained and that she has consistent information on which to base the decisions about her organization.

Exercise 11.1

1 Give two examples of top-down drivers for changes to an information system.
2 What is meant by a bottom-up driver to changes to an information system?
3 If Amy appoints a new employee with responsibility for her accounts, why might the information requirements of the finance system change?
4 Is the introduction of an online ordering system an example of incremental or transformational change? Why?
5 What is the difference between a method and a methodology?
6 Why is the traditional systems development life cycle referred to as the waterfall approach?
7 List three criticisms of the waterfall approach to systems development.
8 What is the difference between low-fidelity and high-fidelity prototypes?

9 Why are prototypes useful in determining information requirements?

10 Why are methodologies needed to develop an information system?

11 Why is the process determining information requirements critical in developing an information system?

12 List at least six barriers which hinder the ability to determine the information requirements of an information system.

13 Give an example of a functional requirement and a nonfunctional requirement for Amy's ordering system.

14 What are the benefits of observation as a means of determining information requirements?

15 Why are models important in information systems development?

16 What is the relationship between event models and process models?

17 What is meant by a black box approach to analysing an information system?

18 How can a prototyping approach be used to determine information requirements?

19 From Figure 11.6, what seven business processes are needed to manage information relating to customer orders?

20 What information management issues need to be considered when making changes to an existing information system and why?

Link 11.4
Answers to Exercise 11.1

Activities 11.1

1 Table 11.1 shows the components of an information system. Amy plans to introduce the process *order status tracking* to enable her customers to find out whether their orders are being produced or have been dispatched. Specify the roles for human, physical, and technological resources to support this process.

2 Section 11.3 lists a number of barriers that affect the ability to determine the information requirements of an information system. Suggest how each barrier may be overcome.

3 Develop a set of scenarios of how Amy's online ordering system may be used by potential customers.

4 Apply Table 11.7 to determine the full information requirements for Amy's online order capturing system using the information provided in Figures 11.2 and 11.3. List additional questions to ask Amy to clarify the requirements.

5 Develop a lo-fi prototype for Amy's online ordering system. Check that the prototype includes the information content listed for prototypes in Table 11.8.

6 Use the scenarios developed for Activity 11.1.3 to assess the completeness of the prototype developed in Activity 11.1.5.

Discussion Questions 11.1

1 As a model is an abstraction of reality, to what extent can a model be regarded as being complete?

2 The reductionist paradigm advocates reducing an object (or problem) into its smallest parts. What are the benefits and limitations of reductionism in information systems development?

3 Why can it be difficult to determine the requirements of a new information system?

4 Which of the following approaches is most suited to determining the information requirements of a) a new information system, b) changes to an existing information system, and c) both new and existing information systems.
   i Reverse engineering.
   ii Exchange-driven.
   iii Goal-oriented.
   iv Process-driven.
   v Scenario-driven.
   vi Context-driven.

5 Consider the relative merits of document analysis, interviews, focus groups, and observations and discuss in what circumstances each should be used to determine information requirements.

6 What is the role of notation in modelling techniques? Why do notations differ?

7 Why does the business have to be involved in analysing the integration of information between information systems?

8 Review the business rules represented in the data model in Figure 11.4. What changes may need to be made to these rules to allow, for example, monthly payment of an order?

12

CHANGING INFORMATION TECHNOLOGY

Scenario

Changing Software Packages in Match Lighting

The IT manager of Match Lighting, Mr Cook, opened the meeting by outlining the situation. 'We have been contacted by Code-IT, the organization that supplies us with the Talk2 software package that you use for contact management. They released a new version of the software last month, Talk3, and they have informed us that they will no longer provide updates and support for Talk2. We therefore need to purchase and install Talk3.'

'I met with a sales representative from Code-IT recently and saw a demonstration of the new software,' explained Ms Bevan, the sales manager. 'It contains some new features that we would not want to use. The new version extends the functionality of Talk2 from managing contacts to analysing the value of orders placed by individual contacts. We use a separate package, C.Rate, to analyse the value of contacts. Talk3 would need to be linked with our ordering system and this is not required

as C.Rate currently provides this link. We are happy with Talk2 and do not want to upgrade to Talk3.'

'I accept that,' replied Mr Cook, 'however, Code-IT have been sending us security updates to Talk2 regularly and the lack of further updates may mean that the contact data are put at risk from unauthorized access. Also, we are migrating the IT architecture to a new operating system next year and Talk2 will not work on this platform but Talk3 is compatible.'

Ms Bevan began to feel that the new package was being forced upon her team. 'We chose Talk2 because it allows staff to include private notes about contacts as well as the formal contact details. This is important to us in developing relationships with key customers and this feature has been removed in Talk3. It does not meet our needs,' she said.

What should Match Lighting do?
What are the information management issues that need to be considered?

Learning Outcomes

The learning outcomes of this chapter are to:

○ Identify drivers for changes to IT systems.
○ Outline types of IT-led organization transformation.
○ Assess information issues arising from IT migration.
○ Introduce an approach to compare information requirements of packaged systems.
○ Define the options for managing information in legacy systems.
○ Define the information management issues relating to the compatibility and integration of IT systems.

Introduction

An information technology (IT) system comprises a number of components to implement an information system. Technology is needed to capture data, store data, transmit data, and perform actions on data. IT systems incorporate hardware such as data capture devices (for example, keyboards, netbooks, sensors), storage devices (for example, disks, memory sticks), and processing devices (for example, servers). IT systems also include software such as:

○ Application software, relating to the purpose of the specific information system. This will include, for example, program code to display the data input fields on a screen, capture the data entered in each field via a keyboard, and store the data entered in a database.

○ Operations software, which coordinates the internal actions of the computing technology.

○ Network software, which coordinates the secure transmission of data between internal and external devices in the computer system.

IT has driven the need for continual change in organizations and has changed the way people interact with information. Technology is both an enabler and a barrier to organizational change (Avison & Fitzgerald, 2006). This chapter explores both of these roles of IT and emphasizes the importance of assessing the impact on information management when changing IT in an organization.

The chapter first identifies the drivers for changes to IT and how change in IT affects information throughout the information life cycle. Migrating data, that is, moving data from one IT device to another, is then considered. Organizations may choose to implement packaged software solutions and the specific challenges with integrating software and hardware are discussed. The options available for managing legacy IT systems are then outlined and the chapter concludes by discussing the information management challenges initiated by changes to IT.

12.1 Overview of Information Technology Transformation

IT provides organizations with new opportunities for using information, changing the requirements and expectations of the information resource. Business processes and practices need to change to meet these changing requirements, which affect the people and the skills needed to perform the processes in the organization.

12.1.1 Capture Information

IT provides a technical device for capturing and transmitting data. The information system provides the business rules that are implemented using IT, determining what data to capture and in what form. Developments in IT offer new ways of capturing data and interacting with the source of the data. The specific technology used to capture data affects the:

○ Type of data that can be captured.

○ Characteristics of data that can be captured, including accuracy, frequency of data collection, quantity of data collected, and error reduction.

○ Way data are captured and from where the data are captured.

For example, Match Lighting previously tracked stock through the manufacturing and distribution processes using barcodes. Pallets of light fittings, marked with a barcode, were manually scanned as the pallets moved around the organization. Match Lighting replaced the barcodes with RFID tags and scanners tracked the pallets without manual intervention. The data captured were the same but the characteristics of the data changed. The automated tracking of the pallets enabled data to be captured more frequently. This meant that the data were more up to date as there were no delays in capturing the data when a pallet was moved. The greater frequency with which the data could be captured improved the level of detail of the data and facilitated closer tracking of the pallets. The change of data capture device improved the quality of the data.

When changes are proposed to data capture devices information management needs to consider whether the changes will affect the:

○ Attributes of the data collected. Match Lighting needed to collect four data items: pallet identifier, location, date, and time. Figure 12.1 shows the data dictionary entries for these data items. The data owner needs to assess whether changing the data capture device will change any of the information in the data dictionary. For example, will the *location_code*

Entity Name: PALLET_LOCATION

Entity Definition: The physical location of a pallet at a specific instance in time determined by the location of the reading device at which the pallet identifier was recognized and recorded.

Attribute Name	Attribute Definition	Attribute Length and Type	Attribute Structure
Pallet_id	Identifies a pallet.	9(9)	String of numbers.
Location_code	Identifies where the data was captured.	X(6)	String of characters.
Date	Gregorian calendar.	9(8)	DD-MM-YYYY
Time	Universal time.	9(6)	HH:MM:SS

Figure 12.1 Extract from Data Dictionary for Pallet Information

still be captured as a string of six characters? If not, the impact on information systems that use the *location_code* will need to be assessed.

o Use of the information. The more frequent capture of data provides the opportunity to track pallets more closely; however, the improved frequency of data collection is only of value to Match Lighting if the information is used. The ability of the existing information systems to make use of the more frequent information therefore needs to be assessed. Changing the way data are captured may mean that the existing *location_codes* are insufficient to represent the location of the pallet. The data owners may need to consider whether additional attributes are needed to make use of the data. This may require changes to be made to existing information systems to capture and use additional data attributes.

12.1.2 Store and Retrieve Information

IT provides a means of securely storing the data captured in a form that will allow the data to be retrieved by authorized personnel when required. IT storage devices differ in terms of portability, capacity, and speed of access. When changing the storage device consideration needs to be given to how the change may affect the organization's ability to store data securely, the volume of data that can be stored, and the time taken to access data from the device.

It is also important to assess how changes in the way data are stored and retrieved in the future may affect the organization's ability to restore and access archived data. IT provides a means to store archived data so data can be retrieved when needed. When organizations replace old storage devices care is needed to ensure that the data that have been archived using these devices can still be accessed with the replacement technology if necessary. Data storage media can quickly become obsolete and it is essential that archived data can still be retrieved when needed, irrespective of the IT storage media used.

Changes to storage devices can change the business practices used to store and retrieve data. For example, portable storage devices allow data to be taken away from the organization. While this has benefits, it also introduces problems in areas such as:

o Data security, as the data can be lost, stolen, or accessed by unauthorized parties.
o Data consistency, as changes to the data stored on the portable device may not get propagated to the central data storage of the organization and vice versa.

When IT storage devices are changed the information manager will need to ensure that the data can be stored in accordance with the requirements specified in the data dictionary. Where the data are geographically stored is also a concern of the information manager as different legislation may be applicable. This is particularly relevant to developments in cloud computing (discussed in Chapter 13).

12.1.3 Use, Generate, Share, and Maintain Information

IT enables different areas of the organization to access different views of the data stored on IT devices. Changes to IT may introduce tools to manipulate and present data in different ways, which can change how business processes use the data. For example, data analytics tools enable organizations to gain insights into their data to support customer relationship management strategies. Changes to IT can also provide new opportunities for sharing data with others. For example, e-business systems transform the way organizations share information internally and externally.

Opportunities to change working practices need to be assessed in terms of the impact on the organization's information resource. Consideration needs to be given to the:

o Data definitions: Data definitions are agreed to and defined in the data dictionary. Proposed changes to how the data are to be used in the organization need to be considered in terms of the degree to which the change of use adheres with the agreed upon definition of the data. Using the data in different ways could cause confusion and result in misunderstandings and misinformation.
o Legal and ethical implications: Changing the way data are used or shared may not be permissible or acceptable.
o Security issues: The classification of the data defines the permitted access level for each category of data. Care is needed to ensure that the security of data is not compromised as opportunities are seized to share data more widely.

12.1.4 Drivers for Changing Information Technology

IT-led change is driven by changes to the hardware or software used in the IT system. For example:

o Hardware may change as a result of malfunction or the need to upgrade or replace the hardware with a new device to improve its efficiency, effectiveness, reliability, or security.
o Software may change if a problem (bug) is found in the software. Small upgrades are made to improve the

software (such as to make it more secure). Large-scale changes require a new version of the software to be installed or a complete replacement of the software to improve functionality.

○ Application software changes will be driven by the need to upgrade software, replace packaged software systems, or make changes to legacy systems.

○ Operations software change as new operating systems are developed; previous operating systems become obsolete and are no longer supported. Upgrades to software and hardware will therefore need to use the new operating systems and organizations are forced to change to the newer systems. Changing the operating system may mean that some applications software may have to be changed to ensure compatibility. Changes to operations software are unlikely to impact on the information resource directly.

○ Network software change to improve the secure transmission of data. Changes to network software are unlikely to impact on data directly, though it is necessary to ensure that any changes to the network do not expose the data resource to potential security risks.

Table 12.1 categorizes drivers for changes to IT systems.

Ongoing maintenance of existing IT systems consumes a considerable amount of an organization's annual IT expenditure. It includes upgrades to IT that may seem to have no impact on the organization, however, upgrades are necessary in order to:

○ Protect the organization's data from unauthorized access by a third party.

○ Respond to the needs of the organization to store and process increasing volumes of data.

○ Maintain the ability to capture, store, retrieve, and process data in a changing environment.

The IT resource must support the information needs of the organization and satisfy the expectations of the wider community. For example, customers expect to be able to access information about an organization via the Internet using an increasing range of Internet-enabled devices. The organization needs to continually develop its IT infrastructure to meet these demands.

12.1.5 ▶ Information Technology Transformation Dimensions

Much of the IT resource is invisible to the organization. Staff need to be confident that the information they require to make decisions and perform business processes will be available to them when they need the information. Activities such as upgrading the capacity of a database may not seem to have a direct and immediate impact on the organization, however, the upgrade will ensure that the organization's demand to store and access an increasing volume of information can be supported.

The depth of transformation initiated by changes to IT range significantly from having a minimal perceivable direct impact on the organization through to initiating complete transformation of an organization. The scale of change to IT can relate to:

○ Fixing, maintaining, upgrading, or replacing an IT device to improve the robustness, reliability, and capability of the organization's IT systems.

○ Changes to the IT architecture, which change how data are captured, accessed, processed, and shared.

Changes to IT may require changes to be made to:

○ The organizational strategy to change the way the organization interacts with its market, performs its processes, or uses the data to make decisions.

○ Information systems to facilitate the use of IT to support business processes.

○ Business processes which use IT to capture, access, or use information.

○ People who use and maintain the IT, and the skills they need.

○ Security procedures to maintain the integrity and confidentiality of the information captured, stored, and transmitted with the IT.

These changes may be initiated directly by the introduction of the technology or by the information that is

Table 12.1 ▶ Drivers for Changes to IT Systems

Limitations of Existing IT	Mandatory Changes to IT	Opportunities Provided by Advances in IT
Malfunction of IT.	Satisfy regulatory requirements.	Improve the efficiency or effectiveness of existing information processes.
Breakdown of IT.	Adhere to industry standards.	Transform business processes.
Obsolescence, where the IT is no longer supported by vendor.	Comply with market or industry expectations.	Integrate information from partners in the supply chain.
Incompatibility with other IT.	Ensure compatibility between partner organizations.	Develop a competitive advantage.

made available by the IT. For example, mobile technology provides the opportunity for Match Lighting to improve the tracking of its products on pallets. Customers can be informed of the status of their orders and monitor orders being delivered, improving visibility in the supply chain. But changes to information systems and business processes are needed to use the tracking information and address security issues.

12.1.6 ▶ Role of Information Management in Information Technology Transformation

The impact of changes to IT on the information can range from having no discernible direct effect through to impacting, positively or negatively, the:

- Speed with which data can be accessed or processed.
- Ease of access to data.
- Organization's ability to integrate data from different sources.
- Organization's capacity for data storage or processing.
- Format of the data stored.
- Security of the data.
- Way the data can be aggregated, shared, and used.

Changes to the information resource initiated by changes to IT can be negative or positive. For example, a mandatory change to an IT system may require the format of a data item to change, which will require changes to be made to the information systems that use the data item. The change to the IT system may be seen as having a negative impact on the organization. In contrast, the additional flexibility that changing an IT system may offer the organization, such as providing opportunities for new ways of working, may be regarded as a positive impact.

Information management is needed to:

- Assess the implications of changes to IT systems on the information resource.
- Contribute to identifying the changes needed in the organization to improve how information is used, building on the opportunities offered by changes to IT.
- Ensure that changes to the information resource are documented in the data dictionary.
- Maintain the quality, security, and integrity of the information resource.

The role of information management therefore includes:

- Identifying the data that might be affected by the change to the IT.
- Clarifying if the change will affect the data and how (such as changes to the structure, availability, security, and use of the data).

- Determining whether current data definitions, structures, and formats documented in the data dictionary can still be supported.
- Identifying the information systems affected by changes to data definitions, structures, and formats with reference to the information architecture.
- Discussing the implications of the changes to the IT systems with the appropriate data owners.
- Agreeing on approaches to address any changes required to data.
- Considering how the changes to data affect the quality and accessibility of the information available to the organization.
- Exploring how the changes could affect the way information is used in the organization.
- Contributing to the review of any organizational transformation initiated by the change.
- Updating the data dictionary and information architecture to reflect any agreed upon changes to the data definition, format, or usage.

12.2 ▶ Migrating Data

The introduction of new IT into an organization does not always mean the development of a new information system. IT can be used to enhance the performance of existing information systems, overcome problems with technical implementations (such as malfunctions or security concerns), or implement new standards. In such cases the existing information systems need to be migrated to the new technology.

DEFINITION: Migration is the complete transfer of data or applications to a different IT device or technical platform.

For example, if the Director of Match Lighting, Mr Alvis, replaces his laptop, the IT department will migrate the data and applications from the old laptop to the new laptop.

12.2.1 ▶ Types of Data Migration

Data migration refers to the transfer of data to different:

- Storage devices: Data may need to be transferred to a different storage device to improve the speed at which the data can be retrieved, or due to space limitations on the existing device, or as a result of device malfunction.
- Storage formats: When data are moved to a different storage device it may be necessary to change the format in which the data are stored on the physical device. Changes to data storage formats at the

physical level should not have a significant impact on the information systems. Information management is needed to assess any impact on information systems integration and the organization's resource.

○ IT systems: When an IT system is introduced to replace an existing information system, whether developed in-house or purchased as an application package, the data from the existing information systems need to be transferred to the new system. This may require the storage format of the data to be changed and integration issues to be addressed (discussed in Chapter 8).

12.2.2 Stages of Data Migration

Data migration involves a number of stages:

○ Define the scope of the migration. Scott (2004) recommends that a detailed topology of the source data needs to be specified, which includes the IT devices where the source data are located, the specifics of the migration process (including any conversion required), protocols, and security issues that need to be addressed. The volume of data to be migrated also needs to be established.

○ Design a mapping between the original source data and the destination. Migration involves the translation of data models (Ceccato *et al.*, 2009). Data models of the source and target data are needed, specifying the structure and format of the data, to ensure that data integrity is maintained during the migration process.

○ Extract the data from the original source. A plan is needed of how to capture the source data. This will involve creating a copy of the data so that if necessary the original data can be restored for use.

○ Clean the data. Data migration provides the opportunity to clean data and avoid loading inaccurate or incomplete data into the new system or storage device. Data cleaning is discussed in Chapter 8.

○ Convert the data from the source format into the format required by the destination device. Chapter 8 discussed problems that may arise with data integration and the need to convert data formats.

○ Load the data into the new storage device or system in the converted format.

○ Verify that the all the data have been transferred correctly.

○ Develop a test plan to check that the migration has been successful.

The main priority in migration projects is to ensure business continuity both during and after the migration. The migration process should be planned to minimize the impact on the business. This includes:

○ Completing as much preparatory work as possible before the migration process starts.

○ Scheduling the migration to take place at a time when it will have least impact on the organization.

○ Creating backups of the existing data to ensure that the existing implementation can be reinstated if necessary.

○ Developing milestones in the migration plan to determine points at which the migration can be rolled back (reversed) if necessary.

12.2.3 Role of Information Management in Migrating Data

Morris (2006) emphasizes that data migration is a business issue as it is the business that understands the meaning of data that must be preserved during the data migration.

Information management is needed in all stages of data migration to:

○ Assist in the mapping of source and destination data models.

○ Consult data owners about the impact of changes proposed.

○ Clean the data before data are migrated.

○ Design integration procedures.

○ Assess the impact on information systems integration where conversion processes are applied to the source data.

○ Address any issues relating to data integrity.

○ Ensure that the business rules are retained and enforced in the migrated system.

○ Confirm that data security is maintained throughout the process.

○ Conduct tests to check that the data are complete and accessible following the migration.

○ Document any changes to data formats in the data dictionary.

12.3 Implementing Packaged Software

Some common information requirements exist among organizations. For example, all organizations need to manage their finances, assets, and staff. Standard IT application packages are available to meet these information processing requirements. Organizations can purchase off-the-shelf software packages to satisfy their information systems requirements, rather than developing their own information systems. For example, Microsoft Word is an example of a proprietary application package providing software for word processing. Organizations purchase this application package rather than developing their own word processing system. Packaged applications offer the advantage of purchasing ready-made information systems that have been tested both during development and in practice by other customers.

DEFINITION: An **application package** is a suite of software programs which perform a set of tasks. The application package is acquired with a licence that outlines permissions and restrictions of how the package may be used.

Proprietary packaged software, also referred to as closed source software, is licensed software that prevents organizations from changing the software code; the code is the intellectual property of the vendor. The licence prevents organizations changing how information is captured, stored, displayed, accessed, or processed in the packaged software.

Open source software provides organizations with the program code so that the code can be changed by organizations to meet their specific needs. Table 12.2 outlines some of the differences between open and closed source software. Examples of open source application packages include the word processing package Open Office and the Internet browser Firefox (Damsgaard & Karlsbjerg, 2010). Open source software is developed and maintained by a community of software engineers who develop and share program code. Open source software can lack the formal technical support that proprietary software vendors are expected to provide to their customers. However, the community approach to open source software development enables any errors in the software to be identified and corrected more quickly than proprietary vendors. Organizations choose between branded closed source software from corporations and open source software offered by communities of software developers (Figure 12.2).

Table 12.2 Comparison of Closed Source and Open Source Software

Criteria	Closed Source	Open Source
Philosophy	Software is a commodity. Software is owned by an organization.	Software code should be freely accessed and freely distributed. Detailed criteria for open source software defined by Perens (1999) has been adopted by the Open Source Initiative (OSI) http://www.opensource.org/docs/OSD
Control	Software is controlled by vendor.	Software evolves within a community of developers and users.
Licence	The licence restricts how the software can be used.	Licences are unrestrictive and nonproduct-specific.
Software Code	Software code is not available to customers to change.	Software code is made available to be changed by customers.
Development Approach	Software is developed by staff employed by or contracted to a commercial organization.	Software is developed by a community of volunteer software engineers.
Technology	Specific technology is required to use the software, which can force organizations to only use specific vendor technology.	The software is technology-neutral, that is, no specific technology is required to use the software which facilitates interoperability of IT.
Maintenance	Some maintenance to the software may be provided but sometimes organizations may need to wait until the next version of software is released for sale before changes are addressed.	The community of software developers maintains and develops the software as required.
Support	Support for installing and using the software is provided to a customer at a price.	Support for using the software is volunteered by the software developer community but some organizations have been established from which formalized support can be purchased.
Cost	Software is sold at a price for restricted usage specified in the terms of the licence.	Software is volunteered and participation in its development is encouraged.

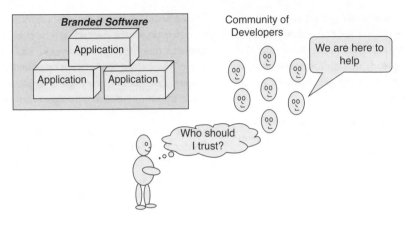

Figure 12.2 Open Source or Closed Source Application?

12.3.1 Introducing Packaged Software

The purchase of a packaged software application usually includes the software code that is ready to be installed in an organization, technical documentation relating to compatibility and installation requirements, and supporting documentation of how to use the software. By purchasing a proprietary software package, the organization does not need to develop the software themselves. This can reduce the time taken to implement the system in the organization.

The process of introducing packaged software into the organization includes the following activities:

○ Determining the information requirements of the organization. This involves the same methods and techniques that are used in the information systems development process for developing bespoke systems.

○ Identifying potential application packages. A range of packaged applications may be available to meet the organization's defined requirements.

○ Evaluating the identified application packages. The potential packaged applications identified are assessed to determine the extent to which they satisfy the organization's requirements.

○ Selecting the application package. An application package is chosen from the evaluation of potential packages. This may involve weighting individual elements of the evaluation criteria in terms of importance and the organization may have to compromise on some of its requirements.

○ Implementing the package. The implementation of the chosen package will involve installing the application software, integrating the software with the existing information systems in the organization, and may also involve migrating data

from an existing system. Installing an application package is likely to require some bridging software programs to be written that integrate information from existing systems with the packaged system. Figure 12.3 shows a bridge program converting data to and from the C.Rate package in Match Lighting in order to integrate the package with the order processing system. The bridge program may include restructuring or reformatting information provided by existing systems into the requirements of the application package and vice versa.

○ Testing the application package. A test plan is developed to ensure that the application is fully installed and operating as required.

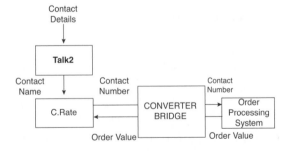

The Converter Bridge takes the contact number output (999999) from C.Rate and converts it into the customer number (XX9999) that is input into the Order Processing System.

The Converter Bridge takes the order value in the form 999v99 output from the Order Processing System and converts it into the form 999 that is input into the C.Rate package.

Figure 12.3 Bridging Software to Integrate Packaged Software in the Information Systems Architecture

12.3.2 Evaluating Packaged Software

Vendors offer a range of packaged applications for sale to organizations. Organizations evaluate the packages available to determine which is most suitable to meet their specific requirements. The evaluation considers the organization's information requirements, functional requirements, and nonfunctional requirements (such as speed of processing and technical compatibility). In addition to evaluating the suitability of the packaged software to meet the business process requirements identified, Avison and Fitzgerald (2006) suggest that the following areas should also be considered:

○ The resources required for implementing and using the application package.

○ The number and type of organizations that are using the package and their views about the package (including its installation, use in practice, and limitations).

○ The quality of the documentation provided with the application relating to how to implement, use, and maintain the application.

An application package is unlikely to exactly meet the specific requirements of the organization. Decisions therefore have to be taken about to what extent aspects of the organization can or should change to accommodate the requirements of the application package. In addition to assessing the extent to which a package system meets the current requirements of the organization, consideration needs to be given to the extent to which the system may limit the ability of the organization to change in the future. Although the vendor may offer regular upgrades to the packaged software, the organization cannot modify the functionality of closed software as its requirements change. The benefits of purchasing a tested and ready-to-use information system therefore need to be weighed against the lack of flexibility of proprietary packaged systems to be able to respond to the changing needs of the organization. The application package could become a barrier preventing the organization changing business processes as information requirements change.

Table 12.3 provides criteria against which packaged application software can be evaluated.

12.3.3 Information in Packaged Software

Packaged application software provides a quick means of implementing a predefined information system, but the way information is used in the system and the data required by the system is unlikely to exactly match the needs of the organization and compromises usually have to be made. The vendor needs to provide the organization

with data models and file specifications in order for the organization to understand how data are used in the application and to assess the implications of implementing the package.

For example, if Match Lighting uses different attribute structures from those used in the application package it plans to purchase, Match Lighting has three options. Option one is not to purchase the package and develop the system in-house or purchase an alternative package. Developing the system in-house is likely to take some time and buying an alternative package may require Match Lighting to compromise on functional requirements. Option two is to create a bridging program to convert the attribute structures when integrating data into the package and back again (Figure 12.3). Option three is to change all attribute structures in the organization to those used in the application package. This would involve changing existing information systems and ensuring that archived data could still be retrieved if necessary. The impact of this option could be extensive.

If a packaged application does not quite meet the information needs of the organization and is implemented, staff are likely to develop workarounds to cope with the situation. However, this may lead to further problems in the future. For example, a previous delivery system used by Match Lighting had a field on the data input screen that allowed short notes to be added relating to the delivery of an order. These notes were printed on the dispatch labels to help the driver delivering the order, for example, 'delivery area at back of premises' or 'parking restrictions, phone ahead to confirm access is available'. The system was replaced by an application package that did not provide this facility. However, the new system did provide eight lines for a delivery address (the previous system only used six lines) so operators used the additional lines of the address to add notes to drivers. In the short term this worked fine. A year later the requirements for a new finance system were defined. Since the output from the delivery system application was an eight-line address, eight-line addresses were specified as the format for addresses to be input into the finance system. This meant that the delivery instructions appeared on all finance documents. Problems then arose due to validation errors that the finance system applied to specific lines of the address.

12.3.4 Role of Information Management in Implementing Packaged Software

The role of information management in the evaluation of packaged information systems is to ensure that the potential impact of the package on the organization's

Table 12.3 Criteria for Evaluating Packaged Software

Information	What data does the package require as input? What data does it produce as output? What format are the data in? What is the structure of data items? (For example, what format is used for dates?) What is the data model of the package? What files are created and used by the package? What are the key data items used in the package? What are the attributes of the data items? What integrity constraints are enforced to maintain the quality of the data? What security controls are implemented in the package to maintain the security of the data? Which data items are mandatory in the package? Which data items are optional?
Business Processes	What reporting tools are included? Can customized reports be produced? What processes are supported in the package? Are all functions mandatory? Can some functions be disabled? What are the average response times for processes? What is the maximum capacity of data and transactions that can be stored and processed by the system? What standards and regulations are embedded into the processing (for example, taxation regulations and accepted currencies)? What auditing features are included? What archiving options are available? What processes are not supported by the package?
Technical Specification	What hardware is required? What technical platform is required? What network protocols are required? What storage devices are required? What are the processing requirements? What devices are supported (for example, are mobile devices supported)? How many concurrent users can be supported? Can the application be accessed remotely? Is it compatible with other packages? What standards are used in the package?
Interface	How easy is the package to use? How are different functions accessed? How does a user move around the different functions? How meaningful are the menu options and button labels? What terminology is used in the screen designs? Are options well spaced to avoid the wrong option being selected? How easy it to correct mistakes? How intuitive is the system to use? What accessibility options are available? (For example, is it possible to change font size and colour? Is it compatible with screen readers?) Are there quick path keys to access commonly used options?
Implementation	How easy it is to implement the package? What technical resources are required to implement the package? What human resources, including specialist skills, are needed for the implementation? How long will it take to implement the package? What data are needed to populate the files used by the package? What actions will be needed to migrate the existing data into the package? What changes will need to be made to existing systems to accommodate the package? How will the vendor support the implementation process? Will it be possible to run the package in parallel with the existing systems during the changeover process? How will the implementation be tested?

Table 12.3 Continued

Customer base	How many organizations are using the software?
	What industries are using it?
	What size of organization currently uses the software?
	Which organizations are using it?
	Can an existing customer's site be visited?
	How long have organizations been using the package?
	In what countries is the package being used?
	What is the take-up rate of the software?
	Do customers purchase more than one type of product from the vendor?
	How does the vendor interact with the customer base? (For example, is there a customer forum?)
Customer Opinion	What do organizations that use the package think about it?
	Did they have any problems installing the package?
	Have they had any problems in using the package?
	Is there anything they wished they had known before they had purchased the package?
	With the benefit of hindsight, would they purchase the package again?
	How does the vendor respond to customer feedback?
	How quickly are bugs in the software addressed?
	How reliable is the software?
	How flexible is the application package?
	What problems have arisen while using the package?
Documentation	What documentation is provided with the package (such as systems documentation, user guide)?
	How many copies are provided?
	Is the documentation accurate?
	Is the documentation complete?
	How frequently is the documentation updated?
	How thorough is the documentation?
	What form is the documentation in (for example, online, paper)?
	Can the documentation be tailored to meet the needs of the customer? (For example, can the user manual be edited to reflect how the product will be used in a specific organization?)
	Can additional documentation be generated?
	What form of training is available?
Contract	What is the pricing structure? (For example, is the software leased or licensed?)
	How many sites can use the package?
	Can the package be used across international sites?
	What is included in the package?
	How many licences are included?
	Is training included?
	What support is provided? In what form? For what period of time?
	What maintenance is provided?
	What updates are provided and for how long?
	What are the costs of seeking to end the contract early?
Vendor	How many years has the vendor been trading?
	What is the size of the organization?
	How many staff work on product development?
	How old is the product?
	When was the product last updated?
	How frequently is the product updated?
	What are the vendor's future plans for the product?
	How is the product evolving?
	What other products and services does the vendor provide?
	Is the vendor cooperative and trustworthy?

information resource is fully considered. The information manager therefore needs to explore how information is defined, structured, and used in the package and to what extent this differs from the way information is defined and used in the organization's data dictionary. This will involve:

○ Reviewing the data structure and data formats used in the system.

○ Comparing the data structures with the data dictionary entries.

○ Identifying the format, structure, and type of data required as input to the package.

○ Identifying the format, structure, and type of data output from the package.

○ Using the information architecture to identify the information systems that need to integrate with the package system.

○ Identifying how the information used in the package differs from the current information used in the organization.

○ Assessing the implications of any differences in how information is used.

○ Proposing changes needed to current business processes and practices to accommodate the differences in information usage.

○ Working with IT staff to assess the changes needed to existing information systems and IT systems.

○ Defining potential options to accommodate the needs of the package.

○ Ensuring that if the package is implemented, its use of information is documented in the data dictionary.

○ Participate in the external community of other organizations that use the application package, working with the vendor to improve the package, establish industry standards, and develop further compatible application packages (Damsgaard & Karlsbjerg, 2010).

Application packages increase the complexity of the information management task. It can be difficult to acquire detailed information about how data relationships are managed in the package due to the vendor's desire to sell their support services and protect their intellectual property. The problem is further compounded when bridge programs are needed to convert data going into and out of the application. However, it is important that the data items used in the package are also documented in the data dictionary and information architecture to support information integration and impact analysis of changes to information proposed in the future.

12.4 ▶ Integrating Information

The information needed in an organization is distributed across a range of information systems. Organizations need seamless access to the information resource irrespective of how or where the information is located. This requires information from individual information systems to be integrated through the integration of IT systems in which the underlying data are stored and processed. However, the information needed is held not just in disparate internal systems but in the systems of customers and suppliers (Evgeniou, 2002). Integration of information is essential for intraorganizational business processes sharing information and coordinating activities (Tripathi & Gupta, 2012).

Gulledge (2006) distinguishes between two extremes of integration, providing a scale in which to position forms of integration. These are *Big I*, where all data are stored only once and shared by all systems, and *Little I*, where data can pass between systems via interfaces (requiring data to be cleaned and harmonized from different sources). Tripathi and Gupta (2012) distinguish integration and interoperability; integration involves combining information and processes whereas interoperability refers to being able to work together efficiently. Interoperability of IT enables the integration of information and businesses processes to take place.

12.4.1 ▶ Levels of Information Integration

The enterprise architecture (introduced in Chapter 4) comprises four levels: organizational architecture, information architecture, information systems architecture, and IT architecture. Each of these architectures has a role in facilitating information integration. Table 12.4 identifies some of the challenges that need to be addressed at each level of the enterprise architecture to support information integration. At the organizational level, differences in working practices and departmental cultures can hinder access and integration of information. Issues arising from different information definitions, measuring units, and data structures were discussed in Chapters 7 and 8. Within the IT architecture, information integration can be hindered due to issues arising with the compatibility of the physical IT devices and operations software used by a device.

Figure 12.4 shows the influence of people-related and technology-related factors affecting the ability to integrate information at different levels in the enterprise architecture. People-related factors affect integration in the organization architecture, whereas technological issues affect integration in the IT architecture.

The organization needs unified access to consistent and accurate information irrespective of where information is created and stored in the extended organization. This requires issues of information integration, data compatibility, and technical interoperability to be considered:

Information integration involves the aggregation of data. It is important to understand the source of the

Table 12.4 Challenges to Information Integration in the Enterprise Architecture

	Barriers	**Challenges to Overcome**
Organizational Architecture	People and practice.	Organizational and departmental boundaries.
		Mistrust of information received from other teams, departments, or organizations.
		Cultural unwillingness to share information.
		Inconsistent quality practices.
Information Architecture	Information and processes.	Information semantics.
		Different interpretations of information.
		Different requirements for information.
Information Systems Architecture	Semantic and structure.	Inconsistencies in information due to conflicting definitions, coding systems, and structures.
IT Architecture	Technology interoperability.	Balancing heterogeneity and interoperability of IT by using consistent data formats, standards, and messaging protocols.

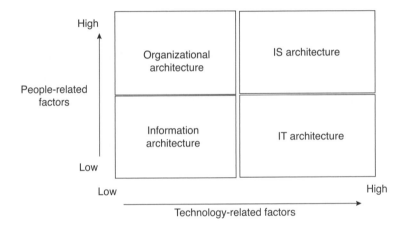

Figure 12.4 Factors Affecting Information Integration in the Enterprise Architecture

data to ensure that similar data are being aggregated. If different data definitions have been applied this will affect how the data can be interpreted and used; it may lead to inaccurate interpretations and decisions that are based on inaccurate data. Issues of data compatibility need to be addressed to support information integration.

Data integration involves the collection, comparison, and aggregation of data (Evgeniou, 2002), which is achieved through a mapping between the target and source data models (Lenzerini, 2002). Issues arising with the compatibility of data were discussed in Chapter 8.

Technical interoperability refers to the need for the physical IT devices, used to store and process the organization's data, to be able to work together to provide the information required by the organization. The IT infrastructure of an organization evolves over time, influenced by the need to implement the latest IT trends in order

to remain competitive (Evgeniou, 2002). A growth in disparate systems can lead to the infrastructure becoming fragmented with incompatible heterogeneous platforms (Badii & Sharif, 2003). This can limit the ability to access data and integrate information from different systems, which may lead to data duplication, incurring unnecessary costs and potential inconsistency of data.

12.4.2 Interoperability of Information

IT manufacturers develop proprietary standards enabling their hardware and software to work together effectively. This encourages organizations to rely on a specific IT provider to supply their IT needs, reassured that the equipment will work together, facilitating information integration. However, there are risks associated with being locked in to one supplier (such as the supplier going out of business, high price increases, and limited choice of products). Organizations have to balance their need for equipment and software from different vendors, with potential problems of IT interoperability.

Interoperability enables two or more devices to work together, irrespective of the manufacturer of the equipment or the systems and applications running on the IT equipment. This requires manufacturers to agree to the use of common standards. Standards stipulate a specification to ensure devices will work together (Sutor, 2011) and provide the basis for integrating exchanged information (Kosanke, 2005). This avoids organizations becoming reliant on a single manufacturer. However, standards take time to develop and a range of standards often coexist until one becomes the de facto standard or technology evolves such that the standards are superseded.

Compatibility between IT systems can be considered from a number of levels, including: application interfaces, software platforms, data formats, data standards, and network protocols. Kubicek and Cimander (2009) outline four levels of interoperability:

- Organizational interoperability enables processes to be linked via workflows. This is particularly important to enable organizations to work effectively with their trading partners in the extended enterprise. It can be achieved through the standardization of processes.
- Semantic interoperability enables information exchanged between IT devices to be interpreted and processed appropriately. This is achieved through the use of agreed upon information definitions.
- Syntactic interoperability enables data to be exchanged between IT devices. It is achieved through the standardization of the format used for exchanging data, such as XML (discussed in Chapter 3).
- Technical interoperability enables the complete and secure transfer of data signals between IT devices. It is achieved through the standardization of communication protocols used in the transmission of data.

DEFINITION: Protocols are the rules used to send and receive data signals between IT devices.

12.4.3 ▶ Role of Information Management in Integrating Information

Information management is concerned with ensuring that the organization's information resource is secure and accessible irrespective of how and where the information is physically stored, and the specific technology used to manage the data. Changes to the IT architecture, such as the introduction or replacement of IT equipment or operating software platforms, can affect the accessibility of data. When changes

are proposed to the IT architecture it is therefore important to assess the potential impact of the change on the ability to integrate data held in different IT systems. Information management needs to:

- Identify the data stored in the IT system which is to be changed.
- Define the current format of the data.
- Determine the format of the data used by the proposed IT system.
- Compare the current data formats with the formats used by the proposed system.
- Assist IT staff to assess the compatibility of the proposed IT system with the current IT architecture.
- Assist IT staff to assess any constraints imposed on the future development of the IT architecture by the proposed IT system.
- Document the format of the data to be used in the proposed IT system.

12.5 ▶ Managing Legacy Systems

Most organizations have some legacy IT systems. Legacy systems evolve over time as a system is modified through a series of upgrades and extensions to its existing functionality and technical implementation (Scherpereel & Lefebvre, 2006). This results in a complex system (Reddy & Reddy, 2002), which may include obsolete hardware and software, making it difficult to implement changes to the system. Legacy systems can be costly to maintain, such that it may become cheaper to replace the system (Scherpereel & Lefebvre, 2006). In such cases, IT may become a barrier to organizational change.

A legacy system incorporates application software and systems hardware; application data used by the system; and knowledge of business policies and business rules embedded in the system implementing the business processes (Rodriguez et al., 2009). The term *legacy system* conjures ideas of age, incompatibility, and obsolescence. However, legacy systems often perform critical functions in the organization (Rodriguez et al., 2009) and there can be a reluctance to replace the system. This is partly driven by the need to protect the day-to-day operation of the business and partly driven by reluctance to address the complexity of the system. This has led to what Scherpereel and Lefebvre (2006) refer to as the *legacy mindset*, that is, an approach to continually extend and maintain existing systems rather than replace them.

12.5.1 ▶ Perspectives on Legacy Systems

Alderson and Shah (1999) propose four perspectives of legacy systems: developmental, operational, organizational, and strategic. In the developmental perspective legacy systems are identified as an information system for which information systems development has been completed. If changes are needed to the system in order to meet the evolving organizational requirements, the changes will be approached via a maintenance programme. This will evaluate the direct and indirect costs of the maintenance task against the potential benefits to the organization of performing the maintenance and the potential costs to the organization of not performing the maintenance.

The operational perspective uses the term *legacy* to refer to out-of-date IT or software that is no longer part of the organization's current information systems and IT strategy. It recognizes that changes to the legacy system will require knowledge, expertise, and skills that the organization may no longer possess and significant investment may be required to migrate the information systems to a different technical platform.

The organizational perspective identifies legacy systems as systems that constrain the organization's ability to make necessary changes to business processes to support the evolving organizational strategy. The term *legacy* here refers to outdated business processes embedded in the organization's information systems; this means that changes to the business processes cannot be undertaken quickly.

In the strategic perspective, legacy systems are identified as systems which are no longer cost-effective; the cost of operating and maintaining the system exceeds the value of the system to the business. This perspective also considers the costs to the organization resulting from the organization's inability to easily and quickly make changes to information systems to adapt to changing business needs.

The perspective on legacy systems adopted influences on how legacy systems are managed in the organization.

12.5.2 Strategies for Managing Legacy Systems

Colosimo *et al.* (2009) suggest that there are five main options, which are not mutually exclusive, for maintaining legacy systems:

- Modify the legacy system.
- Replace the legacy system.
- Incorporate the legacy system as a component in a new information system.
- Engage in a programme of preventative maintenance.
- Conduct business process re-engineering.

These options can be broadly encompassed in two main approaches for addressing the challenges of legacy systems. The first approach is to undertake maintenance, redevelopment, or replacement of the legacy system to meet the changing needs of the business or technology. The second approach is to develop a wrapper around the legacy system so that the legacy system can be integrated with other systems. A wrapper is software code which surrounds the legacy system, providing an interface to and from the system so that the system can be regarded as a black box (Figure 12.5). Other information systems can send information to and receive information from the legacy system through the wrapper, but no changes are made to the legacy system itself. This enables the legacy system to be incorporated as a component in a new information system.

Figure 12.6 considers the options for maintaining or replacing legacy systems, from technological and organizational perspectives, based on the degree of change of business processes and technology, since the system was developed.

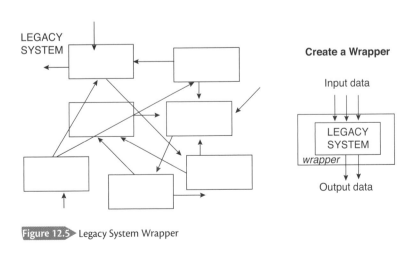

Figure 12.5 Legacy System Wrapper

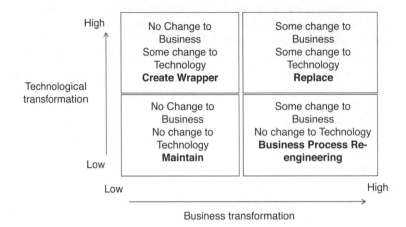

Figure 12.6 Assessing the Strategic Options for Legacy System

Figure 12.6 can be used to inform decisions from the strategic viewpoint relating to legacy systems. For example:

○ If there has been no, or limited, change to business processes and the technology used in the organization, then it may be cost-effective to continue maintaining the legacy system.

○ If there has been no, or limited, change to business processes and there is significant change to the technology used in the organization, then it may be appropriate to develop a wrapper around the legacy system to enable it to be effectively integrated with newer systems in the organization.

○ If there has been significant change to business processes and there has also been significant change to the technology used in the organization, then it may be appropriate to completely replace the existing information systems.

○ If there has been significant change to business processes and there has been no, or limited, change to the technology used in the organization, business process re-engineering may be required to ensure that the information system can meet the changing needs of the organization.

The purpose of Figure 12.6 is to offer general guidance to decision-makers, rather than prescribing courses of action; decision-makers will also need to consider other strategic and operational issues. For example, the potential impact on the availability of business information during the change process will need to be compared with the technical arguments to justify changes to the system.

12.5.3 Role of Information Management in Managing Legacy Systems

The role of information management differs depending on the strategy implemented for managing legacy systems shown in Figure 12.6.

Replacement Strategy

The replacement of a legacy system will involve either the development of a new information system or the purchase of a packaged application. Both approaches will require the information and functional requirements of the system to be identified and modelled. The role of information management is to assist in determining the information needs of the organization and to ensure that the integrity of the information resource is maintained. For example, information in the replacement system will need to adhere to the agreed upon definitions and information management policies in the organization.

Wrapping Strategy

The creation of a wrapper around the legacy system requires the data input to the system and output from the system to be fully understood. Data owners and IT staff need to work together to fully document the data inputs and outputs of the legacy system. This will provide the information requirements for other systems that need to integrate with the legacy system.

Maintenance Strategy

Maintaining a legacy system involves:

○ Determining the degree of the change required (such as a minor change to the presentation of information through to changes in functionality).

○ Identifying the type of change required to the system (such as data structures, business processes, technical implementation).

○ Assessing the impact on data in the information system.

○ Assessing the impact on the data required by the information system and the data output from the system to other systems.

○ Planning the maintenance.

○ Completing the maintenance and testing the information system.

Maintenance may be difficult due to the complexity of the information system design which has evolved over time. Changes to the legacy system may lead to unanticipated effects that require further investigation to resolve. The role of information management is to assess the impact of the maintenance on the information resource used by the information system and on other systems with which it is integrated. Data owners can assist the maintenance activity by documenting changes to the information system and explaining to IT staff how data are used and processed by the information system.

Re-engineering Strategy

Re-engineering a legacy system involves working backward from the current operational system to create the models and documentation normally produced during the development of an information system. Re-engineering helps to understand the legacy system in terms of its technical implementation, business processes, and information processes. The original documentation may no longer exist or may be out of date as changes may have been made to the system that may not have been thoroughly documented. Pérez-Castilo et al. (2010) suggest that business patterns can be used to identify business knowledge embedded in legacy systems. The patterns include structural patterns relating to the sequence of business processes, data patterns relating to the relationship between data and the inputs and outputs of processes, and event patterns such as conditional sequences and exception handling (Pérez-Castilo et al., 2010).

The role of information management in re-engineering legacy systems is to:

○ Create a data model showing the relationships between data items in the systems.

○ Determine the business rules to maintain the integrity of the data in the system.

○ Define the data that are input to and output from the system.

○ Assist in defining the processes that are performed on the data in the system.

○ Document the use of data in the system.

○ Identify any anomalies with how the data are used in the system and elsewhere in the organization.

When an understanding of the data and processes in the legacy system has been attained, changes needed to the system can be identified. The changes will then be implemented through information systems development processes.

12.6 Information Management Challenges with Changing Information Technology

Changes to IT can have a significant immediate impact on an organization and may influence or prevent the organization changing in the future. It is therefore essential that the business is actively involved in assessing the implications that may arise when changes to IT are proposed. Changes to IT may affect the availability and accessibility of information in the organization and need to be considered within the context of information management.

Information management is needed to:

○ Identify the information to be used by the technology.

○ Identify information systems affected in the information architecture.

○ Define the information requirements of information systems that use the technology.

○ Determine the scope of changes proposed to the information resource.

○ Assess the impact on the information resource.

○ Assess the legal and ethical implications of using the technology to access information.

○ Assess the potential security risks to information posed by the technology.

○ Review the issues relating to the accessibility and characteristics of information used by the technology, such as limited screen size of a mobile device or change in length of a data field.

○ Assess the impact on the flexibility and interoperability of the IT infrastructure.

○ Document agreed upon changes in the data dictionary and information architecture.

IT may change how data are stored and accessed in information systems. This may increase the risk to information security and may affect the interoperability of information systems. Changing IT may require business processes to change to take advantage of opportunities (such as remote working) or to accommodate the requirements of application packages. These changes to business processes may require changes to be made to the staff and skills needed to conduct the processes. This could range from the need to train staff in how to use a new application package through to the development of new skill sets. IT can also be used to support and direct the organization's strategy. For example, improvements to Match Lighting's contact management system may help support the organization's objective to improve relationships with potential partners. At the other extreme, e-business initiatives transform all aspects of the organization, facilitating new ways of working and new opportunities for engaging with external parties. Figure 12.7 reflects the impact of IT on organizational transformation. As technology continues to advance, each new development needs to be assessed in terms of the opportunities and threats that it offers to organizations. Figure 12.7 identifies a number of organizational dimensions to consider when exploring the impact of new technology on organizations and the areas of transformation needed to accommodate the technology.

Link 12.1
Checklist for Assessing Information Management Challenges with Changes to Information Technology

Summary

IT provides the means for implementing the processes required by information systems. IT is continually changing and ideally changes to the IT architecture should be invisible to the organization. Incremental changes to improve the way data are physically stored or processed are usually invisible to the organization, though the availability of information and the performance of information systems may be affected while the change is being implemented.

Open source or closed source software application packages provide ready-made information systems for organizations. Although packaged systems avoid the costs of information systems development, work is needed to assess the package and integrate the package with existing systems in the organization. Legacy information systems pose specific challenges to information integration. Legacy systems may be replaced, maintained, re-engineered, or wrapped to facilitate integration with other systems in the organization.

IT has the potential to transform the way organizations conduct their business and influence their strategic position in the marketplace. Advances in technology continue to remove barriers to accessing, processing, and sharing information, but to maximize the opportunities offered by IT requires organizations to change business processes and their use of information. A range of technological themes, and their impact on information management, are discussed in the following chapter.

Reviewing Scenario 12.1

There are a number of options for Match Lighting to consider:

○ Do nothing and keep using Talk2. Talk2 meets the current information requirements of the sales team but the vendor is no longer developing the software. Further improvements to the design and functionality of Talk2 will not be made in the future. Although the package meets Ms Bevan's current requirements, the software may not meet future requirements. There is

Figure 12.7 ▶ Information Technology–led Organizational Transformation

also concern that the lack of further upgrades could put the security of the data captured and stored using the software at risk. The current package is not compatible with the future platform requirements of the IT department. If Talk2 still needed to be used by the organization after the operating system was upgraded, Talk2 would need to be treated as a legacy system.

○ Upgrade to Talk3. This option would require a detailed analysis of the information requirements and functionality of the package to be assessed to determine how the package would integrate with the existing information systems. It may be possible to disable some of the functions that Ms Bevan does not need. If this is not possible, the installation of the package may require considerable work to be undertaken to integrate it with the existing ordering system and it may also replace other packages used, such as C.Rate. This will require data from C.Rate to be migrated to Talk3.

○ Investigate other packages. Other packages available on the market for managing contacts could be identified and evaluated to replace Talk2. As Talk3 does not seem to meet the requirements of the sales team, Match Lighting could try to find an alternative application package. This will require a list of requirements to be developed against which potential packages can be assessed.

○ Develop a new information system in Match Lighting to meet the specific information and functional requirements of the sales team in relation to contact management. The development of a new information system will take time and in the interim period data security issues may arise using Talk2. However, developing the system will enable the specific information requirements of Match Lighting to be met and the system could be modified in the future to support the changing needs of the organization.

Information management issues to consider include the:

○ Risk to data security of continuing to use Talk2.
○ Legal and ethical implications of maintaining personal notes about contacts. Talk2 may have removed this feature as the information captured would have to be disclosed if demanded by a request under the Freedom of Information Act.

○ Information required as input to Talk3 and produced as output of Talk3 to assess how the application would need to integrate with the existing systems.

○ Information required as input to other packages and produced as output for other packages that Match Lighting might consider using as a replacement for Talk2.

○ Information required as input to C.Rate.

○ Information requirements of the sales team.

○ Extent to which the information used in Talk3 or other packages adheres to the organization's use of the information documented in the data dictionary.

○ Changes required to information and its use in existing information systems to integrate Talk3 or another package into the organization's architecture.

○ Migration of data from Talk2 to the replacement system.

○ Need to ensure that information archived from Talk2 can be retrieved if needed.

Cloze Exercise 12.1

Complete the following paragraph by choosing the correct word from Table 12.5 to fill in each gap.

An IT system comprises a number of components to implement an _____ . It provides the _____ and software to capture, store, transmit, and process data securely. Changes to an IT system may be needed due to breakdown or _____ of equipment. Mandatory changes to IT may be required to satisfy _____ requirements and industry standards. Other changes to IT may be implemented to improve the efficiency and effectiveness of existing information processes to support development of competitive _____ .

Upgrading IT equipment may increase the _____ of data that can be stored and processed but may also require changes to be made to data structures and formats. _____ refers to the transfer of data from one IT device to another. The process provides the opportunity

Table 12.5 Words to Complete Cloze Exercise 12.1

Access	Closed	Integration	Obsolescence	Protocols
Advantage	Evaluated	Interoperability	Open	Regulatory
Barrier	Hardware	Legacy	Package	Resource
Capacity	Information	Loaded	People	Verification
Clean	Information System	Migration	Proprietary	Wrapper

to _____ data before data are converted and transferred to the new device. When the data has been _____ into the new IT, _____ is needed to check that all the data has been transferred correctly.

An application _____ is a set of software programs that can be purchased to perform business functions. Proprietary software is _____ source software where the program code is the intellectual property of the vendor. _____ source software is developed by a community of software developers who make the program code available for others to modify and improve. When purchasing software the initial stages of information systems development are still needed to determine the _____, functional, and nonfunctional requirements of the software. Potential software that may satisfy the organization's requirements is thoroughly _____ . It is unlikely that _____ software will exactly meet the organization's requirements and compromises may need to be made. The extent of changes to the information _____ needed to accommodate the software package must be thoroughly investigated. This includes assessing the impact on information _____ .

Barriers to information integration in the enterprise architecture can be _____-related and technology-related. Technical _____ refers to the need for IT devices to work together. _____ are needed which define rules to standardize data communication between IT. A _____ system evolves over time as systems are maintained to meet the needs of the organization. The systems become more complex and can become a _____ to organizational change. Although it may be cheaper to replace such systems rather than maintain them, this can be difficult, so a _____ may be developed around the system. This enables it be integrated as a component in a new information system. Proposals to change IT can affect the future flexibility of the IT architecture and may hinder the ability to _____ information needed by the organization.

Link 12.2
Answers to Cloze Exercise 12.1

Activities 12.1

1   Table 12.3 lists a range of criteria for evaluating software packages. How should the criteria be weighted?

2   Identify the factors that Match Lighting should consider in deciding whether to upgrade to Talk3.

3   List the potential business benefits to Match Lighting of replacing barcodes on pallets with RFID tags. Identify the changes needed to the business processes in Match Lighting in order to take advantage of these benefits.

4   Using Figure 12.7, explain the dimensions of organizational change initiated by the replacement of barcodes on pallets in Match Lighting.

5   For each driver of IT change listed in Section 12.1.4, identify the source of the driver from the business model introduced in Chapter 1.

6   Compare the relative advantages and disadvantages of open source and closed source software.

7   With reference to the four perspectives of legacy systems, assess whether Talk2 is a legacy system.

8   If Talk2 was an in-house legacy system, what strategy, from Figure 12.6 should be used to manage the system?

Discussion Questions 12.1

1   Packaged systems provide an organization with key functionality. Should an organization seek to use the same packaged software as its competitors? What are the advantages and disadvantages of this strategy?

2   Open source software offers a number of advantages to organizations, so why is it that some organizations are hesitant to adopt an open source strategy?

3   What are the relative advantages and disadvantages of basing an organization's IT architecture on the hardware offered by a single manufacturer?

4   Legacy systems evolve in response to the changing needs of the organization and wider technological environment. What factors should be considered when deciding whether to modify or replace a legacy system?

5   Why does the information manager need to be involved in the migration of data between IT storage devices?

6   To what extent is organizational change driven by changes to IT?

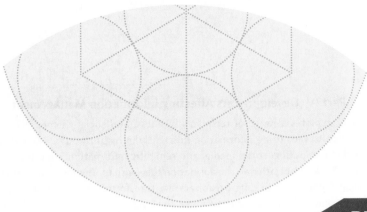

DEVELOPMENTS AFFECTING INFORMATION MANAGEMENT

Part IV Developments Affecting Information Management

Part IV explores a range of technical, business, and social themes that offer opportunities for using information differently in organizations. Themes such as cloud computing, social media, and semantic information are discussed in terms of the organizational transformation they initiate. The role of information management in facilitating organizational transformation is considered and the ongoing information management challenges that need to be addressed through collaboration between the business and IT functions are identified.

Chapter 13 Technological Themes

Chapter 13 discusses a range of technology in terms of the impact of the technology on the organizational architecture. It provides an introduction to cloud computing, outlining the risks and benefits to the organization. The information management issues in applications of mobile computing, smart homes, smart cities, and intelligent buildings are discussed. The integration of information in enterprise resource planning and enterprise content management systems is explained.

Chapter 14 Business Themes

Chapter 14 explores how themes in business management impact the organization and the information management strategy. It explains the relationship between information and knowledge, outlining the processes in knowledge management and identifying types of business innovation. Social network analysis is introduced and the impact of social media on the organizational architecture is considered. The chapter discusses the role of information management in business intelligence.

Chapter 15 Information Themes

Chapter 15 discusses the challenges of indexing and retrieving semantically rich information. It demonstrates an approach to indexing multimedia information and explains the semantic web with examples of RDF and OWL. The difference between customization and personalization is considered and the challenges of personalized information are discussed. A funnel-and-filter model of information retrieval is presented. The chapter defines the primary and secondary contexts of information and presents a model for exploring the context of information.

Chapter 16 Future of Information Management

Chapter 16 identifies common complaints about information in organizations and explains how business and IT functions can work together to improve information management. Barriers and facilitators of information quality are identified and the technological and human challenges affecting information management are discussed. The chapter summarizes the stages of information management and identifies key information management issues that need to be addressed, such as information consumption, pollution, and sustainability.

TECHNOLOGICAL THEMES

Introducing an ERP System in Match Lighting

The domestic light fitting manufacturer Match Lighting has been bought by Watts Electrical UK. The IT manager, Mr Cook, has been instructed to prepare a plan to implement Watts Electrical's ERP and ECM systems at Match Lighting as soon as possible. Match Lighting's managing director, Mr Alvis, is concerned about the impact that the systems will have on the organization and has asked Mrs Winters, the information manager to assess the potential impact of the systems.

What issues should the information manager include in her report?

Learning Outcomes

The learning outcomes of this chapter are to:

○ Identify the information management challenges of cloud computing.

○ Define information applications of mobile computing.

○ Analyse the context of information in pervasive computing environments.

○ Assess the impact of enterprise resource planning on the information resource.

○ Outline the role of information management in enterprise content management.

○ Determine the information management issues of technological developments.

Introduction

Information technology (IT) is continually changing and the information management strategy developed in Part II must be sufficiently robust to deal with future technological changes in the organization. This chapter explores a range of current technologies. Although technology continues to evolve, IT focuses on the way data are captured, stored, and used. IT may change how individuals interact with information and initiate the transformation of business processes. Technological developments can pose new challenges for the way in which information is managed in organizations and requires changes to be made to the information management strategy. This chapter first considers cloud computing, mobile technology, and pervasive technology, which change where data are captured, stored, and accessed. Two enterprise systems are then discussed which aim to improve the consistency and integration of data in the organization. The chapter concludes by presenting a set of frameworks to assess the impact on information management of changes to IT in an organization.

13.1 ▶ Cloud Computing

In traditional computing environments an organization's data and computer programs (the software code that runs the business applications) are stored on IT equipment (servers) located on the organization's premises. The storage and information processing capacity of the organization is determined by the number and size of the servers that it owns. Increasing IT capacity can take several months to source, install, and set up additional equipment. An organization needs sufficient capacity to deal with peaks of demand and have spare capacity in case of hardware failure. This means that some capacity remains unused for long periods of time.

In a cloud computing environment, an organization leases storage and processing capacity on servers, which are located away from the organization's premises and are accessed via the Internet. *CLOUD* is an acronym for

Common Location Independent, Online Utility on Demand (Cervone, 2010).

DEFINITION: Cloud computing is the provision of an IT infrastructure that is accessible via the Internet and may be managed and maintained by a service provider. Organizations rent use of the infrastructure and can quickly increase or decrease the capacity rented to meet their changing needs.

Cloud computing offers a new paradigm in access and distribution of IT services (Low *et al.*, 2011). It has been described as utility computing and on-demand computing, which reflects the provision of IT services as a metered pay-for-usage service (Thomas, 2011). There are two key advantages of cloud computing. First, the IT capacity available to an organization is dynamic and the changing needs of the organization can be quickly accommodated. For example, additional storage capacity can usually be sourced and ready to use in 30 minutes. This means that an organization can achieve cost savings by only renting the capacity it needs and extending or reducing its rented capacity as needs change. Second, the direct costs of installing and maintaining IT equipment are passed to the host provider.

13.1.1 ▶ Types of Cloud Computing

Cloud computing differs in terms of the type of IT service provided (referred to as service models) and who can access the services (referred to as deployment models).

Cloud computing has three service models:

○ **Cloud Infrastructure as a Service (IaaS)** enables an organization to use Internet technologies to access a scalable IT infrastructure to support its information processing requirements. This replaces the need for the organization to develop and maintain its own physical IT infrastructure located on its premises (Figure 13.1). The cloud infrastructure is flexible, enabling further storage or processing capacity to be added when needed to satisfy increases in demand. This provides the opportunity for an organization to reduce its IT costs while improving the flexibility and scalability of its IT infrastructure (Low *et al.*, 2011).

○ **Cloud Platform as a Service (PaaS)** provides software development environments that organizations can rent. The environments may be used by the internal IT department of the organization for writing and testing software applications. The platform providers can also host applications created by the organization. Figure 13.2 shows a provider offering a web hosting service in the cloud. An organization can develop its website

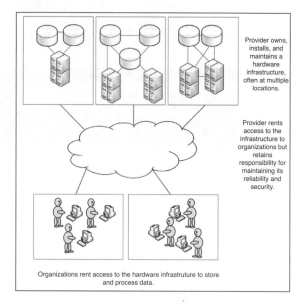

Organizations rent access to the hardware infrastructure to store and process data.

Figure 13.1 ▶ Cloud Infrastructure as a Service

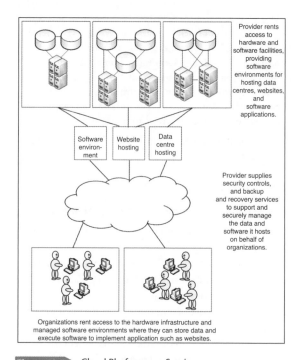

Organizations rent access to the hardware infrastructure and managed software environments where they can store data and execute software to implement application such as websites.

Figure 13.2 ▶ Cloud Platform as a Service

and then upload it to the web hosting service rented from the provider. The provider stores the website on its hardware and provides the security, backup, and recovery services to ensure that the website is secure. The provider may also offer additional services, such as email provision and tools to assist organizations in managing the services. IT departments have to address the issue of how to integrate cloud-based application systems with non-cloud-based systems in the organization.

○ **Cloud Software as a Service (SaaS)** enables organizations to access complete software applications using a web browser rather than installing software on their own hardware. Organizations rent access to software systems instead of purchasing a packaged software application. The cloud provides a range of ready-to-rent software applications (Figure 13.3). Individual departments in an organization can easily purchase SaaS, bypassing the IT department. This can mean that the IT department does not know what applications are being used by the organization and cannot control proliferation and duplication. The IT department therefore needs to provide a list of approved prepaid services that can be made available across the organization (Petri, 2010).

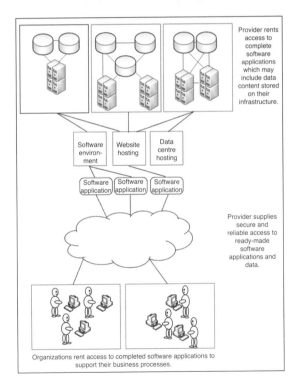

Figure 13.3 Software as a Service

Cloud computing has four deployment models:

○ **Private cloud** is an IT infrastructure dedicated for the use of one organization. A private cloud addresses concerns relating to, for example, data theft in the cloud, but the organization has to invest in the

maximum capacity that it may require. The potential to make savings by varying capacity is therefore lost.

○ **Community cloud** is an IT infrastructure that is shared by a number of organizations. Costs are shared by organizations in the community. Access to the cloud is limited while still providing the potential for cost savings to be made.

○ **Public cloud** provides resources that are available for anyone to use, adopting either a free-of-charge or pay-per-usage model.

○ **Hybrid cloud** integrates two or more clouds with different deployment models which remain separate but work together.

Quiz 13.1
Cloud Computing

Table 13.1 outlines some of the main benefits associated with cloud computing.

Table 13.1 Benefits of Cloud Computing

Cost Savings	Cloud computing enables IT resources to be shared, changing the costing model of computing from capital expenditure to operational expenditure. The total cost of IT ownership is reduced through reductions in direct in-house hardware, software, and licences, in addition to reducing costs associated with installation, maintenance, and support. The responsibility for maintenance is passed to the cloud provider (Cervone, 2010). This is particularly important due to the need to continually upgrade hardware and software (Sultan, 2011).
Increased Speed of Deployment	Development time is shorter due to the ease with which access can be gained to additional processing and storage capacity that is ready to use. In addition, SaaS means that an organization can adopt ready-to-use applications that are available in the cloud and being used by other organizations.
Greater Flexibility	The speed with which additional IT capacity can be attained offers greater flexibility to organizations, responding to peaks and troughs in demand.

Table 13.1 ▶ Continued

Ease of Access	Data and applications can be accessed anywhere via the Internet (Thomas, 2011).
Added Value	SaaS provides added value in the form of information content included with the software functionality. For example, some human resource departments are using LinkedIn or Plaxo applications to maintain details of their staff. This is because the self-maintained employee profiles in such applications are usually more up to date than the details held by internal organizational systems (Petri, 2010).

Table 13.2 outlines some of the risks associated with cloud computing.

Table 13.2 ▶ Risks of Cloud Computing

Privacy Issues	The terms and conditions offered by service providers need to be assessed to ensure that the privacy of data stored in the cloud is maintained.
Legal Issues	The organization needs to know in what country the data are held as local laws will apply.
Vendor Reliance	Some warn of the risk of being locked into proprietary systems of specific cloud-computing vendors (Sultan, 2011), however, the integration of PaaS prevents organizations being locked into one service provider (Petri, 2010).
Service Unavailability	Consideration needs to be given to what would happen if the cloud provider could no longer offer the required services. For IAAS, workload could be moved to a different vendor but for SAAS portability can be more difficult and organizations need to assess the degree of business continuity they need. For smaller organizations the availability of the Internet may be the greatest concern.
Data Loss or Theft	Cloud data centres are physically and procedurally more closed off than enterprise data centres. Some argue that vendors can provide better security and reliability than in-house staff (Sultan, 2011), however, organizations need to understand the encryption and backup measures being taken by the provider.

Source: Based on Petri (2010).

13.1.2 ▶ Transformation Dimensions of Cloud Computing

The adoption of cloud computing, particularly infrastructure as a service, changes the role of the IT function. It becomes more focused on forecasting the information-processing requirements of the organization and planning the demand for cloud services, as opposed to maintaining the in-house IT architecture. The processes undertaken in the IT department and the staff skills required in the department are changed.

Elsewhere in the organization staff benefit from the ability to access information and information systems via the Internet. New information systems can be deployed more quickly or purchased via software as a service. The revised costing model for IT provision changes the way IT is perceived in the organization. However, it is important that while embracing the utility service payment model for IT, the strategic role of IT in the organization does not become overshadowed. The potential impact of cloud computing on the organization is summarized in Table 13.3.

13.1.3 ▶ Role of Information Management in Cloud Computing

Cloud computing provides an IT infrastructure in which data can be stored and processed. It further increases the level of transparency between the organization's use of information and the technological platform that facilitates the management and processing of the underlying data resource. While relinquishing management of the IT infrastructure to a third party can be cost-effective, the organization still retains *responsibility* for the secure management of the information resource. Information management therefore needs to consider the impact of cloud computing on the information resource, including the:

○ Geographic location of the data and the location of the data that the provider replicates for backup purposes. Data centres are typically located where buildings, utilities, and labour are cheapest. The applications and data are subject to the laws and policies of the country where the data are physically stored. The legal implications of storing data in different countries must be considered.

○ Data replication strategies applied. Cloud providers automatically replicate data to reduce data loss and improve data availability. Replication strategies may affect the durability of the data (Abadi, 2009) and may lead to inconsistency and inaccuracy in the data stored.

○ Security controls that are implemented to protect the data from unauthorized access and disclosure. European data protection legislation stipulates that the responsibility for data lies with the organization

Table 13.3 ▶ Organizational Transformation Initiated by Cloud Computing

Formal Organization Architecture	Informal Organization Architecture	Impact on Organization Architecture
Technology	Socio-technical	Cloud computing changes the location of the IT architecture which facilitates the business applications and stores the organization's data.
Security	Trust	Ownership and responsibility for the maintenance of the technical infrastructure and IT services used by the organization is transferred to the cloud provider. However, legally the organization retains responsibility for the security of its data and the availability of its business operations. The transfer of data and its replication by the cloud provider introduces risks to the security of the data which need to be addressed. Security breaches will adversely affect the organization's position in its markets. Both staff in the organization and external parties (such as customers, suppliers, and partners) need to trust that the cloud provider is adequately securing the organization's data.
People	Skills	Renting access to IT hardware changes the skills required by the IT staff in the organization. Skill in maintaining hardware is replaced by a need for skill in predicting capacity requirements; skill in developing systems is replaced by skill in evaluating cloud services provision.
Strategy	Vision	Cloud computing changes the finance model for IT provision and changes how IT is perceived in the organization.
Processes	Practices	Although the processes performed by the IT function change, the main impact on other business processes is the ability to conduct the processes via the Internet. This enables unrestricted mobility in accessing the organization's information and information systems.
Systems	Human Activity Systems	Software as a service provides a range of information systems that are available in the cloud for the organization to use.
Culture	Values	Cloud computing changes the role of IT in an organization, which is reflected in a cultural change in relation to the organization's use of IT services. It offers new ways of working for the organization but the opportunities need to be evaluated in relation to the organization's core values.

to ensure that the cloud service provider is adequately securing the data. Key questions to consider include: Who has access to the data? How is the physical facility secured? How often are routine checks and security audits conducted?

○ Deduplication techniques applied by the cloud provider. Deduplication techniques are used by cloud providers to ensure that only one copy of redundant data are stored (Harnik *et al.*, 2010). This reduces the cost of storing multiple copies of the same data and reduces the processing required to ensure that all copies of the data are updated. Although there are security risks associated with deduplication techniques, cloud providers can use strategies such as encryption, limiting data uploads, and uploading all files before applying deduplication techniques to reduce the risks (Harnik *et al.*, 2010).

○ Stability and reliability of the services provided to ensure that the accuracy and integrity of data can be maintained. A service level agreement is needed which outlines the acceptable levels of performance and availability of the services rented. This will affect the access and availability of information systems in the organization.

○ Standards used by the provider which may affect the ability of the organization to transfer data to another cloud provider.

○ Ability to integrate information from both cloud- and non-cloud-based applications in the organization.

○ Ease with which changes to the data structures can be implemented.

○ Ability of the cloud services to meet the data quality standards demanded to meet the information requirements of the organization.

○ Contingency plans that have been put in place to ensure business continuity and access to accurate data.

13.2 ▶ Mobile Computing

Mobile computing provides both remote and mobile access to information and information systems:

○ Remote access refers to the ability to access, store, and change information that is stored at another location using information systems that are also stored at another location (as opposed to being stored on the mobile device).

○ Mobile access refers to the ability to continue to access and use information systems while moving, removing the need to remain stationary.

As information and information systems no longer need to be stored on a mobile computing device, the device used to provide access to information can be smaller and lighter. This has led to developments of smart mobile telephones, netbooks, tablet computers, and internet tablets. Improvements in the quality of smartphone displays and touch-screen interfaces have also contributed to the increased use of mobile telephones (White, 2010), establishing them as prominent information communication tools.

DEFINITION: Mobile computing is the ability to access and process information, that may be stored at another location, while at a different location or in transit.

Mobile computing can increase the distance between the data and the user of the data, enabling information processing to be undertaken remotely. It can also be used to enable data to be captured locally, closer to the source.

13.2.1 ▶ Applications of Mobile Computing

Mobile computing enables an organization's staff, their customers (and their potential customers), and business partners to access the organization's information systems wherever there is an appropriate Internet connection. This facilitates the remote collection of data, location-based information services, m-commerce and mobile working.

Remote Data Capture

Direct data capture enables data to be collected by a device and transferred to a central database to enable wider access to the data stored (Welker, 2007). Capturing data at the original source improves data accuracy, reducing the potential for transcription errors or facts to be forgotten. It also enables data to be captured quickly, supporting the timely provision of information. For example, Match Lighting issued delivery drivers with devices to electronically capture the signature of the individual taking receipt of a delivery. The data provides timely information to support the tracking of deliveries. Ashar et al. (2010) suggest that electronic data capture is more structured than paper-based systems as it is structured for automated upload to databases to support analysis, enabling data to be combined from different sources. However, this requires data integration, software

compatibility issues, and technical differences relating to the devices used to be addressed (Welker, 2007).

Location-based Services

Mobile computing provides the opportunity to offer information that is directly relevant to the current location of an individual. This requires an awareness of the current location, the information available in that area, and the information that may be of value to the individual in that location at the specific time. There are two approaches to determining the location of a device: a geometric model uses global-positioning system (GPS) coordinates, and symbolic modelling uses real-world entities such as streets and buildings (Lee et al., 2002). When the location has been established, Lee et al. (2002) suggest that there are three types of queries that can be made:

○ Simple queries, such as find the nearest hotel.

○ Spatially bound queries, such as find all the hotels in a 10-mile radius.

○ Nonspatially bound queries, such as find hotels with rooms under £10.

Information delivery can follow a push or pull model; information can be pushed to the device based on the device's location or the information system could wait for the person using the device to request information. In addition to assessing the potential information needs of the individual, consideration also needs to be given to the specific device that is being used to access the information. This includes the limitations of screen size, data transmission volumes, and the data formats supported by mobile devices. Location-dependent information services provide a number of challenges to information delivery, such as restricted bandwidth, risk of network disconnection, and the mobility of the device (Lee et al., 2002).

M-Commerce

M-commerce refers to electronic transactions associated with e-business conducted using mobile computing devices. Shankar et al. (2010) suggest that m-commerce facilitates a paradigm shift in commerce in that it allows the seller to enter the consumer's environment using the mobile device, rather than waiting for the consumer to enter the seller's environment. The success of m-commerce therefore requires organizations to have a good understanding of customer segmentation to enable content to be personalized (Martin et al., 2012). Personalization is a prerequisite of mobile customer relationship management (MCRM) due to the personal nature of the receiving mobile device, requiring individuals to be identified and their needs and preferences understood (Sinisalo et al., 2007). MCRM needs to be considered from two aspects: how mobile technology can be used to improve relationships with customers and capture information about the relationship, and how the ability of staff to access CRM information remotely can improve decision-making.

Mobile Working

Staff in organizations need to be able to work on the move, which requires the ability to access enterprise applications remotely (Ranjan & Bhatnagar, 2009). However, staff do not need to access the whole intranet, just sections of it, when travelling (White, 2010). Key information that may need to be accessed using mobile devices therefore needs to be identified.

The ability to conduct work remotely, away from the normal working environment, removes the geographical boundaries between work life and home life and poses new challenges within the context of maintaining a healthy work–life balance (Cox, 2009). Institutionalization of anytime, anywhere availability is exasperated as mobile telephone numbers tend to be more widely distributed to colleagues who would not have access to home telephone numbers (Prasopoulou *et al.*, 2006). The growing acceptability of this work–family interference establishes new organizational norms and raises social issues (Cox, 2009).

Context-sensitive computing technology incorporates features that can be used to moderate the anytime, anywhere availability. For example, a mobile phone can be set not to ring if the electronic schedule indicates that a person is in a meeting (Colbert & Livingstone, 2006) or has finished work for the day. Mobile technologies empower individuals with greater freedom to choose when, where and how to balance the demands of their work and home lives but although employees *can* work at home, they should not be *expected* to do so (Cox, 2009). Organizations need to determine how to deal with

the convergence of work life and home life facilitated by technology (Townsend & Batchelor, 2005).

13.2.2 ▶ Transformation Dimensions of Mobile Computing

Mobile devices pose particular challenges in information presentation, version control, and security. Mobile computing requires the context in which the information is presented to be considered from two perspectives. First, the information requirements of the recipient need to be identified, including their location, task objectives, and preferences. Second, at the technical level, the requirements and limitations of the specific device used to access the information have to be established. Limitations of mobile devices include a small display, lack of pointing device, low text input rate, low bandwidth, limited colour, and lack of support for data formats (Vigo *et al.*, 2009). The delivery of the information needs to be tailored to meet the specific requirements of the accessing device. For example, the presentation of an intranet page must be adapted to enable it to be displayed on the smaller screen of a mobile phone.

While technical controls can be implemented to maintain the security of data, the portability of IT devices means that authorized users provide the greatest risk to data security. Risks include the loss or theft of the mobile device and lack of care taken when using the device. Conducting private conversations and transactions in public places has the potential for confidential information to be overheard, for data entered to be observed by a third party and for the data to be intercepted on unsecured networks. The potential impact of mobile computing on the organization is summarized in Table 13.4.

Table 13.4 ▶ Organizational Transformation Initiated by Mobile Computing

Formal Organization Architecture	Informal Organization Architecture	Impact on Organization Architecture
Technology	Socio-technical	Mobile computing demands remote access and delivery of information. The IT architecture needs to incorporate mobile technology and address the technical challenges such as data compatibility, data volumes, and transmission capabilities. Mobile devices offer the potential for empowering individuals through wider access to information via personal computing devices, changing the use of the technology, and introducing additional challenges such as interface design and accessibility.
Security	Trust	Mobile computing introduces risks to the security of information, both from technical and human perspectives. As the means of accessing data are increased, there is an associated increased risk of unauthorized access to the data. Enabling data to be accessed in unregulated environments requires organizations to trust that staff will not unwittingly disclose information through, for example, being overheard, or leaving devices unattended.

Table 13.4 Continued

Formal Organization Architecture	Informal Organization Architecture	Impact on Organization Architecture
People	Skills	Training may be required about how to use mobile devices and access information. Training will relate to the security and safe use of the device.
Strategy	Vision	A range of opportunities are offered by mobile computing in relation to how data are captured, information accessed, the conduct of business processes, and the way the organization interacts with customers, suppliers, and partners. These opportunities need to be assessed to inform the organization's strategy and vision.
Processes	Practices	The ability to capture data and access information remotely changes the way business processes can be conducted. Business processes are changed to accommodate and act upon the data captured. Business practices are changed to make use of the mobile computing devices.
Systems	Human Activity Systems	Information systems may need to be changed to address the information accessibility issues of mobile devices and to enable the data captured remotely to be validated, stored, and used. The use of mobile devices facilitates new ways of working through which informal practices will be revised and evolve.
Culture	Values	Increasing the mobility of information changes how information is used and perceived in the organization and impacts upon the culture of the organization. Widening access to information facilitates, for example, home working. This may challenge the organizational culture from one of being expected to be in the office between specified hours to one of more flexible working. However, cultural change can have a negative effect on individuals in terms of work–life balance.

13.2.3 Role of Information Management in Mobile Computing

Mobile devices extend the ability to capture, access, and modify the information resource. While this provides opportunities for capturing data at source and widens the availability of information, it introduces further challenges in information management, including:

○ Security of information. This includes both the technical controls implemented to protect data access and the wider security policies relating to the use of mobile computing.

○ Privacy of information. For example, Match Lighting asks their customers a range of security questions to confirm the authenticity of the customer before discussing their accounts. If the customer's responses are overheard, the security of their account becomes threatened.

○ Accessibility of information. There is a need to balance the ease with which information can be accessed by authorized personnel against the need to prevent unauthorized access.

○ Ease of use of information. As IT becomes smaller and lighter, this introduces challenges for data input and data output. The suitability of keyboards, touch screens, and voice commands for accurately entering

data have to be considered. The screen size (and processing capacity) limits the volume and format of information that can be effectively displayed to the recipient.

○ Validity and verification of information captured remotely. While mobile devices offer the ability to capture data remotely, the remote environment and the technical design of the device can impede data entry. For example, the environment may be noisy, dirty, crowded, with a range of media and people competing for attention. In such circumstances accurate data entry can be difficult, therefore controls are needed to check that the information entered is valid (appropriate or reasonable values) and verified (accurately entered).

○ Volume and demand of information. Chapter 7 referred to the problem of information overload. Mobile devices increase information's demand for attention and policies are needed to limit the impact of this on staff and their work–life balance.

13.3 Pervasive Technology

The term *pervasive technology*, also referred to as 'ubiquitous technology', reflects the ability to embed IT in electronic equipment. The Internet of Things refers to the vision of allocating an Internet Protocol (IP) address to things, connecting them to the Internet in order to send and receive data.

DEFINITION: An **Internet Protocol (IP)** address is a numerical identifier assigned to a device on a computer network. It enables the device to be recognized for sending and receiving data on the network.

Sensors can be embedded in equipment to capture data and transmit data via the Internet, to provide information on the status of the equipment. This enables the development of smart devices that can adapt and respond to data. Pervasive technology provides a means of extending the capability of electrical equipment by enabling data about the status of the equipment to be reported via Internet technologies. Examples include a production line malfunction, the energy usage recorded on a utility meter, and a vending machine that needs replenishing. These examples of smart devices offer opportunities for organizations to reduce costs and increase process efficiency.

13.3.1 ▶ Applications of Pervasive Technology

Pervasive technology increases the range of devices that can be used to capture data and respond to changes identified in the data. The challenge of pervasive technology is how to integrate the high volume of data that can be captured from multiple devices and process the data to provide meaningful information that can be acted upon.

Smart Home

Pervasive technology is being used in the home to support home security, home automation, energy conservation, and assisted living. These applications require data from a variety of devices such as cameras, motion sensors, temperature sensors, and pressure sensors to be captured and managed. A generic framework is needed to integrate data from these different devices which use different hardware standards (While *et al.*, 2008). The data then need to be analysed to identify activities taking place in the environment in order to prompt an appropriate response to the data received (Chen & Nugent, 2009).

Smart City

The term *smart city* has a range of definitions in different fields. Giffinger *et al.* (2007) identify six characteristics of a smart city which reflect this diversity: smart living (quality of life), smart environment (natural resources), smart mobility (transport and IT), smart governance (participation), smart people (social and human capital), and smart economy (competitiveness). The role of IT is generally considered in terms of the availability of a computer network infrastructure to support business-led

development in the city. It refers to the opportunities to use technology to transform aspects of the city life and the way technology can become embedded (Hollands, 2008). Examples of smart city initiatives include smart energy metering and intelligent traffic management systems.

Intelligent Buildings

An intelligent building adapts to the needs of occupants to create and maintain a suitable safe and conducive environment in which the activities of the organization can take place. It assists an organization in managing its resources efficiently and effectively (Clements-Croome, 1997). Building controls are based on two dimensions: manual or automatic operation; reactive or anticipatory response (Clements-Croome, 1997). Figure 13.4 shows how these controls can be used to control lighting in an organization. Automatic

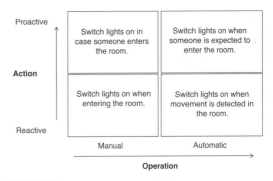

Figure 13.4 ▶ Intelligent Control of Lighting

control of lighting can reduce energy consumption by ensuring that lights are switched off when not needed.

Sensors can track movement in corridors to anticipate when and where lights need to be switched on. In Figure 13.5, when the motion sensor at point A is triggered, the building system automatically switches the light on in area 1. When the motion sensor at point B is triggered, the building system anticipates that a person will enter area 2 and the system proactively switches on the light in area 2. Patterns need to be identified in the sensor data collected to determine the rules used by the building control system to establish the appropriate response to the real-time data received from sensors in the building.

Intelligent Systems

All open systems (systems that take input from their environment) have the potential to adapt their behaviour in response to the data received. In Figure 13.5, when the building management system receives input data from a

Key: 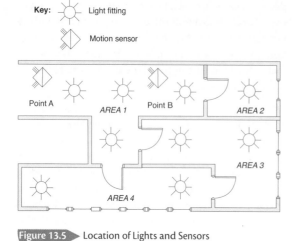 Light fitting

Motion sensor

Point A

AREA 1   Point B

AREA 2

AREA 3

AREA 4

Figure 13.5 Location of Lights and Sensors

motion sensor indicating that movement is detected, it responds by switching lights on in a specific area. In such systems the rules are written into the software of the system. An intelligent system is one that learns how to adapt its behaviour over time in response to changing situations.

13.3.2 Transformation Dimensions of Pervasive Technology

Pervasive technology provides the means to capture data about the status of equipment, processes, and locations.

This requires the development of additional systems to manage the data collected. The potential impact of pervasive technology on the organization is summarized in Table 13.5.

13.3.3 Role of Information Management in Pervasive Technology

Pervasive technology increases the opportunities for collecting data. Although technical skills are required to connect the equipment to computer networks to capture data, staff in the organization need to be able to interpret the data and act appropriately on the information derived. The context within which the data are collected needs to be understood in order to derive meaningful information from the data. In addition, business processes need to be implemented to enable the information to be acted upon.

Link 13.1
Example Analysis of Pervasive Context

Using the data captured by pervasive technology provides opportunities for the organization to reduce its costs and improve performance, but introduces further challenges in information management, including:

Table 13.5 Organizational Transformation Initiated by Pervasive Technology

Formal Organization Architecture	Informal Organization Architecture	Impact on Organization Architecture
Technology	Socio-technical	Pervasive technology increases the means for data capture in the organization. This increases the requirements for staff to engage with technology.
Security	Trust	Technology provides a means to improve security of people, data, buildings, and tangible assets, however, each device connected to the Internet also has the potential for its data to be accessed via unauthorized means. The deployment of devices to capture data which monitor the movement and actions of staff in the organization requires staff to trust that they are fully aware of the data collected and that the data are only used for legitimate purposes.
People	Skills	As more equipment uses pervasive technology, more people in the organization need to develop the skills required to interact with the technology.
Strategy	Vision	Pervasive technology increases the organization's ability to collect data. If appropriate processes are developed to use the data effectively, it provides opportunities for the organization to improve its efficiency and effectiveness. The areas in which these improvements can be achieved need to be aligned with the organization's strategy and used to inform the direction of the strategy.
Processes	Practices	New processes are needed to capture, manage, and act upon the data collected from the pervasive technology. Current working practices need to be adapted to respond to the data captured.

Table 13.5 Continued		
Formal Organization Architecture	**Informal Organization Architecture**	**Impact on Organization Architecture**
Systems	Human Activity Systems	New information systems are needed to capture and process the data collected from the pervasive technology devices. Staff have to adapt to new ways of working to respond to the data captured.
Culture	Values	Technology, such as cameras and door-access cards are used to deter and record unauthorized activity. However, the data captured can be used to monitor individual behaviour and this raises ethical issues. The use of technology can therefore challenge the cultural values in an organization relating to trust and responsibility.

○ Data volume: The amount of data that can be captured from devices can quickly escalate. For example, domestic energy monitors can capture and transmit energy usage data every six seconds. Each transmission will include details of the date and time of the reading, the monitor identifier, and the energy used. As more pervasive devices are added to collect data, the volume of data raises issues of storage and accessibility. Procedures therefore need to be devised to aggregate data into meaningful groupings to inform decisions.

○ Sense-making: Data from one device has limited information potential. For example, if a temperature sensor collects data every two seconds about the temperature in a room, over time it will be possible to identify any fluctuations in the temperature recorded. However, further data will be needed from other sources to assist in determining the potential causes of the fluctuations. Contextual frameworks are therefore needed to assist in making sense of the data collected.

○ Data integration: Wide-scale data collection from a range of devices raises issues relating to the ability to compare and integrate the data collected. For example, energy usage can be recorded in a range of measures such as units, kilowatts per hour, cubic meters, and cubic feet. Data cleaning, conversion, and integration therefore need to be undertaken before the data can be used.

13.4 Enterprise Resource Planning

Enterprise resource planning (ERP) provides an interoperable set of application modules, providing functionality and software to support specific aspects of the organization. Each module is an application package with business functionality and business rules embedded into the design of the software. A module is therefore unlikely to exactly meet the requirements of a specific organization and may need to be:

○ Configured to reflect the specific business rules in the organization. This may involve deactivating some rules or functions in the package and incorporating the organization's financial and control structures into the package.

○ Customized by making changes to the ERP system such as adding or changing program code to change the way the system operates to meet the requirements of the organization. This provides the opportunity for organizations to differentiate their processes from others using the same ERP system, however, it further increases the complexity of the system.

○ Extended by purchasing further application packages, often from a different vendor to the ERP system, which are compatible with the ERP system and provide additional functionality. Extensions can provide access and reporting tools to provide the organization with greater ability to access and analyse the data stored in the ERP system.

DEFINITION: An **Enterprise Resource Planning System (ERP)** is a set of software application modules in which business functionality is embedded, that work together to coordinate business activities across the organization (and between supply chain partners) through the integration of data.

ERP systems are large-scale IT systems integrating value-chain activities in the organization, and linking the activities with the value chains of external partners in the supply chain. Examples of ERP modules are listed in Table 13.6. They focus on the flow of resources through the supply chain with the overall aim to improve the integration of information throughout the organization and between parties in the supply chain.

Table 13.6	Example Modules in an ERP System	
Primary Activities	**Support Activities**
Production planning.	Financial accounting.
Material management.	Human resource management.
Manufacturing management.	Quality management.
Sales.	Supply chain management.
Distribution.	Customer relationship management.
Logistics.	
Customer service.	

13.4.1 Complexity of Enterprise Resource Planning

By coordinating business processes, ERP offers the potential to support the integration of information across the organization. Benefits of this integration include both tangible benefits such as reduced inventory levels and intangible benefits arising from the ability to share information, such as improvements in customer service (Dezdar & Ainin, 2011). However, many organizations have found that the implementation of ERP systems is challenging due to the scale of the work involved. Issues include:

○ Interoperability: Although the modules are interoperable, when an organization implements one module it needs to integrate the module with its existing information systems, which can be difficult.

○ Integration testing: Testing of individual modules prior to implementation is usually focused on testing the technical module system. Additional testing is needed of business processes that capture the information to be used in the module and use the information generated by the module.

○ Data quality: Data are the means by which the modules of the ERP system are integrated. The purchase of an ERP system is often regarded as a solution to data management problems in the organization, particularly in relation to the quality of the data.

One of the factors affecting data quality is that the same data are often stored and maintained in different systems (Haug *et al.*, 2009) resulting in inconsistent data. ERP systems aim to address this problem by helping organizations to standardize data formats and integrate processes across functional boundaries (Dezdar & Ainin, 2011), providing one source of data for all the ERP modules to use. The implementation of the ERP system highlights problems with the quality of data in an organization, particularly in relation to inconsistent and incomplete data values. The implementation therefore forces organizations

to undertake data cleaning and data definition activities to ensure that only accurate, clean data are migrated into the system. This takes time and the scale of the task can be underestimated. The scale and complexity of ERP systems challenge every aspect of the organizational architecture.

13.4.2 Transformation Dimensions of Enterprise Resource Planning

The purchase of an ERP system results in the purchase of business processes embedded in the system. The implementation of the system therefore includes the implementation of new processes and different ways of working. It requires a programme of organizational change to be undertaken to facilitate the transition and to understand the practical implications of the degree of transformation required. The potential impact of an ERP system on the organization is summarized in Table 13.7.

13.4.3 Role of Information Management in Enterprise Resource Planning

In ERP systems, modules are integrated by the flow of data between the modules. It is therefore essential that the data are clean and accurate as the effects of any problems with the data quality will not be limited to one area of the organization. Information management is core to the successful implementation of ERP systems and is needed to:

○ Define the data and business rules to assist in the selection of the ERP system and to identify the configuration required to ensure that the system meets the information needs of the organization.

○ Clean the data before data are migrated into the ERP system. The effectiveness of the ERP system is dependent upon the quality of the data that it uses.

○ Migrate the data from existing systems to the ERP system. This involves developing a migration plan and testing to ensure that all the data has been accurately migrated.

○ Ensure the data are defined and business rules understood by staff entering data into the system in order to keep the data clean. This will involve working

Table 13.7 Organizational Transformation Initiated by Enterprise Resource Planning

Formal Organization Architecture	Informal Organization Architecture	Impact on Organization Architecture
Technology	Socio-technical	An ERP system requires existing IT systems to be replaced with ERP compatible modules. The replacement will require data to be cleaned and migrated to the new system. The new system will need to be configured, and possibly customized and extended, to meet the specific requirements of the organization. The implementation and maintenance of any packaged application is challenging as there is limited information available about how the system works.
Security	Trust	The ERP system facilitates the sharing of data throughout the organization. Controls therefore need to be implemented to ensure that only authorized personnel can access, modify, and delete data, as determined by the data security classifications.
People	Skills	Staff across the organization will be affected by the implementation of the ERP system as each module replaces existing systems. Business staff will need training in how to use the system and IT staff will need training in how to maintain the system. This may require additional skills to be developed.
Strategy	Vision	The integration of information and business processes across the organization provides the opportunity to improve the efficiency and effectiveness of its operations and its communications with partners in the supply chain. However, the organization needs to consider how this specifically relates to its strategy and how it can differentiate itself from other organizations that use the same ERP system.
Processes	Practices	The ERP system is developed by the vendor to include business processes. These are unlikely to exactly match the requirements of the organization, therefore either the software or the processes in the organization have to change. Although a degree of customization is possible, it is likely that business processes will need to change to fit the requirements of the software. This requires staff to make changes to how work is performed in the organization.
Systems	Human Activity Systems	The ERP system may be implemented in separate modules so the replacement of existing systems will take place over a period of time. The introduction of the new system requires staff to adopt news ways of working.
Culture	Values	A standard interface reflects the standardization of business processes enforced within the ERP system. This can challenge the cultural values of different areas of the organization. A programme of change management is needed to facilitate the successful implementation, acceptance of the system, and the new ways of working it requires. The organizational values need to be incorporated into the configuration and customization of the system in order to increase its acceptability and maintain the values which underpin the organization's strategy and vision.

with IT staff to develop system controls to reduce the ability to enter inaccurate data.

O Develop information management policies to ensure that the quality of the data is maintained. This will include defining how free-text fields should be used (if they cannot be avoided) to ensure data consistency. It will also include policies to limit the ability to store copies of data locally or on portable storage devices. Reducing the potential for multiple copies of the data to be held increases the security of data and reduces the potential for inconsistent data to be used by different areas of the organization.

O Promote a culture of individual responsibility for data quality. In addition to training new staff in the rules to

be followed when entering data, continuous training is needed to maintain staff awareness of the implications of entering incorrect data.

O Continually take action to clean data; cleaning data is not a one-off activity. A programme of continual improvement is needed to develop business rules and formatting standards, implemented through IT controls, to reduce the potential for inaccurate data to be entered and to correct inaccuracies when they arise.

O Establish the data archiving policies to be implemented in the ERP system. Selecting data for archiving in ERP systems is challenging due to the extensive integration of the data throughout the system (Mensching & Corbitt, 2004). Particular attention should be given to the historic data that may be required to generate reports by the system.

13.5 ▶ Enterprise Content Management

Enterprise content management (ECM) refers to the capture, storage, coordination, and control of structured and unstructured information represented on paper documents and digital media in the organization. Documents are social artefacts that provide a wrapping for the content of communication; the wrapping is embedded with the rules governing interaction with the document, such as not opening a letter addressed to someone else (Forbes-Pitt, 2006). Information is derived from content from external parties (such as supplier policies and customer letters), content provided by the organization for external parties (such as product catalogue and installation instructions), and content provided by the organization for internal use (such as the information management strategy). Electronic communication enables the content of documents to be extracted from their wrapping and repackaged to meet the requirements of a different media.

The term *enterprise CMS* reflects the implementation of a system that is used by the whole organization.

DEFINITION: An **Enterprise Content Management System (ECMS)** is a software package that provides tools and workflow processes to manage the creation, use, storage, and archiving of information content in an electronic repository across the organization.

A key challenge with the vast volumes of content in an organization is how to ensure consistency of information content across different communication channels and media. For example, Match Lighting needs to ensure that the information about its light fittings provided in its online catalogue is consistent with the information stated in the newsletter emailed to its retailers and with the paper instruction sheet provided with each light fitting. Problems can arise as the authors of these different forms of communication may not work together, may use different information from which to create their content, and may be required to produce similar content (such as a product description) for different purposes (such as press release, catalogue entry, packaging description). This can lead to inaccurate and inconsistent information being communicated, as well as inefficiency as time is spent writing the same information.

13.5.1 ▶ Features of Enterprise Content Management Systems

Enterprise content management systems (ECMS) aim to improve the consistency and quality of information content in the organization and have the following general features:

○ Single source. The ECMS provides a centralized repository for the storage and retrieval of content in the organization. The development of a single source of content enables staff to access, for example, the latest policy documents in an organization preventing out-of-date policies being used.

○ Audit. The implementation of an ECMS requires a content audit to be undertaken. A content audit identifies the content used in the organization and explores opportunities for reusing content created in one in area of the organization in other areas.

○ Reuse. Documents can be deconstructed into their individual elements, which are stored in the ECMS and then reused to construct a range of different documents. The elements can comprise text, images (such as a brand logo), sound recordings, videos, and other media elements.

○ Templates. The structural elements of information products, such as newsletters and instruction sheets, are defined to create templates into which the reusable content can be automatically inserted. The templates are referred to as document type definitions in XML (discussed in Chapter 3).

○ Systematic reuse. Systematic reuse enables content to be automatically inserted into new content and information products being created. The reusable content may be locked, where the content must be reused as it is without any changes, or the content may be derivative, enabling minor changes to be made to the reusable content (such as tenses and spelling) to meet the needs of the target audience (Rockley *et al.*, 2003).

○ Security. Although the ECMS is used by the entire organization, privilege controls are set to restrict different levels of access to specific content. For example, all staff in Match Lighting can read the IT strategy document in the ECMS but only Mr Cook has authorization to publish a new version of the strategy. Security controls also include digital rights management. These are technical controls, such as encryption, digital signatures, and watermarks used to verify authenticity and prevent unauthorized use of intellectual property.

○ Version control. Version-control mechanisms are procedures to check-out documents from the ECMS before they are changed and then to check-in the modified document. This provides an audit of the changes made to a document and ensures that the latest version of a document is accessed.

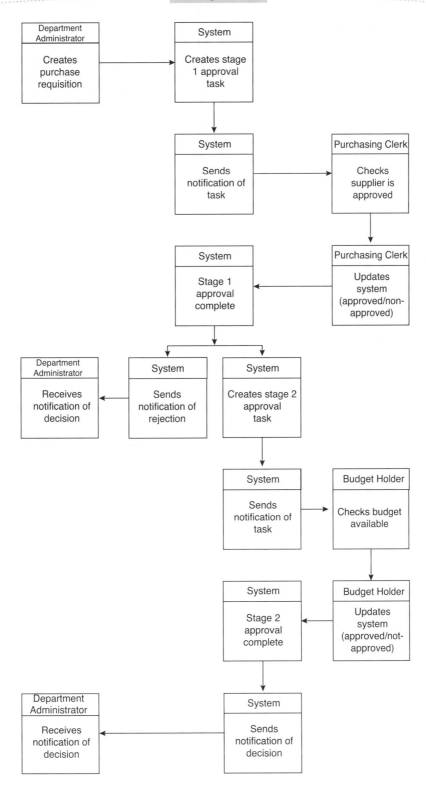

Figure 13.6 Example of Workflow in an Enterprise Content Management System

○ Workflow. Process-routing procedures are the organizational procedures to, for example, approve the purchase of some equipment or create a press release. A workflow comprises the tasks in the procedure and the staff role completing each task (Rockley *et al.*, 2003). The system automatically assigns tasks to designated individuals to inform them that the previous task has been completed and that their action (such as approval) is now sought. An example of a workflow is shown in Figure 13.6. Workflows are also used in content creation to ensure that appropriate approvals have been acquired before materials are published.

Link 13.2
Description of Workflow
Requisition Process

Table 13.8 outlines content created about a product and Table 13.9 shows how different parts of the single source of content are reconfigured to meet the needs of different audiences. The structural templates for each of the communications shown in Table 13.9 contain links to the product elements in Table 13.8. This means that when product element content is modified, the changes to the content are automatically reflected in the documents which use the content. For example, if the size of the

product changes, the new size is automatically included in Match Lighting's packaging and brochure. Structured writing is needed to facilitate content reuse. Structured writing involves creating individual units of information (chunks) which can be combined, clearly labelling information content and focusing on relevance and consistency of information (Rockley *et al.*, 2003).

13.5.2 ▸ Transformation Dimensions of Enterprise Content Management Systems

An ECMS is a software application package which assists organizations to manage the information content that is incorporated in paper-based and electronic documents and media. As an application package, the software is based on generalized business rules and procedures which may not reflect the working practices in Match Lighting. The implementation of an ECMS provides the opportunity to improve the way content is created and used in an organization and therefore has the potential to impact on a number of areas of the organization shown in Table 13.10.

13.5.3 ▸ Role of Information Management in Enterprise Content Management

Inaccurate and inconsistent content can have significant implications for an organization, such as dissatisfied customers and legal issues. Information management is therefore needed to contribute to:

Table 13.8 ▸ Single Source of Content for Product

Product Element	Product Element Content
Overview	A glass bell pendant.
Aesthetic Description	The bell pendant provides a touch of elegance to a room with its clear-cut lines and timeless style. It is etched with a stunning floral motif to complement the décor of any home.
Material	Made from handblown glass in a traditional red house cone.
Size	The bell measures 25cm in height with a diameter of 45cm.
Fitting	It can be used with a ceiling rose with up to a 15cm pendant lamp holder.

Table 13.9 ▸ Reconfigured Content for Product

Packaging	Brochure	Newsletter	Instruction
A glass bell pendant. The bell measures 25cm in height with a diameter of 45cm.	A glass bell pendant. The bell pendant provides a touch of elegance to a room with its clear-cut lines and timeless style. It is etched with a stunning floral motif to complement the decor of any home. Made from handblown glass in a traditional red house cone. The bell measures 25cm in height with a diameter of 45cm. It can be used with a ceiling rose with up to a 15cm pendant lamp holder.	A glass bell pendant. Made from handblown glass in a traditional red house cone. It is etched with a stunning floral motif to complement the decor of any home.	A glass bell pendant. The bell measures 25cm in height with a diameter of 45cm. It can be used with a ceiling rose with up to a 15cm pendant lamp holder.

Table 13.10 ► Organizational Transformation Initiated by Enterprise Content Management

Formal Organization Architecture	Informal Organization Architecture	Impact on Organization Architecture
Technology	Socio-technical	The implementation of an ECMS introduces a new software application into the organization, which provides a single repository for content. All staff in the organization will be expected to use the repository to locate information they need. Some staff will also be required to use the system to locate content to reuse in their work, and the workflow of some activities will be tracked by the system. The impact of the system is therefore widespread, changing the way content is created, accessed, and used in the organization with technology.
Security	Trust	A single source for content requires changes to be made to security controls. As the ECMS will be accessed by all staff in the organization, security controls will need to be implemented at the level of individual content. The system will only be effective if staff trust the quality of the content in it. The workflow controls are intended to improve the quality of content, directing activity and providing an audit of the events during the life cycle of content. However, the workflow may be regarded as a way of monitoring staff actions and trust must be promoted that the information provided by the audit will be used appropriately.
People	Skills	The introduction of an ECMS requires additional roles in the organization to oversee the content strategy and define content structures. The use of an ECMS requires new skills to be developed to define structures of documents, identify content elements that can be reused, and writing in a structured manner to facilitate reuse of material.
Strategy	Vision	A single source of content in an ECMS enables an organization to address the accuracy and consistency of both the content and presentation of information in its internal and external communications. This can contribute to improving the quality of external relationships in the supply chain, and improve efficiency and effectiveness of business processes.
Processes	Practices	An ECMS may include workflow patterns to direct activities such as content creation through the organization creating and confirming completion of tasks required in the activity. The implementation of the workflows may require changes to be made to existing business processes or may change how staff are notified about the start and end of a required activity. The ECMS provides an audit trail of tasks and changes the way tasks are monitored. The implementation of templates, style sheets, and content reuse changes how content is created, reducing redundant content creation. It also provides a single source of content, changing the way staff in the organization search for information.
Systems	Human Activity Systems	ECMS is a new system in the organization and needs to be integrated with existing technical systems such as authoring tools, publishing tools, and e-business systems. It changes the way content is created and used in the organization, requiring changes to be made to how staff engage with content.
Culture	Values	The standardization of content is sometimes criticized as reducing the creativity in content creation to content configuration. The reuse of content requires a change in the way content is perceived within the organizational culture. It may challenge existing views of authorship and ownership of content. It is therefore important that the organizational values such as quality, integrity, and branding are embedded in the templates and workflows of the ECMS.

○ Formulating a content strategy to improve the quality and accessibility of information in the organization. Policies governing the use of content need to be sufficiently broad to incorporate content developed in social media technologies and future technological developments.

○ Content requirements analysis and content audits determine what content is needed and to what extent content can be shared.

○ Identifying the source of data which will be included in the content.

○ Developing templates to ensure content elements are captured in a consistent manner to provide a single source of content materials. The formation of document structures enables common elements to be inserted into different forms of communication, ensuring consistency.

○ Specification of workflow patterns to improve the quality of content through appropriate review and approval controls.

○ Defining metadata to improve the ability to locate content when needed.

○ Establishing a content repository provides a single source for content in the organization. It includes elements that can be reused in the development of communication materials and the definitive source of information in the organization about, for example, policies and procedures.

○ Developing version controls to improve the security and robustness of the content. This also includes the development of legal and technical controls required for digital rights management.

○ Establishing archiving procedures to ensure that previously used content is available in the event of query at a later time.

○ Implementing the content retention policies required by the organization.

13.6 ▶ Assessing Impact of Changing Technology on Information Management

Advances in IT continue to change how information is captured, managed, and used in the organization. Due to the complexity and obscurity of terms such as cloud computing there is a tendency to delegate responsibility for assessing the value and impact of technological developments to the IT department. However, any changes to the way in which information is managed needs to be assessed in terms of its potential impact on the organization and the information management strategy. The

implementation of, for example, an enterprise content management system, will change how content is used and reused in the organization, impacting processes, practices, skills, people, and the organization's information management strategy.

Table 13.11 presents a framework to assist organizations in assessing the impact of IT on the information management strategy. The middle area of the table focuses on the specific activities that take place in the data life cycle. The first column identifies the different elements which form the context in which the life cycle activities are conducted. Questions are suggested to determine which areas of the life cycle may be affected by IT. The last column identifies areas in information management that may need to be changed to accommodate the changes identified to the life cycle.

Link 13.3
Application of Table 13.11 to Assess Impact of Cloud Computing on Information Management

Summary

IT provides the means to implement processes to support each stage of the information life cycle. Changes in technology offer innovative ways to access data and interact with information. Cloud computing changes where data are stored. Mobile technology changes where data are captured and used. Pervasive technology changes where data are captured and can respond to the data to facilitate intelligent systems. Enterprise resource planning integrates data through integrated application modules in the organization. Enterprise content management systems standardize data to improve consistency of information. Although each of these technologies offers advantages to organizations, they can also pose threats to data integrity and security. Advances in technology will continue to offer new ways of acquiring, accessing, and using information; however, it is necessary to explore the impact of each new technology on the fundamental processes of information management.

Reviewing Scenario 13.1

Enterprise resource planning and enterprise content management are both types of software application packages. This may lead to the misconception that the responsibility for implementing these systems lies with the IT department. The systems are complex and the technical

Table 13.11 Guidelines to Assess the Impact of Changing IT on Information Management Policies

Contextual Elements	Activities in the Life Cycle				Area of Impact
	Capture	Store and Retrieve	Use, Share, and Maintain	Archive and Destroy	
Actors: Roles and individuals involved in each stage of the life cycle.	Who is the source of the data? Who captures the data?	Who stores the data? Who can retrieve the data?	Who can use the data? Who can share the data? Who can maintain the data?	Who can archive the data? Who can delete the data?	Changes affect people in the organization and the skills required. Changes may be needed to the roles of data owners, authors, and maintainers.
Data: The data entities and attributes that underpin information.	What data are captured?	What data are stored? What data are retrieved?	What data can be used? What data can be shared? What data can be maintained?	What data are archived? What data are deleted?	Changes affect the information architecture, data dictionary, and data retention policy.
Location: The geographical and functional position where stages in the life cycle take place.	Where is the source of the data? Where is the data captured?	Where are the data stored? Where can the data be retrieved from?	Where can the data be used? Where can the data be shared? Where can the data be maintained?	Where are the data archived? Where are the data deleted?	Changes may affect the information architecture, and will need to be documented in the data dictionary.
Date/Time: When activities in the life cycle take place.	When are the data captured?	When are the data stored? When are the data retrieved?	When are the data used? When are the data shared? When are the data maintained?	When are the data archived? When are the data deleted?	Changes will need to be reflected in the data definitions and archive policy.
Strategy: The rationale for activities in the life cycle taking place in this specific context.	Why are the data captured? Why are the data captured in this way?	Why are the data stored? Why are the data stored in this way? Why are the data retrieved?	Why are the data used? Why are the data shared? Why are the data maintained?	Why are the data archived? Why are the data archived in this way? Why are the data deleted?	Changes impact the way information is used to support the organization's strategy and will need to be reflected in the information management strategy.
Means: Tasks required to complete actions in the life cycle.	How are the data captured?	How are the data stored? How are the data retrieved?	How are the data used? How are the data shared? How are the data maintained?	How are the data archived? How are the data deleted?	Changes affect the processes and practices of the organization. Changes may need to be made to the data dictionary and information architecture.

challenges of system implementation are increased by the wide-scale use and impact of these enterprise systems. The technical challenges include:

○ Understanding how the software systems operate and the data that are needed as input to and output from the systems.
○ Integrating the systems with existing IT and information systems in the organization.
○ Cleaning and migrating existing data into the systems.
○ Managing the changeover to using the new systems while minimizing the impact on day-to-day operations of Match Lighting.
○ Testing the systems.

It is a mistake to solely regard the introduction of enterprise systems as being merely technical projects. An information system has business rules and processes embedded in its design which were identified during the initial phases of the information systems development process. A packaged application also has business rules and processes embedded in its design; however, these are unlikely to match the current working of Match Lighting exactly. IT staff need to work with the software vendors (or the staff at Watts Electrical) to determine the business rules that are embedded in the packaged systems. When the processes and systems are understood, the impact on the existing business processes and practices at Match Lighting can be assessed.

The adoption of an application package changes how staff in Match Lighting work in two ways. First, procedures are changed to reflect the use of the system. For example, if the ECM system is adopted as the single source of information in Match Lighting, the IT manager will need to ensure that all training manuals are made available in the ECM system. This will replace his current practice of uploading an electronic copy of the manuals to the intranet and circulating copies to staff via email when requested. Secondly, the systems are likely to demand changes in the way work is currently conducted in order to accommodate the requirements of the package. This can be a way for Watts Electrical to enforce standards and improve upon current practices at Match Lighting. For example, providing one source of data for the training manuals ensures that all staff can access up-to-date manuals when necessary. The process of designing the training manuals can also be improved through the:

○ Ability to reuse standard content (such as how to report IT problems to the IT help desk which may be included in all manuals), reducing the time taken to prepare and maintain the manuals.

○ Formalization of verification procedures to ensure that the manuals are accurate, complete, and consistent before they are published.
○ Version controls which clearly show the evolution of the manuals.
○ Standardization of content, improving the accessibility of the information in them.

The process of creating the manuals is changed in that the:

○ Activities involved in preparing the manuals are monitored by the workflow of the ECM system.
○ Use of standard templates for the manuals is enforced.
○ Existing information content is automatically inserted.
○ Manuals have to progress through verification procedures before they are published.
○ Sections of the manual have to be written as structured elements that can be reused.

Changes to the way business processes are conducted in Match Lighting are likely to meet resistance from some staff. They may not trust the accuracy of the reusable content and may feel threatened, controlled, or too restricted by the workflow activities.

An ERP system, if installed in its entirety, replaces all the IT systems in the organization, resulting in widespread change. It enables integration of information throughout the organization as business processes are coordinated in the ERP system. This integration is reliant upon quality data flowing through the organization. Match Lighting will therefore need to ensure that its data have been cleaned and that procedures are developed to ensure that the integrity of data is maintained as data are migrated to the ERP system.

The introduction of enterprise systems therefore requires consideration of the following issues:

○ An understanding of the rules and processes embedded in the application and the changes needed to organizational processes to accommodate them.
○ An awareness of the data requirements of the enterprise systems and how they will integrate with existing systems.
○ Identification of the new skills required to operate and maintain the systems.
○ Consideration of how the systems relate to the culture and values in the organization.
○ An assessment of the impact of the system on the existing information management strategy.
○ Formulation of strategies and policies to accommodate the systems, such as the introduction of a policy for reusing information content in the organization.

Exercise 13.1

1 What does the acronym *cloud* stand for?
2 Why is cloud computing referred to as on-demand computing?
3 Which is more secure, a private cloud or a public cloud? Why?
4 Which is the most cost-effective, a private cloud or a public cloud? Why?
5 What is the difference between Infrastructure as a Service and Software as a Service?
6 How does remote access differ from mobile access?
7 What is m-commerce?
8 List three features of a mobile telephone that need to be considered when using it to access large documents.
9 What type of location-based query is 'find the nearest café'?
10 How is a location determined in location-based services?
11 What is meant by the *Internet of Things*?
12 What are the two dimensions of building controls?
13 What ethical issues arise from the installation of a swipe card in a building?
14 Is an enterprise resource planning system one system or a set of modules?
15 Why does the implementation of an ERP system often require business processes to change?
16 What is the difference between configuring an ERP system and customizing an ERP system?
17 Why is the quality of data important in an ERP system?
18 What is the difference between a document management system and a content management system?
19 What is meant by systematic reuse?
20 What are three advantages of adopting a single-source strategy?

Link 13.4
Answers to Exercise 13.1

Activities 13.1

1 Draw a diagram to show how moving to cloud computing could affect Match Lighting.

2 Prepare a list of the advantages and disadvantages of mobile working.
3 Add motion sensors to Figure 13.5 to control the lights in area 4.
4 Explain how cameras, motion sensors, temperature sensors, and pressure sensors could be used in a domestic property to create a smart home.
5 Draw a value chain and map the ERP modules listed in Table 13.6 to illustrate the scope of an ERP system.
6 Use Table 13.11 to assess the potential impact of the introduction of an ECMS on information management at Match Lighting.

Discussion Questions 13.1

1 The IT infrastructure is fundamental to the operation of many organizations so to what extent should organizations devolve responsibility for their infrastructure to cloud providers?
2 If Match Lighting were to implement cloud computing, would information management be easier or more difficult?
3 Mobile technology provides the means for business processes to be undertaken remotely; however, this raises issues of security and privacy. When should transactions and conversations not be conducted on mobile technology?
4 In a shopping centre, should organizations adopt a mobile strategy of information pull or information push? Why?
5 Pervasive technology is used in assisted living applications to enable vulnerable adults to live with a degree of safety and independence. When does technology become an invasion of privacy as opposed to a means of security?
6 What should an intelligent building be able to do in order to demonstrate its intelligence? To what extent can a building be intelligent?
7 An ERP system provides a standard set of IT modules. How does this affect the potential for an organization to attain competitive advantage using IT?
8 Forbes-Pitt (2006) describes a document as a wrapping which conveys the rules for interacting with the content in the document. Comparing emails, text messages, and tweets, have the rules of paper-documents been transferred to the electronic medium or have new rules been developed?

BUSINESS THEMES

Scenario 14.1

Social Media in Amy's Candles

Amy came into the office to talk to Brian about the monthly accounts and noticed that he was looking at his mobile phone. 'What are you doing?' she asked.

'I am reading some tweets about a new camera being developed. It has mixed reviews so far,' replied Brian putting the phone away quickly. Curious, Amy asked Brian to explain more about tweets.

'Tweets are microblogs, short messages posted online by staff from the manufacturer and journalists about the design of the camera. Everyone is talking about the camera design, posting their own opinions about the design. Some like the proposed design, others think the controls are too close together. Can't wait to see what the final design will look like when the camera is finally launched.'

'So the designers are using the tweets to get feedback during the design process?' asked Amy.

'Yes, and generating interest from potential customers for a product that is not yet available to buy.'

'Perhaps we could do something similar,' suggested Amy.

How could Amy use social media to develop relationships with her customers?

In what other ways could Amy use social media to develop and share knowledge within the supply chain?

Learning Outcomes

The learning outcomes of this chapter are to:

○ Explain the relationship between information management and knowledge management.

○ Identify opportunities for leveraging the value of information in social networks.

○ Define the role of information in different types of business innovation.

○ Outline the stages of business intelligence.

○ Demonstrate how information is used in business simulations.

○ Determine the information management issues arising from business development.

Introduction

Business management develops concepts to leverage the value of the information resource in organizations. This chapter discusses a range of business concepts and assesses their impact on both the organization and the role of information management in the organization. Knowledge management is defined and the relationship between knowledge and information is explained. The role of social media to share knowledge is then considered. Business innovation is the creative application of knowledge. Different types of business innovation that focus on different areas of the business model are defined. The previous chapter outlined innovative ways that information technology (IT) could be used to capture data. Business intelligence is a collection of processes and tools which aim to extract meaning from data. The stages of business intelligence are explained. As a greater understanding of the factors affecting organizational systems is gained from analysis of data, simulation models can be developed to explore time-related scenarios. A range of simulation models are introduced and the role of information management in creating simulation models is discussed. The chapter concludes by presenting a framework that can be used to assess the impact of business management concepts on information management.

14.1 ▶ Knowledge Management

Organizations can use similar resources and follow similar processes to deliver similar products and services but organizations differ in the staff they employ. The unique-ness of individuals provides a key source of differentiation and competitive advantage for organizations. When staff leave the organization they take their knowledge with them. The organization loses valuable knowledge, which is potentially acquired by another organization. Knowledge management processes aim to capture and share knowledge to maximize the potential of this unique resource and reduce the risk of knowledge being lost from the organization.

DEFINITION: Information is derived from the interpreta-tion of data in context; **knowledge** is derived from information by adding meaning to the information, usually gained from experience.

Davenport and Prusak (1998) suggest that knowledge can be generated by adding value to information in four ways: by comparing information, exploring the consequences that may arise from the information, connecting informa-tion with what is already known, and discussing informa-tion with others in conversation.

14.1.1 ▶ Relationship between Information and Knowledge

Nonaka and Takeuchi (1995) distinguish between the Western and Japanese views of knowledge. The Western view is that knowledge is explicit and can be docu-mented; it is therefore closely related to information. In contrast, the Japanese view knowledge as being tacit, personal skills gained through experience, reflection, and learning. Polanyi (1966) argues that all knowledge is rooted in tacit knowledge as explicit knowledge is generated through internal processes. Within these two extremes of explicit knowledge and tacit knowledge, Blackler (1995) outlined a taxonomy of knowledge comprising:

○ Embrained knowledge, which includes shared visions and personal insights.

○ Embodied knowledge, practical knowledge of a situation acquired through engaging in procedures and processes.

○ Encultured knowledge, a socially constructed shared understanding that is dependent on a shared language.

○ Embedded knowledge, which is incorporated into routines and procedures.

○ Encoded knowledge, defined in manuals and codes of practice.

Components of knowledge include: know-what, know-how, and know-why (Garud, 1997), to which a fourth component of know-who can be added:

○ Know-what: By applying information about the different characteristics of candles, Amy *knows what* different categories of candles exist.

○ Know-how: Amy *knows how* to make candles. She has read and internalized explicit knowledge embedded in written procedures for making candles. Amy has also developed implicit knowledge gained from the experience of making candles over time. This includes, for example, knowledge of the best consistency of wax for different candles and the optimum time to remove candles from their moulds.

○ Know-why: By combining knowing-what and knowing-how through reasoning processes knowledge of why situations arise is generated. For example, Amy *knows what* different waxes there are and that different waxes have different properties. She *knows how* to make the candles by heating the wax, pouring it into moulds, and allowing the wax to cool. From experience Amy therefore *knows why* a candle is the wrong size (because paraffin wax shrinks when cooling).

○ Know-who: Amy *knows who* to approach for advice; for example, Brian is knowledgeable about accounting procedures. Directories and knowledge maps can be used to help to identify and locate individuals in the organization who have knowledge about specific topics.

Although organizations agree that information manage-ment is an enabler of knowledge management, the differ-ence between the terms remains confusing (Kruger & Johnson, 2010). The confusion is perhaps partly fuelled by the use of IT to develop knowledge management systems to provide support for one or more aspects of knowledge, such as storing explicit knowledge and enabling tacit knowledge to be shared. Singh (2007) differentiates information management as documenting and retrieving explicit knowledge, and knowledge management as the process of generating value from knowledge assets, that is, the collection and distribution of knowledge.

14.1.2 ▶ Processes of Knowledge Management

The phrase 'knowledge management' is misleading as knowledge itself cannot be managed (Kakabadse *et al.*,

Table 14.1 ▶ Knowledge Management Processes in the Life Cycle

Create	Capture	Store and Retrieve	Use, Share, and Maintain	Destroy
Acquire knowledge (employ staff, hire consultants, acquire or merge with another organization). Dedicate resources to create knowledge through research and development activities. Facilitate knowledge creation through organizational learning and communities of practice.	Capture external knowledge, such as competitor intelligence. Capture internal knowledge in, for example, reports and examples of best practice. Elicit knowledge using questioning techniques.	Codify knowledge so that it can be retrieved. Map knowledge to enable sources and locations of knowledge to be identified. Store knowledge.	Use knowledge. Disseminate knowledge. Share knowledge. Update knowledge. Retain knowledge.	Knowledge is lost through: Staff leaving. Being forgotten. Being unused. Losing relevance. Encoded knowledge being destroyed. Routines and processes being replaced.

2003), only the processes in the knowledge life cycle can be managed. Assundani (2005) refers to knowledge as being a resource that is input to an organization through the human capital joining the organization with their know-how and knowledge of the industry or processes. This knowledge is used and shared to create knowledge as a resource that is output from the organization through its products and processes and patents. Table 14.1 identifies a number of processes in the knowledge life cycle. The knowledge management life cycle is cyclic as knowledge is used to facilitate the creation of new knowledge.

The term *learning organization* refers to an organization that is committed to using knowledge to share best practice and learn from experience by developing mechanisms to capture and exploit knowledge. The organization's ability to make use of knowledge is referred to as its *absorptive capacity*. Learning organizations adopt processes to promote knowledge creation such as the adoption of double-loop learning. Single-loop learning refers to the detection and correction of an error; double-loop learning refers to the detection and correction of an error followed by an investigation into why the error occurred and changes to procedures or policies to avoid the error reoccurring (Argyris, 1991).

Through experience the organization develops an *organizational memory*. This includes knowledge and skills, lessons learnt and experience gained, documented in procedures, embedded in the design of systems and processes, and held in the heads of the employees in the organization. A shared language is needed to support the evolution and utilization of the organizational memory. The language of knowledge is important as it provides the context for knowledge, aiding elicitation, and stimulating thinking (Snowden, 2003).

Knowledge is shared and new knowledge emerges from engagement in communities of practice. Communities

of practice are informal, self-organized networks that may become formalized over time. People with a shared interest are brought together within the network to share expertise and solve problems. The communities may be within organizations but are often formed outside organizations. Online discussion forums enable communities of practice to be formed and maintained, removing global barriers and enabling knowledge-sharing. The rise of social media networks demonstrates the growth in the use of IT as a means of communication and as vehicle for knowledge creation and knowledge-sharing.

14.1.3 ▶ Transformation Dimensions of Knowledge Management

Knowledge management aligns organizational strategy and performance by identifying the knowledge that the organization needs to achieve its vision (Wenger, 2004). Three elements needed to facilitate effective knowledge management in organizations are:

○ Processes to enable knowledge management activities to take place.

○ People who are willing and able (that is, have access to tools and processes) to share knowledge. The organizational culture needs to be conducive to knowledge-sharing.

○ Tools to:

- Create repositories to store explicit knowledge so that it can be shared and used.
- Maintain directories of people and documents where knowledge can be located.
- Facilitate communication networks (such as online forums) to provide the opportunity to share and generate tacit knowledge through discussions.

Table 14.2 outlines the impact on the organizational architecture of knowledge management initiatives.

Table 14.2 ▶ Organizational Transformation Initiated by Knowledge Management

Formal Organization Architecture	Informal Organization Architecture	Impact on Organization Architecture
Technology	Socio-technical	Although a specific knowledge management system may be implemented, the existing information systems and IT can be used to support knowledge management processes. Technology provides a means to access and share knowledge. The implementation of a knowledge management strategy therefore requires changes to the way staff use IT to generate and share knowledge.
Security	Trust	Sharing knowledge is core to knowledge management; however, to some extent the design of the IT architecture focuses on restricting the ability to share knowledge. Security controls, such as firewalls, can become a barrier to sharing knowledge outside the organization. Organizations need to secure their internal knowledge but also need to share knowledge with external partners. A social barrier to sharing knowledge relates to fear about how the knowledge will be used (for example, if an employee shares his or her knowledge will he or she become redundant?). Trust therefore has to be developed that knowledge-sharing will be rewarded and reciprocated.
People	Skills	People are fundamental to knowledge management. Knowledge can only be volunteered, forcing people to share knowledge results in camouflage behaviour where the knowledge is shared but in an unusable manner or conformance behaviour where only the minimum knowledge is shared (Snowden, 2003). Staff need to develop skill in how to acquire and share knowledge effectively using the tools available in the organization.
Strategy	Vision	Although the knowledge management strategy is initially aligned with the organization's strategy, as knowledge emerges it provides opportunities to influence the organization's strategy. Knowledge management requires leadership to secure resources and cultivate a culture conducive to knowledge management.
Processes	Practices	Knowledge management processes have to be introduced to formalize the acquisition, codification, and sharing of knowledge. Existing business processes have to be adapted to ensure that the knowledge is used. This will require changes to work practices to share and leverage knowledge in the organization.
Systems	Human Activity Systems	Although a specific knowledge management system may be implemented, existing systems can be used to support knowledge management processes. Knowledge working requires a change of practice, providing time for reflection, and knowledge creation and dissemination.
Culture	Values	Culture can be the main obstacle or facilitator of knowledge management. The culture must be supportive of the knowledge management strategy and embrace learning, reflection, continuous improvement, and knowledge-sharing. Knowledge management initiatives need to be aligned with the core values of the organization to be successful. Sharing lessons learnt can also provide a means of reinforcing rituals and routines in organizations (Davenport & Prusak, 1998).

14.1.4 ▶ **Role of Information Management in Knowledge Management**

Despite the confusion between information and knowledge, knowledge is encoded in information artefacts and embedded into the processes that use information. Information provides the foundation for knowledge, facilitating the communication needed for sharing and generating knowledge. The shared meanings of information documented in data dictionaries reflect the encultured knowledge that has evolved in the organization. The role of information management in facilitating and supporting knowledge management processes includes ensuring that:

○ The organization captures the information needed for organizational learning.
○ Information is presented in an appropriate form to facilitate knowledge generation.
○ Suitable standards of information quality are maintained so that information can be trusted.
○ Information is accessible when required by authorized staff in a meaningful format.

o Information definitions are agreed upon and applied consistently to ensure that information can be shared and interpreted accurately to support creation of organizational memory.

o Encoded knowledge is categorized to facilitate accessibility and dissemination.

o Information management processes adopt best practice and are continually reviewed to identify opportunities for improvement.

o Information contributes to developing and maintaining the organizational memory.

14.2 ▶ Social Networking

Communication networks enable information to be passed among devices that are connected together. In a social network, communication passes among individuals who are connected together in some way through their social bonds, common interests, and social interaction. Social networks have always existed, however, advances in IT have increased both the speed and reach of communication, fuelling and empowering social networks. While customers may have previously shared their experience of poor service from an organization with a few local people over a period of a few weeks, now their experience can be communicated worldwide in seconds. Organizations are therefore seeking ways to harness the power of social networks.

DEFINITION: A **social network** comprises a number of individuals who are connected in some way through, for example, shared interests or experiences and who engage in direct communication to one or more individuals within the network.

14.2.1 ▶ Social Network Analysis

Social network analysis explores the relationships in social structures. The analysis provides a means to visualize communication patterns to support reflection on how individuals and teams work together. An audit is first conducted to identify the formal and informal channels of communication. The frequency of communication among individuals in the channels is then analysed. Table 14.3 provides an extract from a social network analysis at Amy's Candles.

A diagram forms a visual representation of the social network. Figure 14.1 shows the formal communication paths between staff at Amy's Candles and Figure 14.2 shows the informal communication flows. Analysis of the communication paths can show where sources of information are centred and help to identify

Table 14.3 ▶ Audit of Social Networks in Amy's Candles

Audit for Brian (Accounts)		
Individual or Department	**Sends Information**	**Engages in Informal Discussions**
Amy (Owner)	Weekly	Daily
Bob (Computer Consultant)	Never	Never
Chris (Shop)	Never	Daily
Louise (Temporary Staff)	Never	Never
Audit for Chris (Shop)		
Individual or Department	**Sends Information**	**Informal Discussions**
Amy (Owner)	Daily	Daily
Bob (Computer Consultant)	Never	Never
Brian (Accounts)	Never	Daily
Louise (Temporary Staff)	Daily	Daily
Audit for Amy (Owner)		
Individual or Department	**Sends Information**	**Informal Discussions**
Bob (Computer Consultant)	Monthly	Never
Brian (Accounts)	Weekly	Daily
Chris (Shop)	Daily	Daily
Louise (Temporary Staff)	Daily	Daily

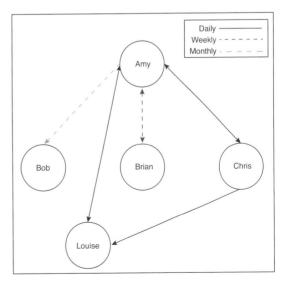

Figure 14.1 ▶ Formal Communication Flows in Amy's Candles

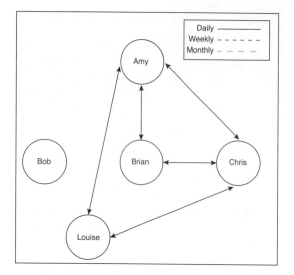

Daily ————
Weekly – – – – –
Monthly – — –

Amy
Bob
Brian
Chris
Louise

Figure 14.2 Informal Communication Flows in Amy's Candles

where communication could be improved. For example, Figure 14.1 shows that Amy is a key node in the network of formal information flow and Figure 14.2 shows that Bob is omitted from all informal discussions. Social network analysis can be applied to communications between the organization and external parties, or between external parties such as the activities within social media networks.

14.2.2 Social Media in Organizations

Social media refers to the use of technology to support the creation and dissemination of information in social networks. It encompasses three elements: content, community, and Web 2.0 technology (Ahlqvist et al., 2010). IT provides the means for anyone to easily create information content, which can then be shared with others in their social networks.

Social media sites differ in a number of areas shown in Table 14.4.

Kaplan and Haenlein (2010) differentiate social media using two dimensions:

○ Self-disclosure: the degree to which an individual, organization, or association offers information about themselves.
○ Media richness: the means of presenting information to create a social presence.

For example, a personal blog facilitates a high degree of self-disclosure; in contrast, virtual gaming worlds use a high degree of media but require limited self-disclosure.

Sharing information to develop and sustain social relationships is at the heart of social media. Active engagement in social relationships is critical to the successful use of social media in organizations. Adams (2009) differentiates between *connections* and *interactions* in social networks; a person may have many connections in their social network but only regularly interact with a few of them.

Adams (2009) defines three levels of social relationship:

○ Temporary ties are created to address an immediate requirement, such as the need for specific information, after which the ties are broken.
○ Weak ties are loose connections, such as friends of friends, where connections may be based on, for example, shared interests.
○ Strong ties are trusted connections with contacts that have been well established.

Consumers trust the views of other members of their social network, therefore a *network neighbour*, someone linked to an existing customer in a social network, is more likely to adopt the same product or service than someone outside the network (Beynon-Davies, 2009). Direct and indirect connections in the network of interactions quickly result in a vast international communication network. Viral marketing harnesses the

Table 14.4 Characteristics of Social Media Sites

Target Audience	Purpose of the Site	Information Content
○ Age-related; for example, aimed at children, teenagers, or adults. ○ Subject-related; for individuals with common interests in areas such as sports, computing, or the environment. ○ Experience-related; for individuals in similar situations such as specific illnesses or stages of life.	○ Acting as repositories to share content in a community. ○ Social networking, connecting people for social or business purposes. ○ Facilitating collaboration among individuals for specific projects, such as Wikipedia. ○ Simulated environments, virtual worlds to facilitate learning, collaboration, and gaming.	○ Microblogs. ○ Blogs. ○ Music. ○ Photographs. ○ Videos.

potential reach of social networks to support organizational marketing. It involves creating content such as a game or video which sufficiently appeals to people that they circulate it to others in their social networks. The marketing material rapidly spreads through and among social networks around the world. The power of relationships in social networks should not be neglected as negative issues can also soon snowball in the same way. It is therefore critical that organizations respond promptly to any negative issues that may arise (Cox, 2013).

Social media provides a means of enabling conversations in the marketplace to help build relationships (Booth & Matic, 2011). It can be used to:

○ Support marketing and customer relationship management.
○ Provide a forum for customer queries and complaints.
○ Support internal communication.
○ Facilitate collaboration with internal and external groups of people.

Social media technology enables organizations to use multimedia rich content to gain access to individuals in other stages of the supply chain. For example, it provides a means of disintermediation in the supply chain, allowing manufacturers direct access to communicate with the consumers of their products and services (Cox, 2013). However, social media should not be seen as another channel to distribute existing information (Hall, 2010). It has changed the role of individuals from being just consumers of information to taking a prominent active role in content creation (Bateman *et al.*, 2011). This requires organizations to develop strategies for engaging with consumers using social media (Kietzmann *et al.*, 2011).

14.2.3 Transformation Dimensions of Social Media

Social media can transform the way an organization interacts with its customers and consumers, providing the opportunity to actively engage in rich communication about the needs and demands of the marketplace. The organizational architecture needs to be able to:

○ Adapt to proactively engage in social media with partners in its supply chain.
○ Use the information content created in social media networks to inform the design and delivery of its products and services.
○ Respond quickly to information about the organization in social media networks.

Committing resources to engage in this communication requires social media to become embedded as an integral part of the organization's communication infrastructure. Responsibility for social media should not reside entirely in marketing, customer service, or corporate communication functions (Cox, 2013). New processes need to be developed to create, respond to, and use social media communications promptly and accurately.

Organizations have reported that the use of social media has led to an increase in malware in their computer systems (He, 2012). Malware is malicious software that is introduced into computer systems for the purpose of collecting private data or disrupting the computer system. It is therefore important that organizations ensure that their security controls are maintained to reduce the threat and potential impact of malware affecting information in their systems through interaction with social media sites.

Table 14.5 outlines the impact on the organizational architecture of social media initiatives.

Table 14.5 Organizational Transformation Initiated by Social Media

Formal Organization Architecture	Informal Organization Architecture	Impact on Organization Architecture
Technology	Socio-technical	Social media technology has become well established and the main impact on the organization is encountered by staff adapting to the demands of social media communication. Social media requires organizations to interact with public websites and therefore technical security controls need to be maintained to minimize risks from malware adversely affecting the organization.
Security	Trust	Despite the increase in malware, the greatest security risk in social networking arises from employees maliciously or accidentally releasing unauthorized information. Staff need to be trained to ensure that the disclosure of information is consistent with the data security classifications. The information presented by the organization must be trusted by staff as well as the external audience.

Table 14.5 Continued

Formal Organization Architecture	Informal Organization Architecture	Impact on Organization Architecture
People	Skills	Staff need to be trained in the technical aspects of how to use the social media tools, given guidance about the range of information that can be disclosed, and how to communicate effectively in social media. In addition to the technical skills needed to proactively create social media content, skills are needed to engage effectively in online communication.
Strategy	Vision	The use of social media in the organization needs to be aligned with the strategic objectives relating to engagement within the marketplace and supply chain. Information gained from social media can be used to inform and direct the organizational strategy to ensure that the needs of customers are met. The closer interaction with external parties facilitated by social media provides the opportunity to transform the relationship between the organization and its customers. For example, it provides the means for customers to contribute to the design of new products and services.
Processes	Practices	Business processes need to be in place to provide information to respond to queries received through social media. Processes are also needed to review, respond to, use, and create social media content. Business practices need to change to embed the use of social media information into the organization's activities.
Systems	Human Activity Systems	The creation of new content to be posted online may be considered to be an extension of the existing services provided by the marketing function. However, systems need to be adapted to ensure that information gathered from social media is appropriately integrated into relevant systems so that it can be used. This requires the organization to change the way it currently operates and how it relates to those outside the organization.
Culture	Values	Social media communities have high expectations in relation to acceptable response times to queries raised. The organizational culture needs to adapt to meet these expectations. Social media changes relationships in the marketplace and the power of consumers. This may challenge the values held by the organization, particularly during the initial introduction of social media as the relationships with consumers are established and trust develops.

14.2.4 Role of Information Management in Social Media

Social media provides a means by which organizations can directly communicate with individuals and organizations externally. This provides three sources of information that need to be managed, the information:

○ Provided by the organization to external parties via social media.

○ Gathered through direct communication between the organization and external parties via social media.

○ About the organization which external parties post via social media.

The role of information management in social networking therefore includes:

○ Supporting analysis of information flows in social networks to improve the management and communication of information in the organization.

○ Monitoring social media networks for information about the organization.

○ Providing a means to capture and use the information from social media.

○ Ensuring adherence to information security categories to avoid the unauthorized disclosure of information.

○ Providing training in information management security.

○ Raising and maintaining awareness of the information management security issues that can arise when engaging with social media.

○ Identifying where information is held to enable it to be accessed when needed to respond to issues that may arise in social media.

○ Providing access to accurate information to enable customer queries to be addressed promptly.

○ Ensuring information management policies are sufficiently flexible to address the management of information in social media.

○ Identifying opportunities for using social media to communicate both proactively and reactively.

14.3 ▶ Business Innovation

Business innovation is derived from people and the application of their knowledge to differentiate the organization from competitors.

DEFINITION: **Business innovation** involves the application of information, knowledge, and creativity to identify opportunities for the development or improvement of products, services, or business processes.

Innovation involves change; this may be change of a product design, change of a business process, or a change in the way an organization interacts and engages with external parties in the market and wider business environment. Innovation can take three general forms that relate to the extent of the change proposed:

- Incremental change builds on what currently exists and seeks to improve it in some way. The change takes place within the current boundaries of the process. For example, Amy may experiment with different additives in the wax mixture to improve the colour or burning time of her candles. This involves a minor change to the existing production process to improve the existing product.
- Radical change seeks to challenge one or more of the current boundaries of concepts and processes in the organization. Amy currently makes her candles by melting wax, pouring it into moulds, and then leaving the wax to cool before removing it from the mould. If Amy devised a way to mould the wax without melting, pouring, and cooling the wax it would radically change the way she produces candles.
- Transformational change challenges all the boundaries of concepts and processes that underpin the use, design, and creation of a product or service. It disrupts the market, changing how society thinks about something, and can make previous products or ways of working obsolete. For example, the development of the light bulb transformed lighting, resulting in the decline and market repositioning of candles.

Ortt and van der Duin (2008) outline four approaches to innovation that historically have developed in response to different social and organizational contexts:

- Technology push, seeking commercialization of technology.
- Market pull, seeking to develop economies of scale, and diversification to meet market needs.
- Market pull and technology push combined, using knowledge about technological development and

interaction with the market requirements to feed into the innovation process.
- Innovation alliance and new business development, through collaboration with external partnerships.

14.3.1 ▶ Types of Business Innovation

Different types of innovation impact different areas of the business mode shown in Figure 14.3. These include:

- Customer relationship innovation. This changes how the organization interacts with its customers and potential customers, seeking to maintain profitable relationships.
- Marketing innovation. This changes how the products and services offered by an organization are presented to potential customers, including packaging design, product promotion, and advertising. Viral marketing is an example of using social media to innovate organizational marketing.
- Experiential innovation. This focuses on how to improve the experience of the product or service for the customer, such as through personalization (Moore, 2006).
- Positioning innovation. This considers how the organization's current products and services could be offered in a different market. It is also known as application innovation as it focuses on identifying new uses and new markets for existing offerings. For example, the markets for Amy's products could include lighting, decoration, health and well-being, and gifts.
- Product innovation. This includes improvements to existing products and the design of new products. Line-extension innovation occurs where subcategories are created from the existing product range (Moore, 2006).
- Paradigm innovation. This refers to transformational changes in how a perceived consumer need could be satisfied. It involves a major change in thinking.
- Platform innovation. This involves change to the foundation or infrastructure on which a generation of products or services are based.
- Process innovation. This changes the way an organization operates, including the processes involved in the design, production, and delivery of products and services.
- Operational excellence. This has a broader focus than process innovation, changing the business processes that support the primary activities of the organization to reduce costs and increase perceived value. It

also seeks to change the organization's structure, management, and culture to create an environment that is conducive to optimum performance.

○ Alliance innovation. This changes the relationships between the organization and other organizations in the supply chain. It includes, for example, corporate merger and the use of collaborative systems.

○ Political innovation. This includes government and social policies that change the business climate in which the organization and its markets operate.

○ Technological innovation. This changes equipment, tools, and methods which impact the organization directly in terms of the design and development of products and services, or indirectly in terms of changes to processes.

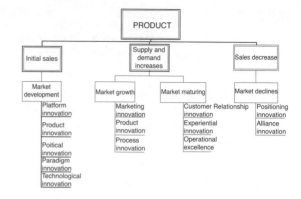

Figure 14.4 Types of Innovation in the Product Life Cycle

Source: Based on Moore (2006).

Figure 14.3 Business Innovation in the Business Model

Moore (2006) suggests that different types of innovation are needed at different positions in the life cycle of the product or service. In Figure 14.4 types of innovation have been added to the product life cycle introduced in Chapter 2. The life cycle is initiated by product, platform, paradigm, political, or technological innovation. Market growth is sustained by marketing innovation, and innovations in product or process. As the market declines, positioning or alliance innovation is needed to maximize sales of the existing products before a new cycle is initiated.

14.3.2 Transformation Dimensions of Business Innovation

The emphasis of business innovation is on change, either relating to the offerings of the organization or the how

the organization operates. Business innovation will therefore require the organization to change in some way. The extent of the change will depend on the form of change (incremental, radical, or transformational). The areas of the organization that may be impacted will depend on the specific type of innovation. For example:

○ Customer relationship innovation will include changes to business processes, the skills required to interact with customers, and the culture of how customers are treated.

○ Marketing innovation may include changes to business processes, technology, and staff skills to change how the organization's offerings are presented to potential customers.

○ Experiential innovation may require changes to systems and processes to improve the customer experience.

○ Positioning innovation will require people with the knowledge and skills of the new market to be entered.

○ Product innovation will require changes to the processes and skills used in the creation of the organization's products.

○ Operational excellence may require changes to the strategy and culture of the organization to facilitate wider organizational change of vision and practice.

Link 14.1
Knowledge and Innovation in Practice

Table 14.6 outlines the potential impact on the organizational architecture of business innovation.

Table 14.6 ▶ Organizational Transformation Initiated by Business Innovation

Formal Organization Architecture	Informal Organization Architecture	Impact on Organization Architecture
Technology	Socio-technical	Technological, platform, and paradigm innovation may require the organization to adopt new technology or use it in a different way. Other forms of innovation such as marketing, customer relationship, and process innovation may require technology to be used to change the way key business processes are conducted.
Security	Trust	Changes to business processes that change the way technology is used to communicate information may pose additional risks to information security. For example, the use of social media as a means of marketing innovation may increase potential security risks. Change can be met with resistance and therefore trust needs to be established in the organization that the innovation is feasible and will have a positive impact on the organization.
People	Skills	Innovation is facilitated and implemented by people. People will therefore be required to change the way they work to implement business innovation. This may require staff to develop new skills; for example, staff may need to learn about the requirements of a new platform that will provide the foundation of the next generation of products.
Strategy	Vision	Opportunities for radical or transformational innovation may provide the basis for the organization to review its strategy. The business opportunities initiated by paradigm, platform, technological, and alliance innovation will need to be reflected in changes to the organization's vision.
Processes	Practices	A number of types of innovation require changes to the existing business processes and practices in the organization. This may include the introduction of new processes or changing the way in which existing processes are conducted. In addition, new processes may be needed to collect and analyse data to facilitate the generation of innovative ideas in the organization.
Systems	Human Activity Systems	All forms of innovation, particularly those with an external focus, such as marketing, experiential, customer relationship, and positioning innovation, may require changes to be made to the existing systems in the organization. For example, positioning innovation will require information about new markets to be captured and managed.
Culture	Values	Innovation may challenge the existing culture of the organization. For example, operational excellence requires a culture of continual improvement to be adopted. A balance is needed between maintaining the core values of the organization's identity and enabling the organization to evolve through innovation.

14.3.3 ▶ Role of Information Management in Business Innovation

Information is needed to facilitate and implement business innovation. Information will need to be collected and presented in an appropriate manner from internal and external sources to initiate innovation. This will include capturing information and knowledge to support business intelligence to generate innovative ideas, which can be explored in business simulations. The role of information management in business innovation includes:

○ Identifying the information available that can be used to develop and evaluate ideas and providing access to the information. For example, customer queries may generate ideas for product innovation.

○ Capturing and managing information to identify the life cycle stage of current products and services.

○ Identifying and protecting intellectual property generated by the organization, including the registration of trademarks and patents.

○ Maintaining the privacy and security of commercially sensitive business information.

○ Restricting the dissemination of confidential information.

○ Identifying the information requirements of specific types of innovation. For example, positioning innovation will require additional information to be captured relating to the potential new market in which the organization may offer its existing products.

○ Identifying the information management issues that may arise in implementing the specific innovation.
○ Capturing and managing information to monitor the implementation and impact of innovations.
○ Integrating new information captured resulting from, for example, alliance or platform innovation.
○ Ensuring information management policies are sufficiently flexible to address the requirements of the innovation proposed.

14.4 Business Intelligence

Business intelligence refers to the processes and tools for extracting meaningful information from data that can be converted to knowledge to gain insights into the organization and its market. It involves collecting, analysing, and presenting information to support organizational decision-making. Business intelligence provides the basis for knowledge discovery and process improvement, identifying opportunities for the organization to gain competitive advantage. This includes monitoring operational activity, such as stock levels and transport delays, to enable an organization to be proactive in ensuring that appropriate facilities are in place to address situations when they arise (Howson, 2008).

DEFINITION: **Business intelligence** involves the collection, aggregation, analysis, synthesis, and presentation of data, which can be interpreted within the context of existing knowledge, to support organizational decisions.

Green (2007) suggests that business intelligence can be derived from business information gained from an understanding of how organizational performance is affected by social interactions among individuals, the abilities of individuals, and the wider organizational environment. Social interaction is facilitated by social networks, supporting knowledge creation; organizational performance is improved through innovation of organizational excellence and the formal and informal organizational architecture provides the environment for organizational activity.

Business intelligence focuses on improving business reporting and access to data to maximize the usefulness of the organization's data (Janeert, 2011). Data analytics is a subset of business intelligence (Davenport & Harris, 2007) that focuses on extensive analysis of data, either by human or automated analysis. It moves beyond the provision of standard alerts and reporting cycles to querying data and creating forecasts and predictions. Reporting tools focus on the presentation of data and organize the results from standard queries for dissemination. Reporting

enables data to be pushed to the right staff when they need the data but relies on organizational directories that define what data may be needed by which staff. In contrast, querying tools enable data values at a specific point in time to be presented and provide a means of structuring questions to interrogate the data. Querying data enables staff to pull data when needed.

14.4.1 Stages of Business Intelligence

Business intelligence involves the following stages to collect, prepare, analyse and present data to support organizational decisions:

Defining key performance indicators: Green (2007) explains that 'asking the right questions' is needed to collect the appropriate information to make effective decisions in the organization. Key performance indicators (KPI) measure what is important for the organization and are derived from the organizational strategy. They are the key measures that the organization needs to monitor. For Amy, key performance indicators may include: number of customers this week, types of candles sold, percentage sales from different product ranges, and number of candles made. These data can be used to compare performance among organizations and identify areas to sustain or improve.

Data cleaning: Data cleaning is needed to ensure that the data on which the analysis is based are complete and consistent. This includes removing corrupt data, applying consistency checks to standardize values, and addressing problems with any missing values.

Data aggregation: The organization needs to explore data generated by different processes and operating divisions. The data from different systems therefore need to be aggregated. Enterprise resource planning systems facilitate the integration of business processes and the standardization of data, which provides a common data resource. Data marts store data in databases for a single department. Data warehouses aggregate data from different databases in the organization that can be used to support business intelligence. Data aggregation requires data definitions to be used consistently in different information systems to ensure that meaningful information can be derived from the data collected from different areas of the organization.

Data mining: Data mining refers to computational techniques that are used to gain insight from data. It provides the ability to extract information to facilitate knowledge discovery from the organization's databases.

Multidimensional modelling: This organizes data in terms of, for example, product and market or product, market, and region to enable relationships between data to be identified. Real-time business intelligence is used in e-business systems where customer data are continually analysed to present customers with more buying options based on their browsing and purchase history.

OnLine Analytical Processing (OLAP): OLAP tools enable multidimensional modelling of data. A data cube is created which can be explored by aggregating data, drilling down into the data, or slicing a section of the data. This enables potential relationships between data to be explored (discussed in Chapter 3).

Data visualization tools: A range of tools are available to improve the communication and analysis of large volumes of complex data. These include charts, graphs, geometric shapes, vector graphics, and spatial visualizations that create maps of the data to aid comparison between, for example, customer sales and satisfaction in different geographical regions. Tools enable data to be visually represented in a meaningful real-world context.

Dashboards provide a visual means of monitoring KPI using graphics such as meters, gauges, and speedometers. Dashboards differ in terms of the scope of data (such as function or organization), the frequency of updates (for example, real-time, hourly, weekly), and the ability to interact with the dashboard by drilling down into more detail or applying further filtering criteria to explore the factors influencing the performance reported. The metrics displayed on the dashboard reflect the factors that are important for the organization to monitor its performance. The factors are derived from the relationships defined in the business model, the strategic objectives, critical success factors, and the core values of the organization. Common features of dashboards include comparisons between regions, time periods, and forecasts, highlighting any anomalies. The challenge of dashboard design is how to represent potentially large volumes of information on a single display screen (Few, 2006). It is therefore important to understand the value of information to the organization.

Figure 14.5 shows how visual measures can be used to present information to Amy.

14.4.2 Transformation Dimensions of Business Intelligence

Business intelligence involves gathering data, making decisions, evaluating the decisions, and learning from the results. Software packages can be purchased to support these activities but it is important to ensure that the people who will use the data understand and

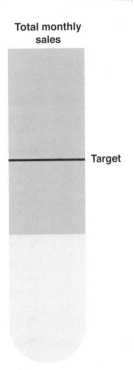

Total monthly sales

Target

Figure 14.5 Sales Performance Indicator

trust the source data that are used by the business intelligence tools. Training is needed in how to use the tools and how to incorporate the use of tools into business processes so that information is used and actioned. IT has a role to enable the data to be gathered, analysed, and presented but the organization needs to act on the data within a culture where the practice of creating and acting upon insights is developed. It requires a measurement approach to the strategic objectives of the organization. Insights gained through data analytics must be in a form where they can be used to have an impact on the organization at some level in order to have a value to the organization. Table 14.7 outlines the impact of business intelligence initiatives on the organizational architecture.

14.4.3 Role of Information Management in Business Intelligence

Business intelligence is dependent on the:

○ Source and quality of data.
○ Extraction of data from individual systems and the cleaning required to enable the data to be aggregated.
○ Data warehouse and data dimensions that can be supported.
○ Tools available to analyse and present the data.

Table 14.7 Organizational Transformation Initiated by Business Intelligence

Formal Organization Architecture	Informal Organization Architecture	Impact on Organization Architecture
Technology	Socio-technical	Software tools to support business intelligence are implemented in the organization that must be integrated with the existing data warehouses and databases. The tools need to be used to assist in organizational decision-making.
Security	Trust	Staff in the organization need to trust the accuracy of data presented by the tools and trust that the tools provide an accurate representation of the data. Security controls are needed to ensure data integrity is maintained and data are not disclosed to unauthorized staff through the business intelligence tools.
People	Skills	Additional skills are needed to install, maintain, and use the business intelligence tools. Training will include guidance on how to interpret data presented in a range of visual formats and how the tools can be used to explore multiple data dimensions.
Strategy	Vision	The tools should be aligned with the strategy of the organization, reporting key performance indicators that are consistent with the organization's vision. Insights gained from the business intelligence will provide information with which to monitor and improve performance and may identify opportunities to influence the direction of the organizational strategy.
Processes	Practices	Processes are required to access and make use of the data using the business intelligence tools. Existing practices will therefore need to be modified to accommodate the tools.
Systems	Human Activity Systems	The business intelligence tools will need to be integrated into the existing organizational information systems. This will require changes to existing systems.
Culture	Values	The potential benefits that may result from improved access and visualization data are dependent on the tools being used. The organizational culture therefore needs to adapt to the introduction of the tools. The design of the business intelligence system and KPI need to reflect the values of the organization.

Business intelligence tools provide a means of accessing data in different ways. The results of business intelligence can reveal unexpected relationships between data items from different systems.

Business intelligence starts by considering the type of business questions that need to be addressed. It is then necessary to consider what data are available in the organization and establish the:

O Scope of the data gathering. For example, data could be collated by function to support the fine tuning of daily processes in each function. Alternatively, data could be collected across business functions, which requires cooperation to share data among teams.

O Level of organizational decisions to be supported by the data analysed (such as strategic or operational).

O Timeline, that is, whether the purpose is to explore historic data, monitor current performance, or create future forecasts.

If the data required are not available it does not mean that data have not been collected as, for example, data might have been aggregated with other data (Janeert, 2011).

The role of information management in business intelligence includes:

O Contributing to determining what information the business needs and how this can be facilitated by business intelligence tools.

O Identifying the information that is available to be extracted from individual information systems to support business intelligence activities using the information architecture.

O Defining information so that it can be used and interpreted appropriately in multidimensional modelling using the data dictionary.

O Agreeing upon and implementing business integrity rules with data owners to provide a coherent and consistent data resource for business intelligence.

○ Cleaning data to ensure that the data are complete and consistent.

○ Ensuring accurate data of appropriate quality is available when needed.

○ Communicating the importance of data quality at the point of capture to support effective analysis of the data with business intelligence tools.

○ Maintaining the security of the data and the insights generated through business intelligence analysis.

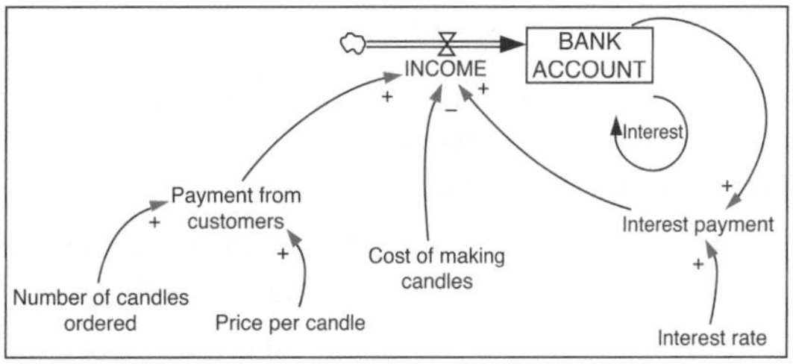

Figure 14.6 Simulation Model for Income Generation

14.5 Business Simulation

Although business innovation is important for an organization to remain competitive, the effectiveness of innovation can only be demonstrated in practice over a period of time. Business simulations provide a means of experimenting with potential *what if* time-related scenarios using models. Simulation models enable an accurate visual simulation of the performance of a system to be created. Dynamic models are used to represent the behaviour of systems to analyse the potential effectiveness of actions over time. Simulation models enable the effect of variables to be investigated using visualization and animation (Doomun & Jungum, 2008).

DEFINITION: A **simulation model** is an accurate model of a system in which the value of variables can be changed to visualize changes to the system over a period of time. It requires the factors that affect the performance of the system to be captured in the model.

Simulation enables potential scenarios to be explored with minimum cost and without impacting upon the current operation of the organization. Software packages are available which incorporate industry-specific simulation models. The models support critical evaluation in different future scenarios and provide a visual representation of the effects of changes to plans to support prediction through experimentation.

14.5.1 Types of Business Simulation

Feinstein and Parks (2002) categorize simulations as symbolic simulations, analytical simulations, instructional simulations used for training, and visual, auditory, or kinaesthetic representations such as flight simulators and video games.

Symbolic simulations replicate systems through mathematical processes in spreadsheets. Although spreadsheets provide a means to explore data, the realism of the simulation is limited.

Analytical simulations represent a phenomenon to support decision-making. Kleijnen and Smits (2003) identify two types of analytical simulation: systems dynamics

and discrete-event dynamic systems. Systems dynamics represent complex systems using interconnected feedback loops. Discrete-event dynamic systems explore a system as a series of sequential events. This type of simulation enables individual events to be explored with a range of uncertain variables (Kleijnen, 2005).

Business games have been used since World War I to provide opportunities to practice and develop skills such as decision-making in realistic contexts (Gilgeous & D'Cruz, 1996). A game is a structured activity providing entertainment which includes elements of challenge and interaction. Serious gaming adds a layer of multimedia animation over the simulation model (Cox, 2008). There is debate about whether animation adds value to a simulation. Some argue that it is the underlying mathematical model that is important, enabling the effect of changes to variables to be explored. Others argue that society increasingly has high expectations about the quality of multimedia resources and visual animation provides a richer and more realistic representation. Games provide the realism of considering a large number of interacting variables while at the same time allowing participants to gain insight into the effects of their actions within a changing and uncertain environment. Business games can provide a rich simulated environment in which to explore the potential impact of decisions and actions.

Simulation models can be used to:

○ Demonstrate the impact of a change in variables over time; the timeline is a key element of the model.

○ Facilitate causal tracing, identifying the variables that cause other variables to change.

○ Support system optimization.

○ Enable forecasting and risk analysis.

For example, Amy is considering using social media to market her products. She could use simulation models to explore a range of scenarios which support her strategic objectives. For example, Figure 14.6 shows an initial simulation model of income generation. Amy can explore her

Table 14.8 Organizational Transformation Initiated by Business Simulation

Formal Organization Architecture	Informal Organization Architecture	Impact on Organization Architecture
Technology	Socio-technical	A software package needs to be acquired in which to create and execute the simulation models. Use of the software needs to become integrated into decision-making processes.
Security	Trust	The simulation model comprises commercially sensitive information and therefore appropriate physical and technical security controls are needed to maintain confidentiality of the organization's plans. Staff are also trusted not to disclose the information to unauthorized parties.
People	Skills	The creation and use of a simulation model requires the ability to apply system dynamics to create business models. Training is needed in using the specific simulation software and skill is needed in creating, experimenting with, and evaluating realistic scenarios.
Strategy	Vision	The simulation model should relate to an aspect of business performance that is aligned with the organizational strategy. Analysis of potential scenarios may provide information that will require changes to the organizational strategy to reflect innovation or address external threats.
Processes	Practices	Changes are required to the existing decision-making processes in the organization to incorporate the development and use of simulation models. This will require staff to change their current practices in assessing plans and addressing problems. Additional actions may be required to capture the data needed to enter into the simulation model.
Systems	Human Activity Systems	The simulation model represents one or more current systems in the organization and changes may be required to systems as a result of the simulation analysis. The model enables the data going into systems to be explored and manipulated in the model to inform business plans.
Culture	Values	The simulation model provides a clinical representation of processes. The results of the simulation therefore need to be assessed within the cultural framework and values of the organization.

pricing strategy and develop the model to include special offers for customers interacting with her through social media. Amy can experiment by adding and changing variables to see how they might affect her income.

Simulation models provide a means of communication (Doomun & Jungum, 2008) to explore business options. However, issues to consider in simulation models include validation and verification of the model, the degree of sensitivity and robustness of the analysis, optimization of the model, and the degree of uncertainty (Kleijnen, 2005).

Link 14.2
Building a Simulation Model

14.5.2 Transformation Dimensions of Business Simulation

The use of business simulation requires the purchase of computer software in which to create the

simulation model and experiment with different scenarios.

The creation of a simulation model involves:

- Specifying the purpose of the model.
- Defining the boundaries of the system to be modelled.
- Collecting data.
- Developing the simulation model.
- Testing the model.
- Experimenting with variable values.
- Formulating proposals.
- Assessing proposals.

Human behaviour is more difficult to model than economic processes (Kleijnen, 2005). A limitation of simulation models is that they represent processes with limited consideration for the human element. It is therefore important to consider the results of the simulation in the broader cultural context of the organization. Table 14.8 outlines the potential impact on the organizational architecture of business simulation.

Table 14.9 Guidelines to Assess the Impact of Business Themes on Information Management

	Activities in the Life Cycle				Quality Characteristics	Integration Issues	Security Concerns
	Capture	Store and Retrieve	Use, Share, and Maintain	Archive and Destroy			
Key Questions	Is any additional information required? Are there changes to the way existing information is captured?	Are there any additional data to be stored? Will the existing storage and retrieval methods need to change?	How will data be used? Who will the data be shared with? How will the data be maintained?	How will the data be archived? How will the data be deleted?	Are the existing quality characteristics of the information sufficient?	Will any new information be integrated with existing information?	How is the security of information affected?

Table 14.10 Impact of Business Themes on Information Management

	Activities in the Life Cycle				Quality Characteristics	Integration Issues	Security Concerns
	Capture	Store and Retrieve	Use, Share, and Maintain	Archive and Destroy			
Knowledge Management	Need to introduce processes to capture explicit knowledge and a means of facilitating generation of tacit knowledge.	Need a means of storing and retrieving knowledge.	Need to use and share knowledge.	Need to archive explicit knowledge.	Information definitions need to be consistent to enable information to be shared.	No.	Need to ensure that information is only shared with authorized staff.
Social Media	Additional information will be captured from social media and will be created for use in social media.	Social media information will need to be stored and retrieved.	Processes are needed to use the social media information captured.	Processes needed to archive social media information.	Information presented on social media must be accurate.	Need to integrate social media data so that the data can be used.	Need to ensure that only authorized data are disclosed via social media.
Business Innovation	May need to capture additional information about external markets.	May need to store additional information. Innovative information generated will need to be stored.	Need to analyse information to assist in generation of new ideas.	Need to archive innovations.	Accurate information is needed to provide the foundation for innovation.	No.	Need to ensure confidentiality of commercially sensitive information.
Business Simulation	May need to capture additional information about external processes or internal processing statistics.	May need to store additional information. Need to store models developed.	Need to use existing information in the formation and testing of the simulation model.	Simulation models will need to be archived.	Information on which the models are developed needs to be accurate and consistent.	Existing information from different systems will need to be used in the simulation models.	Need to ensure security controls are maintained as information is integrated and that the confidentiality of the resulting analysis is maintained.

14.5.3 ► Role of Information Management in Business Simulation

The value of the simulation model is dependent on the quality and reliability of the information on which the model is built. Accurate and consistent information is therefore needed. The simulation may require additional internal or external information to be collected to be incorporated into the model. The role of information management in business simulation includes:

- Ensuring that quality information is available that can be used to develop the simulation model.
- Advising on data definitions to ensure that data are used appropriately in the simulation model.
- Identifying additional information that may be required by the simulation model.
- Defining information required by the model and adding it to the data dictionary.
- Capturing information required by the simulation.
- Integrating information collected with existing information sources.
- Categorizing information from the simulation as commercially sensitive.
- Establishing policies for the management of simulation data.

14.6 ► Assessing Impact of Business Themes on Information Management

Themes in business management focus on different approaches to generate and use information to improve decision-making. This may be through harnessing existing knowledge, generating information through activities (such as using social media), using tools to analyse information to gain new insights (such as business intelligence tools), or exploring potential scenarios (using simulation models). The impact on information management will therefore depend on which area of the information life cycle is affected. A framework is presented in Table 14.9 to assess the impact of business themes on information management. An example of how the framework may be applied to assess the impact of business themes discussed in this chapter on information management is presented in Table 14.10.

Summary

Information documents explicit knowledge. Knowledge management is a set of processes to create, share, and apply knowledge to support the learning organization. Social networks are communities that share information

and knowledge. Social media uses IT to facilitate communication in social networks. Analysis of social networks can identify where information is located and highlight communication flows that could be improved.

Business innovation is the creative application of knowledge to leverage value for organizations. There are a range of types of business innovation, affecting different aspects of the business model. Business innovation requires the organization to change, which may change the organization's requirements for information, and change how information is captured and used in the organization. Business intelligence is a set of processes and tools to extract meaning from data and is dependent on effective information management practices. Business intelligence tools provide a means of accessing data in different ways. Simulation models enable time-related scenarios to be developed. All these business developments are dependent on the availability of consistent and reliable data. In addition, the developments offer new ways of interacting with data and information, therefore the impact on information management needs to be considered at each stage in the information life cycle.

Reviewing Scenario 14.1

Social media is a powerful tool for engaging directly with customers and potential customers. There is a range of social media options which vary in terms of the type of information exchanged. Examples of how Amy could use social media include:

- Keeping customers up to date with new arrivals such as 'new spring shades just arrived' or 'a batch of sky blue pillar candles with a star design are now ready for sale' via a blog.
- Providing information about how Amy makes her candles via social media websites.
- Seeking feedback on her designs via a forum.
- Creating a game, such as how many candles can be lit in a time limit, which could be downloaded from her website.
- Informing customers that their order is ready for collection or has been dispatched, by instant messages.

Amy could also use social media with her suppliers, for example, to

- Discuss issues with mould designs.
- Collaborate on the design and development of new types of mould.
- Provide feedback on the popularity of colours and types of wax.

○ Identify the need for new colours of wax to be added to the range.

○ Report problems with the quality of products.

Cloze Exercise 14.1

Complete the following paragraph by choosing the correct word from Table 14.11 to fill in each gap.

data when needed. Both types of tool rely on clean and consistent data to be available for _____.

Key performance indicators can be used to monitor the progress of the organizational _____. The indicators can be visually represented using _____. IT can be used to capture, analyse, and present data but _____ needs to be taken in response to the information generated. The

Table 14.11 ▸Words to Complete Cloze Exercise 14.1

Action	Context	Knowledge	Practice	Simulation
Analysis	Dashboards	Language	Pull	Spreadsheet
Boundaries	Explicit	Learning	Push	Strategy
Business	Innovation	Media	Richness	Tacit
Communication	Intelligence	Networks	Security	Transformational

Knowledge involves the interpretation of information within the _____ of what is already known. A _____ organization is committed to using knowledge to learn from experience. _____ knowledge refers to knowledge which is difficult to put into words and _____ knowledge includes the documentation of procedures within which knowledge gained from experience is embedded and encoded. This requires a shared _____ of terms to provide the context for knowledge to be shared and used. Information technology provides the tools to store explicit knowledge and share tacit knowledge with others within communities of _____.

Social _____ emerge through connections among individuals to share information. Analysis of social networks can show where the _____ of information may be improved. Social _____ networks use Web 2.0 technology to create online communities where information content can be created and shared. The informality of social media networks poses a threat to information _____ as there is a risk that staff may unwittingly disclose unauthorized information in these networks.

Business _____ is achieved by the creative application of knowledge. This may result in incremental changes to existing products or processes, or _____ change, which challenges existing _____ of concepts and processes. Different types of innovation target different aspects of the _____ model. Business _____ involves extracting information from data to generate knowledge and facilitate business innovation. It requires data to be interpreted within the context of existing _____. Reporting tools _____ data, alerting staff when specified situations arise. Querying tools enable staff to interrogate and _____

potential impact of taking, or not taking, action can be explored using _____ models. An example of a symbolic simulation is a _____ which enables limited *what if* analysis on mathematical data. Serious games add a layer of animation over the simulation model, increasing the _____ of information in the scenario.

Link 14.3
Answers to Cloze Exercise 14.1

Activities 14.1

1   Consider an area in which you are knowledgeable and give an example of how the concepts of know-what, know-how, know-why, and know-who apply to your knowledge.

2   Apply the knowledge management processes from Table 14.1 to Amy's Candles.

3   Provide an example of single-loop learning and double-loop learning from Amy's Candles.

4   Create an audit of the interactions among individuals in a group with which you are familiar and draw a diagram to support analysis of the interactions (similar to Figure 14.1).

5   Find examples of different social media sites and compare how they facilitate the creation and sharing of information content.

6   Give an example of customer relationship innovation from an organization of which you are a customer.

7 Design a dashboard to enable Amy to monitor some of the key performance indicators mentioned in Section 14.4.1.

8 Figure 14.6 provides a basic simulation model. What additional factors may affect Amy's income generation and need to be included in the model?

Discussion Questions 14.1

1 Can an organization learn or can only individuals learn?

2 Is there one IT-based knowledge management system or do all IT-based systems contribute to knowledge management in the organization?

3 For each type of innovation shown in Figure 14.3, consider whether they are most likely to be driven by: technology push, market pull, market pull and technology push, or collaboration.

4 To what extent can the complexity of organizational performance be captured in a visual dashboard? What are their limitations?

5 Which form of social media is most suitable for Amy to engage with her customers and why?

6 How can simulation models be used to aid strategic organizational decisions? What are the limitations of simulation models?

INFORMATION THEMES

Scenario 15.1

Personalized Information at Bright Spark

Larry Hughes, the owner of the Bright Spark retail light fitting chain, is reviewing the organization's website. The marketing team conducted a pilot study of sending emails to existing customers to advertise special offers. Although this prompted customers to browse the website, it did not have a significant impact on sales. The information provided to customers on the website therefore needs to be improved. Larry has seen how other companies have used personalized information on their websites and is considering how this might be used at Bright Spark.

What changes will Bright Spark need to make in order to provide a personalized shopping experience for their customers?

Learning Outcomes

The learning outcomes of this chapter are to:

- Outline the challenges of multimedia information.
- Introduce the semantic web.
- Identify the elements of personalized information.
- Define models for exploring the context of information.
- Assess the challenges of providing remote access to information.
- Determine the information management issues arising from information developments.

Introduction

Organizations need to be able to retrieve meaningful information on demand to support business processes and strategic decisions. This chapter explores a number of information themes which strive to provide individuals with more meaningful information. Multimedia information is first considered; this poses particular challenges in how information is indexed and retrieved. The semantic web is then introduced which aims to encode meaning to provide richer information from search requests.

Sets of factors are identified determining the characteristics of the context in which information is requested to assist in providing more personalized information in response to search requests. A context box is then presented to explore the elements which construct the context in which information is interpreted and given meaning. Location is one aspect of context and the challenges of providing remote access to information are considered. The chapter concludes by providing guidelines to assess the impact on information management of these information themes.

15.1 ▶ Multimedia Information

The term *multimedia* literally means more than one media component, but the term is often used to refer to any nontext-based material such as photographs and sound recordings. The term *multimedia object* refers to an artefact that incorporates one or more of the following: audio, visual, or interactive elements. Organizations increasingly need to create and manage a range of multimedia objects, such as logos, product images, product demonstrations, and promotional videos that can be incorporated into Internet-based resources. The core principles of information management apply to multimedia information though nontext-based content introduces additional challenges, particularly in relation to storage and retrieval.

15.1.1 Challenges of Managing Multimedia Information

Structured data in a database comprise a series of fields defined in the data dictionary; each field stores a data value as shown in Figure 15.1. The fields enable data to be retrieved in response to queries such as: What media objects were captured in March 2013? How many media objects relate to the location 'Oxford'? Who has captured photographs?

A multimedia object comprises:

○ A data element, which refers to the physical representation of the object, (such as file type) and provenance of the object (such as the date of creation) shown in Figure 15.1.
○ An information element that relates to the content of the object. This is subjective and therefore more difficult to define.

A key issue is how to describe the content of a multimedia object so that the object can be located when needed. An index provides information about the data or information element of a multimedia object, predicting the search criteria that someone may use to locate the multimedia object.

Indexing and retrieving multimedia objects involve translations:

○ The indexer seeks to identify the characteristics of the multimedia content that may be used to describe it and translates these characteristics into keywords.

○ The retriever seeks to define the required characteristics of the content they need and translates their requirements into terms that can be used to search for the multimedia object.

Figure 15.2 shows that assigning responsibility for specifying the index to one individual requires their perception of the object to be representative of the way in which an individual will later search for the object. The concepts of semantic and articulatory distance were introduced in Chapter 4. Articulatory distance refers to the abstraction (loss of information content) between reality and a model of reality. Richness is also lost between an individual's perception of reality and the ability to represent that perception using a modelling language (referred to as the semantic distance). The processes of indexing and retrieving information involve minimizing these distances.

Multimedia objects can be indexed by (1) their creator, (2) the individuals using the objects, (3) an information professional using tools such as the Library of Congress Thesaurus for Graphic Materials, or (4) automated tools. Automated indexing tools include vision systems, neural network, and markup languages (Rafferty & Hidderley, 2005).

Vision systems identify and classify objects in an image using object recognition. An object is located in an image and the attributes of the object are compared against predefined attributes. In contrast to this approach of defining the attributes of an object, neural networks

Entity Name: MEDIA_OBJECT			
Entity Definition: Multimedia artefacts that are licensed for use by Bright Spark.			
Attribute Name	**Attribute Definition**	**Attribute Length and Type**	**Attribute Structure**
Date_created	This is the date the media object was created.	9(6)	DD:MM:YY
Created_by	Person creating the object.	X(15)	Surname, Initial.
Media_type	Type of media (such as photograph or video).	X(10)	String of characters.
Location	Locality where media object was created.	X(20)	String of characters.
Example Data Values of MEDIA_OBJECT			
Date_created	**Created_by**	**Media_type**	**Location**
080513	Hughes, L.	Photograph	Oxford

Figure 15.1 Structured Data

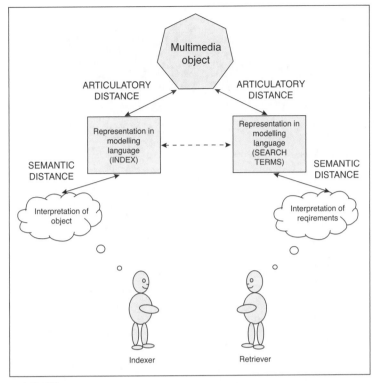

Figure 15.2 Indexing and Retrieving Information

discover the attributes of an object through a learning process. A neural network is trained to recognize objects from a set of example images. The neural network identifies generalizations from the examples presented and applies the generalizations it has learnt when presented with a new object to recognize the type of object. Neural networks are used to identify diseases using medical images. An alternative approach to indexing is the use of markup languages, such as XML discussed in Chapter 3, that provide a structured means to index and retrieve multimedia objects. Examples include markup languages for music (Steyn, 2013), image (Lober *et al.*, 2001), and video (Zhou & Jin, 2003).

The value of information depends on its accessibility and availability when needed but the need for information is subjective and dynamic which increases the difficulty of indexing media objects. Rafferty and Hidderley (2005, p. 179) propose a three-level template for indexing still and moving images. The first level of the template refers to biographical elements of the image (the data elements of the image such as provenance) and structural elements (such as significant objects in the image and their relationship). The second level classifies the objects identified in level one. The third

level interprets the mood of the overall image and the objects in the image. The template is used for democratic indexing where individuals using the multimedia objects contribute to the indexing task. Table 15.1 provides an example of how the template may be used to index the image in Figure 15.3.

Link 15.1
Making Sense of Data Poster

Additional challenges to managing multimedia information are posed by the size and nature of the media. Media files can be very large to store and transmit, and a range of file types may be used. The file type used to store media needs to be considered in terms of the availability of the hardware and software required to view, hear, or interact with the media object.

Multimedia information can be acquired and shared quickly and easily via the Internet. This has advantages for organizations seeking to promote their products and services but legal issues must be considered. While an understanding of the legal issues surrounding personal data are becoming established in organizations, the ease

Figure 15.3 Example Image

Table 15.1 Application of Indexing Template to Figure 15.3

Level and Category	Example Indexing of Figure 15.3
1.1 Biographical	Author: Cox, S. Designer: Easthope, C. Title: Making Sense of Data. Date: 18 July 2012. Presented at: Annual Research Conference at Birmingham City University, UK.
1.2 Structural Contents	2 Robots. Context Box, bottom right. Logo.
2.1 Overall Content	Cartoon.
2.2 Object Content	2 Freestyle Robots. Birmingham City University Logo.
3.1 Interpretation of Whole Image	Fun, colourful.
3.2 Interpretation of Objects	Robot puzzled. Robot menacing.

of access to nontextual information can lead to staff placing less significance on the legality of using multimedia information. For example, images on the Internet can be easily copied into presentations with little thought given to the ownership of the image and whether the organization has a legal right to use the image. Organizations need to ensure staff use multimedia information within the legal constraints and protect the multimedia information that it owns through the use of digital rights management methods. Digital rights management methods use technology to:

○ Authenticate access by requiring, for example, persistent online connectivity to identify the devices accessing the material. This is often used by game providers to ensure that only licensed copies are used.

○ Limit access by restricting the number of times material can be accessed; for example, software purchased online may only be downloaded a defined number of times.

○ Demonstrate ownership and hinder usage of material through the use of watermarks, for example, in images.

15.1.2 Transformation Dimensions of Multimedia Information

Multimedia objects provide a means to communicate information and facilitate interaction. For example, Bright Spark could develop a video game to be included on their website to encourage interaction with customers. Changes are needed in organizations to create and use multimedia objects effectively. Table 15.2 outlines the impact on the organizational architecture of multimedia information.

15.1.3 Role of Information Management in Multimedia Information

Multimedia provides a means to communicate information and offers the opportunity to convey greater semantic richness of information, exceeding the limits of textual information. The fundamental elements of information management to capture, securely store, and provide access to information apply to multimedia information. The specific challenges of managing multimedia information relate to the technical use of the media and the greater potential for the information

Table 15.2 Organizational Transformation Initiated by Multimedia Information

Formal Organization Architecture	Informal Organization Architecture	Impact on Organization Architecture
Technology	Socio-technical	IT is needed to create, index, retrieve, play and use multimedia objects. Staff will need training in the use of the technology and guidance on how to index and retrieve multimedia objects.
Security	Trust	Legal issues relating to digital rights management must be considered. This includes the use of technology to protect the organization's digital assets and trust that staff will not use materials that the organization is not authorized to use.
People	Skills	The creation of multimedia objects requires technical and creative skills in specific media. Skill is also necessary to use multimedia to effectively communicate, engage, and interact both with staff in the organization and with external parties such as customers.
Strategy	Vision	The use of multimedia information needs to be consistent with the organization's strategy. Multimedia can be used, for example, to support a strategy of improved communication with customers using viral marketing.
Processes	Practices	Additional processes may be required to create, index, retrieve, and use multimedia objects. Changes to practice will be needed to incorporate the use of multimedia information into existing communication-based activities.
Systems	Human Activity Systems	Content management systems enable multimedia objects to be easily and consistently incorporated into information content. This requires commitment to use the available media.
Culture	Values	Multimedia information must convey information that is consistent with the values of the organization. Cultural change may be needed to raise the profile of multimedia information and use multimedia effectively in the organization.

to meet diverse and unpredictable needs. Information management needs to:

- Assist in defining the organization's requirement for multimedia information.
- Provide guidelines relating to the creation and use of multimedia objects to facilitate content management.
- Define the approach to be used for indexing multimedia objects.
- Provide guidance on how to search for multimedia information in the organization.
- Develop standards for the creation and use of media file types to address issues of compatibility and interoperability of media content.
- Contribute to the development of the organization's digital rights management processes.
- Ensure that the use of multimedia content adheres to the relevant legal requirements.
- Implement appropriate measures to protect the organization's digital media assets.

15.2 Semantic Information

Floridi (2005) defines information as a set of data that is well formed, meaningful, and truthful. Semantics is the study of meaning; in information management semantics are concerned with how meaning is derived from data. Information management seeks to provide access to information that is semantically rich. Semantic richness refers to the amount of meaning that is embedded in, and can be derived from, information. Kounios *et al.* (2009) define semantic richness as the amount of meaning associated with a concept in the brain. Pexman *et al.* (2007) suggest that semantic richness can be measured by the number of:

- Descriptive features of a concept.
- Associations that can be made from the concept.
- Semantic neighbours (words with a similar meaning such as *customer* and *client*).

From a neurological perspective it has been found that information that is semantically rich is quicker and easier for humans to process. However, there is debate as to whether this is due to improved cognitive activation (Pexman *et al.*, 2007) or decision processing (Kounios *et al.*, 2009). The semantics of information requires humans to interpret and make sense of information. This is achieved through shared languages, shared experiences, and identifying the context of the situation within which the information should be interpreted.

15.2.1 Semantic Information Models

Communication of information requires a shared language within which meanings are understood by the individuals

creating, indexing, searching, and using the information. Although words are the most common vehicle for communicating information, words can have different meanings in different contexts. For example:

- Heteronyms are words that are spelt the same but are pronounced differently and have different meanings. For example, *content* can mean a level of happiness (the owner of Bright Spark was content with the performance of the company) or the constitute elements of something (the information content of the report).
- Homonyms are words that are either spelt or pronounced the same but have different meanings, such as *read* (the owner asked the accountant to read the report; the accountant read the report), and *reed* (the reed grew [plant]; a reed instrument [music]; a reed switch [electronics]).

Textual language is one example of a modelling language used to communicate ideas, instructions and information. Multimedia provides the opportunity to enrich communication through additional layers of meaning. Table 15.3 provides examples of interpretive characteristics which may be used to make sense of a meeting between Larry Hughes and one of his employees. Observing the meeting or an audio-visual recording of the meeting provides the opportunity for auditory and visual clues to be interpreted, providing a richer understanding of the communication in the meeting.

Multimedia can convey greater richness of information than is possible in textual information because while powerful, words can be misinterpreted and only represent one level of communication. Sound and image offer the potential to communicate ideas in a manner which is closer to the real world. For example, a video of the meeting described in Table 15.3 can communicate more information than a textual description of the same meeting. A detailed description would be long and probably incomplete. An image can also convey more strongly the atmosphere and context within which the meeting took place. However, multimedia is interpreted and can therefore be misinterpreted.

15.2.2 Semantic Web

In searching for multimedia objects, the accuracy of the search results is determined by the perceived relevance of the results returned by the search query (Rafferty & Hidderley, 2005). Encoding semantic information provides a means of encoding knowledge about a domain into a form that can be used by information technology (IT) to retrieve information. The Internet can be regarded as a network of pages of documents. When searching for information on the Internet, documents containing the specified search terms are retrieved. These documents

Table 15.3 Examples of Layers of Meaning

Element of Communication	Interpretive Characteristics	Example Narrative
Text	Words used. Consistency. Repetition. Flow.	Tone of phrases used in the meeting expressing the level of seriousness of situation.
Speech	Intonation. Volume. Flow (smoothness, speed).	Tone in which the words are expressed, such as frustration.
Sound	Pitch. Volume. Intensity. Quality.	Emotional expression such as angry or apologetic.
Nonverbal	Facial expression. Body language. Gestures. Behaviour.	Expressions such as sternness and worry. Crossed arms suggesting employee is defensive. Finger-pointing to emphasize a point.
Actions	Movement. Interaction. Response. Speed. Flow.	Writing notes to document the meeting. Standing to indicate the meeting has ended. Leaving the room quickly to escape the situation.
Relationships	Positional. Role (for example, authority, power). Nature (for example, supportive, confrontational, competitive).	Location of people (for example, sitting separated by a desk). Hierarchical (for example, manager and subordinate). Reprimanding.
Context	Background. Location. Circumstances.	Events that happened before the meeting (such as a customer complaint). Where the meeting is taking place. Perceived significance of events (for example, customers have previously complained about the member of staff).

are then interpreted by the individual conducting the search to identify the information required.

The semantic web is a vision in which data on the Internet are defined so that computers can understand the relationships between data in a similar way to humans. It seeks to structure meaningful content (Berners-Lee et al., 2001) and establish a network of data rather than a network of documents. This would improve the ability to search for related information about a topic.

DEFINITION: The **semantic web** aims to encode data so that information technology (IT) can search and retrieve data in a meaningful way. Data are decoupled from web pages so that data, rather than web pages, are retrieved in response to information searches.

A number of technologies can be used to encode meaning, such as the resource description framework (RDF).

RDF enables meaning of data to be encoded within a structure of triples, defining the relationship between sets of three elements (Berners-Lee et al., 2001). A triple statement comprises (1) the concept being described (the subject of the statement), (2) the properties of the concept (the predicate), and (3) the values of the properties (the object), shown in Table 15.4. RDF is written using the markup language XML (introduced in Chapter 3). An example RDF statement is shown in Table 15.5.

Table 15.4 Example of a Triple Statement

Subject:	Poster
Predicate:	Creator
Object:	Cox
The triple describes a *poster* as having a *creator* called *Cox*.	

Table 15.5 Example RDF Statement

RDF	Comment
<?xml version="1.0"?>	Statement of the version of XML being used.
<rdf:RDF xmlns:rdf="http://www.w3.org/1999/02/22-rdf-syntax-ns#"	Opening RDF Tag.
xmlns:poster=http://www.ISDABS.co.uk/poster>	Any tag beginning with *poster* is referring to the vocabulary defined at this namespace.
<rdf:Description rdf:about= "http://www.ISDABS.co.uk/poster#Poster – making_sense_of_data">	The poster identified as *making sense of data* is going to be described.
<poster:creator>Cox</poster:creator>	The poster has a creator identified as *Cox*.
</rdf:Description>	End of description.
</rdf:RDF>	Closing RDF Tag.

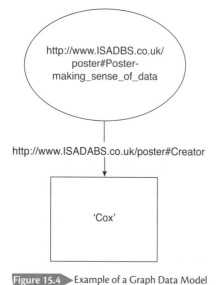

Figure 15.4 Example of a Graph Data Model

RDF enables the features of data to be described but the features can also be shown in a graph data model (Figure 15.4). Recchia and Jones (2012) suggest that the descriptive features are important for describing concrete concepts but the meaning of abstract concepts is more reliant on the associations with other words in a context.

Ontologies classify concepts and the relationships between them in a specific domain, providing an agreed use of terms to capture, index and retrieve information. The Web Ontology Language (known as OWL) is a set of languages which can be used to describe classes of concepts and the relationships between them in an ontology. It is an extension of RDF and is based on first-order predicate logic enabling the implications of facts to be discovered. In a standard database, the facts represented in the database are returned in response to a query. In contrast, OWL draws inferences from the data. OWL adopts the open world assumption, which states that a

statement is only known to be false if it can be proven that the statement is false. This means that if a statement is not proven to be true, it is not assumed to be false. In contrast, the closed world assumption adopts the stance that if a statement is not known to be true, then the statement is assumed to be false. Table 15.6 provides an example of two classes described in OWL which are represented graphically in Figure 15.5. It is known that Mrs Lewis is

Table 15.6 Example of Classes in OWL

OWL	Comment
<owl:Class rdf:ID="Bright_Spark"/>	There is a class of objects that is identified as Bright Spark.
<owl:Class rdf:ID="accountants"/>	There is a class of objects that is identified as accountants.
<owl:Accountants rdf:ID="Mrs Lewis"/>	Mrs Lewis is in the class of accountants (that is, Mrs Lewis is an accountant).

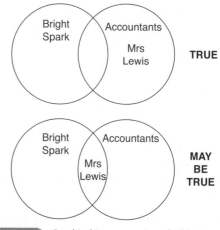

Figure 15.5 Graphical Representation of Table 15.6

Table 15.7 Comparison of OWL and Traditional Database Response to Queries

Query	Traditional Database Response	OWL Response
Is Mrs Lewis an accountant?	Yes	Yes
Is Mrs Lewis employed by Bright Spark?	No	Maybe

in the class accountant, but it is not known (in the OWL statements) whether she is an accountant at Bright Spark. Table 15.7 demonstrates how OWL inferences differ from traditional database queries in dealing with this situation. OWL provides a means of representing, reasoning with and exchanging knowledge.

15.2.3 Transformation Dimensions of Semantic Information

Improving the semantic richness of information in organizations requires four main challenges to be addressed.

First, organizations need to develop a rich understanding of information and the relationships between information in their specific domain. Second, this understanding needs to be encoded through the development of ontologies and RDF descriptors. Third, organizations need to develop appropriate processes and practices to make use of the information. Fourth, consideration needs to be given to exploring ways in which information can be communicated and used beyond the traditional use of text. This includes, for example, the use of multimedia and effective content management tools. Table 15.8 outlines the impact on the organizational architecture of addressing these challenges of encoding semantic information.

15.2.4 Role of Information Management in Semantic Information

Information management has a primary role in establishing the infrastructure to facilitate the encoding of semantic information. This includes:

○ Assisting data owners in the development of domain ontologies.

Table 15.8 Organizational Transformation Initiated by Encoding Semantic Information

Formal Organization Architecture	Informal Organization Architecture	Impact on Organization Architecture
Technology	Socio-technical	Technologies such as ontologies and RDF need to be introduced to encode the meaning of information and relationships between information in the organization.
Security	Trust	Encoding the meaning of information enables technology to be used to interpret information content. Business sensitive information may be encoded and it is essential that appropriate security controls are in place to avoid unauthorized access to the information. Staff in the organization need to trust the information that is retrieved by IT systems, otherwise the information will not be used.
People	Skills	People in organizations interpret information and endow it with meaning. Individuals need to be willing to encode their understanding of the information and develop skill in translating the meaning of information into appropriate modelling languages.
Strategy	Vision	The process of encoding the meaning of information may help to improve the understanding of information in the organization and improve the accessibility of information. This may result in information being identified which provides further insight into the organization and influences the direction of the organization's strategy.
Processes	Practices	Additional processes will be needed in the organization to define, agree upon, and encode the meaning of information. Current practices may need to change to use IT to search for information that has been encoded and to ensure that information is used appropriately to support decision-making.
Systems	Human Activity Systems	New IT systems may be introduced, or existing systems changed, to facilitate improved access to information. Current organizational systems may need to be changed to make use of the ability to locate and use related information when needed.
Culture	Values	The semantic web seeks to improve access to information and this may challenge the culture of how information is accessed and the role of IT in the organization. It is therefore important that the encoding of meaning of information is aligned with the values of the organization.

○ Seeking agreement of the technologies (such as RDF, OWL) to be used in encoding meaning.

○ Developing standards for the format and structure of information to be encoded.

○ Arranging training in the use of modelling languages for indexing and retrieving semantic information.

○ Providing guidance on how semantic information can be used to improve the retrieval of related information.

○ Facilitating the integration of externally available data with existing internal ontologies.

○ Assisting in formulating queries, translating business requirements into search queries.

○ Ensuring appropriate security classifications are used to secure the business sensitive information.

15.3 ▶ Personalized Information

Important information can be overlooked in the vast volumes of information available in the organization. Personalized information is one approach to address the problem of information overload. Information retrieval searches for core information that satisfies the requirements specified in a request for information. Personalizing information uses additional layers to filter the core information that satisfies the initial information request to ensure that the information presented meets the specific requirements of an individual. The ability to personalize information requires browsing agents to understand the semantic contents of web pages and match content to personal interests (Antoniou et al., 2012).

Personalization and customization are approaches to segment a domain to more closely target the specific information requirements of an individual. Personalization is a continuous activity adapting to additional information collected about the individual and the larger community with similar profiling aspects to the individual. In contrast, customization is a discrete activity enabling an individual to select from a static set of variables.

Personalization is initiated by the organization and customization is initiated by the customer (Arora et al., 2008), the individual requesting the information. In the context of online shopping, an organization may provide personalized recommendations to a customer based on their purchase history and that of other customers who have purchased the same product and have similar buying patterns. A customer may customize the organization's offerings to meet their specific needs by selecting optional features available in the manufacture of a product. Personalizing information is part of customer relationship management. It can be used to develop and sustain a relationship with existing customers to encourage repeat business.

Personalization and customization also to apply information requests. A request for the last quarter's regional sales figures may return information *personalized* for the specific region of the manager requesting the information. The manager may then *customize* the presentation of the information by selecting attributes such as product type or product price across the region.

15.3.1 ▶ Personalization Characteristics

There are a number of factors that affect the information an individual requires and an individual's satisfaction with the information provided to them. Personalizing information responds to an individual's request for information by considering elements relating to the context within which the information is requested.

Figure 7.1 presented three interrelated sets of elements which form the context for information requirements: (1) characteristics of the recipient, (2) characteristics of the device used to form the request, and (3) characteristics of the information available. Nicholas and Herman (2009) and Herman and Nicholas (2010) identify a number of factors that determine the need for information. These factors (and others) have been grouped in Table 15.9 in relation to the individual profile, the information profile, and the device profile to inform the context of the information request.

The context profile of the information request is used to personalize the information presented to an individual. Figure 15.6 illustrates a coffee pot approach to information retrieval. Indexed information that an individual has authorized access to is funnelled into a series of filters. The filters remove information that is unwanted or nonessential, allowing richer, more personalized information to be collected for consumption. Information to which an individual has access is funnelled through a series of filters that include the ontology of terms in the domain, the information that others with a similar profile have accessed, the personal preferences of the individual, and the specific context of the information request.

15.3.2 ▶ Challenges of Personalization

Personalization aims to provide more relevant information to an individual in response to their request for information. This will reduce the time taken to search for the required information and reduce the volume of information presented to an individual to use. Personalization also reduces the time taken in decision-making (de Pechpeyrou, 2009). However, there is a risk

Table 15.9 Factors Affecting Information Need

Individual Profile	Information Profile	Device Profile	Context Profile
Age. Country of origin and cultural background. Gender. Personality traits. Work role and tasks.	Date and currency. Information availability and accessibility. Intellectual level. Nature of the information. Place of publication or origin. Processing and packaging of the information. Quality and authority. Quantity. Subject of the information. Viewpoint.	Type. Screen size. Input method. Data transmission method. Data transmission speed. Storage capacity. Processing capacity.	Date and time. Location. Cost. Function for which information is to be used. Resources available. Speed of delivery. Time available.

Source: Based on Nicholas and Herman (2009) and Herman and Nicholas (2010).

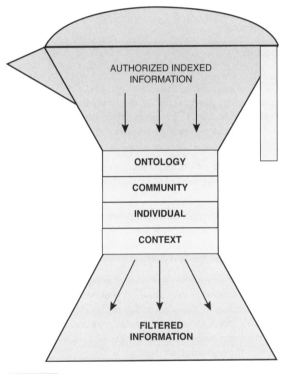

Figure 15.6 Funnel and Filter Information

that information that the individual may perceive as being valuable is rejected by the filtering process and not presented to them. The process of narrowly defining individual profiles risks limiting flexibility and does not consider the potential value of how something different can challenge and influence human thinking. For example, if a customer purchased a lilac lampshade from Bright Spark's website, the next time the customer returned to the website they may be shown other lilac lampshades or other lilac light fittings. Personalization helps customers

find items that meet their needs and has a positive impact on the consumer experience (de Pechpeyrou, 2009). However, the customer may have made the purchase for a specific reason (such as a present for someone) and may no longer be interested in similar purchases. The perception of poor or inappropriate purchase recommendations can lead to customer dissatisfaction and lack of trust in the retailer.

As personalization tailors information provision to individuals, it relies on the willingness of the individual to share information and the organization's ability to capture and use the information (Chellappa & Sin, 2005). Consumer policies are needed to build trust, enabling consumers to control what personal data are collected about them and how the data are used. Zhou (2011) recommends that in order to mitigate consumer concerns about their privacy, practices need to be regulated and consumers need to be informed about how their privacy is protected, for example, by displaying privacy statements on websites. The benefits of personalized information need to be considered against the degree of privacy that is lost.

15.3.3 Transformation Dimensions of Personalized Information

Personalization includes three stages:

○ Creating the individual profile by collecting the characteristics of the individual and their specific information requirements. This may be based on the current requirement, the profile of the individual developed over time, and the information needs of individuals with a similar historic profile.

○ Creating the information profile by describing data using characteristics that may be needed to search and filter related information.

○ Matching the individual profile and the information profile with the device profile.

This requires related work in information retrieval, ontologies, and contextual information to be brought together. Table 15.10 outlines the impact on the organizational architecture of addressing these challenges of personalizing information.

15.3.4 ▶ **Role of Information Management in Personalized Information**

Personalizing information delivery requires an understanding to be developed about the factors that add perceived value to information delivered to an individual. Characteristics of information that can be used to identify information that may be of interest in specific circumstances need to be defined and documented, enabling the characteristics to be used to search and filter potential information. Information management can assist an organization in personalizing information delivery by:

○ Defining characteristics of information that can be used in searching for information.
○ Ensuring that the information architecture is sufficiently flexible to facilitate personalization.
○ Establishing procedures for documenting information in a manner to improve information retrieval.
○ Formulating standards for describing characteristics of information using, for example, RDF.
○ Identifying the individual characteristics that influence the requirements for information which need to be included in a personal profile.

Table 15.10 ▶ Organizational Transformation Initiated by Personalizing Information

Formal Organization Architecture	Informal Organization Architecture	Impact on Organization Architecture
Technology	Socio-technical	Some changes may be needed to technology (such as cookies) to capture the information needed to develop and maintain personal profiles. This requires individuals to accept the use of such technology and be willing to provide personal information that can be used to develop and maintain personal profiles.
Security	Trust	Individuals will need to trust that information will not be collected or used without their prior permission and changes to security may be needed to ensure that the security of the information collected will be maintained.
People	Skills	People need to be willing to provide the information needed to develop profiles. Skills are needed to identify the aspects of context and individual preferences that could contribute to developing a personal profile. Skills in data mining are needed to identify patterns of activity that can be used in personalizing information delivery.
Strategy	Vision	The collection of information about customer and purchases may provide a rich source of data that can be used to improve understanding of the customer's relationship with the organization that may identify new directions for the organization to consider. It can also support the organization's strategy in relation to being customer-focused; improving the provision of information to staff in the organization may improve decision-making and overall effectiveness towards achieving the organization's vision.
Processes	Practices	Additional processes are needed to capture information to create profiles, filter information against profiles, and assess the effectiveness of the personalized information provided. This may require changes to current ways of working to capture the information requirements.
Systems	Human Activity Systems	Changes to information systems may be needed to enable information about individuals to be captured and maintained. This information then needs to be used to improve the delivery of information that meets an individual's requirements. Further information then needs to be collected to assess whether the personalized information provided meets the individual's requirements and whether it has an impact on decision-making and overall organizational performance.
Culture	Values	Personalizing information delivered to customers provides a more customer-focused culture and requires customers to be viewed as individuals with similar profiles. The information captured and used to filter information needs to be consistent with the values of the organization.

- Assisting the organization in the formulation of meaningful search requests.
- Advising on the use of tools to assist individuals in customizing information reports and using configurable interfaces.
- Developing processes to assess the effectiveness of the personalized information retrieved.
- Formulating policies for the ethical use of personal information.
- Providing guidance on legal issues relating to the collection of personal data.

15.4 Contextual Information

Vast volumes of data can be collected, either input from individuals or captured using sensors such as temperature sensors and energy-monitoring devices. The challenge is how to make sense of the data and use the data to inform decision-making. This requires an understanding of both the context in which the data were captured and the context in which the information derived is to be used.

The word *context* is widely used in information management as it is at the heart of the definition of information. Information is derived from interpreting data within a context; information only has meaning, and is only given meaning, in a particular context. It is taken for granted that *context* is understood, but the definition of the term and, more precisely, how to define a specific context is still elusive. In the broadest sense, context is defined by keywords that are related to the data being collected, providing clues about how to interpret the data.

Context emerges from a set of conditions within which meaning can be interpreted. The business model provides an overall context for organizational information. Context is a dynamic setting comprising a number of elements that affect the interpretation and value of information. In contrast, a situation is a set of contextual variables with a given state at a specific time.

Contextual information is an extension of personalized information and uses IT to capture data about the environment in which an individual is currently situated. Context-based systems identify and predict the information needs of an individual by extracting key features of the individual and his or her current context to search for potentially relevant information. This requires information systems to be context-aware and adapt to changes as appropriate.

Information is presented to the individual based on the values of predefined factors, defining the context in which the information is needed. This requires the factors that define a context to be identified and the interrelationship

between them understood. In Section 15.3.1, context was identified as being influenced by three profiles: the individual, the information, and the device. The context of the information request emerges from the interaction between the individual and other factors such as the time, role, and goals of the individual.

Defining a context provides a series of filters through which to refine the presentation of information to an individual. Location-based systems are an example of context awareness, defining context using attributes such as location and time. They respond to changes in an individual's location and adapt the information that can be pushed or pulled to the individual, for example, tourist systems provide information about local attractions in the area. Although location-based systems can identify an individual's current location, they cannot always accurately determine the role they are adopting at the time. This means that subsequent information needs cannot be accurately predicted through the identification of their current location. The underlying issue remains of how to define a specific context. A problem with context-based information systems is that an individual has a number of roles.

15.4.1 Context Models

Typical context models adopt a top-down approach and take a static snapshot of a situation. Attention is given to the main characteristics that can be identified in a context, such as identifying the individual, the time, location, and IT device available. This has led to the development of rule-based systems that push information to an individual if predefined conditions are met. Simplistic context-aware systems do not capture the richness that *emerges* from the *interaction* between the objects and actors in the situation. If approaches to context analysis are too simplistic, this can lead to computer applications that push unwanted information onto people.

Figure 15.7 shows an example of a rule-based context system that makes simplistic assumptions about the information to be pushed to an individual. In Figure 15.7, the system assumes that previous customers of Bright Spark will want to receive a text message offering them a discount when they are identified as being within a 100-metre range of a Bright Spark store. This assumption may or may not be true. For example, maybe the person is in a hurry and unable to stop at the store; maybe the store is closed; maybe they made a purchase from the store some time ago and were dissatisfied by the experience. A richer approach to understanding context is needed. Grønli and Ghinea (2010) enrich rule-based systems by taking into consideration an individual's planned activity from their personal calendar. The rule-based system considers context as comprising the task, location, and social context. The social context includes work activities (such as travelling, meeting), travel methods (such as train, car, bus), and leisure activities (such as shopping, cinema). The additional layer of social context aims to improve the relevance of information provided to an individual, demonstrating a greater sensitivity to their current context.

```
If       PERSON = Customer
and
         LOCATION = 100 metres from Bright Spark store
and
         OBJECT = mobile telephone
then
         ACTION = Send SMS of discount to be spent in store.
```

Figure 15.7 Rule-based Context Awareness

Dey and Abowd (2000) suggest there is a primary context and a secondary context. The primary context comprises location, time, identity, and activity, addressing the who, what, when, and where of a situation. The definition of the primary context provides the ability to identify related information which forms the secondary context (Dey & Abowd, 2000). Table 15.11 provides an example of how secondary contextual elements can be derived from an initial primary context. The primary context identifies the person in the context as Larry Hughes. The name Larry Hughes can be used as an identifier to search for further information about the person and therefore develop a richer understanding of the context.

When the identity of the individual in the primary context is established, this can be used to determine their individual profile in the secondary context. Some of the characteristics for the information profile and context profile of Table 15.9 can be derived from the specification

of the activity, time, and location defined in the primary context. However, the activity element only explores what action is being taken; it does not consider how the activity is being performed or why. These additional factors are included in the formation of the context box.

In creative thinking, advice is given to think out of the box. This involves breaking out of the existing box, which constrains the current context, and climbing into a different box. However, in order to think out of the box it is first necessary to define the box to think outside of. The context box adds further dimensions to the primary context defined by Dey and Abowd (2000). The context box (Figure 15.8) aims to provide a generic template for defining and analysing a context which is defined in Table 15.12.

DEFINITION: The **context box** is a structure in which to analyse how culture emerges from the interactions between individuals and objects within bounded physical and conceptual structures.

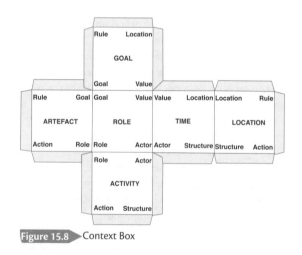

Figure 15.8 Context Box

Table 15.11 Primary and Secondary Contexts

Primary Contextual Element (Dey & Abowd, 2000)	Example Primary Context	Secondary Context
Location	London	London is a city in England and therefore under the jurisdiction of the UK law.
Time	16.45	The activity is taking place in the afternoon.
Identity	Larry Hughes	Company records show that Larry is the owner of Bright Spark. His credit card shows that he purchased a train ticket at 16.00 at Paddington station.
Activity	Boards train	The train timetable indicates that the train on the platform is the 16.48 train travelling from London to Birmingham.

Table 15.12 Context Box Defined

Sides of the Context Box	Intersections of the Context Box
Activity: The set of permissible actions that can take place within the boundary defined by role, artefact, rules, and structure.	Action: The activities being undertaken by an actor from the set of potential activities.
Artefacts: The human, physical, and technical resources available for use by the permitted actions within the constraints of the rules and structure.	Actor: Individual or group of individuals in the context and their skill sets.
Goal: An objective of one or more actors that has priority.	Rule: The legal and socially constructed regulations which limit the acceptable actions and behaviours in the context.
Location: The geographic or logical position in which the context is situated. This provides the structure in which the activity can take place and the position in the structure.	Structure: The physical or conceptual boundaries which restrict actions.
Role: This is a uniquely identifiable individual or group of individuals. An individual may adopt a number of different roles (such as manager, parent, customer) and values which influence and limit their behaviour.	Value: The standards of acceptable behaviour that guide the actions of the actor.
Time: The date and time when the context occurs.	

The context box defines the limits of a specific context in order for the context to be effectively analysed. The box separates the context from the wider environmental factors, allowing the factors that affect the specific context to be examined. In reality, a context box exists inside another box inside another box ad infinitum. The context box therefore provides a scalable structure for exploring context. Contexts can be explored through constructing a series of boxes and identifying how they interrelate. Table 15.13 shows three examples of how a context can be defined within the box. In the first example, Larry Hughes is travelling and wants to review the sales figures before a meeting. The information delivered to him should satisfy his requirement for detailed, quantitative information but also needs to consider the location of the request. It would not be appropriate, for example, to deliver large files containing all the sales data for the previous 12 months. In contrast, large volumes of sales data can be presented and re-presented in different ways to aid the development of the sales presentation in example two. The third example considers a different context where the actor is the train and the structure is the surroundings of the train at its current location.

Quiz 15.1
Context Models

The context box aims to provide a model in which context can be considered to facilitate discussion about the information needed in different contexts. The box does not prescribe or restrict the information that may be delivered to an individual.

Link 15.2
Making Sense of Data Using the Context Box

15.4.2 Transformation Dimensions of Context Models

The provision of contextual information incorporates four elements. First, the variables that influence changes to contextual states need to be identified and the relationship between them understood. Second, technology is needed to capture the data that provide the current state of specific variables, influencing the contextual environment. Third, the data captured must be analysed to make sense of the data and understand the context being depicted. Finally, the description of the context needs to be used in some way to trigger action or improve decision-making. Table 15.14 outlines the impact on the organizational architecture of implementing these elements to capture and use contextual information.

15.4.3 Role of Information Management in Context Models

Contextual information incorporates the following elements:

○ Identify data to be captured to define a specific context.

Table 15.13 Applications of the Context Box

Context Box Element	Example 1	Example 2	Example 3
Action	Check the sales reports.	Create presentation.	Stationary.
Activity	Permissible actions include: Reading. Using laptop.	Permissible actions include: Editing data. Preparing documents.	Permissible actions include: Stationary. Moving. Accelerating. Decelerating.
Actor	Larry Hughes.	Larry Hughes.	Train number 1684.
Artefact	Laptop. Mobile telephone. Briefcase. Fire extinguisher.	Desktop PC. Large monitor.	Engine. Carriages. Driver. Communication system.
Goal	Travel to Birmingham safely. Prepare for meeting.	Prepare sales presentation for meeting.	Transport passengers safely and arrive at scheduled stations on time.
Location	16.45 train from London to Birmingham, carriage C, seat 42.	Office 146.	Point 75.4 from Paddington station.
Role	Managing Director of Bright Spark. Customer of Amy's Candles.	Managing Director of Bright Spark. Chair of sales meeting.	Transport passengers.
Rule	Do not disturb other passengers. Code of conduct for train passengers.	Information can be accessed but not changed.	Transport regulations.
Structure	Train carriage with seats and tables.	Sales data are structured by product, store, region, and sales period.	Limited access to track.
Time	14 February 2013, 16.58.	15 February 2013, 09.32.	14 February 2013, 17.08.
Value	Quiet. Quality. Accuracy. Detailed quantitative information.	Quality. Accuracy. Detailed quantitative information. Up-to-date information.	Safety.

Table 15.14 Organizational Transformation Initiated by Contextual Information

Formal Organization Architecture	Informal Organization Architecture	Impact on Organization Architecture
Technology	Socio-technical	Technology may need to be installed to capture data that can be used to derive the context, such as location detectors or temperature sensors. This challenges the relationship between people and technology as capturing data may be regarded as an invasion of privacy.
Security	Trust	Additional security controls may be needed to ensure that the data captured cannot be intercepted. Trust will need to be developed that the data captured will not be misused and will be acted on appropriately.
People	Skills	The installation of technology may require additional staff to be employed with skills in areas such as sensor technologies. However, existing staff will need to develop skill in analysing the data and taking appropriate actions triggered by the data.

Table 15.14 Continued

Formal Organization Architecture	Informal Organization Architecture	Impact on Organization Architecture
Strategy	Vision	Capturing data to facilitate improved understanding of the organizational context and providing more context-specific information enables the organization to develop more meaningful relationships between trading partners. It can facilitate integration of information aligned with the vision and strategy of the organization.
Processes	Practices	Additional processes are needed to capture, analyse, and take action on the data received. This will require changes to current working practices to analyse and respond to the changing organizational context.
Systems	Human Activity Systems	Technical systems will be needed to capture and manage the data and resulting information. This will require a greater understanding to be developed about the potential causes, impacts, and significance of factors that influence the context in which information is interpreted.
Culture	Values	Factors that trigger change in a context need to be monitored and aligned with the values of the organization. Monitoring and responding to changes in context needs to be accepted in the culture of the organization.

- Analyse the data captured to gain an understanding of the context.
- Determine the information needed in the defined context.
- Retrieve and present the information required.

The role of information management in supporting these elements includes:

- Supporting the exploration of the information needs in different contexts.
- Contributing to the identification of the factors that define the context of different types of information.
- Assisting in making sense of the data collected to define a specific context.
- Ensuring that the information architecture supports contextual information.
- Advising on the characteristics of information that need to be considered in different contexts.
- Developing individual profiles to be used in context-specific information delivery.
- Evaluating the effectiveness of information delivery in context-aware information systems.
- Advising on legal and ethical issues relating to privacy.

15.5 Remote Access to Information

One aspect of context is the location where information is needed. The use of mobile devices has driven the need for organizations to provide access to information systems which were previously only available to staff while they were located in the organization's premises. When access to information was restricted to the organization's premises, the physical entry to the building provided an additional level of security to information. Organizations focused on securing the data resource in the organization and remained alert for attempts to gain access to the data from external sources. Now organizational staff and authorized partners need to be able to access the organization's data using a range of devices from multiple locations. This provides additional technical challenges to ensure that the data are only accessed and modified by those authorized to do so.

15.5.1 Challenges of Providing Remote Access to Information

Organizations need to increasingly enable employees and trading partners to access the data resource from outside the organization's internal data communications network. This can increase the risk of unauthorized access to the organization's data by direct or indirect means. Technical controls need to be implemented to be able to distinguish between an authorized and an unauthorized attempt to access data. This includes authentication methods such as identification and password controls. However, poor choice of passwords or the use of the same password for different systems weakens data security. Data communication outside the confines of the organization uses public communication networks over which the organization has limited control. This creates the potential for data communications to be intercepted. Encryption techniques can be used to authenticate and transmit data. Although such technical measures can be maintained by the IT staff, authorized personnel remain the most significant risk factor affecting data security.

Accessing information remotely requires individuals to assess the indirect risks associated with accessing the information in their current location. This includes consideration of:

○ Privacy: Can access be gained to the information safely? Can anyone nearby see the screen and view the identification and password details being used?

○ Confidentiality: Can the information being accessed be seen or heard by anyone else? Conversations can be overheard and people nearby may be able to read information displayed.

○ Secure storage: If the information is downloaded to a mobile device, is the device protected against unauthorized use? For example, if the device was left unattended could anyone else see the information that has been accessed?

○ Secure access: Are the details used to gain access to remote systems stored on the remote device? If the device was left unattended could anyone log into the organization's systems and gain access to information?

As the range of information that can be accessed using mobile devices increases, the need to take personal responsibility for the devices also needs to increase. For example, a lost mobile telephone can be replaced, but its loss may expose the organization's data to unnecessary risk.

15.5.2 Transformation Dimensions of Remote Access to Information

The ability to provide remote access to information provides benefits to organizations, employees, customers, and trading partners but the risks associated with the access provision need to be considered. Table 15.15 outlines the impact on the organizational architecture of implementing remote access to information.

Table 15.15 Organizational Transformation Initiated by Remote Access to Information

Formal Organization Architecture	Informal Organization Architecture	Impact on Organization Architecture
Technology	Socio-technical	The technological infrastructure will need to change to facilitate and maintain secure access to information. The way information is accessed and used will need to be accepted by staff.
Security	Trust	Security procedures will need to be increased to facilitate authorized access to information. Staff will be trusted to use the remote facility appropriately and not to put the organization at unnecessary risk of unauthorized information access.
People	Skills	Remote access provides greater freedom to the way work can be undertaken and this will require a period of adaptation. Training will be required both in how to access information remotely and how to assess potential risks that may arise.
Strategy	Vision	Remote access to information can provide opportunities for new ways of working with external partners and customers. This can help to develop collaborations that can support and influence the organization's strategy. Remote information provision removes the physical organizational boundary and the impact of this on the future vision for the organization should be considered.
Processes	Practices	Additional security processes may be needed to maintain the security of the organization's information. Remote access will facilitate new ways of working, changing current working practices. The impact of the changing practices need to be considered.
Systems	Human Activity Systems	Existing information systems may need to be adapted to ensure that they work effectively on a range of IT devices. The ability to complete tasks remotely can change the dynamics and power structures in the organization. The potential positive and negative impacts on work–life balance need to be addressed.
Culture	Values	The ability to work remotely changes the culture of the organization as the social networks in organization evolve. Organizational values are challenged in relation to hours of working and the extent to which a person needs to be physically present in the organization.

15.5.3 ▶ Role of Information Management in Remote Access to Information

The provision of remote access to information requires authorized personnel to be identified and information to which they have access to be presented to them in an appropriate manner. Information management can support this by:

○ Defining levels of individual access profile.
○ Ensuring that individual access profiles correspond with the documented information security categories.
○ Checking that the security requirements of the information will not be adversely affected by the proposed access.
○ Advising on the legal issues in the IT policy relating to data access.
○ Providing guidance on the risks associated with remote access to information.
○ Collaborating with IT specialists to ensure that appropriate measures are taken to maintain data security.
○ Developing appropriate standards for the secure access of information.
○ Ensuring that access logs are stored and archived to maintain a record of who has accessed information.

15.6 ▶ Assessing Impact of Information Themes on Information Management

The ability to quickly access large volumes of data using a range of IT fuels the demand for more relevant and more valuable information. The relevance of information is determined by individual preferences and requirements in different contexts. Information management needs to capture and make sense of data about an individual, their role, and current context in order to determine what information may be most relevant to them. Relevance is one factor that influences the perceived value of information, but other factors such as richness of the information also need to be addressed. Multimedia information is considered to be richer than textual information as more information content can be communicated and interpreted by nontextual means. This however creates challenges for the way the requirements for information are specified and how information is indexed to enable the information to be retrieved when required. The demand for richer information poses both technical and social challenges in information management as shown in Table 15.16.

Table 15.16 ▶ Guidelines to Assess the Impact of Information Themes on Information Management

Contextual Profiles	Activities in the Life Cycle			
	Capture	Store and Retrieve	Use, Share, and Maintain	Archive and Destroy
Individual Profile	What information about the individual needs to be captured? How is the information about an individual captured? When is the information about an individual captured?	How will the individual profile be stored? How will the individual profile be retrieved?	How will the individual profile be used to support information retrieval? Who will have access to the profile? How will it be updated (for example, static or dynamic profile)?	How long will the individual profile be stored? When can the individual profile be destroyed?
Information Profile	What additional data need to be captured that can then be matched to individual or context profile requirements? How will the data be represented (for example, RDF)? Who will capture the data semantics?	How will the data be stored? (For example, what format should be used for multimedia?) How will the information be retrieved?	How will the information be used? How will indexes be changed?	How will the data be archived? How will the data be destroyed?

Table 15.16 Continued

Contextual Profiles	Activities in the Life Cycle			
	Capture	**Store and Retrieve**	**Use, Share, and Maintain**	**Archive and Destroy**
Device Profile	What data need to be captured about the device being used to access the information? How will the data be captured? When will the data be captured? Who will capture the data?	How will the device profile be stored? How will the device profile be retrieved?	How will the device profile be used to support information retrieval? Who will have access to the profile? How will the profile be updated?	How long will the device profile be stored? How will the device profile be archived? How will the data be destroyed?
Context Profile of Information Requirements	What information about the context needs to be captured? How is the information about the context captured? When is the information about the context captured?	How will the context profile be stored? How will the context profile be retrieved?	How will the context profile be used to support information retrieval? Who will have access to the profile? How will the profile be updated (a static or dynamic profile)?	How long will the individual profile be stored? When can the individual profile be destroyed?

Summary

As advances in IT facilitate access to data, there is pressure for IT to deliver more meaningful information. Multimedia objects are embedded with more meaning than text documents but consist of data and information elements. Data elements representing the physical object can be indexed and retrieved easily, however, the information element refers to the content of the object which is more difficult to define. The semantic network uses ontologies to encode domain knowledge and facilitate richer information retrieval.

Personalized information explores the information requirements derived from the individual profile, information profile, and device profile that form the context in which information is requested. The profiles provide filters through which potentially relevant information is funnelled to provide more useful information that meets the specific needs of an individual at a point in time. Context emerges from the interactions between people and objects in a bounded structure. The context box provides a model in which to explore the information needs arising in a specific context. As humans give meaning to information, limitations in the ability to articulate how information is given meaning need to be addressed to facilitate more meaningful information retrieval.

Reviewing Scenario 15.1

Personalizing the shopping experience for customers will require Bright Spark to make changes to existing information systems. Factors about customers and purchasing patterns will be captured to develop shopping profiles which can be used to filter information presented to customers. However, changes may also be needed to product and sales data so that filters can be applied to data displayed to customers.

Customers will need to give consent for personal information to be collected. Customers need to be willing to provide the information needed to develop profiles. This requires individuals to trust that information will not be collected or used without their prior permission and changes to security may be needed to ensure that the security of the information collected will be maintained.

Customer purchase history data could be used to offer a customer personalized product recommendations. The recommendations will be based on their purchase history and the purchase history of customers who have purchased the same or similar products. The collection of information about customers and their purchases may provide a rich source of data that can be used to improve understanding of the customer's relationship with the organization and enable Bright Spark to target product recommendations and special offers to specific customers. However, it is important that the information provided to customers does meet their needs as poor recommendations can adversely affect a customer's opinion of Bright Spark. Personalizing information delivered to customers will require Bright Spark to identify the factors that affect the purchasing decision of retail light fittings. Profiles will need to be maintained and dynamically updated to adapt to product sales.

Exercise 15.1

1 What is the difference between the data element and the information element of a multimedia object?
2 What is meant by the provenance of a multimedia object?
3 Explain the relationship between indexing and retrieval.
4 List three challenges that need to be addressed in managing multimedia information.
5 Give an example of how Bright Spark may use digital rights management methods to prevent photographs of its stores being used by other retailers.
6 What is meant by semantic richness?
7 Name two ways in which semantic richness can be measured.
8 What is a homonym?
9 What is OWL?
10 How does the semantic web differ from the Internet?
11 What is an ontology?
12 Using the open world assumption, if a statement is not proven to be true, is the statement assumed to be false?
13 What is the difference between personalization and customization?
14 List three risks associated with personalizing information.
15 What are the three stages of personalizing information?
16 What is the aim of context-specific information?
17 What is meant by location-based information systems?
18 If a context-based system is too simplistic, what may be the result?
19 How does context differ from a situation?

20 Explain how the primary context is used to define the secondary context.

Link 15.3
Answers to Exercise 15.1

Activities 15.1

1 Apply Table 15.1 to a photograph and then ask someone else to apply the table to the same photograph and compare the results.
2 Draw a diagram to show how Figure 15.5 would appear if an additional class *sales staff* were added to the OWL in Table 15.6 and John was a member of the class *sales staff*.
   ```
   <owl:Class rdf:ID="sales_staff"/>
   <owl:Sales_Staff rdf:ID="John"/>
   ```
3 Complete Table 15.17 to show how OWL would respond to the queries relating to the new class *sales staff*.

Table 15.17 ▶ OWL Reponses to Information Queries

Query	OWL Response
Is John a member of the class *sales staff*?	
Is Mrs Lewis a member of the class *accountants*?	
Is Mrs Lewis a member of the class *sales staff*?	
Is John a member of the class *Bright Spark*?	
Is John a member of the class *accountants*?	

Link 15.4
Answers to Activity 15.1.3

4 List the characteristics of a personal profile that Bright Spark might collect to develop a profile of a customer.
5 Use Table 15.9 to identify the information needs of Mrs Lewis, an accountant at Bright Spark.
6 Develop a context box to represent your current context by replacing the labels in Figure 15.8.

Discussion Questions 15.1

1 How has the Internet affected the use of multimedia in organizations and in everyday life?

2 Do you agree with Floridi (2005) who argues that information can only be derived from a data set that is truthful, or can information be derived from data irrespective of whether the data are truthful?

3 Discuss the advantages and disadvantages of the open world assumption.

4 Personalizing information delivered to an individual reduces the volume and breadth of information provided to them. What are the disadvantages of this?

5 To what extent do the benefits of personalization outweigh the intrusion upon individual privacy?

6 Are all sides of the context box equally important or are some more important than others in defining a context?

7 How does each side of the context box affect the content, type, quality, or format of the information required in a specific context?

8 As IT enables information to be accessed from anywhere with an Internet connection, how important is location in determining the potential relevance of information?

FUTURE OF INFORMATION MANAGEMENT

Scenario 16.1

Information Management Conference

'That concludes the presentation of the current developments affecting information management. After lunch the next speaker will outline the key challenges of managing information in organizations today.'

'The challenge is how to make sense of all this information about how to manage information that they talk about at these business events,' moaned Larry Hughes, the owner of Bright Spark, a light fittings retailer. 'We know what the problems are, it is knowing how to solve them that is the real problem.' As they sat down for lunch he continued, 'What I don't understand is this: information from around the world can be accessed in a few key strokes, so why does it take so long to access information in my own company?'

'I know what you mean,' agreed Mr Alvis, the Director of Match Lighting. 'I hired an information manager to try to help sort out the problems

we have in trying to access information in the company. She just keeps telling me how big a problem it is and she seems to keep finding even more problems!'

'I just want to focus on designing and making candles,' explained Amy. 'I know I need to keep detailed records but there seems to be so much information I have to keep on top of.'

Larry nodded in agreement. 'When I opened my first shop I felt the same and now with the Internet, smartphones, and social media there is just so much information. I can't cope with it all. I can spend the whole day going through emails and still not manage to clear my inbox.'

'I thought technology was supposed to make life easier but it seems to be a way of enabling more people to demand my attention and provides access to information that I haven't got time to look at,' said Mr Alvis.

'So, where do we go from here?' asked Amy.

Learning Outcomes

The learning outcomes of this chapter are to:

○ Review the key issues in information management.

○ Assess the challenges to effective information management.

○ Outline future trends affecting the management of information in organizations.

○ Determine the responsibilities for managing information in organizations.

○ Define an approach to managing information effectively.

Introduction

Managing the information resource to provide meaningful, quality, and timely information to inform actions and decisions in organizations remains problematic. This chapter first reviews key issues of information management. Challenges to managing information are then discussed, including cultural issues, both in the organization and in wider society, which demand quicker access to more relevant information. Advances in information technology (IT) facilitate the fast transmission of data, but the speed of technological development has outpaced the conceptual understanding of how data are interpreted and used in different contexts. The future challenges of information management are then considered, such as information consumption, pollution, and sustainability. The chapter concludes by emphasizing the need for the business and IT functions to share responsibility for information and presents an approach to managing information which brings together the information presented in earlier chapters.

16.1 ▶ Key Issues in Information Management

Developments in IT have led to increased expectations of society in terms of the quality and availability of information. Table 16.1 outlines some common complaints relating to information in organizations.

Core themes in the problems listed in Table 16.1 include access to information, quantity of information that can be accessed, quality of information available, and usability of information available when needed. Table 16.2

Table 16.1 ▶ Common Complaints about Information

Information Theme	Complaint
Quantity	Too much information to absorb and act upon. Insufficient information to make a decision.
Quality	Incorrect information that may lead to inappropriate decisions. Irrelevant information that diverts attention away from the issue being considered. Information is incomplete. Inconsistencies are identified in information from different sources.
Source	Unknown provenance of information. Untrusted source of information.
Semantics	Information is interpreted in a different way from that in which it is defined.
Access	Information cannot be accessed when needed.
Availability	Lack of understanding about whether the information needed exists, or where it exists, and how it can be accessed. Information is not available in the form required.
Usability	Information cannot be integrated with information from other sources. The presentation of the information does not meet requirements.

shows that both the business functions and IT function can contribute to addressing these four themes.

16.1.1 ▶ Access to Information

Problems relating to the inability to access information incorporate three components:

Table 16.2 ▶ Roles to Address Key Information Management Issues

Theme	Role of the Organization	Role of Information Technology
Access to information.	Establish the information needs of the organization. Determine who needs access to specific information.	Facilitate authorized access to information. Restrict unauthorized access to information.
Quantity of information.	Define policies to manage the capture, creation, archive, and destruction of information that satisfies the information needs of the organization and fulfils legal requirements.	Provide tools to support the authorized capture, creation, storage, archive, and secure destruction of information, contributing to the volume of information available.
Quality of information.	Agree on information definitions and formulate business rules. Adhere to definitions and rules agreed to by promoting a culture of responsibility for maintaining information quality.	Provide controls to impose information integrity controls. Implement validation and verification procedures defined in business rules.
Usability of information.	Develop policies to minimize information fragmentation. Specify characteristics of information required.	Integrate information from different information systems. Apply procedures such as aggregation to present information in the form required.

○ Physical and technical restrictions imposed by IT systems.

○ Cultural barriers to sharing information between functions and departments.

○ Contextual barriers preventing information from being interpreted appropriately.

In spite of the range of developments in IT to improve access to information, technology can become a barrier to information access. Some barriers are needed, such as authorization controls to prevent information being accessed by unauthorized staff. Other barriers, such as incompatible data and fragmented information captured and stored in a range of incompatible and inaccessible information systems, provide unnecessary restrictions to information access.

The barriers to accessing information in different information systems are not limited to technical controls. Many organizations do not know what information they have and different departments may capture copies of the same information due to the lack of ability to access current information. Incompatible systems and duplicated information evolve in an organization as information systems are allowed to be developed to meet the individual needs of a specific area of the organization rather than the needs of the organization as whole. This action results in disparate information systems incurring unnecessary costs and data duplication, which can lead to inaccurate and inconsistent information.

Cultural barriers between different areas of the organization hinder the willingness and ability to share information. Dingley *et al.* (2000) suggest that areas within the organization adopt tribal behaviour to establish membership of a *we* group and separation of the group from other areas of the organization. The cultural separation of us and them between functions, departments, and teams contributes to an unwillingness to share information with others and an unwillingness to use information generated by others. This is derived from a general mistrust of those in other departmental tribes.

Information is interpreted within the context of departments and business processes. Different areas of the organization define information terms differently to meet the specific needs of different contexts. For example, the sales department at Match Lighting may define a *part* as 'an identifiable item that is made available for retailers to purchase and includes manufactured products and promotional merchandise'. In contrast, the manufacturing department may define a *part* as 'an object purchased from a supplier that is used in the manufacture of a product'. The differences in definition will be used by the

sales and manufacturing departments to demonstrate that they cannot share information and need different information systems to meet their specific information requirements. Accurate interpretation and use of information requires such contextual barriers to be addressed. Although different areas of the organization have specific needs for information, agreed upon consistent information definitions can be used to enable information to be shared and integrated with other information to meet the wider needs of the organization.

16.1.2 Volume of Information

Complaints about the volume of information in an organization relate to the availability of too much information or the lack of access to a sufficient volume of information. Both technological and human factors need to be considered to address these problems. The continual bombardment of information and demands for information from different sources has, for many people, become unmanageable both at a personal level and an organizational level. Too much information becomes a hindrance (Bawden, 2001) to effective working practices. Information overload leads to stress and despondency, as individuals feel inadequate about their lack of ability to cope with information. It can also lead organizations to overlook key information that they need to act upon. Problems with information overload continue until a crisis occurs, then while resources are diverted to address the current crisis, the foundations of the next crisis are often being built elsewhere.

As vast volumes of data are being captured and created every day, technology is now being used to try to assist in making sense of the data. This includes the use of algorithms to discover trends in the data and highlight threats and anomalies requiring immediate attention. Work is also being undertaken to encode semantic information into a form that can be used by technology to assist in retrieving more meaningful information (Chapter 15).

Email is a key contributor to individual information overload. Email interrupts concentration and reduces effectiveness in the workplace, increasing the time it takes to complete tasks (Marulanda-Carter & Jackson, 2012). While technology provides the means to send and receive email, the decisions to write, circulate, and read email are taken by individuals. Some employees can exhibit characteristics of addicted behaviour with respect to email, such as feeling preoccupied with email to the extent that attempts to reduce email usage are unsuccessful (Marulanda-Carter & Jackson, 2012). The volume of emails circulated can be reduced by training to improve the clarity of communication within emails and guidance on when email communication should and should not be used (Burgess *et al.*, 2005).

Complaints relating to insufficient information in organizations require further investigation to determine whether or not the information exists, as it may be a problem of accessibility rather than availability. Figure 16.1 summarizes the potential situations relating to complaints of insufficient information:

○ If the information does not exist and cannot be derived from the existing data, changes need to be made to existing business processes and IT systems to capture (or purchase) the data required.

○ If the information is not known to exist but could be derived from the existing data, changes may be needed to IT systems to provide access to the data and changes will be needed in the organization to inform staff that the information required is available.

○ If the information is known to exist but cannot currently be accessed, the organizational and technical barriers inhibiting access to the information need to be reviewed. These may include reluctance to share information among areas of the organization or incompatible technical issues which need to be resolved.

16.1.3 ▶ Quality and Integrity of Information

Lack of access to information may be caused by poor quality data which do not provide a sufficient basis for the information required by an individual at a specific point in time. Information quality includes aspects such as accuracy, semantic interpretation, and integrity.

The accuracy of information content remains a primary concern of organizations. Inaccurate information may be caused by mistakes in data capture or may arise due to inconsistent copies of the data being maintained

by different information systems in different parts of the organization. Validation and verification controls can be implemented in IT systems to enforce standards and improve the accuracy of the data captured. For example, validation controls can be used to ensure that a post code entered is a valid UK post code and verification checks can be used to check that the post code corresponds to the address entered. However, the accuracy of the address entered is the responsibility of the individual entering the address into the computer system. While technology can be used to implement validation checks and controls, a cultural change is also needed: staff in the organization need to accept responsibility for the way in which information is captured, created, maintained, and used. This requires discipline to ensure that staff entering data into systems do not add inappropriate information to data fields. Such problems can be avoided if the design of the initial information system provides the means for all the required data to be captured appropriately. This extends a responsibility to everyone in the organization to ensure that the accuracy of information is maintained.

Information may be perceived as being inaccurate because the way in which the information has been defined when captured does not relate to the way in which the information is defined by the person who later uses the information. Semantic interpretation is a fundamental problem in organizations and requires agreed upon data definitions to be used consistently throughout the organization. However, the problem of semantics is not restricted to information circulated internally in the organization. Differences in how terms are used within the supply chain need to be identified so that information is correctly interpreted.

From a governance perspective, information integrity refers to qualities of accuracy and completeness (Flowerday & von Solms, 2007). Completeness of information requires coherence within the underlying data held within the organization. For example, an order needs to be associated with a valid customer account. Information integrity requires business rules to be established that meet the needs of the whole organization. These rules then need to be embedded in the information systems developed to ensure that data items are appropriately defined and linked together. This will ensure that data can be integrated from different information systems to attain a holistic view of the information in the organization.

Link 16.1
Examples of Information Interpretation

Figure 16.1 ▶ Causes of Insufficient Information

(Figure 16.1 chart: X-axis "Information known to exist?" with NO/YES; Y-axis "Information accessible?" with NO/YES)

- YES, NO: Business processes needed to inform staff of data available.
- YES, YES: Information known to exist and can be accessed from available data.
- NO, NO: Business processes and IT needed to capture or create data.
- NO, YES: Investigate barriers to data access.

16.1.4 Usability of Information

The usability of information refers to the ease with which the information can be interpreted correctly and used to inform future actions. Information may be available but may not be in the form needed by an individual at a specific point in time and is therefore regarded as unusable. This may be because the information is of poor quality or it may relate to issues of semantic definition. Factors that hinder the usability of information include:

- Comprehension factors: the ability to clearly interpret the data accurately. This is influenced by the use of headings and labels that are meaningful for the specific task for which the information is to be used.
- Level of granularity: the ability to drill into the detail or roll up the data to see higher-level summaries.
- Conversion factors: the ability to convert the data into different units (for example, to be able to convert prices into different currencies).
- Format of the information: the ability to incorporate the information easily into documents and communications (for example, the ability to copy part of a table to include in a presentation).
- Presentation of the information: the ability to change formats (such as tables to graphs), sequence (such as change order of columns in a table), or view (such as choose which columns of a table to include) of the information.

Information can be fragmented in organizations, stored in a range of incompatible and inaccessible information systems. Outside the organization, individuals are able to connect information from different sources using Internet technologies quickly and easily. The same type of connectivity and integration needs to be reflected in how information is managed inside organizations.

Table 16.3 summarizes how technical tools and human factors can influence the themes in information management discussed.

Haug *et al.* (2013) identify 12 barriers to data quality listed in Table 16.4. Information management policies to address these problems have been mapped to the problems identified.

16.2 Challenges for Information Management

Information management faces a range of technical and social challenges that continue to influence the problems and perceptions of information quality and accessibility.

Table 16.3 Technological and Human Factors Affecting Information Management

Theme	Technical Tools	Human Factors
Access	Prevent unauthorized access. Fragment data across incompatible systems.	Reluctance to share information. Inability to share information due to different information definitions.
Volume: Excessive	Captures data that are not needed. Data mining techniques can be used to identify trends in data. Dashboards can be used to summarize data.	Creating emails adds to the volume of information to be processed.
Volume: Insufficient	Data are not captured. Data captured but cannot be accessed due to fragmented or incompatible data.	Unaware the information exists. Reluctance to share information.
Quality: Accuracy	Validation and verification controls can be implemented. Multiple inconsistent copies of data being maintained. Implementation of business rules to maintain information integrity.	Errors can occur when data are entered by individuals. Unwillingness to share data. Misinterpret information.
Quality: Semantics	Encode semantic information for use by IT systems.	Different definitions of information terms.
Quality: Integrity	Implement business rules.	Misuse of data collection mechanisms.
Usability	Tools to drill down and roll up the data. Provide different views of the data. Convert data into different formats.	Information may be interpreted incorrectly.

Table 16.4 ▶ Barriers and Facilitators of Data Quality

Barriers to Data Quality Identified by Haug *et al.* (2013)	Tools to Address Barriers	Chapter
Missing placement of responsibilities for specific types of master data.	Data Ownership.	5.2
Lack of clarity of roles in relation to data creation, use, and maintenance.	Data Owners, Data Authors, and Data Maintainers.	5.2
Inefficient organizational procedures.	Information Management Processes.	7 and 8
Lack of management focus in relation to data quality.	Data Quality Strategy.	7
Lack of data quality measurements.	Data Quality Characteristics.	7
Lack of rewards/reprimands in relation to data quality.	Information Management Strategy.	6
Lack of training and education of data users.	Information Management Strategy.	6
Lack of written data quality policies and procedures.	Data Quality Strategy. Information Management Strategy.	7 6
Lack of emphasis on the importance of data quality from managers.	Information Management Strategy Critical Success Factors.	7
Lack of IT systems for data management.	Information Management Tools.	8
Lack of possibilities for input in existing IT systems.	Data Definition. Information Architecture.	7 4
Poor usability of IT systems.	Development Plan for Information Management Strategy. Cleaning Data and Consolidating Information.	6 8

16.2.1 ▶ Cultural Expectations of Information

In 2012 it was estimated that there were one billion smartphones, and six billion subscriber identity module (SIM) cards in mobile phones and other IT devices that provide access to information. The ease with which requests for information can be issued via email, tweets, and social media forums increases the expectation for a response to be provided just as quickly. The cultural expectations relating to the accessibility of information and the time taken in providing a response to requests for information from sources, both internal and external to the organization, need to be managed.

The term *Google generation* refers to individuals born after 1993 (Rowlands *et al.*, 2008). This generation is also referred to as *generation Z* or *digital natives* (Menou, 2010), representing the first generation who have not experienced life without the widespread accessibility of IT. The Google generation therefore has high expectations of technology, prefers interactivity, and favours visual information over text-based information (Menou, 2010). Society is becoming more visually aware and this may be fuelled by the ease which which digital sounds and images can be captured and shared using technology. As the expectations of society for information to be delivered using high-quality multimedia increases, this places greater pressure on organizations to create and manage nontext-based information. This requires methods for indexing and retrieving nontext-based content to be incorporated into an organization's information management strategy.

Although the generation of digital natives has greater access to IT, studies suggest that information literacy has not improved (Rowlands *et al.*, 2008). While this generation has the skills and tools to access information quickly, typically it is not able to assess the relevance or reliability of the information retrieved (Rowlands *et al.*, 2008). This is supported in a further study by Nicholas *et al.* (2011) which found that the Google generation finds information quickly on the Internet but is less confident about the quality of the information retrieved, accepting the first search result. Menou (2002) suggests that a new culture of information needs to be developed to address the limitations information literacy.

The Google generation trusts information provided by members of their social networks. Social media has enabled the phenomena of user-generated content to grow at an amazing rate. It has removed the barriers of editing and publishing, allowing anyone to publish their views and opinions with limited review being exercised by, for example, forum moderators. Mobile devices enable content to be quickly captured and uploaded and for the responses to the information content uploaded to be received very quickly at any time and place. It removes the barriers of waiting to access email to find out whether someone has responded to information circulated. User-generated content has increasing value to organizations and should not be neglected in information management strategies. It provides a potentially valuable source of information about consumers and the wider society within which the organization operates. The information management strategy needs to include the information generated through social networking activities. Organizations also need to introduce procedures to ensure that the information captured is used.

Rowlands *et al.* (2008) identified that researchers adopt squirrel behaviour, downloading copies of information in case the information is needed at a later date. This contrasts with using the information in situ and hoping to retrieve the information again if necessary. This reflects a shift from *just in case* to *just in time* information acquisition strategies which rely on the ability to find information again. It also reflects a view of information as a more disposable commodity that is used and discarded, rather than one in which information is used and retained. This change of perception may be due to the speed that information is being generated and perhaps reflects that information has a shorter life cycle before it is replaced with more up-to-date information that may be perceived as being more valuable. The perceptions of information value need to be considered in the information management strategy and the strategy may need to initiate change in the way in which information is valued.

16.2.2 ▶ Role of Information Technology in Information Management

IT has enabled the creation of volumes of information and contributes to complaints of too much or too little information as shown in Table 16.1. Carroll and Rosson (1992) assert that the nature of a task influences the requirements of the artefacts needed to perform the task, and that the artefact used changes how the task is performed, changing the nature of the task itself. IT is changing how information is created and consumed in organizations and in society.

For the Google generation, constant connectivity is essential (Nicholas *et al.*, 2011). Ashraf (2009) reports that a Facebook user describes the connectivity as being able to talk to someone as if they were in the same room rather than talking via a screen. The technology becomes invisible as the participants engage in communication. Norman (1998) argues that technology should be invisible; tools should be simply designed to enable the operator to focus on the task rather than the tool being used. When individuals become immersed in communication, the technology facilitating the communication becomes invisible, until something goes wrong. For example, if an Internet connection is temporarily lost, attention is diverted from the communication and back to the technology being used; the technology becomes visible again.

IT can have different roles within the organization. For example, technology is often marketed as the solution, but the nature of the problem for which technology is the solution is not always defined. There are some instances where technology is the solution. For example:

Problem:	How can thousands of customer records be stored so that the data can be accessed quickly from any location?
Solution:	Store the records in a database with remote access.

As a solution, technology provides a means to support specific aspects of the information life cycle.

Sometimes technology offers ways to improve existing services. For example, email is a faster way of communicating than via the postal system. Both allow messages to be transmitted, but the use of technology reduces the time lapse in the communication. The same service is therefore provided more quickly and efficiently. The email system (the artefact) has changed the task of communicating messages. The advantages of speed offered by email has increased the volume of messages transmitted and changed the task of communication. Email is a powerful communication tool, but it has evolved to include information storage, personal scheduling, and task management. These additional functions encourage the continual usage of email programs throughout the day, changing work practices. Technology has changed the way in which information is communicated and changed the requirements for how information is managed.

Sometimes technology is a solution looking for a problem that has not yet been identified; it enables a need to be satisfied that few realized existed. For example, 20 years ago few people thought there was a need to provide a facility to enable customers to shop 24x7 from any location, yet e-business has become firmly embedded in daily life for many people. The artefact of e-business has changed the task of shopping and changed the demand for information.

Sometimes technology is developed and humans are provided with this new tool that at first they are unsure what to do with; behaviour is then adapted to find a use for it. For example, social behaviour is adapting to the opportunities offered by developments in mobile devices. Consumers seek uses for new technological devices (such as tablet computers) and adapt their behaviour to make use of technology (such as social networking). The use of technology emerges from practice and each new technological development provides a new artefact, changing the way in which information is created, stored, delivered, or consumed. Business processes then need to change to adapt to the new ways of working and interacting with information that emerges from the use of the technology. Information management strategies need to be regularly reviewed to ensure that they address issues that arise as employees, customers, and suppliers adapt their behaviour to make use of new technology.

16.2.3 ▶ Information in Information Technology

As technology becomes more elegant and innovative it is easy to become enthralled by the sleek devices that are becoming readily available. Information technology provides the means to capture, store, transmit, retrieve, use, and delete information and the information in information technology can become overlooked. This can lead to a lack of consideration being given to using information responsibly. For example, staff may circulate information electronically that they would not have previously circulated to the same audience on paper.

Each new technological development provides further challenges to how information is managed in organizations. Personal IT devices provide powerful means to create, engage with, and transmit information. With this power comes responsibility; responsibility to use technology to assist in the effective management of information. It should also be remembered that technology can also be used to gain unauthorized access to information, corrupt information, and contribute to information overload.

Information is meant to instigate action, to influence the behaviour of the recipient, but too often the volume of information immobilizes rather than stimulates action. Personalization attempts to address this problem by seeking to filter and target information appropriately. This requires further consideration about what information is really needed in a specific context. Individuals therefore need to be aware of their role in information management and take responsibility for the increased volume of information.

For information to be actioned, it needs to have meaning to the recipient. Information has meaning within a context. IT has removed the traditional boundaries for time and place which previously restricted access to information and specified the requirements for information. The information needs within a specific situation are defined by the values of dynamic states which form a snapshot in time. Context emerges from the interactions among a series of dynamic states. This has given rise to the concept of interactive awareness. For example, two people can be situated in the same room, but if one is engrossed in a task, there is no awareness of the other in the room. Meaningful interaction is important and the information needed for meaningful interaction needs to be defined.

DEFINITION: **Interactive awareness** occurs when two or more entities are alert to the existence of one another and change their behaviour in response to data received to directly engage with each other.

The rule-based approach to context analysis focuses on static snapshots of situations. More interactive awareness is needed to adapt information to the changing needs of an individual in a specific context. This requires data to be captured about the specific states at a point in time. These states then need to be analysed swiftly to determine meaningful responses. The context box facilitates holistic analysis of data within a bounded structure rather than responding to the individual discrete data values such as location.

16.3 ▶ Future Themes in Information Management

As information management strives to address the problems and challenges outlined in the previous sections, it does so within an evolving environment. Innovations in technology, society, and business practice promote new ways in which information can be consumed. Alongside this demand for information there are concerns relating to sustainability. Data captured using IT has a key role in informing decisions about the responsible use of resources, however, the creation and use of IT itself incurs environmental costs. Information management therefore needs to identify ways in which the information resource can be used effectively while minimizing the environmental impact.

16.3.1 ▶ Information Consumption

Developments in IT increase cultural expectations relating to information communication and the use of information to support smarter interaction with the surrounding environment. This influences how information will be created and consumed in the future. IT continues to become cheaper, faster, and smaller. This will continue to increase the demand for information to be delivered promptly irrespective of location or device used to make the request for information. The size of the device requires consideration to be given to the way in which information is presented and the volume of information that is returned from queries. This drives the need for more semantic information to be captured in order to aim to deliver information that is directly relevant to a specific query or request for information.

The ease and speed with which data can be accessed using standard Internet search engines, accompanied by the constant stream of social media updates, continues to increase demand for rapid response to queries and immediate access to internal data. This requires processes to automate relevant swift responses, rather than the standard 'thank you for your email, we will endeavour to respond to your enquiry within 3 days'. This requires further understanding of the different information needs of parties represented in the generic business model.

Chapter 15 introduced approaches to encode semantic meaning into a form that can be processed by technology to improve the ability to search and retrieve meaningful information. This enables automated responses and actions to be generated in response to information received with reduced human intervention. The ability to interpret semantic information requires an understanding of the context from which information derives its meaning.

The development of smart homes and intelligent cities requires immense quantities of data to be captured, stored, analysed, and actioned. Approaches to manage these vast volumes of data are needed. These include:

○ Secure communication systems to facilitate the fast and secure transmission of high-volume data.
○ Large-scale storage media in which data can be indexed and retrieved in an acceptable time frame.
○ Approaches to make sense of the data and the relationships between them in order to identify appropriate actions required in response to the data analysed.
○ Security systems to ensure that the data are only accessed and modified by authorized means.

Technology can assist in capturing and securely storing data. However, the challenge remains of how to make sense of the data captured so that information generated can be used to inform decision-making.

As technology becomes cheaper, it becomes more disposable. The security of information must be considered, both in terms of any information stored on the device and in terms of whether there is any information remaining on the device which can facilitate access to information held elsewhere. Simply deleting data does not remove data from the device; data must be forensically removed to ensure that data cannot be retrieved. A cultural change is needed which recognizes that while the purchase price of technology is falling, the value of information that can be potentially accessed from a mobile device is increasing. For example, the cost of losing a mobile telephone is not just the cost of a replacement and the inconvenience caused; it is the cost of the consequences resulting from the unauthorized access to information stored on the telephone or to information that is accessible using the telephone.

16.3.2 ▶ Information Pollution

Toffler (1970) predicted that there would come a time when there would be too much information available to be processed effectively. Rogerson (2008) has suggested that the powerful resource of information, the lifeblood of organizations, has become polluted through concerns relating to its accuracy and reliability, in addition to the volume of information available. Technological advances continue to improve mechanisms to capture, store, and retrieve data but fail to address the problems of information management. Rogerson (2008) suggests that in order to address the pollution of information improvements are needed to the integrity and provenance of information. Data ownership, defined in Chapter 5, moves towards this by promoting responsibility for information. However, rather than more accurate information, what is really needed is more meaningful information. This requires greater understanding of the information required and the specific quality characteristics of the information to be defined. Data definitions and business rules can then be specified which can be implemented in information systems to improve the quality of data captured, providing the foundation for quality information.

16.3.3 ▶ Information Sustainability

Sustainabilty refers to utilizing natural resources responsibly to ensure that the environmental conditions required to support human life are maintained in the long term. This requires consideration to be given to both the sustainability of information and the information needed for sustainability. Information sustainability refers to the ability to secure the timely provision of accurate and relevant information in the long term without adversely affecting the resources in the natural environment. The current demand for immediate information and the trend to fuel the faster creation of information through user-generated content cannot be sustained. The fast turnover of information and the ability to find information again when required poses challenges for information management. However, while focusing on the immediate demand for information, the continued challenges lie in the ability to retrieve information about past events and to make sense of them in order to try to identify, for example, whether processes have been appropriately followed. The continued maintenance of historic information must not be overlooked in the information management strategy. Applications such as data mining use large volumes of data to identify potential trends and patterns that may emerge in the data and provide insightful intelligence upon which the organization can act. Data mining requires the data to be clean, accurate, and trusted; it also incurs considerable costs in relation to data storage. Archiving and retention can be neglected areas in information management; however, corporate governance and the need to respond to legal issues, such as freedom of information requests, require information to be retained and to be retained in an accessible form. Many organizations archive information and do not test their ability to recover the information until the situation arises when they are forced to attempt to recover the information.

A key concern is the adverse effect on the environment caused by the manufacture of technology. Green computing aims to reduce the energy required to manufacture and operate IT equipment, alongside the increasing demand for electronic information. Energy usage in data centres accounts for a large percentage of an organization's IT budget. Despite work being undertaken in green IT, Judge (2012) reports that the energy consumption of data centres is increasing rather than decreasing. Green IT focuses on energy reduction, whereas sustainable IT services aims to generate value for the organization, consumers, and society (Harman et al., 2012). Sustainability encompasses social, economic, and environmental factors. Technology can be used to support sustainability by enabling resources to be used effectively (Menou, 2010) and to provide information to inform decisions about how resources should be used. For example, energy consumption data can be analysed to inform decisions on how energy consumption may be reduced.

16.3.4 Technology of the Future

The Techcast project (www.techcast.org) collects and analyses technological predictions from experts in a range of fields. It then predicts when a technology will become mainstream, that is, when there will be a minimum of 30 per cent adoption of the technology. Historically, the predictions are accurate to within three years. Table 16.5 lists some of the predictions from Techcast.

Such forecasts introduce new challenges to information management. For example, interaction and communication in 3D virtual environments raise issues such as how to capture information and how to respond to the information using smart sensors, robots, or virtual elements.

These forecasts provide new contexts for information systems and consideration needs to be given to:

○ What information will be needed?
○ Why will the information be needed?
○ How will information be captured, transmitted, stored, retrieved, used, and communicated using IT in these new contexts?

Halal (2008) suggests that IT improves the ability to acquire knowledge; knowledge facilitates innovation and innovation improves IT. Information is at the heart of this cycle. Information is used in IT and information of how IT is being used provides the basis for knowledge, which can facilitate innovation. Information of innovation can be used to provide the requirements of further technology and identify new ways information can be shared and used within society. Information needs to be managed to facilitate the duel learning that takes place within this cycle. Information management strategies need to evolve to ensure that they are sufficient for current and future information needs.

16.3.5 Morphing Organizations

Morphing organizations have changed their structure, location, way of working, staff roles, resources, and interaction with customers, suppliers, and partners. However,

Table 16.5 ▶ Technology Forecasts (based on: www.techcast.org)

Estimated Year	Prediction
2017	Space tourism (Halal, 2013).
2017	Life in 3D virtual environments (Fernández, 2007).
2018	Smart sensors.
2019	Intelligent interfaces.
2024	Smart machines used for routine, mental tasks (Pupo, 2013).
2027	Smart robots.

certain features, structures, and properties must remain unchanged for an organization to retain its original identity (for example, core values, traits, and beliefs). Information enables morphing organizations to meet new challenges in changing socio-technical contexts. Information management needs to respond to changes in organizations but it also has a key role helping organizations to retain their identity.

Information management enables morphing organizations to adapt to future challenges by:

- Identifying the information that individuals really need, that is aligned with the organizational values.
- Exploring the socio-technical context which gives information meaning.
- Providing a flexible information architecture in which information needs can be aligned with the changing business context.
- Establishing policies to ensure the integrity, quality, and availability of meaningful information.
- Defining processes to manage information throughout the life cycle to meet the changing needs of the organization.
- Assessing the impact on the information resource of developments in IT and the business environment.

16.4 ▶ Transformation Dimensions of Information Management

The acknowledgement of the importance of information management in the organization and the decision to make a commitment to managing information must be strategic. Without substantial and sustained support from senior management, information management initiatives are likely to be ad hoc, addressing specific information requirements in one area of the organization that are likely to cause further problems to other areas of the organization. This will reduce the potential for information to be effectively integrated with other areas of the organization or result in information being duplicated, leading to inconsistencies and unnecessary cost. Commitment to managing information therefore needs to be reflected in the organizational strategy to facilitate the investment of resources required. An information management strategy then needs to be formulated.

The information management strategy requires the infrastructure and architecture to be developed to provide the support structures in which information management can then take place. The framework of policies developed in the information management strategy provides the infrastructure for information management, focusing on areas such as security, legality and the processes in the information life cycle. The infrastructure will also identify the roles and responsibilities required to implement the information management strategy.

People are the most important element in the information management strategy as they define the information, specify the need for information, capture the information, use the information, and are therefore responsible for its accuracy. People also carry out the activities required to identify and implement the changes needed to the management of information documented in the information management strategy. This includes the initial work to clean the data, develop processes to address existing problems, and implement practices to ensure that data remain clean in the future.

Information management initiates a change of culture in the organization. In many organizations there is a culture of blame, blaming other teams, departments, and functions for the current inadequacies of information. Behavioural change is needed that recognizes the importance of information in the organization and both acknowledges and accepts the role of the individual in improving and maintaining the quality of the information resource. This cultural change will take time and will require the vision of information management to be effectively communicated and promoted.

Training will need to be provided to assist staff in developing the skills required to implement the information management strategy. This will require, for example, the development of facilitation skills to assist in the formulation of agreed upon definitions of data. It will require training in the use of systems and technology introduced to implement the business rules that have been agreed on to ensure that data remain clean, secure, and can be accessed when needed. Training is also needed to explain how everyone in the organization has a role in information management, highlighting the importance of adhering to data input fields, definitions, and security procedures. Business processes will be introduced or changed to implement the information management policies and support the stages of the information life cycle. The changes to business processes will be reflected in changes to information systems and IT.

Security controls will be affected at three levels. First, technical changes will be needed to continually maintain data security, responding to developments in technology and evolving threats. Second, changes to security processes may be needed to ensure that appropriate authentication is conducted to allow only authorized individuals to access and change data, determined by defined security categories. Finally, security procedures require a change in behaviour, requiring individuals to consider the potential

Table 16.6 Organizational Transformation Initiated by Information Management

Formal Organization Architecture	Informal Organization Architecture	Impact on Organization Architecture
Technology	Socio-technical	Changes to technology will need to be implemented to facilitate authorized access to information and implement controls to maintain integrity of business rules. A change in how staff perceive IT is needed to promote ownership and responsibility for the information.
Security	Trust	Technical controls must be implemented to maintain information security. Behavioural changes are also necessary to raise awareness of potential risks to information security. As information management reduces data duplication, different areas of the organization have to share data, which requires trust to be developed that the data captured are accurate.
People	Skills	Staff in the organization will clean the data and develop processes to address existing problems. Training should be provided to assist staff in developing the skills required to implement the information management strategy.
Strategy	Vision	Commitment to managing information must be reflected in the organizational strategy in order to facilitate the investment of resources required. Effective information management can be used to support the organizational strategy and facilitate opportunities to use the information resource more effectively.
Processes	Practices	Processes will be introduced or changed to implement the information management policies and support the stages of the information life cycle. This will require current working practices to change to accommodate the new processes.
Systems	Human Activity Systems	Existing information systems will need to change to reflect the data definitions and business rules defined in the data dictionary and data security classifications. Human activity systems will need to reflect the responsibility and accountability promoted in the information management strategy.
Culture	Values	A culture of responsibility towards information management will need to be promoted, highlighting the role of the individual in creating and using quality information. Alignment is required between the values of the organization and the values on which the information management strategy is based.

risks related to their access and use of data, particularly in relation to the use of mobile devices.

IT can be seen to create some of the problems with information management, such as threats to security. It also provides the potential to improve the way information can be used in organizations. It is therefore important that information management is addressed in partnership with the IT department and business functions.

Quality information requires individuals to trust that the information is accurate. This is an ongoing challenge. Trust takes a long while to develop but is easily lost. The ease with which information can be accessed and shared devalues how information is perhaps perceived by individuals. The ethics relating to the access and use of information therefore require further consideration.

The environment in which the organization operates is continually changing and information management must maintain awareness of changes that take place and

identify how they will impact the organization's need for information. Chapter 9 explored types of organizational transformation such as capacity building and acquisition, which initiate transformational changes in structure and strategy affecting information management. Changes in IT can be a driver for transformational change, evidenced with e-business (Chapter 10). Information management must therefore be addressed within the framework of a morphological organization.

Table 16.6 summarizes the impact on the organizational architecture of information management initiatives.

16.5 Responsibility for Information Management

The responsibility for managing information lies with everyone. Responsibility cannot be delegated to the business, or to the IT function, or to an external service provider; each has a role to play in information management but cannot work in isolation.

16.5.1 ▶ Responsibility of Business Functions

Information is captured and stored to provide the organization with the information required to achieve the organizational strategy and to monitor progress towards the strategy. Information records business transactions and informs the actions to be taken in business functions. The business is therefore responsible for:

○ Clearly defining the information required to support business processes.
○ Identifying who needs access to specific information.
○ Defining the business rules that will ensure the quality and integrity of information is retained.
○ Adhering to the agreed upon business rules to maintain the quality of information.
○ Establishing the processes for managing information throughout the life cycle to meet the requirements of the whole organization.
○ Specifying policies to maintain the privacy and security of different types of information to satisfy ethical and legal requirements.

16.5.2 ▶ Responsibility of Information Technology Function

The IT function is responsible for satisfying the information requirements specified by business functions by implementing business rules accurately in the information systems developed. The IT function also has a responsibility to help the business to understand the implications of the business rules defined. The IT function is responsible for:

○ Implementing the business rules defined by the business to maintain the quality and integrity of information.
○ Implementing controls to ensure that information is captured, transmitted, and stored securely, preventing unauthorized access.
○ Ensuring that information is accessible when required by authorized personnel.
○ Providing a technical infrastructure so that data can be shared among different business functions.
○ Defining hardware and software policies to integrate information from different information systems, avoiding the purchase of incompatible technologies.
○ Providing tools such as content management systems and business intelligence tools to assist the organization in managing and using information effectively.

16.5.3 ▶ Responsibility of External Service Providers

Organizations may be tempted to delegate some of the responsibility for information management to external service providers. For example, cloud computing (discussed in Chapter 13) provides the opportunity for organizations to rent an IT infrastructure and data storage facilities. Although cloud computing provides benefits such as reduced IT costs and a scalable infrastructure, the ultimate responsibility for the organization's information lies with the organization and not with an organization contracted to provide secure storage for the information. Organizations therefore need to ensure that service level agreements with the external service provider are aligned with the requirements of their information strategy. Procedures also need to be in place for transferring storage of the data to a different provider if necessary at short notice.

16.5.4 ▶ Responsibility of the Individual

Every individual has a responsibility for information. Everyone creates information with each tweet, blog, email, posting on social networking sites and the Internet, document and report written, photograph and video taken. Each time these artefacts are created, information is created, contributing to the volume of information to be managed. Everyone therefore has a responsibility to think about the potential effect of their actions.

Just because we CAN send information, does not mean that we SHOULD send information.

Each person capturing information has a responsibility to capture the information accurately, reflecting the definitions and business rules agreed to in the organization. For example, a sales assistant may enter a comment in an address field about what to do with a delivery if there is no one home to receive the delivery, because a field for delivery comments has not been provided. This works around the problem of how to capture the delivery comments but dirties the data. The address field now contains an invalid address, which is likely to cause problems when the data are aggregated with data from other information systems in the data warehouse. While in this example the IT staff may accuse the sales assistant of acting irresponsibly, the assistant is merely trying to deliver the best service to the customer, working with the inadequacies of the IT system provided. So who is to blame? The IT department for not providing a means for information about a delivery to be captured or the sales assistant for entering data in the wrong field? The information systems provided by the IT department need to satisfy the business needs, but in order to achieve this, the business must ensure that the

Table 16.7 Stages of Information Management

Stage	Activities
Stage 1	Commit to addressing the challenge of managing information. Accept that managing information, as with the management of any resource, is an ongoing activity and not a one-off project.
Stage 2	Identify the information that is really needed in the organization. This will include examining the inadequacies of existing systems and forming an ideal vision. Conduct an initial audit to establish the scale of the problem.
Stage 3	Define the need for the information management strategy and the business benefits. Formulate an information management strategy which includes: ○ Developing a framework of policies. ○ Specifying roles and responsibilities. ○ Identifying statutory compliance measures. ○ Defining performance measures.
Stage 4	Develop and maintain information management plans with scheduled prioritized projects. Invest time and resources in communicating the importance of information to everyone. Initiate a change of culture promoting responsibility for data creation and usage.
Stage 5	Define data definitions to avoid misunderstandings. Clean existing data. Establish procedures for ensuring that data remain clean.
Stage 6	Identify opportunities to maximize the potential of information through specific projects (such as business intelligence, content management, and knowledge management).
Stage 7	Maintain awareness of the ethical and legal issues relating to information management. Regularly review performance and adapt to changes in the organizational and technological environments.

IT department understands what business information needs to be captured in the IT systems.

Staff working in all areas of the business are responsible for ensuring that data are accurately captured and that business rules, embedded in IT systems, are followed. The IT department is responsible for ensuring that business rules are implemented accurately in the systems developed and for helping the business to understand the implications of the business rule defined.

16.5.5 Approach to Managing Information Responsibly

The challenges of information management should be addressed from organizational, technological, and cultural perspectives.

○ The organizational perspective includes establishing the requirements for information in the organization and agreeing to definitions of the information, attributes, and business rules that are necessary for the organization to operative effectively.
○ The technological perspective encompasses the design and development of information systems and IT, which embed the organization's business rules

and ensure that the information resource is accurate, robust, reliable, accessible, and secure.
○ The cultural perspective recognizes that the quality and management of information lies with the staff in the organization. Staff at all levels in the organization must accept their responsibility for the information that they create, capture, use, and share with others. This means confirming that information is captured accurately in accordance with business rules, used appropriately, taking into account issues of privacy and integrity, and that the creation of new information is considered carefully. The thoughtless creation of information contributes to information overload and may mean that information is unnecessarily duplicated in different areas of the organization.

These perspectives are incorporated into the stages of information management in Table 16.7.

Summary

Despite (or perhaps because of) advances in IT, key issues in information remain: how to provide timely access to quality, usable information. The means to capture, store, transmit, and receive high volumes of data quickly fuels expectations about access to meaningful information, but technical, cultural, and contextual barriers to information management still remain. Technology challenges how information is created and used; society has to adapt to new ways of working and new opportunities for interaction. IT changes information consumption and, when unchallenged, IT contributes to information pollution. Technological innovation can overshadow the information aspect of IT but it is individuals who give meaning to information and determine the requirements for information. Every individual has responsibility for the information they create, maintain, and use. IT makes creating information easier, but it does not absolve the individual of responsibility for the quality and integrity of the information. Managing information in organizations requires everyone in the organization to understand their responsibilities towards information, and requires the business and IT functions to work in partnership to effectively manage the information resource.

Reviewing Scenario 16.1

Where do we go from here?

The volume and complexity of information can be overwhelming. As Mr Alvis notes, when the problems of information management in an organization are investigated, more problems are identified. Amy is just starting her business so she can establish good information management practices to try to avoid problems arising in the future. However, both Match Lighting and Bright Spark are organizations that have evolved over time through growth and mergers, resulting in a complex mix of legacy systems and inconsistent and potentially incompatible information.

Each organization needs to demonstrate commitment to addressing the ongoing challenge of managing information and allocate resources to this element of the organization. An audit can be undertaken of the information required in the organization and the current problems experienced. An information management

strategy can then be formulated and implemented. This will include establishing a framework of policies within which information can be managed. Specific projects can be prioritized to address the current problems with information quality and accessibility, while processes are changed to ensure that the problems do not reoccur. The three owners need to recognize that information management is not a one-off task and that continued investment is needed to manage the information resource. In committing to improving information management in the organization, the owners need to appreciate that a partnership is required between the business and IT functions in the organization. In addition, cultural change is needed to ensure that all staff appreciate their role in contributing to the effective management of information in the organization.

Cloze Exercise 16.1

Complete the following paragraph by choosing the correct word from Table 16.8 to fill in each gap.

Information _____ is an external driver for information management. Information needs to be managed to ensure that it is accessible to meet the internal and external information needs of the _____. Access to information can be hindered by technical, _____, and contextual barriers. Groups within the organization adopt _____ behaviour, and use language as a means to separate themselves from other parts of the organization.

Problems with information _____ relate to having too much or too little information. Information is intended to _____ the behaviour of the recipient but too much information prevents action from being taken. Complaints relating to insufficient information in organizations require further investigation to determine whether the problem relates to information _____ rather than availability. Accuracy and completeness are qualities of information _____. The accuracy of information is affected by mistakes in data _____, inconsistent copies of the data, and misinterpretation of the information. Information overload and concerns relating to the

---

Table 16.8 ▶ Words to Complete Cloze Exercise 16.1

Accessibility	Consumed	Everyone	Information	Polluted
Artefact	Cultural	Google	Integrity	Sense
Capture	Data	Governance	Literacy	Strategic
Centres	Delegated	Green	Management	Sustainability
Change	Environmental	Inform	Organization	Tribal

quality of information have contributed to concerns that the information resource has become _____ .

The _____ generation has high expectations for information accessibility. However, while access to information has improved, information _____ has not improved. IT is an _____ which changes the way in which a task is performed and changes the requirements for managing information. The _____ component of IT can become overlooked and this can result in a lack of consideration being given to using information responsibly. Innovations in technology, society, and business practice promote new ways in which information can be _____. _____ can be captured from sensors and then analysed, triggering a preprogrammed response such as switching on a light, to facilitate smart interaction within the home environment. Approaches to make _____ of the data captured are needed to identify appropriate actions to be taken in response to the data.

Information _____ refers to the ability to ensure the timely provision of accurate and relevant information in the long term without adversely affecting the resources in the natural environment. IT provides access to information to inform decisions relating to sustainability; however, the creation and use of IT incurs _____ costs. _____ computing seeks to reduce the energy required to manufacture and operate IT equipment. For example, data _____ use large amounts of energy to store an organization's data.

The decision to make an ongoing commitment to managing information must be _____ to facilitate investment of resources. Behavioural _____ is needed which acknowledges the role of the individual in improving and maintaining the quality of the information resource. The responsibility for managing information lies with _____ and cannot be _____ to business functions, the IT department, or to an external service provider.

Link 16.2
Answers to Cloze Exercise 16.1

Activities 16.1

1 Choose a website with which you are familiar and use the information themes listed in Table 16.2 to assess the information provided on the website.

2 Identify any additional problems with information that can be added to Table 16.1.

3 Table 16.4 identifies barriers to information quality. Categorize each barrier in terms of whether it is a technical barrier, organizational barrier, or cultural barrier.

4 Give an example of how technology can become invisible.

5 Use the task–artefact cycle to explain how email has changed the task of corresponding with an organization.

6 Create a diary of your activities for a day and calculate how many times information is created.

7 Email and social media are key contributors to information overload. How can such information be managed more effectively?

8 The Techcast project predicts that intelligent interfaces will be adopted by 2019. List the factors that would make an interface intelligent and identify the information that would be captured and processed to enable this intelligence.

Discussion Questions 16.1

1 Does the opportunity for anyone to share their views on the Internet have a positive or negative impact on information management?

2 What is the biggest barrier to information quality?

3 How has IT changed the way in which information is created, accessed, and used?

4 To what extent has information become polluted?

5 How can a partnership be established between the business and IT functions in an organization to manage information?

6 What factors will affect how information is consumed in the future?

REFERENCES

Abadi, D. (2009), 'Data Management in the Cloud: Limitations and Opportunities', *IEEE Data Engineering Bulletin*, **32**(1), pp. 3–12.

Ackerman, P. L. (2007), 'New Developments in Understanding Skill Performance', *Current Directions in Psychological Science*, **16**(5), pp. 235–239.

Ackerman, M. S. & Halverson, C. (2000), 'Reexamining Organisational Memory', *Communications of the ACM*, **43**(1), pp. 58–64.

Adams, P. (2009), 'Designing for Social Interaction', *Boxes and Arrows*, 9 April, http://boxesandarrows.com, date accessed 21 August 2013.

Adelman, S., Moss, L. & Abai, M. (2005), *Data Strategy*, Addison Wesley Professional, Canada.

Aerts, A. T. M., Goossenaerts, J. B. M., Hammer, D. K. & Wortmann, J. C. (2004), 'Architectures in Context: On the Evolution of Business, Application Software, and ICT Platform Architectures', *Information & Management*, **41**(6), pp. 781–794.

Ahlqvist, T., Bäck, A., Heinonen, S. & Halonen, M. (2010), 'Road-Mapping the Societal Transformation Potential of Social Media', *Foresight: The Journal of Future Studies, Strategic Thinking and Policy*, **12**(5), pp. 3–26.

Alderson, A. & Shah, H. (1999), 'Viewpoints on Legacy Systems', *Communications of the ACM*, **42**(3), pp. 115–116.

Anonymous (2006), 'Lifecycle Transformations: Looking Beyond the IT', *Strategic Direction*, **22**(3), pp. 33–35.

Antoniou, G., Groth, P., Van Harmelen, F. & Hoekstra, R. (2012), *A Semantic Web Primer*, Third Edition, MIT Press, Cambridge, MA.

Anumba, C. J., Baugh, C. & Khalfan, M. M. A. (2002), 'Organisational Structures to Support Concurrent Engineering in Construction', *Industrial Management and Data Systems*, **102**(5), pp. 260–270.

Argyris, C. (1991), 'Teaching Smart People How to Learn', *Harvard Business Review*, **69**(3), pp. 99–109.

Arora, N., Dreze, X., Ghose, A., Hess, J. D., Iyengar, R., Jing, B., Joshi, Y., Kumar, V., Lurie, N., Neslin, S., Sajeesh, S., Su, M., Syam, N., Thomas, J. & Zhang, Z. J. (2008), 'Putting One-to-One Marking to Work: Personalization, Customization and Choice', *Marketing Letters*, **19**(3/4), pp. 305–321.

Ashar, R., Lewis, S., Blazes, D. L. & Chretien, J. P. (2010), 'Applying Information and Communications Technologies to Collect Health Data from Remote Settings: A Systematic Assessment of Current Technologies', *Journal of Biomedical Informatics*, **43**(2), pp. 332–341.

Ashley, V. & Ashley, S. (2007), *Business and Administration: Student Handbook: Level 2: To Support All Level 2 Vocational Qualifications in Business and Administration*, Second Edition, Council for Administration, London.

Ashraf, B. (2009), 'Teaching the Google-Eyed YouTube Generation', *Education and Training*, **51**(5/6), pp. 343–352.

Assudani, R. H. (2005), 'Catching the Chameleon: Understanding the Elusive Term "Knowledge"', *Journal of Knowledge Management*, **9**(2), pp. 31–44.

Avison, D. & Fitzgerald, G. (2006), *Information Systems Development: Methodologies, Techniques and Tools*, Fourth Edition, McGraw-Hill, Maidenhead, UK.

Bacon, T. R. (2007), 'Driving Cultural Change through Behavioral Differentiation at Westinghouse', *Business Strategy Series*, **8**(5), pp. 350–357.

Badii, A. & Sharif, A. (2003), 'Information Management and Knowledge Integration for Enterprise Innovation', *Logistics Information Management*, **16**(2), pp. 145–155.

Balkau, F. & Sonnemann, G. (2010), 'Managing Sustainability Performance through the Value Chain', *Corporate Governance*, **10**(1), pp. 46–58.

Baptista, J. (2009), 'Institutionalisation as a Process of Interplay Between Technology and Its Organisational Context of Use', *Journal of Information Technology*, **24**(4), pp. 305–319.

Barbaroux, P. (2011), 'A Design-Oriented Approach to Organizational Change: Insights from a Military Case Study', *Journal of Organizational Change Management*, **24**(5), pp. 626–639.

Barratt, M. (2004), 'Understanding the Meaning of Collaboration in the Supply Chain', *Supply Chain Management: An International Journal*, **9**(1), pp. 30–42.

Bass, B. M. (1990), 'From Transactional to Transformational Leadership: Learning to Share the Vision', *Organizational Dynamics*, **18**(3), pp. 19–31.

Bateman, P. J., Pike, J. C. & Butler, B. S. (2011), 'To Disclose or Not: Publicness in Social Networking Sites', *Information Technology and People*, **24**(1), pp. 78–100.

Batley, S. (2007), 'The I in Information Architecture: The Challenge of Content Management', *ASLIB Proceedings: New Information Perspectives*, **59**(2), pp. 139–151.

Batra, D., Hoffer, J. A. & Bostrom, R. P. (1990), 'Comparing Representations with Relational and EER Models', *Communications of the ACM*, **33**(2), pp. 126–139.

Bawden, D. (2001), 'Information and Digital Literacies: A Review of Concepts', *Journal of Documentation*, **57**(2), pp. 218–259.

Bensaou, M. (1999), 'Portfolios of Buyer-Supplier Relationships', *Sloan Management Review*, **40**(4), pp. 35–44.

Bergeron, B. (2002), *Essentials of CRM: A Guide to Customer Relationship Management*, Wiley, Chichester.

Bergman, O., Beyth-Marom, R. & Nachmias, R. (2006), 'The Project Fragmentation Problem in Personal Information Management', *Proceedings of the SIGCHI Conference on Human Factors in Computing Systems*, 22–27 April, Montreal, Canada, pp. 271–274.

Bernard, R. (2007), 'Information Lifecycle Security Risk Assessment: A Tool for Closing Security Gaps', *Computers and Security*, **26**(1), pp. 26–30.

Berners-Lee, T., Hendler, J. & Lassila, O. (2001), 'The Semantic Web', *Scientific American*, May, pp. 29–37.

Berson, A. & Dubov, L. (2011), *Master Data Management and Data Governance*, Second Edition, McGraw-Hill, London.

Bettini, C., Mascetti, S., Wang, S., Freni, D. & Jajodia, S. (2009), 'Anonymity and Historical Anonymity in Location-Based Services', in: Bettini, C., Jajodia, S., Samarati, P. & Wang, S. X. (eds.), (2009), *Privacy in Location-based Services: Research Issues and Emerging Trends*, Springer, London, pp. 1–30.

Beynon-Davies, P. (2009), *Business Information Systems*, Palgrave, Basingstoke.

Blackler, F. (1995), 'Knowledge, Knowledge Work and Organizations: An Overview and Interpretation', *Organization Studies*, **16**(6), pp. 1021–1046.

Boisant, M. H., MacMillan, I. C. & Han, K. S. (2007), *Explorations in Information Space: Knowledge, Agents and Organization*, Oxford University Press, Oxford.

Boisot, M. (1994), *Information and Organizations: the Manager as Anthropologist*, Harper Collins, London.

Boldrin, M. & Levine, D. (2002), 'The Case Against Intellectual Property', *The American Economic Review*, **92**(2), pp. 209–212.

Booth, N. & Matic, J. A. (2011), 'Mapping and Leveraging Influencers in Social Media to Shape Corporate Brand Perceptions', *Corporate Communications: An International Journal*, **16**(3), pp. 184–191.

Bott, F. (2005), *Professional Issues in Information Technology*, The British Computer Society, Swindon.

Brancheau, J. C., Schuster, L. & March, S. T. (1989), 'Building and Implementing an Information Architecture', *ACM SIGMIS Database Archive*, **20**(2), pp. 9–17.

Brown, A. (1998), *Organisational Culture*, Second Edition, Pitman, London.

Bryson, J. (2011), *Managing Information Services: A Sustainable Approach*, Third Edition, Ashgate, Farnham.

Buchanan, S. & Gibb, F. (1998), 'The Information Audit: An Integrated Strategic Approach', *International Journal of Information Management*, **18**(1), pp. 29–47.

Buchanan, S. & Gibb, F. (2007), 'The Information Audit: Role and Scope', *International Journal of Information Management*, **27**(3), pp. 159–172.

Buckland, M. K. (1991), 'Information as a Thing', *Journal of the American Society of Information Science*, **42**(5), pp. 351–360.

Bull, C. (2010), 'Customer Relationship Management (CRM) Systems, Intermediation and Disintermediation: The Case of INSG', *International Journal of Information Management*, **30**(1), pp. 94–97.

Burgess, A., Jackson, T. & Edwards, J. (2005), 'Email Training Significantly Reduces Email Defects', *International Journal of Information Management*, **25**(1), pp. 71–83.

By, R. T. (2005), 'Organizational Change Management: A Critical Review', *Journal of Change Management*, **5**(4), pp. 369–380.

Cadbury Committee (1992), 'Report of the Committee on The Financial Aspects of Corporate Governance', The Committee on the Financial Aspects of Corporate Governance, Gee Publishing, London.

Capurro, R. (2008), 'Intercultural Information Ethics: Foundations and Applications', *Journal of Information, Communication and Ethics*, **6**(2), pp. 116–126.

Carroll, J. M. & Rosson, M. B. (1992), 'Getting Around the Task-Artifact Cycle: How to Make Claims and Design by Scenario', *ACM Transactions on Information Systems*, **10**(2), pp. 181–212.

Carter, R., Martin, J., Mayblin, B. & Munday, M. (1984), *Systems, Management and Change*, Paul Chapman Publishing, London.

Ceccato, M., Dean, T. R. & Tonella, P. (2009), 'Recovering Structured Data Types from a Legacy Data Model with Overlays', *Information and Software Technology*, **51**(10), pp. 1454–1468.

Cenfetelli, R. T. & Benbasat, I. (2002), 'Measuring the E-Commerce Customer Service Life Cycle', *Proceedings of the European Conference on Information Systems*, Poland, pp. 696–705.

Cervone, H. F. (2010), 'An Overview of Virtual and Cloud Computing', *OCLC Systems and Services*, **26**(3), pp. 162–165.

Chaffey, D. (2006), *E-Business and E-Commerce Management: Strategy, Implementation and Practice*, Third Edition, Pearson Education, Harlow.

Checkland, P. (1981), *Systems Thinking, Systems Practice*, Wiley, Chichester.

Chellappa, R. K. & Sin, R. G. (2005), 'Personalization versus Privacy: An Empirical Examination of the Online Consumer's Dilemma', *IT and Management*, **6**(2–3), pp. 181–202.

Chelsom, J. V., Payne, A. C. & Reavill, L. R. P. (2005), *Management for Engineers, Scientists and Technologists*, Second Edition, Wiley, Chichester.

Chen, L. & Nugent, C. (2009), 'Ontology-based Activity Recognition in Intelligent Pervasive Environments', *International Journal of Web Information Systems*, **5**(4), pp. 410–430.

Chen, S-H., Lee, H. T. & Wu, Y-F. (2008), 'Applying ANP Approach to Partner Selection for Strategic Alliance', *Management Decision*, **43**(3), pp. 449–465.

Cho, G., Lee, S. & Cho, J. (2010), 'Review and Reappraisal of Smart Clothing', in: Cho, G. (ed.), (2010), *Smart Clothing Technology and Applications*, CRC Press, New York, pp. 1–36.

Chou, S. (2011), 'Management of Systems Development Knowledge: A Cognitive Approach', *Behaviour and Information Technology*, **30**(3), pp. 389–401.

Chow, W. S. & Ha, W. O. (2009), 'Determinants of the Critical Success Factor of Disaster Recovery Planning for Information Systems', *Information Management and Computer Security*, **17**(3), pp. 248–275.

Chun, M. & Whitfield, G. (2008), 'Social Constraints to Integrating Information Systems, Knowledge, and Firm Capabilities Following a Corporate Merger', *Journal of Systems and Information Technology*, **10**(2), pp. 135–158.

Clarke, R. (1988), 'Information Technology and Dataveillance', *Communications of the ACM*, **31**(5), pp. 498–512.

Clarke, R. (1994), 'Dataveillance by Governments: The Technique of Computer Matching', *Information Technology and People*, **7**(2), pp. 46–85.

Clements-Croome, T. D. J. (1997), 'What Do We Mean By Intelligent Buildings?', *Automation in Construction*, **6**(5–6), pp. 395–400.

Coakes, E. & Bradburn, A. (2005), 'What is the Value of Intellectual Capital?', *Knowledge Management Research and Practice*, **3**(2), pp. 60–68.

Colbert, M. & Livingstone, D. (2006), 'Important Context Changes for Talking and Text Messaging During Homeward Commutes', *Behaviour & Information Technology*, **25**(5), pp. 433–441.

Collette, R. & Gentile, M. (2006), 'Overcoming Obstacles to Data Classification', *Computer Economics*, April, http://www.computereconomics.com, date accessed 1 June 2013.

Colosimo, M., De Lucia, A., Scanniello, G. & Tortora, G. (2009), 'Evaluating Legacy System Migration Technologies Through Empirical Studies', *Information and Software Technologies*, **51**(2), pp. 433–447.

Cox, S. (2008), *Guide to Using Case Studies for Active Learning*, HE Academy, http://www.heacademy.ac.uk, date accessed 21 August 2013.

Cox, S. A. (2009), 'Assessing the Impact of Mobile Technologies on Work-Life Balance', in: Torres-Coronas, T. & Arias-Oliva, M. (eds.), (2009), *Encyclopedia of Human Resources Information Systems: Challenges in e-HRM*, IGI Global, New York, pp. 63–69.

Cox, S. A. (2013), 'E-Business Planning in Morphing Organizations: Maturity Models of Business Transformation', in: Li, E. Y., Loh, S., Evans, C. & Lorenzi, F. (eds.), (2013), *Organizations and Social Networking: Utilizing Social Media to Engage Consumers*, IGI Global, New York, pp. 286–312.

Cox, S. & King, D. (2006), 'Skill Sets: An Approach to Embed Employability in Course Design', *Education and Training*, **48**(4), pp. 262–274.

Cox, S. A., Perkins, J. & Green, P. (2001), 'A Positioning Framework for Developing an E-Business Strategy', *Proceedings of the Eighth European Conference on Information Technology Evaluation*, Oxford, UK, 17–18 September.

Cox, S. A., Shah, H. U. & Golder, P. A. (2005), 'Research Methods for Information Systems Research', *Working Paper*, University of Central England, UK.

Cox, S. A., Krasniewicz, J. A., Perkins, J. S. & Cox, J. A. (2006), 'Modelling the Organisational Transformation Associated with Implementing E-Business Collaborative Systems in the Supply Chain',

Proceedings of the British Academy of Management Conference, 12–14 September 2006, Belfast.

Cross, M. & Shinder, D. L. (2008), *Scene of the Cybercrime*, Second Edition, Elsevier, MA.

Curtis, G. & Cobham, D. (2008), *Business Information Systems: Analysis, Design and Practice*, Sixth Edition, Prentice Hall.

Damsgaard, J. & Karlsbjerg, J. (2010), 'Seven Principles for Selecting Software Packages', *Communications of the ACM*, **53**(8), pp. 63–71.

Date, C. J. (2004), *An Introduction to Database Systems*, Eighth Edition, Pearson, London.

Davenport, T. & Prusak, L. (1998), *Working Knowledge: How Organizations Manage What They Know*, Harvard Business School Press, Boston.

Davenport, T. H. & Harris, J. G. (2007), *Competing on Analytics: The New Science of Winning*, Harvard Business School, Boston.

Delbridge, R. (2008), 'An Illustrative Application of Soft Systems Methodology (SSM) in a Library and Information Service Context: Process and Outcome', *Library Management*, **29**(6/7), pp. 538–555.

de Pechpeyrou, P. (2009), 'How Consumers Value Online Personalization: A Longitudinal Experiment', *Direct Marketing: An International Journal*, **3**(1), pp. 35–51.

de Wit, B. & Meyer, R. (2010), *Strategy: Process, Content, Context. An International Perspective*, Fourth Edition, Cengage Learning EMEA, Andover.

Dey, A. K. & Abowd, G. D. (2000), 'Towards a Better Understanding of Context and Context-Awareness', *Proceedings of the CHI 2000 Workshop on The What, Who, Where, When, and How of Context-Awareness*, The Hague, April 2000, date accessed 21 August 2013.

Dezdar, S. & Ainin, S. (2011), 'The Influence of Organizational Factors on Successful ERP Implementation', *Management Decision*, **49**(6), pp. 911–926.

Dingley, S. (1996), 'A Composite Framework for the Strategic Alignment of Information Systems Development', *Ph.D. thesis*, Aston University in Birmingham, UK.

Dingley, S. & Perkins, J. (1999), 'Tempering Links in the Supply Chain with Collaborative Systems', *Proceedings of the Ninth Annual Conference of BIT: Generative Futures*, Manchester, document 37.

Dingley, S. & Perkins, J. (2000), 'Engaging in Collaborative Systems: Lessons from the Field', *Proceedings of the Second International Conference on Enterprise Information Systems*, Stafford University, 5–7 July, pp. 424–428.

Dingley, S., Shah, H. & Golder, P. (2000), 'Tribes of Users and Systems Developers', *Australian Journal of Information Systems*, **7**(2), pp. 20–31.

Dixon, S. E. A., Meyer, K. E. & Day, M. (2010), 'Stages of Organizational Transformation Economies: A Dynamic Approach', *Journal of Management Studies*, **47**(3), pp. 416–436.

Doherty, N. F., Anastasakis, L. & Fulford, H. (2011), 'Reinforcing the Security of Information Resources: A Critical Review of the Role of the Acceptable Use Policy', *International Journal of Information Management*, **31**(3), pp. 201–209.

Doomun, R. & Jungum, N. V. (2008), 'Business Process Modelling Simulation and Reengineering: Call Centres', *Business Process Management Journal*, **14**(6), pp. 838–848.

Dunphy, D. & Stace, D. (1993), 'The Strategic Management of Corporate Change', *Human Relations*, **46**(8), pp. 905–918.

Earl, M. J. (1989), *Management Strategies for Information Technology*, Prentice Hall, London.

Earl, M. J. (1996), 'Integrating IS and the Organization: A Framework of Organizational Fit', in: Earl, M. J. (ed.), (1996), *Information Management: The Organizational Dimension*, Oxford University Press, Oxford, pp. 485–502.

Ellis, P. & Desouza, K. C. (2009), 'On Information Management, Environmental Sustainabilty, and Cradle to Cradle Mentalities', *Business Information Review*, **26**(4), pp. 257–264.

Elmasri, R. & Navathe, S. B. (2010), *Fundamentals of Database Systems*, Sixth Edition, Pearson Education, London.

Engeström, Y. (1987), *Learning by Expanding: An Activity-Theoretical Approach to Developmental Research*, Orienta-Konsulti, Helsinki.

Engeström, Y. (2001), 'Expansive Learning at Work: Toward an Activity Theoretical Reconceptualisation', *Journal of Education and Work*, **14**(1), pp. 133–156.

EU (2006), 'Directive 2006/24/EC of the European Parliament and of the Council of 15 March 2006', *Official Journal of the European Union*, **L 105**, pp. 54–63.

Eurostat (2003), 'Assessment of Quality in Statistics', *Working Group Sixth Meeting*, Luxembourg, 2–3 October 2003, http://epp.eurostat.ec.europa.eu, date accessed 1 June 2013.

Eurostat (2008), 'NACE Rev. 2 Statistical Classification of Economic Activities in the European Community',

European Commission Publication, http://epp .eurostat.ec.europa.eu, date accessed 25 March 2013.

Evgeniou, T. (2002), 'Information Integration and Information Strategies for Adaptive Enterprises', *European Management Journal*, **20**(5), pp. 486–494.

Ezeife, C. I. & Barker, K. (1995), 'A Comprehensive Approach to Horizontal Class Fragmentation in a Distributed Object Based System', *International Journal of Distributed and Parallel Databases*, **3**(3), pp. 247–273.

Fallis, D. (2007), 'Information Ethics for Twenty-First Century Library Professionals', *Library Hi-Tech*, **25**(1), pp. 23–36.

Farbey, B., Land, F. F. & Targett, D. (1995), 'A Taxonomy of Information Systems Applications: The Benefits' Evaluation Ladder', *European Journal of Information Systems*, **4**(1), pp. 41–50.

Feinstein, A. H. & Parks, S. J. (2002), 'The Use of Simulation in Hospitality as an Analytic Tool and Instructional System: A Review of the Literature', *Journal of Hospitality & Tourism Research*, **26**(4), pp. 396–421.

Fernández, M. (2007), 'The Metaverse Life in 3D Virtual Environments', *Techcast LLC*, http://www.techcast.org, date accessed 21 August 2013.

Ferran, N., Mor, E. & Minguillón, J. (2005), 'Towards Personalization in Digital Libraries Through Ontologies', *Library Management*, **26**(4/5), pp. 206–217.

Few, S. (2006), *Information Dashboard Design: The Effective Visual Communication of Data*, O'Reilly Media, California.

Finnegan, D. & Willcocks, L. (2007), *Implementing CRM: From Technology to Knowledge*, Wiley, Chichester.

Fisher, M. (2004), 'Developing an Information Model for Information- and Knowledge-based Organisations', in: Gilchrist, A. & Mahon, B. (2004), *Information Architecture: Designing Information Environments for Purpose*, Facet Publishing, London, pp. 5–26.

Floridi, L. (2005), 'Is Semantic Information Meaningful Data?', *Philosophy and Phenomenological Research*, **70**(2), pp. 351–370.

Flowerday, S. & von Solms, R. (2007), 'What Constitutes Information Integrity?', *South African Journal of Information Management*, **9**(4), http://www.sajim .co.za, date accessed 21 August 2013.

Foltz, C. B., Schwager, P. H. & Anderson, J. E. (2008), 'Why Users (Fail to) Read Computer Usage Policies', *Industrial Management and Data Systems*, **108**(6), pp. 701–712.

Forbes-Pitt, K. (2006), 'A Document for Document's Sake: A Possible Account for Document System Failures and a Proposed Way Forward', *Records Management Journal*, **16**(1), pp. 13–20.

Galliers, R. D. (1992), 'Soft Systems, Scenarios, and the Planning and Development of Information Systems', *Systemist*, **14**(3), pp. 146–159.

Garfinkel, S. L., Juels, A. & Pappu, R. (2005), 'RFID Privacy: An Overview of Problems and Proposed Solution', *IEEE Security and Privacy*, **3**(3), pp. 34–43.

Garrison, C. P. & Ncube, M. (2011), 'A Longitudinal Analysis of Data Breaches', *Information Management and Computer Security*, **19**(4), pp. 216–230.

Garud, R. (1997), 'On the Distinction between Know-How, Know-Why and Know-What', *Advances in Strategic Management*, **14**, pp. 81–101.

Gayton, C. M. (2006), 'Beyond Terrorism: Data Collection and Responsibility for Privacy', *VINE: The Journal of Information and Knowledge Management Systems*, **36**(4), pp. 377–394.

Gerstein, M. S. (1992), 'From Machine Bureaucracies to Networked Organizations: An Architectural Journey', in: Nadler, D. A., Gerstein, M. C., Shaw, R. B. & Associates (eds.), (1992), *Organizational Architecture: Designs for Changing Organizations*, Jossey-Bass Publishers, San Francisco, pp. 11–38.

Giffinger, R., Fertner, C., Kramar, H., Kalasek, R., Pichler-Milanović, N. & Meijers, E. (2007), 'Smart Cities: Ranking of European Medium-Sized Cities', *Centre of Regional Science*, Vienna University of Technology, http://www.smart-cities.eu, date accessed 21 August 2013.

Gilgeous, V. & D'Cruz, M. (1996), 'A Study of Business and Management Games', *Management Development Review*, **9**(1), pp. 32–39.

Graham, G. & Hardaker, G. (2000), 'Supply-Chain Management Across the Internet', *International Journal of Physical Distribution and Logistics*, **30**(34), pp. 286–296.

Granlund, M. (2003), 'Management Accounting System Integration in Corporate Mergers', *Accounting, Auditing & Accountability Journal*, **16**(2), pp. 208–243.

Green, A. (2007), 'Business Information – A Natural Path to Business Intelligence: Knowing What to Capture', *VINE: The Journal of Information and Knowledge Management Systems*, **37**(1), pp. 18–23.

Greenwood, R., Suddaby, R. & Higgins, C. R. (2002), 'Theorizing Change: The Role of Professional Associations in the Transformation of Institutionalized Fields', *Academy of Management Journal*, **45**(1), pp. 58–80.

Gregor, S., Martin, M., Fernandez, W., Stern, S. & Vitale, M. (2006), 'The Transformational Dimension in the Realization of Business Value from Information Technology', *Journal of Strategic Information Systems*, **15**(3), pp. 249–270.

Griffin, J. (2010), 'Implementing a Data Governance Initiative: The Road to Effective Data Governance Starts with Choosing to Formalize the Practice of Managing Corporate Data', *Information Management*, **20**(2), pp. 27–30.

Grønli, T-M. & Ghinea, G. (2010), 'Three-Dimensional Context-Aware Tailoring of Information', *Online Information Review*, **34**(6), pp. 892–906.

Gulledge, T. (2006), 'What is Integration?', *Industrial Management and Data Systems*, **106**(1), pp. 5–20.

Halal, W. E. (2008), *Technology's Promise*, Palgrave, Basingstoke.

Halal, H. (2013), 'Space Tourism – Introduction', http://www.techcast.org, date accessed 21 August 2013.

Hall, H. (2010), 'Relationship and Role Transformations in Social Media Environments', *The Electronic Library*, **29**(4), pp. 421–428.

Hannula, M. & Pirttimäki, V. (2005), 'A Cube of Information', *Journal of Competitive Intelligence and Management*, **3**(1), pp. 34–40.

Hanseth, O. & Braa, K. (2000), 'Globalization and "Risk Society"', in: Ciborra, C. U. & Associates (eds.), (2000), *From Control to Drift: The Dynamics of Corporate Information Infrastructures*, Oxford University Press, Oxford, pp. 41–55.

Harbury, C. & Lipsey, R. G. (1993), *An Introduction to the UK Economy*, Fourth Edition, Blackwell Publishers, Oxford.

Harman, R. D., Demirkan, H. & Raffo, D. (2012), 'Roadmapping the Next Wave of Sustainable IT', *Foresight*, **14**(2), pp. 121–138.

Harnesk, D. & Lindstrőm, J. (2011), 'Shaping Security Behaviour Through Discipline and Agility: Implications for Information Security Management', *Information Management and Computer Security*, **19**(4), pp. 262–276.

Harnik, D., Pinkas, B. & Shulman-Peleg, A. (2010), 'Side Channels in Cloud Services: Deduplication in Cloud Storage', *Security and Privacy*, **8**(6), pp. 40–47.

Haug, A. & Arlbjørn, J. S. (2011), 'Barriers to Master Data Quality', *Journal of Enterprise Information Management*, **24**(3), pp. 288–303.

Haug, A., Arlbjørn, J. S. & Pederesen, A. (2009), 'A Classification Model of ERP System Data Quality', *Industrial Management & Data Systems*, **109**(8), pp. 1053–1068.

Haug, A., Arlbjørn, J. S., Zachariassen, F. & Schlichter, J. (2013), 'Master Data Quality Barriers: An Empirical Investigation', *Industrial Management & Data Systems*, **113**(2), pp. 234–249.

He, W. (2012), 'A Review of Social Media Security Risks and Migration Techniques', *Journal of Systems and Information Technology*, **14**(2), pp. 171–180.

Hedman, J. & Kalling, T. (2003), 'The Business Model Concept: The Theoretical Underpinnings and Empirical Illustrations', *European Journal of Information Systems*, **12**(1), pp. 49–59.

Herman, R. & Nicholas, D. (2010), 'The Information Enfranchisement of the Digital Consumer', *Aslib Proceedings*, **62**(3), pp. 245–260.

Hewett, W. G. & Whitaker, J. (2002), 'Data Protection and Privacy: The Australian Legislation and Its Implications for IT Professionals', *Logistics Information Management*, **15**(5/6), pp. 369–376.

Hitchman, S. & Bennetts, P. (1994), 'The Strategic Use of Data Modelling and Soft Systems Thinking', in: Lissoni, C., Richardson, T., Miles, R., Wood-Harper, T. & Jayaratna, N. (eds.), (1994), *Information Systems Methodologies*, Proceedings of the Second Conference on Information Systems Methodologies, 31 August–2 September 1994, Edinburgh, British Computer Society, London, pp. 331–336.

Hollands, R. G. (2008), 'Will the Real Smart City Please Stand Up? Intelligent, Progressive or Entrepreneurial?', *City*, **12**(3), pp. 303–320.

Holmes, J. (2003), 'Formulating an Effective Computer Use Policy', *Information Strategy: The Executive's Journal*, **20**(1), pp. 26–33.

Holsapple, C. W. & Singh, M. (2000), 'Toward a Unified View of Electronic Commerce, Electronic Business, and Collaborative Commerce: A Knowledge Management Approach', *Knowledge and Process Management*, **7**(3), pp. 151–164.

Howson, C. (2008), *Successful Business Intelligence: Secrets to Making BI a Killer App.*, McGraw-Hill, New York.

Hugos, M. H. (2011), *Essentials of Supply Chain Management*, Third Edition, Wiley, New Jersey.

ICO (2008), 'CCTV Code of Practice Revised Edition 2008', *Information Commissioner's Office*, http://www.ico.gov.uk, date accessed 1 June 2013.

Inmon, W. H. (1996), *Building the Data Warehouse*, Second Edition, Wiley, Chichester.

Inmon, W. H., Welch, J. D. & Glassey, K. L. (1997), *Managing the Data Warehouse*, Wiley, Chichester.

Inmon, W. H., Rudin, K., Buss, C. K. & Sousa, R. (1999), *Data Warehouse Performance*, Wiley, Chichester.

IRM (2002), *A Risk Management Standard*, Airmic, http://www.theirm.org, date accessed 1 June 2013.

ISO (2008), 'Introduction to ISO 27005', http://www.27000.org, date accessed 1 June 2013.

Ives, B. & Learmonth, G. P. (1984), 'An Information System as a Competitive Weapon', *Communications of the ACM*, **27**(12), pp. 1193–1201.

James, S. (2004), 'Adding Value: The Presentation of Business Information', *Business Information Review*, **21**(4), pp. 44–52.

Janeert, P. K. (2011), *Data Analysis with Open Source Tools*, O'Reilly Media, California.

Jayaratna, N. (1994), *Understanding and Evaluating Methodologies, NISMAD: A Systemic Framework*, McGraw-Hill, Maidenhead.

Jenkins, M. & McDonald, M. (1997), 'Market Segmentation: Organizational Archetypes and Research Agendas', *European Journal of Marketing*, **31**(1), pp. 17–32.

Johnson, G., Scholes, K. & Whittington, R. (2008), *Exploring Corporate Strategy: Text and Cases*, Eighth Edition, Pearson Education, Harlow.

Jones, W. & Anderson, K. M. (2011), 'Many Views, Many Modes, Many Tools & One Structure', *Proceedings of the 22nd ACM Conference on Hypertext and Hypermedia*, Eindhoven, The Netherlands, pp. 113–122.

Judge, P. (2012), 'Data Centre Power Surges 63 Percent', *Techweek Europe*, 8 October 2012, http://www.techweekeurope.co.uk, date accessed 21 August 2013.

Kakabadse, N., Kakabadse, A. & Kouzmin, A. (2003), 'Reviewing the Knowledge Management Literature: Towards a Taxonomy', *Journal of Knowledge Management*, **7**(4), pp. 75–91.

Kaplan, A. M. & Haenlein, M. (2010), 'Users of the World, Unite! The Challenges and Opportunities of Social Media', *Business Horizons*, **53**(1), pp. 59–68.

Khatri, V. & Brown, C. V. (2010), 'Designing Data Governance', *Communications of the ACM*, **53**(1), pp. 148–153.

Kietzmann, J. H., Hermkens, K., McCarthy, I. P. & Silvestre, B. S. (2011), 'Social Media? Get Serious! Understanding the Functional Building Blocks of Social Media', *Business Horizons*, **54**(3), pp. 181–288.

Klausegger, C., Sinkovics, R. R. & Zou, H. (2007), 'Information Overload: A Cross-National Investigation of Influence Factors and Effects', *Marketing Intelligence and Planning*, **25**(7), pp. 691–718.

Kleijnen, J. P. C. (2005), 'Supply Chain Simulation Tools and Techniques: A Survey', *International Journal of Simulation & Process Modelling*, **1**(1/2), pp. 82–89.

Kleijnen, J. P. C. & Smits, M. T. (2003), 'Performance Metrics in Supply Chain Management', *Journal of the Operational Research Society*, **54**(5), pp. 507–514.

Ko, D. & Fink, D. (2010), 'Information Technology Governance: An Evaluation of the Theory-Practice Gap', *Corporate Governance*, **10**(5), pp. 662–674.

Kooper, M. N., Maes, R. & Lindgreen, E. E. O. R. (2011), 'On the Governance of Information: Introducing a New Concept of Governance to Support the Management of Information', *International Journal of Information Management*, **31**(3), pp. 195–200.

Kosanke, K. (2005), 'ISO Standards for Interoperability: A Comparison', in: Konstantas, D., Bourrières, J-P., Léonard, M. & Boudjilida, N. (eds.), (2005), *Interoperability of Enterprise Software and Applications*, Proceedings of INTERO-ESA, 23–25 February, Geneva, Springer, London, pp. 55–64.

Kounios, J., Green, D. L., Payne, L., Fleck, J. I., Grondin, R. & McRae, J. (2009), 'Semantic Richness and the Activation of Concepts in Semantic Memory: Evidence from Event-Related Potentials', *Brain Research*, **1282**(28 July), pp. 95–102.

Kruger, C. J. & Johnson, R. D. (2010), 'Information Management as an Enabler of Knowledge Management Maturity: A South African Perspective', *International Journal of Information Management*, **30**(1), pp. 57–67.

Kubicek, H. & Cimander, R. (2009), 'Three Dimensions of Organizational Interoperability', *European Journal of ePractice*, **6**, pp. 3–14.

Kuntz, J. R. C. & Gomes, J. F. S. (2012), 'Transformational Change in Organisations: A Self-Regulation Approach', *Journal of Organizational Change Management*, **25**(1), pp. 143–162.

Lacey, D. (2010), 'Understanding and Transforming Organizational Security Culture', *Information Management & Computer Security*, **18**(1), pp. 4–13.

Lee, K-H. & Cheong, I-M. (2011), 'Measuring a Carbon Footprint and Environmental Practice: The Case of Hyundai Motors Co. (HMC)', *Industrial Management and Data Systems*, **111**(6), pp. 961–978.

Lee, D. L., Xu, J., Zheng, B. & Lee, W-C. (2002), 'Data Management in Location-Dependent Information Services', *IEEE Pervasive Computing*, **1**(3), pp. 65–72.

Lenzerini, M. (2002), 'Data Integration: A Theoretical Perspective', *ACM Symposium on Principles of Database Systems*, 3–6 June, Wisconsin, pp. 233–246.

Levitt, T. (1965), 'Exploit the Product Life Cycle', *Harvard Business Review*, **43**(November/December), pp. 81–94.

Lewis, P. J. (1993), 'Linking Soft Systems Methodology with Data-Focused Information Systems Development', *Journal of Information Systems*, **3**(3), pp. 169–186.

Lewis, P. J. (1994), *Information-Systems Development*, Pitman Publishing, London.

Lin, L-H. & Lu, I-Y. (2005), 'Adoption of Virtual Organization by Taiwanese Electronics Firms: An Empirical Study of Organization Structure Innovation', *Journal of Organizational Change Management*, **18**(2), pp. 184–200.

Linder, J. C. (1996), 'Mergers: The Role of Information Technology', in Earl, M. J. (ed.), (1996), *Information Management: The Organizational Dimension*, Oxford University Press, Oxford, pp. 295–314.

Lipsey, R. G. & Chrystal, K. A. (2011), *Economics*, Twelfth Edition, Oxford University Press, Oxford.

Liu, H-Y. & Hsu, C. W. (2011), 'Antecedents and Consequences of Corporate Diversification: A Dynamic Capabilities Perspective', *Management Decision*, **49**(9), pp. 1510–1534.

Lober, W. B., Trigg, L. J., Bliss, D. & Brinkley, J. M. (2001), 'IML: An Image Markup Language', *Proceedings of the Annual Symposium of the American Medical Informatics Association*, 3–7 November, Washington, pp. 403–407.

Lomas, E. (2010), 'Information Governance: Information Security and Access within a UK Context', *Records Management Journal*, **20**(2), pp. 182–198.

Loshin, D. (2010), *The Practitioner's Guide to Data Quality Improvement*, Morgan Kaufmann, MA.

Low, C., Chen, Y. & Wu, M. (2011), 'Understanding the Determinants of Cloud Computing Adoption', *Industrial Management and Data Systems*, **111**(7), pp. 1006–1023.

Lucey, T. (2004), *Management Information Systems*, Ninth Edition, Cengage Learning, EMEA, Andover.

Lussier, R. N. & Achua, C. F. (2009), *Leadership: Theory, Application and Skill Development*, Fourth Edition, South Western Cengage Learning, USA.

Lynch, R. (2006), *Corporate Strategy*, Fourth Edition, Pearson, Harlow.

Ma, Y., Fox, E. A. & Conçalves, M. A. (2007), 'Personal Digital Library: PIMP Through 5s Perspective', *Proceedings of the ACM First Ph.D. Workshop In CIKM*, 9 November, Lisbon, pp. 117–124.

Macdonald, J. (1994), 'Service Is Different', *The TQM Magazine*, **6**(1), pp. 5–7.

Maciej, J. & Vollrath, M. (2009), 'Comparison of Manual vs. Speech-based Interaction with In-Vehicle Information Systems', *Accident Analysis & Prevention*, **41**(5), pp. 924–930.

Mahboubi, H. & Darmont, J. (2008), 'Data Mining-Based Fragmentation of XML Data Warehouses', *Proceedings of the ACM 11th International Workshop on Data Warehousing and OLAP*, 26–30 October, CA, pp. 9–16.

Manning, C. D., Raghavan, R. & Schűtze, H. (2008), *An Introduction to Information Retrieval*, Cambridge University Press, Cambridge.

Martin, C. (1999), *Net Future*, McGraw-Hill, New York.

Martin, A., Dmitriev, D. & Akeroyd, J. (2010), 'A Resurgence of Interest in Information Architecture', *International Journal of Information Management*, **30**(1), pp. 6–12.

Martin, S. S., López-Caralán, B. & Ramón-Jerónimo, M. A. (2012), 'Factors Determining Firms' Perceived Performance of Mobile Commerce', *Industrial Management and Data Systems*, **112**(6), pp. 946–963.

Martins, E. C. & Hester, M. (2012), 'Organizational and Behavioral Factors that Influence Knowledge Retention', *Journal of Knowledge Management*, **16**(1), pp. 77–96.

Martins, E. C. & Martins, N. (2011), 'The Role of Organisational Factors in Combating Tacit Knowledge Loss in Organisations', *South African Business Review*, **15**(1), April, pp. 49–69.

Marulanda-Carter, L. & Jackson, T. W. (2012), 'Effects of E-mail Addiction and Interruptions on Employees', *Journal of Systems and Information Technology*, **14**(1), pp. 82–94.

Mason, R. (1986), 'Four Ethical Issues of the Information Age', *Management Information Systems Quarterly*, **10**(1), pp. 5–12.

Masrek, M. M., Karim, N. S. A. & Hussein, R. (2008), 'The Effect of Organizational and Individual Characteristics on Corporate Intranet Utilizations', *Information Management and Computer Security*, **16**(2), pp. 89–112.

Matthews, G., Smith, Y. & Knowles, G. (2009), *Disaster Management in Archives, Libraries and Museums*, Ashgate, Surrey.

Mayo, A. (2006), *Human Value of the Enterprise: Valuing PEOPLE as Assets – Monitoring, Measuring, Managing*, Second Edition, Nicholas Brealey International, London.

McDonald, M. & Dunbar, I. (2012), *Market Segmentation: How to Do It, How to Profit from It*, Fourth Edition, Wiley, Chichester.

McDonough, W. & Braungart, M. (2002), *Cradle to Cradle: Remaking the Way We Make Things*, North Point Press, New York.

McGarry, K. J. (1981), *The Changing Context of Information: An Introductory Analysis*, Clive Bingley Ltd., London.

Meglio, C. E. & Kleiner, B. H. (1990), 'Managing Information Overload', *Industrial Management and Data Systems*, **90**(1), pp. 23–26.

Melville, N., Kraemer, K. & Gurbuxani, V. (2004), 'Review: Information Technology and Organizational Performance: An Integrative Model of IT Business Value', *MIS Quarterly*, **28**(2), pp. 283–322.

Menou, M. J. (2002), 'Information Literacy in National Information and Communications Technology (ICT) Policies: The Missed Dimension, Information Culture', *White Paper Prepared for UNESCO, the U.S. National Commission on Libraries and Information Science, and the National Forum on Information Literacy*, for use at the Information Literacy Meeting of Experts, Prague. Washington, DC: National Commission on Libraries and Information Science, http://citeseerx.ist.psu.edu, date accessed 21 August 2013.

Menou, M. J. (2010), 'Information Behaviour of the "Google Generation" as a Factor in Sustainability for Mexican Cities', *Aslib Proceedings; New Information Perspectives*, **62**(2), pp. 165–174.

Mensching, J. & Corbitt, G. (2004), 'ERP Data Archiving – A Critical Analysis', *The Journal of Enterprise Information*, **17**(2), pp. 131–141.

Meredith, J. R. (1992), *The Management of Operations*, Wiley, Chichester.

Miczka, S. & Größler, S. (2010), 'Merger Dynamics: Using System Dynamics for the Conceptual Integration of a Fragmented Knowledge Base', *Kybernetes*, **39**(9/10), pp. 1491–1512.

Miller, G. A. (1956), 'The Magical Number Seven, Plus or Minus Two: Some Limits on Our Capacity for Processing Information', *Psychological Review*, **63**(2), pp. 81–97.

Mingers, J. (1988), 'Comparing Conceptual Models and Data Flow Diagrams', *The Computer Journal*, **31**(4), pp. 376–379.

Mitropoulos, D., Karakoidas, V., Louridas, P. & Spinellis, D. (2011), 'Countering Code Injection Attacks: A Unified Approach', *Information Management and Computer Security*, **19**(3), pp. 177–194.

Monks, R. A. G. & Minow, N. (2011), *Corporate Governance*, Wiley, Chichester.

Moore, F. (2004), 'Information Life Cycle Management', *Zjournal*, April/May, pp. 8–11, http://enterprisesystemsmedia.com, date accessed 8 March 2013.

Moore, G. A. (2006), *Dealing with Darwin: How Great Companies Innovate at Every Phase of Their Evolution*, Penguin Group, New York.

Moreira, E. D. S., Martimiano, A. F., Brandão, A. J. D. S. & Bernardes, M. C. (2008), 'Ontologies for Information Security Management and Governance', *Information Management and Computer Security*, **16**(2), pp. 150–165.

Morris, J. (2006), *Practical Data Migration*, British Computer Society, Swindon.

Morville, P. & Rosenfield, L. (2007), *Information Architecture for the World Wide Web*, O'Reilly Media Inc., California.

Mullins, C. S. (2010a), 'Managing Data Storage', *Database Trends and Applications*, 7 September 2010, http://www.dbta.com, date accessed 8 March 2013.

Mullins, L. J. (2010b), *Management and Organisational Behaviour*, Ninth Edition, Prentice Hall, Harlow.

Myerson, J. M. (2007), *RFID in the Supply Chain: A Guide to Selection and Implementation*, Auerbach Publications, New York.

Nadler, D. A. (1992), 'Introduction: Organizational Architecture: A Metaphor for Change', in: Nadler, D. A., Gerstein, M. C., Shaw, R. B. & Associates (eds.), (1992), *Organizational Architecture: Designs for Changing Organizations*, Jossey-Bass Publishers, San Francisco, pp. 1–10.

NAICS (2007), 'North American Industry Classification System', *U. S. Census Bureau*, http://www.census.gov/eos/www/naics/index.html, date accessed 25 March 2013.

Nguyen, H. & Kleiner, B. H. (2003), 'The Effective Management of Mergers', *Leadership and Organizational Development Journal*, **24**(8), pp. 447–454.

Nicholas, D. & Herman, E. (2009), *Assessing Information Needs in the Age of the Digital Consumer*, Routledge, London.

Nicholas, D., Rowlands, I., Clark, D. & Williams, P. (2011), 'Google Generation II: Web Behaviour Experiments with the BBC', *Aslib Proceedings: New Information Perspectives*, **63**(1), pp. 28–45.

Nielsen, J. (1994), *Usability Engineering*, Morgan Kaufmann, San Francisco.

Nolan, R. L. (1973), 'Managing the Computer Resource: A Stage Hypothesis', *Communications of the ACM*, **16**(7), pp. 399–405.

Nolan, R. L. (1979), 'Managing the Crises in Data Processing', *Harvard Business Review*, **57**(March), pp. 115–126.

Nonaka, I. & Takeuchi, H. (1995), *The Knowledge Creating Company*, Oxford University Press, Oxford.

Norman, D. A. (1998), *The Invisible Computer: Why Good Products Can Fail, the Personal Computer Is So Complex and Information Applications Are the Solution*, MIT Press, Cambridge, MA.

O'Donoghue, J., O'Kane, T., Gallagher, J., Courtney, G., Aftab, A., Casey, A., Torres, J. & Angove, P. (2011), 'Modified Early Warning Scorecard: The Role of Data/Information Quality within the Decision Making Process', *The Electronic Journal Information Systems Evaluation*, **13**(3), pp. 100–109.

Olson, J. E. (2003), *Data Quality: The Accuracy Dimension*, Morgan Kaufmann, Burlington, MA.

Oppenheim, C. (2011), 'Legal Issues for Information Professionals in IX: An Overview of Recent Developments in the Law, in Relation to the Internet', *Journal of Documentation*, **64**(6), pp. 938–955.

Ortt, J. R. & van der Duin, P. A. (2008), 'The Evolution of Innovation Management Towards Contextual Innovation', *European Journal of Innovation Management*, **11**(4), pp. 522–538.

Öztayşi, B., Sezgin, S. & Özok, A. F. (2011), 'A Measurement Tool for Customer Relationship Management Processes', *Industrial Management and Data Systems*, **111**(6), pp. 943–960.

Papadakis, V. M. (2005), 'The Role of Broader Context and the Communication Program in Merger and Acquisition Implementation Success', *Management Decision*, **43**(2), pp. 236–255.

Parnell, N. (2001), 'Managing Information Overload', *Business Information Review*, **18**(1), pp. 45–50.

Parsons, G. L. (1983), 'Information Technology: A New Competitive Weapon', *Sloan Management Review*, **25**(1), pp. 3–14.

Parum, E. (2006), 'Corporate Governance and Corporate Identity', *Corporate Governance*, **14**(6), pp. 558–567.

Pedersen, C. & Nagengast, J. (2008), 'The Virtual Organization', *Strategic HR Review*, **7**(3), pp. 19–25.

Perens, B. (1999), 'The Open Source Definition', in: Dibona, C., Ockman, S. & Stone, M. (eds.), (1999), *Open Sources: Voices from the Open Source Revolution*, O'Reilly Media, California, pp. 171–188.

Pérez-Castilo, R., Rodriguez de Guzmán, I. G. & Piattini, M. (2010), 'On the Use of Patterns to Recover Business Processes', *Proceedings of the 2010 ACM Symposium on Applied Computing*, 22–26 March, Sierre, Switzerland, pp. 165–166.

Perkins, J. & Cox, S. A. (2004), 'Sharing Knowledge in Communities of Practice: Taxonomies for Enabling Inter and Intra Organisational Collaboration', *Fifth European Conference on Knowledge Management*, 30 September–1 October 2004, France.

Pessi, K., Magoulas, T. & Hugoson, M-Å. (2011), 'Enterprise Architecture Principles and Their Impact on the Management of IT Investments', *The Electronic Journal Information Systems Evaluation*, **14**(1), pp. 53–62.

Peters, C. & Bradbard, D. A. (2010), 'Web Accessibility: An Introduction and Ethical Implications', *Journal of Information, Communication and Ethics in Society*, **8**(2), pp. 206–232.

Peters, T. J. & Waterman Jr., R. H. (2004), *In Search of Excellence: Lessons from America's Best Run Companies*, Second Edition, Harper Collins, New York.

Petri, G. (2010), *Shedding Light on Cloud Computing*, Smashwords Edition, Los Gatos, CA.

Pexman, P., Hargreaves, I.S., Edwards, J. D., Henry, L. C. & Goodyear, B. G., (2007), 'The Neural Consequences of Semantic Richness', *Psychological Science*, **18**(5), pp. 401–406.

Pietraszek, T. & Berghe, C. V. (2005), 'Defending Against Injection Attacks Through Context-Sensitive String Evaluation', in: Valdes, A. & Zamboni, D. (eds.), (2006), *Recent Advances in Intrusion Detection, Proceedings of the Eighth International Symposium*, RADI, 7–9 September, Seattle, *Lecture Notes in Computer Science*, **3858**, Springer, pp. 124–145.

Polanyi, M. E. (1966), *Personal Knowledge: Towards a Post-Critical Philosophy*, University of Chicago Press, Chicago.

Popper, K. R. (1968), 'Epistemology Without a Knowing Subject', in: van Rootselaar, B. (ed.), (1968), *Logic, Methodology and Philosophy of Science III*, North-Holland, Amsterdam, pp. 333–373.

Porter, M. E. (1980), *Competitive Strategy Technique for Analyzing Industries and Competitors*, Free Press, New York.

Porter, M. E. (2008), 'The Five Competitive Forces that Shape Strategy', *Harvard Business Review*, **86**(1), pp. 86–104.

Porter, M. E. & Millar, V. E. (1985), 'How Information Gives you Competitive Advantage', *Harvard Business Review*, **63**(4), pp. 149–160.

Prasopoulou, E., Pouloudi, A. & Panteli, N. (2006), 'Enacting New Temporal Boundaries: The Role of Mobile Phones', *European Journal of Information Systems*, **15**(3), pp. 277–284.

Preece, R. (1994), *Starting Research: An Introduction to Academic Research and Dissertation Writing*, Pinter, London.

Presidents & Fellows of Harvard College (2009), 'What Makes a Profession?', Harvard Business School, http://

www.hbs.edu/centennial/im/inquiry/sections/1/, date accessed 25 March 2013.

Professions Australia (1997), 'Definition of a Profession', http://www.professions.com.au, date accessed 25 March 2013.

Pupo, A. (2013), 'AI – 30%', http://www.techcast.org, date accessed 21 August 2013.

Quality Research International (2009), 'Regulatory Body', http://www.qualityresearchinternational.com, date accessed 25 March 2013.

Quinn, J. B., Anderson, P. & Finkelstein, S. (1996), 'Managing Professional Intellect: Making the Most of the Best', *Harvard Business Review*, **74**(2), pp. 71–80.

Raben, C. S. (1992), 'Building Strategic Partnerships: Creating and Managing Effective Joint Ventures', in: Nadler, D. A., Gerstein, M. C., Shaw, R. B. & Associates (eds.), (1992), *Organizational Architecture: Designs for Changing Organizations*, Jossey-Bass Publishers, San Francisco, pp. 81–109.

Radicati, S. (2010), 'Email Statistics Report 2010', *The Radicati Group Inc.*, http://www.radicati.com, date accessed 17 July 2013.

Rafferty, P. & Hidderley, R. (2005), *Indexing Multimedia and Creative Works: The Problems of Meaning and Interpretation*, Ashgate, Aldershot.

Rajola, F. (2012), *Customer Relationship Management: Organizational and Technological Perspectives*, Springer, New York.

Ranjan, J. & Bhatnagar, V. (2009), 'A Holistic Framework for mCRM – Data Mining Perspective', *Information Management and Computer Security*, **17**(2), pp. 151–165.

Recchia, G. & Jones, M. N. (2012), 'The Semantic Richness of Abstract Concepts', *Frontiers in Human Neuroscience*, **6**(315), November, pp. 1–16.

Reddy, S. B. & Reddy, R. (2002), 'Competitive Agility and the Challenge of Legacy Information Systems', *Industrial Management & Data Systems*, **102**(1), pp. 5–16.

Reimer, Y. J., Bubnash, M., Hagedal, M. & Wolf, P. (2009), 'Helping Students with Information Fragmentation, Assimilation and Notetaking', *Proceedings of the Ninth ACM/IEE-CS Joint Conference on Digital Libraries*, 14–19 June, TX, pp. 15–18.

Rockley, A., Kostur, P. & Manning, S. (2003), *Managing Enterprise Content: A Unified Content Strategy*, New Riders, Berkeley.

Rodgers, S. & Sheldon, K. (2002), 'An Improved Way to Characterize Internet Use', *Journal of Advertising Research*, **42**(5), pp. 85–89.

Rodriguez, A., Caro, A. & Fernández-Medina, E. (2009), 'Towards Framework Definition to Obtain Secure Business Process From Legacy Information Systems', *Proceedings of the First International Workshop on Model Driven Service Engineering and Data Quality and Security*, 2–6 November, Hong Kong, pp. 17–24.

Rogerson, S., (2008), 'Information – Lifeblood or Pollution?', *IT Now*, **50**(3), pp. 14–15.

Rose, A., Eichel, D. & Krueger, T. (2009), 'A Comparison of Gesture and Speech in Intraoperative-near Environment', *Fourth European Conference of the International Federation for Medical and Biological Engineering*, **22**(11), pp. 1574–1576.

Rowlands, I., Nicholas, D., Williams, P., Huntington, P., Fieldhouse, M., Gunter, B., Withey, R., Jamali, H. R., Dobrowolski, T. & Tenopir, C. (2008), 'The Google Generation: The Information Behaviour of the Researcher of the Future', *Aslib Proceedings: New Information Perspectives*, **60**(4), pp. 290–310.

Rowley, J. (1998), 'Towards a Framework for Information Management', *International Journal of Information Management*, **18**(5), pp. 359–369.

Royal Mail Group Ltd. (2011), 'Postcode Address File (PAF®)', http://www.postcodeaddressfile.co.uk, date accessed 5 June 2013.

Sahay, B. S. (2003), 'Supply Chain Collaboration: The Key to Value Creation', *Work Study*, **52**(2), pp. 76–83.

Samarati, P. & di Vimercati, S. de C. (2010), 'Data Protection in Outsourcing Scenarios: Issues and Directions', *Proceedings of the ACM Symposium on Information, Computer and Communications Security*, 13–16 April, Beijing, pp. 1–14.

Sarsfield, S. (2009), *The Data Governance Initiative*, IT Governance Publishing, Cambridgeshire.

Saucer, C. & Willcocks, L. (2004), 'Strategic Alignment Revisited: Connecting Organizational Architecture and IT Infrastructure', *Proceedings of the 37th Hawaii International Conference on System Sciences*, 5–8 January, Hawaii, pp. 1–10.

Savolainen, R. (2007), 'Filtering and Withdrawing: Strategies for Coping with Information Overload in Everyday Contexts', *Journal of Information Science*, **33**(5), pp. 611–621.

Schein, E. H. (2010), *Organizational Culture and Leadership*, Fourth Edition, Wiley, San Francisco.

Scherpereel, C. M. & Lefebvre, J. R. (2006), 'Shocking the Legacy Mindset™: Management Development and the Internet', *Journal of Management Development*, **25**(3), pp. 232–248.

Scofield, M. (1998), 'Issues of Data Ownership', *Information Management Magazine*, November, http://www.information-management.com, date accessed 1 June 2013.

Scott, C. R. (2004), *Project Management for Data Conversions: A Data Conversion Methodology and Guide to Converting Data for Mission Critical Applications*, Author House, Indiana.

Seadle, M. (2004), 'Copyright in a Networked World: Ethics and Infringement', *Library Hi-Tech*, **22**(1), pp. 106–110.

Senior, B. & Swailes, S. (2010), *Organisational Change*, Fourth Edition, Pearson Education, Harlow.

Shankar, V., Venkatesh, A., Hofacker, C. & Naik, P. (2010), 'Mobile Marketing in the Retailing Environment; Current Insights and Future Research Avenues', *Journal of Interactive Marketing*, **24**(2), pp. 111–120.

Shekleton, J. F. (1991), 'Aristotle, the Entity Model and Neurosis', *Boxes and Arrows*, **92**, pp. 11–14.

Shepherd, E. (2006), 'Why are Records in the Public Sector Organizational Assets?', *Records Management Journal*, **16**(1), pp. 6–12.

Shepherd, E. & Ennion, E. (2007), 'How Has the Implementation of the UK Freedom of Information Act 2000 Affected Archives and Records Management Services?', *Records Management Journal*, **17**(1), pp. 32–51.

Sherif, M. A, (1988), *Database Projects: A Framework for Effective Management*, Ellis Horwood Ltd., Chichester.

Shirtz, D. & Elovici, Y. (2011), 'Optimizing Investment Decisions in Selecting Information Security Remedies', *Information Management and Computer Security*, **19**(2), pp. 95–112.

SIC (2007), 'Standard Industry Classification System', *Office for National Statistics*, http://www.ons.gov.uk, date accessed 25 March 2013.

Silvola, R., Jaaskelainen, O., Kropsu-Vehkapera, H. & Haapaslo, H. (2011), 'Managing One Master Data – Challenges and Preconditions', *Industrial Management and Data Systems*, **111**(1), pp. 146–162.

Singh, S. P. (2007), 'What Are We Managing – Knowledge or Information?', *VINE: The Journal of Information and Knowledge Management Systems*, **37**(2), pp. 169–179.

Singh, T. & Hill, M. E. (2003), 'Consumer Privacy and the Internet in Europe: A View from Germany', *Journal of Consumer Marketing*, **20**(7), pp. 634–651.

Sinisalo, J., Salo, J., Karjaluoto, H. & Leppäniemi, M. (2007), 'Mobile Customer Relationship Management: Underlying Issues and Challenges', *Business Process Management Journal*, **13**(6), pp. 771–787.

Snowden, D. (2003), 'Knowing What We Know: Language and Tools for Knowledge Mapping', in: Evans, C. (2003), *Managing for Knowledge: HR's Strategic Role*, Butterworth Heinemann, Oxford, pp. 186–208.

Soparnot, R. (2011), 'The Concept of Organizational Change Capacity', *Journal of Organizational Change Management*, **24**(5), pp. 640–661.

Srinivasan, S. R., Ramakrishnan, S. & Grasman, S. E. (2005), 'Identifying the Effects of Cannibalization on the Product Portfolio', *Marketing Intelligence & Planning*, **23**(4/5), pp. 359–371.

Stanton, J. M., Stam, K. R., Mastrangelo, P. & Jolton, J. (2005), 'Analysis of End-User Security Behaviours', *Computers and Security*, **24**(2), pp. 124–133.

Steyn. J. (ed.) (2013), *Structuring Music Through Markup Language: Designs and Architectures*, IGI Information Science Reference, New York.

Sudalaimuthu, S. & Raj, A. S. (2009), *Logistics Management for International Business: Text and Cases*, PHI Learning Private Limited, New Delhi.

Sultan, N. A. (2011), 'Reaching for the "Cloud": How SME's Can Manage', *International Journal of Information Management*, **31**(3), pp. 272–278.

Sun, J., Ahluwalia, P. & Koong, K. S. (2011), 'The More Secure the Better? A Study of Information Security Readiness', *Industrial Management and Data Systems*, **111**(4), pp. 570–588.

Susman, G. I. & Evered, R. D. (1978), 'An Assessment of the Scientific Merits of Action Research', *Administrative Science Quarterly*, **23** (December), pp. 582–603.

Sutor, R. S. (2011), 'Software Standards, Openness and Interoperability', in: DeNardis, L. (ed.), (2011), *Opening Standards: The Global Politics of Interoperability*, MIT Press, Cambridge, MA, pp. 209–218.

Tallon, P. T. & Scannell, R. (2007), 'Information Life Cycle Management', *Communications of the ACM*, **50**(11), pp. 65–69.

Tarzey, B. (2010), 'A Business Case for Network Security', *Computer Weekly*, 27 April–3 May, p. 16.

Tavani, H. T. (2011), *Ethics and Technology*, Third Edition, Wiley, Chichester.

Thomas, G. (2011a), '"Flavors" of Data Governance', Data Governance Institute, Florida, http://www.datagovernance.com, date accessed 1 June 2013.

Thomas, P. Y. (2011b), 'Cloud Computing: A Potential Paradigm for Practising the Scholarship of Teaching and Learning', *The Electronic Library*, **29**(2), pp. 214–224.

Toffler, A. (1970), *Future Shock*, The Bodley Head, London.

Tonkin, C., Ouzts, A. D. & Duchowski, A. T. (2011), 'Eye Tracking within the Packaging Design Workflow: Interaction with Physical and Virtual Shelves', *Proceedings of the First Conference on Novel Gaze-Controlled Applications*, Sweden, 26–27 May, article 3.

Townsend, K. & Batchelor, L. (2005), 'Managing Mobile Phones: A Work/Non-Work Collision in Small Business', *New Technology, Work and Employment*, **20**(3), pp. 259–267.

Tripathi, R. & Gupta, M. P. (2012), 'Interoperability Adoption Amongst Government and Corporate Portals in India: A Study', *Journal of Enterprise Information Management*, **25**(2), pp. 98–122.

Tsichritzis, D. C. & Lochovsky, F. H. (1982), *Data Models*, Prentice Hall, New York.

Umar, A., Karabatis, G., Ness, L. & Horowitz, B. (1999), 'Enterprise Data Quality: A Pragmatic Approach', *Information Systems Frontiers*, **1**(3), pp. 279–301.

van Eijk, N., Helberger, N., Kool, L., van der Plas, A. & van der Sloot, B. (2012), 'Online Tracking: Questioning the Power of Informed Consent', *Info*, **14**(5), pp. 57–73.

Vigo, M., Aizpurua, A., Arrue, M. & Abascal, J. (2009), 'Automatic Device-Tailored Evaluation of Mobile Web Guidelines', *New Review of Hypermedia and Multimedia*, **15**(3), pp. 223–244.

Vigon, B. W., Tolle, D. A., Cornaby, B. W., Latham, H. C., Harrison, C. L., Boguski, T. L., Hunt, R. G. & Sellers, J. D. (1993), *Life-Cycle Assessment: Inventory Guidelines and Principles*, CRC Press, Florida.

Vlachos, V., Minou, M., Assimakopouos, V. & Toska, A. (2011), 'The Landscape of Cybercrime in Greece', *Information Management and Computer Security*, **19**(2), pp. 113–123.

Wagner, B. A., Fillis, I. & Johansson, U. (2003), 'E-Business and E-Supply Strategy in Small and Medium Sized Businesses (SMEs)', *Supply Chain Management: An International Journal*, **8**(4), pp. 343–354.

Wang, F. & Head, M. M. (2001), 'A Model for Web-based Information Systems in E-Retailing', *Internet Research: Electronic Networking Applications and Policy*, **11**(4), pp. 310–321.

Ward, J., Griffiths, P. & Whitmore, P. (1996), *Strategic Planning for Information Systems*, Second Edition, Wiley, Chichester.

Warren, A. (2002), 'Right to Privacy The Protection of Personal Data in UK Public Organizations', *New Library World*, **103**(1182/1183), pp. 446–456.

Webb, P., Pollard, C. & Ridley, G. (2006), 'Attempting to Define IT Governance: Wisdom or Folly?', *Proceedings of 39th Hawaii International Conference on Systems Sciences*, **8**, IEEE Computer Society Press, pp. 3126–3136.

Weil, P. & Ross, J. W. (2004), *IT Governance: How Top Performers Manage IT Decision Rights for Superior Results*, Harvard Business School Press, Boston.

Welker, J. A. (2007), 'Implementation of Electronic Data Capture Systems: Barriers and Solutions', *Contemporary Clinical Trials*, **28**(3), pp. 329–336.

Wenger, E. (2004), 'Knowledge Management as a Doughnut: Shaping Your Knowledge Strategy through Communities of Practice', *Ivey Business Journal Online*, January/February, pp. 1–8.

While, D., Krasniewicz, J. & Cox, S. (2008), 'The Development of a Unified API for Smart Home Systems', *The Internet of Things and Services, 1st International Research Workshop co-located with EuroTRUSTAmi 2008 Conference*, 18–19 September, Sophia-Antipolis, French Riviera.

White, M. (2010), 'Information Anywhere, Any When: The Role of the Smartphone', *Business Information Review*, **27**(4), pp. 242–247.

Willis, A. (2005), 'Corporate Governance and Management of Information and Records', *Records Management Journal*, **15**(2), pp. 86–97.

Wilson, B. (1990), *Systems: Concepts, Methodologies and Applications*, Second Edition, Wiley, Chichester.

Wilson, D. W. (2000), 'Maturity Models and Information Systems: From S-Curves to E-commerce', *Proceedings of the Fifth Conference of the UK Academy of Information Systems*, Cardiff, 26–28 April, pp. 628–633.

Wilson, B. (2001), *Soft Systems Methodology*, Wiley, Chichester.

W3C (2011), *Web Accessibility Initiative*, http://www.w3c.org/wai, date accessed 1 June 2013.

Yang, H-L. & Tang, J-H. (2005), 'Key User Roles on Web-Based Information Systems Requirements', *Industrial Management & Data Systems*, **105**(5), pp. 577–595.

Zhou, T. T. (2011), 'The Impact of Privacy Concern on User Adoption of Location-based Services', *Industrial Management and Data Systems*, **111**(2), pp. 212–226.

Zhou, T. T. & Jin, J. S. (2003), 'Principles of Video Annotation Markup Language (VAML)', in: Piccardi, M., Hintz, T., He, S., Huang, M. L. & Feng, D. D. (eds.), (2003), *Proceedings of the Pan-Sydney Area Workshop on Visual Information Processing 2003*, **36**, Sydney, pp. 123–127.

INDEX

Note: *Page numbers referring to tables and illustrations are represented in bold.*